The Essential
EatingWell
Cookbook

823A Ferry Road, P.O. Box 1010, Charlotte, VT 05445
www.eatingwell.com

Library of Congress Cataloging-in-Publication Data

The essential Eating well cookbook : good carbs, good fats, great flavor / edited by Patsy Jamieson.
p. cm.
Includes index.
ISBN 0-88150-630-3
1. Cookery, International. 2. Low-fat diet--Recipes. 3. Menus. I. Jamieson, Patricia. II. Eating well.
TX725.A1E843 2004
641.5'638--dc22

2004052730

Editorial Director: James M. Lawrence **Editor:** Patsy Jamieson **Managing Editor:** Wendy S. Ruopp

Nutrition Consultants: Sylvia Geiger, M.S., R.D.; Robin Edelman, M.S., R.D., C.D.E.
Contributing Writer & Editor: Lee Ann Cox
Test Kitchen: Jim Romanoff, Mariana Velasquez, Katie Webster
Recipe Analysis & Editorial Support: Alesia Depot, Katherine Robinson, Bridget Cummings, Beth Hatem
Production Director: Alice Z. Lawrence **Proofreader:** Anne C. Treadwell

Designer: Susan McClellan **Photographer:** Ken Burris

Front cover photographs: South Pacific Shrimp (*page 264*); Grilled Tofu & Vegetable Kebabs (*page 182*); Honey-Lavender Plum Gratin (*page 330*); Grilled Pork Chops with Rhubarb Chutney (*page 283*); Whole-Wheat Fusilli with Beef Ragu (*page 172*); Chocolate-Hazelnut Cake (*page 356*)

Published by
The Countryman Press, P.O. Box 748, Woodstock, Vermont 05091
Distributed by
W.W. Norton & Company, Inc., 500 Fifth Avenue, New York, New York 10110

PRINTED IN THE UNITED STATES OF AMERICA

10 9 8 7 6 5 4 3 2 1

The Essential EatingWell Cookbook

Good Carbs | Good Fats | Great Flavors

Edited by Patsy Jamieson

THE COUNTRYMAN PRESS
WOODSTOCK, VERMONT

ACKNOWLEDGMENTS

AT THE HEART OF EATINGWELL Magazine is a hardworking test kitchen, where for more than a dozen years, many fine cooks have sharpened their knives and honed the thousands of recipes that make up the library from which this book has been selected. Jim Romanoff, Mariana Velasquez and Katie Webster make up the current crew, with invaluable help from time to time from testers Deidre Stapleton, Judy Woods, Jessica Price, Susan Buchanan and Stephanie Browner. Former test kitchen staffers Susan Herr, Susanne Davis and Ruth Cousineau contributed numerous recipes and ideas to this collection. Along the way, we have had assistance from a talented group of cooks, including Beth-Ann Bove, Carolyn Casner, Stacy Fraser, Maria Kourebanas, Alison Frye, Melissa McClelland, Elizabeth Lowe, Thy Tran, Jennifer Armentrout, Catherine Jones. In addition, former food editors Rux Martin and Susan Stuck helped forge the EATINGWELL recipe style.

Special thanks go to all the food writers who created recipes for EATINGWELL. (Specific recipe contributions can be found on page 416.) We would also like to thank all the readers who shared their recipes in the magazine's "Kitchen to Kitchen" and "Rx for Recipes" departments.

For the mouthwatering photographs, we would like to thank our photo team: photographer Ken Burris, art director Susan McClellan, prop stylist Jeanne Peech Santiago, food stylist Kate Hays.

Without the efforts of our capable managing editor, Wendy Ruopp, who orchestrated the entire production and tied myriad pieces together, this book would not have been possible. We are grateful for production director Alice Lawrence's careful eye for detail. Special thanks go to Lee Ann Cox, who wrote chapter introductions, and Joyce Hendley, who wrote about beans and grains. Thanks to Alesia Depot, Katherine Robinson, Beth Hatem and Bridget Cummings for recipe analysis. We appreciate the editorial support of James Lawrence, Allison Cleary and Anne Treadwell, and the enthusiasm and encouragement of our in-house marketing team, Paula Joslin, Laura Carlsmith, Judy Bunten and Caroline Biddle McKenzie.

Nutrition advisor Sylvia Geiger, M.S., R.D., from the University of Vermont, translated the nutrition-analysis numbers into useful nutrition tips and created the Healthy Weight-Loss Index and nutrition "star" icon system found throughout the book. Our thanks to Robin Edelman, M.S., R.D., C.D.E., and Jane Kirby, R.D., for their guidance on nutrition matters. We would also like to thank Julie Stillman for her invaluable role in the formative stages of this project.

We are sincerely grateful for the enthusiasm of Kermit Hummel at The Countryman Press in helping make this project a reality. David Corey and Jennifer Thompson, also at Countryman, made our first collaboration a joy, and we are indebted to the many wonderful people at W.W. Norton who share our love of books and standards of excellence.

The Essential EatingWell Cookbook is dedicated to the memory of our late founding nutrition editor, Elizabeth Normand Hiser. Betsy exemplified the EATINGWELL life and motivated countless readers, students and colleagues to eat wisely and joyfully. Her indomitable spirit continues to inspire us daily.

CONTENTS

INTRODUCTION

As the recipes in this collection will attest, EatingWell lives and cooks at the intersection where the culinary world meets the realm of nutritional wellness.

In more than a decade of creating and publishing recipes, EatingWell, The Magazine of Food & Health, has established a reputation for creatively balancing good taste and good health—something often easier said than done.

The secrets come from an inventive team of cooks—some classically trained, others self-taught—nutritionists, award-winning editors, far-flung food writers, collectors of exotic foreign recipes, an international network of cutting-edge health professionals and hundreds of thousands of demanding, food-loving readers. The nexus for all this energy is the well-seasoned EatingWell test kitchen, located in the lakeside town of Charlotte, Vermont (Pop. 3,569).

This collection represents more than 350 of our favorite recipes—those that have migrated to the top of an elite heap of new and classic EatingWell dishes numbering well into the thousands. These are the must-have recipes our own staff members take home at night, alongside time-tested winners that our readers call and write to request over and over again. All are freshly updated, with improved nutritional analyses and an eye to today's fast-evolving nutritional guidelines.

We believe that the essential flavors and goodness of food can be enjoyed without detracting from good health. Consider the South Pacific Shrimp on the cover of this book: it's a quick and simple recipe (*page 264*) enlivened with a near-magical confluence of ginger, coconut and lime, with a subtle touch of tropical heat from minced peppers.

All our recipes are scrutinized by highly respected dietitians and can be unstintingly recommended for a lifetime of healthful eating. The majority fit perfectly with a wide range of popular weight- and health-maintenance plans, from Atkins to the South Beach Diet to The Zone, with uniquely useful recipes for enthusiastic cooks who want heart-healthy, low-saturated-fat, lower-carbohydrate and vegetarian ideas.

What to Eat?

The leading consumer magazine devoted to both cooking and nutrition, EatingWell is not in the business of prescribing weight-loss diets. With the constant involvement of trustworthy nutrition experts, physicians, food researchers and some of the most creative home chefs in the country, we provide our readers with the latest advice on what to eat, accompanied by recipes that can be served with confidence, pride and an assurance that they fit the current standards for a lifetime of healthy food choices.

Naturally, it is not possible to talk about intelligent eating without noting the sea change currently taking place in the nutrition world. Thanks in part to the phenomenon of many tens of millions of people adopting low-carbohydrate weight-loss or weight-management diets, the academic and scientific nutrition communities have begun to react. If more than a century of dieting history tells us anything, extreme diets of any kind will prove to be a passing fad.

Still, we suspect that some of the best aspects of these diets are here to stay. Clearly, ours is a society in which the consumption of nutrient-stripped carbohydrates has gotten out of control. By substituting better foods—including better choices of carbohydrates—for highly sugared drinks and high-glycemic starches, many people report being able to achieve and sustain a healthy weight loss.

Diet Tools

SOME NEW TOOLS ARE INCORPORATED INTO this book to help cooks find recipes that fit their particular needs. Designed by Sylvia Geiger, M.S., R.D., a University of Vermont faculty member and an EATINGWELL associate editor, the star icons described on page 8 quickly and simply highlight those recipes most appropriate for healthy weight loss, for carbohydrate-monitoring diets or for plans that emphasize fiber content. The Healthy Weight-Loss Index (*page 400*) will be a godsend to people who need to find a guilt-free recipe in a hurry. These recipes all have 350 calories or less per serving, 33 grams or less of carbohydrates and are also low in saturated and total fat. Most are also high in fiber and lower in sodium.

At EATINGWELL, we work hard to feature natural, nutritious ingredients and to serve foods that deliver true, intense flavors and aromas and satisfying textures without the excesses that have led to health woes for so many modern families. Underlying all our recipes are some tenets of what we believe should be the real hallmarks of informed eating and cooking today: good carbohydrates, good fats and great flavors.

The secret of EATINGWELL *recipes is to test, retest and test again until a dish achieves reliability and great flavor. The Charlotte, Vermont-based test kitchen staff: Patsy Jamieson, Mariana Velasquez, Katie Webster, Jim Romanoff.*

Nutrition Stars & Bonuses

Our nutritionists have highlighted recipes likely to be of interest to those following various dietary plans. Recipes that meet specific guidelines are marked with one to three stars (*right*).

If a recipe provides 15% or more of the **Daily Value** (DV) of a nutrient, it is listed as a Nutrition Bonus. These values—identical to those found on food labels—are FDA benchmarks for adults eating 2,000 calories per day.

Recipe has reduced calories, carbohydrates, fats, saturated fats. (*See page 400 for specific levels.*)

Recipe has 22 grams or less of carbohydrates per serving.

Recipe provides 5 grams or more of fiber per serving.

Good Carbs

EatingWell recipes focus on using natural, unprocessed, whole foods with all their goodness intact. Not only are such foods more nutrient-dense in terms of vitamins and minerals, but they also tend to be lower-glycemic index (GI) foods. The glycemic index measures the speed and height that a particular food raises blood sugar (glucose). Higher-GI foods trigger a quick and large insulin response that, among other things, tells the body to start storing fat. There are a number of predicted long-term health risks associated with eating large amounts of high-GI foods ("bad carbs") and many diet advisors are steering their patients away from these refined grains, starches and concentrated sugars.

Moderating the glycemic response by choosing lower-GI foods is currently considered by some to be an exciting new route to weight loss, vitality and better health. While the scientific jury is still deliberating this, no one disputes the benefits of eating "good carbs" in the form of whole grains, legumes, vegetables and fruits. This collection of recipes is packed with smart carbohydrate choices, and readers will discover many recipes that fall into the different stages of carbohydrate-moderating eating plans.

Good Fats

One of the great food phobias in recent memory had us spurning all fats, lumping lard with extra-virgin olive oil, bacon with eggs, deep-frying fat with salad dressings. Confusion reigned, and masses of well-intentioned consumers embraced low-fat products and regimens.

According to Dr. Walter Willett of the Harvard School of Public Health, interviewed in EatingWell Magazine, the most damaging piece of eating advice given to the American public was "the 'all-fats-are-bad' message that we should be eating large amounts of starch and minimizing fat…"

We now know that the type of fats eaten is as important as the amount of fat in foods. In EatingWell's test kitchens we use olive oil, canola oil and various nut and seed oils. The use of these oils, along with the overall reduction in high-calorie fat content and/or the modification of cooking techniques, enables us to create recipes that are consistent with current recommendations for heart-healthy eating. Saturated fat, strongly linked with cardiovascular disease, is kept in moderation in all recipes.

The oils used in our recipes provide richness and flavor, maintain a healthy balance of essential omega-3 to omega-6 fatty acids, and are rich in healthy monounsaturated and polyunsaturated fats. Trans fats, now clearly linked to cardiovascular disease, are nonexistent in our recipes because we do not use margarine or other highly processed ingredients with hydrogenated fats. Butter, although high in saturated fats, is a unique flavoring agent and for that reason we use it judiciously in some recipes. An overwhelming number of recipes in this book are low in fat and come in under 20 grams total fat and under 10 grams saturated fat.

Great Flavor

In EatingWell recipes, good taste and the genuine enjoyment of food always come first. We take it as an article of faith that a recipe must taste wonderful or it will be abandoned by most cooks or shunned by those for whom they cook.

Unlike so many "health" cookbooks, this volume does not simply resort to the usual tricks of stripping out taste and texture and joy to make things "light." Inventive substitutions, often discovered only after repeated testing sessions, are a hallmark of EatingWell recipes. A moist, decadent-tasting chocolate cake, for example, might derive its richness from a simple puree of dates. A plain lamb stew might be elevated to greatness by replacing potatoes with flavorful, nutritious turnips, carrots and pearl onions. A turkey stuffing might be wonderfully transformed by using whole grains and chopped hazelnuts.

Throughout this collection, there are numerous classic recipes that have been given the highly acclaimed EatingWell "Rx" makeover treatment. For example, the Sunday Sausage Strata (*page 20*) started out as an ultra-rich egg-and-cheese casserole. Through numerous revisions in our test kitchen, it dropped from almost 400 calories per serving down to a trim 256, while saturated fat was cut by more than 60 percent and fiber content doubled. The creative substitutions involved replacing fatty pork with leaner turkey sausage, using cheese in just the right proportion and upping the flavor complexity with sautéed onions, red peppers and whole-wheat bread. The result is an enlightened, festive dish that strata lovers find both delicious and satisfying.

In keeping with growing concerns about the salt content in modern foods, all recipes in this book deliver abundant good taste while keeping the sodium level reasonable. With the exception of a few recipes, the majority of dishes in this collection are lower in sodium than their conventional counterparts, and close to two-thirds of these recipes have less than 360 milligrams sodium per serving.

Rarely do the words "wonderful" and "healthful" end up in the same sentence, but they are a fitting description of this collection of recipes. For anyone who loves to cook, who thinks about what they eat and what they feed to family and friends, we commend these recipes. We trust you will find them appealing, a pleasure to cook and as rewarding to eat and serve as we have. We're sure that many will become favorites in your own home collection of essential, trustworthy, beloved recipes. To your health!

—Patsy Jamieson
Charlotte, Vermont

SEASONAL MENUS

QUICK CHICKEN DINNER

Chicken Sauté with Provençal Sauce (*page 236*)
Whole-Wheat Couscous (*page 101*)
Steamed asparagus or green beans
Instant Strawberry Frozen Yogurt (*page 384*)

SIMPLY VEGETARIAN

Crostini with Cannellini Beans,
Arugula & Tomatoes (*page 36*)
Roasted Vegetable Pasta (*page 162*)
Mixed greens with Walnut Oil Vinaigrette (*page 85*)
Balsamic Vinegar-Spiked Strawberries (*page 339*)

EASY TASTE OF INDIA

Warm chapatis or naan bread with
Cucumber-Mint Raita (*page 291*)
Ginger-Coconut Chicken (*page 225*)
Rice Pilaf with Lime & Cashews (*page 94*)
Sautéed spinach
Broiled Pineapple (*page 340*)

ELEGANT SPRING BRUNCH

Mango Splash cocktails (*page 39*)
Twice-Baked Goat Cheese Soufflés on
a Bed of Mixed Greens (*page 22*)
Turkey Rollups (*page 49*)
Blueberry Danish (*page 310*)
Chocolate- & Biscotti-Dipped
Strawberries (*page 339*)

SPRING CELEBRATION

Leek, Asparagus & Herb Soup (*page 64*)
Braised Lamb with a Garden-Vegetable
Medley (*page 285*)
Insalata Mista with
Buttermilk-Chive Dressing (*page 75*)
Whole-wheat rolls
Ruffled Phyllo Tart with Spring Fruit (*page 350*)

SUMMER PICNIC TABLE

Chili Burgers (*page 141*)
Grilled Corn on the Cob (*page 110*)
Creamy Potato Salad (*page 82*)
Three-Bean Salad (*page 79*)
Sliced tomatoes
Peach-Blackberry Compote
with Basil Syrup (*page 337*)

HARVEST SUPPER

Curried Chicken with
Sweet Potatoes & Cauliflower (*page 208*)
Brown rice (*page 101*)
Arugula & Pear Salad (*page 70*)
Apple-Oatmeal Cookies (*page 373*)

HOLIDAY OPEN HOUSE

Cumin-Roasted Almonds (*page 38*)
Hot Artichoke Dip (*page 44*)
Toasted Pita Crisps (*page 47*)
Shrimp Spring Rolls (*page 40*)
Crudités
Roasted Vegetable Galette with
Olives (*page 180*)
The Big Salad (*page 73*)
Chocolate-Dipped Dried Fruit (*page 338*)

A CHILI NIGHT

Black Bean Dip (*page 47*)
Tortilla Chips (*page 47*)
Ultimate Beef Chili (*page 277*)
Wholesome Cornbread (*page 313*)
Spinach Salad with
Warm Maple Dressing (*page 71*)
Mango-Lime Sorbet (*page 387*)

HOLIDAY MENUS

TRADITIONAL THANKSGIVING

Fireside Mulled Cider (*below*)

Figs Stuffed with Gorgonzola (*page 37*)

Curried Roasted Squash & Pear Soup (*page 62*)

Roast Turkey with Madeira Gravy (*page 240*)

Cornbread & Apple Stuffing (*page 103*)

Green Beans with Caramelized Red Onions (*page 107*)

Glazed Carrots with Currants (*page 110*)

Marbled Pumpkin Cheesecake (*page 369*) *or* Classic Pumpkin Pie (*page 347*)

Assorted seasonal fruits: pomegranates, pears, apples, grapes

VEGETARIAN FEAST

Fireside Mulled Cider (*below*)

Edamame-Feta Dip (*page 48*)

Toasted Pita Crisps (*page 47*)

Squash-Stuffed Roasted Poblano Peppers (*page 114*)

Barley Pilaf with Mushrooms, Red Peppers & Spinach (*page 95*)

Bitter Lemon, Honey & Sweet Simmered Greens (*page 123*)

Shades of Autumn Pie (*page 343*)

Fireside Mulled Cider

PREP TIME: 10 MINUTES

START TO FINISH: 35 MINUTES

EASE OF PREPARATION: EASY

Reducing fruit juice with spices and fragrant seasonings intensifies the flavors, creating a beverage that will warm your heart and soul.

- 6 cups apple cider *or* juice
- 2 orange slices
- 1 lemon slice
- 1 slice fresh ginger, smashed
- 2 cinnamon sticks
- 10 whole cloves

In a large saucepan, combine all ingredients. Bring to a boil over high heat. Cook, stirring occasionally, until cider has reduced to 4 cups, about 25 minutes. Remove fruit and spices with a slotted spoon.

MAKES 4 SERVINGS, 1 CUP EACH.

PER SERVING: 206 CALORIES; 1 G FAT (0 G SAT, 0 G MONO); 0 MG CHOLESTEROL; 50 G CARBOHYDRATE; 0 G PROTEIN; 0 G FIBER; 11 MG SODIUM.

NUTRITION BONUS: 10 MG VITAMIN C (15% DV).

BREAKFAST & BRUNCH

1

For so many of us, breakfast is the launching point of the day, where a good start sets us sailing off full of vitality and immune to the proliferating temptations of Krispy Kremes, Cinnabons and behemoth bagels. We know now that high-glycemic breakfasts—sugary cereals, pastries, sweet drinks—leave most people prone to energy crashes within hours and likely to overeat during the rest of the day. From a Greek omelet to hearty, nutty-tasting whole-grain cereals or French Toast Pudding, the recipes here are designed for breakfast lovers and engineered for good health. Break your fast intelligently or plan a creative brunch suffused with good nutrition and great flavors.

BRUNCH

BREAKFAST

HEALTHY-START BEVERAGES

High Fiber

Artichoke & Red Pepper Frittata

PREP TIME: 20 MINUTES | **START TO FINISH:** 35 MINUTES | **EASE OF PREPARATION:** EASY

For an impromptu supper, nothing beats a frittata, the Italian version of an omelet. This one relies on the convenience of canned artichokes, which are a good, delicious source of fiber.

- **2 teaspoons extra-virgin olive oil, divided**
- **1 medium red bell pepper, diced**
- **2 cloves garlic, minced**
- **¼ teaspoon crushed red pepper**
- **4 large eggs**
- **1 14-ounce can artichoke hearts, rinsed and coarsely chopped**
- **¼ cup freshly grated Parmesan cheese**
- **1 teaspoon dried oregano**
- **¼ teaspoon salt, or to taste**
- **Freshly ground pepper to taste**

1. Heat 1 teaspoon oil in a 10-inch nonstick skillet over medium heat. Add bell pepper and cook until tender, about 2 minutes. Add garlic and crushed red pepper; cook, stirring, for 30 seconds. Transfer to a plate. Wipe out the pan.
2. Whisk eggs in a medium bowl. Stir in artichoke hearts, Parmesan, oregano, salt, pepper and the bell pepper mixture.
3. Set a rack about 4 inches from the heat source; preheat the broiler.
4. Brush the pan with the remaining 1 teaspoon oil; heat over medium heat. Pour in the egg mixture and tilt to distribute evenly. Reduce the heat to medium-low and cook until the bottom is light golden, lifting the edges to allow uncooked egg to flow underneath, 3 to 4 minutes. Place the pan under the broiler and cook until the top is set, 1½ to 2½ minutes. Slide the frittata onto a platter and cut into wedges.

MAKES 2 SERVINGS.

PER SERVING: 305 CALORIES; 18 G FAT (6 G SAT, 8 G MONO); 432 MG CHOLESTEROL; 18 G CARBOHYDRATE; 21 G PROTEIN; 6 G FIBER; 734 MG SODIUM.

NUTRITION BONUS: 126 MG VITAMIN C (200% DV), 140 MCG FOLATE (35% DV), 227 MG CALCIUM (23% DV).

Mexican Potato Omelet

PREP TIME: 15 MINUTES | **START TO FINISH:** 25 MINUTES | **EASE OF PREPARATION:** EASY

Whip up this simple, tasty omelet on those nights when it seems the refrigerator is bare. Frozen hash browns are perfect for such occasions—just look for a brand with little or no fat. And while the cheese adds some fat, it also provides almost a third of your daily calcium needs.

- **2 teaspoons extra-virgin olive oil, divided**
- **¾ cup frozen hash-brown potatoes *or* diced cooked potatoes**
- **1 4½-ounce can chopped mild green chiles**
- **4 large eggs**
- **½ teaspoon hot sauce, such as Tabasco**
- **¼ teaspoon salt, or to taste**
- **Freshly ground pepper to taste**
- **½ cup grated pepper Jack *or* Cheddar cheese**
- **¼ cup chopped scallions**
- **¼ cup coarsely chopped fresh cilantro *or* parsley**

1. Heat 1 teaspoon oil in a 10-inch nonstick skillet over medium-high heat. Add potatoes and cook until golden brown, shaking the pan and tossing the potatoes from time to time, 3 to 5 minutes. Stir in chiles and transfer to a plate. Wipe out the pan.
2. Blend eggs, hot sauce, salt and pepper with a fork in a medium bowl. Stir in cheese, scallions, cilantro (or parsley) and the potato mixture.
3. Set a rack about 4 inches from the heat source; preheat the broiler.
4. Brush the pan with the remaining 1 teaspoon oil; heat over medium heat. Pour in the egg mixture and tilt to distribute evenly. Reduce the heat to medium-low and cook until the bottom is light golden, lifting the edges to allow uncooked egg to flow underneath, 3 to 4 minutes. Place the pan under the broiler and cook until the top is set, 1½ to 2½ minutes. Slide the omelet onto a platter and cut into wedges.

MAKES 2 SERVINGS.

PER SERVING: 342 CALORIES; 24 G FAT (9 G SAT, 7 G MONO); 453 MG CHOLESTEROL; 11 G CARBOHYDRATE; 21 G PROTEIN; 2 G FIBER; 753 MG SODIUM.

NUTRITION BONUS: 31 MG VITAMIN C (52% DV), 309 MG CALCIUM (30% DV).

Greek Omelet

PREP TIME: 10 MINUTES | **START TO FINISH:** 20 MINUTES | **EASE OF PREPARATION:** EASY

With flavors reminiscent of the classic Greek spanakopita, this easy omelet is just right for a light dinner or brunch. Frozen leaf spinach makes it ultra-quick.

- **¼ cup cooked spinach**
- **4 large eggs**
- **½ cup crumbled feta cheese (2 ounces)**
- **2 scallions, thinly sliced**
- **2 tablespoons chopped fresh dill**
- **Freshly ground pepper to taste**
- **2 teaspoons extra-virgin olive oil**

1. Squeeze spinach to remove any excess water. Blend eggs with a fork in a medium bowl. Add feta, scallions, dill, pepper and the spinach; mix gently with a rubber spatula.
2. Set a rack about 4 inches from the heat source; preheat the broiler.
3. Heat oil in a 10-inch nonstick skillet over medium heat. Pour in the egg mixture and tilt to distribute evenly. Reduce the heat to medium-low and cook until the bottom is light golden, lifting the edges to allow uncooked egg to flow underneath, 3 to 4 minutes. Place the pan under the broiler and cook until the top is set, 1½ to 2½ minutes. Slide the omelet onto a platter and cut into wedges.

MAKES 2 SERVINGS.

PER SERVING: 271 CALORIES; 19 G FAT (7 G SAT, 7 G MONO); 438 MG CHOLESTEROL; 4 G CARBOHYDRATE; 19 G PROTEIN; 2 G FIBER; 432 MG SODIUM.

NUTRITION BONUS: 27% DV VITAMIN A.

Omelet Essentials

PREP TIME: 5 MINUTES | **START TO FINISH:** 10 MINUTES | **EASE OF PREPARATION:** EASY

THE FASTEST MEAL ON THE PLANET is a simple folded French-style omelet. Once you have mastered the technique, as long as you have a few eggs on hand you will be able to whip up a healthful, satisfying repast that's perfect anytime. Here are the basics:

- Use 2 eggs to make an omelet for one serving, 4 eggs to make an omelet for two. Never make an omelet with more than 5 eggs. If you are serving four people, make two omelets back to back. They're that fast.
- Use a heavy 7- to 10-inch nonstick or well-seasoned skillet with low, sloping sides and a comfortable sturdy handle that won't get hot. A small flexible spatula is essential; we like a heat-resistant rubber spatula.
- Have the filling all prepared and warmed, if it was refrigerated. Don't overstuff: figure ¼ cup filling for a 2-egg omelet. The filling can be just about anything (*see "Filling Ideas," right*).

1. Gently whisk the eggs or mix with a fork just until blended. Add about ½ tablespoon water per egg, if desired: the water will turn to steam as the eggs heat and make the omelet a little fluffier. The classic omelet is made without any additions other than a pinch of salt and a grinding of pepper.

2. Heat 1 teaspoon olive oil in a 7- to 10-inch skillet over medium-high heat until hot. Tilt to coat the pan with oil. Pour the eggs into the pan and immediately stir with a heat-resistant rubber spatula or fork for 5 to 10 seconds. Then push the cooked portions at the edge toward the center, tilting the pan to allow uncooked egg to fill in around the edges. When no more egg runs to the sides, continue to cook until almost set and the bottom is light golden. (The omelet will continue to cook as it is filled and folded.) This whole step takes about 1 minute.

3. Remove the pan from the heat and spoon filling onto the center third of the omelet perpendicular to the handle. Use the spatula to fold the third of the omelet closest to the handle over the filling. Then, grasping the handle from underneath and using the spatula as a guide, tip the omelet onto a warm plate so that it lands folded in thirds, seam-side down.

FILLING IDEAS

- Grated cheese and chopped cooked broccoli (use frozen for convenience)
- Sautéed mushrooms
- Vine-ripened tomatoes, diced, and slivers of fresh basil
- Sautéed chopped onion and Canadian bacon
- Sliced smoked salmon, reduced-fat cream cheese and dill
- Sautéed potatoes and onions

Broccoli-Cheese Pie

PREP TIME: 30 MINUTES | **START TO FINISH:** 1¼ HOURS | **TO MAKE AHEAD:** PREPARE THROUGH STEP 4. COVER AND REFRIGERATE FOR UP TO 12 HOURS. | **EASE OF PREPARATION:** EASY

If you want to give this a fancy name, call it a crustless quiche. For a vegetarian version, simply omit the Canadian bacon.

- **2 tablespoons plain dry breadcrumbs**
- **4 large eggs**
- **1¼ cups 1% milk**
- **½ teaspoon hot sauce, such as Tabasco**
- **¼ teaspoon salt, or to taste**
- **Freshly ground pepper to taste**
- **2 cups cubed whole-wheat country bread (about 2 slices, crusts removed)**
- **3 cups broccoli florets**
- **2 teaspoons extra-virgin olive oil**
- **4 slices Canadian bacon, diced (about 2½ ounces)**
- **1 medium onion, chopped**
- **1 cup grated Monterey Jack *or* part-skim mozzarella cheese (4 ounces)**

1. Preheat oven to 350°F. Coat a 9-inch deep-dish pie pan (6-cup capacity) with cooking spray. Add breadcrumbs, tilting to coat bottom and sides.

2. Whisk eggs, milk, hot sauce, salt and pepper in a large bowl. Add bread and stir to coat. Set aside in the refrigerator.

3. Steam broccoli until just tender, 3 to 4 minutes. Refresh under cold water and drain well. Chop coarsely.

4. Heat oil in a medium nonstick skillet over medium-high heat. Add bacon and onion; cook, stirring often, until softened and light golden, 3 to 5 minutes. Add onion mixture and broccoli to the egg mixture; stir in cheese. Pour into the prepared pan, spreading evenly.

5. Bake the pie until light golden and set, 45 to 50 minutes. Let cool slightly, cut into wedges and serve.

MAKES 6 SERVINGS.

PER SERVING: 226 CALORIES; 13 G FAT (5 G SAT, 3 G MONO); 172 MG CHOLESTEROL; 14 G CARBOHYDRATE; 15 G PROTEIN; 3 G FIBER; 479 MG SODIUM.

NUTRITION BONUS: 36 MG VITAMIN C (60% DV), 227 MG CALCIUM (28% DV).

Lower Carbs

Cheese & Scallion Puff

PREP TIME: 35 MINUTES | **START TO FINISH:** 1¼ HOURS
TO MAKE AHEAD: PREPARE THROUGH STEP 2. COVER AND REFRIGERATE FOR UP TO 2 DAYS. RETURN TO ROOM TEMPERATURE BEFORE CONTINUING. | **EASE OF PREPARATION:** MODERATE

This savory egg and cheese puff is more akin to a pudding than a soufflé, so don't dismay when it loses some of its height.

- **3 cups 1% milk**
- **1¼ cups finely chopped scallions**
- **¾ cup yellow cornmeal**
- **2 large eggs, separated**
- **½ cup freshly grated Parmesan cheese**
- **½ cup grated extra-sharp Cheddar cheese**
- **1 teaspoon salt, divided**
- **¼ teaspoon freshly ground pepper**
- **5 large egg whites, at room temperature (*see Tip, page 22*), or 10 teaspoons dried egg whites (*see Ingredient Note, page 394*), reconstituted according to package directions**

1. Preheat oven to 375°F. Coat a 3-quart soufflé dish or similar baking dish with cooking spray.
2. Bring milk and scallions to a simmer in a heavy medium saucepan over medium heat. Whisking constantly, slowly sprinkle in cornmeal. Cook, whisking constantly, until mixture has thickened, about 5 minutes. Remove from heat and let cool for 10 minutes. Whisk in egg yolks, Parmesan, Cheddar, ½ teaspoon salt and pepper.
3. About 45 minutes before serving, beat the 7 egg whites and remaining ½ teaspoon salt in a large mixing bowl with an electric mixer on high speed until soft peaks form. Whisk one-fourth of the beaten whites into the cornmeal mixture. With a rubber spatula, fold in remaining whites. Spoon batter into the prepared baking dish and smooth the top.
4. Bake the puff until puffed and golden brown, 30 to 35 minutes. Serve immediately.

MAKES 8 SERVINGS.

PER SERVING: 160 CALORIES; 6 G FAT (3 G SAT, 1 G MONO); 68 MG CHOLESTEROL; 15 G CARBOHYDRATE; 12 G PROTEIN; 2 G FIBER; 508 MG SODIUM.

NUTRITION BONUS: 231 MG CALCIUM (23% DV).

Healthy Weight

Lower Carbs

Sunday Sausage Strata

PREP TIME: 30 MINUTES | **START TO FINISH:** 3¼ HOURS (INCLUDING 2 HOURS STANDING TIME)
TO MAKE AHEAD: PREPARE THROUGH STEP 4 THE NIGHT BEFORE SERVING. | **EASE OF PREPARATION:** EASY

The "strata" in this classic casserole are layers of bread, cheese and sausage baked in an egg-rich pudding.

- ½ pound turkey breakfast sausage (four 2-ounce links), casing removed
- 2 medium onions, chopped (2 cups)
- 1 medium red bell pepper, seeded and diced (1½ cups)
- 12 large eggs
- 4 cups 1% milk
- 1 teaspoon salt, or to taste
- Freshly ground pepper to taste
- 6 cups cubed, whole-wheat country bread (about 7 slices, crusts removed)
- 1 tablespoon Dijon mustard
- 1½ cups grated Swiss cheese (4 ounces)

What We Did

To make a healthful version, we replaced pork sausage with turkey sausage, using half as much and making up the difference with flavorful sautéed onions and red peppers. We also switched to whole-wheat bread and used just enough *real* cheese to achieve a rich taste. Although we tested the recipe with reduced-fat cheese, the flavor and texture didn't measure up.

1. Coat a 9-by-13-inch baking dish (or similar shallow 3-quart baking dish) with cooking spray.
2. Cook sausage in a large nonstick skillet over medium heat, crumbling with a wooden spoon, until lightly browned, 3 to 4 minutes. Transfer to a plate lined with paper towels to drain. Add onions and bell pepper to the pan and cook, stirring often, until softened, 3 to 4 minutes.
3. Whisk eggs, milk, salt and pepper in a large bowl until blended.
4. Spread bread in the prepared baking dish. Scatter the sausage and the onion mixture evenly over the bread. Brush with mustard. Sprinkle with cheese. Pour in the egg mixture. Cover with plastic wrap and refrigerate for at least 2 hours or overnight.
5. Preheat oven to 350°F. Bake the strata, uncovered, until puffed, lightly browned and set in the center, 55 to 65 minutes. Let cool for about 5 minutes before serving hot.

RECIPE RX

Original Strata:
399 calories
13 grams saturated fat
1 gram fiber

EW Strata:
256 calories
5 grams saturated fat
2 grams fiber

MAKES 12 SERVINGS.

PER SERVING: 256 CALORIES; 13 G FAT (5 G SAT, 4 G MONO); 236 MG CHOLESTEROL; 19 G CARBOHYDRATE; 17 G PROTEIN; 2 G FIBER; 522 MG SODIUM.

NUTRITION BONUS: 43 MG VITAMIN C (72% DV), 225 MG CALCIUM (23% DV).

VEGETARIAN VARIATION: Substitute ½ pound soy sausage or crumbles, such as Gimme Lean, for the turkey sausage in Step 2; cook in 1 teaspoon olive oil and add an additional 1 teaspoon oil to the skillet before adding onions and bell pepper.

Chile-Cheese Brunch Casserole

PREP TIME: 25 MINUTES | **START TO FINISH:** 1 HOUR 20 MINUTES | **TO MAKE AHEAD:** THE CASSEROLE WILL KEEP IN THE REFRIGERATOR FOR UP TO 2 DAYS. REHEAT BEFORE SERVING. | **EASE OF PREPARATION:** MODERATE

Zesty and cheesy, this casserole is easy to make ahead of time for entertaining.

- **6 corn tortillas**
- **4 large eggs**
- **⅓ cup all-purpose flour**
- **1 teaspoon baking powder**
- **½ teaspoon salt, or to taste**
- **6 large egg whites, or ¼ cup dried egg whites (*see Ingredient Note, page 394*), reconstituted according to package directions**
- **2 16-ounce containers low-fat cottage cheese**
- **2½ cups grated extra-sharp Cheddar cheese**
- **4 4½-ounce cans chopped mild green chiles**
- **1 cup prepared tomato salsa**

1. Preheat oven to 350°F. Coat a 9-by-13-inch baking dish with cooking spray.

2. Toast tortillas: place one at a time directly on a burner (gas or electric) set at medium heat. Toast, turning frequently with tongs, until golden, 30 to 60 seconds. Cut tortillas into 1-inch-wide strips.

3. Whisk 2 whole eggs in a large bowl until foamy. Add flour, baking powder and salt; whisk until smooth. Add remaining 2 whole eggs and egg whites and whisk until smooth. Add cottage cheese, Cheddar cheese, chiles and tortilla strips and mix with a rubber spatula. Pour into the prepared baking dish.

4. Bake the casserole until set in the center and golden on top, 40 to 50 minutes. Let cool for 5 to 10 minutes. Cut into squares. Serve with salsa.

RECIPE RX

Original Casserole:
335 calories
25 grams fat

EW Casserole:
236 calories
10 grams fat

MAKES 12 SERVINGS.

PER SERVING: 236 CALORIES; 10 G FAT (6 G SAT, 1 G MONO); 95 MG CHOLESTEROL; 15 G CARBOHYDRATE; 21 G PROTEIN; 3 G FIBER; 763 MG SODIUM.

NUTRITION BONUS: 238 MG CALCIUM (24% DV).

What We Did

THE ORIGINAL VERSION of this casserole oozed with saturated fat. Our test kitchen lightened it up by using a mixture of whole eggs and egg whites and replacing the mild Cheddar with a mixture of low-fat cottage cheese and extra-sharp Cheddar for maximum impact.

Twice-Baked Goat Cheese Soufflés on a Bed of Mixed Greens

PREP TIME: 30 MINUTES | **START TO FINISH:** 2 HOURS 40 MINUTES (INCLUDING 1 HOUR CHILLING TIME)
TO MAKE AHEAD: PREPARE THROUGH STEP 6. COVER AND REFRIGERATE FOR UP TO 24 HOURS.
EASE OF PREPARATION: MODERATE

If you'd love to wow your guests with a soufflé, but can't stand the last-minute heat, this is your recipe. The soufflés bake once, fall, and revive on a second round in the oven. They emerge modestly puffed, soft and tender. If you are entertaining a group, the recipe can be easily doubled.

SOUFFLES

- Fine dry breadcrumbs (about 1½ tablespoons)
- 1 tablespoon unsalted butter *or* extra-virgin olive oil
- 1½ tablespoons all-purpose flour
- ½ cup 1% milk
- ½ teaspoon Dijon mustard
- ¼ teaspoon salt, or to taste
- Freshly ground pepper to taste
- 2 large egg yolks
- ½ cup crumbled creamy goat cheese (2½ ounces)
- 3 large egg whites, at room temperature (*see Tip*)
- ⅛ teaspoon cream of tartar

SALAD & DRESSING

- 1 clove garlic, halved
- 1 tablespoon lemon juice
- 1 tablespoon honey
- ¼ teaspoon salt, or to taste
- Freshly ground pepper to taste
- 8 cups lightly packed mixed salad greens
- ½ cup crumbled goat cheese (2½ ounces)

1. To prepare soufflés: Position rack in lower third of oven; preheat to 400°F. Coat four 6-ounce (¾ cup) ramekins or custard cups with cooking spray. Lightly coat with breadcrumbs; shake out excess. Put a kettle of water on to boil for the water bath.

2. Melt butter (or heat olive oil) in a small saucepan over low heat; stir in flour. Cook, stirring constantly, for 1 minute. Gradually whisk in milk. Increase heat to medium-high and cook, whisking constantly, until the mixture boils. Reduce heat to low and simmer, whisking constantly, for about 3 minutes. Stir in mustard, salt and pepper. Remove from the heat. The sauce will be very thick.

3. Whisk egg yolks in a medium bowl until blended. Whisk in the sauce until blended. Gently stir in goat cheese.

4. Place egg whites in a large clean bowl. Add cream of tartar. Beat the whites with an electric mixer on medium speed until soft peaks form; increase speed to high and continue beating until stiff and glossy peaks form. Using a rubber spatula, gently fold whites in 3 additions into the cheese sauce until blended.

5. Spoon the soufflé mixture into the prepared ramekins. Run a fingertip (or chopstick) around the inside of the rim so the soufflés will form a high hat as they puff up. Place the ramekins in a baking pan.

> **TO BRING COLD EGGS TO ROOM TEMPERATURE QUICKLY:** Place in a mixing bowl and set it in a larger bowl of warm water for a few minutes; the eggs will beat to a greater volume.

The Essential Egg

THERE IS NOTHING in the kitchen both as basic and brilliant as the egg. Packed with protein, rich in nutrients, eggs do round-the-clock duty. They're the bedrock of a busy cook, a foundation for flavors from Italy to Mexico, the scaffolding that lifts a soufflé skywards. Whether you're looking for a comforting casserole for a casual brunch, an impress-your-guests centerpiece or a simple, healthful supper, eggs are versatile, inexpensive, and easily transformed into a hot, wholesome meal. Now that nutritionists have brought them back from fat-phobic oblivion, we can relax and know that, with eggs around, there's always something good to eat.

6. Place the baking pan in the oven and carefully add enough boiling water to come halfway up the sides of the ramekins. Bake the soufflés until puffed and browned, 25 to 30 minutes. Remove from the oven and let stand in the water bath for 20 minutes. (The soufflés can be eaten right out of the oven, if desired, with salad on the side.)

7. Transfer the soufflés to a rack and let cool to room temperature; they will shrink. Cover and refrigerate (for up to 24 hours) until ready to reheat.

8. About 40 minutes before serving, position rack in center of oven; preheat to 350°F. Coat a baking sheet with cooking spray. Using a thin spatula, carefully loosen the sides of the soufflés. Lift them out (they will be surprisingly sturdy) and place, right-side up, on the prepared baking sheet. (If any soufflé bits stick to a ramekin, loosen with the spatula and press back into place.) Bake the soufflés until puffed and golden, 20 to 25 minutes.

9. **Meanwhile, to prepare salad & dressing:** Rub a large bowl with the cut side of the garlic; discard garlic. Add lemon juice, honey, salt and pepper; whisk to blend. When the soufflés are ready, add salad greens to the bowl and toss to coat with the dressing. Divide salad among 4 plates. Sprinkle with goat cheese. Using a wide spatula, place a warm soufflé in the center of each salad. Serve immediately.

MAKES 4 SERVINGS.

PER SERVING: 266 CALORIES; 16 G FAT (10 G SAT, 4 G MONO); 141 MG CHOLESTEROL; 15 G CARBOHYDRATE; 15 G PROTEIN; 3 G FIBER; 604 MG SODIUM.

NUTRITION BONUS: 145 MCG FOLATE (36% DV), 35% DV VITAMIN A, 224 MG CALCIUM (23% DV).

Multi-Grain Waffles

PREP TIME: 30 MINUTES | **START TO FINISH:** 45 MINUTES

TO MAKE AHEAD: WRAP ANY LEFTOVERS INDIVIDUALLY IN PLASTIC WRAP AND REFRIGERATE FOR UP TO 2 DAYS OR FREEZE FOR UP TO 1 MONTH. REHEAT IN A TOASTER OR TOASTER OVEN. | **EASE OF PREPARATION:** MODERATE

Traditional waffles are a butter-laden, high-carb indulgence, but they make the transition to good fats and smart carbs beautifully, yielding crisp, nutty-tasting waffles with all the sweet pleasure of the original. The batter can also be used for pancakes. (*Photo: page 209.*)

- 2 cups buttermilk
- ½ cup old-fashioned rolled oats
- ⅔ cup whole-wheat flour
- ⅔ cup all-purpose flour
- ¼ cup toasted wheat germ *or* cornmeal
- 1½ teaspoons baking powder
- ½ teaspoon baking soda
- ¼ teaspoon salt
- 1 teaspoon ground cinnamon
- 2 large eggs, lightly beaten
- ¼ cup packed brown sugar
- 1 tablespoon canola oil
- 2 teaspoons vanilla extract

TOPPING SUGGESTIONS

Blackberry Sauce (*page 392*)
Raspberry Sauce (*page 391*)
Vanilla Cream (*page 390*)
Seasonal fresh fruit

1. Mix buttermilk and oats in a medium bowl; let stand for 15 minutes.

2. Whisk whole-wheat flour, all-purpose flour, wheat germ (or cornmeal), baking powder, baking soda, salt and cinnamon in a large bowl.

3. Stir eggs, sugar, oil and vanilla into the oat mixture. Add the wet ingredients to the dry ingredients; mix with a rubber spatula just until moistened.

4. Coat a waffle iron with cooking spray and preheat. Spoon in enough batter to cover three-fourths of the surface (about ⅔ cup for an 8-by-8-inch waffle iron). Cook until waffles are crisp and golden brown, 4 to 5 minutes. Repeat with remaining batter.

RECIPE RX

Traditional Waffles:
248 calories
13 grams total fat
9 grams saturated

EW Multi-Grain Waffles:
188 calories
4 grams total fat
1 gram saturated

MAKES 8 SERVINGS, 2 WAFFLES EACH.

PER SERVING: 188 CALORIES; 4 G FAT (1 G SAT, 2 G MONO); 55 MG CHOLESTEROL; 30 G CARBOHYDRATE; 8 G PROTEIN; 3 G FIBER; 328 MG SODIUM.

NUTRITION BONUS: 144 MG CALCIUM (14% DV).

FOR PANCAKES: Coat a large nonstick skillet with cooking spray; heat over medium heat. Using about ¼ cup batter for each pancake, cook until the bottoms are golden and small bubbles start to form on the tops, about 3 minutes. Flip and cook until pancakes are browned and cooked through, 1 to 2 minutes longer.

MAKES 16 PANCAKES.

German Apple Pancake

PREP TIME: 30 MINUTES | **START TO FINISH:** 1 HOUR 10 MINUTES
TO MAKE AHEAD: THE TOPPING WILL KEEP, COVERED, IN THE REFRIGERATOR FOR UP TO 2 DAYS. REHEAT BEFORE SERVING. | **EASE OF PREPARATION:** MODERATE

Whether your family calls it a Dutch bunny, a Dutch baby or an *Apfelpfannkuchen,* this baked pancake is a breakfast classic. The topping—sautéed apples glazed with apple cider syrup—is wonderful on oatmeal, waffles and frozen yogurt too.

APPLE TOPPING

- 1½ teaspoons butter
- 1½ teaspoons canola oil
- 4 Granny Smith apples, peeled and sliced
- 3 tablespoons sugar
- ½ teaspoon vanilla extract
- ¼ teaspoon ground cinnamon
- 1 cup apple cider

PANCAKE

- 3 large eggs
- ¼ cup all-purpose flour
- 2 teaspoons sugar
- ¼ teaspoon salt
- ¾ cup 1% milk
- Confectioners' sugar for dusting

1. **To prepare topping:** Heat butter and oil in a large nonstick skillet over medium heat until melted. Add apples and sugar; cook, stirring, until the apples are tender and golden, about 20 minutes. Stir in vanilla and cinnamon.
2. Meanwhile, bring cider to a boil in a medium saucepan over medium-high heat. Cook until reduced to ⅓ cup, 10 to 15 minutes. Stir into the sautéed apples. Set aside.
3. **To prepare pancake:** Preheat oven to 400°F. Coat a 12-inch cast-iron or other ovenproof skillet with cooking spray.
4. Whisk eggs, flour, sugar and salt in a mixing bowl until smooth. Gradually add milk, whisking until smooth. Pour the batter into the prepared skillet.
5. Bake the pancake for 15 minutes. Reduce oven temperature to 350°; bake until the pancake is golden and puffed, 15 minutes more. (The pancake will deflate when removed from the oven.)
6. Meanwhile, gently reheat the apple topping, if necessary. Dust the pancake with confectioners' sugar and cut into wedges. Serve immediately, with warm apple topping.

MAKES 4 SERVINGS.

PER SERVING: 271 CALORIES; 7 G FAT (3 G SAT, 3 G MONO); 165 MG CHOLESTEROL; 45 G CARBOHYDRATE; 8 G PROTEIN; 3 G FIBER; 224 MG SODIUM.

Mixed-Grain Cereal with Apricots & Almonds

PREP TIME: 10 MINUTES | **START TO FINISH:** 20 MINUTES | **EASE OF PREPARATION:** EASY

Using a combination of grains—in this case oats and cornmeal—creates an appealing variety of textures that makes a hot cereal anything but bland.

- 2½ cups calcium-fortified orange juice
- 1 cup water
- ½ teaspoon ground cinnamon
- ¼ teaspoon salt, or to taste
- 1 cup dried apricots *or* figs, diced
- ⅔ cup rolled oats
- ⅔ cup cornmeal
- ¾ cup low-fat *or* nonfat plain yogurt
- 6 tablespoons maple syrup
- 6 tablespoons sliced almonds

Combine orange juice, water, cinnamon and salt in a medium saucepan. Bring to a boil over medium-high heat; stir in apricots (or figs) and oats. Gradually add cornmeal, whisking constantly. Reduce heat to low and cook, stirring, until thickened, about 5 minutes. Divide the porridge among 6 bowls. Top with yogurt, maple syrup and almonds. Serve immediately.

MAKES 6 SERVINGS, GENEROUS ½ CUP EACH.

PER SERVING: 309 CALORIES; 6 G FAT (1 G SAT, 3 G MONO); 2 MG CHOLESTEROL; 60 G CARBOHYDRATE; 8 G PROTEIN; 5 G FIBER; 124 MG SODIUM.

NUTRITION BONUS: 46 MG VITAMIN C (77% DV), 254 MG CALCIUM (25% DV).

Wheat & Dried Fruit Porridge

PREP TIME: 10 MINUTES | **START TO FINISH:** 10 MINUTES | **EASE OF PREPARATION:** EASY

This high-fiber hot cereal offers a delightfully nutty change from oatmeal. Bulgur is a quick-cooking form of wheat that has been parboiled and dried. Don't confuse it with cracked wheat, which needs longer cooking.

- ⅓ cup dried apricots, sliced
- ⅓ cup currants
- 1 tablespoon honey, or to taste
- ¼ teaspoon ground cinnamon, plus more for garnish
- Pinch of salt
- 2 cups water
- ⅔ cup bulgur (*see Ingredient Note, page 394*)

Combine apricots, currants, honey, cinnamon, salt and water in a saucepan. Bring to a simmer over medium heat. Stir in bulgur; cook, stirring constantly, until the bulgur starts to thicken, 1 to 2 minutes. Remove from the heat, cover and let stand until most of the liquid is absorbed and the fruit is tender, about 3 minutes. Divide between 2 bowls, dust with a little cinnamon and serve.

MAKES 2 SERVINGS, ABOUT 1 CUP EACH.

PER SERVING: 312 CALORIES; 1 G FAT (0 G SAT, 0 G MONO); 0 MG CHOLESTEROL; 76 G CARBOHYDRATE; 7 G PROTEIN; 12 G FIBER; 90 MG SODIUM.

NUTRITION BONUS: 48% DV FIBER, 30% DV VITAMIN A.

Banana-Walnut Oatmeal

PREP TIME: 5 MINUTES | **START TO FINISH:** 10 MINUTES | **EASE OF PREPARATION:** EASY

Fruit and nuts wake up ordinary oatmeal with a boost of flavor, texture and nutrition. Here, mashed banana lends both sweetness and potassium, while walnuts add omega-3 fatty acids along with an appealing crunch.

- 1 cup 1% milk
- ¾ cup water
- Pinch of salt
- 1 cup quick oats
- 1 very ripe banana, mashed
- 1 tablespoon maple syrup
- 1 tablespoon chopped walnuts

Combine milk, water and salt in a medium saucepan; heat until almost boiling. Add oats and cook, stirring, until creamy, 1 to 2 minutes. Remove from the heat and stir in mashed banana and maple syrup. Divide between 2 bowls, sprinkle with walnuts and serve.

MAKES 2 SERVINGS, ABOUT 1 CUP EACH.

PER SERVING: 306 CALORIES; 7 G FAT (1 G SAT, 2 G MONO); 8 MG CHOLESTEROL; 54 G CARBOHYDRATE; 11 G PROTEIN; 6 G FIBER; 142 MG SODIUM.

NUTRITION BONUS: 22% DV FIBER, 391 MG POTASSIUM (20% DV), 184 MG CALCIUM (18% DV).

Blue Hill Granola

PREP TIME: 20 MINUTES | **START TO FINISH:** 1 HOUR | **TO MAKE AHEAD:** THE GRANOLA WILL KEEP, IN AN AIRTIGHT CONTAINER, AT ROOM TEMPERATURE FOR UP TO 1 WEEK. | **EASE OF PREPARATION:** EASY

Made at The Blue Hill Inn in Maine, this granola bears little resemblance to clumped-up, sugary varieties.

- 4 cups rolled oats
- ¼ cup brown sugar
- ½ cup walnuts, coarsely chopped
- ¼ cup sunflower *and/or* pumpkin seeds
- 2 teaspoons ground cinnamon
- ½ cup apple juice concentrate, thawed
- 2 tablespoons honey
- 2 tablespoons vanilla extract
- ½ cup dried blueberries *or* dried cranberries
- ⅓ cup raisins
- ⅓ cup thinly sliced dried apricots

1. Preheat oven to 400°F. Stir together oats, brown sugar, walnuts, seeds and cinnamon in a large bowl. Mix apple juice concentrate, honey and vanilla in a small bowl. Drizzle over the oat mixture and stir to coat. Spread the mixture onto a large baking sheet with sides.

2. Bake the granola, stirring every 5 to 7 minutes, until it is crisp and golden, 20 to 25 minutes. Transfer to a bowl and stir in dried fruits. Let cool completely.

MAKES 10 SERVINGS, ½ CUP EACH.

PER SERVING: 345 CALORIES; 8 G FAT (1 G SAT, 1 G MONO); 0 MG CHOLESTEROL; 60 G CARBOHYDRATE; 8 G PROTEIN; 7 G FIBER; 8 MG SODIUM.

NUTRITION BONUS: 28% DV FIBER.

French Toast Pudding with Winter Fruits

PREP TIME: 30 MINUTES | **START TO FINISH:** 1¼ HOURS | **EASE OF PREPARATION:** EASY

Crisp French toast tops a fragrant compote of apples, pears and prunes for a great breakfast treat or comforting dessert.

- 1 cup low-fat vanilla yogurt
- 1½ cups apple cider
- 2 apples, peeled and sliced
- 1 firm but ripe pear, peeled and sliced
- 1½ cups pitted prunes (½ pound)
- 1 cinnamon stick
- 1 teaspoon freshly grated lemon zest
- 2 tablespoons lemon juice
- 10 slices whole-wheat sandwich bread, crusts trimmed
- 2 large eggs
- ⅔ cup 1% milk
- 1 teaspoon vanilla extract
- 2 tablespoons sugar
- ½ teaspoon ground cinnamon

1. Preheat oven to 400°F. Line a sieve with cheesecloth or a coffee filter and set it over a bowl. Spoon in yogurt, cover and let drain in the refrigerator for 30 minutes to 1 hour.

2. Combine cider, apples, pear, prunes, cinnamon stick, lemon zest and lemon juice in a large saucepan; bring to a simmer, stirring occasionally. Discard the cinnamon stick and pour the fruit mixture into a 7-by-11-inch or similar 2-quart baking dish.

3. Cut each bread slice in half diagonally. Whisk eggs, milk and vanilla in a shallow dish. Immerse the bread in the egg-milk mixture, carefully turning the slices for even soaking. Arrange the slices in overlapping rows on top of the fruit. Combine sugar and cinnamon and sprinkle over the bread.

4. Bake the pudding until the top is crisp and golden, 20 to 25 minutes. Let cool slightly; serve with the drained yogurt.

MAKES 8 SERVINGS.

PER SERVING: 253 CALORIES; 2 G FAT (1 G SAT, 1 G MONO); 3 MG CHOLESTEROL; 56 G CARBOHYDRATE; 7 G PROTEIN; 6 G FIBER; 216 MG SODIUM.

NUTRITION BONUS: 24% DV FIBER.

Hot Chocolate

PREP TIME: 5 MINUTES | **START TO FINISH:** 5 MINUTES | **EASE OF PREPARATION:** EASY

Our hot cocoa is rich and chocolaty without the overly sweet taste of some packaged mixes. We give it a luxurious froth with a whisk or blender—or use a cappuccino frother if you have one.

- **2 tablespoons sugar**
- **4 teaspoons unsweetened cocoa powder**
- **1 cup 1% milk, divided**
- **¼ teaspoon vanilla extract**
- **Pinch of ground cinnamon**

1. Mix sugar, cocoa and 2 tablespoons cold milk in a mug until smooth. Heat the remaining milk in a small saucepan on the stovetop or in a 2-cup glass measure in the microwave until steaming hot but not boiling. Stir in the cocoa mixture and vanilla.

2. To froth the hot chocolate, whirl a whisk in it by rubbing your hands back and forth. (*Alternatively, pour the hot chocolate into a blender, cover with the lid and a kitchen towel and blend until frothy.*) Pour it back into the mug and sprinkle with cinnamon.

MAKES 1 SERVING, 1 CUP.

PER SERVING: 227 CALORIES; 3 G FAT (2 G SAT, 1 G MONO); 15 MG CHOLESTEROL; 42 G CARBOHYDRATE; 10 G PROTEIN; 3 G FIBER; 132 MG SODIUM.

NUTRITION BONUS: 312 MG CALCIUM (31% DV).

VARIATION: Use vanilla soymilk, reduce sugar to 4 teaspoons and omit vanilla extract.

PER SERVING: 181 CALORIES; 4 G FAT (1 G SAT, 0 G MONO); 0 MG CHOLESTEROL; 31 G CARBOHYDRATE; 7 G PROTEIN; 2 G FIBER; 97 MG SODIUM.

NUTRITION BONUS: 311 MG CALCIUM (31% DV).

Banana-Berry Smoothie

PREP TIME: 5 MINUTES | **START TO FINISH:** 5 MINUTES | **EASE OF PREPARATION:** EASY

This bright and easy breakfast packs two servings of fruit plus soy protein and fiber.

- 1¼ cups calcium-fortified orange juice
- 1 ripe medium banana, peeled and sliced
- 1 cup frozen blueberries, blackberries *or* raspberries
- ½ cup silken tofu
- 2 ice cubes, crushed
- 1 tablespoon sugar (optional)

Combine orange juice, banana, berries, tofu and crushed ice in a blender; cover and blend until smooth and frothy. Sweeten with sugar, if desired. Serve immediately.

MAKES 3 SERVINGS, 1 CUP EACH.

PER SERVING: 135 CALORIES; 2 G FAT (0 G SAT, 0 G MONO); 0 MG CHOLESTEROL; 27 G CARBOHYDRATE; 4 G PROTEIN; 3 G FIBER; 18 MG SODIUM.

NUTRITION BONUS: 50 MG VITAMIN C (80% DV), 152 MG CALCIUM (15% DV).

TEST KITCHEN TIP:
An easy way to crush ice is to place cubes in a heavy-duty plastic bag and break them with a rolling pin.

Strawberry Smoothie

PREP TIME: 5 MINUTES | **START TO FINISH:** 5 MINUTES | **EASE OF PREPARATION:** EASY

Reminiscent of an old-fashioned strawberry milkshake, this smoothie blends that cold, creamy luxury with the healthful benefits of fresh fruit.

- 1 cup fresh strawberries, rinsed and hulled, *or* frozen strawberries, partially thawed
- ¾ cup buttermilk
- ½ cup frozen cranberry juice concentrate
- 2 ice cubes, crushed
- 1 teaspoon sugar (optional)

Combine strawberries, buttermilk, cranberry juice concentrate and crushed ice in a blender; cover and blend until smooth and frothy. Sweeten with sugar, if desired. Serve immediately.

MAKES 2 SERVINGS, ABOUT 1 CUP EACH.

PER SERVING: 206 CALORIES; 1 G FAT (1 G SAT, 0 G MONO); 4 MG CHOLESTEROL; 47 G CARBOHYDRATE; 4 G PROTEIN; 1 G FIBER; 101 MG SODIUM.

NUTRITION BONUS: 76 MG VITAMIN C (127% DV).

Mango-Passion Fruit Smoothie

PREP TIME: 5 MINUTES | **START TO FINISH:** 5 MINUTES | **EASE OF PREPARATION:** EASY

The sweetness level of mangoes varies considerably. Start with the lesser amount of passion fruit juice and add more to taste.

- **1 ripe mango, peeled and diced (1 cup)**
- **⅔ cup nonfat vanilla yogurt**
- **⅓-½ cup frozen passion fruit juice concentrate**
- **¼ cup water**
- **2 ice cubes, crushed**

Combine mango, yogurt, ⅓ cup juice concentrate, water and crushed ice in a blender; cover and blend until smooth and frothy. Add more concentrate, if desired. Serve immediately.

MAKES 2 SERVINGS, 1 CUP EACH.

PER SERVING: 215 CALORIES; 1 G FAT (0 G SAT, 0 G MONO); 1 MG CHOLESTEROL; 44 G CARBOHYDRATE; 7 G PROTEIN; 1 G FIBER; 90 MG SODIUM.

NUTRITION BONUS: 37 MG VITAMIN C (62% DV), 155 MG CALCIUM (15% DV).

Cranberry-Grapefruit Cooler

PREP TIME: 15 MINUTES | **START TO FINISH:** 15 MINUTES | **TO MAKE AHEAD:** COMBINE JUICES, COVER AND REFRIGERATE FOR UP TO 12 HOURS. | **EASE OF PREPARATION:** EASY

Give this tart, pretty drink a sparkle by adding a little club soda or seltzer. The juice proportions may be varied according to taste.

- **3 cups pink *or* white grapefruit juice (3 large grapefruit)**
- **2¼ cups cranberry juice**
- **6 orange slices for garnish**

Combine grapefruit juice and cranberry juice in a pitcher. Pour into tall glasses half-filled with ice cubes. Garnish with orange slices.

MAKES 6 SERVINGS, GENEROUS ¾ CUP EACH.

PER SERVING: 92 CALORIES; 0 G FAT (0 G SAT, 0 G MONO); 0 MG CHOLESTEROL; 23 G CARBOHYDRATE; 1 G PROTEIN; 0 G FIBER; 3 MG SODIUM.

NUTRITION BONUS: 56 MG VITAMIN C (93% DV).

APPETIZERS & SNACKS

2

In the world of dietary downfalls, snacking is its own continent. Be it in front of the television, the computer or the inevitable string of holiday buffets, it's easy to succumb to the salty and the crisp, the rich and the creamy, all in safe, single nibbles that somehow seem to multiply into a full-fledged feast. The impulse may never go away, but it can easily be managed with recipes that offer the same irresistible satisfactions without crossing the borders of healthy eating. From all-American standards to finger foods gathered from around the globe, here are some of our secrets to snacking smart.

Baked Stuffed Portobello Caps

PREP TIME: 20 MINUTES | **START TO FINISH:** 1¾ HOURS (INCLUDING MARINATING TIME)
EASE OF PREPARATION: MODERATE

Red pepper, garlic and herbs add bright color and flavor to earthy portobello mushrooms. Serve them with crusty bread for a hearty appetizer. The mushrooms also make a great accompaniment for grilled meat or fish.

- **2 tablespoons extra-virgin olive oil**
- **½ teaspoon minced garlic**
- **¼ teaspoon crushed red pepper**
- **6 portobello mushrooms, about 4 inches in diameter** (*see Ingredient Note, page 396*)
- **1 teaspoon coarse salt, divided**
- **½ cup finely diced red bell pepper**
- **1 tablespoon finely chopped fresh parsley**
- **1 teaspoon chopped fresh thyme leaves**
- **¼ teaspoon freshly ground pepper**
- **Arugula leaves *or* parsley sprigs for garnish**

1. Combine oil and garlic in a small skillet. Cook over very low heat until soft and aromatic, not browned, 2 to 4 minutes. Add crushed red pepper and remove from the heat.

2. Hold each mushroom upright and tap to dislodge dirt. Clean with a soft brush. Holding each mushroom upright, gently cut the stem flush with the cap; reserve the stem. Paint the caps sparingly with about half of the oil mixture, outside then inside. Set gill-side up on a baking sheet. Sprinkle with ½ teaspoon salt.

3. With a paring knife, peel the mushroom stems, cut them into fine dice and place in a small bowl. Stir in bell pepper, parsley and thyme. Add the remaining oil mixture, remaining ½ teaspoon salt and pepper. Let stand until somewhat juicy, about 1 hour, tossing occasionally.

4. Position rack in upper third of oven; preheat to 450°F. Divide the stuffing among the caps, spreading evenly. Bake until tender throughout, 10 to 15 minutes. Transfer to a warm platter and garnish with arugula or parsley. Serve hot.

MAKES 6 SERVINGS, 1 CAP EACH.

PER SERVING: 66 CALORIES; 5 G FAT (1 G SAT, 4 G MONO); 0 MG CHOLESTEROL; 5 G CARBOHYDRATE; 2 G PROTEIN; 2 G FIBER; 389 MG SODIUM.

Bruschetta with Roasted Peppers & Mozzarella

PREP TIME: 10 MINUTES | **START TO FINISH:** 15 MINUTES | **EASE OF PREPARATION:** EASY

Roasting peppers intensifies their natural sweetness and gives them a depth of flavor that marries beautifully with the mild cheese in this pretty antipasto.

- 4 roasted bell peppers, peeled, seeded and sliced (2 cups)
- 2 tablespoons finely chopped fresh basil
- 1 tablespoon balsamic vinegar
- Salt & freshly ground pepper to taste
- 8 ½-inch-thick slices whole-wheat country bread
- 1 clove garlic, peeled and cut in half
- 2 ounces fresh mozzarella, cut into thin strips
- 2 teaspoons extra-virgin olive oil

1. Preheat broiler.
2. Combine peppers, basil and vinegar in a medium bowl. Season with salt and pepper.
3. Toast or grill bread slices lightly. Rub both sides of the bread with the cut sides of the garlic. Place bread on a baking sheet; top with roasted peppers. Lay mozzarella strips on a diagonal over the peppers and drizzle with oil.
4. Broil bruschetta, 6 inches from the heat source, until the cheese melts and starts to brown. Serve hot.

MAKES 8 SERVINGS.

PER SERVING: 96 CALORIES; 3 G FAT (1 G SAT, 1 G MONO); 6 MG CHOLESTEROL; 13 G CARBOHYDRATE; 3 G PROTEIN; 1 G FIBER; 163 MG SODIUM.

NUTRITION BONUS: 58 MG VITAMIN C (97% DV), 40% DV VITAMIN A.

How to Oven-Roast Peppers

1. Preheat oven to 450°F. Place a wire rack on a large baking sheet. Arrange whole bell peppers on the rack.
2. Roast peppers in the center of the oven, turning occasionally with tongs, until blackened in places, 30 to 40 minutes.
3. Transfer the peppers to a large bowl and cover with plastic wrap. Let steam for 10 minutes. Uncover and let cool.
4. With a paring knife, remove stems, skins and seeds. If serving as antipasto, combine accumulated juices with peppers.

Crostini with Cannellini Beans, Arugula & Tomatoes

PREP TIME: 10 MINUTES | **START TO FINISH:** 25 MINUTES | **EASE OF PREPARATION:** EASY

The creamy richness of white beans is a lovely foil for slightly bitter greens like arugula in this classic appetizer of southern Italy. Do as Italian cooks do and take advantage of what you have on hand, substituting other beans or greens for the varieties suggested here.

- 2-3 cloves garlic, peeled
- 1 tablespoon extra-virgin olive oil
- 2 cups cooked *or* canned cannellini beans (*see "Essential Bean-Cooking Guide," page 93*)
- ½ cup water
- Salt & freshly ground pepper to taste
- 12 ½-inch-thick slices whole-wheat country bread
- 1 cup stemmed and chopped arugula *or* watercress
- 2 tomatoes, seeded and chopped (1½ cups)

1. Mince one garlic clove. Combine it with the oil in a medium saucepan. Stir over low heat until golden, about 2 minutes. Add beans, water, salt and pepper. Bring to a simmer over low heat and cook, stirring often, until the mixture is thickened, 8 to 10 minutes.
2. Toast or grill bread slices. Rub one side of each bread slice with the remaining garlic cloves.
3. Top each bread slice with some of the beans, followed by arugula (or watercress) and tomatoes. Serve immediately.

MAKES 12 CROSTINI.

PER CROSTINI: 158 CALORIES; 1 G FAT (0 G SAT, 1 G MONO); 0 MG CHOLESTEROL; 28 G CARBOHYDRATE; 6 G PROTEIN; 3 G FIBER; 253 MG SODIUM.

Figs Stuffed with Gorgonzola

PREP TIME: 40 MINUTES | **START TO FINISH:** 40 MINUTES | **TO MAKE AHEAD:** THE APPETIZERS WILL KEEP, COVERED, IN THE REFRIGERATOR FOR UP TO 8 HOURS. | **EASE OF PREPARATION:** MODERATE

Gorgonzola cheese meets dried figs poached in port. The result: a thoroughly elegant holiday appetizer.

- 16 dried Mission figs (about 8 ounces)
- ½ cup port
- 1 tablespoon balsamic vinegar
- ¼ cup crumbled Gorgonzola cheese (2 ounces)
- ¼ cup reduced-fat cream cheese, softened (2 ounces)
- 1 teaspoon chopped fresh rosemary
- 2 ounces sliced prosciutto, trimmed of fat
- Coarsely ground pepper to taste

1. Snip the stem off each fig and make a crisscross cut two-thirds of the way down to partially open the fig. Trim the base of each fig so it will sit upright when finished.
2. Place the figs, port and vinegar in a small saucepan; cook, uncovered, over low heat, shaking the pan occasionally, until the figs are plumped and softened and most of the liquid is reduced, 10 to 15 minutes. Set aside until cool enough to handle.
3. Meanwhile, combine Gorgonzola, cream cheese and rosemary in a small bowl; blend with a fork. Cover and refrigerate until the figs are cooled. Cut prosciutto into ¼-inch-wide ribbons.
4. Using a teaspoon, melon baller or small spoon, place a dollop of cheese mixture in the opening of each fig. Garnish each appetizer with a ribbon of prosciutto. Dust with a grinding of pepper.

MAKES 16 PIECES.

PER PIECE: 76 CALORIES; 2 G FAT (1 G SAT, 0 G MONO); 7 MG CHOLESTEROL; 11 G CARBOHYDRATE; 2 G PROTEIN; 2 G FIBER; 109 MG SODIUM.

Goat Cheese Kisses

PREP TIME: 15 MINUTES | **START TO FINISH:** 35 MINUTES | **TO MAKE AHEAD:** THE KISSES WILL KEEP, COVERED, IN THE REFRIGERATOR FOR UP TO 4 DAYS. | **EASE OF PREPARATION:** EASY

Each of these bite-size savory treats has a bit of dried fruit tucked inside for a slightly sweet surprise. They make wonderful holiday gifts as well as elegant little hors d'oeuvres.

- **3 tablespoons hazelnuts *or* pistachios (¾ ounce), finely chopped**
- **6 ounces creamy goat cheese**
- **6 dried apricots *or* dried figs, each cut into quarters**

Line a plate or small tray with wax paper. Place nuts in a shallow dish. Scoop a heaping ½ teaspoon goat cheese and press a piece of dried apricot (or fig) into the center. Wrap the cheese around the dried fruit to form a ball. Roll the ball in the chopped nuts to create a crust; set on the plate or tray. Repeat with remaining goat cheese, dried fruit and nuts.

MAKES ABOUT 2 DOZEN PIECES.

PER PIECE: 28 CALORIES; 2 G FAT (1 G SAT, 1 G MONO); 3 MG CHOLESTEROL; 1 G CARBOHYDRATE; 1 G PROTEIN; 0 G FIBER; 26 MG SODIUM.

Cumin-Roasted Almonds

PREP TIME: 5 MINUTES | **START TO FINISH:** 30 MINUTES | **TO MAKE AHEAD:** THE ALMONDS WILL KEEP IN AN AIRTIGHT CONTAINER FOR UP TO 3 DAYS. | **EASE OF PREPARATION:** EASY

Lower Carbs

Spiced almonds make a simple irresistible nibble to accompany cocktails, such as the ones on page 39.

- **2 cups whole blanched almonds**
- **2 teaspoons extra-virgin olive oil**
- **2 teaspoons ground cumin**
- **½ teaspoon salt, or to taste**
- **¼ teaspoon freshly ground pepper**

1. Preheat oven to 300°F.

2. Place almonds in a baking pan; toss with oil, cumin, salt and pepper. Bake until lightly toasted, about 25 minutes. Let cool on a wire rack.

MAKES 2 CUPS.

PER TABLESPOON: 58 CALORIES; 5 G FAT (0 G SAT, 0 G MONO); 0 MG CHOLESTEROL; 2 G CARBOHYDRATE; 2 G PROTEIN; 1 G FIBER; 37 MG SODIUM.

VARIATION: Use curry powder and cayenne pepper in place of cumin and black pepper.

Cocktails

KIR

PREP TIME: 5 MINUTES | **START TO FINISH:** 5 MINUTES
EASE OF PREPARATION: EASY

A French bistro favorite, this aperitif turns an everyday white wine into a festive cocktail. To really make it an occasion, use sparkling wine.

- **4 tablespoons crème de cassis (black currant liqueur) *or* black currant syrup**
- **16 fluid ounces (2 cups) chilled dry white wine *or* sparkling wine**
- **Twists of lemon *or* orange zest for garnish**

Spoon 1 tablespoon crème de cassis (or black currant syrup) into each 8-ounce wineglass. Fill with white wine and add a twist of lemon or orange zest.

MAKES 4 SERVINGS.

PER SERVING: 122 CALORIES; 0 G FAT (0 G SAT, 0 G MONO); 0 MG CHOLESTEROL; 6 G CARBOHYDRATE; 0 G PROTEIN; 0 G FIBER; 6 MG SODIUM.

PASSION FRUIT PUNCH

PREP TIME: 5 MINUTES | **START TO FINISH:** 5 MINUTES
EASE OF PREPARATION: EASY

Buy frozen lemon juice for easy squeezing.

- **¼ cup frozen passion fruit juice concentrate**
- **2 tablespoons lemon juice**
- **2 tablespoons light rum**
- **1 cup crushed ice**

Combine passion fruit concentrate, lemon juice and rum in a 12-ounce glass. Add ice; stir until chilled.

MAKES 1 SERVING.

PER SERVING: 108 CALORIES; 1 G FAT (0 G SAT, 0 G MONO); 0 MG CHOLESTEROL; 14 G CARBOHYDRATE; 2 G PROTEIN; 0 G FIBER; 27 MG SODIUM.

NUTRITION BONUS: 18 MG VITAMIN C (30% DV), 30% DV VITAMIN A.

MANGO SPLASH

PREP TIME: 15 MINUTES | **START TO FINISH:** 20 MINUTES
TO MAKE AHEAD: THE MANGO PUREE WILL KEEP, COVERED, IN THE REFRIGERATOR FOR UP TO 8 HOURS.
EASE OF PREPARATION: MODERATE

Whatever the occasion, toast your guests with this fresh, fruity cocktail. Be sure to buy mangoes that have a pleasant, sweet aroma. For the bubbles, choose a not-too-sweet sparkling wine, such as a French *crémant de Bourgogne* or an Italian *prosecco.* For a nonalcoholic cocktail, mix with ginger ale or soda water.

- **4 ripe mangoes**
- **⅓ cup curaçao *or* other orange-flavored cordial**
- **3 tablespoons fresh lime juice**
- **3 tablespoons sugar**
- **2 bottles sparkling white wine, chilled**
- **Lime wedges for garnish**

Remove mango flesh from skin and pit (*see Tip, page 397*). Place flesh in a food processor or blender and puree. Add curaçao, lime juice and sugar; pulse until blended. Pour about 2 tablespoons mango puree into each glass, top with sparkling wine, garnish with a lime wedge and serve.

MAKES 12 SERVINGS.

PER SERVING: 147 CALORIES; 0 G FAT (0 G SAT, 0 G MONO); 0 MG CHOLESTEROL; 17 G CARBOHYDRATE; 0 G PROTEIN; 1 G FIBER; 8 MG SODIUM.

NUTRITION BONUS: 19 MG VITAMIN C (30% DV).

Shrimp Spring Rolls

PREP TIME: 50 MINUTES | **START TO FINISH:** 50 MINUTES | **EASE OF PREPARATION:** MODERATE

Rice-paper wrappers—translucent round or triangular sheets made from rice flour—are widely used in Vietnamese and Thai cooking. Dipped in warm water, the delicate wrappers become soft and pliable in seconds. It just takes a few times working with them to master the technique.

- 1 cup Thai Sauce (*page 294*)

MARINADE & SHRIMP

- 1 tablespoon rice wine *or* medium-dry sherry
- 1 tablespoon fish sauce (*see Ingredient Note, page 395*)
- ½ tablespoon lemon juice
- 1 tablespoon chopped fresh cilantro
- 1 small fresh red chile pepper, such as Fresno, seeded and minced (2 tablespoons)
- 3 cloves garlic, minced
- 2 teaspoons minced fresh ginger
- 20 medium shrimp (30-40 per pound), peeled and deveined

FILLING & WRAPPERS

- 1 large apple *or* peach, peeled and diced
- 4 scallions, green part only, thinly sliced
- 1 small red bell pepper, seeded and diced
- 1 small yellow bell pepper, seeded and diced
- 1 tablespoon rice vinegar
- ½ tablespoon toasted sesame oil
- 1 tablespoon canola oil
- 20 8-inch rice-paper wrappers (*see Ingredient Note, page 396*)
- 20 fresh basil leaves *or* mint leaves

1. Make Thai Sauce. Cover and refrigerate.
2. **To prepare marinade:** Combine rice wine (or sherry), fish sauce, lemon juice, cilantro, chile pepper, garlic and ginger in a medium bowl. Add shrimp and toss to coat. Cover and marinate in the refrigerator for 30 minutes.
3. **To prepare filling:** Combine apple (or peach), scallion greens, bell peppers, vinegar and sesame oil in a medium bowl; toss to coat.
4. Heat a large nonstick skillet over medium-high heat. Add canola oil and tilt pan to coat it evenly. Add shrimp and marinade; stir-fry until shrimp turn pink, 1 to 2 minutes. Remove from heat.
5. **To assemble rolls:** Dip a wrapper in warm water for a few seconds. Carefully transfer it to a clean work surface and let stand until soft, about 1 minute. Center 1 basil leaf (or mint leaf) in the bottom third of the wrapper; top with a shrimp and 2 tablespoons of the filling. Fold the wrapper over the filling and roll into a tight cylinder, folding in the sides about halfway. Assemble the remaining spring rolls the same way. Keep the finished rolls covered with a damp cloth to prevent them from drying out. Serve with Thai Sauce.

MAKES 20 SPRING ROLLS.

PER ROLL: 87 CALORIES; 2 G FAT (0 G SAT, 1 G MONO); 9 MG CHOLESTEROL; 14 G CARBOHYDRATE; 3 G PROTEIN; 1 G FIBER; 237 MG SODIUM.

NUTRITION BONUS: 21 MG VITAMIN C (35% DV).

Lower Carbs

Pan-Fried Dumplings

PREP TIME: 40 MINUTES | **START TO FINISH:** 1 HOUR | **TO MAKE AHEAD:** PREPARE THROUGH STEP 2. COVER AND REFRIGERATE THE SAUCE FOR UP TO 4 DAYS, THE FILLING FOR UP TO 1 DAY. | **EASE OF PREPARATION:** MODERATE

Crisp pan-fried dumplings don't have to be loaded with fat. Cooking them in a mixture of water and oil lets the filling heat through while the outside becomes delightfully crisp and golden.

- ¾ cup Chile-Garlic Dipping Sauce (*page 293*)

FILLING

- ½ pound lean ground pork, beef *or* turkey
- 3 large napa cabbage leaves, stemmed and minced (2 cups)
- 4 fresh shiitake mushroom caps *or* oyster mushrooms, wiped clean and diced (¼ cup)
- 1 medium leek (white part only), washed (*see Cooking Tip, page 397*) and minced
- 2 scallions, minced
- 1 tablespoon minced fresh ginger
- 2 tablespoons reduced-sodium soy sauce
- 1 tablespoon lemon juice
- 1 tablespoon canola oil
- 1 tablespoon rice wine *or* medium-dry sherry
- 2 teaspoons toasted sesame oil
- ¼ teaspoon freshly ground pepper

DUMPLINGS

- 36 wonton wrappers (10 ounces) (*see Ingredient Note, page 396*)
- 2 tablespoons canola oil, divided
- ¾ cup water, divided

1. Make Chile-Garlic Dipping Sauce.
2. **To prepare filling:** Mix all filling ingredients in a large bowl.
3. **To assemble dumplings:** Organize your work area with a bowl of cold water, stack of wonton wrappers (cover with a damp cloth while assembling dumplings) and a floured plate to hold the dumplings.
4. Using a 3½-inch round cookie cutter (or clean can), cut wonton wrappers into circles (they need not be perfectly round). Using a pastry brush, brush the edges of a circle with water. Spoon 1 heaping teaspoon of filling into the center. Fold the wrapper over to form a half-moon shape, pressing the edges together to seal. Repeat with remaining wrappers and filling. Keep dumplings covered with a damp cloth while working to prevent them from drying out.
5. Preheat oven to 200°F.
6. Combine 1 tablespoon oil and ¼ cup water in a large nonstick skillet over medium heat. Place one-third of the dumplings in the skillet so that they are not touching; cover and cook until dumplings puff up and are light brown on the bottom, 4 to 5 minutes. Carefully flip with tongs and cook, covered, until the other side is light brown and the filling is no longer pink in the center, about 1 minute more. Transfer dumplings to a baking sheet and place in the oven to keep warm. Repeat the procedure with half the remaining dumplings, the remaining 1 tablespoon oil and another ¼ cup water. Then, cook remaining dumplings in the remaining ¼ cup water. (There is enough oil left in the skillet for the final batch.) Serve hot, with dipping sauce.

MAKES 36 DUMPLINGS.

PER DUMPLING: 53 CALORIES; 2 G FAT (0 G SAT, 1 G MONO); 5 MG CHOLESTEROL; 6 G CARBOHYDRATE; 2 G PROTEIN; 0 G FIBER; 139 MG SODIUM.

Phyllo Cheese Triangles

PREP TIME: 30 MINUTES | **START TO FINISH:** 1 HOUR 10 MINUTES

TO MAKE AHEAD: PREPARE THROUGH STEP 4. FREEZE IN A SINGLE LAYER, THEN STACK IN A CONTAINER AND COVER TIGHTLY. THE UNBAKED TRIANGLES WILL KEEP IN THE FREEZER FOR UP TO 2 MONTHS. DO NOT THAW BEFORE BAKING.

EASE OF PREPARATION: MODERATE

Reminiscent of the ever-popular cheese straws, these savory, flaky cheese bites are a guaranteed hit for any occasion.

- **2 tablespoons extra-virgin olive oil**
- **½ teaspoon Dijon mustard**
- **¼ teaspoon salt**
- **⅛ teaspoon cayenne pepper**
- **4 sheets phyllo dough (14x18 inches), thawed**
- **⅓ cup freshly grated Parmesan cheese**

1. Preheat oven to 350°F. Coat 2 baking sheets with cooking spray.
2. Stir together oil, mustard, salt and cayenne in a small bowl.
3. Lay 1 sheet of phyllo on a work surface. (Keep remaining phyllo covered with plastic wrap and a damp kitchen towel.) Dampen a pastry brush with water and use it to brush the phyllo lightly with the oil mixture. Sprinkle with about 1½ tablespoons Parmesan. Lay another sheet of phyllo on top. Lightly brush with more oil mixture and sprinkle with Parmesan. Repeat with the remaining phyllo, oil mixture and Parmesan.
4. Cut the phyllo stack crosswise into 4 strips. Cut each strip into 7 triangles. Transfer the triangles to the prepared baking sheets.
5. Bake the triangles, 1 sheet at a time, for 6 to 10 minutes, or until golden and crisp. Transfer to a wire rack to cool.

TEST KITCHEN TIP:
Thaw frozen phyllo dough, in its original wrapper, overnight in the refrigerator. Let stand at room temperature for 2 hours before using.

MAKES 28 TRIANGLES.

PER TRIANGLE: 21 CALORIES; 1 G FAT (0 G SAT, 1 G MONO); 1 MG CHOLESTEROL; 1 G CARBOHYDRATE; 1 G PROTEIN; 0 G FIBER; 51 MG SODIUM.

Quesadillas con Frijoles Refritos

PREP TIME: 10 MINUTES | **START TO FINISH:** 25 MINUTES | **EASE OF PREPARATION:** EASY

These easy tortilla snacks, filled with refried beans, salsa, corn and cheese, satisfy your Tex-Mex cravings with a fraction of the fat and calories of the usual fare.

- 1 cup fat-free refried beans
- 2 tablespoons prepared hot salsa, plus more for dipping
- 12 6-inch corn tortillas
- 1 cup frozen corn, thawed
- ⅓ cup chopped fresh cilantro
- ⅓ cup chopped scallions
- ¾ cup finely grated Monterey Jack cheese (3 ounces)

1. Preheat oven to 400°F. Line a baking sheet with foil.
2. Mix refried beans and 2 tablespoons salsa together.
3. Place a tortilla directly on a stovetop burner (gas or electric), set at medium, and toast, turning frequently with tongs, until softened, about 30 seconds. Wrap in a kitchen towel to keep warm while you soften the remaining tortillas in the same manner.
4. Lay 6 of the softened tortillas on the prepared baking sheet. Divide the bean mixture among these tortillas, spreading evenly. Sprinkle each with corn, cilantro and scallions, then cheese. Top with the remaining softened tortillas and press to seal.
5. Bake until lightly crisped and browned, about 10 minutes. Cut each quesadilla into 4 wedges. Serve hot, with additional salsa for dipping.

MAKES 6 SERVINGS, 4 WEDGES EACH.

PER SERVING: 237 CALORIES; 6 G FAT (3 G SAT, 2 G MONO); 13 MG CHOLESTEROL; 38 G CARBOHYDRATE; 10 G PROTEIN; 6 G FIBER; 354 MG SODIUM.

PER WEDGE: 59 CALORIES; 1 G FAT (1 G SAT, 0 G MONO); 3 MG CHOLESTEROL; 10 G CARBOHYDRATE; 3 G PROTEIN; 1 G FIBER; 89 MG SODIUM.

Lower Carbs

Hot Artichoke Dip

PREP TIME: 10 MINUTES | **START TO FINISH:** 20-30 MINUTES | **TO MAKE AHEAD:** PREPARE THROUGH STEP 1. COVER AND REFRIGERATE FOR UP TO 2 DAYS. | **EASE OF PREPARATION:** EASY

Cheesy, rich and delicious, this update of an entertaining classic delivers all the fabulous flavor with far less fat. Serve with Toasted Pita Crisps (*page 47*) or toasted slices of crusty whole-wheat bread.

- 2 14-ounce cans artichoke hearts, rinsed
- 2 cups plus 2 tablespoons freshly grated Parmesan cheese
- ½ cup reduced-fat mayonnaise
- 2 cloves garlic, minced
- 2 teaspoons freshly grated lemon zest, preferably organic
- Cayenne pepper to taste
- Salt & freshly ground pepper to taste

1. Preheat oven to 400°F. Chop artichoke hearts in a food processor. Add 2 cups Parmesan, mayonnaise, garlic, lemon zest and cayenne; puree until smooth. Season with salt and pepper. Place in two gratin or shallow baking dishes (2-cup capacity). Sprinkle each dish with 1 tablespoon Parmesan.

2. Bake the dip until golden on top and heated through, 10 to 20 minutes.

MAKES ABOUT 2⅔ CUPS.

PER TABLESPOON: 31 CALORIES; 2 G FAT (1 G SAT, 0 G MONO); 3 MG CHOLESTEROL; 3 G CARBOHYDRATE; 2 G PROTEIN; 1 G FIBER; 109 MG SODIUM.

Turkish Red Pepper Spread

PREP TIME: 15 MINUTES | **START TO FINISH:** 15 MINUTES | **EASE OF PREPARATION:** EASY

Enriched with walnuts and olive oil, a jar of roasted peppers quickly turns into *muhammara*, a spread from southeast Turkey. Serve on Toasted Pita Crisps (*see page 47*) or crisp sesame crackers.

- ¼ cup chopped walnuts
- 1 7-ounce jar roasted red peppers, rinsed
- ½ cup fresh breadcrumbs (*see Tip*)
- 1 large clove garlic, crushed
- 1 tablespoon extra-virgin olive oil
- 1 tablespoon lemon juice, or to taste
- 1½ teaspoons ground cumin
- ¼ teaspoon crushed red pepper
- Salt to taste

1. Toast walnuts in a small dry skillet over medium heat, stirring, until fragrant, 2 to 3 minutes. Transfer to a small bowl and let cool.

2. Combine all ingredients in a food processor and process until smooth. Adjust seasoning with more lemon juice and salt, if desired.

MAKES ABOUT ¾ CUP.

PER TABLESPOON: 41 CALORIES; 3 G FAT (0 G SAT, 1 G MONO); 0 MG CHOLESTEROL; 4 G CARBOHYDRATE; 1 G PROTEIN; 1 G FIBER; 65 MG SODIUM.

TO MAKE FRESH BREADCRUMBS: Trim crusts from firm sandwich bread. Tear bread into pieces and process in a food processor until coarse crumbs form. One slice of bread makes about ⅓ cup crumbs.

Hummus

PREP TIME: 10 MINUTES | **START TO FINISH:** 30 MINUTES | **TO MAKE AHEAD:** THE HUMMUS WILL KEEP, COVERED, IN THE REFRIGERATOR FOR UP TO 2 DAYS. | **EASE OF PREPARATION:** EASY

An easy initiation into the versatility of tofu: serve this rich, brightly seasoned hummus with Toasted Pita Crisps (*page 47*) and/or fresh bell pepper and carrot strips.

- 1 15½-ounce can chickpeas, rinsed (1½ cups)
- 1 clove garlic, minced
- ¾ cup silken tofu
- 3 tablespoons lemon juice
- 1½ tablespoons tahini (*see Note*)
- 1 tablespoon extra-virgin olive oil
- 1½ teaspoons ground cumin
- Salt & freshly ground pepper to taste
- Paprika for garnish (optional)

1. Combine chickpeas, garlic, tofu, lemon juice, tahini, oil and cumin in a food processor or blender; puree until very smooth. Season with salt and pepper.

2. Transfer to a serving bowl and cover. Let sit at room temperature for 20 to 30 minutes before serving. Garnish with paprika, if desired.

INGREDIENT NOTE: Tahini is a paste made from ground sesame seeds. Look for it in natural-foods stores and some supermarkets.

MAKES ABOUT 2 CUPS.

PER TABLESPOON: 24 CALORIES; 1 G FAT (0 G SAT, 1 G MONO); 0 MG CHOLESTEROL; 2 G CARBOHYDRATE; 1 G PROTEIN; 1 G FIBER; 35 MG SODIUM.

Roasted Garlic Bagna Caulda

PREP TIME: 5 MINUTES | **START TO FINISH:** 1 HOUR | **TO MAKE AHEAD:** THE BAGNA CAULDA WILL KEEP, TIGHTLY COVERED, IN THE REFRIGERATOR FOR UP TO 2 DAYS. | **EASE OF PREPARATION:** EASY

The name of this traditional sauce from the Piedmont region of Italy means literally "warm bath." Serve warm with plenty of fresh vegetables and bread for dipping.

- 1 head garlic, roasted (*see Tip, page 80*)
- 1 cup extra-virgin olive oil
- 1 2-ounce can anchovies, rinsed
- Pinch of crushed red pepper

1. When garlic is cool enough to handle, squeeze cloves out of their skins into a small bowl. Mash with a fork.

2. Combine garlic, oil and anchovies in a small saucepan. Simmer over low heat, stirring often, until the garlic and anchovies have broken down completely, about 15 minutes. Stir in crushed red pepper. Serve warm.

MAKES 1¼ CUPS.

PER TABLESPOON: 112 CALORIES; 12 G FAT (2 G SAT, 9 G MONO); 2 MG CHOLESTEROL; 1 G CARBOHYDRATE; 1 G PROTEIN; 0 G FIBER; 104 MG SODIUM.

Lower Carbs

Tuna-Caper Spread

PREP TIME: 10 MINUTES | **START TO FINISH:** 10 MINUTES | **TO MAKE AHEAD:** THE SPREAD WILL KEEP, COVERED, IN THE REFRIGERATOR FOR UP TO 2 DAYS. | **EASE OF PREPARATION:** EASY

Delicious, easy, inexpensive; serve as a sandwich filling or an hors d'oeuvre with whole-grain crackers or triangles of rye bread.

- **1 6-ounce can light tuna in water, drained (*see Note*)**
- **4 ounces reduced-fat cream cheese (½ cup)**
- **1 tablespoon extra-virgin olive oil**
- **2 teaspoons lemon juice**
- **⅛ teaspoon cayenne pepper, or more to taste**
- **3 tablespoons capers, rinsed and chopped**
- **2 tablespoons chopped fresh parsley**
- **1½ teaspoons chopped fresh thyme *or* ½ teaspoon dried thyme leaves**

Combine tuna, cream cheese, oil, lemon juice and cayenne in a food processor and process until smooth. Transfer to a serving bowl; stir in capers, parsley and thyme.

MAKES 1 CUP.

PER TABLESPOON: 39 CALORIES; 3 G FAT (1 G SAT, 1 G MONO); 9 MG CHOLESTEROL; 0 G CARBOHYDRATE; 3 G PROTEIN; 0 G FIBER; 112 MG SODIUM.

INGREDIENT NOTE:
"Light" canned tuna has very low levels of mercury in comparison to "white" canned tuna and tuna steaks. (*See "Essential EatingWell Seafood Guide," page 260.*)

Black Bean Dip

PREP TIME: 10 MINUTES | **START TO FINISH:** 10 MINUTES | **TO MAKE AHEAD:** THE DIP WILL KEEP, COVERED, IN THE REFRIGERATOR FOR UP TO 2 DAYS. | **EASE OF PREPARATION:** EASY

This lively dip can be made in minutes. Serve with baked tortilla chips (*below*).

- **1 19-ounce *or* 15½-ounce can black beans, rinsed**
- **½ cup prepared salsa, hot *or* mild**
- **2 tablespoons fresh lime juice**
- **2 tablespoons chopped fresh cilantro**
- **¼ teaspoon ground cumin**
- **Salt & freshly ground pepper to taste**

Combine black beans, salsa, lime juice, cilantro and cumin in a food processor. Process until smooth. Season with salt and pepper.

MAKES ABOUT 1½ CUPS.

PER TABLESPOON: 17 CALORIES; 0 G FAT (0 G SAT, 0 G MONO); 0 MG CHOLESTEROL; 3 G CARBOHYDRATE; 1 G PROTEIN; 1 G FIBER; 65 MG SODIUM.

Dippers

PREP TIME: 5 MINUTES | **START TO FINISH:** 15 MINUTES

TO MAKE AHEAD: BOTH CHIPS AND CRISPS WILL KEEP, IN AN AIRTIGHT CONTAINER AT ROOM TEMPERATURE, FOR UP TO 1 WEEK OR IN THE FREEZER FOR UP TO 2 MONTHS. | **EASE OF PREPARATION:** EASY

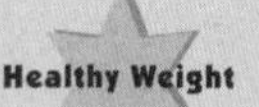

TORTILLA CHIPS

Lower Carbs

It's definitely worth making your own—fresh-baked low-fat chips have a more pronounced corn flavor than store-bought.

Preheat oven to 400°F. Lightly brush one side of 4 corn tortillas with about ¼ teaspoon canola oil each and sprinkle with a pinch of salt. Stack the tortillas and cut into 8 wedges; arrange on lightly oiled baking sheets. Bake until crisp, 8 to 10 minutes.

MAKES 32 TORTILLA CHIPS.

PER CHIP: 8 CALORIES; 0 G FAT (0 G SAT, 0 G MONO); 0 MG CHOLESTEROL; 2 G CARBOHYDRATE; 0 G PROTEIN; 0 G FIBER; 23 MG SODIUM.

TOASTED PITA CRISPS

Healthy Weight

Lower Carbs

A basket of low-fat pita crisps provides the perfect scoop for dips and spreads.

Preheat oven to 425°F. Cut 4 whole-wheat pita breads into 4 triangles each. Separate each triangle into 2 halves at the fold. Arrange, rough side up, on a baking sheet. Spritz lightly with olive oil cooking spray or brush lightly with olive oil. Bake until crisp, 8 to 10 minutes.

MAKES 32 PITA CRISPS.

PER CRISP: 23 CALORIES; 0 G FAT (0 G SAT, 0 G MONO); 0 MG CHOLESTEROL; 4 G CARBOHYDRATE; 1 G PROTEIN; 1 G FIBER; 43 MG SODIUM.

Lower Carbs

Edamame-Feta Dip

PREP TIME: 20 MINUTES | **START TO FINISH:** 1 HOUR (INCLUDING ½ HOUR RESTING TIME)
TO MAKE AHEAD: THE DIP WILL KEEP, COVERED, IN THE REFRIGERATOR FOR UP TO 2 DAYS.
EASE OF PREPARATION: EASY

This mint-green Mediterranean-flavored dip is inspired by the Greek spread known as *skordalia.* Be sure to use the best, fruitiest olive oil in your pantry, because its flavor will really come through. Serve with Toasted Pita Crisps (*page 47*). The dip also makes a delicious sandwich filling spread on whole-grain bread and topped with fresh vegetables.

- **2 cups frozen shelled edamame** (*see Ingredient Note, page 394*)
- **3 cloves garlic, peeled**
- **½ cup crumbled feta cheese**
- **2½ tablespoons lemon juice**
- **2 tablespoons extra-virgin olive oil**
- **¼ teaspoon salt, or to taste**
- **¼ teaspoon freshly ground pepper**

1. Bring a large saucepan of lightly salted water to a boil. Add edamame and garlic; return to a boil. Reduce heat to medium-low and simmer until edamame are tender, about 5 minutes. Drain, reserving ½ cup cooking liquid.

2. Place the edamame, garlic, ¼ cup of the cooking liquid, feta, lemon juice, oil, salt and pepper in a food processor or blender. Puree, scraping down the sides as needed, until completely smooth. Transfer to a serving bowl or storage container.

3. Place plastic wrap directly on the surface of the dip and let stand for 30 minutes at room temperature to allow flavors to blend. Thin with additional cooking liquid to desired consistency, if necessary. Serve at room temperature.

MAKES 1¾ CUPS.

PER TABLESPOON: 31 CALORIES; 2 G FAT (1 G SAT, 1 G MONO); 2 MG CHOLESTEROL; 2 G CARBOHYDRATE; 2 G PROTEIN; 1 G FIBER; 55 MG SODIUM.

6 Smart Snacks

Noshing and nutrition go hand-in-hand with these easy, healthful snacks.

GORP: Combine equal amounts of whole unpeeled almonds, unsalted dry-roasted peanuts, dried cranberries and chopped pitted dates. Toss in a handful of chocolate chips for a treat.

CHEESY POPCORN: Toss hot popcorn with grated Parmesan, 1 tablespoon extra-virgin olive oil and a pinch of cayenne pepper.

EGGCETERA: Dip slices of hard-cooked egg (*see box, page 82*) in extra-virgin olive oil and sprinkle with kosher salt and paprika.

SARDINES ON CRACKERS: Top whole-grain Scandinavian-style crackers (Wasa, Ry Krisp, Ryvita, Kavli) with canned sardines, preferably packed in olive oil. Finish with a squeeze of lemon.

SESAME CARROTS: Toss 2 cups of baby carrots with 1 tablespoon toasted sesame seeds and a pinch each of dried thyme and kosher salt.

TURKEY ROLLUPS: Spread slices of deli turkey breast with honey mustard or mango chutney and season with freshly ground pepper. Wrap turkey around breadsticks. For a snappy touch, tie with a blanched chive.

Marinated Olives

PREP TIME: 10 MINUTES | **START TO FINISH:** 10 MINUTES | **EASE OF PREPARATION:** EASY

When you need an easy, make-ahead hors d'oeuvre, just toss olives with one of these three quick marinades.

GARLIC-HERB: Combine 1 tablespoon dried oregano, 6 peeled and smashed garlic cloves, ½ cup red-wine vinegar and 2 teaspoons extra-virgin olive oil. Toss with 2 cups Kalamata olives.

MAKES 16 SERVINGS.

PER SERVING: 68 CALORIES; 6 G FAT (1 G SAT, 5 G MONO); 0 MG CHOLESTEROL; 3 G CARBOHYDRATE; 0 G PROTEIN; 0 G FIBER; 348 MG SODIUM.

ROSEMARY-LEMON: Combine 4 teaspoons fresh rosemary leaves, 5 strips lemon zest (preferably organic), 4 peeled and smashed garlic cloves, 1 teaspoon whole black peppercorns, ½ cup lemon juice and 2 teaspoons extra-virgin olive oil. Toss with 2 cups cracked green olives.

MAKES 16 SERVINGS.

PER SERVING: 40 CALORIES; 4 G FAT (1 G SAT, 3 G MONO); 0 MG CHOLESTEROL; 2 G CARBOHYDRATE; 0 G PROTEIN; 1 G FIBER; 331 MG SODIUM.

ZESTY ORANGE: Combine 2 teaspoons crushed cumin seeds, 1 teaspoon caraway seeds, ½ teaspoon crushed red pepper, 3 strips orange zest (preferably organic), ½ cup fresh orange juice and 2 teaspoons extra-virgin olive oil. Toss with 2 cups oil-cured olives.

MAKES 16 SERVINGS.

PER SERVING: 110 CALORIES; 9 G FAT (2 G SAT, 0 G MONO); 0 MG CHOLESTEROL; 5 G CARBOHYDRATE; 0 G PROTEIN; 0 G FIBER; 596 MG SODIUM.

SOUPS

3

"Between soup and love," goes an old Spanish saying, "the first is better." Perhaps, but we tend to think that the two go hand-in-hand, that tending a pot of homemade soup is love, an unmistakable offering of comfort and care. And there's hardly a better vehicle for eating well. Soups, by their very nature, are steeped in the stuff of good health—fresh vegetables and wholesome grains, beans, chicken and seafood. The specifics depend on what's on hand and the fancy of the cook. Here are a few of our favorites, guaranteed to be nourishing and delicious. Where they fall on the soup-love spectrum, we'll leave to you.

SOUPS

Chicken Noodle Soup with Dill

PREP TIME: 20 MINUTES | **START TO FINISH:** 50 MINUTES | **TO MAKE AHEAD:** THE SOUP WILL KEEP, COVERED, IN THE REFRIGERATOR FOR UP TO 2 DAYS. | **EASE OF PREPARATION:** EASY

This recipe for "grandma's penicillin" has a long lineage. Passed from mother to daughter, friend to friend, on to EATINGWELL recipe tester Deidre Senior, each cook has given the recipe her own touch, resulting in a superb healing antidote to any winter chill.

- **10 cups chicken broth, homemade (*page 67*) *or* reduced-sodium canned**
- **3 medium carrots, peeled and diced**
- **1 large stalk celery, diced**
- **3 tablespoons minced fresh ginger**
- **6 cloves garlic, minced**
- **4 ounces dried egg noodles (3 cups)**
- **4 cups shredded cooked skinless chicken (about 1 pound)**
- **3 tablespoons chopped fresh dill**
- **1 tablespoon lemon juice, or to taste**

1. Bring broth to a boil in a Dutch oven. Add carrots, celery, ginger and garlic; cook, uncovered, over medium heat until vegetables are just tender, about 20 minutes.

2. Add noodles and chicken; continue cooking until the noodles are just tender, 8 to 10 minutes. Stir in dill and lemon juice.

MAKES 9 SERVINGS, ABOUT 1 CUP EACH.

PER SERVING: 191 CALORIES; 4 G FAT (2 G SAT, 1 G MONO); 64 MG CHOLESTEROL; 14 G CARBOHYDRATE; 24 G PROTEIN; 1 G FIBER; 182 MG SODIUM.

NUTRITION BONUS: 50% DV VITAMIN A.

Moroccan Chicken Soup

PREP TIME: 25 MINUTES | **START TO FINISH:** 45 MINUTES | **TO MAKE AHEAD:** THE SOUP WILL KEEP, COVERED, IN THE REFRIGERATOR FOR UP TO 2 DAYS. | **EASE OF PREPARATION:** EASY

To make this soup more like a stew, serve in shallow bowls over couscous. For a spicy finish, pass your favorite hot sauce at the table.

- **1 tablespoon sweet paprika**
- **2 teaspoons ground cumin**
- **½ teaspoon ground coriander**
- **1 pound boneless, skinless chicken breasts, trimmed**
- **1 tablespoon extra-virgin olive oil**
- **2 onions, chopped**
- **2 cloves garlic, minced**
- **½ teaspoon saffron threads, crushed (optional)**
- **¼ teaspoon cayenne pepper**
- **1 cinnamon stick**
- **6 cups reduced-sodium chicken broth**
- **½ small butternut squash, peeled and diced (1 cup)**
- **1 red bell pepper, seeded and diced**
- **1 zucchini, diced**
- **1 carrot, grated**
- **2 tablespoons lemon juice**
- **¼ cup chopped fresh mint *or* parsley for garnish**

1. Combine paprika, cumin and coriander in a small bowl. Cut chicken into ½-inch strips. Transfer to a bowl and toss with 1 tablespoon of the spice mixture.

2. Heat oil in a Dutch oven or large pot over medium heat. Add chicken and cook until browned, 3 to 4 minutes. Transfer to a plate.

3. Add onions and garlic to the pot and cook, stirring, until softened, about 5 minutes. Add saffron (if using), cayenne, cinnamon stick and the remaining spice mixture; cook, stirring, for 1 minute. Add broth, squash, bell pepper and the chicken. Bring to a boil. Reduce heat to low and simmer, uncovered, for 10 minutes. Add zucchini and carrot and simmer until the vegetables are tender and the chicken is cooked through, about 5 minutes. Discard cinnamon stick. Stir in lemon juice. Ladle the soup into bowls and garnish with mint (or parsley).

MAKES 6 MAIN-DISH SERVINGS, 2 CUPS EACH.

PER SERVING: 197 CALORIES; 5 G FAT (1 G SAT, 2 G MONO); 48 MG CHOLESTEROL; 16 G CARBOHYDRATE; 23 G PROTEIN; 3 G FIBER; 173 MG SODIUM.

NUTRITION BONUS: 140% DV VITAMIN A, 60 MG VITAMIN C (100% DV).

Thai Chicken & Coconut Soup

PREP TIME: 10 MINUTES | **START TO FINISH:** 45 MINUTES | **TO MAKE AHEAD:** THE SOUP WILL KEEP, COVERED, IN THE REFRIGERATOR FOR UP TO 2 DAYS. | **EASE OF PREPARATION:** EASY

Rich coconut milk and chicken broth infused with lemongrass, chiles and ginger combine to give this fragrant, spicy soup authentic Asian flavor.

- **2 stalks fresh lemongrass (*see Note*)**
- **6 coin-size slices fresh ginger, unpeeled**
- **2 cloves garlic, unpeeled**
- **2 fresh chile peppers, such as serrano *or* jalapeño**
- **2 14-ounce cans reduced-sodium chicken broth**
- **½ pound boneless skinless chicken breasts, trimmed of fat**
- **½ cup "lite" coconut milk (*see Ingredient Note, page 184*)**
- **3 tablespoons cornstarch**
- **2-3 tablespoons fresh lime juice, plus 4 thin lime slices for garnish**
- **1-2 teaspoons fish sauce (*see Ingredient Note, page 395*) *or* reduced-sodium soy sauce**
- **2 scallions, trimmed and sliced**
- **¼ cup fresh cilantro leaves**

1. Trim lemongrass stalks of root ends, outer leaves and grassy tops. Cut into 2-inch lengths. Smash each piece with the flat of a chef's knife. Crush ginger and garlic (do not peel) with the knife. Trim stems from chiles, cut in half lengthwise and smash (for maximum heat do not remove the seeds).

2. Place the crushed lemongrass, garlic, ginger and chiles in a wide pan and pour in broth. Bring to a simmer, skimming off any foam that rises to the surface.

3. Add chicken breasts to the broth. Cover and simmer gently over low heat just until the chicken is cooked through, 10 to 12 minutes. With tongs, transfer the chicken to a cutting board and set aside.

4. Bring the broth to a lively boil and boil for about 5 minutes to intensify the flavors. Strain the broth into a saucepan, pressing on the solids to extract all the juices. Stir in coconut milk and heat through over medium heat.

5. Stir together cornstarch, 2 tablespoons lime juice and 1 teaspoon fish sauce (or soy sauce) in a small bowl. Add to the soup and cook, stirring, until simmering and slightly thickened, 2 to 3 minutes.

6. Thinly slice the poached chicken and add to the soup. Season with additional lime juice and fish sauce (or soy sauce). Ladle the soup into bowls and float a lime slice, some scallions and cilantro leaves in each one.

INGREDIENT NOTE:
Lemongrass is an aromatic tropical grass used to add a pungent, lemony flavor to Asian dishes. It is available fresh at large supermarkets and Asian groceries.

MAKES 4 SERVINGS, SCANT 1 CUP EACH.

PER SERVING: 152 CALORIES; 4 G FAT (2 G SAT, 0 G MONO); 36 MG CHOLESTEROL; 12 G CARBOHYDRATE; 17 G PROTEIN; 0 G FIBER; 200 MG SODIUM.

Chickpea & Pasta Soup

PREP TIME: 15 MINUTES | **START TO FINISH:** 50 MINUTES | **TO MAKE AHEAD:** PREPARE THROUGH STEP 1. THE SOUP WILL KEEP, COVERED, IN THE REFRIGERATOR FOR UP TO 2 DAYS. | **EASE OF PREPARATION:** EASY

This easy soup with its full, rich flavor is hearty enough to make a meal. The shape of the pasta is important to the final texture of the soup. Ditalini and tubetti are very short macaroni that can be found in most supermarkets.

- **1 15½-ounce *or* 19-ounce can chickpeas, rinsed (*see page 93*)**
- **5 cups reduced-sodium chicken broth**
- **½ cup canned diced tomatoes (*not* drained)**
- **2 tablespoons extra-virgin olive oil, plus 2 teaspoons for garnish**
- **1 large clove garlic, minced**
- **1 teaspoon chopped fresh rosemary**
- **Pinch of crushed red pepper**
- **¼ teaspoon salt, or to taste**
- **Freshly ground pepper to taste**
- **½ cup short pasta, such as ditalini *or* tubetti**

1. Combine chickpeas, broth, tomatoes, 2 tablespoons oil, garlic, rosemary and crushed red pepper in a 4- to 6-quart Dutch oven or soup pot. Bring to a boil over high heat. Reduce heat to medium-low and simmer for 20 minutes.

2. Transfer half the soup to a blender or food processor and process until smooth. Return the pureed soup to the pot; season with salt and pepper. Bring to a boil over high heat. Add pasta and cook, stirring frequently to prevent it from sticking to the bottom, until the pasta is just tender, about 10 minutes. Drizzle ½ teaspoon oil over each serving and serve immediately.

MAKES 4 SERVINGS, 1 CUP EACH.

PER SERVING: 280 CALORIES; 10 G FAT (2 G SAT, 5 G MONO); 5 MG CHOLESTEROL; 38 G CARBOHYDRATE; 11 G PROTEIN; 6 G FIBER; 628 MG SODIUM.

NUTRITION BONUS: 99 MCG FOLATE (25% DV), 22% DV FIBER.

Lower Carbs

Mushroom-Barley Soup

PREP TIME: 25 MINUTES | **START TO FINISH:** 55 MINUTES | **TO MAKE AHEAD:** THE SOUP WILL KEEP, COVERED, IN THE REFRIGERATOR FOR UP TO 2 DAYS. | **EASE OF PREPARATION:** EASY

Cooking a nutritious barley soup like this one was once unthinkable on a busy weeknight. But with quick-cooking grains and good canned broth available, this simple, comforting dinner can be on the table in under an hour.

- 1 tablespoon extra-virgin olive oil
- 2 onions, chopped
- 3 cloves garlic, minced
- 1 pound mushrooms, wiped clean and sliced (6 cups)
- 1½ tablespoons all-purpose flour
- 6 cups reduced-sodium chicken broth *or* vegetable broth
- ½ butternut squash, peeled and diced (about 1½ cups)
- 1 red bell pepper, diced
- 1 cup quick-cooking barley (*see Note*)
- ¼ cup medium-dry sherry
- 4 tablespoons chopped fresh dill, divided
- ¼ teaspoon salt, or to taste
- Freshly ground pepper to taste
- ⅓ cup reduced-fat sour cream *or* nonfat plain yogurt (optional)

1. Heat oil in a Dutch oven or large pot over medium heat. Add onions and garlic; cook, stirring, until softened, about 5 minutes. Increase heat to high; add mushrooms and cook, stirring often, until browned and liquid has evaporated, about 7 minutes more.
2. Reduce heat to medium and sprinkle flour over vegetables; cook, stirring constantly, for 1 minute. Add broth, squash, bell pepper, barley and sherry. Bring to a boil, reduce heat to low and simmer, partially covered, until barley is tender, 15 to 20 minutes. Add 2 tablespoons dill and season with salt and pepper.
3. Ladle soup into bowls and garnish with sour cream (or yogurt), if using, and the remaining 2 tablespoons dill.

INGREDIENT NOTE: Quick-cooking barley is rolled thinner than traditional pearl barley, so the cooking time is about 20 to 30 minutes shorter. It can be found in supermarkets and health-food stores.

MAKES 10 SERVINGS, ABOUT 1 CUP EACH.

PER SERVING: 132 CALORIES; 3 G FAT (1 G SAT, 1 G MONO); 2 MG CHOLESTEROL; 22 G CARBOHYDRATE; 6 G PROTEIN; 3 G FIBER; 128 MG SODIUM.

NUTRITION BONUS: 80% DV VITAMIN A, 34 MG VITAMIN C (60% DV), 14% DV FIBER.

Southwestern Tomato & Pinto Bean Soup

PREP TIME: 25 MINUTES | **START TO FINISH:** 50 MINUTES | **TO MAKE AHEAD:** THE SOUP WILL KEEP, COVERED, IN THE REFRIGERATOR FOR UP TO 2 DAYS. | **EASE OF PREPARATION:** EASY

Roasted poblano chiles lend a smoky depth of flavor to a soup that's as good to eat as it is good for you. The spicy broth gets its body—and nutrition—from lycopene-rich tomatoes and fiber- and protein-packed pinto beans. (*Photo: page 210.*)

- 2 corn tortillas
- 1 poblano chile (*see Note*) *or* one 4½-ounce can chopped green chiles
- 2 15½-ounce cans pinto beans, rinsed
- 2 teaspoons extra-virgin olive oil
- 1 medium onion, chopped
- 2 cloves garlic, minced
- 3 cups vegetable broth *or* reduced-sodium chicken broth
- 1 14½-ounce can diced tomatoes, preferably fire-roasted (*not* drained)
- 1 teaspoon ground cumin
- ⅓ cup reduced-fat sour cream for garnish
- 2 tablespoons coarsely chopped fresh cilantro for garnish
- 2 limes, cut into wedges, for garnish

1. Preheat oven to 425°F. Stack tortillas and cut crosswise into thirds, then rotate 90° and cut into ¼-inch-wide strips; scatter in a baking pan. Toast until browned and crisp, stirring once, about 10 minutes.

2. Meanwhile, if using a fresh poblano, roast it over a gas burner, turning often with tongs, until the skin is blackened, about 10 minutes. (*Alternatively, cut it in half and broil, skin-side up, for 15 minutes.*) Place in a bowl, cover with plastic wrap and let steam for 5 minutes to loosen skin. Scrape off the charred skin; core and remove seeds and inner membranes; cut poblano into ½-inch dice.

3. Mash 1 cup of beans in a small bowl with a fork.

4. Heat oil in a soup pot or Dutch oven over medium heat; add onion and cook, stirring often, until softened, 3 to 4 minutes. Add garlic and cook, stirring, until fragrant, 30 seconds to 1 minute. Add broth, tomatoes, cumin, diced poblano (or green chiles), mashed and whole beans to the pot; bring just to a boil. Reduce heat to low and simmer, uncovered, for 10 minutes.

5. To serve, ladle the soup into bowls and garnish each serving with a dollop of sour cream, a sprinkling of cilantro, toasted tortilla strips and a lime wedge.

INGREDIENT NOTE: The dark green poblano chile turns reddish brown as it ripens. The flavor ranges from mild to pungent. Dried, it is known as an ancho or mulato. Fresh poblanos are sold in Mexican markets and many supermarkets.

MAKES 6 SERVINGS, ABOUT 1 CUP EACH.

PER SERVING: 193 CALORIES; 2 G FAT (0 G SAT, 1 G MONO); 0 MG CHOLESTEROL; 34 G CARBOHYDRATE; 9 G PROTEIN; 10 G FIBER; 291 MG SODIUM.

NUTRITION BONUS: 39% DV FIBER, 3 MG IRON (15% DV), 56 MG MAGNESIUM (14% DV).

Italian Peasant Soup with Cabbage, Beans & Cheese

PREP TIME: 20 MINUTES | **START TO FINISH:** 40 MINUTES | **TO MAKE AHEAD:** PREPARE THROUGH STEP 2. COVER AND REFRIGERATE FOR UP TO 2 DAYS. REHEAT ON THE STOVETOP. | **EASE OF PREPARATION:** EASY

A well-stocked pantry (*see page 398*) is a good starting point for making a hearty homemade soup like this one—just add some fresh vegetables, bread and cheese and you've got dinner (and tomorrow's lunch).

- **2 19-ounce *or* 15½-ounce cans cannellini beans, rinsed, divided**
- **3 tablespoons extra-virgin olive oil, divided**
- **1 medium onion, halved and sliced**
- **4 cups shredded Savoy cabbage (½ medium head)**
- **3 cloves garlic, minced, plus 1 clove garlic, halved**
- **3 14½-ounce cans reduced-sodium chicken broth *or* 5¼ cups vegetable broth (*see page 67*)**
- **Freshly ground pepper to taste**
- **8 ½-inch-thick slices day-old whole-wheat country bread**
- **1 cup grated fontina cheese *or* ½ cup Parmesan cheese**

1. Mash 1½ cups beans with a fork.
2. Heat 1 teaspoon oil over medium heat in a Dutch oven or soup pot. Add onion and cook, stirring often, until softened and lightly browned, 2 to 3 minutes. Add cabbage and minced garlic; cook, stirring often, until the cabbage has wilted, 2 to 3 minutes. Add broth, mashed beans and whole beans; bring to a simmer. Reduce heat to medium-low, partially cover and simmer until the cabbage is tender, 10 to 12 minutes. Season with pepper.
3. Shortly before the soup is ready, toast bread lightly and rub with the cut side of the garlic clove (lightly or heavily depending on taste). Divide toast among 8 soup plates. Ladle soup over the toast and sprinkle with cheese. Drizzle about 1 teaspoon oil over each serving. Serve immediately.

MAKES 8 SERVINGS, 1 CUP EACH.

PER SERVING: 303 CALORIES; 12 G FAT (4 G SAT, 5 G MONO); 18 MG CHOLESTEROL; 38 G CARBOHYDRATE; 14 G PROTEIN; 12 G FIBER; 552 MG SODIUM.

NUTRITION BONUS: 47% DV FIBER, 245 MG CALCIUM (25% DV), 69 MCG FOLATE (17% DV).

Split Pea Soup

PREP TIME: 20 MINUTES | **START TO FINISH:** 1 HOUR | **TO MAKE AHEAD:** PREPARE THROUGH STEP 1. COVER AND REFRIGERATE FOR UP TO 2 DAYS. | **EASE OF PREPARATION:** EASY

Sit down to the hearty old-fashioned comfort of split pea soup in just an hour.

- **2 teaspoons extra-virgin olive oil**
- **2 carrots, diced**
- **1 onion, chopped**
- **1 all-purpose potato, peeled and diced**
- **1 sweet potato, peeled and diced**
- **2 cloves garlic, minced**
- **6 cups reduced-sodium chicken broth *or* vegetable broth**
- **1 cup green split peas, rinsed**
- **Freshly ground pepper to taste**
- **4 slices reduced-fat bacon *or* turkey bacon, diced (optional)**
- **1½ cups Rye Croutons (*recipe follows*)**

1. Heat oil in a Dutch oven or large pot over medium-high heat. Add carrots, onion, potato, sweet potato and garlic; cook, stirring, until softened, about 3 minutes. Add broth and split peas and bring to a boil. Reduce heat to low and simmer, partially covered, until the vegetables are tender and the split peas have broken down, about 40 minutes. Season with pepper.
2. Meanwhile, cook bacon (if using) in a small skillet over medium heat, stirring, until crisp, 3 to 5 minutes. Drain on paper towels.
3. Ladle the soup into bowls and garnish with bacon and croutons.

MAKES 6 SERVINGS, GENEROUS 1 CUP EACH.

PER SERVING: 240 CALORIES; 6 G FAT (1 G SAT, 3 G MONO); 4 MG CHOLESTEROL; 43 G CARBOHYDRATE; 13 G PROTEIN; 11 G FIBER; 346 MG SODIUM.

NUTRITION BONUS: 120% DV VITAMIN A, 45% DV FIBER.

RYE CROUTONS

PREP TIME: 5 MINUTES | **START TO FINISH:** 20 MINUTES | **EASE OF PREPARATION:** EASY

- **1 tablespoon extra-virgin olive oil**
- **1 clove garlic, minced**
- **¼ teaspoon salt, or to taste**
- **¼ teaspoon freshly ground pepper**
- **1 tablespoon chopped fresh dill *or* 1 teaspoon dried**
- **3 slices rye *or* pumpernickel bread, crusts removed, cut into ½-inch cubes (2 cups)**

1. Preheat oven to 350°F.
2. Combine oil, garlic, salt, pepper and dill in a medium bowl. Add bread cubes and toss to coat. Spread on a baking sheet.
3. Bake the croutons until lightly browned and crisp, about 15 minutes. (*The croutons are best served the day they are baked.*)

MAKES 6 SERVINGS, ABOUT ¼ CUP EACH.

PER SERVING: 64 CALORIES; 3 G FAT (0 G SAT, 2 G MONO); 0 MG CHOLESTEROL; 8 G CARBOHYDRATE; 1 G PROTEIN; 1 G FIBER; 203 MG SODIUM.

Oyster Bisque

PREP TIME: 25 MINUTES | **START TO FINISH:** 1 HOUR
TO MAKE AHEAD: PREPARE THROUGH STEP 3. STORE THE VEGETABLE GARNISH AND PUREE IN SEPARATE, COVERED CONTAINERS IN THE REFRIGERATOR FOR UP TO 8 HOURS. | **EASE OF PREPARATION:** MODERATE

Pureed rice thickens the bisque, giving it a soft flavor that marries well with the sweet oysters.

- 2 carrots, cut into 2-inch-long julienne strips (1 cup)
- 2 leeks, trimmed, washed (*see Cooking Tip, page 397*) and cut into 2-inch-long julienne strips (1 cup)
- 1 tablespoon canola oil
- 2 onions, finely chopped
- ½ cup long-grain white rice
- 6 cups fish stock (*recipe follows*) *or* 3 cups clam juice diluted with 3 cups water, divided
- 1 cup 1% milk
- 1 pint shucked oysters with their liquor
- Salt & freshly ground pepper to taste

1. Blanch carrots and leeks in boiling salted water until tender, 1 to 2 minutes. Drain and refresh under cold running water. Spread the julienned vegetables on paper towels and pat dry; set aside.

2. Heat oil in a large (4-quart) saucepan over medium-high heat. Add onions and cook, stirring often, until softened, about 2 minutes. Stir in rice and cook for about 2 minutes. Pour in 4 cups fish stock (or diluted clam juice) and increase heat to high. Bring to a boil, stirring often, then reduce heat to medium-low. Cover and cook for 25 minutes, or until the rice is very soft.

3. Puree the mixture in a blender or food processor until very smooth. Return the puree to the pan; pour in milk and the remaining 2 cups stock (or diluted clam juice). Bring to a simmer over medium-high heat. Stir in oysters and their liquor and cook gently for 3 minutes, or until the oysters are curled at the edges. Season with salt and pepper. Ladle the bisque into bowls and garnish with the julienned carrots and leeks.

MAKES 10 SERVINGS, ABOUT ¾ CUP EACH.

PER SERVING: 137 CALORIES; 4 G FAT (1 G SAT, 1 G MONO); 29 MG CHOLESTEROL; 16 G CARBOHYDRATE; 9 G PROTEIN; 1 G FIBER; 362 MG SODIUM.

NUTRITION BONUS: 35% DV VITAMIN A, 4 MG IRON (20% DV).

Fish Stock

1. Place 2 pounds fish heads and bones (from nonoily whitefish) in a colander and rinse well under cold running water. Set aside.

2. In a large pot, heat 2 teaspoons olive oil over medium heat. Add 2 chopped onions and cook until translucent, about 5 minutes. Add 2 chopped celery stalks and 1 chopped leek and cook for 1 minute. Add fish heads/bones and cook for 1 minute.

3. Add 1½ cups dry white wine, 1½ quarts water, ½ teaspoon white peppercorns, 1 bay leaf and 1 teaspoon chopped fresh thyme. Bring to a slow simmer. Simmer for 30 minutes, skimming off foam as it rises. Remove from heat and let stand for 10 minutes.

4. Strain through a fine sieve lined with cheesecloth into a bowl. Let cool. Refrigerate for up to 2 days or freeze for up to 6 months. Makes about 1½ quarts.

Smoky Corn & Lobster Stew

PREP TIME: 1½ HOURS | **START TO FINISH:** 2½ HOURS | **EASE OF PREPARATION:** CHALLENGING

Dreaming of the Maine coast on a breezy summer night? Savor a bowl of this stew and you're there.

- 2 large ears corn, unhusked
- 7 cups water
- 1 cup dry white wine
- 1 small bay leaf
- 2 medium leeks, white and light green parts only, washed (*see Cooking Tip, page 397*), divided
- 2 live lobsters, 1-1¼ pounds each
- 4 plum tomatoes, halved lengthwise and seeded (¾ pound)
- 1 medium red onion, peeled and quartered
- 6 small red potatoes, scrubbed and cut into 1-inch cubes (½ pound)
- Salt & freshly ground pepper to taste
- 1 tablespoon chopped fresh basil
- Hot pepper sauce to taste

1. Soak corn in a bowl of cold water for 30 minutes.
2. Meanwhile, bring 7 cups water, wine, bay leaf and 1 leek to a boil in a large pot. Add lobsters and cover. Cook until the lobsters turn bright red, about 10 minutes. Transfer the lobsters to a cutting board. Reserve cooking liquid.
3. When the lobsters are cool enough to handle, twist off tails and claws. Using kitchen shears, cut the underside of the tail shells in half; pull out meat. Crack the claws with a nutcracker or hammer and remove meat. Cut the lobster meat into ½-inch pieces; place in a bowl, cover and refrigerate. Return shells to the cooking liquid.
4. Prepare a charcoal fire or preheat a gas grill. Oil the grill rack.
5. Drain the corn and grill with the remaining leek, tomatoes and onion, turning occasionally, until charred, 4 to 5 minutes. Remove leek, tomatoes and onion. Grill corn 3 to 4 minutes longer.
6. Husk the corn. Cut the kernels from the cobs and add to the reserved lobster meat. Add husks and cobs to the reserved liquid.
7. Remove skins from the tomatoes; add the skins to the reserved liquid along with half the onion. Coarsely chop the tomato flesh, grilled leek and remaining onion and place in a small bowl. Cover and refrigerate.
8. Bring the cooking liquid to a boil over high heat. Cook until reduced to 4 cups, 25 to 30 minutes. Strain into a 4-quart pot.
9. Add potatoes, the chopped grilled vegetables, salt and pepper. Cook over medium heat until the potatoes are tender, 15 to 20 minutes. Add the reserved lobster and corn, reduce heat to low and simmer until heated through, about 2 minutes. Season with salt and pepper. Stir in basil. Serve in wide bowls, passing hot sauce separately.

MAKES 6 SERVINGS, ABOUT 1 CUP EACH.

PER SERVING: 160 CALORIES; 1 G FAT (0 G SAT, 0 G MONO); 28 MG CHOLESTEROL; 24 G CARBOHYDRATE; 11 G PROTEIN; 3 G FIBER; 196 MG SODIUM.

NUTRITION BONUS: 21 MG VITAMIN C (35% DV).

Curried Roasted Squash & Pear Soup

PREP TIME: 25 MINUTES | **START TO FINISH:** 1½ HOURS | **TO MAKE AHEAD:** THE SOUP WILL KEEP, COVERED, IN THE REFRIGERATOR FOR UP TO 2 DAYS. | **EASE OF PREPARATION:** MODERATE

A fruit or vegetable's best nature is revealed by roasting. It caramelizes the sugars and forms an irresistible golden-brown crust. The result is a warmly spiced soup rich with the sweet earthy flavors of autumn.

- 1 butternut squash (1½ pounds), peeled, seeded and cut into ¾-inch cubes
- 6 ripe but firm Bartlett pears, peeled, cored and cut into ¾-inch cubes
- 2 tablespoons extra-virgin olive oil, divided
- 1 teaspoon granulated sugar
- ¼ teaspoon salt, or to taste
- Freshly ground pepper to taste
- ½ cup water
- ⅓ cup finely chopped shallots
- 1 tablespoon dark brown sugar
- 1 2½-inch cinnamon stick
- 2 teaspoons curry powder, preferably Madras (*see Ingredient Note, page 394*)
- ½ teaspoon ground cardamom
- ¼ teaspoon ground coriander
- 6 cups reduced-sodium chicken broth
- 2 tablespoons slivered fresh mint *or* cilantro leaves

1. Preheat oven to 400°F.
2. Toss squash and pears with 1 tablespoon oil and granulated sugar on a large baking sheet with sides. Season with salt and pepper. Drizzle with water.
3. Roast squash and pears until both are tender, 30 to 40 minutes. (Add a little more water if necessary to prevent burning.) Remove any pears that are done before squash. Measure 1 cup pears and cut each cube in half; set aside.
4. In batches if necessary, puree squash and remaining pears in a food processor or blender until smooth. (Add a little chicken broth if necessary.)
5. Heat the remaining 1 tablespoon oil in a Dutch oven or soup pot over medium heat. Add shallots and cook, stirring, until softened but not browned, 3 to 5 minutes. Add brown sugar, cinnamon stick, curry powder, cardamom and coriander. Cook, stirring, for 2 minutes more.
6. Add squash-pear puree and chicken broth. Bring to a simmer. Reduce heat to low and simmer, stirring occasionally, for 25 to 30 minutes. Season with salt and pepper. Discard cinnamon stick. Add reserved pears and simmer until heated through. Ladle into warmed soup bowls and garnish with mint (or cilantro). Serve immediately.

MAKES 8 SERVINGS, ABOUT 1 CUP EACH.

PER SERVING: 181 CALORIES; 5 G FAT (1 G SAT, 3 G MONO); 3 MG CHOLESTEROL; 34 G CARBOHYDRATE; 4 G PROTEIN; 6 G FIBER; 161 MG SODIUM.

NUTRITION BONUS: 180% DV VITAMIN A, 24 MG VITAMIN C (40% DV), 24% DV FIBER.

Lower Carbs

Roasted Tomato Soup

PREP TIME: 15 MINUTES | **START TO FINISH:** 3 HOURS (INCLUDING 2½ HOURS CHILLING TIME)
TO MAKE AHEAD: THE SOUP WILL KEEP, COVERED, IN THE REFRIGERATOR FOR UP TO 2 DAYS.
EASE OF PREPARATION: EASY

Roasting tomatoes gives them an intense, sweet flavor and also makes them very easy to peel. The soup is then chilled, making a refreshing first course on a hot summer night.

- **8-10 ripe tomatoes (3 pounds), cut in half and seeded**
- **1½ teaspoons extra-virgin olive oil**
- **2 red onions, chopped**
- **1 clove garlic, minced**
- **3 cups reduced-sodium chicken broth**
- **3 tablespoons chopped fresh basil**
- **Salt & freshly ground pepper to taste**

1. Preheat broiler. Coat a baking sheet with cooking spray.
2. Place tomatoes on the prepared baking sheet, cut-side down. Broil until skins are blistered, about 10 minutes. Set aside to cool. Slip off the skins and chop the tomatoes coarsely.
3. Meanwhile, heat oil in a medium saucepan over medium-low heat. Add onions and cook, stirring often, for 5 minutes. Add garlic and cook, stirring, until the onions are very soft, about 5 minutes longer. Stir in tomatoes and cook, stirring, for 1 minute.
4. Transfer the mixture to a food processor or blender and process until smooth; return to the saucepan. Stir in broth and bring to a boil. Reduce heat to low and simmer for 5 minutes. Remove from the heat and stir in basil. Season with salt and pepper. Cover loosely and refrigerate until chilled, 2½ to 3 hours.

MAKES 6 SERVINGS, ABOUT ¾ CUP EACH.

PER SERVING: 90 CALORIES; 3 G FAT (1 G SAT, 1 G MONO); 2 MG CHOLESTEROL; 15 G CARBOHYDRATE; 4 G PROTEIN; 3 G FIBER; 124 MG SODIUM.

NUTRITION BONUS: LOW SODIUM, LYCOPENE, 62 MG VITAMIN C (103% DV), 30% DV VITAMIN A.

Lower Carbs

Leek, Asparagus & Herb Soup

PREP TIME: 15 MINUTES | **START TO FINISH:** 40 MINUTES | **TO MAKE AHEAD:** PREPARE THROUGH STEP 3. COVER AND REFRIGERATE FOR UP TO 8 HOURS. | **EASE OF PREPARATION:** MODERATE

Like a bouquet of fresh vegetables, this light but soothing soup is just the thing on a cool spring evening. It is important to cut the green vegetables into small pieces so they cook quickly, while retaining their bright color.

- 1 tablespoon extra-virgin olive oil
- 2 medium leeks, trimmed, washed (*see Cooking Tip, page 397*) and finely chopped (1½ cups)
- 2 cloves garlic, minced
- ½ pound new potatoes, scrubbed and diced (about 1⅔ cups)
- 2 cups reduced-sodium chicken broth *or* vegetable broth
- 1 pound fresh asparagus, trimmed and cut into ½-inch pieces (1½-2 cups)
- ⅔ cup snow peas *or* sugar snap peas, stemmed and cut into ½-inch dice
- 3 tablespoons chopped fresh chives, divided
- 2 tablespoons chopped fresh flat-leaf parsley
- 1 tablespoon chopped fresh dill
- 2 teaspoons chopped fresh chervil (*see Note*) *or* flat-leaf parsley, plus sprigs for garnish
- 2 cups 1% milk
- 1 tablespoon lemon juice
- ¼ teaspoon salt, or to taste
- Freshly ground pepper to taste
- ⅓ cup low-fat plain yogurt for garnish

1. Heat oil in a large saucepan over medium-low heat. Add leeks and cook, stirring often, until softened but not browned, about 5 minutes. Add garlic and cook, stirring, for 1 minute.
2. Add potatoes and broth; bring to a simmer over medium-high heat. Cover and reduce heat to medium-low. Simmer, stirring occasionally, until the potatoes are tender, 10 to 15 minutes.
3. Increase heat to medium-high and stir in asparagus and peas; simmer, covered, stirring 2 or 3 times, until just tender, 3 to 4 minutes. Remove from heat; stir in 1 tablespoon chives, parsley, dill and chopped chervil (or parsley). Transfer the soup to a blender and blend until smooth. (Use caution when pureeing hot liquids.)
4. Return the soup to the pan. Add milk and bring to just below a simmer, stirring, over medium heat. Stir in lemon juice, salt and pepper. Ladle into soup bowls. Garnish each serving with a dollop of yogurt, a sprinkling of the remaining chopped chives and a sprig of chervil (or parsley).

INGREDIENT NOTE: Chervil (from the Greek for "herb of rejoicing") has a mild flavor between those of parsley and anise. It doesn't dry well, so is best used fresh.

MAKES 6 SERVINGS, ABOUT 1 CUP EACH.

PER SERVING: 132 CALORIES; 4 G FAT (1 G SAT, 2 G MONO); 7 MG CHOLESTEROL; 18 G CARBOHYDRATE; 7 G PROTEIN; 2 G FIBER; 195 MG SODIUM.

NUTRITION BONUS: 21 MG VITAMIN C (33% DV).

Lower Carbs

High Fiber

Turkey-Barley Soup

PREP TIME: 20 MINUTES | **START TO FINISH:** 4½ HOURS (INCLUDING MAKING TURKEY BROTH) | **TO MAKE AHEAD:** THE SOUP WILL KEEP, COVERED, IN THE REFRIGERATOR FOR UP TO 2 DAYS. | **EASE OF PREPARATION:** EASY

Nutty barley and earthy, sweet root vegetables supplement leftover turkey to create a homey soup with an old-fashioned flavor. To shorten cooking time, substitute quick-cooking barley for pearl barley; add carrots and parsnips with the barley and simmer the soup for about 20 minutes total.

- 2 teaspoons extra-virgin olive oil
- 1 large onion, chopped (2 cups)
- 3 cloves garlic, minced
- ½ cup pearl barley
- 6 cups Turkey Broth (*page 241*) *or* reduced-sodium chicken broth
- 2 carrots, peeled and diced (1 cup)
- 2 medium parsnips, peeled and diced (1 cup)
- 2 cups diced skinless cooked turkey (8 ounces)
- ⅓ cup chopped fresh dill
- 2 teaspoons lemon juice
- ¼ teaspoon freshly ground pepper
- ½ teaspoon salt (optional)

1. Heat oil in heavy soup pot (4- to 6-quart capacity) over medium heat. Add onion and cook, stirring, until softened, 2 to 3 minutes. Add garlic and cook, stirring, for 30 seconds. Add barley and stir to coat. Add broth and bring to a simmer. Reduce heat to low. Skim off any froth. Cover and simmer for 20 minutes.

2. Add carrots and parsnips. Cover and simmer until the barley and vegetables are just tender, 15 to 20 minutes. Add turkey and simmer until heated through, 3 to 4 minutes more. Add dill, lemon juice and pepper. Taste and add salt, if needed. Serve hot.

MAKES 8 SERVINGS, 1 CUP EACH.

PER SERVING: 171 CALORIES; 4 G FAT (1 G SAT, 2 G MONO); 27 MG CHOLESTEROL; 19 G CARBOHYDRATE; 16 G PROTEIN; 4 G FIBER; 238 MG SODIUM.

NUTRITION BONUS: 35% DV VITAMIN A, 444 MG POTASSIUM (22% DV).

High Fiber

Vegetarian Hot Pot

PREP TIME: 15 MINUTES | **START TO FINISH:** 45 MINUTES | **EASE OF PREPARATION:** EASY

Quick to prepare, this Asian-style noodle soup has all the makings of a one-pot meal. To punch up the heat, add a dab of chile-garlic sauce.

- **5¼ cups vegetable broth *or* reduced-sodium chicken broth**
- **4 ¼-inch-thick slices fresh ginger, peeled**
- **2 cloves garlic, crushed and peeled**
- **2 teaspoons canola oil**
- **1¾ cups shiitake mushrooms, stemmed, wiped clean and sliced (4 ounces)**
- **¼ teaspoon crushed red pepper, or to taste**
- **1 small bok choy (¾ pound), cut into ½-inch pieces, stems and greens separated**
- **3½ ounces Chinese wheat noodles *or* rice sticks (*see Note*)**
- **1 14-ounce package firm tofu (*see Ingredient Note, page 396*), drained, patted dry and cut into ½-inch cubes**
- **1 cup grated carrots (2 large)**
- **4-6 teaspoons rice vinegar**
- **2 teaspoons reduced-sodium soy sauce**
- **1 teaspoon toasted sesame oil**
- **¼ cup chopped scallions for garnish**

1. Combine broth, ginger and garlic in a Dutch oven; bring to a simmer. Simmer, partially covered, over medium-low heat for 15 minutes. Discard the ginger and garlic.

2. Meanwhile, heat oil in a large nonstick skillet over medium-high heat. Add mushrooms and crushed red pepper; cook, stirring often, until tender, 3 to 5 minutes. Add bok choy stems; cook, stirring often, until tender, 3 to 4 minutes.

3. Add the mushroom mixture to the broth. Add noodles, reduce heat to medium-low and simmer for 3 minutes. Add bok choy greens and tofu; simmer until heated through, about 2 minutes. Stir in carrots, vinegar to taste, soy sauce and sesame oil. Serve garnished with scallions.

INGREDIENT NOTE: Chinese wheat noodles and rice sticks (dried rice noodles) are quick-cooking and can be found in the Asian-food section of your supermarket.

MAKES 5 MAIN-DISH SERVINGS, ABOUT 1½ CUPS EACH.

PER SERVING: 230 CALORIES; 9 G FAT (1 G SAT, 1 G MONO); 0 MG CHOLESTEROL; 26 G CARBOHYDRATE; 14 G PROTEIN; 5 G FIBER; 706 MG SODIUM.

NUTRITION BONUS: 130% DV VITAMIN A, 29 MG VITAMIN C (50% DV), 179 MG CALCIUM (20% DV), 20% DV FIBER.

Stock Essentials

CHICKEN BROTH

PREP TIME: 15 MINUTES | **START TO FINISH:** 2 HOURS 35 MINUTES | **TO MAKE AHEAD:** THE BROTH WILL KEEP, COVERED, IN THE REFRIGERATOR FOR UP TO 2 DAYS OR IN THE FREEZER FOR UP TO 3 MONTHS.
EASE OF PREPARATION: EASY

Nothing soothes, nourishes and comforts like homemade chicken broth. Canned broth is a handy standby for quick soups, but homemade delivers maximum flavor while contributing minimal calories.

- **1 3-pound chicken (or use parts, such as wings and backs)**
- **4 stalks celery (with leaves), trimmed and cut into 2-inch pieces**
- **4 medium carrots, peeled and cut into 2-inch pieces**
- **1 medium onion, peeled and quartered**
- **6 cloves garlic, peeled**
- **1 small bunch fresh parsley, washed**
- **6 sprigs fresh thyme *or* 1 teaspoon dried**
- **1 teaspoon kosher salt, or to taste**
- **4 quarts cold water**

1. Combine all ingredients in a large stockpot and bring to a boil over medium-high heat. Reduce heat to medium-low and simmer, partially covered, until the chicken is falling apart, about 2 hours. Skim the foam from the surface as it builds up.

2. Strain the broth through a large sieve or colander into a large bowl. Use a wooden spoon to press on the solids to extract as much of the broth as possible. (Reserve the chicken and vegetables to eat separately, if desired.) Divide the broth among several shallow containers so it will cool quickly. Cover loosely and refrigerate overnight. Use a spoon to remove the fat that congeals on the surface.

MAKES ABOUT 2 QUARTS.

VEGETABLE BROTH

PREP TIME: 15 MINUTES | **START TO FINISH:** 45 MINUTES
TO MAKE AHEAD: THE BROTH WILL KEEP, COVERED, IN THE REFRIGERATOR FOR UP TO 2 DAYS OR IN THE FREEZER FOR UP TO 6 MONTHS.
EASE OF PREPARATION: EASY

Making and freezing vegetable broth is well worth the minimal effort. While there are some commercial broths we like (*see page 396*), nothing beats the fresh clean flavor of homemade.

- **4 quarts water**
- **4 carrots, peeled and chopped**
- **2 medium onions, chopped**
- **2 leeks, trimmed, washed (*see Cooking Tip, page 397*) and chopped**
- **2 stalks celery, left whole**
- **8 mushrooms, trimmed, wiped clean and sliced**
- **1 tomato, quartered**
- **5 sprigs fresh parsley**
- **3 sprigs fresh thyme *or* ½ teaspoon dried**
- **½ teaspoon kosher salt, or to taste**
- **1 bay leaf**

Place all ingredients in a large stockpot. Bring to a boil over medium heat and cook, uncovered, for 30 minutes, skimming foam. Strain through a fine sieve.

MAKES ABOUT 4 QUARTS.

ANALYSIS NOTE:
After straining and skimming, broth has negligible calories and nutrients except sodium (240 mg per cup for the chicken, 120 mg per cup for the vegetable).

SALADS & DRESSINGS

4

"I'll just have a salad" is a common refrain from dispirited weight watchers, resigning themselves to yet another bowl of lettuce. Just a salad? If salad seems like punishment, you've got the wrong recipe. Sure, have salad for dinner, but make it intensely flavorful grilled vegetables with a lemony vinaigrette and garlic croutons. Going for greens? Spike them with fennel and oranges. Salads are a terrific vehicle for getting your five-a-day, as well as good fats in the form of dressings and additions like nuts and olives. Our essential salad repertoire brings all the color, texture and taste that make eating a pleasure. Choose a salad with soul.

Arugula & Pear Salad

PREP TIME: 15 MINUTES | **START TO FINISH:** 25 MINUTES | **TO MAKE AHEAD:** THE DRESSING WILL KEEP, COVERED, IN THE REFRIGERATOR FOR UP TO 2 DAYS. | **EASE OF PREPARATION:** EASY

Besides giving this salad a nutty crunch, walnuts are a rich source of omega-3 fatty acids, as well as vitamins, minerals, protein and antioxidants. For an added flavor dimension, crumble some Gorgonzola cheese over each salad.

DRESSING

- 2 tablespoons finely chopped shallot
- 3 tablespoons vegetable broth (*see Ingredient Note, page 396*)
- 3 tablespoons extra-virgin olive oil
- 1½ tablespoons balsamic vinegar
- ½ teaspoon Dijon mustard
- ¼ teaspoon salt, or to taste
- Freshly ground pepper to taste

SALAD

- ½ cup chopped walnuts
- 2 firm red Bartlett pears
- 5 cups butterhead lettuce (Bibb *or* Boston), torn into bite-size pieces
- 4 cups arugula, trimmed

1. To prepare dressing: Whisk shallot, broth, oil, vinegar, mustard, salt and pepper in a small bowl.

2. To prepare salad: Toast walnuts in a small dry skillet over medium-low heat, stirring, until fragrant, 2 to 3 minutes. Transfer to a small bowl and let cool.

3. Just before serving, cut pears into 16 slices each. Place in a large bowl. Spoon on 1 tablespoon of the dressing and toss to coat. Add lettuce, arugula and the remaining dressing; toss well. Divide among 8 plates. Top with the walnuts.

MAKES 8 SERVINGS, ABOUT 1 CUP EACH.

PER SERVING: 132 CALORIES; 10 G FAT (1 G SAT, 5 G MONO); 0 MG CHOLESTEROL; 10 G CARBOHYDRATE; 2 G PROTEIN; 2 G FIBER; 94 MG SODIUM.

NUTRITION BONUS: 30% DV VITAMIN A.

Spinach Salad with Warm Maple Dressing

PREP TIME: 15 MINUTES | **START TO FINISH:** 20 MINUTES | **EASE OF PREPARATION:** EASY

Pure maple syrup, as opposed to artificially flavored and colored "pancake" syrup, is an extraordinary cooking ingredient. Here it adds body as well as rich flavor to the dressing, providing a perfect counterpoint to the smoked cheese.

- **2 tablespoons chopped pecans**
- **1 10-ounce package fresh spinach, torn, *or* 12 cups baby spinach**
- **1 cucumber, peeled, seeded and cut into ¼-inch slices**
- **2 teaspoons extra-virgin olive oil**
- **1 shallot, finely chopped**
- **¼ cup cider vinegar**
- **2 tablespoons pure maple syrup**
- **Salt & freshly ground pepper to taste**
- **¼ cup shredded smoked cheese, such as Gouda *or* Cheddar**

1. Toast pecans in a small dry skillet over low heat, stirring often, until fragrant, 2 to 3 minutes. Transfer to a small bowl and let cool.
2. Toss spinach and cucumber in a salad bowl.
3. Heat oil in a small skillet over medium-low heat. Add shallot and cook, stirring, until softened, about 4 minutes. Add vinegar and maple syrup and bring to a boil. Season with salt and pepper.
4. Immediately pour dressing over the spinach and cucumber. Toss well and sprinkle with cheese and toasted pecans.

MAKES 4 SERVINGS, ABOUT 2 CUPS EACH.

PER SERVING: 164 CALORIES; 12 G FAT (2 G SAT, 7 G MONO); 7 MG CHOLESTEROL; 12 G CARBOHYDRATE; 4 G PROTEIN; 2 G FIBER; 182 MG SODIUM.

NUTRITION BONUS: 130% DV VITAMIN A, 146 MCG FOLATE (37% DV), 22 MG VITAMIN C (35% DV).

High Fiber

Mixed Lettuce, Fennel & Orange Salad with Black Olive Vinaigrette

PREP TIME: 25 MINUTES | **START TO FINISH:** 30 MINUTES | **TO MAKE AHEAD:** THE VINAIGRETTE WILL KEEP, COVERED, IN THE REFRIGERATOR FOR UP TO 2 DAYS. WASHED, DRIED LETTUCE WILL KEEP IN A PLASTIC BAG IN THE REFRIGERATOR FOR UP TO 8 HOURS. KEEP PREPARED ORANGES AND FENNEL IN SEPARATE CONTAINERS IN THE REFRIGERATOR FOR UP TO 8 HOURS. | **EASE OF PREPARATION:** MODERATE

This colorful salad offers a symphony of flavors and textures. Savory black olives, sweet orange slices and crisp, licorice-flavored fennel balance the slightly bitter tastes of chicory, radicchio and Belgian endive.

BLACK OLIVE VINAIGRETTE

- 1 tablespoon red-wine vinegar
- 1 tablespoon lemon juice
- 1 teaspoon Dijon mustard
- 2 cloves garlic, minced
- 1/8 teaspoon salt, or to taste
- Freshly ground pepper to taste
- 1/4 cup extra-virgin olive oil
- 1/2 cup Kalamata olives, pitted and coarsely chopped
- 1 tablespoon chopped fresh parsley

SALAD

- 3 medium navel *or* Valencia oranges
- 10 cups mixed lettuces (3 small heads), such as chicory, radicchio and leaf lettuce, torn into bite-size pieces
- 2 heads Belgian endive, sliced
- 2 bulbs fennel, trimmed and sliced

1. **To prepare vinaigrette:** Whisk vinegar, lemon juice, mustard, garlic, salt and pepper in a small bowl. Slowly whisk in oil. Stir in olives and parsley.
2. **To prepare salad:** Using a sharp knife, remove peel and white pith from oranges. Quarter the oranges; slice pieces crosswise.
3. Just before serving, combine lettuces, endive, fennel and the orange slices in a large bowl. Drizzle the vinaigrette over the salad and toss to coat well.

MAKES 8 SERVINGS, 1¾ CUPS EACH.

PER SERVING: 167 CALORIES; 10 G FAT (1 G SAT, 7 G MONO); 0 MG CHOLESTEROL; 18 G CARBOHYDRATE; 4 G PROTEIN; 7 G FIBER; 274 MG SODIUM.

NUTRITION BONUS: 100% DV VITAMIN A, 58 MG VITAMIN C (100% DV), 296 MCG FOLATE (74% DV), 30% DV FIBER.

Lower Carbs

High Fiber

The Big Salad

PREP TIME: 15 MINUTES | **START TO FINISH:** 20 MINUTES | **EASE OF PREPARATION:** EASY

Big flavors, big benefits. Loaded with vitamins and minerals, antioxidants and fiber—not to mention color, crunch and great taste—starting a meal with this salad is a healthy habit you could really live with.

- **3 tablespoons coarsely chopped walnuts**
- **4 tablespoons Mustard-Balsamic Vinaigrette (*recipe follows*)**
- **1 15½-ounce can chickpeas, rinsed**
- **1 small red onion, thinly sliced**
- **1 red bell pepper, seeded and sliced**
- **1 cup shredded carrots**
- **1 cup cauliflower florets, coarsely chopped**
- **12 Kalamata olives, pitted and finely chopped**
- **12 cups mixed salad greens**
- **½ cup crumbled feta cheese**

1. Toast walnuts in a small dry skillet over medium heat, stirring, until fragrant, 2 to 3 minutes. Transfer to a small bowl and let cool.
2. Prepare Mustard-Balsamic Vinaigrette.
3. Combine chickpeas, onion, bell pepper, carrots, cauliflower and olives in a medium bowl. Add 2 tablespoons of the vinaigrette; toss to coat. Toss greens with the remaining 2 tablespoons vinaigrette in a large bowl. Divide among 6 plates and top with the vegetable mixture. Sprinkle with feta and the walnuts. Serve immediately.

MAKES 6 SERVINGS, 2⅓ CUPS EACH.

PER SERVING: 210 CALORIES; 11 G FAT (2 G SAT, 5 G MONO); 3 MG CHOLESTEROL; 22 G CARBOHYDRATE; 8 G PROTEIN; 7 G FIBER; 393 MG SODIUM.

NUTRITION BONUS: 140% DV VITAMIN A, 83 MG VITAMIN C (140% DV), 150 MCG FOLATE (38% DV), 30% DV FIBER.

MUSTARD-BALSAMIC VINAIGRETTE

PREP TIME: 5 MINUTES | **START TO FINISH:** 5 MINUTES | **TO MAKE AHEAD:** THE VINAIGRETTE WILL KEEP, COVERED, IN THE REFRIGERATOR FOR UP TO 1 WEEK. | **EASE OF PREPARATION:** EASY

Here is a tasty all-purpose "house" dressing. Shake up a batch to keep on hand to help streamline weeknight meal preparation.

- **½ cup balsamic vinegar**
- **¼ cup extra-virgin olive oil**
- **¼ cup canola oil**
- **2 tablespoons coarse mustard**
- **1 tablespoon pure maple syrup *or* 1½ teaspoons brown sugar**
- **1 teaspoon dried basil**
- **Salt & freshly ground pepper to taste**

Combine all ingredients in a jar with a tight-fitting lid and shake well. Adjust seasoning with salt and pepper.

MAKES 1¼ CUPS.

PER TABLESPOON: 59 CALORIES; 6 G FAT (1 G SAT, 4 G MONO); 0 MG CHOLESTEROL; 2 G CARBOHYDRATE; 0 G PROTEIN; 0 G FIBER; 47 MG SODIUM.

High Fiber

Caesar Salad with Tofu Dressing

PREP TIME: 15 MINUTES | **START TO FINISH:** 20 MINUTES | **TO MAKE AHEAD:** THE DRESSING WILL KEEP, COVERED, IN THE REFRIGERATOR FOR UP TO 2 DAYS. | **EASE OF PREPARATION:** EASY

The creamy richness of this popular dressing comes from tofu, rather than the usual raw egg, eliminating food-safety worries. It's so good that you may want to make a double batch; for best results, because it becomes thicker and more garlicky by the day, use half the garlic and thin the dressing with a little water before using.

DRESSING

- 2½ ounces reduced-fat firm tofu
- 1 clove garlic, minced
- 3½ tablespoons freshly grated Parmigiano-Reggiano *or* Pecorino Romano cheese
- 2½ tablespoons lemon juice
- 2 tablespoons light mayonnaise
- 1 tablespoon Dijon mustard
- 1 teaspoon anchovy paste (optional)
- ¼ teaspoon Worcestershire sauce

SALAD

- 8 cups torn romaine lettuce leaves
- 1 cup Whole-Wheat Croutons (*recipe follows*) *or* store-bought
- 2 tablespoons grated or shaved Parmigiano-Reggiano *or* Pecorino Romano cheese (*see Tip*)
- Freshly ground pepper to taste

1. To prepare dressing: Combine tofu, garlic, cheese, lemon juice, mayonnaise, mustard, anchovy paste (if using) and Worcestershire in a food processor or blender. Pulse, scraping down the sides as needed, until smooth.

2. To prepare salad: Place lettuce and croutons in a large salad bowl; top with dressing and toss to coat well. Sprinkle with cheese and pepper and serve immediately.

TEST KITCHEN TIP: Use a vegetable peeler to shave curls off a block of Parmigiano-Reggiano or Pecorino Romano cheese.

MAKES 4 SERVINGS, 2 CUPS EACH.

PER SERVING: 132 CALORIES; 7 G FAT (2 G SAT, 3 G MONO); 8 MG CHOLESTEROL; 13 G CARBOHYDRATE; 6 G PROTEIN; 5 G FIBER; 267 MG SODIUM.

NUTRITION BONUS: 130% DV VITAMIN A, 32 MG VITAMIN C (50% DV), 154 MCG FOLATE (39% DV).

WHOLE-WHEAT CROUTONS

PREP TIME: 5 MINUTES | **START TO FINISH:** 25-30 MINUTES | **EASE OF PREPARATION:** EASY

- 1 cup cubed whole-wheat country bread
- 2 teaspoons extra-virgin olive oil

Preheat oven to 350°F. Toss cubed bread with oil. Spread on a baking sheet and bake until golden brown, turning once during baking, 20 to 25 minutes.

MAKES 4 SERVINGS, ¼ CUP EACH.

PER SERVING: 49 CALORIES; 3 G FAT (0 G SAT, 2 G MONO); 0 MG CHOLESTEROL; 7 G CARBOHYDRATE; 1 G PROTEIN; 2 G FIBER; 38 MG SODIUM.

Insalata Mista with Buttermilk-Chive Dressing

PREP TIME: 15 MINUTES | **START TO FINISH:** 15 MINUTES | **TO MAKE AHEAD:** THE DRESSING WILL KEEP, COVERED, IN THE REFRIGERATOR FOR UP TO 2 DAYS. | **EASE OF PREPARATION:** EASY

A simple "mixed salad" is irresistible with our healthful version of everybody's favorite buttermilk dressing.

DRESSING

- **1 clove garlic, unpeeled**
- **1 tablespoon reduced-fat mayonnaise**
- **¼ cup buttermilk *or* nonfat plain yogurt**
- **1 tablespoon extra-virgin olive oil**
- **1 teaspoon tarragon vinegar *or* white-wine vinegar**
- **¼ teaspoon honey *or* sugar**
- **2 tablespoons snipped fresh chives *or* scallion greens**
- **Salt & freshly ground pepper to taste**

SALAD

- **1 large *or* 2 small heads butterhead lettuce (Bibb *or* Boston), torn into bite-size pieces**
- **¼ pound fresh mushrooms, wiped clean and sliced**
- **2 medium carrots, peeled and coarsely grated**

1. To prepare dressing: Skewer garlic clove with a fork. Place mayonnaise in a small bowl. Using the skewered garlic to stir, gradually blend in buttermilk (or yogurt), oil, vinegar and honey (or sugar). Gently stir in chives (or scallions). Season with salt and pepper. Leave the garlic in the dressing until ready to toss salad, then discard.

2. To prepare salad: Just before serving, combine lettuce, mushrooms and carrots in a large salad bowl. Add dressing and toss to coat well. Taste and adjust seasonings.

MAKES 4 SERVINGS, ABOUT 2 CUPS EACH.

PER SERVING: 79 CALORIES; 5 G FAT (1 G SAT, 3 G MONO); 2 MG CHOLESTEROL; 7 G CARBOHYDRATE; 3 G PROTEIN; 2 G FIBER; 137 MG SODIUM.

NUTRITION BONUS: 120% DV VITAMIN A.

Tricolor Coleslaw

PREP TIME: 20 MINUTES | **START TO FINISH:** 20 MINUTES | **TO MAKE AHEAD:** THE COLESLAW WILL KEEP, COVERED, IN THE REFRIGERATOR FOR UP TO 2 HOURS. | **EASE OF PREPARATION:** EASY

Red and green cabbage and bright orange carrots make a colorful, healthful combination. For an especially nutty flavor, use Savoy instead of regular green cabbage.

- **3 tablespoons reduced-fat mayonnaise**
- **3 tablespoons nonfat plain yogurt**
- **1 tablespoon Dijon mustard**
- **2 teaspoons cider vinegar**
- **1 teaspoon sugar**
- **½ teaspoon caraway seed *or* celery seed (optional)**
- **Salt & freshly ground pepper to taste**
- **2 cups shredded red cabbage (¼ of a small head)**
- **2 cups shredded green cabbage (¼ of a small head)**
- **1 cup grated carrots (2 medium)**

Combine mayonnaise, yogurt, mustard, vinegar and sugar in a large bowl. Add caraway seed (or celery seed), if using. Season with salt and pepper. Add cabbage and carrots and toss well.

MAKES 6 SERVINGS, ABOUT ¾ CUP EACH.

PER SERVING: 49 CALORIES; 2 G FAT (0 G SAT, 1 G MONO); 2 MG CHOLESTEROL; 7 G CARBOHYDRATE; 1 G PROTEIN; 1 G FIBER; 153 MG SODIUM.

NUTRITION BONUS: 50% DV VITAMIN A, 22 MG VITAMIN C (35% DV).

Lower Carbs

Cool Zucchini Slaw

PREP TIME: 15 MINUTES | **START TO FINISH:** 45 MINUTES | **EASE OF PREPARATION:** EASY

Summertime—and zucchini is taking over your garden. Turn the bounty into a crisp, colorful salad.

- **1½ pounds zucchini (3 medium), grated**
- **1 medium sweet onion, such as Vidalia *or* Walla Walla, very thinly sliced**
- **1½ teaspoons coarse kosher salt**
- **1 small red bell pepper, diced**
- **¼ cup cider vinegar**
- **3 tablespoons frozen apple juice concentrate**
- **2 tablespoons chopped fresh basil**
- **Salt & freshly ground pepper to taste**

1. Place zucchini and onion in a colander set over a bowl. Add salt and toss to coat. Let drain at room temperature for 30 minutes. Rinse vegetables and squeeze to remove as much moisture as possible.

2. Transfer vegetables to a medium bowl. Add bell pepper, vinegar, apple juice concentrate and basil; toss well. Season with salt and pepper. Serve immediately.

MAKES 6 SERVINGS, ABOUT ⅔ CUP EACH.

PER SERVING: 61 CALORIES; 0 G FAT (0 G SAT, 0 G MONO); 0 MG CHOLESTEROL; 14 G CARBOHYDRATE; 2 G PROTEIN; 2 G FIBER; 534 MG SODIUM.

NUTRITION BONUS: 61 MG VITAMIN C (100% DV), 30% DV VITAMIN A.

Carrot Salad with Cumin

Lower Carbs

PREP TIME: 15 MINUTES | **START TO FINISH:** 15 MINUTES | **TO MAKE AHEAD:** THE SALAD WILL KEEP, COVERED, IN THE REFRIGERATOR FOR UP TO 1 DAY. | **EASE OF PREPARATION:** EASY

Since carrots are great keepers, this simple salad is a practical option when you haven't had time to shop for fresh leafy greens. With its bright taste and crunchy texture, the salad also adds super appeal—as well as a nice nutrition boost—to sandwiches and wraps.

- **1 pound carrots (about 6), peeled and coarsely grated**
- **½ cup chopped fresh parsley**
- **1 tablespoon lemon juice**
- **2 tablespoons extra-virgin olive oil**
- **1 clove garlic, minced**
- **½ teaspoon ground cumin**
- **¼ teaspoon salt, or to taste**
- **Freshly ground pepper to taste**

Combine all ingredients in a medium bowl; toss to mix.

MAKES 4 SERVINGS.

PER SERVING: 115 CALORIES; 7 G FAT (1 G SAT, 5 G MONO); 0 MG CHOLESTEROL; 12 G CARBOHYDRATE; 1 G PROTEIN; 4 G FIBER; 228 MG SODIUM.

NUTRITION BONUS: 290% DV VITAMIN A, 19 MG VITAMIN C (30% DV).

Green Bean Salad with Corn, Basil & Black Olives

PREP TIME: 20 MINUTES | **START TO FINISH:** 45 MINUTES

TO MAKE AHEAD: PREPARE THROUGH STEP 2. STORE GREEN BEANS AND CORN SEPARATELY, IN PLASTIC BAGS LINED WITH PAPER TOWELS, IN THE REFRIGERATOR FOR UP TO 8 HOURS. | **EASE OF PREPARATION:** EASY

This vibrant summer salad goes well with just about any entree. Be sure to get ultra-fresh beans and corn and blanch them just long enough to tenderize them and bring out their color. If they are available, use salt-cured black olives, which provide the best complement to the crisp vegetables.

- 2 pounds green beans, trimmed
- 3 ears corn, husked
- ½ small red bell pepper, finely chopped
- 1 small red onion, finely chopped
- ⅔ cup black olives, preferably salt-cured, halved and pitted
- ⅓ cup chopped fresh basil
- ¼ cup extra-virgin olive oil
- 3 tablespoons balsamic vinegar
- 3 tablespoons lemon juice
- 2 cloves garlic, minced
- Hot sauce, such as Tabasco, to taste
- Salt & freshly ground pepper to taste

1. Put a large pot of water on to boil. Fill another large pot half full with ice water. Blanch about half the green beans in the boiling water just until tender, 1 to 2 minutes. Remove with a slotted spoon and plunge into the ice water. Transfer to a large bowl. Repeat with the remaining beans.
2. Return the water to a boil. Add corn and blanch until tender but still crisp, about 3 minutes. Drain and immediately plunge into the ice water. Cut the kernels off the cobs.
3. Add the corn to the beans in the bowl. Add bell pepper, onion, olives, basil, oil, vinegar, lemon juice and garlic; toss to mix well. Season with hot sauce, salt and pepper.

MAKES 8 SERVINGS.

PER SERVING: 155 CALORIES; 8 G FAT (1 G SAT, 5 G MONO); 0 MG CHOLESTEROL; 18 G CARBOHYDRATE; 3 G PROTEIN; 6 G FIBER; 147 MG SODIUM.

NUTRITION BONUS: 28 MG VITAMIN C (45% DV), 15% DV VITAMIN A.

Three-Bean Salad

PREP TIME: 20 MINUTES | **START TO FINISH:** 30 MINUTES | **TO MAKE AHEAD:** PREPARE THROUGH STEP 2. COVER AND REFRIGERATE FOR UP TO 8 HOURS. | **EASE OF PREPARATION:** EASY

You'll forsake all previous recipes for three-bean salad once you've tried this fresh, tangy-sweet version.

- **1/3 cup cider vinegar**
- **3 tablespoons light corn syrup**
- **1 tablespoon coarse-grained mustard**
- **1 teaspoon canola oil**
- **1/2 teaspoon salt, or to taste**
- **Freshly ground pepper to taste**
- **1 small red onion, diced**
- **1 15-ounce can black-eyed peas *or* chickpeas, rinsed**
- **1 10-ounce package frozen baby lima beans *or* shelled edamame (*see Ingredient Note, page 394*)**
- **1 pound green beans, trimmed and cut diagonally into 1-inch pieces**
- **2 tablespoons chopped fresh parsley**

1. Put a large saucepan of lightly salted water on to boil. Fill a large bowl half full with cold water.
2. Whisk vinegar, corn syrup, mustard, oil, salt and pepper in a large bowl until blended. Add onion and black-eyed peas (or chickpeas); toss to coat.
3. Cook lima beans (or edamame) in the boiling water until tender, about 5 minutes. Remove with a slotted spoon and refresh in the cold water. Pat dry and add to the onion mixture.
4. Cook green beans in the boiling water until just tender, 3 to 6 minutes. Drain and refresh in the cold water. Pat dry and add to the salad along with parsley; toss well. Adjust seasoning with salt and pepper.

MAKES 6 SERVINGS, ABOUT 1 CUP EACH.

PER TABLESPOON: 176 CALORIES; 2 G FAT (0 G SAT, 1 G MONO); 0 MG CHOLESTEROL; 34 G CARBOHYDRATE; 8 G PROTEIN; 8 G FIBER; 485 MG SODIUM.

NUTRITION BONUS: 13 MG VITAMIN C (20% DV).

Grilled Vegetable Salad with Roasted Garlic Vinaigrette

PREP TIME: 25 MINUTES | **START TO FINISH:** 1¼ HOURS | **TO MAKE AHEAD:** THE VINAIGRETTE WILL KEEP, COVERED, IN THE REFRIGERATOR FOR UP TO 1 DAY. | **EASE OF PREPARATION:** MODERATE

The flavors of Tuscany inspired this hearty main-course salad, perfect for a late-summer supper. We also like this garlicky dressing on a Greek salad of tomatoes, cucumbers and feta.

VINAIGRETTE

- 2 large heads garlic
- ⅓ cup lemon juice
- 4 teaspoons extra-virgin olive oil
- 3 tablespoons water
- ¼ cup coarsely chopped parsley
- Salt & freshly ground pepper to taste

SALAD

- 5 small red potatoes
- 2 plum tomatoes, halved lengthwise
- 1 red bell pepper, quartered lengthwise and seeded
- 1 medium Vidalia *or* other sweet onion, cut into ½-inch-thick slices
- 1 small eggplant, cut into ½-inch-thick rounds
- 1 tablespoon extra-virgin olive oil
- Salt & freshly ground pepper to taste
- ⅓ cup pitted and chopped Kalamata *or* other briny black olives
- 8 cups torn romaine lettuce leaves
- 2 cups garlic croutons, store-bought *or* homemade (*page 74*), optional

1. To prepare vinaigrette: Roast garlic (*see Tip*). When the garlic is cool enough to handle, squeeze the cloves out of their skins into a blender or food processor. Add lemon juice, oil and water and blend until smooth. Transfer to a small bowl, stir in parsley and season with salt and pepper.

2. Preheat grill to medium-high.

3. To prepare salad: Place potatoes in a saucepan, cover with water and bring to a boil. Cook until just tender, about 10 minutes. Transfer to a large bowl. Add tomatoes, bell pepper, onion and eggplant. Add oil, salt and pepper and toss gently. Grill the vegetables until softened and browned, about 5 minutes per side, removing them as they are done. When cool enough to handle, cut into bite-size pieces.

4. Toss the vegetables and olives with half the vinaigrette in a bowl. Toss romaine with the remaining vinaigrette on a platter. Mound the vegetables on the lettuce and top with croutons, if using.

TO ROAST GARLIC: Preheat oven to 350°F. Place each head of garlic on a piece of foil, drizzle with 1 teaspoon oil and wrap into a package. Place the packages directly on the oven rack and roast until cloves are soft, 30 to 40 minutes.

MAKES 6 SERVINGS.

PER SERVING: 227 CALORIES; 8 G FAT (1 G SAT, 6 G MONO); 0 MG CHOLESTEROL; 36 G CARBOHYDRATE; 6 G PROTEIN; 7 G FIBER; 254 MG SODIUM.

NUTRITION BONUS: 110 MG VITAMIN C (180% DV), 130% DV VITAMIN A, 157 MCG FOLATE (39% DV).

Lower Carbs

Grilled Tomato Salad

PREP TIME: 10 MINUTES | **START TO FINISH:** 20 MINUTES | **EASE OF PREPARATION:** EASY

Grilling the tomatoes adds depth to a simple summer salad. Serve with hunks of rustic bread for soaking up the vibrant dressing.

- **1 tablespoon extra-virgin olive oil**
- **1 tablespoon lemon juice**
- **2 cloves garlic, minced**
- **1 serrano chile, seeded and minced**
- **3 dashes Worcestershire sauce**
- **¼ cup chopped fresh basil**
- **½ teaspoon kosher salt**
- **½ teaspoon freshly ground pepper**
- **4 large tomatoes, quartered**

1. Preheat grill.

2. Whisk oil, lemon juice, garlic, chile and Worcestershire sauce in a medium bowl. Add basil and set aside.

3. Combine salt and pepper and sprinkle over tomatoes. When the grill is hot, sear the tomato wedges, turning them frequently, until browned on all sides, 3 to 4 minutes.

4. Toss tomatoes with the reserved basil mixture. Divide among 4 salad plates.

MAKES 4 SERVINGS, ABOUT ¾ CUP EACH.

PER SERVING: 70 CALORIES; 4 G FAT (1 G SAT, 3 G MONO); 0 MG CHOLESTEROL; 8 G CARBOHYDRATE; 2 G PROTEIN; 2 G FIBER; 247 MG SODIUM.

NUTRITION BONUS: 27 MG VITAMIN C (45% DV), 35% DV VITAMIN A.

Creamy Potato Salad

PREP TIME: 30 MINUTES | **START TO FINISH:** 1¼ HOURS (INCLUDING ½ HOUR CHILLING TIME) | **TO MAKE AHEAD:** THE SALAD WILL KEEP, COVERED, IN THE REFRIGERATOR FOR UP TO 2 DAYS. | **EASE OF PREPARATION:** EASY

Tossing potatoes with a little good vinegar while they are still warm infuses them with flavor. Capers, gherkins and a touch of anchovy give this old-fashioned salad a piquant finish, while red bell pepper and celery give it an appealing crunch.

- **2 large eggs**
- **1½ pounds fingerling *or* other small waxy thin-skinned potatoes (about 10), scrubbed**
- **½ cup reduced-fat mayonnaise *or* soy mayonnaise**
- **½ cup low-fat plain yogurt**
- **1 tablespoon extra-virgin olive oil**
- **1 teaspoon anchovy paste**
- **Freshly ground pepper to taste**
- **2 tablespoons white-wine vinegar *or* rice vinegar**
- **½ teaspoon salt, or to taste**
- **1 medium red bell pepper, seeded and diced (1½ cups)**
- **½ cup finely diced red onion**
- **½ cup chopped celery (1-2 stalks)**
- **¼ cup chopped fresh parsley**
- **2 tablespoons diced gherkin pickles**
- **2 tablespoons drained capers, rinsed**
- **1 tablespoon chopped fresh chives**

1. Hard-cook eggs (*see box*). Peel eggs and chop coarsely.
2. Meanwhile, place potatoes in a large saucepan, cover with lightly salted water and bring to a simmer over medium-high heat. Reduce heat to medium and cook, covered, until just tender, 15 to 20 minutes. Drain; let cool for about 10 minutes.
3. Meanwhile, whisk mayonnaise, yogurt, oil, anchovy paste and pepper in a small bowl until smooth.
4. Cut potatoes into cubes and place in a large bowl. Add vinegar and salt; toss gently to coat. Add bell pepper, onion, celery, parsley, gherkins, capers, chives, chopped eggs and the mayonnaise mixture; toss to coat well. Cover and refrigerate until chilled, at least 30 minutes.

RECIPE RX

Original Potato Salad:
245 calories
21 g total fat
3 g saturated fat

EW Creamy Potato Salad:
119 calories
5 g total fat
1 g saturated fat

MAKES 12 SERVINGS, ½ CUP EACH.

PER SERVING: 119 CALORIES; 5 G FAT (1 G SAT, 2 G MONO); 40 MG CHOLESTEROL; 14 G CARBOHYDRATE; 4 G PROTEIN; 1 G FIBER; 321 MG SODIUM.

NUTRITION BONUS: 42 MG VITAMIN C (70% DV), 20% DV VITAMIN A.

To Make Hard-Cooked Eggs

PLACE EGGS IN A SINGLE LAYER in a saucepan; cover with water. Bring to a simmer over medium-high heat. Reduce heat to low, cover and cook at the barest simmer for 10 minutes. Pour off hot water and run cold water over the eggs until completely cooled. To peel, crack the shell, then roll egg between your palms to loosen shell. Peel, starting at the large end. Rinse under cold water or dip in water to remove bits of shell.

Sesame, Snow Pea & Noodle Salad

PREP TIME: 30 MINUTES | **START TO FINISH:** 40 MINUTES | **EASE OF PREPARATION:** EASY

This sophisticated Asian noodle salad is high in flavor thanks to its miso-ginger dressing and high in fiber thanks to snow peas, which are a good source of protein and magnesium as well.

- 4 cups small snow peas (3/4 pound), trimmed of stem ends and strings
- 1/2 pound daikon radish, cut into julienne (2 cups)
- 8 ounces soba noodles (*see Ingredient Note, page 396*)
- 2 tablespoons rice vinegar
- 1 tablespoon miso (*see Ingredient Note, page 395*) mixed with 1 tablespoon hot water
- 1 tablespoon canola oil
- 2 teaspoons sugar
- 1 teaspoon grated fresh ginger
- 1 tablespoon finely chopped fresh cilantro
- Salt to taste
- Hot sauce to taste
- 1 red bell pepper, thinly sliced
- 1 tablespoon sesame seeds, toasted (*see Note*)

1. Put a large pot of lightly salted water on to boil. Halve snow peas on the diagonal. Cook the peas in the boiling water until bright green, about 1 minute. Add daikon and immediately remove vegetables with a slotted spoon; refresh in cold water. Blot dry.
2. Return water to a boil and cook noodles until al dente, 3 to 5 minutes. Drain and refresh under cool water.
3. Whisk vinegar, miso mixture, oil, sugar and ginger in a large bowl until blended. Stir in cilantro. Season with salt and hot sauce. Add bell pepper, snow peas, daikon and noodles and toss to coat. Sprinkle with sesame seeds and serve.

TEST KITCHEN TIP:
To toast sesame seeds, heat a small dry skillet over low heat. Add sesame seeds and stir constantly until golden and fragrant, about 2 minutes. Transfer to a small bowl and let cool.

MAKES 4 SERVINGS, ABOUT 1 3/4 CUPS EACH.

PER SERVING: 345 CALORIES; 9 G FAT (0 G SAT, 3 G MONO); 0 MG CHOLESTEROL; 55 G CARBOHYDRATE; 14 G PROTEIN; 6 G FIBER; 310 MG SODIUM.

NUTRITION BONUS: 151 MG VITAMIN C (250% DV), 80% DV VITAMIN A, 5 MG IRON (30% DV), 97 MG MAGNESIUM (24% DV).

Red-Hot Sesame Dressing

PREP TIME: 10 MINUTES | **START TO FINISH:** 10 MINUTES | **TO MAKE AHEAD:** THE DRESSING WILL KEEP, COVERED, IN THE REFRIGERATOR FOR UP TO 1 WEEK. | **EASE OF PREPARATION:** EASY

Fiery chile-garlic sauce, nutty sesame seeds, soy sauce and brown sugar meet in this Asian-inspired dressing to add a salty-sweet punch to rice and noodle salads.

- **1½ teaspoons sesame seeds**
- **⅓ cup reduced-sodium soy sauce**
- **¼ cup rice vinegar**
- **1 tablespoon toasted sesame oil**
- **2 cloves garlic, minced**
- **1 tablespoon light brown sugar**
- **½-1 teaspoon chile-garlic sauce (*see Ingredient Note, page 394*)**
- **¼ cup chopped scallions**

1. Heat a small dry skillet over low heat. Add sesame seeds and stir constantly until golden and fragrant, about 2 minutes. Transfer to a small bowl and let cool.

2. Whisk soy sauce, vinegar, oil, garlic, sugar and chile-garlic sauce in another small bowl until the sugar dissolves. Stir in scallions and sesame seeds.

MAKES ABOUT ¾ CUP.

PER TABLESPOON: 22 CALORIES; 1 G FAT (0 G SAT, 0 G MONO); 0 MG CHOLESTEROL; 2 G CARBOHYDRATE; 0 G PROTEIN; 0 G FIBER; 247 MG SODIUM.

Fresh Tomato Vinaigrette

PREP TIME: 10 MINUTES | **START TO FINISH:** 10 MINUTES | **EASE OF PREPARATION:** EASY

Grating tomatoes is a terrific technique for getting body into the dressing without adding a lot of oil. Toss this summery dressing with romaine or spinach.

- **2 vine-ripened tomatoes, halved and seeded**
- **1 small clove garlic, peeled**
- **1 tablespoon red-wine vinegar**
- **1 tablespoon extra-virgin olive oil**
- **1 tablespoon finely chopped fresh parsley *or* basil**
- **Salt & freshly ground pepper to taste**

1. Set a box grater over a shallow bowl. Rub the cut side of a tomato half against the coarse holes to squeeze out tomato flesh. Discard skin. Repeat with remaining tomato halves.

2. Skewer garlic clove with a fork and use it to vigorously mix vinegar into the grated tomato. Still mixing, slowly drizzle in oil. Add parsley (or basil) and season with salt and pepper. Discard garlic.

MAKES ABOUT ½ CUP.

PER TABLESPOON: 23 CALORIES; 2 G FAT (0 G SAT, 1 G MONO); 0 MG CHOLESTEROL; 2 G CARBOHYDRATE; 0 G PROTEIN; 0 G FIBER; 39 MG SODIUM.

Lower Carbs

Walnut Oil Vinaigrette

PREP TIME: 5 MINUTES | **START TO FINISH:** 5 MINUTES | **EASE OF PREPARATION:** EASY

Common in Indian and Middle Eastern cooking, pomegranate molasses is a sweet-yet-tart sauce made from reduced pomegranate juice. Combined with walnut oil, it makes a zesty dressing, perfect for sweet greens like Bibb lettuce and sugar snap peas. Toasted walnuts are a natural topping.

- **1 tablespoon red-wine vinegar**
- **2 teaspoons pomegranate molasses (*see Cooking Tip, page 397*) *or* frozen cranberry juice concentrate**
- **1/8 teaspoon salt, or to taste**
- **Freshly ground pepper to taste**
- **1/3 cup walnut oil *or* extra-virgin olive oil**

Whisk vinegar, pomegranate molasses (or cranberry juice concentrate), salt and pepper in a small bowl. Slowly whisk in oil.

MAKES ABOUT 1/2 CUP.

PER TABLESPOON: 82 CALORIES; 9 G FAT (1 G SAT, 2 G MONO); 0 MG CHOLESTEROL; 1 G CARBOHYDRATE; 0 G PROTEIN; 0 G FIBER; 37 MG SODIUM.

Apricot Dressing

Lower Carbs

PREP TIME: 5 MINUTES | **START TO FINISH:** 5 MINUTES | **TO MAKE AHEAD:** THE DRESSING WILL KEEP, COVERED, IN THE REFRIGERATOR FOR UP TO 1 DAY. | **EASE OF PREPARATION:** EASY

This dressing takes off from the Middle East, where apricots have long been a favorite and parsley is the herb of choice. Try it on mixed bitter greens and grilled chicken.

- **1/3 cup apricot nectar**
- **3 tablespoons minced dried apricots**
- **3 tablespoons balsamic vinegar**
- **3 tablespoons coarsely chopped fresh parsley**
- **2 tablespoons extra-virgin olive oil**
- **2 teaspoons minced garlic**
- **2 teaspoons grainy mustard**
- **1 teaspoon sugar**
- **Salt & coarsely ground pepper to taste**

Whisk apricot nectar, apricots, vinegar, parsley, oil, garlic, mustard, sugar, salt and pepper in a bowl.

MAKES ABOUT 3/4 CUP.

PER TABLESPOON: 38 CALORIES; 3 G FAT (0 G SAT, 2 G MONO); 0 MG CHOLESTEROL; 4 G CARBOHYDRATE; 0 G PROTEIN; 0 G FIBER; 77 MG SODIUM.

BEANS & GRAINS

5

In Praise of Beans Be it ever so humble, the benevolent bean is hard not to love. Besides being delicious and accepting of just about any flavoring, virtually all types of beans are nutrient powerhouses—rich in protein, folic acid, magnesium and protective phytochemicals. (Choose darker-colored beans, and you'll benefit even more; recent research confirms that black, red and brown beans are richest in heart-healthy, cancer-protective antioxidants.) Most beans are high in both soluble and insoluble fiber, and the carbohydrates they contain are slowly digested, with a gentler effect on blood-sugar levels. That makes beans especially filling and satisfying, even though they're fairly low in calories—about 100 to 125 calories per half-cup serving.

But perhaps the most important gift beans bring to the healthy table is their ability to substitute for, or extend, meat. Hearty, protein-packed and toothsome, beans closely match meat's nutrition and flavor profile, without the accompanying dose of saturated fat.

The Goodness of Whole Grains When you choose a whole grain over its refined counterpart—say, opting for brown rice over white—you are most certainly trading up. Not only are you treating yourself to more complex flavors and interesting textures, you're also getting a substantial nutritional bonus. Whole grains contain all the B vitamins, vitamin E, zinc, iron and protective phytochemicals they were born with, rather than having these nutrients removed in a refining process. By contrast, most refined grains are basically just starch. (It's true that some of the stripped nutrients are frequently replaced—white rice and flour, for example, are enriched with B vitamins and iron—but some critical components, like fiber, are not added back.) Just like the beans, whole grains take more time to digest and absorb, so they produce a more gradual rise in blood sugar than refined grains do. They'll keep you feeling full longer.

These days, it's easy to make the switch to superior grains, as supermarkets and natural-foods stores are stocking more whole-grain options. Use the recipes in this chapter, and the basic techniques in the chart (*page 101*), to experiment with new and different grains. Like an artist who adds more colors to her palette, you'll find ever more opportunities to be creative.

BEANS (& A FEW GRAINS)

GRAINS

Black Beans & Barley

PREP TIME: 15 MINUTES | **START TO FINISH:** 35 MINUTES | **EASE OF PREPARATION:** EASY

Quick-cooking barley replaces rice in this classic Caribbean combo. Barley is rich in soluble fiber and makes a good whole-grain choice because it is digested slowly, leaving you feeling satisfied longer.

- **2 teaspoons canola oil**
- **1 medium onion, chopped**
- **½ red bell pepper, chopped**
- **2 cloves garlic, minced**
- **¼ teaspoon ground cumin**
- **1½ cups reduced-sodium chicken broth *or* vegetable broth**
- **¾ cup quick-cooking barley**
- **½ teaspoon dried oregano**
- **1 15½-ounce *or* 19-ounce can black beans, rinsed**
- **2 tablespoons chopped fresh cilantro (optional)**

1. Heat oil in a large nonstick skillet over medium heat. Add onion, bell pepper and garlic; cook, stirring frequently, until onion is barely tender, about 5 minutes. Add cumin and cook for 30 seconds more.

2. Add broth, barley and oregano; increase heat and bring to a boil. Reduce heat to low; cover and simmer until the barley is tender and most of the liquid has been absorbed, about 10 minutes.

3. Gently stir in beans and heat through. Sprinkle with cilantro (if using) just before serving.

MAKES 4 SERVINGS, 1 CUP EACH.

PER SERVING: 279 CALORIES; 4 G FAT (1 G SAT, 1 G MONO); 1 MG CHOLESTEROL; 49 G CARBOHYDRATE; 12 G PROTEIN; 13 G FIBER; 384 MG SODIUM.

NUTRITION BONUS: 51% DV FIBER, 32 MG VITAMIN C (50% DV), 4 MG IRON (20% DV).

What About the Glycemic Index?

RATHER THAN RATE CARBOHYDRATES in the old terms of "simple" or "complex," the glycemic index (GI) provides a new assessment tool. It measures the glycemic response or, put simply, the speed and height that a particular food raises blood sugar (glucose). For example, a slice of white bread has a value of 70 (considered high) while a slice of Multi-Grain Whole-Wheat Bread (*page 315*) has a value of about 53 (considered low). Higher-GI foods can cause rapid spikes in blood sugar, while lower-GI foods raise blood sugar gradually, which is thought to be better for the body and for appetite control.

Whole grains, legumes and vegetables fit nicely with the carb-watcher's eating style. Barley, bulgur, pinto beans and oats come in just slightly higher but far below a slice of white bread. And the carbohydrates in fruits convert to blood sugar slowly. Cooking methods and ingredient choices can also affect a food's index: pasta cooked al dente (just tender—and not overcooked) and waxy potatoes (not starchy) are lower-GI choices.

Studies indicate that a low-GI diet may reduce the risk of obesity and the related health problems of diabetes and heart disease, making the GI index worth considering when making carbohydrate choices.

—*Robin Edelman,* M.S., R.D.

Beans & Rice

PREP TIME: 10 MINUTES | **START TO FINISH:** 15 MINUTES | **EASE OF PREPARATION:** EASY

The combination of whole-grain brown rice and fiber-rich beans makes this a nutritionally super side dish. And because we use instant brown rice and canned beans, it's also super-fast. Try it with pork or chicken, or sprinkle with cheese and wrap in a flour tortilla for lunch or a vegetarian supper.

- **1 cup instant brown rice (*see Note*)**
- **2 teaspoons extra-virgin olive oil**
- **1 medium onion, chopped (1 cup)**
- **1 medium red bell pepper, seeded and diced (2 cups)**
- **2 cloves garlic, minced**
- **1 19-ounce can black beans *or* dark red kidney beans, rinsed**
- **¼ cup reduced-sodium chicken broth *or* vegetable broth**
- **1 tablespoon cider vinegar**
- **¼ teaspoon hot sauce, such as Tabasco**
- **⅛ teaspoon freshly ground pepper**
- **⅓ cup chopped fresh cilantro**

1. Cook rice according to package directions.

2. Meanwhile, heat oil in large nonstick skillet over medium-high heat. Add onion; cook, stirring often, for 2 minutes. Add bell pepper and garlic; cook, stirring often, until softened, 2 to 3 minutes. Add beans, broth, vinegar, hot sauce and pepper; cook until heated through, 1 to 2 minutes. Add the hot rice and cilantro; mix well.

MAKES 4 SERVINGS, 1 CUP EACH.

PER SERVING: 252 CALORIES; 4 G FAT (0 G SAT, 2 G MONO); 0 MG CHOLESTEROL; 42 G CARBOHYDRATE; 10 G PROTEIN; 10 G FIBER; 429 MG SODIUM.

NUTRITION BONUS: 40 MG VITAMIN C (70% DV), 39% DV FIBER, 3 MG IRON (20% DV).

INGREDIENT NOTE: When waiting for 45 minutes for brown rice to cook seems just too long, instant brown rice—ready in 10 minutes—is a convenient alternative. Look for it in the rice aisle of your supermarket.

Lentil & Bulgur Pilaf with Green & Yellow Squash

PREP TIME: 20 MINUTES | **START TO FINISH:** 45 MINUTES | **EASE OF PREPARATION:** EASY

Based on a traditional Lebanese Lenten dish, this recipe makes a terrific meatless meal. Serve with warm whole-wheat flatbread or pita and a dollop of tangy plain yogurt.

- **4½ cups reduced-sodium chicken broth *or* vegetable broth**
- **1¼ cup brown lentils, rinsed**
- **1 medium onion, chopped**
- **1 bay leaf**
- **¼ teaspoon salt**
- **½ teaspoon ground allspice**
- **Freshly ground pepper to taste**
- **¾ cup coarse bulgur** (*see Ingredient Note, page 394*)
- **2 tablespoons lemon juice**
- **1 tablespoon extra-virgin olive oil**
- **1 small zucchini, halved lengthwise and cut into ¼-inch-thick slices**
- **1 small yellow squash, halved lengthwise and cut into ¼-inch-thick slices**
- **1 clove garlic, minced**
- **2 teaspoons freshly grated lemon zest**
- **¼ cup chopped fresh parsley**
- **¼ cup chopped fresh cilantro *or* dill**

1. Combine broth, lentils, onion, bay leaf, salt, allspice and pepper in a 3-quart saucepan. Bring to a boil over medium heat. Reduce heat to low, cover, and cook until the liquid is absorbed and the lentils are tender, about 20 minutes. Add bulgur and cook for 15 to 20 minutes more. Remove the pilaf from the heat, discard the bay leaf and stir in lemon juice.

2. Meanwhile, heat oil in a large nonstick skillet over medium heat. Add zucchini, squash, garlic and lemon zest; sauté for 5 minutes. Stir in parsley and cilantro (or dill). Season with pepper. Stir into the pilaf. Serve hot.

MAKES 6 SERVINGS, 1 CUP EACH.

PER SERVING: 260 CALORIES; 4 G FAT (1 G SAT, 2 G MONO); 3 MG CHOLESTEROL; 42 G CARBOHYDRATE; 17 G PROTEIN; 17 G FIBER; 190 MG SODIUM.

NUTRITION BONUS: 67% DV FIBER, 194 MCG FOLATE (49% DV), 18 MG VITAMIN C (30% DV), 4 MG IRON (25% DV).

Lemony Lentil Salad with Feta

PREP TIME: 30 MINUTES | **START TO FINISH:** 30 MINUTES | **TO MAKE AHEAD:** THE SALAD WILL KEEP, COVERED, IN THE REFRIGERATOR FOR UP TO 8 HOURS. | **EASE OF PREPARATION:** EASY

Serve this Middle Eastern-inspired salad with whole-wheat pitas and melon wedges.

- ⅓ cup lemon juice
- ⅓ cup chopped fresh dill
- 2 teaspoons Dijon mustard
- ¼ teaspoon salt, or to taste
- Freshly ground pepper to taste
- ⅓ cup extra-virgin olive oil
- 2 15-ounce cans lentils, rinsed, *or* 3 cups cooked brown *or* green lentils (*see box*)
- 1 cup crumbled feta cheese (about 4 ounces)
- 1 medium red bell pepper, seeded and diced (about 1 cup)
- 1 cup diced seedless cucumber
- ½ cup finely chopped red onion

Whisk lemon juice, dill, mustard, salt and pepper in a large bowl. Gradually whisk in oil. Add lentils, feta, bell pepper, cucumber and onion; toss to coat.

MAKES 6 SERVINGS, 1 CUP EACH.

PER SERVING: 280 CALORIES; 16 G FAT (4 G SAT, 10 G MONO); 7 MG CHOLESTEROL; 24 G CARBOHYDRATE; 13 G PROTEIN; 10 G FIBER; 535 MG SODIUM.

NUTRITION BONUS: 46 MG VITAMIN C (80% DV), 41% DV FIBER, 15% DV VITAMIN A.

Lentil Essentials

FRENCH GREEN LENTILS are smaller and firmer than brown lentils, and cook more quickly. They can be found in natural-foods stores and some larger supermarkets. **To cook lentils:** Place lentils in a medium saucepan, cover with water and bring to a boil. Cook until just tender, about 20 minutes for French green lentils and 30 minutes for brown. Drain and rinse under cold water.

Slow-Cooker Yankee Bean Pot

PREP TIME: 20 MINUTES | **BEAN-SOAKING & SLOW-COOKER TIME:** 5¼ HOURS
TO MAKE AHEAD: THE BEANS WILL KEEP, COVERED, IN THE REFRIGERATOR FOR UP TO 4 DAYS.
EASE OF PREPARATION: EASY

We've updated this old-fashioned American favorite, taking advantage of the gentle, uniform heat of a slow cooker. Instead of the traditional salt pork, this recipe uses lean Canadian-style bacon.

- 1 pound dried navy *or* great northern beans
- 1 teaspoon canola oil
- 2 medium onions, chopped
- 4 ounces Canadian-style bacon, diced (¾ cup)
- 6 cloves garlic, minced
- 1 teaspoon dried thyme leaves
- Pinch of crushed red pepper
- ¼ cup pure maple syrup *or* molasses
- ¼ cup ketchup
- 2 tablespoons Worcestershire sauce
- 1 tablespoon dry mustard
- ½ pound smoked ham hock, pork neck bones *or* turkey wings (optional)
- 3 cups boiling water
- 2 bay leaves
- 1-2 tablespoons cider vinegar
- Hot sauce, such as Tabasco, to taste
- ¼ teaspoon salt, or to taste
- Freshly ground pepper to taste

1. Place beans in a large bowl and cover with cold water. Let soak for at least 8 hours or overnight. (*Alternatively, place beans and 2 quarts water in a large pot. Bring to a boil. Boil for 2 minutes. Remove from the heat and let stand for 1 hour.*)

2. Drain and rinse beans. Place in a slow cooker.

3. Heat oil in a large nonstick skillet over medium-high heat. Add onions and bacon; cook, stirring often, until onions are softened and light golden, about 5 minutes. Add garlic, thyme and crushed red pepper; cook, stirring, for 1 minute more. Add to the beans.

4. Add maple syrup (or molasses), ketchup, Worcestershire and mustard to the beans; stir to combine. Bury ham hock (or neck bones or turkey wings), if using, in the beans. Add boiling water and top with bay leaves.

5. Cover and cook until the beans are tender, about 4¼ hours on high or about 11 hours on low. Remove the bay leaves and bones. Season with vinegar, hot sauce, salt and pepper. Serve hot.

MAKES 8 SERVINGS, ABOUT ¾ CUP EACH.

PER SERVING: 279 CALORIES; 3 G FAT (1 G SAT, 1 G MONO); 7 MG CHOLESTEROL; 49 G CARBOHYDRATE; 17 G PROTEIN; 15 G FIBER; 411 MG SODIUM.

NUTRITION BONUS: 60% DV FIBER, 212 MCG FOLATE (53% DV), 5 MG IRON (25% DV).

Essential Bean-Cooking Guide

Cooking dried beans from scratch gives you the firmest texture and best flavor, and it's easy to do with a little advance planning. But there's no denying that canned beans are wonderfully convenient, and you're more likely to eat beans regularly if there are canned beans in your cupboard. So we're advocates of having both types on hand.

When you use canned beans in a recipe, be sure to rinse them first in a colander under cold running water, as their canning liquid often contains a fair amount of sodium.

Equivalents

A pound of dried beans will yield 2 to 2½ cups cooked beans.

One 19-ounce can will also yield about 2 cups of cooked beans; a 15-ounce can, about 1½ cups.

Soaking

Our preferred method for cooking most types of dried beans is to soak them first, to shorten their cooking time. (Lentils and split peas do not need to be soaked, as they cook quickly.) For the best results, use the overnight soaking method; if you're in a hurry and don't mind risking a few burst bean skins, use the quick-soak method.

Overnight Soak: Rinse and pick over the beans, then place in a large bowl with enough cold water to cover them by 2 inches. Let soak for at least 8 hours or overnight. Drain.

Quick Soak: Rinse and pick over the beans, then place them in a large pot with enough cold water to cover them by 2 inches. Bring to a boil. Boil for 2 minutes. Remove from the heat and let stand, covered, for 1 hour; drain.

Cooking

Conventional Method: Place the soaked beans in a large pot and add enough cold water to cover them by 2 inches (about 2 quarts of water for 1 pound of beans). Bring to a boil, skimming off any debris that rises to the surface. Reduce the heat to low and simmer gently, stirring occasionally, until the beans are tender (cooking time will vary with the type and age of the bean). Wait until the end of the cooking time to add salt or acidic ingredients, such as tomatoes, vinegar or molasses; these ingredients prevent the beans from softening.

Slow-Cooker Method: Soak 1 pound beans by the overnight or quick-soak method; drain. Place in a slow cooker and pour in 5 cups boiling water. Cover and cook on high until tender, 2 to 3½ hours. Add salt, if using, and cook 15 minutes more.

Rice Pilaf with Lime & Cashews

PREP TIME: 10 MINUTES | **START TO FINISH:** 1 HOUR (INCLUDING SOAKING TIME) | **EASE OF PREPARATION:** EASY

In southern India, this fragrant dish is served during the harvest season. We've made it the traditional way using white rice (though brown rice is nutritionally superior, it is rarely used in India because the oils in the bran cause it to deteriorate faster, reducing its shelf life). If you are committed to eating only whole grains, you can use brown basmati rice (*see Variation*).

- 1 cup basmati rice
- 1½ cups cold water
- 1 tablespoon canola oil
- 1 teaspoon black *or* yellow mustard seeds
- 2 tablespoons coarsely chopped cashews
- 2-3 tablespoons lime juice
- 2 tablespoons finely chopped fresh cilantro *or* 12 fresh kari leaves (*see Note*), chopped
- 2-3 fresh Thai, cayenne *or* serrano chiles *or* 1 jalapeño pepper, seeded and minced
- ¼ teaspoon turmeric
- ¼ teaspoon salt, or to taste

INGREDIENT NOTE:
Olive-green kari leaves (also called curry leaves), a distant cousin to the citrus family, have a delicate aroma and flavor and are available in the produce section of Indian grocery stores. They last up to 3 weeks in the refrigerator or in the freezer for up to a month. Do not use the dried (and highly insipid) version of these leaves—substitute cilantro instead.

1. Place rice in a medium saucepan with enough water to cover by about 1 inch. Gently swish grains in the pan with your fingertips until the water becomes cloudy; drain. Repeat 3 or 4 times, until the water remains almost clear. Cover with 1½ cups cold water; let soak for 30 minutes.
2. Bring the rice and water to a boil over medium-high heat. Cook, uncovered, stirring occasionally, until most of the liquid evaporates from the surface, 4 to 6 minutes. Cover the pan and reduce the heat to the lowest setting; cook for 5 minutes. Remove from the heat and let sit undisturbed for 5 minutes.
3. Meanwhile, heat oil in a small skillet over medium-high heat; add mustard seeds. When the seeds begin to pop, cover the skillet until the popping stops. Reduce heat to medium; add cashews and cook, stirring, until golden brown, 30 seconds to 1 minute. Remove from the heat; add lime juice, cilantro (or kari leaves), chiles (or jalapeño), turmeric and salt. Add the mixture to the cooked rice; mix well.

MAKES 6 SERVINGS, ABOUT ½ CUP EACH.

PER SERVING: 161 CALORIES; 4 G FAT (1 G SAT, 2 G MONO); 0 MG CHOLESTEROL; 29 G CARBOHYDRATE; 3 G PROTEIN; 0 G FIBER; 101 MG SODIUM.

BROWN-RICE VARIATION: If using brown basmati rice, rinse as directed in Step 1 then soak in 2 cups water. In Step 2, bring rice and water to a boil over medium-high heat. Reduce the heat to low, cover and simmer until the water is absorbed and the rice is tender, 25 to 30 minutes. Remove from the heat and let sit for 5 minutes. Proceed with Step 3.

Barley Pilaf with Mushrooms, Red Peppers & Spinach

PREP TIME: 25 MINUTES | **START TO FINISH:** 30 MINUTES-1 HOUR
TO MAKE AHEAD: THE PILAF WILL KEEP, COVERED, IN THE REFRIGERATOR FOR UP TO 2 DAYS. REHEAT IN A COVERED CASSEROLE IN A MODERATE OVEN OR IN THE MICROWAVE. | **EASE OF PREPARATION:** EASY

Flecks of sweet red pepper and spinach add festive flair to the classic mushroom and barley combo. You can use either convenient quick-cooking barley or pearl barley, but note that the amount of liquid and the cooking times will vary.

- **4 teaspoons extra-virgin olive oil *or* canola oil, divided**
- **1½ cups chopped onion (1 large or 2 medium)**
- **1¾ cups quick-cooking *or* pearl barley (*see Ingredient Note, page 394*)**
- **1 clove garlic, minced**
- **1 teaspoon dried thyme leaves**
- **3-4 cups reduced-sodium chicken broth *or* vegetable broth**
- **12 ounces assorted mushrooms (cremini, shiitake *and/or* button), wiped clean, trimmed and sliced (4 cups)**
- **1½ cups diced red bell pepper (1 large or 2 medium)**
- **¼ teaspoon salt, or to taste**
- **Freshly ground pepper to taste**
- **4 cups spinach leaves, thinly sliced**
- **1 tablespoon balsamic vinegar, or to taste**

1. Heat 2 teaspoons oil in a large heavy pot or Dutch oven over medium heat. Add onion and cook, stirring often, until softened, 2 to 3 minutes. Add barley, garlic and thyme and cook, stirring, for 30 to 60 seconds. Pour in broth (3 cups if using quick-cooking barley, 4 cups if using pearl barley) and bring to a simmer. Cover and simmer over low heat until the barley is tender and the liquid has been absorbed, 10 to 12 minutes for quick-cooking barley or about 45 minutes for pearl barley.
2. Meanwhile, heat the remaining 2 teaspoons oil in a nonstick skillet over high heat. Add mushrooms and bell pepper, season with salt and pepper and sauté until just tender, 2 to 3 minutes. Add spinach leaves and stir just until they have wilted, about 1 minute.
3. Add the sautéed vegetables to the cooked barley and stir gently to mix. Season with vinegar, salt and pepper.

MAKES 12 SERVINGS, ABOUT ⅔ CUP EACH.

PER SERVING: 121 CALORIES; 3 G FAT (0 G SAT, 1 G MONO); 1 MG CHOLESTEROL; 22 G CARBOHYDRATE; 5 G PROTEIN; 3 G FIBER; 86 MG SODIUM.

NUTRITION BONUS: 31 MG VITAMIN C (50% DV), 25% DV VITAMIN A.

High Fiber

Barley, Asparagus & Mushroom Salad

PREP TIME: 20 MINUTES | **START TO FINISH:** 50 MINUTES

TO MAKE AHEAD: THE DRESSING WILL KEEP IN AN AIRTIGHT CONTAINER IN THE REFRIGERATOR FOR UP TO 2 DAYS. THE SALAD WILL KEEP, COVERED, IN THE REFRIGERATOR FOR UP TO 2 HOURS. | **EASE OF PREPARATION:** EASY

Barley provides the base for this colorful Asian-inspired salad. Add strips of chicken, chunks of salmon, cooked shrimp or cubed tofu for a main-course offering.

DRESSING

- 3 tablespoons canola oil
- 2 tablespoons plus 1 teaspoon rice vinegar
- 2 tablespoons reduced-sodium soy sauce
- 2 teaspoons toasted sesame oil
- 2 teaspoons minced fresh ginger
- 2 cloves garlic, minced
- ½ teaspoon chile-garlic sauce (*see Ingredient Note, page 394*)

SALAD

- ¾ cup barley (quick-cooking *or* pearl) (*see Ingredient Note, page 394*)
- ½ pound asparagus, trimmed, cut into 1-inch pieces (2 cups)
- 2 teaspoons canola oil
- 6 ounces shiitake mushrooms, stemmed, wiped clean and sliced (about 2½ cups)
- 1 red bell pepper, seeded and cut into ½-inch dice
- ½ cup chopped scallions

1. **To prepare dressing:** Whisk canola oil, vinegar, soy sauce, sesame oil, ginger, garlic and chile-garlic sauce in a small bowl.
2. **To prepare salad:** Cook barley according to package directions: 10 to 12 minutes for quick-cooking; about 45 minutes for pearl. (*See "Essential Grain-Cooking Guide," page 101.*)
3. Meanwhile, blanch asparagus in boiling water until crisp-tender, 3 to 4 minutes. Drain and refresh under cold water. Heat oil in a large nonstick skillet over medium heat. Add mushrooms and cook, stirring occasionally, until tender, about 5 minutes.
4. Combine bell pepper, scallions, barley, asparagus and mushrooms in a large bowl. Add dressing and toss to coat well.

MAKES 6 SERVINGS, ABOUT 1 CUP EACH.

PER SERVING: 205 CALORIES; 11 G FAT (1 G SAT, 6 G MONO); 0 MG CHOLESTEROL; 25 G CARBOHYDRATE; 4 G PROTEIN; 5 G FIBER; 207 MG SODIUM.

NUTRITION BONUS: 42 MG VITAMIN C (70% DV), 18% DV FIBER, 15% DV VITAMIN A.

Lower Carbs

High Fiber

Tabbouleh with Grilled Vegetables

PREP TIME: 45 MINUTES | **START TO FINISH:** 1 HOUR
TO MAKE AHEAD: THE SALAD WILL KEEP AT ROOM TEMPERATURE FOR UP TO 1 HOUR.
EASE OF PREPARATION: MODERATE

Grilled vegetables add a layer of rich, complex flavors to the popular Middle Eastern salad of bulgur and herbs. Serve with whole-wheat pita bread or use as a sandwich filling.

- **1 cup bulgur** (*see Ingredient Note, page 394*)
- **¾ teaspoon salt, divided**
- **1 cup boiling water**
- **2 medium zucchini, cut lengthwise into ½-inch-thick slabs**
- **2 sweet onions, such as Vidalia, cut into ½-inch-thick rounds**
- **3 large portobello mushroom caps, wiped clean**
- **2 cups cherry tomatoes**
- **3 tablespoons extra-virgin olive oil, divided**
- **Freshly ground pepper to taste**
- **¼ cup chopped walnuts**
- **3 tablespoons lemon juice**
- **½ cup chopped fresh parsley**
- **½ cup chopped fresh mint**

1. Place bulgur and ½ teaspoon salt in a large bowl. Add boiling water and stir. Cover with plastic wrap and let soak until tender and liquid has been absorbed, about 30 minutes.

2. Meanwhile, preheat grill to medium-high. Place a fine-mesh nonstick grill topper on the grill to heat.

3. Place zucchini, onions, portobellos and tomatoes in a single layer on a baking sheet. Brush both sides with 1 tablespoon oil and sprinkle with remaining ¼ teaspoon salt and pepper. Working in batches, grill the vegetables until tender, turning once or twice. Allow 8 to 10 minutes for zucchini and onions, 6 to 8 minutes for mushrooms, and 2 to 3 minutes for tomatoes.

4. Toast walnuts in a small dry skillet over medium-low heat, stirring constantly, until fragrant, 2 to 3 minutes. When the vegetables are cool enough to handle, coarsely chop the zucchini, onions and mushrooms. Cut the tomatoes in half.

5. When the bulgur is tender, add the remaining 2 tablespoons oil, lemon juice, parsley and mint; toss to mix. Add the vegetables and toss. Sprinkle with walnuts.

VARIATION:
For a nonvegetarian, main-course version, add 2 cups diced cooked chicken.

MAKES 8 SERVINGS, ABOUT 1 CUP EACH.

PER SERVING: 167 CALORIES; 8 G FAT (1 G SAT, 5 G MONO); 0 MG CHOLESTEROL; 21 G CARBOHYDRATE; 5 G PROTEIN; 6 G FIBER; 232 MG SODIUM.

NUTRITION BONUS: 27 MG VITAMIN C (45% DV), 23% DV FIBER, 20% DV VITAMIN A, 60 MG MAGNESIUM (15% DV).

Baked Risotto Primavera

PREP TIME: 25 MINUTES | **START TO FINISH:** 1 HOUR 10 MINUTES | **EASE OF PREPARATION:** MODERATE

This updated spring classic calls for nutty-tasting short-grain brown rice instead of the traditional white arborio. Because the cooking time is longer with whole-grain rice, this risotto is cooked in the oven rather than on the stovetop, eliminating the need for almost constant stirring. (*Photo: page 219.*)

- 1 tablespoon extra-virgin olive oil
- 2 medium onions, chopped (about 1½ cups)
- 1 cup short- *or* medium-grain brown rice (*see Note*)
- 3 cloves garlic, minced
- ½ cup dry white wine
- 2 14½-ounce cans reduced-sodium chicken broth *or* 3½ cups vegetable broth
- 8 ounces asparagus, ends trimmed, cut into 1-inch pieces (2 cups)
- 1 cup sugar snap peas *or* snow peas, trimmed, cut into 1-inch pieces
- 1 cup diced red bell pepper (1 medium)
- 1½ cups freshly grated Parmesan cheese (3½ ounces)
- ¼ cup chopped fresh parsley
- ¼ cup chopped fresh chives
- 1-2 teaspoons freshly grated lemon zest, preferably organic
- Freshly ground pepper to taste

1. Preheat oven to 425°F.
2. Heat oil in a Dutch oven or ovenproof deep sauté pan over medium heat. Add onions and cook, stirring occasionally, until softened, 3 to 5 minutes. Stir in rice and garlic; cook, stirring, 1 to 2 minutes. Stir in wine and simmer until it has mostly evaporated. Add broth and bring to a boil. Cover the pan and transfer to the oven.
3. Bake until the rice is just tender, 50 minutes to 1 hour.
4. Shortly before the risotto is done, steam asparagus, peas and bell pepper until crisp-tender, about 4 minutes.
5. Fold the steamed vegetables, Parmesan, parsley, chives, lemon zest and pepper into the risotto. Serve immediately.

INGREDIENT NOTE: Use short- or medium-grain brown rice to achieve the characteristic creamy risotto texture.

MAKES 6 SERVINGS, ABOUT 1 CUP EACH.

PER SERVING: 267 CALORIES; 8 G FAT (3 G SAT, 3 G MONO); 11 MG CHOLESTEROL; 35 G CARBOHYDRATE; 12 G PROTEIN; 3 G FIBER; 607 MG SODIUM.

NUTRITION BONUS: 65 MG VITAMIN C (110% DV), 30% DV VITAMIN A, 253 MG CALCIUM (25% DV).

Mushroom Risotto

PREP TIME: 20 MINUTES | **START TO FINISH:** 1 HOUR 20 MINUTES | **EASE OF PREPARATION:** MODERATE

Although traditional risottos use refined arborio rice and require constant stirring, you can achieve excellent results with this oven-baked version using short-grain brown rice, taking advantage of its whole-grain benefits.

- 1 ounce dried porcini mushrooms (1½ cups)
- 1½ cups hot water
- 4 teaspoons extra-virgin olive oil, divided
- 1 medium leek, trimmed, washed (*see Cooking Tip, page 397*) and sliced (1 cup)
- 1 cup short-grain brown rice (*see Ingredient Note, page 98*)
- 2 cloves garlic, minced
- 1 tablespoon chopped fresh thyme *or* 1 teaspoon dried
- ½ cup dry white wine
- 3 cups reduced-sodium chicken broth
- 4 ounces cremini *or* baby bella mushrooms, wiped clean, stemmed and quartered (*see Note*)
- ½ cup freshly grated Parmesan cheese
- ¼ cup chopped fresh parsley, divided
- 2 teaspoons balsamic vinegar
- ¼ teaspoon salt, or to taste
- Freshly ground pepper to taste

1. Combine porcini and hot water in a small bowl. Let stand for 30 minutes. Strain, reserving the liquid. Rinse the mushrooms well under cool water; drain and chop finely. Strain the reserved liquid through a coffee filter or paper towel to remove any sand or dirt. Set aside.
2. Preheat oven to 425°F.
3. Heat 2 teaspoons oil in a Dutch oven or ovenproof deep sauté pan over medium heat. Add leek and the porcini; cook, stirring often, until the leek is tender, 2 to 3 minutes. Add rice, garlic and thyme; stir to coat well. Add wine and cook until almost all evaporated, 2 to 4 minutes. Add broth and the reserved porcini liquid. Bring to a boil. Cover the pan and transfer to the oven.
4. Bake until the rice is just tender but still has a little resistance and a creamy consistency, 40 to 50 minutes. If the risotto seems soupy, place it on the stovetop over medium heat and simmer for a few minutes, stirring, until it reaches the desired consistency.
5. While the risotto is baking, heat the remaining 2 teaspoons oil in a nonstick skillet over medium-high heat. Add cremini and cook, stirring occasionally, until tender and browned, 5 to 7 minutes.
6. When the risotto is ready, stir in the cremini, Parmesan, 2 tablespoons parsley, vinegar, salt and pepper. Sprinkle the remaining parsley on top and serve immediately.

INGREDIENT NOTE: Cremini mushrooms (sometimes called baby bella mushrooms) are a strain of button mushrooms prized for their dark hue, firm texture and rich flavor.

MAKES 4 SERVINGS, ABOUT 1 CUP EACH.

PER SERVING: 350 CALORIES; 10 G FAT (3 G SAT, 4 G MONO); 11 MG CHOLESTEROL; 47 G CARBOHYDRATE; 14 G PROTEIN; 4 G FIBER; 404 MG SODIUM.

NUTRITION BONUS: 3 MG IRON (20% DV), 18% DV FIBER, 173 MG CALCIUM (15% DV).

Gingered Couscous with Chickpeas

PREP TIME: 15 MINUTES | **START TO FINISH:** 25 MINUTES | **EASE OF PREPARATION:** EASY

Whole-wheat couscous is as fast and easy to prepare as regular couscous. Here, it makes a delightful simple side dish or stuffing for baked winter squash halves.

- 1 tablespoon extra-virgin olive oil
- ½ teaspoon cumin seeds (*see Ingredient Note, page 394*)
- 1 tablespoon grated fresh ginger
- 2 teaspoons curry powder, preferably Madras
- 1 15½-ounce *or* 19-ounce can chickpeas, rinsed
- 1 tomato, diced
- 1½ teaspoons honey
- 1 cup water
- ⅛ teaspoon salt, or to taste
- Freshly ground pepper to taste
- 1 cup whole-wheat couscous (*see Ingredient Note, page 394*)
- ⅓ cup chopped fresh cilantro *or* parsley

Heat oil in a large saucepan over medium-high heat. Add cumin seeds and stir until they begin to pop, about 1 minute. Add ginger and stir until fragrant, about 30 seconds. Add curry powder and stir until it is toasted, about 30 seconds longer. Add chickpeas, tomatoes, honey, water, salt and pepper; bring to a boil. Stir in couscous; remove from the heat and cover. Let stand until the liquid has been absorbed, about 5 minutes. With a fork, fluff the couscous and stir in cilantro (or parsley).

NUTRITION NOTE: Chickpeas, also called garbanzo beans, are a good source of plant protein and fiber.

MAKES 8 SERVINGS, ½ CUP EACH.

PER SERVING: 177 CALORIES; 3 G FAT (0 G SAT, 2 G MONO); 0 MG CHOLESTEROL; 32 G CARBOHYDRATE; 7 G PROTEIN; 6 G FIBER; 99 MG SODIUM.

NUTRITION BONUS: 24% DV FIBER.

Essential Grain-Cooking Guide

Directions are for 1 cup of grain.

GRAIN	LIQUID (water/broth)	DIRECTIONS	YIELD	PER ½-CUP SERVING
BARLEY				
Quick-cooking	1¾ cups	Bring liquid to a boil; add barley. Reduce heat to low and simmer, covered, 10-12 minutes.	2 cups	86 CALORIES; 1 G FAT (0 G SAT, 0 G MONO); 0 MG CHOLESTEROL; 19 G CARBOHYDRATE; 3 G PROTEIN; 3 G FIBER; 2 MG SODIUM.
Pearl	2½ cups	Bring barley and liquid to a boil. Reduce heat to low and simmer, covered, 35-50 minutes.	3-3½ cups	117 CALORIES; 0 G FAT; 0 MG CHOLESTEROL; 26 G CARBOHYDRATE; 3 G PROTEIN; 5 G FIBER; 6 MG SODIUM.
BROWN RICE	2½ cups	Bring rice and liquid to a boil. Reduce heat to low and simmer, covered, until tender and most of the liquid has been absorbed, 40-50 minutes. Let stand 5 minutes, then fluff with a fork.	3 cups	98 CALORIES; 1 G FAT (0 G SAT, 0 G MONO); 0 MG CHOLESTEROL; 20 G CARBOHYDRATE; 2 G PROTEIN; 1 G FIBER; 3 MG SODIUM.
BULGUR	1½ cups	Bring bulgur and liquid to a boil. Reduce heat to low and simmer, covered, until tender and most of the liquid has been absorbed, 10-15 minutes.	2½-3 cups	96 CALORIES; 0 G FAT; 0 MG CHOLESTEROL; 21 G CARBOHYDRATE; 3 G PROTEIN; 5 G FIBER; 7 MG SODIUM.
COUSCOUS (WHOLE-WHEAT)	1¾ cups	Bring liquid to a boil; stir in couscous. Remove from heat and let stand, covered, 5 minutes. Fluff with a fork.	3-3½ cups	140 CALORIES; 1 G FAT (0 G SAT, 0 G MONO); 0 MG CHOLESTEROL; 30 G CARBOHYDRATE; 5 G PROTEIN; 5 G FIBER; 1 MG SODIUM.
MILLET	2½ cups	Bring liquid to a boil; add millet. Reduce heat to low and simmer, covered, until tender, 20-25 minutes.	3 cups	126 CALORIES; 1 G FAT (0 G SAT, 0 G MONO); 0 MG CHOLESTEROL; 24 G CARBOHYDRATE; 4 G PROTEIN; 3 G FIBER; 3 MG SODIUM.
QUINOA	2 cups	Rinse in several changes of cold water. Bring quinoa and liquid to a boil. Reduce heat to low and simmer, covered, until tender and most of the liquid has been absorbed, 15-20 minutes. Fluff with a fork.	3 cups	106 CALORIES; 2 G FAT (0 G SAT, 0 G MONO); 0 MG CHOLESTEROL; 20 G CARBOHYDRATE; 4 G PROTEIN; 2 G FIBER; 8 MG SODIUM.
WILD RICE	At least 4 cups	Cook rice in a large saucepan of lightly salted boiling water until tender, 35-55 minutes. Drain.	2-2½ cups	82 CALORIES; 0 G FAT; 0 MG CHOLESTEROL; 17 G CARBOHYDRATE; 3 G PROTEIN; 1 G FIBER; 4 MG SODIUM.

Bulgur Stuffing with Dried Cranberries & Hazelnuts

PREP TIME: 15 MINUTES | **START TO FINISH:** 40 MINUTES
TO MAKE AHEAD: THE STUFFING WILL KEEP, COVERED, IN THE REFRIGERATOR FOR UP TO 2 DAYS. TO REHEAT, PLACE IN A BAKING DISH AND ADD ½ CUP WATER. COVER AND MICROWAVE ON HIGH FOR 10 TO 15 MINUTES. (ALTERNATIVELY, BAKE AT 350°F FOR 25 TO 30 MINUTES.) | **EASE OF PREPARATION:** EASY

For a change of pace from traditional bread stuffing, try this elegant, nutty-tasting pilaf, which features quick-cooking whole-grain bulgur.

- **1 tablespoon extra-virgin olive oil**
- **3 cups chopped onions (2 large)**
- **1 cup chopped celery (2-3 stalks)**
- **1 clove garlic, minced**
- **½ teaspoon ground cinnamon**
- **¼ teaspoon ground allspice**
- **2 cups bulgur (*see Ingredient Note, page 394*), rinsed**
- **3 cups reduced-sodium chicken broth**
- **1 bay leaf**
- **¼ teaspoon salt, or to taste**
- **⅔ cup dried cranberries**
- **¼ cup orange juice**
- **⅔ cup chopped hazelnuts (2 ounces)**
- **½ cup chopped fresh parsley**
- **Freshly ground pepper to taste**

1. Heat oil in a Dutch oven over medium heat. Add onions and celery; cook, stirring often, until softened, 5 to 8 minutes. Add garlic, cinnamon and allspice; cook, stirring, for 1 minute. Add bulgur and stir for a few seconds. Add broth, bay leaf and salt; bring to a simmer. Reduce heat to low, cover and simmer until the bulgur is tender and liquid has been absorbed, 15 to 20 minutes.
2. Meanwhile, combine dried cranberries and orange juice in a small microwave-safe bowl. Cover with vented plastic wrap and microwave on high for 2 minutes. (*Alternatively, bring dried cranberries and orange juice to a simmer in a small saucepan on the stovetop and remove from heat.*) Set aside to plump.
3. Toast hazelnuts in a small dry skillet over medium-low heat, stirring constantly, until light golden and fragrant, 2 to 3 minutes. When the bulgur is ready, discard the bay leaf. Add the cranberries, toasted hazelnuts, parsley and pepper; fluff with a fork.

> **TIP:**
> **To stuff a turkey, prepare the recipe and let cool completely. Place about 5 cups of the stuffing loosely in turkey cavities; heat the remainder separately.**

MAKES 10 SERVINGS, ¾ CUP EACH.

PER SERVING: 210 CALORIES; 7 G FAT (1 G SAT, 5 G MONO); 1 MG CHOLESTEROL; 35 G CARBOHYDRATE; 6 G PROTEIN; 7 G FIBER; 105 MG SODIUM.

NUTRITION BONUS: 11 MG VITAMIN C (27% DV), 64 MG MAGNESIUM (16% DV).

Lower Carbs

Cornbread & Apple Stuffing

PREP TIME: 40 MINUTES | **START TO FINISH:** 2 HOURS 50 MINUTES
TO MAKE AHEAD: PREPARE THROUGH STEP 2. THE TOASTED CORNBREAD WILL KEEP, IN AN AIRTIGHT CONTAINER, AT ROOM TEMPERATURE FOR UP TO 1 WEEK. | **EASE OF PREPARATION:** MODERATE

Why load your holiday feasts with fat and calories when there are healthful recipes that offer all the pleasure and traditional flavors you look forward to? It's not necessary, for instance, to add a cup of butter to keep stuffing moist—chicken broth and fruit juice do the job quite nicely.

- Wholesome Cornbread (*page 313*)
- 1 tablespoon extra-virgin olive oil
- 1 small onion, chopped (1 cup)
- 1 large stalk celery, diced (½ cup)
- 2 red apples, such as Cortland, diced
- ½ cup golden raisins
- 2 cloves garlic, minced
- 1 tablespoon chopped fresh sage *or* 1 teaspoon dried rubbed sage
- 1 tablespoon chopped fresh thyme *or* 1 teaspoon dried thyme leaves
- 1 cup reduced-sodium chicken broth *or* vegetable broth, divided
- ¼ teaspoon salt
- Freshly ground pepper to taste
- ½ cup apple cider *or* apple juice

1. Prepare Wholesome Cornbread.
2. When the cornbread has cooled, crumble into rough chunks (you should have about 6 cups). Spread the chunks and crumbs out on a large baking sheet. Toast in the oven, stirring occasionally, until crisp but not browned, 25 to 30 minutes. Let cool.
3. Meanwhile, heat oil in a large nonstick skillet over medium heat. Add onion and celery; cook, stirring, until softened, about 5 minutes. Add apples, golden raisins, garlic, sage and thyme; cook, stirring, for 2 minutes. Add ½ cup broth and cook until most of the liquid has evaporated, 5 to 6 minutes. Season with salt and pepper. Transfer to a large bowl.
4. Add the toasted cornbread and toss to mix. Drizzle cider (or juice) and the remaining ½ cup broth over the mixture and toss until evenly moistened. (*To stuff a turkey, let the mixture cool completely. Place about 5 cups of it loosely in turkey cavities; heat the remainder of the stuffing separately.*)
5. Transfer the stuffing to a 3-quart baking dish coated with cooking spray. Cover with foil. Bake for 35 to 45 minutes, or until heated through. For a crisp top, remove the foil for the last 15 minutes.

MAKES 12 SERVINGS, ABOUT ⅔ CUP EACH.

PER SERVING: 70 CALORIES; 2 G FAT (0 G SAT, 1 G MONO); 2 MG CHOLESTEROL; 14 G CARBOHYDRATE; 1 G PROTEIN; 1 G FIBER; 86 MG SODIUM.

VEGETABLES

6

If you've strolled aisles of glossy sweet peppers and dewy greens at the farmers' market, toted baskets of freshly dug potatoes from a friend's garden or picked through piles of corn and ripe tomatoes, snap beans and squash at any of the countless roadside stands that beckon lovers of old-fashioned tastes, you know the irresistible lure of vegetables. From their humble, dirt-bound origins, they offer an endless adventure for cooks, as well as a feast of vitamins, minerals and phytochemicals that can help fight cancer and heart disease. Here we've tapped the timeless appeal, versatility and nutrition of vegetables, creating recipes to live with, season after season.

High Fiber

Braised Green Beans & Tomatoes

PREP TIME: 15 MINUTES | **START TO FINISH:** 55 MINUTES | **EASE OF PREPARATION:** EASY

When you've enjoyed your fill of summer's ripe, raw tomatoes and crisp-tender veggies, try this Italian-inspired braise, where the vegetables surrender into a succulent (lycopene-rich) stew of flavors.

- **8 ripe tomatoes**
- **1 pound green beans, trimmed**
- **2 teaspoons extra-virgin olive oil**
- **4 cloves garlic, thinly sliced**
- **1 tablespoon fennel seeds, crushed**
- **¼ teaspoon crushed red pepper**
- **Salt & freshly ground pepper to taste**

1. Bring a large saucepan of lightly salted water to a boil. Dip tomatoes in boiling water. Peel and seed (*see box*), then chop.
2. Cook green beans in the boiling water until just tender, 3 to 4 minutes. Drain and refresh with cold water.
3. Heat oil in a large nonreactive saucepan or Dutch oven over medium-low heat. Add garlic and cook, stirring, until fragrant, about 1 minute. Add fennel seeds and crushed red pepper; cook, stirring, for 30 seconds more. Add tomatoes and the green beans. Cover and cook, stirring often, until the tomatoes form a sauce and the beans are soft, about 30 minutes. Season with salt and pepper. Serve hot or at room temperature.

MAKES 6 SERVINGS, ¾ CUP EACH.

PER SERVING: 79 CALORIES; 2 G FAT (0 G SAT, 1 G MONO); 0 MG CHOLESTEROL; 14 G CARBOHYDRATE; 3 G PROTEIN; 6 G FIBER; 35 MG SODIUM.

NUTRITION BONUS: LYCOPENE, 32 MG VITAMIN C (50% DV), 35% DV VITAMIN A, 679 MG POTASSIUM (34% DV), 22% DV FIBER.

To Peel Tomatoes:

MAKE A SMALL X in the bottom of each tomato and plunge into boiling water for a few seconds. Remove with a slotted spoon and slip off the skin, beginning at the X.

To Seed Tomatoes:

PLACE A STRAINER over a bowl. Cut tomatoes in half horizontally and, holding one section cut-side down, squeeze gently but firmly into the strainer, which will catch the seeds and allow the flavorful juices to drain through (add them to the recipe if you like).

Green Beans with Caramelized Red Onions

PREP TIME: 10 MINUTES | **START TO FINISH:** 35 MINUTES

TO MAKE AHEAD: PREPARE THROUGH STEP 2. COVER AND REFRIGERATE ONIONS FOR UP TO 2 DAYS. REFRESH BEANS UNDER COLD RUNNING WATER; COVER AND REFRIGERATE FOR UP TO 2 DAYS. | **EASE OF PREPARATION:** EASY

For an attractive presentation, trim the stem ends of the beans, leaving the pointed ends intact. Most fresh beans today do not require stringing, as the fibrous string has been bred out of them.

- **1 tablespoon extra-virgin olive oil**
- **3 medium red onions (about 1¾ pounds), cut into 16 wedges each**
- **1 pound green beans, trimmed**
- **½ cup vegetable broth**
- **1 tablespoon balsamic vinegar**
- **2 teaspoons light brown sugar**
- **¼ teaspoon salt, or to taste**
- **Freshly ground pepper to taste**

1. Heat oil in a large skillet over medium heat. Add onions and cook, stirring occasionally, until golden, 10 to 15 minutes.

2. Meanwhile, bring a large saucepan of lightly salted water to a boil. Add green beans and cook, uncovered, until crisp-tender, 6 to 7 minutes. Drain.

3. Add broth to the onions; cook for 5 minutes. Stir in vinegar, brown sugar, salt and pepper. Add the beans, cover and cook for 2 minutes. Serve warm.

MAKES 8 SERVINGS, ABOUT ⅔ CUP EACH.

PER SERVING: 82 CALORIES; 2 G FAT (0 G SAT, 1 G MONO); 0 MG CHOLESTEROL; 16 G CARBOHYDRATE; 2 G PROTEIN; 3 G FIBER; 108 MG SODIUM.

NUTRITION BONUS: 16 MG VITAMIN C (25% DV).

Broccoli with Caramelized Onions & Pine Nuts

PREP TIME: 15 MINUTES | **START TO FINISH:** 25 MINUTES | **EASE OF PREPARATION:** EASY

Broccoli's impressive nutritional profile (think folate, vitamins C and A, fiber, phytochemicals) puts it high on the list of foods to eat more of, an inviting task when you toss it with crunchy pine nuts, soft, sweet onions and tangy balsamic vinegar.

- 3 tablespoons pine nuts *or* chopped slivered almonds
- 2 teaspoons extra-virgin olive oil
- 1 cup chopped onion (about ½ large)
- ¼ teaspoon salt, or to taste
- 4 cups broccoli florets
- 2 teaspoons balsamic vinegar
- Freshly ground pepper to taste

1. Toast pine nuts (or almonds) in a medium dry skillet over medium-low heat, stirring constantly, until lightly browned and fragrant, 2 to 3 minutes. Transfer to a small bowl to cool.

2. Add oil to the pan and heat over medium heat. Add onion and salt; cook, stirring occasionally, adjusting heat as necessary, until soft and golden brown, 15 to 20 minutes.

3. Meanwhile, steam broccoli until just tender, 4 to 6 minutes. Transfer to a large bowl. Add the nuts, onion, vinegar and pepper; toss to coat. Serve immediately.

MAKES 4 SERVINGS, ¾ CUP EACH.

PER SERVING: 102 CALORIES; 7 G FAT (1 G SAT, 3 G MONO); 0 MG CHOLESTEROL; 9 G CARBOHYDRATE; 3 G PROTEIN; 3 G FIBER; 166 MG SODIUM.

NUTRITION BONUS: 69 MG VITAMIN C (110% DV), 45% DV VITAMIN A, 62 MCG FOLATE (16% DV).

Lower Carbs

Cajun Corn Sauté

PREP TIME: 15 MINUTES | **START TO FINISH:** 55 MINUTES | **TO MAKE AHEAD:** THE SAUTÉ WILL KEEP, COVERED, IN THE REFRIGERATOR FOR UP TO 2 DAYS. | **EASE OF PREPARATION:** EASY

A taste of summer, Louisiana-style. Serve this zesty sauté with grilled chicken or fish. When fresh corn is not in season, substitute frozen.

- 3 medium ears of corn, husked
- 2 teaspoons extra-virgin olive oil
- 1 small onion, chopped
- 1 stalk celery, chopped
- 1 small green bell pepper, seeded and chopped
- 1 clove garlic, minced
- 1 large ripe tomato, seeded and chopped
- 1 cup okra, trimmed and cut into 1-inch lengths
- ½ teaspoon Cajun seasoning
- ½ cup reduced-sodium chicken broth
- 1 tablespoon chopped fresh parsley
- Salt & freshly ground pepper to taste

1. Cut corn from cobs (*see box*). You should have about 2 cups.
2. Heat oil in a nonstick skillet over medium heat. Add onion, celery, bell pepper and garlic; cook, stirring, until the vegetables soften and begin to brown, 5 to 7 minutes. Add tomato, okra, Cajun seasoning and the corn; cook, stirring frequently, for 10 minutes.
3. Add broth. Reduce heat to low and simmer, stirring occasionally, until the corn is tender, about 10 minutes more. Stir in parsley and season with salt and pepper. Serve hot.

MAKES 6 SERVINGS, ABOUT ⅔ CUP EACH.

PER SERVING: 77 CALORIES; 2 G FAT (0 G SAT, 1 G MONO); 0 MG CHOLESTEROL; 14 G CARBOHYDRATE; 3 G PROTEIN; 3 G FIBER; 112 MG SODIUM.

NUTRITION BONUS: 22 MG VITAMIN C (35% DV).

Removing Corn from the Cob

STAND AN UNCOOKED EAR of corn on its stem end in a shallow bowl and slice the kernels off with a sharp, thin-bladed knife. This technique produces whole kernels that are good for adding to salads and salsas. If you want to use the corn kernels for soups, fritters or puddings, you can add another step to the process. After cutting the kernels off, reverse the knife and, using the dull side, press it down the length of the ear to push out the rest of the corn and its milk.

Grilled Corn on the Cob

PREP TIME: 30 MINUTES | **START TO FINISH:** 45 MINUTES | **EASE OF PREPARATION:** EASY

Sweet corn grilled in the husk is so tender and good that it needs no butter.

- 4 **ears of corn, unhusked**

1. Preheat grill. Carefully peel back husks but do not detach. Remove as much silk as possible. Pull the husks back over the corn and secure the end by tying with a strip of husk. Soak the corn in cold water for 20 minutes. Remove from the water, shaking off excess.

2. Grill the ears of corn, periodically rolling them for even cooking, until the kernels are tender when pierced with a fork, 15 to 20 minutes. Remove the husks before serving.

MAKES 4 SERVINGS.

PER SERVING: 77 CALORIES; 1 G FAT (0 G SAT, 0 G MONO); 0 MG CHOLESTEROL; 17 G CARBOHYDRATE; 3 G PROTEIN; 2 G FIBER; 14 MG SODIUM.

Glazed Carrots with Currants

PREP TIME: 10 MINUTES | **START TO FINISH:** 40 MINUTES | **EASE OF PREPARATION:** EASY

We eat so many raw carrots, it's easy to forget how excellent they can be cooked. Try them glazed in honey and spiked with cumin and cayenne for a good reminder.

- ½ **tablespoon extra-virgin olive oil**
- 1 **teaspoon cumin seeds**
- 3 **pounds carrots of similar size, peeled and cut into ½-inch-thick diagonal slices**
- ½ **teaspoon salt**
- ⅛ **teaspoon cayenne pepper**
- ¾ **cup water**
- 2 **tablespoons honey**
- ¼ **cup currants**

1. Heat oil in a large deep sauté pan or Dutch oven over medium heat. Add cumin seeds; cook, stirring, until fragrant, about 30 seconds. Add carrots, salt and cayenne and cook, stirring, for 3 minutes. Add water and honey; bring to a boil. Reduce heat to low, cover and simmer until the carrots begin to soften, about 10 minutes.

2. Add currants; increase heat to medium-high. Cook, uncovered, until the carrots are glazed and tender, 8 to 12 minutes more.

MAKES 8 SERVINGS.

PER SERVING: 108 CALORIES; 1 G FAT (0 G SAT, 1 G MONO); 0 MG CHOLESTEROL; 24 G CARBOHYDRATE; 2 G PROTEIN; 5 G FIBER; 264 MG SODIUM.

NUTRITION BONUS: 410% DV VITAMIN A, 22% DV FIBER.

Lower Carbs

High Fiber

Minted Peas & Shallots

PREP TIME: 5 MINUTES | **START TO FINISH:** 15 MINUTES | **EASE OF PREPARATION:** EASY

Peas are high in fiber and a good source of other nutrients. They're also one of our favorite harbingers of spring. Whether you shell your own straight from the garden or go for the convenience of frozen, these sweet minted peas are a celebration of the earth turning green again.

- 2 teaspoons canola oil
- ½ cup chopped shallots
- 3 cups fresh *or* frozen peas
- 1 cup reduced-sodium chicken broth *or* vegetable broth
- Pinch of sugar
- 2 tablespoons shredded fresh mint
- 1 teaspoon butter
- Salt & freshly ground pepper to taste

Heat oil in a large nonstick skillet over medium heat. Add shallots and cook, stirring, until softened and beginning to color, about 3 minutes. Stir in peas, broth and sugar. Increase heat to medium-high and cook until the peas are just tender and most of the liquid has evaporated, 4 to 6 minutes. Stir in mint and butter. Season with salt and pepper and serve.

MARKET TIP: One pound of peas in the pod yields 1 cup shelled peas.

MAKES 4 SERVINGS, ABOUT ¾ CUP EACH.

PER SERVING: 141 CALORIES; 4 G FAT (1 G SAT, 1 G MONO); 3 MG CHOLESTEROL; 20 G CARBOHYDRATE; 7 G PROTEIN; 6 G FIBER; 72 MG SODIUM.

NUTRITION BONUS: 45 MG VITAMIN C (80% DV), 25% DV VITAMIN A, 24% DV FIBER, 80 MCG FOLATE (20% DV).

Mashed Garlicky Potatoes with Portobello Gravy

PREP TIME: 10 MINUTES | **START TO FINISH:** 30 MINUTES
TO MAKE AHEAD: THE POTATOES CAN BE KEPT HOT, COVERED WITH PARCHMENT OR WAX PAPER, OVER A PAN OF BARELY SIMMERING WATER FOR UP TO 1 HOUR. | **EASE OF PREPARATION:** EASY

The creamy texture of these mashed potatoes is achieved without using cream or milk. The secret is to use the cooking liquid to moisten the puree, adding just a small amount of butter or olive oil to provide a luxurious finish. A rich-tasting mushroom gravy adds old-fashioned comfort.

Portobello Gravy (*page 289*)
3¼ pounds russet potatoes (4-5 large), peeled and cut into 2-inch pieces
4 large cloves garlic, peeled
2 tablespoons butter *or* extra-virgin olive oil
½ teaspoon salt, or to taste
Freshly ground pepper to taste

1. Make Portobello Gravy.
2. Place potatoes and garlic in a large pot, cover with lightly salted water and bring to a boil. Cover and cook over medium heat until the potatoes are tender, about 20 minutes. Drain, reserving cooking liquid.
3. Return the potatoes and garlic to the pot. Add butter (or oil). Mash potatoes with a potato masher, adding ½ to 1 cup of the reserved liquid to make a creamy consistency. Season with salt and pepper. Transfer the mashed potatoes to a warmed serving bowl and serve with Portobello Gravy.

MAKES 8 SERVINGS, ABOUT ¾ CUP EACH.

PER SERVING: 217 CALORIES; 5 G FAT (2 G SAT, 1 G MONO); 8 MG CHOLESTEROL; 39 G CARBOHYDRATE; 5 G PROTEIN; 3 G FIBER; 665 MG SODIUM.

NUTRITION BONUS: 38 MG VITAMIN C (60% DV), 875 MG POTASSIUM (44% DV).

Champ (Mashed Potatoes from Ulster)

PREP TIME: 25 MINUTES | **START TO FINISH:** 40 MINUTES | **EASE OF PREPARATION:** EASY

Traditionally, this dish is made with potatoes and scallions and topped with a great deal of butter. Substituting leeks for scallions produces a mellower flavor, one that doesn't require a rich finish. Yukon Golds also add buttery color and flavor.

- **1½ pounds potatoes, preferably Yukon Gold, peeled and cut into chunks**
- **1 cup chopped leeks, washed** (*see Cooking Tip, page 397*)
- **1 cup 1% milk**
- **1 tablespoon extra-virgin olive oil**
- **¼ teaspoon salt, or to taste**
- **Freshly ground pepper to taste**

1. Place potatoes in a saucepan and cover with cold salted water. Bring to a boil and cook, partially covered, until tender, about 15 minutes.
2. Meanwhile, combine leeks and milk in another saucepan. Bring to a simmer over low heat. Cook, partially covered, stirring occasionally, until the leeks are tender, about 15 minutes.
3. Drain the potatoes and return them to the pan. With a potato masher, mash until smooth. Stir in oil and the warm leeks and milk. Season with salt and pepper.

MAKES 4 SERVINGS, ABOUT 1 CUP EACH.

PER SERVING: 213 CALORIES; 4 G FAT (1 G SAT, 3 G MONO); 4 MG CHOLESTEROL; 36 G CARBOHYDRATE; 7 G PROTEIN; 2 G FIBER; 192 MG SODIUM.

NUTRITION BONUS: 39 MG VITAMIN C (60% DV).

Squash-Stuffed Roasted Poblano Peppers

PREP TIME: 1 HOUR 10 MINUTES | **START TO FINISH:** 2¼ HOURS (INCLUDING ROASTING SQUASH)
TO MAKE AHEAD: MAKE SQUASH PUREE UP TO 2 DAYS AHEAD OR PREPARE RECIPE THROUGH STEP 5; COVER AND REFRIGERATE FOR UP TO 2 DAYS. | **EASE OF PREPARATION:** MODERATE TO CHALLENGING

When fresh, poblanos have a wonderful, somewhat sweet heat that makes a terrific vessel for rich-tasting butternut squash stuffing. Accompanied by corn tortillas or rice and beans, this makes a special vegetarian entree. Most of the preparation can be done in advance and the recipe can easily be doubled. Look for dark green poblanos about 5 inches long, with broad shoulders at the stem, tapering to a pointy tip. Wash your hands thoroughly after removing the seeds or wear rubber gloves; most of the chile oils are found in the seeds and connective membranes.

- **1½ cups butternut squash puree (*see page 115*) *or* frozen pureed squash**
- **4 poblano peppers**
- **2 tablespoons yellow cornmeal**
- **1 tablespoon frozen pineapple juice concentrate, thawed**
- **2 teaspoons butter, melted**
- **1 teaspoon ground cumin**
- **1 teaspoon chopped fresh oregano *or* ¼ teaspoon dried**
- **½ teaspoon salt, or to taste**
- **½ cup crumbled *queso blanco* (*see Note*) *or* grated Monterey Jack**
- **½ cup all-purpose flour**
- **1 large egg, lightly beaten**
- **½ cup plain dry breadcrumbs**
- **1 tablespoon canola oil**
- **¼ cup reduced-fat sour cream *or* low-fat plain yogurt**

1. Make squash puree. If using frozen squash, cook according to package directions.
2. Meanwhile, roast peppers: Place over a gas flame and roast, turning as needed, until blackened on all sides, 2 to 3 minutes. (*Alternatively, broil peppers on a baking sheet, turning from time to time, until blackened on all sides, 4 to 8 minutes.*) Transfer to a paper bag and seal or place in a medium bowl and cover with plastic wrap. Set aside for about 10 minutes.
3. Mix the squash puree, cornmeal, pineapple juice concentrate, butter, cumin, oregano and salt in a large bowl until smooth.
4. Peel the peppers and rinse. A few blackened specks left on them will be fine. Make a long incision down one side of each pepper. Gently pry peppers open, then scoop out seeds and membranes, taking care not to tear the soft skin.
5. Carefully spoon about ⅓ cup squash filling into each pepper, followed by 2 tablespoons *queso blanco* (or Monterey Jack). Gently fold peppers closed.
6. Preheat oven to 350°F. Coat a baking sheet with cooking spray. Place flour, egg and breadcrumbs in 3 separate shallow dishes. Dredge each pepper in flour, roll in egg, then coat with breadcrumbs. Heat oil in a large nonstick skillet over medium-high heat. Add the peppers and cook until lightly browned all over, 4 to 6 minutes. Transfer to the prepared baking sheet.
7. Bake the peppers until the cheese has melted and the filling is

INGREDIENT NOTE: *Queso blanco*, also known as *queso fresco*, is a soft, slightly salty fresh Mexican cheese. You can find it in Latin markets and many supermarkets.

Squash Options

Fresh winter squash can be difficult to peel and cut. To soften the skin slightly, pierce squash in several places with a fork. Microwave on high for 45 to 60 seconds, heating it just long enough to slightly steam the skin, not actually cook the flesh. Easier still, buy ready-peeled squash in season or frozen pureed squash.

hot, about 20 minutes. Let cool for 5 minutes. Serve with a dollop of sour cream (or yogurt).

MAKES 4 SERVINGS.

PER SERVING: 305 CALORIES; 12 G FAT (5 G SAT, 4 G MONO); 74 MG CHOLESTEROL; 39 G CARBOHYDRATE; 11 G PROTEIN; 4 G FIBER; 457 MG SODIUM.

NUTRITION BONUS: 70% DV VITAMIN A, 30 MG VITAMIN C (50% DV), 78 MCG FOLATE (20% DV), 16% DV FIBER, 165 MG CALCIUM (15% DV).

◆ TO PUREE WINTER SQUASH

Roast squash (*see page 122*). Let cool slightly, then scoop flesh into a food processor. Pulse until smooth. For a chunkier texture, mash squash with a potato masher. A 2-pound butternut squash yields about 2 cups puree. A 2-pound buttercup or acorn squash yields about 1½ cups puree.

Orange-Scented Sweet Potato-Squash Puree

PREP TIME: 5 MINUTES | **START TO FINISH:** 1 HOUR 10 MINUTES

TO MAKE AHEAD: THE PUREE WILL KEEP, COVERED, IN THE REFRIGERATOR FOR UP TO 1 DAY. REHEAT BEFORE SERVING.

EASE OF PREPARATION: EASY

This elegant orange medley is packed with beta carotene, vitamin C, fiber and other nutrients. Serve it with your holiday turkey, roast chicken or pork. It's also a great accompaniment for Beans & Rice (*page 89*).

- **1½ pounds butternut squash (1 small)**
- **¾ pound sweet potatoes (2 small)**
- **1½ teaspoons freshly grated orange zest**
- **1½ teaspoons orange juice**
- **Salt to taste**

1. Preheat oven to 375°F.
2. Prick squash and sweet potatoes with a fork; roast on a baking sheet for 50 to 60 minutes, or until tender. Cut the vegetables in half; remove and discard squash seeds.
3. When cool enough to handle, scoop the flesh into a bowl. Add orange zest and juice. Mash until smooth. Season with salt.

MAKES 4 SERVINGS, ABOUT ½ CUP EACH.

PER SERVING: 167 CALORIES; 0 G FAT (0 G SAT, 0 G MONO); 0 MG CHOLESTEROL; 41 G CARBOHYDRATE; 3 G PROTEIN; 5 G FIBER; 54 MG SODIUM.

NUTRITION BONUS: 610% DV VITAMIN A, 57 MG VITAMIN C (100% DV), 778 MG POTASSIUM (39% DV), 67 MG MAGNESIUM (17% DV), 20% DV FIBER, 58 MCG FOLATE (15% DV).

Curried Sweet Potatoes

PREP TIME: 10 MINUTES | **START TO FINISH:** 45 MINUTES
TO MAKE AHEAD: THE SWEET POTATOES WILL KEEP, COVERED, IN THE REFRIGERATOR FOR UP TO 2 DAYS. REHEAT ON THE STOVETOP OR IN THE MICROWAVE. | **EASE OF PREPARATION:** EASY

Dried apricots, raisins and curry powder make unusual but delectable partners for sweet potatoes in this old-style Southern recipe. Try it with roasted pork tenderloin, turkey or chicken.

- **4½ pounds sweet potatoes (8 or 9 medium), peeled and cut into 1-inch pieces**
- **1 teaspoon salt, plus more to taste**
- **1 cup dried apricots (3 ounces), cut into ¼-inch slivers**
- **½ cup raisins**
- **1 cup boiling water**
- **1 tablespoon canola oil**
- **1 onion, finely chopped**
- **2 teaspoons curry powder**
- **Freshly ground pepper to taste**

1. Place sweet potatoes in a large pot and add enough cold water to cover by 1 inch. Add 1 teaspoon salt and bring to a boil over high heat. Reduce heat to medium and cook, uncovered, until tender but not mushy, 8 to 12 minutes. Drain well.

2. Meanwhile, combine apricots, raisins and boiling water in a small bowl; let sit until plumped, about 10 minutes.

3. Heat oil in a large wide pot over medium-high heat. Add onion and cook, stirring often, until softened, about 2 minutes. Add curry powder and cook, stirring, until fragrant, about 2 minutes. Add the cooked sweet potatoes, apricots, raisins and the fruit-soaking liquid. Season with salt and pepper. Stir gently over medium-low heat until warmed through.

MAKES 10 SERVINGS.

PER SERVING: 287 CALORIES; 2 G FAT (0 G SAT, 1 G MONO); 0 MG CHOLESTEROL; 65 G CARBOHYDRATE; 4 G PROTEIN; 8 G FIBER; 262 MG SODIUM.

NUTRITION BONUS: 840% DV VITAMIN A, 48 MG VITAMIN C (80% DV), 680 MG POTASSIUM (34% DV), 31% DV FIBER.

Potato & Sweet Potato Torte

PREP TIME: 15 MINUTES | **START TO FINISH:** 1 HOUR

TO MAKE AHEAD: THE TORTE WILL KEEP, COVERED, IN THE REFRIGERATOR FOR UP TO 2 DAYS. REHEAT, COVERED, IN A 350°F OVEN. | **EASE OF PREPARATION:** MODERATE

Layers of potatoes and sweet potatoes meld into an impressive vegetable "cake" that forms a golden crust during baking. Serve as a vegetarian centerpiece or with roast poultry or pork.

- **1 tablespoon extra-virgin olive oil**
- **2 large leeks, trimmed, washed (*see Cooking Tip, page 397*) and thinly sliced**
- **1 tablespoon chopped fresh thyme *or* 1 teaspoon dried thyme leaves**
- **½ teaspoon salt, or to taste**
- **Freshly ground pepper to taste**
- **1 pound sweet potatoes (about 2 small), peeled and cut into ⅛-inch-thick slices**
- **1 pound all-purpose potatoes, preferably Yukon Gold (2-4 medium), peeled and cut into ⅛-inch-thick slices**

1. Position oven rack at the lowest level; preheat to 450°F. Coat a 9½-inch, deep-dish pie pan with cooking spray. Line the bottom with parchment paper or foil and lightly coat with cooking spray.

2. Heat oil in a large nonstick skillet over medium-high heat. Add leeks and thyme; cook, stirring often, until tender, about 5 minutes. (If necessary, add 1 to 2 tablespoons water to prevent scorching.) Season with ⅛ teaspoon salt and pepper.

3. Arrange half the sweet potato slices, slightly overlapping, in the prepared pie pan and season with a little of the remaining salt and pepper. Spread one-third of the leeks over the top. Arrange half the potato slices over the leeks and season with salt and pepper. Top with another third of the leeks. Layer the remaining sweet potatoes, leeks and potatoes in the same manner. Cover the pan tightly with foil.

4. Bake the torte until the vegetables are tender, about 45 minutes. Run a knife around the edge of the torte to loosen it. Invert onto a serving plate. Remove paper or foil and serve.

MAKES 6 SERVINGS.

PER SERVING: 144 CALORIES; 3 G FAT (0 G SAT, 2 G MONO); 0 MG CHOLESTEROL; 30 G CARBOHYDRATE; 4 G PROTEIN; 4 G FIBER; 221 MG SODIUM.

NUTRITION BONUS: 240% DV VITAMIN A, 30 MG VITAMIN C (50% DV), 704 MG POTASSIUM (35% DV), 16% DV FIBER.

Oven-Fried Potatoes & Sweet Potatoes

PREP TIME: 15 MINUTES | **START TO FINISH:** 45 MINUTES | **EASE OF PREPARATION:** EASY

Hungry for fries? Slice potatoes into long thin wedges, toss with a little oil, salt and pepper, and pop them in the oven. They'll crisp to perfection—irresistible.

1 pound all-purpose potatoes, preferably Yukon Gold (2-4 medium), scrubbed
1 pound sweet potatoes (about 2 small), scrubbed
1 tablespoon extra-virgin olive oil
¼ teaspoon paprika
Salt & freshly ground pepper to taste

1. Position rack in upper third of oven; preheat to 450°F. Coat a baking sheet with cooking spray.
2. Cut each potato lengthwise into 8 wedges. Cut sweet potatoes into wedges about the same size. Place potatoes and sweet potatoes in a large bowl and toss with oil, paprika, salt and pepper.
3. Spread potatoes and sweet potatoes on the prepared baking sheet and roast for 20 minutes. Loosen and turn; roast for 10 to 15 minutes longer, or until golden brown. Serve immediately.

MAKES 6 SERVINGS.

PER SERVING: 159 CALORIES; 2 G FAT (0 G SAT, 2 G MONO); 0 MG CHOLESTEROL; 33 G CARBOHYDRATE; 3 G PROTEIN; 4 G FIBER; 47 MG SODIUM.

NUTRITION BONUS: 150% DV VITAMIN A, 30 MG VITAMIN C (50% DV), 637 MG POTASSIUM (32% DV), 16% DV FIBER.

Lower Carbs

Ratatouille

PREP TIME: 20 MINUTES | **START TO FINISH:** 1 HOUR 25 MINUTES | **EASE OF PREPARATION:** MODERATE

Bursting with fresh vegetables, this classic Provençal stew is wonderful with eggs, pasta or grilled fish.

- **2 tablespoons extra-virgin olive oil, divided**
- **2 onions, coarsely chopped**
- **2 red *and/or* yellow bell peppers, seeded and diced**
- **4 cloves garlic, minced**
- **1½ teaspoons fennel seeds, crushed**
- **1 medium eggplant, diced**
- **2 large zucchini, diced**
- **6 medium ripe tomatoes, coarsely chopped**
- **¼ cup finely chopped fresh basil**
- **2 tablespoons finely chopped fresh thyme**
- **Salt & freshly ground pepper to taste**
- **2 tablespoons finely chopped fresh parsley**

1. Preheat oven to 350°F.
2. Heat 1 tablespoon oil in a Dutch oven over medium heat. Add onions and bell peppers; cook, stirring occasionally, until the vegetables begin to brown, 8 to 10 minutes. Add garlic and fennel seeds; cook, stirring, until fragrant, about 1 minute more. Transfer the vegetables to a large bowl.
3. Add ½ tablespoon oil to the pot. Add eggplant and cook, stirring frequently, until browned in places, 7 to 8 minutes. Transfer to the bowl with the vegetables.
4. Add the remaining ½ tablespoon oil to the pot. Add zucchini and cook, stirring frequently, until browned in places, about 5 minutes. Add tomatoes, basil, thyme and the reserved vegetables and bring to a simmer. Cover the pot and transfer to the oven.
5. Bake the ratatouille, stirring occasionally, until the vegetables are tender, 35 to 45 minutes. Season with salt and pepper. Serve hot or at room temperature. Garnish with parsley before serving.

MAKES 10 SERVINGS, GENEROUS ¾ CUP EACH.

PER SERVING: 88 CALORIES; 3 G FAT (0 G SAT, 2 G MONO); 0 MG CHOLESTEROL; 14 G CARBOHYDRATE; 3 G PROTEIN; 4 G FIBER; 30 MG SODIUM.

NUTRITION BONUS: 65 MG VITAMIN C (110% DV), 45% DV VITAMIN A, 18% DV FIBER.

Melange of Roasted Baby Vegetables

PREP TIME: 15 MINUTES | **START TO FINISH:** 50 MINUTES | **EASE OF PREPARATION:** MODERATE

Fresh thyme and a golden maple glaze season this attractive mixture of tiny root vegetables.

- 1½ cups pearl onions
- 2 cups baby carrots (¼ inch of greens left on) *or* mini carrots
- 12 ounces baby turnips, peeled (¼ inch of greens left on) and halved, if large, *or* regular turnips, peeled and cut into ½-inch wedges
- 1 tablespoon extra-virgin olive oil
- 2 teaspoons pure maple syrup, divided
- ½ teaspoon salt, or to taste
- Freshly ground pepper to taste
- 10 sprigs fresh thyme *or* lemon thyme
- 2 teaspoons cider vinegar
- 2 tablespoons chopped fresh flat-leaf parsley, divided

1. Preheat oven to 450°F. Bring a medium saucepan of water to a boil. Add onions and boil for 1 minute. Drain and rinse under cold running water. Using a sharp paring knife, trim root ends and peel.

2. Combine onions, carrots, turnips, oil, 1 teaspoon maple syrup, salt, pepper and thyme sprigs in a large bowl; toss to coat well. Spread the vegetable mixture in a single layer on a large baking sheet with sides. Roast, turning the vegetables twice, until tender and lightly browned in spots, about 30 minutes.

3. Transfer the vegetables to a large bowl; remove thyme stems. Drizzle with the remaining 1 teaspoon syrup, vinegar and 1 tablespoon parsley; toss to coat. Sprinkle with the remaining 1 tablespoon parsley and serve.

MAKES 4 SERVINGS, ¾ CUP EACH.

PER SERVING: 121 CALORIES; 4 G FAT (1 G SAT, 3 G MONO); 0 MG CHOLESTEROL; 21 G CARBOHYDRATE; 2 G PROTEIN; 4 G FIBER; 417 MG SODIUM.

NUTRITION BONUS: 240% DV VITAMIN A, 33 MG VITAMIN C (50% DV), 476 MG POTASSIUM (24% DV), 16% DV FIBER.

Essential Vegetable-Roasting Guide

VEGETABLE	PREP	ROASTING	YIELD	PER SERVING
Asparagus (1 pound)	Trim ends from tender stalks. (Peel stalks if more mature). Toss with 1 tsp. olive oil. After roasting, season with salt and pepper.	450°F; 10 to 15 minutes, or until tender	3 servings	44 CALORIES; 2 G FAT (0 G SAT, 1 G MONO); 0 MG CHOLESTEROL; 6 G CARBOHYDRATE; 3 G PROTEIN; 0 G FIBER; 51 MG SODIUM. ✱ 25% DV VITAMIN A, 20% DV FOLATE, 20% DV IRON.
Beets (2 pounds)	Discard greens; trim the ends. Scrub off thin outer skin with a stiff brush. Cut in quarters or eighths, depending on size, and toss with 1 tsp. olive oil. After roasting, toss with 2 tsp. lemon zest (preferably organic), 1 Tbsp. chopped scallions or chives, and salt and pepper to taste.	400°F; 50 to 60 minutes, or until crispy outside and tender within	4 servings	109 CALORIES; 2 G FAT (0 G SAT, 1 G MONO); 0 MG CHOLESTEROL; 22 G CARBOHYDRATE; 4 G PROTEIN; 7 G FIBER; 214 MG SODIUM. ✱ 62% DV FOLATE, 37% DV POTASSIUM, 20% DV VITAMIN C.
Broccoli (1½ pounds, for 4 cups florets)	Toss with 1 Tbsp. olive oil, ¼ tsp. salt, or to taste, and pepper.	450°F; 10 to 12 minutes, or until tender and blackened on the bottom	4 servings	54 CALORIES; 4 G FAT (1 G SAT, 3 G MONO); 0 MG CHOLESTEROL; 4 G CARBOHYDRATE; 2 G PROTEIN; 2 G FIBER; 165 MG SODIUM. ✱ 120% DV VITAMIN C, 45% DV VITAMIN A.
Carrots & Parsnips (1 pound each)	Peel and cut into matchsticks. Toss with 2 tsp. olive oil. After roasting, toss with 2 tsp. frozen orange juice concentrate and 1 tsp. balsamic vinegar. Season with salt, pepper and chopped parsley.	450°F; 10 to 15 minutes, or until tender and browned, turning midway	6 servings	106 CALORIES; 2 G FAT (0 G SAT, 1 G MONO); 0 MG CHOLESTEROL; 22 G CARBOHYDRATE; 2 G PROTEIN; 5 G FIBER; 84 MG SODIUM. ✱ 180% DV VITAMIN A, 35% DV VITAMIN C, 27% DV POTASSIUM.
Corn on the Cob	Gently peel back husks and remove silk; pull husks back around ears and secure with string. Serve on the cob or cut off with a knife. Season with salt and pepper.	450°F, directly on the oven rack; 20 to 25 minutes, turning midway	1 ear per serving	78 CALORIES; 1 G FAT (0 G SAT, 0 G MONO); 0 MG CHOLESTEROL; 17 G CARBOHYDRATE; 3 G PROTEIN; 2 G FIBER; 159 MG SODIUM.
Eggplant (1 large)	Trim and cut in ⅜-inch-thick slices. Brush slices on both sides with 1 tsp. olive oil. After roasting, season with salt and pepper.	425°F; 20 minutes, or until tender and browned, turning midway	4 servings	46 CALORIES; 1 G FAT (0 G SAT, 1 G MONO); 0 MG CHOLESTEROL; 8 G CARBOHYDRATE; 1 G PROTEIN; 3 G FIBER; 40 MG SODIUM.

VEGETABLE	PREP	ROASTING	YIELD	PER SERVING
Green Beans (1 pound)	Trim; toss with 1 tsp. olive oil. Meanwhile, toast 2 tsp. sesame seeds in a small dry skillet over medium heat, stirring until brown; crush lightly and toss with the roasted beans. Season with salt and pepper.	450°F; about 12 minutes, until wrinkled, brown and tender, stirring midway	4 servings	54 CALORIES; 2 G FAT (0 G SAT, 1 G MONO); 0 MG CHOLESTEROL; 8 G CARBOHYDRATE; 2 G PROTEIN; 4 G FIBER; 43 MG SODIUM. ✶ 30% DV VITAMIN C, 15% DV VITAMIN A.
Leeks (1 pound)	Trim the green tops to within 2 inches of the white part. Halve leeks lengthwise and trim root ends. Keeping each half intact, rinse thoroughly to remove grit. Brush with 1 tsp. olive oil. Wrap leeks in foil, in a single layer, folding to seal. After roasting, sprinkle with 1 Tbsp. freshly grated Parmesan cheese, salt and pepper.	450°F; 15 to 20 minutes, or until tender	4 servings	85 CALORIES; 2 G FAT (0 G SAT, 1 G MONO); 1 MG CHOLESTEROL; 16 G CARBOHYDRATE; 2 G PROTEIN; 2 G FIBER; 78 MG SODIUM. ✶ 40% DV VITAMIN A, 25% DV VITAMIN C, 18% DV FOLATE.
Peppers (*see page 35*)				
Shallots (10 large)	Peel and cut in half lengthwise. Toss with 1 tsp. oil, 1 sprig fresh rosemary and salt and pepper to taste.	450°F; 20 to 25 minutes, stirring often, until tender and browned around the edges	4 servings	69 CALORIES; 1 G FAT (0 G SAT, 1 G MONO); 0 MG CHOLESTEROL; 14 G CARBOHYDRATE; 2 G PROTEIN; 2 G FIBER; 46 MG SODIUM. ✶ 20% DV VITAMIN A.
Squash (Acorn, Buttercup, Butternut) (1 pound)	Cut in half and scrape out seeds and membranes. Oil a baking sheet with sides and place squash on it, cut-side down.	400°F; 35 to 45 minutes for acorn or buttercup, 40 to 50 minutes for butternut, or until soft	3 servings	83 CALORIES; 2 G FAT (0 G SAT, 1 G MONO); 0 MG CHOLESTEROL; 18 G CARBOHYDRATE; 1 G PROTEIN; 2 G FIBER; 54 MG SODIUM. ✶ 25% DV VITAMIN C, 25% DV POTASSIUM.
Sweet Potatoes & Potatoes (*see page 118*)				

Bitter Lemon, Honey & Sweet Simmered Greens

PREP TIME: 20 MINUTES | **START TO FINISH:** 40 MINUTES | **EASE OF PREPARATION:** EASY

You can use any soft, quick-cooking greens, such as spinach or beet greens, for this recipe, but keep in mind that they have slightly different cooking times. (*See "Essential Greens-Cooking Guide," page 124.*)

- **1½-2 pounds Swiss chard (2 bunches)**
- **1½ tablespoons extra-virgin olive oil**
- **½ teaspoon cumin seeds**
- **2 cloves garlic, thinly sliced**
- **4 slices lemon, ⅛ inch thick, seeds removed**
- **¼ cup reduced-sodium chicken broth, vegetable broth *or* water**
- **1 tablespoon honey**
- **¼ teaspoon salt, or to taste**
- **Freshly ground pepper to taste**

1. Separate chard leaves from stems and ribs. Wash leaves thoroughly and roughly chop. If using stems, rinse and finely chop.

2. Heat oil in a deep sauté pan or Dutch oven over medium heat. Add cumin seeds and cook, stirring often, until fragrant, about 1 minute. Add garlic and chard stems, if using; cook, stirring often, for 3 minutes more. Stir in lemon slices. Add the leaves in 2 batches, allowing them to wilt before adding more. Add broth (or water), honey, salt and pepper. Cover and cook until the greens are tender, 1 to 2 minutes more. Serve hot or warm.

MAKES 4 SERVINGS, ABOUT ¾ CUP EACH.

PER SERVING: 103 CALORIES; 6 G FAT (1 G SAT, 4 G MONO); 0 MG CHOLESTEROL; 12 G CARBOHYDRATE; 3 G PROTEIN; 3 G FIBER; 515 MG SODIUM.

NUTRITION BONUS: 190% DV VITAMIN A, 32 MG VITAMIN C (50% DV), 886 MG POTASSIUM (44% DV), 4 MG IRON (20% DV).

Catalan Spinach Sauté

PREP TIME: 5 MINUTES | **START TO FINISH:** 10 MINUTES | **EASE OF PREPARATION:** EASY

In minutes, standard pantry items can transform frozen spinach into a satisfying side dish or omelet filling.

- **2 teaspoons extra-virgin olive oil**
- **1 small onion, chopped**
- **1 clove garlic, minced**
- **1 pound frozen cut-leaf spinach**
- **¼ cup currants**
- **2 tablespoons pine nuts, toasted**
- **Balsamic vinegar to taste**
- **Salt & freshly ground pepper to taste**

Heat oil in a skillet; add onion and garlic and sauté until beginning to soften. Add spinach and cook, stirring occasionally, until heated through. Stir in currants, pine nuts, a splash of balsamic vinegar, salt and pepper.

MAKES 4 SERVINGS, ABOUT ¾ CUP EACH.

PER SERVING: 120 CALORIES; 6 G FAT (1 G SAT, 3 G MONO); 0 MG CHOLESTEROL; 14 G CARBOHYDRATE; 6 G PROTEIN; 5 G FIBER; 122 MG SODIUM.

NUTRITION BONUS: 270% DV VITAMIN A, 29 MG VITAMIN C (50% DV), 155 MCG FOLATE (39% DV), 190 MG CALCIUM (20% DV).

Essential Greens-Cooking Guide

GREEN	PREP	COOKING	YIELD	PER SERVING
Beet Greens (1 pound)	Cut stems 1 inch above beet crown. Trim long stems from large leaves; discard blemished leaves. Wash in several changes of water; drain. Cut crosswise into 1-inch pieces.	Very tender leaves can be cooked like spinach (*see page 125*). Cook larger mature leaves, covered, in a wide pot of 2 cups lightly salted boiling water just until wilted, about 5 minutes. Drain and press out moisture. Be aware that beet greens, like beets, will bleed and discolor accompanying foods.	2 servings, about ½ cup each	48 CALORIES; 0 G FAT (0 G SAT, 0 G MONO); 0 MG CHOLESTEROL; 10 G CARBOHYDRATE; 5 G PROTEIN; 5 G FIBER; 426 MG SODIUM. ✱ 270% DV VITAMIN A, 80% DV POTASSIUM, 70% DV VITAMIN C.
Collards (1 pound)	Pull the leaf from the tough ribs and stems; discard stems. Wash in several changes of water; drain. Cut leaves into 1-inch pieces.	Cook, covered, in 2 cups lightly salted boiling water until tender, 10 to 12 minutes. Drain and press out moisture.	4 servings, about ½ cup each	34 CALORIES; 0 G FAT (0 G SAT, 0 G MONO); 0 MG CHOLESTEROL; 6 G CARBOHYDRATE; 3 G PROTEIN; 4 G FIBER; 21 MG SODIUM. ✱ 210% DV VITAMIN A, 40% DV VITAMIN C.
Kale (1 pound)	Strip leaves from stems; discard stems. Wash in several changes of water; drain. Cut into 1-inch pieces.	Cook large, tough leaves, covered, in 2 cups lightly salted boiling water until tender, 10 to 12 minutes. Drain and press out moisture. Small tender leaves can be steamed in a covered skillet with a little water until wilted.	4 servings, about ½ cup each	33 CALORIES; 0 G FAT (0 G SAT, 0 G MONO); 0 MG CHOLESTEROL; 7 G CARBOHYDRATE; 2 G PROTEIN; 2 G FIBER; 27 MG SODIUM. ✱ 320% DV VITAMIN A, 80% DV VITAMIN C.
Mustard Greens (1 pound)	Trim and discard long stems. Wash in several changes of water; drain. Bunch up leaves and cut into 1-inch pieces.	Cook large mature leaves, covered, in 2 cups lightly salted boiling water until tender, 10 to 12 minutes (add more water if needed). Small tender leaves can be steamed or stir-fried until wilted. Drain and press out moisture.	4 servings, about ½ cup each	14 CALORIES; 0 G FAT (0 G SAT, 0 G MONO); 0 MG CHOLESTEROL; 2 G CARBOHYDRATE; 2 G PROTEIN; 2 G FIBER; 15 MG SODIUM. ✱ 120% DV VITAMIN A, 40% DV VITAMIN C.

GREEN	PREP	COOKING	YIELD	PER SERVING
Spinach (1 pound)	Trim stems. Wash leaves in several changes of water. Cut into 1-inch pieces.	Tender spinach cooks in 1 to 3 minutes. Cook in a steamer basket over an inch of boiling water. Drain excess moisture. Or steam, covered, in a large pot with just the rinse water clinging to the leaves. Or stir-fry in a little olive oil and garlic.	2 servings, about ½ cup each	46 CALORIES; 1 G FAT (0 G SAT, 0 G MONO); 0 MG CHOLESTEROL; 7 G CARBOHYDRATE; 6 G PROTEIN; 6 G FIBER; 167 MG SODIUM. ✶ 270% DV VITAMIN A, 60% DV VITAMIN C, 67% DV FOLATE, 55% DV POTASSIUM, 30% DV IRON.
Swiss Chard (1 pound)	Wash in several changes of water; drain. Strip large leaves from the edible stems. Pull strings from stems; cut stems crosswise into 1-inch lengths. Bunch up leaves and cut into 1-inch pieces.	Cook in 2 cups lightly salted boiling water. Add stems first and cook for 5 minutes, then add leaves. Full-size leaves cook in about 10 minutes. Steam young leaves for 5 minutes. Drain and press out moisture.	4 servings, about ½ cup each	21 CALORIES; 0 G FAT (0 G SAT, 0 G MONO); 0 MG CHOLESTEROL; 4 G CARBOHYDRATE; 2 G PROTEIN; 2 G FIBER; 185 MG SODIUM. ✶ 130% DV VITAMIN A, 30% DV VITAMIN C, 15% DV IRON.

TO WASH GRITTY GREENS:

GENTLY SWIRL in a large bowl of water to loosen any sand or dirt; lift greens from the water to a colander or salad spinner; swirl in two more changes of water to make sure no grit remains.

TO STORE GREENS:

IT IS BEST NOT TO WASH LEAVES before storing because the moisture encourages decay. If greens are sprayed in the market, dry on kitchen towels before wrapping in dry towels and placing in plastic storage bags. Most greens keep in the refrigerator crisper for 3 to 5 days.

BASIC GREENS WITH GARLIC OIL & HOT PEPPER

TO MAKE A SIMPLE SIDE DISH of greens, cook any of the varieties as directed above. Drain; press with the back of a spoon to release excess moisture. Heat some olive oil and thinly sliced garlic in a skillet over low heat until the garlic begins to sizzle. Add a pinch of crushed red pepper and cook, stirring, until the garlic is tender and light golden, 1 to 2 minutes. Add greens and toss with the hot oil until heated through, 1 to 2 minutes. Season with a splash of lemon juice *or* vinegar (cider vinegar, wine vinegar *or* balsamic), and salt and pepper to taste.

SANDWICHES & BURGERS

7

Imagine biting into a juicy burger stuffed with blue cheese for dinner. Or savoring grilled eggplant and peppers on crusty bread, dressed with marinated feta cheese. Imagine pulling out a taste-awakening pita pocket filled with Italian-style tuna-bean salad for lunch instead of the usual insipid deli turkey on a bun. If you've gotten sick of the same old sandwiches, get ready for a revolution. We've gone from the streets of Saigon to the south of France, from the steakhouse to the berry patch, gathering creative inspiration for 16 knock-out recipes you'll want close at hand. Just don't forget the napkins.

Apple, Sauerkraut & Cheddar Quesadillas

PREP TIME: 10 MINUTES | **START TO FINISH:** 30 MINUTES | **EASE OF PREPARATION:** EASY

This combination may seem unusual—until you try it. The sweet-tartness of the apple, creaminess of the cheese and bite of the sauerkraut work together beautifully in this easy hot sandwich. Serve with oven-roasted potatoes (*see page 118*) or a green salad.

- **1 cup sauerkraut, rinsed**
- **½ cup water**
- **2 9-to-10-inch (burrito-size) flour tortillas**
- **1⅓ cups grated reduced-fat Cheddar cheese**
- **1 small Granny Smith *or* other tart, juicy apple, peeled and very thinly sliced**

1. Put sauerkraut and water in a medium nonreactive skillet. Gently heat just until the liquid has evaporated but not so much that the sauerkraut begins to stick to the pan. Remove from the heat.
2. Gradually heat a large cast-iron or nonstick skillet over medium heat. Put one tortilla in the pan and immediately sprinkle ⅓ cup cheese over half of it. Quickly arrange about half the apple slices over the cheese, then top with half the sauerkraut, spreading it evenly. Sprinkle with another ⅓ cup cheese.
3. Fold the tortilla over the filled half and press gently on it with a spatula to seal. Heat the quesadilla until the bottom is golden, about 2 minutes, then carefully flip and lightly brown the other side. Slide the quesadilla onto a cutting board and cut it into halves or quarters. Prepare the second one in the same fashion.

MAKES 2 MAIN-DISH OR 4 APPETIZER SERVINGS.

PER MAIN-DISH SERVING: 306 CALORIES; 9 G FAT (4 G SAT, 2 G MONO); 16 MG CHOLESTEROL; 34 G CARBOHYDRATE; 22 G PROTEIN; 3 G FIBER; 951 MG SODIUM.

NUTRITION BONUS: 398 MG CALCIUM (40% DV), 3 MG IRON (15% DV).

VARIATION: If you like, a little chopped ham tastes wonderful layered in with the other ingredients.

Vegetarian Reubens with Russian Dressing

PREP TIME: 10 MINUTES | **START TO FINISH:** 25 MINUTES | **TO MAKE AHEAD:** THE DRESSING WILL KEEP, COVERED, IN THE REFRIGERATOR FOR UP TO 2 DAYS. | **EASE OF PREPARATION:** EASY

This exceptional sandwich originated at Penny Cluse Café in Burlington, Vermont. The spinach, mushroom and onion filling is so satisfying, you won't even miss the corned beef.

RUSSIAN DRESSING

- **2 tablespoons reduced-fat mayonnaise**
- **2 teaspoons ketchup**
- **2 teaspoons chopped capers**
- **1 teaspoon chopped pickle *or* relish**

SANDWICHES

- **3 teaspoons extra-virgin olive oil, divided**
- **1 small red onion, thinly sliced**
- **1 cup sliced mushrooms**
- **5 cups baby spinach**
- **Freshly ground pepper to taste**
- **4 slices rye bread**
- **½ cup shredded reduced-fat Swiss cheese, such as Jarlsberg Lite *or* Alpine Lace (2 ounces)**
- **½ cup sauerkraut**

1. To prepare Russian dressing: Whisk mayonnaise and ketchup in a small bowl until smooth. Stir in capers and pickle (or relish).

2. To prepare sandwiches: Heat 2 teaspoons oil in a 12-inch nonstick skillet over medium-high heat. Add onion and mushrooms; cook, stirring often, until the onion is softened, 4 minutes. Add spinach and cook, stirring, until it has wilted, 1 to 2 minutes. Transfer the mixture to a plate.

3. Coat the pan with the remaining 1 teaspoon oil and return to medium heat. Add the bread; divide cheese equally among the slices. Divide sauerkraut between 2 slices and divide the spinach mixture between the other 2 slices; cook until the cheese has melted and the bread is golden brown, 4 to 6 minutes. Transfer sandwich halves to a cutting board. Divide the dressing between the spinach halves. Carefully place the sauerkraut halves on top. Cut sandwiches in half and serve.

MAKES 2 SERVINGS.

PER SERVING: 380 CALORIES; 16 G FAT (3 G SAT, 7 G MONO); 15 MG CHOLESTEROL; 44 G CARBOHYDRATE; 16 G PROTEIN; 7 G FIBER; 931 MG SODIUM.

NUTRITION BONUS: 80% DV VITAMIN A, 26 MG VITAMIN C (45% DV), 387 MG CALCIUM (40% DV), 5 MG IRON (25% DV).

Grilled Portobello "Steak" Sandwiches with Blue Cheese Sauce

PREP TIME: 20 MINUTES | **START TO FINISH:** 30 MINUTES | **EASE OF PREPARATION:** EASY

Blue cheese sauce gives these gutsy grilled mushroom sandwiches a classic steakhouse flavor.

- Blue Cheese Sauce (*page 296*)
- **3 teaspoons walnut oil *or* extra-virgin olive oil, divided**
- **4 slices whole-wheat country bread**
- **2 vine-ripened tomatoes, cut into ½-inch-thick slices**
- **4 portobello mushroom caps, 3-4 inches in diameter**
- **1 sweet onion, such as Vidalia, cut into ⅜-inch-thick slices**
- **Salt & freshly ground pepper to taste**
- **2 cups trimmed arugula *or* watercress**
- **2 tablespoons chopped walnuts**

1. Preheat a grill to medium-high.
2. Prepare Blue Cheese Sauce. Set aside.
3. Dip a pastry brush in water, then lightly brush 1 teaspoon oil over both sides of bread. Grill (or toast) the bread, about 1 minute per side. Set aside.
4. Lightly brush tomatoes, mushrooms and onion slices with remaining 2 teaspoons oil. Season with salt and pepper. Oil the grill rack (*see Tip*). Grill the vegetables (or pan-sear in batches) until browned on both sides: about 1 minute per side for tomatoes, 3 to 5 minutes per side for mushrooms and onion. Cut mushrooms into ½-inch-thick slices and separate onion slices into rings.
5. To assemble, spread the reserved cheese sauce over the grilled bread. Divide arugula (or watercress) among the bread slices and arrange the grilled vegetables on top. Sprinkle with walnuts. Serve immediately.

TIP:
To oil a grill: Oil a folded paper towel, hold it with tongs and rub it over the rack. (Do not use cooking spray on a hot grill.) When grilling delicate foods like tofu and fish, it is helpful to spray the food with cooking spray.

MAKES 4 SERVINGS.

PER SERVING: 267 CALORIES; 8 G FAT (2 G SAT, 2 G MONO); 6 MG CHOLESTEROL; 36 G CARBOHYDRATE; 12 G PROTEIN; 6 G FIBER; 356 MG SODIUM.

NUTRITION BONUS: 1,103 MG POTASSIUM (55% DV), 24% DV FIBER.

Roasted Vegetable & Feta Sandwiches

PREP TIME: 30 MINUTES | **START TO FINISH:** 30 MINUTES
TO MAKE AHEAD: THE SANDWICHES WILL KEEP, WELL WRAPPED, IN THE REFRIGERATOR OR A COOLER WITH A COLD PACK FOR UP TO 8 HOURS. | **EASE OF PREPARATION:** EASY

Inspired by that famous New Orleans sandwich, the muffaletta, this jazzy vegetarian version is actually good for you.

- **1 medium eggplant (about 1 pound)**
- **1 tablespoon extra-virgin olive oil, divided**
- **1 7-ounce jar roasted red peppers, rinsed and chopped**
- **Salt & freshly ground pepper to taste**
- **4 ounces feta cheese**
- **2 teaspoons lemon juice**
- **1 teaspoon dried oregano**
- **Pinch of crushed red pepper**
- **1 round loaf whole-wheat country bread (about 9 inches across)**

1. Preheat a grill or the broiler. Cut eggplant crosswise into ½-inch-thick slices. If using a grill, oil the grill rack (*see Tip, page 130*). Brush ½ tablespoon oil over both sides of the slices. Grill or broil the eggplant until lightly browned and tender, 3 to 4 minutes per side. Let cool slightly. Chop the eggplant coarsely and mix with red peppers. Season with salt and pepper.
2. Mash feta with a fork in a small bowl. Add lemon juice, oregano, crushed red pepper and the remaining ½ tablespoon oil; blend until smooth and spreadable. Season with pepper.
3. Slice loaf in half horizontally and scoop out about 1 inch of the soft interior from each half. (Reserve for another use, such as breadcrumbs.) Spread the seasoned feta in the bottom half of the loaf. Spoon the chopped eggplant and peppers over the cheese and replace the bread top firmly. Cut into wedges.

MAKES 6 SERVINGS.

PER SERVING: 226 CALORIES; 6 G FAT (2 G SAT, 2 G MONO); 7 MG CHOLESTEROL; 34 G CARBOHYDRATE; 8 G PROTEIN; 3 G FIBER; 613 MG SODIUM.

NUTRITION BONUS: 20% DV VITAMIN A.

Lower Carbs

Pecan & Mushroom Burgers

PREP TIME: 50 MINUTES | **START TO FINISH:** 1 HOUR | **TO MAKE AHEAD:** PREPARE PATTIES THROUGH STEP 6. WRAP INDIVIDUALLY AND REFRIGERATE FOR UP TO 2 DAYS OR FREEZE FOR UP TO 3 MONTHS. THAW IN THE REFRIGERATOR BEFORE COOKING. | **EASE OF PREPARATION:** MODERATE, BUT LABOR-INTENSIVE

Filled with toasted pecans, vinegar-splashed mushrooms and bulgur, these burgers have an earthy, nutty character that pairs perfectly with the luxurious Blue Cheese Sauce.

- **⅔ cup bulgur**
- **¾ teaspoon salt, divided**
- **1 cup boiling water**
- **6 teaspoons extra-virgin olive oil, divided**
- **3 cups chopped white *or* brown mushrooms, stems trimmed, wiped clean (8 ounces)**
- **1½ cups chopped onion (1 large)**
- **1½ tablespoons balsamic vinegar**
- **¾ cup pecan halves**
- **½ cup Blue Cheese Sauce (*page 296*), optional**
- **1 large egg, lightly beaten**
- **½ cup fine dry breadcrumbs**
- **Freshly ground pepper to taste**
- **8 whole-wheat buns (optional)**
- **Watercress for garnish**

1. Place bulgur and ¼ teaspoon salt in a small bowl. Pour the boiling water over, cover and set aside until the water is absorbed, about 20 minutes. Drain in a sieve, pressing out excess liquid.
2. Meanwhile, heat 2 teaspoons oil in a large nonstick skillet over medium heat. Add mushrooms, onion and remaining ½ teaspoon salt; cook, stirring, until the vegetables are softened, 8 to 10 minutes. Stir in vinegar. Immediately transfer the mixture to a plate and let cool to room temperature, about 30 minutes.
3. Toast pecans in a small dry skillet over medium-low heat, stirring, until fragrant, 4 to 6 minutes. Transfer to a plate to cool.
4. Prepare Blue Cheese Sauce, if using.
5. Combine the vegetable mixture and pecans in a food processor; pulse briefly until coarsely chopped. Add egg and the bulgur; pulse briefly, scraping down the sides if necessary, until the mixture is cohesive but roughly textured. Transfer to a bowl; stir in breadcrumbs and pepper. Mix well.
6. With dampened hands, form the mixture into eight ½-inch-thick patties, using about ½ cup for each.
7. Using 2 teaspoons oil per batch, cook 4 patties at a time in a large nonstick skillet over medium heat until evenly browned and heated through, about 4 minutes per side. Meanwhile, split and toast buns, if using, to serve burgers on. Garnish burgers with watercress and the cheese sauce, if desired.

MAKES 8 SERVINGS.

PER SERVING (WITHOUT BUNS OR GARNISHES): 197 CALORIES; 12 G FAT (1 G SAT, 7 G MONO); 26 MG CHOLESTEROL; 19 G CARBOHYDRATE; 5 G PROTEIN; 4 G FIBER; 281 MG SODIUM.

NUTRITION BONUS: 17% DV FIBER.

Curried Cashew Burgers

PREP TIME: 20 MINUTES | **START TO FINISH:** 1 HOUR | **TO MAKE AHEAD:** PREPARE PATTIES THROUGH STEP 6. WRAP INDIVIDUALLY AND REFRIGERATE FOR UP TO 2 DAYS OR FREEZE FOR UP TO 3 MONTHS. THAW IN THE REFRIGERATOR BEFORE COOKING. | **EASE OF PREPARATION:** MODERATE, BUT LABOR-INTENSIVE

If you're looking for a veggie burger with a great "meaty" feel, these are the ones to try. The secret is toasted cashews, which give them amazing flavor as well as texture. The red lentils cook surprisingly fast, keeping the prep time brief.

- **2 cups plus 2 tablespoons water, divided**
- **1 cup diced peeled carrots (2-4 medium)**
- **½ cup red lentils, rinsed (*see Ingredient Note, page 395*)**
- **¾ teaspoon salt, divided**
- **¾ cup raw cashews**
- **6 teaspoons extra-virgin olive oil, divided**
- **1 cup chopped onion (1 medium)**
- **1 clove garlic, minced**
- **2 teaspoons curry powder**
- **½ cup Cucumber-Mint Raita (*page 291*), optional**
- **¾ cup fine dry breadcrumbs**
- **Freshly ground pepper to taste**
- **6 6-inch whole-wheat pita breads**
- **Lettuce & sliced cucumber for garnish**

1. Combine 2 cups water, carrots, lentils and ¼ teaspoon salt in a saucepan. Bring to a boil. Reduce heat to low. Partially cover and simmer until the lentils are tender and falling apart, 12 to 14 minutes. Drain in a colander, gently pressing out excess liquid. Transfer to a plate; let cool to room temperature, about 20 minutes.
2. Meanwhile, toast cashews in a small dry skillet over medium-low heat, stirring, until golden and fragrant, 2 to 4 minutes. Transfer to a plate to cool.
3. Heat 2 teaspoons oil in a large nonstick skillet over medium heat. Add onion and cook, stirring, until softened, 5 to 8 minutes. Add garlic, curry powder and the remaining 2 tablespoons water; cook, stirring, for 1 minute. Remove from heat and let cool.
4. Prepare Cucumber-Mint Raita, if using.
5. Pulse cashews in a food processor until finely chopped. Add the lentils and the onion mixture; pulse until the mixture is cohesive but still somewhat textured. Transfer to a bowl and stir in breadcrumbs, the remaining ½ teaspoon salt and pepper; mix well.
6. With dampened hands, form the mixture into six ½-inch-thick patties, using about ½ cup for each.
7. Using 2 teaspoons oil per batch, cook 2 to 4 patties at a time in a large nonstick skillet over medium heat until evenly browned and heated through, about 4 minutes per side. Cut small ends off pitas and open the pockets. Serve burgers in pitas, with lettuce, cucumber and the raita, if desired.

MAKES 6 SERVINGS.

PER SERVING: 437 CALORIES; 15 G FAT (3 G SAT, 9 G MONO); 0 MG CHOLESTEROL; 65 G CARBOHYDRATE; 15 G PROTEIN; 9 G FIBER; 755 MG SODIUM.

NUTRITION BONUS: 50% DV VITAMIN A, 38% DV FIBER, 5 MG IRON (25% DV).

Mediterranean Burgers

PREP TIME: 1¼ HOURS | **START TO FINISH:** 1¾ HOURS | **TO MAKE AHEAD:** PREPARE PATTIES THROUGH STEP 6. WRAP INDIVIDUALLY AND REFRIGERATE FOR UP TO 2 DAYS OR FREEZE FOR UP TO 3 MONTHS. THAW IN THE REFRIGERATOR BEFORE COOKING. | **EASE OF PREPARATION:** MODERATE, BUT LABOR-INTENSIVE

These high-fiber veggie burgers get added body and a pleasant mild flavor from millet, a nutrition powerhouse. They get their spectacular punch from Olive Ketchup and feta cheese. (*Photo: page 211.*)

- **4 sun-dried tomatoes (*not* packed in oil)**
- **1½ cups vegetable broth (*see Ingredient Note, page 396*) *or* water**
- **½ cup millet, rinsed (*see Ingredient Note, page 395*)**
- **¼ teaspoon salt**
- **6 teaspoons extra-virgin olive oil, divided**
- **1 large onion, chopped**
- **3 cups lightly packed baby spinach, stems trimmed**
- **2 cloves garlic, minced**
- **½ cup Olive Ketchup (*page 295*), optional**
- **½ cup crumbled feta cheese**
- **1 tablespoon chopped fresh basil**
- **⅔ cup fine dry breadcrumbs**
- **¼ teaspoon freshly ground pepper**
- **7 whole-wheat English muffins *or* whole-wheat buns**
- **Arugula & sliced tomatoes for garnish**

1. Place sun-dried tomatoes in a small saucepan and cover with water. Bring to a boil. Remove from heat and let soak until softened, about 30 minutes. Drain and finely chop; set aside.
2. Meanwhile, bring broth (or water) to a boil in a medium saucepan. Stir in millet and salt; return to a boil. Reduce heat to low, cover and simmer until the millet is tender and liquid is absorbed, 25 to 30 minutes. Let stand, covered, for 10 minutes. Fluff with a fork; transfer to a plate to cool to room temperature, about 20 minutes.
3. While the millet cooks, heat 2 teaspoons oil in a large nonstick skillet over medium heat. Add onion and cook, stirring often, until softened and light brown, 5 to 7 minutes. Gradually stir in spinach; cover and cook, stirring, until the spinach is wilted, 30 to 60 seconds. Add garlic and cook, stirring, until fragrant, about 1 minute more. Transfer to a plate; let cool for about 10 minutes.
4. Prepare Olive Ketchup, if using.
5. Place millet in a food processor and pulse to mix lightly. Add the spinach mixture and pulse until coarsely chopped. Transfer to a large bowl; stir in the feta, basil, breadcrumbs, pepper and the reserved sun-dried tomatoes; mix well.
6. With dampened hands, form the mixture into seven ½-inch-thick patties, using about ½ cup for each.
7. Using 2 teaspoons oil per batch, cook 3 to 4 patties at a time in a large nonstick skillet over medium heat until browned and heated through, about 4 minutes per side. Toast English muffins (or buns). Garnish burgers with arugula, tomatoes and Olive Ketchup, if desired.

MAKES 7 SERVINGS.

PER SERVING: 309 CALORIES; 9 G FAT (3 G SAT, 4 G MONO); 10 MG CHOLESTEROL; 49 G CARBOHYDRATE; 11 G PROTEIN; 7 G FIBER; 735 MG SODIUM.

NUTRITION BONUS: 27% DV FIBER, 270 MG CALCIUM (25% DV), 3 MG IRON (20% DV).

Chicken Salad Wraps

PREP TIME: 40 MINUTES | **START TO FINISH:** 40 MINUTES | **EASE OF PREPARATION:** EASY

Guaranteed crowd-pleasers, these wraps are perfect for leftover grilled chicken. The distinctive salty flavor from the fish sauce is balanced by fresh mint and lemon juice.

- **½ cup lemon juice**
- **⅓ cup fish sauce** (*see Ingredient Note, page 395*)
- **¼ cup sugar**
- **2 cloves garlic, minced**
- **¼ teaspoon crushed red pepper**
- **8 6-inch flour tortillas**
- **4 cups shredded romaine lettuce**
- **3 cups shredded cooked chicken (12 ounces)**
- **1 large ripe tomato, cut into thin wedges**
- **1 cup grated carrots (2 medium)**
- **⅔ cup chopped scallions (1 bunch)**
- **⅔ cup slivered fresh mint**

1. Whisk lemon juice, fish sauce, sugar, garlic and crushed red pepper in a small bowl until sugar is dissolved. Set aside.
2. Preheat oven to 325°F. Wrap tortillas in foil and heat in the oven for 10 to 15 minutes, until softened and heated through. Keep warm.
3. Combine lettuce, chicken, tomato, carrots, scallions and mint in a large bowl. Add ⅓ cup of the reserved dressing; toss to coat.
4. Set out chicken mixture, tortillas and the remaining dressing for diners to assemble wraps at the table. Serve immediately.

TIP:
To warm tortillas in a microwave, stack between two damp paper towels; microwave on high for 30 to 60 seconds, or until heated through.

MAKES 4 SERVINGS.

PER SERVING: 439 CALORIES; 9 G FAT (2 G SAT, 4 G MONO); 89 MG CHOLESTEROL; 49 G CARBOHYDRATE; 40 G PROTEIN; 5 G FIBER; 1,018 MG SODIUM.

NUTRITION BONUS: 140% DV VITAMIN A, 31 MG VITAMIN C (50% DV), 179 MCG FOLATE (45% DV), 4 MG IRON (25% DV).

Vietnamese Chicken Sandwiches

PREP TIME: 15 MINUTES | **START TO FINISH:** 2 HOURS 35 MINUTES (INCLUDING MAKING PICKLED CARROT & RADISH)
TO MAKE AHEAD: THE SANDWICH WILL KEEP, WELL WRAPPED, IN THE REFRIGERATOR OR A COOLER WITH A COLD PACK FOR UP TO 8 HOURS. | **EASE OF PREPARATION:** EASY

Many people are surprised to find sandwiches in Vietnamese cuisine, but this is a popular example of Vietnamese street fare. What makes it distinctive is the use of fresh herbs, hot chiles, pickled vegetables and a zesty dressing of fish sauce and lime juice. Enjoy with a tall glass of jasmine iced tea for an exciting summer lunch.

- **½ cup Pickled Carrot & Radish (*recipe follows*)**
- **1 teaspoon lime *or* lemon juice**
- **½ teaspoon fish sauce (*see Ingredient Note, page 395*)**
- **½ cup thinly sliced cucumber**
- **1 12-inch baguette, halved lengthwise**
- **1 cup thinly sliced cooked chicken**
- **2 scallions, thinly sliced**
- **2 serrano chiles, seeded and finely chopped (1 tablespoon)**
- **A few sprigs fresh cilantro *or* basil leaves**
- **2 teaspoons reduced-fat mayonnaise**

1. Prepare Pickled Carrot & Radish.

2. Combine lime juice (or lemon juice) and fish sauce in a small bowl. Spread cucumber and Pickled Carrot & Radish over the bottom half of baguette. Top with sliced chicken and sprinkle with scallions and chiles. Sprinkle with the fish sauce mixture and top with herbs. Spread mayonnaise on the top half of the baguette; replace top and cut into two 6-inch sandwiches.

MAKES 2 SANDWICHES.

PER SERVING: 252 CALORIES; 5 G FAT (1 G SAT, 1 G MONO); 60 MG CHOLESTEROL; 27 G CARBOHYDRATE; 25 G PROTEIN; 3 G FIBER; 760 MG SODIUM.

NUTRITION BONUS: 60% DV VITAMIN A, 543 MG POTASSIUM (27% DV), 22 MG VITAMIN C (22% DV).

PICKLED CARROT & RADISH

PREP TIME: 10 MINUTES | **START TO FINISH:** 2 HOURS 20 MINUTES (INCLUDING MARINATING TIME)
TO MAKE AHEAD: REFRIGERATE, COVERED, FOR UP TO 2 DAYS. | **EASE OF PREPARATION:** EASY

- **1 cup grated carrot**
- **1 cup grated daikon radish**
- **1 tablespoon salt**
- **2 tablespoons sugar**
- **¼ cup white-wine vinegar**

1. Toss carrot, radish and salt together in a medium bowl. Let stand for 10 minutes. Squeeze the mixture in a dry towel to remove excess water. Transfer to a sieve, rinse and drain.

2. Place carrot and radish in a medium bowl. Add sugar and vinegar; toss to coat. Cover and refrigerate for 2 hours. Serve chilled.

MAKES 1¼ CUPS.

PER TABLESPOON: 10 CALORIES; 0 G FAT (0 G SAT, 0 G MONO); 0 MG CHOLESTEROL; 2 G CARBOHYDRATE; 0 G PROTEIN; 0 G FIBER; 356 MG SODIUM.

Asian Turkey Burgers

PREP TIME: 20 MINUTES | **START TO FINISH:** 35 MINUTES | **TO MAKE AHEAD:** PREPARE PATTIES THROUGH STEP 2. WRAP PATTIES INDIVIDUALLY AND REFRIGERATE FOR UP TO 8 HOURS OR FREEZE FOR UP TO 3 MONTHS. THAW IN THE REFRIGERATOR BEFORE COOKING. | **EASE OF PREPARATION:** EASY

Hoisin sauce gives these burgers a juicy texture, while ginger and garlic provide a burst of flavor, and water chestnuts deliver an appealing crunch. Serve them over tender greens or on toasted whole-wheat buns.

- 2 slices whole-wheat sandwich bread, crusts removed, torn into pieces
- 12 ounces lean ground turkey breast
- 1 8-ounce can sliced water chestnuts, rinsed and chopped
- 2 tablespoons hoisin sauce (*see Ingredient Note, page 182*)
- 2 scallions, trimmed and sliced
- 1 tablespoon minced fresh ginger
- 2 cloves garlic, minced
- ¼ teaspoon salt
- 1½ teaspoons toasted sesame oil
- ¼ cup Sesame Mayonnaise (*page 297*), optional

1. Preheat grill to medium-high.
2. Place bread in a food processor and pulse into fine crumbs. Transfer to a large bowl. Add ground turkey, water chestnuts, hoisin, scallions, ginger, garlic and salt; mix well. (The mixture will be moist.) With dampened hands, form the mixture into four ½-inch-thick patties (*see Cooking Tip, page 141*).
3. Oil the grill rack (*see Tip, page 130*). Brush patties with sesame oil. Grill until browned and no longer pink in the center, about 5 minutes per side. (An instant-read thermometer inserted in the center should register 165°F.)
4. Meanwhile, prepare Sesame Mayonnaise, if desired, to serve with the burgers.

NUTRITION NOTE: Check labels carefully and select ground turkey *breast.* Regular ground turkey, which is a mixture of dark and white meat, has a higher fat content (similar to that of lean ground beef).

MAKES 4 SERVINGS.

PER SERVING: 207 CALORIES; 3 G FAT (1 G SAT, 1 G MONO); 53 MG CHOLESTEROL; 19 G CARBOHYDRATE; 24 G PROTEIN; 4 G FIBER; 405 MG SODIUM.

NUTRITION BONUS: 17% DV FIBER, 292 MG POTASSIUM (15% DV).

Turkey-Mushroom Burgers

PREP TIME: 45 MINUTES | **START TO FINISH:** 1 HOUR | **TO MAKE AHEAD:** PREPARE PATTIES THROUGH STEP 5. WRAP INDIVIDUALLY AND REFRIGERATE FOR UP TO 8 HOURS OR FREEZE FOR UP TO 3 MONTHS. THAW IN THE REFRIGERATOR BEFORE COOKING. | **EASE OF PREPARATION:** MODERATE

Ground turkey is the standard lean alternative to ground beef—and a good one—but burgers made from it can be dry and bland. These turkey burgers are particularly moist and flavorful because mushrooms are used to extend the ground meat.

- **2 slices whole-wheat sandwich bread, crusts removed, torn into pieces**
- **8 ounces white mushrooms, wiped clean**
- **3 teaspoons extra-virgin olive oil, divided**
- **1 medium onion, finely chopped**
- **2 cloves garlic, minced**
- **½ cup Scallion-Lemon Mayonnaise (*page 297*), optional**
- **1 pound lean ground turkey breast (*see Nutrition Note, page 137*)**
- **1 large egg, lightly beaten**
- **3 tablespoons chopped fresh dill**
- **1½ tablespoons coarse-grained mustard**
- **½ teaspoon salt**
- **¼ teaspoon freshly ground pepper**
- **6 whole-wheat buns (optional)**
- **Lettuce leaves & tomato slices for garnish**

1. Place bread in a food processor and pulse into fine crumbs. Transfer to a large bowl. Pulse mushrooms in the food processor until finely chopped.

2. Heat 2 teaspoons oil in a large nonstick skillet over medium-high heat. Add the onion, garlic and mushrooms; cook, stirring occasionally, until tender and liquid has evaporated, about 10 minutes. Add to breadcrumbs and let cool completely, 15 to 20 minutes.

3. Meanwhile, prepare Scallion-Lemon Mayonnaise, if using.

4. Preheat grill to medium-high.

5. Add ground turkey, egg, dill, mustard, salt and pepper to the mushroom mixture; mix well with a potato masher. With dampened hands, form the mixture into six ½-inch-thick patties, using about ½ cup for each (*see Cooking Tip, page 141*).

6. Oil the grill rack (*see Tip, page 130*). Brush the patties with the remaining 1 teaspoon oil. Grill until no longer pink in the center, about 5 minutes per side. (An instant-read thermometer inserted in the center should register 165°F.) Meanwhile, split buns and toast on the grill for 30 to 60 seconds, if using. Serve burgers on buns, garnished with lettuce, tomato and Scallion-Lemon Mayonnaise, if desired.

MAKES 6 SERVINGS.

PER SERVING (WITHOUT BUNS OR GARNISHES): 193 CALORIES; 10 G FAT (2 G SAT, 5 G MONO); 95 MG CHOLESTEROL; 9 G CARBOHYDRATE; 18 G PROTEIN; 2 G FIBER; 418 MG SODIUM.

NUTRITION BONUS: 383 MG POTASSIUM (19% DV).

Lower Carbs

Pan Bagna

PREP TIME: 45 MINUTES | **START TO FINISH:** 45 MINUTES | **TO MAKE AHEAD:** THE SANDWICHES WILL KEEP, WRAPPED IN PLASTIC WRAP, IN THE REFRIGERATOR OR IN A COOLER WITH A COLD PACK FOR UP TO 8 HOURS | **EASE OF PREPARATION:** MODERATE

In the Provençal dialect, "pan bagna" means "moist bread." In this lightened version of the classic Mediterranean sandwich, a filling of hard-boiled eggs is seasoned with pungent black olives, mustard and a subtle hint of anchovy. For a truly great sandwich, use the best-quality bread you can find.

- 3 large eggs
- Salt to taste
- 2 teaspoons extra-virgin olive oil, divided
- 1 large sweet onion, such as Vidalia, Walla Walla *or* Maui, thinly sliced
- Freshly ground pepper to taste
- 1 22-inch-long baguette, preferably whole-grain
- 1 small clove garlic, peeled
- 2 tablespoons reduced-fat mayonnaise
- 2 tablespoons lemon juice
- 2 teaspoons Dijon mustard
- ¾ teaspoon anchovy paste
- 2 tablespoons chopped fresh parsley
- 6 imported black olives, pitted and chopped
- 1 cup mesclun *or* lamb's lettuce (mâche)

1. Hard-cook eggs (*see box, page 82*). Peel when cool enough to handle. Set aside one of the yolks for the dressing. Coarsely chop the remaining eggs; set aside.

2. Meanwhile, heat 1 teaspoon oil in a large nonstick skillet over medium-low heat. Add onion; season with salt and pepper. Cook, stirring often, until very tender and light golden, 10 to 20 minutes. (Add 1 to 2 tablespoons water if onions are browning too quickly.)

3. Cut baguette into 4 equal lengths. Split each piece in half horizontally. Pull out the soft bread from the center of each piece, leaving ½-inch-thick shells. Place soft bread in a food processor or blender and process to form fine crumbs. Measure out ½ cup of crumbs (reserve the rest for another use).

4. With the side of a chef's knife, mash garlic with ¼ teaspoon salt. Transfer to a medium bowl. (*Alternatively, mash garlic and salt in a mortar with a pestle.*) Add reserved egg yolk and mash with a fork. Whisk in mayonnaise, lemon juice, mustard, anchovy paste and remaining 1 teaspoon oil. Fold in parsley, olives, reserved chopped eggs and breadcrumbs. Season with pepper.

5. To assemble sandwiches, spread the caramelized onions over the bread-shell bottoms. Mound the egg mixture over the onions. Top with mesclun (or lamb's lettuce) and replace bread tops.

INGREDIENT NOTE:
You can make your own mesclun by combining your choice of tender greens, both bitter and mild.

MAKES 4 SANDWICHES, FOR 4 SERVINGS.

PER SERVING: 165 CALORIES; 10 G FAT (2 G SAT, 4 G MONO); 163 MG CHOLESTEROL; 11 G CARBOHYDRATE; 6 G PROTEIN; 1 G FIBER; 443 MG SODIUM.

NUTRITION BONUS: 11 MG VITAMIN C (20% DV), 15% DV VITAMIN A.

Tuna & Bean Salad in Pita Pockets

PREP TIME: 15 MINUTES | **START TO FINISH:** 15 MINUTES | **EASE OF PREPARATION:** EASY

Dressing tuna salad with lemon and olive oil lends a bright, fresh note that's a great alternative to mayo. Beans add appealing texture and fabulous nutrition.

- 1 clove garlic, crushed and peeled
- ¼ teaspoon salt, or to taste
- 1 tablespoon lemon juice
- 1 tablespoon extra-virgin olive oil
- ¼ teaspoon crushed red pepper
- 1 15-ounce can great northern beans, rinsed
- 1 3-ounce can tuna packed in water, drained and flaked
- 1 cup arugula leaves, coarsely chopped
- Freshly ground pepper to taste
- 2 6-inch whole-wheat pita breads
- 2-4 large lettuce leaves
- ¼ cup thinly sliced red onion

1. With a chef's knife, mash garlic and salt into a paste. Transfer to a bowl. Whisk in lemon juice, oil and crushed red pepper. Add beans, tuna and arugula; toss to mix. Season with pepper.

2. Cut a quarter off each pita to open the pocket. (*Save the trimmings to make pita crisps, page 47.*) Line the centers with lettuce. Fill with tuna/bean salad and red onion slices.

MAKES 2 SANDWICHES, FOR 2 SERVINGS.

PER SERVING: 454 CALORIES; 10 G FAT (2 G SAT, 6 G MONO); 13 MG CHOLESTEROL; 67 G CARBOHYDRATE; 29 G PROTEIN; 15 G FIBER; 782 MG SODIUM.

NUTRITION BONUS: 59% DV FIBER, 184 MCG FOLATE (48% DV), 842 MG POTASSIUM (42% DV), 131 MG MAGNESIUM (33% DV), 6 MG IRON (30% DV), 133 MG CALCIUM (15% DV), 9 MG VITAMIN C (15% DV), 15% DV VITAMIN A.

Chili Burgers

PREP TIME: 20 MINUTES | **START TO FINISH:** 35 MINUTES | **EASE OF PREPARATION:** EASY

A chili burger without the mess—beans, jalapeños and chili seasonings are mixed right into the ground beef. By bulking up the ground beef with mashed beans, not only do you reduce saturated fat, you increase fiber. Canned beans are fine here; just be sure to drain and rinse them thoroughly before using.

1 teaspoon canola oil
1 small onion, finely chopped
1 clove garlic, minced
1 jalapeño pepper, seeded and finely chopped
2 teaspoons ground cumin
1 cup cooked black beans
12 ounces 90%-lean ground beef
2 tablespoons tomato paste
2 tablespoons chopped fresh cilantro
1 teaspoon dried thyme
½ teaspoon salt, or to taste
½ teaspoon freshly ground pepper
4 whole-wheat Kaiser rolls, split and toasted
Tomato salsa for garnish
Shredded lettuce for garnish

1. Heat oil in a small nonstick skillet over medium heat. Add onion and sauté until light golden, about 3 minutes. Add garlic, jalapeño and cumin; sauté until fragrant, about 2 minutes longer. (If the mixture becomes too dry, add 1 tablespoon water.) Transfer the mixture to a medium bowl.

2. Prepare a grill or preheat the broiler. Add beans to the onion mixture and mash coarsely with a potato masher. Add beef, tomato paste, cilantro, thyme, salt and pepper; mix thoroughly but lightly. Shape the mixture into four ¾-inch-thick patties (*see Tip*).

3. Grill or broil the patties on a lightly oiled rack (*see Tip, page 130*) until browned and cooked through, about 5 minutes per side. Place on rolls and garnish with salsa and lettuce.

COOKING TIP: When forming burger patties, make them thinner at the center to prevent them from steaming as they cook.

MAKES 4 SERVINGS.

PER SERVING: 377 CALORIES; 8 G FAT (3 G SAT, 3 G MONO); 53 MG CHOLESTEROL; 50 G CARBOHYDRATE; 30 G PROTEIN; 7 G FIBER; 705 MG SODIUM.

NUTRITION BONUS: 27% DV FIBER, 4 MG IRON (20% DV), 72 MCG FOLATE (18% DV).

Blueberry-Beef Burgers

PREP TIME: 20 MINUTES | **START TO FINISH:** 30 MINUTES | **EASE OF PREPARATION:** EASY

Whatever the season, burgers remain America's favorite sandwich. If the idea of blueberries in a hamburger sounds farfetched (*see box*), consider classic fruit-and-meat combinations like pork with prunes and chicken with apples.

- **2 slices whole-wheat country bread, crusts removed, torn into pieces**
- **⅓ cup fresh *or* frozen and thawed blueberries**
- **1 tablespoon balsamic vinegar**
- **2 teaspoons Dijon mustard**
- **1 teaspoon Worcestershire sauce**
- **2 cloves garlic, minced**
- **¼ teaspoon salt, or to taste**
- **Freshly ground pepper to taste**
- **12 ounces 90%-lean ground beef**

What We Did

Adding the antioxidant powers of blueberries to ground beef serves several purposes. Researchers are investigating the extent to which antioxidants counter the carcinogens that develop when red meat is grilled. With berries standing in for some of the meat, the fat content is reduced. The berries also supply moisture that leaner cuts of ground beef may lack, ensuring a juicy patty.

1. Place bread in a food processor and pulse into fine crumbs. Transfer to a large bowl. (No need to wash the workbowl.)
2. Add blueberries, vinegar, mustard, Worcestershire, garlic, salt and pepper to the food processor; process until pureed. Scrape into the bowl with the breadcrumbs. Add ground beef and mix well with a potato masher. Divide the mixture into four equal portions; form into ½-inch-thick patties, about 4 inches in diameter (*see Tip, page 141*).
3. Meanwhile, preheat broiler or heat an indoor or outdoor grill to medium-high. If using the broiler, coat a broiler pan with cooking spray. If using a grill, oil the grill rack (*see Tip, page 130*). Cook patties until browned and no longer pink in the center, 4 to 5 minutes per side. An instant-read thermometer inserted in the center should register 160°F. Serve immediately, with or without rolls and toppings.

RECIPE RX

Regular 90%-Lean Beef Burger:
262 calories
6 grams saturated fat
0 grams fiber

EW Blueberry-Beef Burger:
200 calories
4 grams saturated fat
1 gram fiber

MAKES 4 SERVINGS.

PER SERVING: 200 CALORIES; 9 G FAT (4 G SAT, 4 G MONO); 55 MG CHOLESTEROL; 10 G CARBOHYDRATE; 19 G PROTEIN; 1 G FIBER; 351 MG SODIUM.

NUTRITION BONUS: 343 MG POTASSIUM (17% DV), 3 MG IRON (15% DV).

Beef, Watercress & Roquefort Burgers

PREP TIME: 10 MINUTES | **START TO FINISH:** 50 MINUTES | **EASE OF PREPARATION:** EASY

Roquefort cheese, peppery watercress and succulent beef create a deliciously bold burger that meat lovers will rave over. The bulgur stretches the ground beef and boosts the fiber.

- **⅓ cup bulgur (*see Ingredient Note, page 394*)**
- **½ cup warm water**
- **12 ounces 90%-lean ground beef**
- **½ cup coarsely chopped watercress leaves, plus extra sprigs for garnish**
- **½ teaspoon salt**
- **¼ teaspoon freshly ground pepper**
- **3 tablespoons crumbled Roquefort cheese (1 ounce)**
- **4 whole-wheat buns, split and toasted**

1. Combine bulgur and warm water in a medium bowl; let stand until the bulgur is tender and the liquid is absorbed, about 30 minutes.

2. Prepare a grill or preheat the broiler. Add beef, watercress, salt and pepper to the plumped bulgur and mix thoroughly but lightly. Shape the mixture into eight ⅜-inch-thick patties (*see Tip, page 141*). Sandwich cheese between the patties to form 4 stuffed burgers.

3. Grill or broil the patties on a lightly oiled rack (*see Tip, page 130*) until browned and cooked through, 4 to 5 minutes per side. (An instant-read thermometer inserted in the center should register 160°F.) Place burgers on buns and garnish with watercress sprigs.

MAKES 4 SERVINGS.

PER SERVING: 328 CALORIES; 13 G FAT (5 G SAT, 5 G MONO); 61 MG CHOLESTEROL; 31 G CARBOHYDRATE; 24 G PROTEIN; 5 G FIBER; 671 MG SODIUM.

NUTRITION BONUS: 478 MG POTASSIUM (24% DV), 22% DV FIBER, 3 MG IRON (20% DV).

PIZZA

8

"Imagine if all of life were determined by majority rule," wrote journalist P.J. O'Rourke. "Every meal would be a pizza." We know some people—and not just children—who would consider that an excellent use of the democratic process. But not all pizzas are created equal. Pizza has suffered from the ubiquitous American urge to take a good thing and overdo it. Crusts bloated with cheese. Extreme amounts of sausage and pepperoni. At EATINGWELL, we've looked to Italy for inspiration, where a few simple ingredients are set off against a thin, crackling-crisp crust, where flavor is prized over sheer heft. Our pizza collection wins votes from both sides—healthful enough and tasty enough to eat every day.

Caramelized Onion & Olive Pizza

PREP TIME: 25 MINUTES | **START TO FINISH:** 40 MINUTES | **EASE OF PREPARATION:** EASY

Sweet onions get even sweeter when they are sautéed until golden and almost meltingly soft. Tangy goat cheese and good imported black olives provide the perfect flavor balance.

Cornmeal for dusting
12 ounces Whole-Wheat Pizza Dough (*page 147*) *or* other prepared dough
1½ teaspoons extra-virgin olive oil
2 large sweet onions, such as Vidalia *or* Walla Walla, thinly sliced
¼ cup water
3 cloves garlic, minced
1 teaspoon chopped fresh rosemary *or* ½ teaspoon dried
Salt & freshly ground pepper to taste
⅓ cup crumbled creamy goat cheese (2 ounces)
8 imported black olives, pitted and chopped

1. Place a pizza stone or inverted baking sheet on the lowest oven rack (*see "Pizza Essentials," page 148*); preheat oven to 500°F or highest setting. Coat a 12½-inch pizza pan with cooking spray and dust with cornmeal.
2. Prepare Whole-Wheat Pizza Dough, if using.
3. Heat oil in a large nonstick skillet over medium-high heat. Add onions and cook, stirring occasionally, until golden and tender, 10 to 15 minutes. Add water, garlic and rosemary and cook, stirring, until fragrant, 1 to 2 minutes more. Season with salt and pepper.
4. On a lightly floured surface, roll the dough into a 13-inch circle. Transfer to the prepared pan. Turn edges under to make a slight rim. Spread the onion mixture over the dough. Scatter goat cheese and olives over the onions.
5. Place the pizza pan on the heated pizza stone (or baking sheet) and bake the pizza until the edges are golden and the topping is bubbling, 10 to 20 minutes. Slice into wedges and serve.

MAKES ONE 12-INCH PIZZA, FOR 4 SLICES.

PER SLICE: 339 CALORIES; 9 G FAT (3 G SAT, 4 G MONO); 7 MG CHOLESTEROL; 55 G CARBOHYDRATE; 11 G PROTEIN; 6 G FIBER; 691 MG SODIUM.

NUTRITION BONUS: 119 MCG FOLATE (30% DV), 26% DV FIBER, 11 MG VITAMIN C (20% DV), 3 MG IRON (15% DV).

WHOLE-WHEAT PIZZA DOUGH

PREP TIME: 5 MINUTES | **START TO FINISH:** 15 MINUTES | **TO MAKE AHEAD:** THE DOUGH WILL KEEP, IN A PLASTIC BAG COATED WITH COOKING SPRAY, IN THE REFRIGERATOR FOR UP TO 2 DAYS. BRING TO ROOM TEMPERATURE BEFORE USING. | **EASE OF PREPARATION:** MODERATE

To improve the nutritional profile of pizza, include whole-wheat flour in the crust. Using half whole-wheat and half all-purpose yields a light crust with a distinctive nutty taste. Quick-rising yeast shortens rising time to just 10 minutes, making wholesome homemade pizza a possibility for busy weeknights.

A food processor makes fast work of mixing the dough, but you can also use a stand mixer fitted with a paddle attachment, or a little elbow grease to do it by hand. Whichever method you choose, add enough liquid to the dry ingredients to make a soft dough. If kneading by hand, knead for about 10 minutes. Toss, rather than push, the dough onto the counter; this allows the gluten to develop without incorporating too much flour.

TO MAKE 12 OUNCES DOUGH:

- **¾ cup whole-wheat flour**
- **¾ cup all-purpose flour**
- **1 package quick-rising yeast (2¼ teaspoons), such as Fleischmann's RapidRise**
- **¾ teaspoon salt**
- **¼ teaspoon sugar**
- **½-⅔ cup hot water (120-130°F)**
- **2 teaspoons extra-virgin olive oil**

TO MAKE 1 POUND DOUGH:

- **1 cup whole-wheat flour**
- **1 cup all-purpose flour**
- **1 package quick-rising yeast (2¼ teaspoons), such as Fleischmann's RapidRise**
- **1 teaspoon salt**
- **½ teaspoon sugar**
- **¾ cup hot water (120-130°F)**
- **1 tablespoon extra-virgin olive oil**

1. Combine whole-wheat flour, all-purpose flour, yeast, salt and sugar in a food processor; pulse to mix. Combine hot water and oil in a measuring cup. With the motor running, gradually pour in enough of the hot liquid until the mixture forms a sticky ball. The dough should be quite soft. If it seems dry, add 1 to 2 tablespoons warm water; if too sticky, add 1 to 2 tablespoons flour. Process until the dough forms a ball, then process for 1 minute to knead.

2. Transfer the dough to a lightly floured surface. Coat a sheet of plastic wrap with cooking spray and place it, sprayed-side down, over the dough. Let the dough rest for 10 to 20 minutes before rolling.

PER 12 OUNCES: 766 CALORIES; 12 G FAT (2 G SAT, 8 G MONO); 0 MG CHOLESTEROL; 142 G CARBOHYDRATE; 26 G PROTEIN; 16 G FIBER; 1,882 MG SODIUM.

PER 1 POUND: 1,032 CALORIES; 18 G FAT (3 G SAT, 12 G MONO); 0 MG CHOLESTEROL; 189 G CARBOHYDRATE; 33 G PROTEIN; 21 G FIBER; 2,509 MG SODIUM.

Pizza Essentials

One way to ensure a really great pizza crust is to use a wood-burning oven that reaches a temperature of at least 600°F, a feature most home kitchens lack. Fortunately, you can transform your regular oven into a pizza oven by baking directly on a hot pizza stone. The unglazed clay surface absorbs and distributes heat evenly, producing a crisp crust. Here are some tips for adapting the recipes:

USING A PIZZA STONE

- Place a pizza stone in a cold oven on the lowest rack. Allow at least 30 minutes for the stone to heat before baking the pizza.

- Let dough come to room temperature before baking. If cold dough is placed directly on a heated pizza stone, the abrupt change in temperature may cause the stone to crack.

- Because pizza stones are porous, they absorb odors. Avoid using soap to clean them. Wash with warm water and use baking soda to remove stubborn stains.

USING A PIZZA PEEL

- The best way to transfer a pizza to a stone is to use a wooden paddle called a peel—and it is much easier to slide a small pizza from a peel than to slide a large one. To use a peel for recipes that call for 12 ounces of dough, divide the dough in half and roll one piece into a 10-inch circle. Transfer the crust to a cornmeal-dusted pizza peel. Turn edges under to make a slight rim. Assemble the pizza, using half the topping. Make sure the dough slides easily on the peel; add more cornmeal if necessary.

Open the oven door and set the tip of the pizza peel near the back of the stone. Pull the pizza peel toward you, letting the pizza slide onto the stone. Quickly close the door. Baking time for a pizza baked directly on a stone is shorter than for pan pizza: allow 8 to 10 minutes. Assemble the second pizza on the peel with the remaining dough and toppings while the first one bakes.

- To remove the pizza from the oven, use a wide metal spatula to slide the pizza onto a pizza peel or pizza pan.

PIZZA FOR A CROWD

When using a home oven, you will achieve the best results making one pizza at a time. However, if you would like to double any of our recipes, assemble the larger pizza on a 17½-by-12½-inch baking sheet that has been coated with cooking spray and dusted with cornmeal. To help crisp the crust, set the baking sheet in the oven on a heated pizza stone or inverted baking sheet.

Peperonata & Sausage Pizza

PREP TIME: 50 MINUTES | **START TO FINISH:** 1 HOUR 5 MINUTES | **EASE OF PREPARATION:** MODERATE

A melding of sautéed onions, bell peppers and tomatoes, peperonata is often served as an Italian antipasto. (*Photo: page 212.*)

Cornmeal for dusting
12 ounces Whole-Wheat Pizza Dough (*page 147*) *or* other prepared dough
1 link Italian turkey sausage (4 ounces), casing removed

PEPERONATA

3 teaspoons extra-virgin olive oil, divided
1 cup slivered onion (1 medium)
1 cup thinly sliced red bell pepper (½ large)
2 cloves garlic, minced
⅛ teaspoon crushed red pepper
¾ cup diced tomato (1 medium)
2 teaspoons red-wine vinegar
⅛ teaspoon salt
Freshly ground pepper to taste

1 cup grated part-skim mozzarella cheese
¼ cup freshly grated Parmesan cheese

1. Place a pizza stone or inverted baking sheet on the lowest oven rack (*see "Pizza Essentials," page 148*); preheat oven to 500°F or highest setting. Coat a 12½-inch pizza pan with cooking spray and dust with cornmeal.
2. Prepare Whole-Wheat Pizza Dough, if using.
3. Cook sausage in a small nonstick skillet over medium heat, turning from time to time, until browned and cooked through, 10 to 12 minutes. Drain and cut into ¼-inch-thick slices.
4. **Meanwhile, prepare peperonata:** Heat 2 teaspoons oil in a large nonstick skillet over medium heat. Add onion and bell pepper; cook, stirring often, until softened, 4 to 6 minutes. Add garlic and crushed red pepper; cook, stirring, for 1 minute. Add tomato and cook for 3 minutes. Remove from the heat and stir in vinegar, salt and pepper. Transfer to a plate and let cool.
5. On a lightly floured surface, roll the dough into a 13-inch circle. Transfer to the prepared pan. Turn edges under to make a slight rim. Brush the rim with the remaining 1 teaspoon oil.
6. Sprinkle mozzarella over the crust, leaving a ½-inch border. Top with the peperonata and sausage. Sprinkle with Parmesan.
7. Place the pizza pan on the heated pizza stone (or baking sheet) and bake the pizza until the bottom is crisp and golden, 10 to 14 minutes. Serve immediately.

MAKES ONE 12-INCH PIZZA, FOR 4 SLICES.

PER SLICE: 416 CALORIES; 17 G FAT (6 G SAT, 7 G MONO); 37 MG CHOLESTEROL; 46 G CARBOHYDRATE; 22 G PROTEIN; 6 G FIBER; 956 MG SODIUM.

NUTRITION BONUS: 67 MG VITAMIN C (110% DV), 45% DV VITAMIN A, 290 MG CALCIUM (30% DV), 23% DV FIBER, 4 MG IRON (20% DV).

VEGETARIAN VARIATION: Replace the sausage with ¼ cup halved Kalamata olives.

Pizza Margherita

PREP TIME: 15 MINUTES | **START TO FINISH:** 25 MINUTES | **EASE OF PREPARATION:** EASY

This pizza is said to have been a favorite of Margaret of Savoy; supposedly the garlic was left out so that no odor might sully the breath of the Queen of Italy.

- **Semolina *or* cornmeal for dusting**
- **12 ounces Whole-Wheat Pizza Dough (*page 147*) *or* other prepared dough**
- **3 teaspoons extra-virgin olive oil, divided**
- **½ cup prepared tomato sauce *or* Basic Tomato Sauce (*page 169*)**
- **2 ounces mozzarella cheese, sliced ⅛ inch thick**
- **Salt & freshly ground pepper to taste**
- **½ cup loosely packed fresh basil leaves (1 small bunch), rinsed**
- **¼ cup freshly grated Parmesan cheese**

1. Place a pizza stone or inverted baking sheet on the lowest oven rack (*see "Pizza Essentials," page 148*); preheat oven to 500°F or highest setting. Coat a 12½-inch pizza pan with cooking spray and dust with cornmeal.
2. Prepare Whole-Wheat Pizza Dough, if using.
3. On a lightly floured surface, roll the dough into a 13-inch circle. Transfer to the prepared pan. Turn edges under to make a slight rim. Brush the rim with 1 teaspoon oil.
4. Spread tomato sauce over the crust, leaving a ½-inch border. Distribute mozzarella slices over the sauce; season with salt and pepper. Arrange basil leaves over the mozzarella, reserving a few for garnish if you wish. Sprinkle with Parmesan. Drizzle with the remaining 2 teaspoons oil.
5. Place the pizza pan on the heated pizza stone (or baking sheet) and bake the pizza until the bottom is crisp and browned and the top is bubbling, 10 to 14 minutes. Garnish with the reserved basil leaves, if desired.

MAKES ONE 12-INCH PIZZA, FOR 4 SLICES.

PER SLICE: 312 CALORIES; 12 G FAT (4 G SAT, 7 G MONO); 12 MG CHOLESTEROL; 40 G CARBOHYDRATE; 13 G PROTEIN; 5 G FIBER; 715 MG SODIUM.

NUTRITION BONUS: 193 MG CALCIUM (20% DV), 19% DV FIBER, 3 MG IRON (15% DV).

Pizza with Broccoli & Black Olives

PREP TIME: 30 MINUTES | **START TO FINISH:** 45 MINUTES | **EASE OF PREPARATION:** MODERATE

Broccoli, accented by black olives, makes a delicious—and extra healthful—pizza topping. As a variation, substitute Canadian bacon for the olives.

- **Cornmeal for dusting**
- **12 ounces Whole-Wheat Pizza Dough (*page 147*) *or* other prepared dough**
- **2 cups broccoli florets, cut into ¾-inch pieces**
- **½ cup diced red onion**
- **1 tablespoon plus 1 teaspoon extra-virgin olive oil**
- **⅔ cup prepared marinara sauce *or* Basic Tomato Sauce (*page 169*)**
- **¾ teaspoon dried oregano**
- **⅛ teaspoon crushed red pepper**
- **1 cup grated part-skim mozzarella cheese**
- **¼ cup Kalamata olives, pitted and coarsely chopped**

1. Place a pizza stone or inverted baking sheet on the lowest oven rack (*see "Pizza Essentials," page 148*); preheat oven to 500°F or highest setting. Coat a 12½-inch pizza pan with cooking spray and dust with cornmeal.
2. Prepare Whole-Wheat Pizza Dough, if using.
3. Place broccoli in a steamer basket over boiling water, cover and steam until just tender, 2 to 3 minutes. Rinse with cold water to stop cooking; drain well. Transfer to a medium bowl, add onion and 1 tablespoon oil; toss to coat.
4. Combine sauce, oregano and crushed red pepper.
5. On a lightly floured surface, roll the dough into a 13-inch circle. Transfer to the prepared pan. Turn edges under to make a slight rim. Brush the rim with the remaining 1 teaspoon oil.
6. Spread the sauce over the crust, leaving a ½-inch border. Sprinkle with mozzarella. Scatter the broccoli mixture over the cheese. Sprinkle with olives.
7. Place the pizza pan on the heated pizza stone (or baking sheet) and bake the pizza until the bottom is crisp and golden, 10 to 14 minutes. Serve immediately.

MAKES ONE 12-INCH PIZZA, FOR 4 SLICES.

PER SLICE: 374 CALORIES; 15 G FAT (4 G SAT, 9 G MONO); 18 MG CHOLESTEROL; 45 G CARBOHYDRATE; 15 G PROTEIN; 6 G FIBER; 927 MG SODIUM.

NUTRITION BONUS: 37 MG VITAMIN C (60% DV), 92 MCG FOLATE (32% DV), 30% DV VITAMIN A, 268 MG CALCIUM (25% DV), 24% DV FIBER.

Pizza with Potato & Artichoke Topping

PREP TIME: 30 MINUTES | **START TO FINISH:** 45 MINUTES | **EASE OF PREPARATION:** MODERATE

Potatoes may sound like an unusual, somewhat redundant pizza topping, but the combination is much loved in Italy. Artichokes complement the potatoes for a thoroughly satisfying meatless pie.

Cornmeal for dusting
12 ounces Whole-Wheat Pizza Dough (*page 147*) *or* other prepared dough
2 medium potatoes, preferably Yukon Gold, peeled, cut lengthwise into quarters and sliced ¼ inch thick
¾ cup prepared marinara sauce *or* Basic Tomato Sauce (*page 169*)
¼ teaspoon crushed red pepper
1 teaspoon extra-virgin olive oil
1 cup grated part-skim mozzarella cheese
1 14-ounce can artichoke hearts, rinsed and quartered
¼ teaspoon salt
Freshly ground pepper to taste
2 tablespoons chopped fresh parsley
¼ cup freshly grated Parmesan cheese

1. Place a pizza stone or inverted baking sheet on the lowest oven rack (*see "Pizza Essentials," page 148*); preheat oven to 500°F or highest setting. Coat a 12½-inch pizza pan with cooking spray and dust with cornmeal.
2. Prepare Whole-Wheat Pizza Dough, if using.
3. Place potatoes in a steamer basket over boiling water, cover and steam until just tender, 7 to 8 minutes. Rinse with cold water to stop cooking. Pat dry.
4. Combine sauce and crushed red pepper.
5. On a lightly floured surface, roll the dough into a 13-inch circle. Transfer to the prepared pan. Turn edges under to make a slight rim. Brush the rim with oil.
6. Spread the sauce over the crust, leaving a ½-inch border. Sprinkle with mozzarella. Scatter the potatoes and artichokes over the cheese. Season with salt and pepper and sprinkle with parsley. Top with Parmesan.
7. Place the pizza pan on the heated pizza stone (or baking sheet) and bake the pizza until the bottom is crisp and golden, 10 to 14 minutes. Serve immediately.

MAKES ONE 12-INCH PIZZA, FOR 4 SLICES.

PER SLICE: 438 CALORIES; 12 G FAT (5 G SAT, 5 G MONO); 18 MG CHOLESTEROL; 65 G CARBOHYDRATE; 21 G PROTEIN; 10 G FIBER; 1,148 MG SODIUM.

NUTRITION BONUS: 32 MG VITAMIN C (50% DV), 39% DV FIBER, 638 MG POTASSIUM (32% DV), 281 MG CALCIUM (30% DV).

Pizza with White Beans, Prosciutto & Rosemary

PREP TIME: 30 MINUTES | **START TO FINISH:** 45 MINUTES | **EASE OF PREPARATION:** MODERATE

White beans seasoned with fresh rosemary and prosciutto make this rustic pizza an interesting departure from your standard take-out fare. Scattering it with arugula after baking provides a contrasting texture and a fresh, appealing finish. (*Photo: page 212.*)

- Cornmeal for dusting
- 12 ounces Whole-Wheat Pizza Dough (*page 147*) *or* other prepared dough
- 1 cup canned cannellini beans, rinsed
- 1 tablespoon plus 1 teaspoon extra-virgin olive oil
- 1 tablespoon chopped fresh rosemary
- 1 clove garlic, minced
- ¼ teaspoon crushed red pepper
- ⅔ cup prepared marinara sauce *or* Basic Tomato Sauce (*page 169*)
- ½ cup freshly grated Parmesan cheese, divided
- 2 ounces thinly sliced lean prosciutto, diced (½ cup)
- ½ cup diced red onion
- Freshly ground pepper to taste
- 1½ cups lightly packed arugula leaves, torn

1. Place a pizza stone or inverted baking sheet on the lowest oven rack (*see "Pizza Essentials," page 148*); preheat oven to 500°F or highest setting. Coat a 12½-inch pizza pan with cooking spray and dust with cornmeal.
2. Prepare Whole-Wheat Pizza Dough, if using.
3. Combine beans, 1 tablespoon oil, rosemary, garlic and crushed red pepper in a medium bowl; toss to coat.
4. On a lightly floured surface, roll the dough into a 13-inch circle. Transfer to the prepared pan. Turn edges under to make a slight rim. Brush the rim with the remaining 1 teaspoon oil.
5. Spread sauce over the crust, leaving a ½-inch border. Sprinkle with ¼ cup Parmesan. Spread the bean mixture on top. Sprinkle with prosciutto and onion. Top with the remaining ¼ cup Parmesan. Grind pepper over the top.
6. Place the pizza pan on the heated pizza stone (or baking sheet) and bake the pizza until the bottom is crisp and golden, 10 to 14 minutes. Scatter arugula over the pizza and serve immediately.

MAKES ONE 12-INCH PIZZA, FOR 4 SLICES.

PER SLICE: 386 CALORIES; 13 G FAT (3 G SAT, 7 G MONO); 17 MG CHOLESTEROL; 52 G CARBOHYDRATE; 16 G PROTEIN; 8 G FIBER; 1,151 MG SODIUM.

NUTRITION BONUS: 31% DV FIBER, 4 MG IRON (25% DV), 142 MG CALCIUM (15% DV).

Turkish-Style Pizza

PREP TIME: 30 MINUTES | **START TO FINISH:** 45 MINUTES | **EASE OF PREPARATION:** MODERATE

Italians usually get the credit for inventing pizza, but some people believe that Turkish *pide* (flatbreads with toppings) may have come first. This recipe is an adaptation of a pizza discovered in a street-side café in the Mediterranean coastal city of Antalya.

Cornmeal for dusting
12 ounces Whole-Wheat Pizza Dough (*page 147*) *or* other prepared dough
1 teaspoon plus 1 tablespoon extra-virgin olive oil
1½ cups grated fontina *or* Monterey Jack cheese
1½ cups diced tomatoes (2 medium)
1 cup diced sweet onion, such as Vidalia (1 medium)
2 tablespoons minced seeded jalapeño pepper (1 pepper)
2 ounces sliced pastrami, diced (½ cup), optional
Freshly ground pepper to taste
⅓ cup fresh flat-leaf parsley leaves, torn

1. Place a pizza stone or inverted baking sheet on the lowest oven rack (*see "Pizza Essentials," page 148*); preheat oven to 500°F or highest setting. Coat a large baking sheet with cooking spray and dust with cornmeal.

2. Prepare Whole-Wheat Pizza Dough, if using.

3. On a lightly floured surface, roll the dough into a 15-by-10-inch oval. Transfer to the prepared baking sheet. Turn edges under to make a slight rim. Brush the rim with 1 teaspoon oil.

4. Sprinkle cheese over the crust, leaving a ½-inch border. Top with tomatoes, onion, jalapeño and pastrami, if using. Season with pepper. Drizzle with the remaining 1 tablespoon oil.

5. Place the baking sheet on the heated pizza stone (or baking sheet) and bake the pizza until the bottom is crisp and golden, 10 to 14 minutes. Sprinkle with parsley and serve immediately.

TEST KITCHEN TIP:
To bake this recipe directly on a pizza stone, make two 14-by-7-inch oval pizzas.

MAKES ONE 14½-BY-9½-INCH PIZZA, FOR 6 SLICES.

PER SLICE: 286 CALORIES; 14 G FAT (6 G SAT, 6 G MONO); 31 MG CHOLESTEROL; 30 G CARBOHYDRATE; 12 G PROTEIN; 4 G FIBER; 535 MG SODIUM.

NUTRITION BONUS: 20% DV VITAMIN A, 13 MG VITAMIN C (20% DV), 171 MG CALCIUM (15% DV), 15% DV FIBER.

Spinach & Roasted Red Pepper Calzones

PREP TIME: 25 MINUTES | **START TO FINISH:** 40 MINUTES | **EASE OF PREPARATION:** EASY

Using our quick food processor pizza dough (page 147) or purchased dough, these stuffed turnovers are as easy to make as a flat pizza. If you like, serve the calzones with a bowl of extra sauce for dipping.

- Cornmeal for dusting
- 1 pound Whole-Wheat Pizza Dough (*page 147*) *or* other prepared dough
- ¾ cup prepared marinara sauce *or* Basic Tomato Sauce (*page 169*)
- 1 10-ounce package frozen chopped spinach, thawed and drained
- Salt & freshly ground pepper to taste
- 1 7½-ounce jar roasted red peppers, rinsed and sliced (½ cup)
- ¾ cup crumbled feta *or* ricotta salata cheese (3 ounces) (*see Note*)

1. Position rack in lowest position; preheat oven to 450°F. Sprinkle a baking sheet generously with cornmeal.
2. Prepare Whole-Wheat Pizza Dough, if using.
3. On a lightly floured surface, divide the dough into 4 pieces. Roll each piece into an 8-inch circle. Spread 2 tablespoons sauce on the lower half of each circle, leaving a 1-inch border. Season spinach with salt and pepper and distribute it over the sauce. Top with roasted red peppers and cheese.
4. Brush the border with cold water and fold the top half of each circle over the filling. Fold the edges over and crimp with a fork to seal. Transfer the calzones to the prepared baking sheet.
5. Bake the calzones for 12 to 15 minutes, or until golden. Let cool slightly before serving.

INGREDIENT NOTE: Ricotta salata is ricotta cheese that has been aged with salt. Look for it in a specialty cheese shop or gourmet food store.

MAKES 4 CALZONES.

PER CALZONE: 368 CALORIES; 8 G FAT (3 G SAT, 2 G MONO); 8 MG CHOLESTEROL; 61 G CARBOHYDRATE; 16 G PROTEIN; 10 G FIBER; 1,405 MG SODIUM.

NUTRITION BONUS: 190% DV VITAMIN A, 37 MG VITAMIN C (60% DV), 40% DV FIBER, 157 MCG FOLATE (39% DV), 5 MG IRON (30% DV), 233 MG CALCIUM (25% DV).

Grilled Pizza with Eggplant, Tomatoes & Feta

PREP TIME: 30 MINUTES | **START TO FINISH:** 45 MINUTES | **EASE OF PREPARATION:** EASY

For this Greek-style pizza, eggplant slices are grilled, chopped and tossed with fresh tomatoes, feta and mint; the mixture is spread on the pizza to finish cooking.

- 1 pound Whole-Wheat Pizza Dough (*page 147*) *or* other prepared dough
- 1 large eggplant (about 1¼ pounds), trimmed and cut into ½-inch-thick slices
- 2 tablespoons extra-virgin olive oil, divided
- Salt & freshly ground pepper to taste
- 2 large vine-ripened tomatoes, seeded and roughly chopped (about 2 cups)
- ⅓ cup crumbled feta cheese (about 2 ounces)
- 4 tablespoons chopped fresh mint, divided

1. Prepare Whole-Wheat Pizza Dough, if using. Prepare the grill (*see Step 1 in "Pizza on the Grill," page 157*).

2. Toss eggplant slices with 1 tablespoon oil in a large bowl. Sprinkle the slices with salt and pepper and grill, turning often, until tender, about 8 minutes. Let cool; chop coarsely.

3. Combine the chopped eggplant with tomatoes, feta cheese, 2 tablespoons mint and the remaining 1 tablespoon oil in a mixing bowl. Season with salt and pepper.

4. Form and grill the pizzas as described in Steps 2 through 5 (*"Pizza on the Grill"*). In Step 4, distribute the eggplant mixture on the crusts after turning. Just before serving, scatter the remaining 2 tablespoons mint over the pizzas.

MAKES FOUR 6-INCH PIZZAS, FOR 4 SERVINGS.

PER SERVING: 409 CALORIES; 14 G FAT (3 G SAT, 8 G MONO); 5 MG CHOLESTEROL; 61 G CARBOHYDRATE; 13 G PROTEIN; 10 G FIBER; 889 MG SODIUM.

NUTRITION BONUS: 27 MG VITAMIN C (45% DV), 58 MCG FOLATE (29% DV), 553 MG POTASSIUM (28% DV), 22% DV FIBER.

Grilled Pizza with Garden Tomatoes

PREP TIME: 20 MINUTES | **START TO FINISH:** 35 MINUTES | **EASE OF PREPARATION:** EASY

Alternate yellow and red tomatoes on the pizza for a pretty effect. If you don't have *olivada* (black olive spread), use a little prepared tomato sauce and scatter sliced olives over the top.

- 1 pound Whole-Wheat Pizza Dough (*page 147*) *or* other prepared dough
- 4 tablespoons *olivada*
- 2 pounds vine-ripened tomatoes, very thinly sliced (4-6 tomatoes)
- Salt & freshly ground pepper to taste
- 1 cup grated fresh mozzarella cheese (3 ounces)
- ¼ cup chopped fresh basil leaves

1. Prepare Whole-Wheat Pizza Dough, if using. Prepare the grill (*see Step 1, below*).

2. Grill the pizzas as described in Steps 2 through 5 (*below*). In Step 4, spread *olivada* on the crusts after turning, then cover with overlapping tomato slices, sprinkle with salt and pepper and scatter mozzarella over all. Just before serving, sprinkle the pizzas with basil.

TEST KITCHEN TIP: To make grating fresh mozzarella easier, place it in the freezer to firm up for about 20 minutes.

MAKES FOUR 6-INCH PIZZAS, FOR 4 SERVINGS.

PER SERVING: 447 CALORIES; 18 G FAT (4 G SAT, 4 G MONO); 13 MG CHOLESTEROL; 58 G CARBOHYDRATE; 16 G PROTEIN; 8 G FIBER; 911 MG SODIUM.

NUTRITION BONUS: 59 MG VITAMIN C (100% DV), 35% DV VITAMIN A, 554 MG POTASSIUM (28% DV).

TECHNIQUE

Pizza on the Grill

THE FIRST TIME you slide a circle of dough onto a grill rack, you realize this technique really is going to work. We found that a covered grill with a large surface area is best because it allows you to crisp one side of the crust over hot coals, then flip the crust over onto indirect heat to warm the toppings and melt the cheese.

Step 1. To cook pizzas on a charcoal grill, build a medium-hot fire in one half of the grill (two bricks placed end-to-end work well as a divider). For a gas grill with two burners, preheat one burner on high, leaving the other unlit. For a single-burner gas grill, preheat on high, and lower the flame to cook the second side of the pizzas.

Step 2. Roll out the pizza dough into 4 circles and place on a floured cutting board. Bring the dough, toppings and a pair of tongs to grillside.

Step 3. Place 2 of the dough circles on the hot side of the grill. Within 1 minute the dough will puff slightly, and the underside will firm up and be striped with grill marks. Use tongs to flip the crusts over and onto the cooler side of the grill.

Step 4. Spread half of the toppings on the two crusts. Cover the grill and cook, rotating the pizzas once or twice, until the toppings are heated through, about 5 minutes.

Step 5. Remove the pizzas from the grill. Repeat Steps 3 and 4 with the remaining dough and toppings.

PASTA

9

Given its ancient Mediterranean origins, it is impressive how many of us have abandoned pasta in the name of health. But is that necessary? Before you pack away your spaghetti pot, consider what pasta, smartly made, has to offer. In the pages that follow, you'll find recipes rich with antioxidants and omega-3 fatty acids from vegetables, nuts and healthy oils; many are high in protein from seafood and lean meat. And while the carb counts may look high, wherever appropriate, we've used whole-wheat pasta, a significant source of dietary fiber that's dense with trace nutrients and phytochemicals. Because these dishes are satisfying—as well as great-tasting—you'll find it easy to keep portion sizes under control. Add a big salad of leafy greens and set your pasta passions free again.

Carb Control

THE FIBER CONTENT OF WHOLE-WHEAT PASTA makes it a great choice for those counting carbohydrates. Because dietary fiber is undigested, you can simply subtract the grams of dietary fiber from the total grams of carbohydrates. For example, in the Roasted Vegetable Pasta (*page 162*) the carbohydrate count of 49 can be reduced by the fiber count of 9; the remaining 40 grams is then used by someone monitoring their carb intake.

Pasta with Parsley-Walnut Pesto

PREP TIME: 15 MINUTES | **START TO FINISH:** 30 MINUTES | **EASE OF PREPARATION:** EASY

Remaking this classic high-calorie, high-fat pasta sauce was a great success. By adding fresh breadcrumbs to the pesto, we were able to use much less oil. The pesto still coats the pasta nicely and its herbal flavor remains intense and vibrant. Parsley is more than just a garnish—it's a rich source of carotenoids and vitamin C.

- 2 tablespoons walnuts
- 2 slices whole-wheat country bread, crusts trimmed
- 1 cup packed fresh parsley leaves
- 1 clove garlic, peeled and chopped
- 2 tablespoons nonfat plain yogurt
- 2 tablespoons walnut oil (*see Ingredient Note, page 395*) *or* extra-virgin olive oil
- Salt & freshly ground pepper to taste
- 12 ounces whole-wheat fusilli *or* penne (*see "Taste Test," page 161*)
- 2 tablespoons freshly grated Parmesan cheese

1. Put a large pot of lightly salted water on to boil. Toast walnuts in a small skillet over medium heat, stirring, until fragrant, 3 to 4 minutes. Transfer to a plate to cool.

2. Tear bread into large pieces and pulse in a food processor to form fine crumbs. Add parsley, garlic and the walnuts and pulse until finely chopped, scraping down the sides as needed. Add yogurt and oil; process until smooth. Season with salt and pepper.

3. Cook pasta until just tender, 8 to 10 minutes, or according to package directions. Drain and place in a warmed large shallow bowl. Toss with pesto until well coated. Sprinkle with Parmesan and serve.

MAKES 4 SERVINGS.

PER SERVING: 439 CALORIES; 10 G FAT (1 G SAT, 2 G MONO); 2 MG CHOLESTEROL; 75 G CARBOHYDRATE; 13 G PROTEIN; 9 G FIBER; 246 MG SODIUM.

NUTRITION BONUS: 21 MG VITAMIN C (35% DV), 36% DV FIBER, 25% DV VITAMIN A.

Pasta Essentials

TIMING IT RIGHT

ONCE COOKED, pasta will wait for no one—especially a disorganized cook. Most sauces can easily be kept warm for a few minutes while the pasta finishes cooking, but the opposite doesn't hold true. In some cases, such as in Spaghetti with Clams (*page 167*), the sauce cooks in even less time than the pasta. Make sure you have all the ingredients prepped (chopping parsley, mincing garlic, etc.) before you drop the pasta into boiling water.

SHAPES & SAUCES

THE MANY DIFFERENT SHAPES of pasta can overwhelm a cook, but each particular shape has its role in the world of sauces. The nooks and crannies of fusilli, for instance, offer a cozy refuge for nuts and pieces of meat and vegetables. In contrast, smooth tomato sauces, pestos and light cream recipes work best with long thin pastas, such as spaghetti, because they coat the strands evenly.

Fusilli with Garden-Fresh Tomato "Sauce"

PREP TIME: 20 MINUTES | **START TO FINISH:** 35 MINUTES | **TO MAKE AHEAD:** PREPARE SAUCE (STEP 1). COVER AND LET STAND AT ROOM TEMPERATURE FOR UP TO 1½ HOURS. | **EASE OF PREPARATION:** EASY

This easy uncooked sauce is perfect on a hot summer night. You can serve it right away, but it tastes even better if everything marinates for an hour or so. To feed more people, simply add a little more of each ingredient—especially the tomatoes. Halved cherry tomatoes are a nice alternative to field tomatoes.

- 3 cups diced, seeded ripe tomatoes
- ½ cup finely diced green bell pepper
- 2 scallions, white and pale green parts only, thinly sliced
- 1 clove garlic, minced
- ¼ cup extra-virgin olive oil
- 1 cup crumbled feta cheese (4 ounces)
- ½ cup Kalamata olives, pitted and coarsely chopped
- 2 tablespoons chopped fresh flat-leaf parsley
- 2 tablespoons chopped fresh basil
- 2 tablespoons balsamic vinegar
- 1 tablespoon red-wine vinegar
- 1 tablespoon lemon juice
- ⅛ teaspoon salt, or to taste
- Freshly ground pepper to taste
- 12 ounces whole-wheat fusilli *or* other whole-wheat pasta (*see "Taste Test," right*)

1. Combine tomatoes, bell pepper, scallions, garlic and oil in a large bowl; toss to mix well. Add feta cheese, olives, parsley, basil, balsamic vinegar, wine vinegar and lemon juice; toss again. Season with salt and pepper.

2. Put a large pot of lightly salted water on to boil. Shortly before serving, cook pasta according to package directions. Drain and add to the sauce; toss to coat well.

MAKES 6 SERVINGS, 1⅔ CUPS EACH.

PER SERVING: 387 CALORIES; 17 G FAT (5 G SAT, 11 G MONO); 17 MG CHOLESTEROL; 49 G CARBOHYDRATE; 10 G PROTEIN; 7 G FIBER; 513 MG SODIUM.

ANALYSIS NOTE: While this dish is high in fat, it's mostly from heart-healthful monounsaturated fats.

NUTRITION BONUS: 22 MG VITAMIN C (35% DV), 26% DV FIBER.

Taste Test

IN A COMPARISON OF SEVERAL BRANDS of whole-wheat pasta, our tasters gave top marks to Bionaturæ. Others that rated well were Hodgson Mill and Prince Healthy Harvest (not a true whole-wheat pasta, but a blend that includes wheat germ and bran). You can find a selection in the natural-foods section of large markets and in natural-foods stores.

Roasted Vegetable Pasta

PREP TIME: 15 MINUTES | **START TO FINISH:** 35 MINUTES | **EASE OF PREPARATION:** EASY

Inspired by hunger and what's in the garden, this is a quick and flexible dish. For more roasted vegetables, see "Essential Vegetable-Roasting Guide," page 121.

- **1 medium zucchini, diced**
- **1 red *or* yellow bell pepper, seeded and diced**
- **1 large onion, thinly sliced**
- **2 tablespoons extra-virgin olive oil, divided**
- **Salt & freshly ground pepper to taste**
- **2 large tomatoes, chopped**
- **¼ cup chopped fresh basil**
- **2 cloves garlic, minced**
- **12 ounces whole-wheat pasta** (*see "Taste Test," page 161*)
- **½ cup crumbled feta cheese**

1. Preheat oven to 450°F. Put a large pot of lightly salted water on to boil.

2. Toss zucchini, bell pepper and onion with 1 tablespoon oil in a large roasting pan or a large baking sheet with sides. Season with salt and pepper. Roast the vegetables, stirring every 5 minutes, until tender and browned, 10 to 20 minutes.

3. Meanwhile, combine tomatoes, basil, garlic and the remaining 1 tablespoon oil in a large bowl. Season with salt and pepper.

4. Cook pasta until just tender, 8 to 10 minutes. Drain and transfer to the bowl with the tomatoes. Add the roasted vegetables and toss well. Adjust seasoning with salt and pepper. Serve, passing feta cheese separately.

MAKES 6 SERVINGS, ABOUT 1½ CUPS EACH.

PER SERVING: 288 CALORIES; 7 G FAT (2 G SAT, 4 G MONO); 3 MG CHOLESTEROL; 49 G CARBOHYDRATE; 11 G PROTEIN; 9 G FIBER; 177 MG SODIUM.

NUTRITION BONUS: 53 MG VITAMIN C (90% DV), 34% DV FIBER, 25% DV VITAMIN A.

Soba Noodles with Roasted Eggplant

PREP TIME: 20 MINUTES | **START TO FINISH:** 50 MINUTES
TO MAKE AHEAD: THE SALAD WILL KEEP, COVERED, IN THE REFRIGERATOR FOR UP TO 1 DAY. BRING TO ROOM TEMPERATURE BEFORE SERVING. | **EASE OF PREPARATION:** MODERATE

Roasted eggplant makes a creamy sauce that coats pasta quite nicely. Soba (Japanese buckwheat noodles) add a lovely nutty flavor to the dish, but you can also use linguine.

- 1 medium eggplant (1 pound)
- 2 tablespoons sesame seeds
- 8 ounces soba noodles
- 1 teaspoon plus 1 tablespoon peanut oil *or* canola oil, divided
- 2 cloves garlic, crushed and peeled
- ½ teaspoon salt
- 3½ tablespoons rice vinegar
- 2 tablespoons reduced-sodium soy sauce
- 2 tablespoons minced fresh ginger
- 2 tablespoons brown sugar
- 1½ teaspoons chile-garlic sauce
- 3 cups grated carrots (about 5 carrots)
- ½ cup chopped fresh cilantro
- 1 cup diced cucumber

1. Preheat broiler. Cut eggplant in half lengthwise. Place the halves cut-side down on a baking sheet. Broil about 4 inches from the heat until the skin is blackened and the flesh is very soft, 10 to 15 minutes. Set aside to cool.
2. Meanwhile, bring a large pot of lightly salted water to a boil for cooking pasta. Stir sesame seeds in a small skillet over medium-low heat until toasted and fragrant, about 2 minutes. Transfer to a small dish to cool.
3. Cook noodles until just tender, about 3 minutes. Drain and rinse under cold water until cool. Press to remove excess water, transfer to a large bowl and toss with 1 teaspoon oil to keep them from sticking.
4. With a chef's knife, mash garlic and salt into a paste. Transfer to a small bowl and add vinegar, soy sauce, ginger, brown sugar, chile-garlic sauce and the remaining 1 tablespoon oil. Whisk until blended.
5. Peel the cooled eggplant and discard the skin. Chop the eggplant flesh to a coarse puree. Add it to the noodles, along with carrots, cilantro and the sesame seeds. Add the dressing and toss until well combined. Just before serving, garnish with diced cucumber.

TEST KITCHEN TIP:
Raw garlic can have too assertive a flavor if it doesn't have time to mellow and blend with other seasonings. A quick remedy is to mash it with salt, which helps tame the flavor and reduces it to a puree that will quickly blend into the dressing.

MAKES 4 SERVINGS.

PER SERVING: 371 CALORIES; 9 G FAT (1 G SAT, 3 G MONO); 0 MG CHOLESTEROL; 63 G CARBOHYDRATE; 12 G PROTEIN; 6 G FIBER; 711 MG SODIUM.

NUTRITION BONUS: 190% DV VITAMIN A, 5 MG IRON (25% DV), 23% DV FIBER, 13 MG VITAMIN C (20% DV).

Spicy Peanut Noodles

PREP TIME: 5 MINUTES | **START TO FINISH:** 25 MINUTES | **EASE OF PREPARATION:** EASY

When you can't get out to get take-out, make these easy favorites yourself with what's in the pantry.

- 12 ounces whole-wheat pasta
- ½ cup natural peanut butter
- ¾ cup boiling water
- 4 sliced scallions
- 4 tablespoons reduced-sodium soy sauce
- 3 tablespoons rice vinegar
- 1 clove garlic, minced
- ½ teaspoon sugar
- Cayenne pepper to taste
- Sliced cucumber for garnish

Cook pasta in a large pot of lightly salted boiling water until just tender, according to package directions. Whisk peanut butter with ¾ cup boiling water in a bowl until smooth. Stir in scallions, soy sauce, vinegar, garlic, sugar and cayenne. Toss with hot pasta. Garnish with cucumber. Serve hot or at room temperature.

MAKES ABOUT 6 CUPS, FOR 6 SERVINGS.

PER SERVING: 336 CALORIES; 12 G FAT (1 G SAT, 0 G MONO); 0 MG CHOLESTEROL; 48 G CARBOHYDRATE; 14 G PROTEIN; 9 G FIBER; 442 MG SODIUM.

NUTRITION BONUS: 35% DV FIBER.

Penne with Asparagus & Lemon Cream Sauce

PREP TIME: 15 MINUTES | **START TO FINISH:** 35 MINUTES | **EASE OF PREPARATION:** EASY

Strike while the asparagus is fresh—it's loaded with nutrients, and gives this quick pasta the very taste of spring.

- 1 teaspoon extra-virgin olive oil
- 1 pound asparagus, trimmed and cut into 1-inch diagonal pieces
- 2 bunches scallions, trimmed and cut into 1-inch diagonal pieces
- ¾ cup part-skim ricotta cheese
- 2 teaspoons freshly grated lemon zest, preferably organic
- 12 ounces penne
- Salt & freshly ground pepper to taste
- ¼ cup slivered fresh basil

1. Put a large pot of lightly salted water on to boil.
2. Heat oil in a large skillet over medium heat. Add asparagus and scallions and cook, stirring occasionally, until the vegetables are tender and browned in places, 10 to 12 minutes.
3. Meanwhile, whisk ricotta and lemon zest in a large bowl. Cook penne until just tender, about 10 minutes. Measure out ¼ cup of the pasta-cooking water; stir into ricotta mixture until creamy. Drain penne and mix into the ricotta mixture; toss to coat. Add vegetables and toss well. Season with salt and pepper. Serve, garnished with basil.

MAKES 6 SERVINGS.

PER SERVING: 285 CALORIES; 4 G FAT (2 G SAT, 1 G MONO); 10 MG CHOLESTEROL; 49 G CARBOHYDRATE; 13 G PROTEIN; 4 G FIBER; 94 MG SODIUM.

NUTRITION BONUS: 13 MG VITAMIN C (20% DV), 17% DV FIBER, 3 MG IRON (15% DV), 133 MG CALCIUM (15% DV).

Fettuccine Alfredo

PREP TIME: 40 MINUTES | **START TO FINISH:** 50 MINUTES | **EASE OF PREPARATION:** EASY

A rich Alfredo sauce with a fraction of the calories and fat—it's safe to put this popular pasta dish back in your repertoire.

- 2 cups 1% milk
- 8 large cloves garlic, peeled
- Salt & freshly ground pepper to taste
- Pinch of ground nutmeg
- 1 pound fettuccine
- 2 tablespoons reduced-fat cream cheese
- ¾ cup freshly grated Parmesan cheese, divided
- 3 tablespoons chopped fresh parsley

1. Put a large pot of lightly salted water on to boil.
2. Combine milk and garlic in a heavy medium saucepan; bring to a simmer over low heat. Simmer gently until the garlic is tender and the milk has reduced to 1½ cups, 15 to 25 minutes. Let cool slightly.
3. Puree milk and garlic in a blender until smooth. (Use caution when blending hot liquids.) Return to the pan and season with salt, pepper and nutmeg. Keep the sauce warm.
4. Meanwhile, cook fettuccine until just tender, 8 to 10 minutes. Drain and transfer to a warmed large bowl.
5. Whisk cream cheese and ½ cup Parmesan into the sauce. Add to the fettuccine and toss well. Sprinkle with parsley. Serve immediately, passing the remaining ¼ cup Parmesan separately.

MAKES 6 SERVINGS.

PER SERVING: 373 CALORIES; 6 G FAT (3 G SAT, 1 G MONO); 17 MG CHOLESTEROL; 63 G CARBOHYDRATE; 18 G PROTEIN; 3 G FIBER; 265 MG SODIUM.

NUTRITION BONUS: 167 MCG FOLATE (42% DV), 240 MG CALCIUM (25% DV), 3 MG IRON (15% DV).

When to Choose Whole-Wheat

CLEARLY THE BEST NUTRITIONAL CHOICE, whole-wheat pasta can also offer great flavor—if you pair it with the right sauce. We like it with robust sauces containing meat, nuts, greens and other assertive flavors. Delicate cream sauces are best suited to regular pasta.

Linguine with Grilled Shrimp & Black Olives

PREP TIME: 20 MINUTES | **START TO FINISH:** 30 MINUTES
EQUIPMENT: BAMBOO OR METAL SKEWERS | **EASE OF PREPARATION:** MODERATE

The smoky mellowness of grilled shrimp plays against the powerful saltiness of olives in this lively summer pasta.

- **1 pound medium shrimp (30-40 per pound), peeled and deveined**
- **Salt & coarsely ground pepper to taste**
- **12 ounces whole-wheat linguine** (*see "Taste Test," page 161*)
- **1 tablespoon extra-virgin olive oil**
- **6 large cloves garlic, peeled and thinly sliced lengthwise**
- **4 vine-ripened tomatoes, coarsely chopped**
- **½ cup brine-cured black olives, pitted and coarsely chopped**
- **½ cup chopped fresh basil**
- **Freshly ground pepper to taste**
- **½ cup freshly grated Parmesan cheese (optional)**

1. Preheat grill to medium-high. Put a large pot of lightly salted water on to boil.

2. Thread shrimp onto skewers and sprinkle with salt and pepper. Grill until just opaque throughout, 3 to 4 minutes per side. Remove the shrimp from the skewers and cut each into 3 or 4 pieces. Set aside.

3. While the shrimp is grilling, cook linguine until just tender, about 8 minutes. Drain but do not rinse.

4. Meanwhile, heat oil in a large skillet over medium heat until hot but not smoking. Add garlic and cook, stirring frequently, until it just starts to brown, about 2 minutes. Add tomatoes, olives, the grilled shrimp and cooked linguine; cook, tossing, until heated through, 2 to 3 minutes. Transfer to a large bowl, mix in the basil and season with pepper. Top with Parmesan, if using, and serve.

MAKES 4 SERVINGS.

PER SERVING: 522 CALORIES; 11 G FAT (2 G SAT, 6 G MONO); 172 MG CHOLESTEROL; 74 G CARBOHYDRATE; 37 G PROTEIN; 13 G FIBER; 449 MG SODIUM.

NUTRITION BONUS: 52% DV FIBER, 24 MG VITAMIN C (40% DV), 7 MG IRON (35% DV), 35% DV VITAMIN A, 78 MCG FOLATE (20% DV).

Spaghetti with Clams (Spaghetti alle Vongole)

PREP TIME: 15 MINUTES | **START TO FINISH:** 25 MINUTES | **EASE OF PREPARATION:** EASY

When you are tired and hungry and you want to eat fast, this recipe, using convenient canned clams, is a sanity saver. Having toasted breadcrumbs on hand makes it even easier.

- 3 tablespoons Toasted Breadcrumbs (*recipe follows*), divided
- 12 ounces whole-wheat spaghetti *or* thin spaghetti (*see "Taste Test," page 161*)
- 1 tablespoon extra-virgin olive oil
- 2 cloves garlic, minced
- 4 tablespoons finely chopped fresh flat-leaf parsley, divided
- ¼ cup dry white wine
- 2 10-ounce cans baby clams, drained, liquid reserved
- Freshly ground pepper to taste
- 2 teaspoons freshly grated lemon zest, preferably organic

1. Put a large pot of lightly salted water on to boil.
2. Make Toasted Breadcrumbs.
3. Cook pasta until just tender, 9 to 11 minutes, or according to package directions.
4. Meanwhile, heat oil in a large skillet over medium-high heat. Add garlic and 2 tablespoons parsley; cook, stirring, until the garlic is light golden, 1 to 2 minutes. Add wine and 1 cup of the reserved clam liquid. Bring to a boil. Cook for 4 minutes. Add clams and remove from heat. Season with pepper.
5. Drain the pasta. Add to the pan with the sauce. Add lemon zest, 2 tablespoons breadcrumbs and the remaining 2 tablespoons parsley; place over medium-high heat and toss well. Serve immediately, sprinkled with the remaining breadcrumbs.

MAKES 4 SERVINGS, ABOUT 1¾ CUPS EACH.

PER SERVING: 494 CALORIES; 9 G FAT (2 G SAT, 3 G MONO); 113 MG CHOLESTEROL; 72 G CARBOHYDRATE; 36 G PROTEIN; 11 G FIBER; 647 MG SODIUM.

NUTRITION BONUS: 39 MG IRON (220% DV), 45% DV FIBER, 218 MG CALCIUM (20% DV).

TOASTED BREADCRUMBS

TO MAKE AHEAD: KEEP IN A COVERED CONTAINER IN THE REFRIGERATOR FOR UP TO 1 MONTH.

Use these to add a pleasant crunchiness to pasta, thicken a sauce, substitute for grated cheese and top salads.

- 3 tablespoons plain dry breadcrumbs
- 1 teaspoon extra-virgin olive oil

Combine breadcrumbs and oil in a small heavy skillet; toast over medium heat, stirring constantly, until golden brown, 2 to 3 minutes. Transfer to a small bowl and let cool.

MAKES 3 TABLESPOONS.

PER TABLESPOON: 41 CALORIES; 2 G FAT (0 G SAT, 1 G MONO); 0 MG CHOLESTEROL; 5 G CARBOHYDRATE; 1 G PROTEIN; 0 G FIBER; 58 MG SODIUM.

Spaghetti, Streetwalkers' Style (Spaghetti alla Puttanesca)

PREP TIME: 25 MINUTES | **START TO FINISH:** 40 MINUTES | **EASE OF PREPARATION:** EASY

This classic sauce is traditionally made with vermicelli, but it works with any long thin pasta. We've used whole-wheat spaghettini for maximum nutrition. Another tradition-breaker is the addition of sweet peas. Besides taste, they add an attractive emerald accent to the assertive sauce.

- 3 tablespoons Toasted Breadcrumbs (*page 167*), divided
- ⅓ cup fresh flat-leaf parsley
- 16 brine-cured black olives (Sicilian *or* Greek), pitted
- 6 anchovy fillets, rinsed
- 3 tablespoons capers, rinsed
- 1 clove garlic, crushed and peeled
- 1 tablespoon extra-virgin olive oil
- ⅛ teaspoon crushed red pepper
- 1 14½-ounce can diced tomatoes
- 1 cup frozen peas, rinsed under cold water to thaw
- Freshly ground pepper to taste
- 12 ounces whole-wheat thin spaghetti *or* spaghetti (*see "Taste Test," page 161*)

1. Put a large pot of lightly salted water on to boil.
2. Make Toasted Breadcrumbs.
3. Place parsley, olives, anchovies, capers and garlic on a cutting board; mince together with a chef's knife.
4. Heat oil in a large skillet over medium-low heat. Add the parsley mixture and crushed red pepper; cook, stirring, until fragrant, about 3 minutes. Stir in tomatoes. Increase heat to medium-high and bring to a simmer, mashing tomatoes with a wooden spoon or potato masher. Simmer for 3 minutes. Add peas and cook for 1 to 2 minutes. Season with pepper.
5. Meanwhile, cook pasta until just tender, 6 to 10 minutes, or according to package directions. Reserving ⅓ cup of the cooking water, drain the pasta and add to the pan with the sauce. Add 2 tablespoons toasted breadcrumbs and the reserved cooking water; toss well. Serve immediately, sprinkled with the remaining breadcrumbs.

MAKES 4 SERVINGS, ABOUT 1¾ CUPS EACH.

PER SERVING: 439 CALORIES; 10 G FAT (1 G SAT, 6 G MONO); 2 MG CHOLESTEROL; 77 G CARBOHYDRATE; 17 G PROTEIN; 15 G FIBER; 636 MG SODIUM.

NUTRITION BONUS: 58% DV FIBER, 21 MG VITAMIN C (35% DV), 35% DV VITAMIN A, 5 MG IRON (25% DV), 79 MCG FOLATE (20% DV).

Spaghetti with Arugula, Roasted Peppers & Prosciutto

PREP TIME: 15 MINUTES | **START TO FINISH:** 30 MINUTES | **EASE OF PREPARATION:** EASY

The complex flavors of a good Parmesan, such as Reggiano, and a high-quality prosciutto, such as San Danielle, Volpi or di Parma, are essential for this pasta. Less expensive products will often contribute more saltiness than true flavor to the final result. Ask for a sample at the delicatessen when buying—if it tastes good on its own, it will make the dish taste good as well.

- **12 ounces whole-wheat spaghetti** (*see "Taste Test," page 161*)
- **1 tablespoon extra-virgin olive oil**
- **4 cloves garlic, minced**
- **⅛-¼ teaspoon crushed red pepper**
- **2 ounces thinly sliced prosciutto, trimmed of fat and cut into thin strips (½ cup)**
- **1 12-ounce jar roasted red peppers, rinsed and cut into thin strips (1½ cups)**
- **8 cups arugula leaves (8 ounces)**
- **⅔ cup freshly grated Parmesan cheese, divided**
- **Freshly ground pepper to taste**
- **⅓ cup chopped walnuts, toasted** (*see Cooking Tip, page 397*)

1. Cook spaghetti in a large pot of lightly salted boiling water until just tender, 8 to 10 minutes.
2. Meanwhile, heat oil in a large skillet over medium-low heat. Add garlic and crushed red pepper; cook, stirring, until fragrant but not colored, 1 to 2 minutes. Add prosciutto and cook, stirring often, until lightly browned, 2 to 3 minutes. Stir in roasted peppers and arugula; increase heat to medium-high. Cook, stirring often, until the arugula is wilted, 3 to 4 minutes.
3. Reserving ⅓ cup of the cooking water, drain the spaghetti and place in a warmed large bowl. Add the reserved water, arugula mixture, ⅓ cup Parmesan and pepper; toss to coat well. Sprinkle with walnuts and the remaining Parmesan and serve.

MAKES 4 SERVINGS, ABOUT 2 CUPS EACH.

PER SERVING: 496 CALORIES; 16 G FAT (3 G SAT, 4 G MONO); 18 MG CHOLESTEROL; 72 G CARBOHYDRATE; 23 G PROTEIN; 13 G FIBER; 727 MG SODIUM.

NUTRITION BONUS: 90% DV VITAMIN A, 55 MG VITAMIN C (90% DV), 51% DV FIBER, 5 MG IRON (25% DV), 90 MCG FOLATE (24% DV).

VEGETARIAN VARIATION: Omit prosciutto. In Step 2, add 3 cups sliced baby bella mushrooms or sliced portobello mushroom caps and ¼ teaspoon salt to the skillet in place of the prosciutto; cook, stirring occasionally, until tender and browned, 3 to 5 minutes (add a little water to the skillet if the mixture seems dry).

PER SERVING: 479 CALORIES; 14 G FAT (3 G SAT, 4 G MONO); 5 MG CHOLESTEROL; 74 G CARBOHYDRATE; 20 G PROTEIN; 13 G FIBER; 603 MG SODIUM.

NUTRITION BONUS: 90% DV VITAMIN A, 55 MG VITAMIN C (90% DV), 54% DV FIBER, 106 MCG FOLATE (27% DV), 5 MG IRON (25% DV).

Old-Fashioned Spaghetti & Meatballs

PREP TIME: 40 MINUTES | **START TO FINISH:** 1¼ HOURS | **EASE OF PREPARATION:** MODERATE

To coax more flavor from a small quantity of meat, we use spicy Italian sausage instead of ground pork in the meatballs, which are baked rather than fried.

MEATBALLS

- ⅓ cup bulgur
- ½ cup hot water
- 4 ounces lean ground beef
- 4 ounces hot Italian sausage (1 link), casing removed
- 1 onion, very finely chopped
- 2 large egg whites, lightly beaten
- 3 cloves garlic, very finely chopped
- 1 teaspoon dried oregano
- ½ teaspoon salt
- ½ teaspoon freshly ground pepper
- 1 cup fresh breadcrumbs, preferably whole-wheat (*see Cooking Tip, page 396*)

SAUCE & SPAGHETTI

- 4 cups Basic Tomato Sauce (*page 171*) *or* prepared marinara sauce
- ½ cup slivered fresh basil leaves
- 1 pound whole-wheat spaghetti *or* linguine (*see "Taste Test," page 161*)
- ½ cup freshly grated Parmesan *or* Romano cheese (1 ounce)

1. **To prepare meatballs:** Combine bulgur and water in a small bowl. Let stand until the bulgur is tender and the liquid is absorbed, about 30 minutes.
2. Preheat oven to 350°F. Coat a rack with cooking spray and place it over a baking sheet lined with foil.
3. Combine ground beef, sausage, onion, egg whites, garlic, oregano, salt, pepper, breadcrumbs and the soaked bulgur in a mixing bowl. Mix well with your hands or a wooden spoon. Form the mixture into 1-inch meatballs (about 24). Place the meatballs on the rack and bake for 25 minutes. Blot well with paper towel.
4. **To prepare sauce & spaghetti:** Put a large pot of lightly salted water on to boil. Bring sauce to a simmer in a Dutch oven. Add the meatballs to the sauce and simmer, covered, for 20 minutes. Stir in basil. Taste and adjust seasonings.
5. Meanwhile, cook spaghetti (and linguine) until just tender, 8 to 10 minutes. Drain and transfer to a serving bowl. Top with the sauce and meatballs and serve with grated cheese.

MAKES 6 SERVINGS.

PER SERVING: 496 CALORIES; 8 G FAT (3 G SAT, 3 G MONO); 28 MG CHOLESTEROL; 86 G CARBOHYDRATE; 27 G PROTEIN; 18 G FIBER; 568 MG SODIUM.

NUTRITION BONUS: 72% DV FIBER, 20 MG VITAMIN C (35% DV), 5 MG IRON (30% DV), 227 MG CALCIUM (25% DV), 25% DV VITAMIN A.

High Fiber

BASIC TOMATO SAUCE

PREP TIME: 15 MINUTES | **START TO FINISH:** 1 HOUR | **EASE OF PREPARATION:** EASY

This simple but intensely flavored sauce can be used in many Italian recipes. Make a large batch and freeze in small containers for quick reheating.

- **1 tablespoon extra-virgin olive oil**
- **1 medium onion, finely chopped**
- **4 cloves garlic, minced**
- **Pinch of crushed red pepper**
- **2 28-ounce cans diced tomatoes**
- **1 tablespoon tomato paste**
- **1 teaspoon dried oregano**
- **Freshly ground pepper to taste**

Heat oil in a large heavy pan or Dutch oven over medium-low heat. Add onion and cook, stirring often, until softened, about 5 minutes. Add garlic and crushed red pepper; cook for 30 to 60 seconds. Add tomatoes, tomato paste and oregano; mash with a potato masher. Bring to a boil. Simmer, uncovered, over low heat, stirring frequently, until the tomatoes cook down to a thick mass, 45 to 55 minutes. Season with pepper.

MAKES ABOUT 5 CUPS.

PER CUP: 109 CALORIES; 3 G FAT (0 G SAT, 2 G MONO); 0 MG CHOLESTEROL; 20 G CARBOHYDRATE; 3 G PROTEIN; 6 G FIBER; 130 MG SODIUM.

NUTRITION BONUS: 27 MG VITAMIN C (45% DV), 25% DV VITAMIN A, 24% DV FIBER. RICH IN THE ANTIOXIDANT LYCOPENE.

Whole-Wheat Fusilli with Beef Ragu

PREP TIME: 20 MINUTES | **START TO FINISH:** 1 HOUR | **TO MAKE AHEAD:** PREPARE THROUGH STEP 3. COVER AND REFRIGERATE THE SAUCE FOR UP TO 2 DAYS OR FREEZE FOR UP TO 3 MONTHS. | **EASE OF PREPARATION:** EASY

This chunky, full-bodied sauce is a good match for hearty whole-wheat pasta. We've augmented a little lean ground beef with mushrooms to get a rich, meaty sauce that has a minimum of saturated fat.

- 8 ounces 90%-lean ground beef
- 1 teaspoon extra-virgin olive oil
- 2 medium carrots, chopped
- 1 medium onion, chopped
- 1 stalk celery, chopped
- 6 ounces cremini *or* baby bella mushrooms, wiped clean and coarsely chopped (2 cups)
- 2 cloves garlic, minced
- 1 28-ounce can diced tomatoes (*not* drained)
- ½ cup dry red wine
- 1-2 teaspoons fennel seeds, crushed
- Large pinch of crushed red pepper
- ¼ teaspoon salt, or to taste
- 12 ounces whole-wheat fusilli *or* rotini (*see "Taste Test," page 161*)
- 2 tablespoons chopped fresh parsley (optional)
- 6 tablespoons freshly grated Parmesan cheese (optional)

1. Cook meat in a large skillet over medium-high heat, breaking it up with a wooden spoon, until browned, 4 to 5 minutes. Transfer to a strainer or colander and drain off fat.
2. Heat oil in the skillet over medium-high heat. Add carrots, onion and celery; cook, stirring occasionally, until the onion softens and begins to brown, 4 to 5 minutes. Add mushrooms and garlic; reduce heat to medium and cook, stirring occasionally, until the mushrooms begin to soften, 3 to 4 minutes.
3. Add tomatoes and mash with a potato masher. Add wine, fennel seeds, crushed red pepper, salt and the meat; bring to a simmer. Reduce heat to low; cover and cook, stirring occasionally, until the sauce is slightly thickened and the flavors have developed, about 30 minutes.
4. Meanwhile, bring a large pot of lightly salted water to a boil. Cook pasta until just tender, 9 to 11 minutes or according to package directions. Drain and toss with the sauce. Sprinkle with parsley, if desired. Pass Parmesan separately, if using.

PORTION TIPS: If you're only serving 2 or 3 people, toss half the sauce with 6 ounces cooked pasta; freeze the remaining sauce. If you're serving more than 6 or are just feeling industrious, you can easily double the sauce recipe.

MAKES 6 SERVINGS, ABOUT 1⅓ CUPS EACH.

PER SERVING: 318 CALORIES; 3 G FAT (1 G SAT, 1 G MONO); 23 MG CHOLESTEROL; 55 G CARBOHYDRATE; 17 G PROTEIN; 9 G FIBER; 213 MG SODIUM.

NUTRITION BONUS: 60% DV VITAMIN A, 36% DV FIBER, 423 MG POTASSIUM (21% DV).

Updated Mac & Cheese

PREP TIME: 25 MINUTES | **START TO FINISH:** 55 MINUTES | **TO MAKE AHEAD:** PREPARE THROUGH STEP 4. COVER AND REFRIGERATE FOR UP TO 2 DAYS OR FREEZE FOR UP TO 3 MONTHS. THAW IN THE REFRIGERATOR, IF NECESSARY, THEN BAKE FOR 35 TO 45 MINUTES. | **EASE OF PREPARATION:** EASY

Our mac-and-cheese makeover wins raves of approval, having all the comfort and great taste of its predecessors with a substantially more healthful profile. It uses whole-wheat pasta and includes a colorful layer of spinach. It's also a winner for make-ahead convenience.

- 3 tablespoons plain dry breadcrumbs
- 1 teaspoon extra-virgin olive oil
- ¼ teaspoon paprika
- 1 16-ounce *or* 10-ounce package frozen spinach
- 1¾ cups 1% milk, divided
- 3 tablespoons all-purpose flour
- 2 cups grated extra-sharp Cheddar cheese (6 ounces)
- 1 cup low-fat (1%) cottage cheese
- ⅛ teaspoon ground nutmeg
- ½ teaspoon salt, or to taste
- Freshly ground pepper to taste
- 8 ounces (2 cups) whole-wheat elbow macaroni *or* penne (*see "Taste Test," page 161*)

1. Put a large pot of lightly salted water on to boil. Preheat oven to 450°F. Coat an 8-inch square (2-quart) baking dish with cooking spray.
2. Mix breadcrumbs, oil and paprika in a small bowl; set aside. Cook spinach according to package directions. Drain and refresh under cold water; press out excess moisture. Set aside.
3. Heat 1½ cups milk in a large heavy saucepan over medium-high heat until steaming. Whisk remaining ¼ cup milk and flour in a small bowl until smooth; add to the hot milk and cook, whisking constantly, until the sauce simmers and thickens, 2 to 3 minutes. Remove from heat and stir in Cheddar until melted. Stir in cottage cheese, nutmeg, salt and pepper.
4. Cook pasta for 4 minutes, or until not quite tender. (It will continue to cook during baking.) Drain and add to the cheese sauce; mix well. Spread half the pasta mixture in the prepared baking dish. Spoon spinach on top. Top with the remaining pasta; sprinkle with the breadcrumb mixture.
5. Bake the casserole until bubbly and golden, 25 to 30 minutes.

RECIPE RX

Traditional Mac & Cheese:
664 calories
18 grams saturated fat
4 grams fiber

Updated Mac & Cheese:
503 calories
9 grams saturated fat
8 grams fiber

MAKES 4 SERVINGS.

PER SERVING: 503 CALORIES; 17 G FAT (9 G SAT, 2 G MONO); 54 MG CHOLESTEROL; 60 G CARBOHYDRATE; 31 G PROTEIN; 8 G FIBER; 935 MG SODIUM.

NUTRITION BONUS: 200% DV VITAMIN A, 583 MG CALCIUM (60% DV), 107 MCG FOLATE (27% DV).

Classic Lasagna

PREP TIME: 40 MINUTES | **START TO FINISH:** 2 HOURS | **TO MAKE AHEAD:** PREPARE THROUGH STEP 6. REFRIGERATE FOR UP TO 2 DAYS OR FREEZE FOR UP TO 3 MONTHS. THAW BEFORE BAKING. | **EASE OF PREPARATION:** MODERATE

An old-fashioned meat-and-cheese lasagna made lusciously low-fat. If you can find whole-wheat lasagna noodles, they taste great in this recipe.

MEAT SAUCE

- ½ tablespoon extra-virgin olive oil
- 4 ounces hot *or* sweet Italian turkey sausage, casings removed
- 2 onions, finely chopped
- 1 carrot, finely chopped
- 12 ounces mushrooms, wiped clean and chopped
- 2 cloves garlic, minced
- Salt & freshly ground pepper to taste
- ¼ cup dry red wine
- 2 28-ounce cans plum tomatoes, drained and chopped
- ½ cup sun-dried tomatoes (*not* packed in oil), slivered
- 1 teaspoon dried oregano
- 1 teaspoon dried basil
- 1 teaspoon dried thyme
- ¼ teaspoon crushed red pepper, or to taste

PASTA & CHEESE FILLING

- 12 lasagna noodles (12 ounces)
- 2 cups nonfat ricotta cheese
- Salt & freshly ground pepper to taste
- Ground nutmeg to taste
- 1 cup grated part-skim mozzarella cheese
- ½ cup freshly grated Parmesan cheese
- 2 tablespoons chopped fresh parsley

1. To prepare meat sauce: Heat oil in a large heavy pot or Dutch oven over medium-high heat. Add sausage and cook, breaking up clumps, until browned, 3 to 5 minutes. Reduce heat to medium. Add onions and carrot; cook, stirring, until softened, 2 to 3 minutes. Add mushrooms and garlic; season with salt and pepper. Cook, stirring frequently, until mushroom liquid evaporates, 4 to 6 minutes.

2. Stir in wine, plum tomatoes, sun-dried tomatoes, oregano, basil, thyme and crushed red pepper. Bring to a simmer; reduce heat to low, cover and simmer, stirring occasionally, about 45 minutes. Uncover and cook, stirring frequently, until the sauce is very thick, 30 to 45 minutes more. Adjust seasoning with salt and pepper.

3. To prepare filling & assemble lasagna: Bring a large pot of lightly salted water to a boil. Preheat oven to 350°F. Coat a 9-by-13-inch baking dish with cooking spray.

4. Cook noodles until just tender, about 10 minutes. Drain, then cool by plunging noodles into a large bowl of ice-cold water. Lay noodles out on kitchen towels.

5. Season ricotta with salt, pepper and nutmeg. Spread about 1½ cups meat sauce in prepared pan. Layer 3 noodles on top. Spread another 1 cup sauce over noodles. Dot about ⅔ cup ricotta over sauce, then sprinkle with ¼ cup mozzarella and 2 tablespoons Parmesan. Continue layering noodles, sauce and cheeses, finishing with sauce, mozzarella and Parmesan. Sprinkle with parsley; cover with foil.

6. Bake the lasagna for 35 to 40 minutes, or until the sauce is bubbling. Uncover and bake until golden, 5 to 10 minutes more. Let cool for 10 minutes before cutting.

MAKES 8 SERVINGS.

PER SERVING: 361 CALORIES; 8 G FAT (3 G SAT, 2 G MONO); 33 MG CHOLESTEROL; 46 G CARBOHYDRATE; 24 G PROTEIN; 9 G FIBER; 367 MG SODIUM.

NUTRITION BONUS: 36% DV FIBER, 302 MG CALCIUM (30% DV).

Lasagne al Forno

PREP TIME: 45 MINUTES | **START TO FINISH:** 1¾ HOURS | **TO MAKE AHEAD:** PREPARE THROUGH STEP 6. REFRIGERATE FOR UP TO 2 DAYS OR FREEZE FOR UP TO 3 MONTHS. THAW BEFORE BAKING. | **EASE OF PREPARATION:** MODERATE

Mushrooms (*forno*) add depth of flavor and a nice chewy texture to this baked vegetarian pasta.

MUSHROOM SAUCE

- 1½ tablespoons extra-virgin olive oil, divided
- 1 onion, finely chopped
- 1 carrot, finely chopped
- 1 stalk celery, finely chopped
- 12 ounces mushrooms, wiped clean and chopped (4 cups)
- 2 cloves garlic, finely chopped
- ½ cup dry white wine
- 1 28-ounce can diced tomatoes
- 2 sun-dried tomatoes (*not* packed in oil), very finely chopped (2 tablespoons)
- 1 teaspoon dried thyme leaves
- Salt & freshly ground pepper to taste

WHITE SAUCE

- ⅓ cup all-purpose flour
- 3 cups 1% milk
- ¼ teaspoon freshly grated nutmeg

- 1 pound no-boil lasagna noodles
- 8 cups spinach leaves
- 1 cup freshly grated Parmesan cheese (2 ounces), divided

1. **To prepare mushroom sauce:** Heat ½ tablespoon oil in a Dutch oven over medium heat. Add onion, carrot and celery; cook, stirring, until the onion has softened, about 5 minutes. Add mushrooms and garlic; cook until the mushrooms release their liquid, 2 to 3 minutes. Add wine; cook until most of the liquid has evaporated, about 5 minutes.
2. Stir in diced tomatoes, sun-dried tomatoes and thyme; bring to a simmer. Reduce heat to low and simmer, stirring often, until the sauce is thick, about 1 hour. Season with salt and pepper.
3. **To prepare white sauce:** Heat the remaining 1 tablespoon oil in a heavy saucepan over low heat. Add flour and cook, whisking constantly, until the flour starts to turn light brown, about 3 minutes. Remove from the heat and gradually whisk in milk. Return the pan to medium heat and cook, whisking constantly, until the sauce bubbles and thickens. Season with nutmeg and salt to taste.
4. **To assemble & bake lasagna:** Preheat oven to 375°F. Coat an 8-by-11½-inch baking dish with cooking spray.
5. Spread ½ cup of the mushroom sauce in the prepared pan, arrange a layer of noodles on top and spread with another ½ cup of the mushroom sauce. Arrange a layer of spinach over the sauce and drizzle with ⅓ cup of the white sauce. Sprinkle 2 tablespoons Parmesan over the spinach and top with another layer of noodles. Repeat this layering five more times. Spread the remaining white sauce over the top layer of noodles, covering completely. Cover with foil.
6. Bake the lasagna for 30 minutes. Uncover, sprinkle with the remaining Parmesan, and bake until golden, about 20 minutes longer. Let rest for 10 minutes before serving.

MAKES 6 SERVINGS.

PER SERVING: 510 CALORIES; 12 G FAT (4 G SAT, 4 G MONO); 19 MG CHOLESTEROL; 76 G CARBOHYDRATE; 29 G PROTEIN; 17 G FIBER; 413 MG SODIUM.

NUTRITION BONUS: 130% DV VITAMIN A, 66% DV FIBER, 169 MCG FOLATE (42% DV), 422 MG CALCIUM (40% DV), 7 MG IRON (40% DV).

Sweet Potato Ravioli

PREP TIME: 2 HOURS | **START TO FINISH:** 3¾ HOURS (INCLUDING 1 HOUR DOUGH-RESTING TIME) **EQUIPMENT:** PASTA MACHINE OR ROLLING PIN | **TO MAKE AHEAD:** THE PASTA DOUGH WILL KEEP IN THE REFRIGERATOR FOR UP TO 2 DAYS. THE UNCOOKED RAVIOLI WILL KEEP IN THE REFRIGERATOR OVERNIGHT OR IN THE FREEZER FOR UP TO 3 MONTHS. FREEZE IN A SINGLE LAYER, THEN ENCLOSE IN A PLASTIC BAG. DO NOT THAW BEFORE COOKING. | **EASE OF PREPARATION:** CHALLENGING

Handmade ravioli, the pride of Italian grandmothers, is easier to make than you might think. Just keep in mind that the secret to good fresh pasta is not to work it too much. If you would like to enjoy the delicious filling without the fuss of rolling out fresh pasta, you can use wonton wrappers (*see Ingredient Note, page 396*); you'll need about 84 wrappers.

PASTA

- **2 large egg whites (*you'll need 1 yolk for the filling*)**
- **½ cup water**
- **2⅓ cups semolina flour, plus extra for dusting**
- **¼ teaspoon salt**

FILLING

- **1 teaspoon extra-virgin olive oil**
- **2 small leeks, white and light green parts only, washed (*see Cooking Tip, page 397*) and diced**
- **1 medium sweet potato, peeled and cut into 1-inch cubes**
- **½ cup reduced-sodium chicken broth**
- **¼ cup part-skim ricotta cheese**
- **1 ounce prosciutto, trimmed of fat and finely diced (about ¼ cup)**
- **Salt & freshly ground pepper to taste**
- **1 large egg yolk**

1. To prepare pasta dough: Beat egg whites and water in a glass measuring cup. In a food processor, combine semolina and salt. With the motor running, gradually pour the egg-white mixture through the feed tube; process until a smooth ball forms. (If the dough is dry, add a little water; if sticky, add a little semolina.)

2. Turn the dough out onto a semolina-dusted surface and knead several times. Wrap tightly in plastic wrap. Let rest at room temperature for at least 1 hour or in the refrigerator for up to 2 days.

3. To prepare filling: Heat oil in a medium saucepan over medium heat. Add leeks and cook, stirring, until softened, 1 to 2 minutes. Add sweet potato and broth and bring to a boil. Reduce heat to low, cover and simmer until very tender, 8 to 12 minutes.

4. Uncover and shake pan over low heat until liquid has evaporated, 1 to 2 minutes. Off the heat, mash with a potato masher. Return to low heat and stir for about 1 minute. Transfer to a bowl and let cool completely. Stir in ricotta and prosciutto. Season with salt and pepper. Stir in egg yolk.

5. To roll dough & fill ravioli: Divide the dough into 8 pieces. Keeping remaining pieces covered, feed one piece through the widest setting of a pasta machine. (Dust with semolina if sticky.) If the edges appear ragged and torn, fold in thirds crosswise, turn 90° and feed through the widest setting again. Repeat until the edges are smooth.

ROSEMARY SAUCE

- **1 teaspoon extra-virgin olive oil**
- **2 cloves garlic, minced**
- **1½ teaspoons chopped fresh rosemary**
- **3 cups reduced-sodium chicken broth**
- **1 teaspoon butter**
- **¼ cup freshly grated Parmesan cheese**
- **Freshly ground pepper to taste**

6. Feed the pasta strip through successively narrow settings, finishing with the next-to-smallest setting. (Cut the strip in half if it becomes too long to handle.) Lay pasta strip(s) on a semolina-dusted surface, sprinkle with more semolina and cover with plastic wrap. Repeat with the remaining pasta dough. (*Alternatively, roll out pasta with a rolling pin to a thickness of less than ⅛ inch.*)

7. With a pastry brush, lightly brush a pasta strip with water. Drop filling by rounded teaspoonfuls, about 2 inches apart, on the strip. Cover with a second pasta strip, easing it over the filling. With your fingers, press pasta together around mounds of filling.

8. Using a serrated 2½-inch cutter or a pastry wheel, cut out round or square ravioli. Place ravioli on a semolina-dusted baking sheet and cover with plastic wrap. Repeat with remaining pasta strips and filling.

9. **To prepare sauce & cook ravioli:** Put a large wide pot of lightly salted water (at least 4 quarts) on to boil.

10. Heat oil in a large skillet over medium heat. Add garlic and rosemary and cook, stirring, until fragrant, about 30 seconds. Add broth and bring to a boil. Increase heat to high and cook until reduced by half, 6 to 8 minutes. Reduce heat to very low and whisk in butter. Keep the sauce warm over very low heat.

11. Cook the ravioli in boiling water, 15 at a time, until they are tender and float to the surface, about 2 minutes. With a slotted spoon, transfer to the sauce in the skillet. Repeat with the remaining ravioli.

12. Divide the ravioli and sauce among warmed plates. Serve immediately, passing Parmesan and pepper separately.

MAKES 6 SERVINGS, ABOUT 7 RAVIOLI EACH.

PER SERVING: 374 CALORIES; 8 G FAT (3 G SAT, 2 G MONO); 48 MG CHOLESTEROL; 59 G CARBOHYDRATE; 16 G PROTEIN; 4 G FIBER; 399 MG SODIUM.

NUTRITION BONUS: 90% DV VITAMIN A, 195 MCG FOLATE (49% DV), 4 MG IRON (20% DV), 15% DV FIBER.

VEGETARIAN MAIN DISHES

10

If going without meat was once considered a sacrifice self-inflicted by spartan eaters, all that has changed. Vegetarian meals are as exotic, suffused with flavor and satisfying as anything from a mainstream menu. Whether you make vegetarian cooking a way of life or just part of a healthy, balanced eating plan, it's also clear that plant-based meals, rich in fruits, vegetables, whole grains, nuts and legumes, can help fight hypertension, heart disease, obesity, diabetes and some cancers. The recipes here should convince any skeptic. From everyday comfort cuisine to stylish dishes for entertaining, we've assembled some of our all-time best vegetarian dishes, guaranteed to please any appetite.

Roasted Vegetable Galette with Olives

PREP TIME: 45 MINUTES | **START TO FINISH:** 2¼ HOURS | **TO MAKE AHEAD:** THE UNBAKED CRUST WILL KEEP, WELL WRAPPED, IN THE REFRIGERATOR FOR UP TO 2 DAYS. | **EASE OF PREPARATION:** MODERATE

The natural sugar in the vegetables caramelizes during roasting, giving this tart an incredible sweet-savory flavor. Roasted garlic adds a mellow note and moistens the filling. This is a very adaptable recipe: experiment with different vegetables—eggplant, bell peppers, zucchini—and cheeses like fontina or Jarlsberg.

CRUST

- 1¼ cups all-purpose flour
- 1 cup whole-wheat pastry flour (*see Ingredient Note, page 395*)
- 2 teaspoons baking powder
- 1 teaspoon sugar
- ½ teaspoon salt
- ⅓ cup water
- ¼ cup extra-virgin olive oil
- ½ cup finely chopped pitted Kalamata olives

FILLING

- 1½ cups diced peeled carrots (3 medium)
- 1½ cups diced peeled parsnips (3 medium)
- 1½ cups diced peeled butternut squash (½ medium)
- 1 cup diced peeled beet (1 medium)
- 2 tablespoons extra-virgin olive oil, divided
- 2 teaspoons chopped fresh rosemary *or* ½ teaspoon dried
- ½ teaspoon salt, or to taste
- Freshly ground pepper to taste
- 1 head garlic
- 1 cup crumbled creamy goat cheese (4 ounces), divided
- 1 egg mixed with 1 tablespoon water for glazing

1. **To prepare crust:** Combine all-purpose flour, whole-wheat flour, baking powder, sugar and salt in a food processor; pulse several times. Mix water and oil; sprinkle over the dry ingredients and pulse just until blended. Add olives and pulse to mix. (*Alternatively, combine dry ingredients in a large bowl. Make a well in the center and add the water-oil mixture, stirring until well blended. Stir in olives.*) Press the dough into a disk; if it seems dry, add a little more water. Wrap in plastic wrap and refrigerate for 30 minutes or longer.
2. Meanwhile, preheat oven to 400°F. Coat a large baking sheet with cooking spray.
3. **To prepare filling:** Combine carrots, parsnips, squash, beet, 1 tablespoon oil, rosemary, salt and pepper in a large bowl; toss to coat. Spread the vegetables on the prepared baking sheet. Cut the tip off the head of garlic. Set on a square of foil, sprinkle with a tablespoon of water and pinch the edges of the foil together. Place the packet on the baking sheet with the vegetables. Roast, stirring the vegetables every 10 minutes, until they are tender and beginning to brown and the garlic is soft, about 35 minutes. (The garlic may take a little longer.)
4. Transfer the vegetables to a bowl. Unwrap the garlic and let cool slightly. Squeeze the garlic cloves into a small bowl; add the remaining 1 tablespoon oil and mash with a fork. Add the mashed garlic to the roasted vegetables and toss to mix. Add ¾ cup goat cheese and toss to coat.
5. **To assemble galette:** Roll the dough into a rough 14-inch circle about ¼ inch thick. Coat a baking sheet with cooking spray and place the dough on it. Arrange the roasted vegetables on the

TEST KITCHEN TIP:
The vegetables should be cut to a uniform size so they cook evenly. Aim for ¾-inch pieces.

dough, leaving a 2-inch border all around. Fold the border up and over the filling to form a rim, pleating as you go. Scatter the remaining ¼ cup goat cheese over the vegetables. Stir egg and water briskly; brush lightly over the crust.

6. Bake the galette at 400°F until the crust is golden, 30 to 35 minutes. Let cool for 10 minutes. Serve warm.

MAKES 8 SERVINGS.

PER SERVING: 385 CALORIES; 20 G FAT (6 G SAT, 12 G MONO); 41 MG CHOLESTEROL; 42 G CARBOHYDRATE; 10 G PROTEIN; 6 G FIBER; 667 MG SODIUM.

NUTRITION BONUS: 160% DV VITAMIN A, 18 MG VITAMIN C (30% DV), 22% DV FIBER, 423 MCG POTASSIUM (21% DV), 208 MG CALCIUM (20% DV), 81 MCG FOLATE (20% DV).

Spice-Crusted Tofu

Healthy Weight

PREP TIME: 10 MINUTES | **START TO FINISH:** 20 MINUTES | **EASE OF PREPARATION:** EASY

Pantry ingredients and basic spices transform a package of tofu into a quick, simple meal—no slicing and dicing required. (*Photo: page 214.*)

- 3 tablespoons pine nuts
- 1 tablespoon paprika
- 1 teaspoon ground cumin
- 1 teaspoon ground coriander
- ½ teaspoon coarse kosher salt, or to taste
- Freshly ground pepper to taste
- 1 14- to 16-ounce package extra-firm tofu
- 3 tablespoons boiling water
- 2 tablespoons lemon juice
- 4 teaspoons honey
- 1 tablespoon extra-virgin olive oil

1. Toast pine nuts (*see Tip, page 197*); set aside to cool. Mix paprika, cumin, coriander, salt and pepper in a small bowl. Drain tofu and pat dry with paper towels. Cut crosswise into 8 slices, ½ inch thick. Dredge the tofu liberally with the spice mixture, coating all sides. Mix boiling water, lemon juice and honey in a small bowl.

2. Heat oil in a large nonstick skillet over medium-high heat; swirl to coat the bottom. Add tofu and cook on one side until brown and crusty, 4 to 5 minutes; flip and cook for another 3 minutes. Add the honey mixture to the pan (it will bubble up and evaporate very quickly) and shake to coat the tofu. Serve immediately, sprinkled with the toasted pine nuts.

MAKES 4 SERVINGS.

PER SERVING: 206 CALORIES; 15 G FAT (2 G SAT, 4 G MONO); 0 MG CHOLESTEROL; 10 G CARBOHYDRATE; 12 G PROTEIN; 2 G FIBER; 248 MG SODIUM.

NUTRITION BONUS: 15% DV VITAMIN A, 15% DV IRON.

Lower Carbs

Grilled Tofu & Vegetable Kebabs

PREP TIME: 10 MINUTES | **START TO FINISH:** 50 MINUTES (INCLUDING MARINATING TIME)
EQUIPMENT: EIGHT 12-INCH SKEWERS | **EASE OF PREPARATION:** EASY

Grilling imparts a wonderful smoky flavor and meaty texture to tofu. Because it has a tendency to stick to the grill, be sure the grate is clean and well oiled. This makes a good year-round dish—just use the broiler when you can't cook outside. Steamed brown rice makes it a complete meal.

TOFU & MARINADE

- 1 14- to 16-ounce package extra-firm regular tofu
- 3 tablespoons reduced-sodium soy sauce
- 2 tablespoons hoisin sauce (*see Note*)
- 2 tablespoons Chinese rice wine, sake *or* medium-dry sherry
- 1 tablespoon peanut oil *or* canola oil
- 1 tablespoon honey
- ½ teaspoon chile-garlic sauce

KEBABS

- 2 cups broccoli florets
- 1 teaspoon peanut oil *or* canola oil
- 6 scallions, white and light green parts, cut into 2-inch lengths
- 1 cup cherry tomatoes *or* grape tomatoes

INGREDIENT NOTE: Hoisin sauce is a dark brown, thick, spicy-sweet sauce made with soybeans and a complex mix of spices. Look for it in the Chinese section of your supermarket, and in Asian groceries.

1. **To prepare tofu & marinade:** Drain tofu and pat dry with paper towels. Cut into 1½-inch squares; place in a medium bowl. Combine soy sauce, hoisin sauce, rice wine (or sake or sherry), oil, honey and chile-garlic sauce in a glass measuring cup. Gently toss tofu with ¼ cup of the marinade (reserve the remainder). Cover and marinate in the refrigerator for 30 minutes, gently turning the tofu once.
2. **To prepare kebabs:** Steam broccoli until tender-crisp, about 2 minutes. Refresh under cold running water.
3. Preheat grill to medium-high.
4. Thread the tofu onto 4 skewers and brush with oil. Alternately thread broccoli, scallions and tomatoes onto 4 more skewers and brush with some of the reserved marinade. Reserve half the remaining marinade for basting and half for sauce.
5. Lightly oil the grill rack (*see Tip, page 130*). Grill the kebabs, turning carefully with a metal spatula after 2 to 3 minutes and basting with reserved marinade, until the tofu is well scored with grill marks and the vegetables are softened and blackened along the edges. The tofu should take about 6 minutes, the vegetables 7 to 8 minutes. Warm the remaining marinade in a microwave or on the stovetop and serve with the kebabs.

MAKES 4 SERVINGS.

PER SERVING: 213 CALORIES; 12 G FAT (2 G SAT, 2 G MONO); 0 MG CHOLESTEROL; 16 G CARBOHYDRATE; 14 G PROTEIN; 3 G FIBER; 583 MG SODIUM.

NUTRITION BONUS: 47 MG VITAMIN C (80% DV), 30% DV VITAMIN A, 3 MG IRON (20% DV), 296 MG POTASSIUM (15% DV), 123 MG CALCIUM (15% DV).

Sesame-Crusted Tofu with Soba Noodles

PREP TIME: 10 MINUTES | **START TO FINISH:** 55 MINUTES | **EASE OF PREPARATION:** MODERATE

Elegant and full of sophisticated Asian flavors—tofu doesn't get any better than this.

DRESSING

- 2 tablespoons rice wine *or* sake
- 1½ tablespoons prepared black bean sauce
- 1 tablespoon reduced-sodium soy sauce
- 1 tablespoon sugar
- 1 tablespoon water

TOFU & SOBA

- 1 14- to 16-ounce package extra-firm regular tofu
- ¼ cup rice wine *or* sake
- 2 tablespoons reduced-sodium soy sauce
- 2 teaspoons sesame oil, divided
- 8 ounces soba noodles
- 4 cups trimmed watercress, loosely packed
- 1 cup thinly sliced scallions
- 2 tablespoons Chinese fermented black beans, rinsed (optional)
- 3 tablespoons sesame seeds

1. **To prepare dressing:** Combine rice wine (or sake), black bean sauce, soy sauce, sugar and water in a small bowl; stir until the sugar has dissolved. Set aside.
2. **To prepare tofu & soba:** Cut tofu into 8 pieces the size of a playing card.
3. Combine rice wine (or sake), soy sauce and 1 teaspoon sesame oil in a shallow dish just large enough to hold tofu in a single layer. Add tofu; cover and marinate in the refrigerator for 30 minutes, turning once.
4. Meanwhile, cook noodles in a large pot of boiling water until tender, about 5 minutes. Drain and rinse under cold running water. Place in a large bowl. Remove tofu from marinade and pat dry. Mix any marinade not absorbed by tofu into the reserved dressing and add to the noodles along with watercress, scallions and fermented black beans, if using; toss to combine. Set aside.
5. Spread sesame seeds on a small plate. Dip tofu into sesame seeds to coat one side. Heat remaining 1 teaspoon sesame oil in a large nonstick skillet over medium heat. Cook tofu, sesame-seed-side down (in batches, if necessary), until golden, about 1 minute. Turn and cook the other side until golden, 1 to 2 minutes more.
6. Divide the noodles among 4 plates and arrange sesame-crusted tofu on top. Serve immediately.

MAKES 4 SERVINGS.

PER SERVING: 466 CALORIES; 16 G FAT (2 G SAT, 2 G MONO); 0 MG CHOLESTEROL; 51 G CARBOHYDRATE; 26 G PROTEIN; 5 G FIBER; 544 MG SODIUM.

NUTRITION BONUS: 7 MG IRON (40% DV), 35% DV VITAMIN A, 19 MG VITAMIN C (30% DV), 20% DV FIBER.

Lower Carbs

Coconut-Curry Stew

PREP TIME: 20 MINUTES | **START TO FINISH:** 45 MINUTES | **TO MAKE AHEAD:** THE STEW WILL KEEP, COVERED, IN THE REFRIGERATOR FOR UP TO 2 DAYS. | **EASE OF PREPARATION:** MODERATE

Have a taste of this spicy, seemingly rich Thai-style curry and you won't believe it's so low in calories. Serve it over cooked brown rice, if desired.

- 2 bunches scallions
- 1 14-ounce can "lite" coconut milk
- 3-4 tablespoons reduced-sodium soy sauce
- 1½ teaspoons light brown sugar
- 1½ teaspoons curry powder
- 1 teaspoon minced fresh ginger
- 1-2 teaspoons chile-garlic sauce
- 1 14- to 16-ounce package firm *or* extra-firm tofu, drained and cut into ¾-inch cubes
- 4 ripe plum tomatoes, cut into 6 wedges each
- 1 yellow bell pepper, halved and thinly sliced
- 4 ounces mushrooms, such as shiitake *or* white, stemmed and thickly sliced (3 cups)
- ¼ cup fresh basil leaves, coarsely chopped
- 4 cups coarsely chopped bok choy (green part only) *or* spinach
- Salt to taste

1. Cut scallion whites and about 2 inches of the greens into 2-inch diagonal pieces. Finely chop remaining scallion greens; reserve separately.

2. Combine coconut milk, 3 tablespoons soy sauce, brown sugar, curry powder, ginger and 1 teaspoon chile-garlic sauce in a Dutch oven. Bring to a boil over medium-high heat. Add tofu, tomatoes, bell pepper, mushrooms, basil and scallion pieces. Cover and cook, stirring occasionally, for 5 minutes. Add bok choy (or spinach), cover and cook, stirring occasionally, for 5 minutes more, or until the vegetables are tender. Adjust seasonings with soy sauce, chile-garlic sauce and salt. Garnish with the reserved chopped scallion greens. Serve immediately.

INGREDIENT NOTE: Look for reduced-fat coconut milk (labeled "lite") in the Asian section of your market.

MAKES 6 SERVINGS, GENEROUS 1 CUP EACH.

PER SERVING: 123 CALORIES; 6 G FAT (4 G SAT, 0 G MONO); 0 MG CHOLESTEROL; 11 G CARBOHYDRATE; 9 G PROTEIN; 2 G FIBER; 435 MG SODIUM.

NUTRITION BONUS: 68 MG VITAMIN C (110% DV), 60% DV VITAMIN A, 465 MG POTASSIUM (23% DV), 63 MCG FOLATE (16% DV).

North African Vegetable Stew with Poached Eggs

PREP TIME: 10 MINUTES | **START TO FINISH:** 35 MINUTES | **TO MAKE AHEAD:** PREPARE THROUGH STEP 3. THE STEW WILL KEEP, COVERED, IN THE REFRIGERATOR FOR UP TO 2 DAYS. | **EASE OF PREPARATION:** EASY

Fragrant vegetable stews are common all around the Mediterranean. This streamlined version is flavored with a Tunisian spice blend and made simple with the use of precut frozen stir-fry vegetables.

- 2 teaspoons extra-virgin olive oil
- 3 cups frozen pepper stir-fry vegetables
- 1 teaspoon coriander seeds (*see Ingredient Note, page 189*)
- ½ teaspoon caraway seeds
- Pinch of salt
- ¼ teaspoon paprika, plus more for sprinkling
- ⅛ teaspoon cayenne pepper
- 4 cloves garlic, minced
- 1 28-ounce can *or* 2 14½-ounce cans diced tomatoes
- 1 19-ounce *or* 15½-ounce can chickpeas, rinsed
- Freshly ground pepper to taste
- 4 large eggs

1. Heat oil in a large nonstick skillet over medium-high heat. Add stir-fry vegetables; cook, stirring occasionally, until most of the liquid has evaporated, 5 to 7 minutes.
2. Meanwhile, grind coriander seeds, caraway seeds and salt coarsely in a spice mill, a dry blender or in a mortar and pestle. Transfer to a small bowl and stir in ¼ teaspoon paprika and cayenne.
3. Add garlic and the spice mixture to the skillet; cook, stirring, for 30 seconds. Add tomatoes and chickpeas; bring to a simmer. Reduce heat to medium and cook at a lively simmer until slightly thickened, 10 to 15 minutes. Season with pepper.
4. Break eggs into separate quadrants of the stew, taking care not to break the yolks. Reduce heat to medium-low, cover the skillet and cook until the eggs are set, 5 to 7 minutes. Sprinkle eggs with paprika. Carefully transfer an egg and some stew to each plate.

MAKES 4 SERVINGS.

PER SERVING: 277 CALORIES; 10 G FAT (2 G SAT, 4 G MONO); 211 MG CHOLESTEROL; 30 G CARBOHYDRATE; 15 G PROTEIN; 9 G FIBER; 554 MG SODIUM.

NUTRITION BONUS: 30 MG VITAMIN C (50% DV), 35% DV FIBER, 30% DV VITAMIN A, 4 MG IRON (20% DV).

FRESH-VEGETABLE VARIATION: In Step 1, cook 1 medium sliced onion for about 2 minutes; add 2 diced bell peppers and cook for 3 to 5 minutes more. In Step 3, add 3 diced seeded tomatoes.

Slow-Cooker Black Bean-Mushroom Chili

PREP TIME: 25 MINUTES PLUS 1¼ HOURS SOAKING TIME | **SLOW-COOKER TIME:** 5-8 HOURS | **TO MAKE AHEAD:** THE CHILI WILL KEEP, COVERED, IN THE REFRIGERATOR FOR UP TO 2 DAYS OR IN THE FREEZER FOR UP TO 3 MONTHS. THAW IN THE REFRIGERATOR, IF NECESSARY, AND REHEAT ON THE STOVETOP OR IN A MICROWAVE. | **EASE OF PREPARATION:** EASY

Earthy mushrooms, tomatillos and a subtle layering of spices combine to give this full-bodied vegetarian chili a deep complexity of flavor. Note that dried beans need to be soaked before going into the slow cooker. Once that's done, the chili can gently bubble for hours, adding flexibility to your schedule. (*Photo: page 213.*)

- 1 pound dried black beans (2½ cups), picked over and rinsed
- 1 tablespoon extra-virgin olive oil
- ¼ cup mustard seeds
- 2 tablespoons chili powder
- 1½ teaspoons cumin seeds *or* ground cumin
- ½ teaspoon cardamom seeds *or* ground cardamom
- 2 medium onions, coarsely chopped
- 1 pound mushrooms, wiped clean, trimmed and sliced (4½ cups)
- 8 ounces tomatillos, husked, rinsed and coarsely chopped
- ¼ cup water
- 5½ cups mushroom broth *or* vegetable broth, homemade (*page 67*) *or* canned
- 1 6-ounce can tomato paste
- 1-2 tablespoons minced canned chipotle peppers in adobo sauce
- 1¼ cups grated Monterey Jack *or* pepper Jack cheese
- ½ cup reduced-fat sour cream
- ½ cup chopped fresh cilantro
- 2 limes, cut into wedges

1. Soak beans overnight in 2 quarts water. (*Alternatively, place beans and 2 quarts water in a large pot. Bring to a boil. Boil for 2 minutes. Remove from heat and let stand for 1 hour.*) Drain beans, discarding soaking liquid.

2. Meanwhile, combine oil, mustard seeds, chili powder, cumin and cardamom in a 5- to 6-quart Dutch oven. Place over high heat and stir until the spices sizzle, about 30 seconds. Add onions, mushrooms, tomatillos and ¼ cup water. Cover and cook, stirring occasionally, until vegetables are juicy, 5 to 7 minutes. Uncover and stir often until the juices evaporate and the vegetables are lightly browned, 10 to 15 minutes. Add broth, tomato paste and chipotles (with sauce); mix well.

3. Place the beans in a 5- to 6-quart slow cooker. Pour the hot mixture over the beans. Turn heat to high. Put the lid on and cook until the beans are creamy to bite, 5 to 8 hours.

4. To serve, ladle the chili into bowls. Garnish each serving with cheese, a dollop of sour cream and a sprinkling of cilantro. Pass lime wedges at the table.

MAKES 10 SERVINGS, GENEROUS 1 CUP EACH.

PER SERVING: 310 CALORIES; 10 G FAT (4 G SAT, 2 G MONO); 20 MG CHOLESTEROL; 40 G CARBOHYDRATE; 18 G PROTEIN; 13 G FIBER; 414 MG SODIUM.

NUTRITION BONUS: 53% DV FIBER, 187 MCG FOLATE (47% DV), 743 MG POTASSIUM (37% DV), 4 MG IRON (25% DV).

◆ **STOVETOP METHOD:** **START TO FINISH:** 4½ HOURS
In Step 2, increase broth to 8½ cups. Omit Step 3. Add the beans to the Dutch oven; cover and simmer the chili gently over low heat, stirring occasionally, until beans are creamy to bite, about 3 hours.

Winter Vegetable Stew

PREP TIME: 20 MINUTES | **START TO FINISH:** 1¼ HOURS | **TO MAKE AHEAD:** THE STEW WILL KEEP, COVERED, IN THE REFRIGERATOR FOR UP TO 2 DAYS. | **EASE OF PREPARATION:** MODERATE

Serve this robust stew over barley for cozy, casual entertaining.

- 6 large carrots, peeled
- 2 medium potatoes, peeled
- 2 leeks, trimmed and washed (*see Cooking Tip, page 397*)
- 2 onions, peeled
- 2 stalks celery
- ½ small rutabaga, peeled
- 2 small turnips, peeled
- 1 tablespoon extra-virgin olive oil
- 6 large mushrooms, wiped clean and quartered
- ¼ cup all-purpose flour
- ½ cup dry red wine
- 4 cups vegetable broth, homemade (*page 67*) *or* canned
- 1 head garlic, cloves peeled
- 1 teaspoon salt
- ¼ teaspoon freshly ground pepper
- 4 sprigs fresh thyme *or* ½ teaspoon dried thyme leaves
- 1 bay leaf
- 6 juniper berries (*see Note*), crushed (optional)
- 2 tablespoons chopped fresh parsley

1. Cut carrots, potatoes, leeks, onions, celery and rutabaga into 1½- to 2-inch lengths. Cut turnips into quarters.

2. Cook the rutabaga in a large pot of boiling salted water for 1 minute. Add the turnips and cook for 1 minute more. Drain.

3. Heat oil in a Dutch oven over medium-high heat. Add mushrooms, the carrots and potatoes. Cook, stirring occasionally, until lightly browned, 5 to 10 minutes. Sprinkle flour over the vegetables and cook, stirring, for 1 minute. Add wine and cook, stirring, until the liquid is absorbed, about 30 seconds. Add broth and bring to a boil, stirring constantly.

4. Add cloves of garlic, the reserved rutabaga and turnips, leeks, onions, celery, salt and pepper. Tie together thyme, bay leaf and juniper berries, if using, in a cheesecloth bag and add to the stew. Return to a boil. Reduce heat to low, cover and simmer until the vegetables are tender, 35 to 40 minutes.

5. Discard the cheesecloth bag. Adjust seasoning with salt and pepper. Ladle the stew into shallow bowls, garnish with parsley and serve immediately.

INGREDIENT NOTE: Familiar to most as the flavoring in gin, the blue-black berries of the evergreen juniper bush are often used to spice up game dishes. You can find juniper berries in specialty stores.

MAKES 4 SERVINGS, GENEROUS 2 CUPS EACH.

PER SERVING: 299 CALORIES; 4 G FAT (1 G SAT, 3 G MONO); 0 MG CHOLESTEROL; 58 G CARBOHYDRATE; 8 G PROTEIN; 10 G FIBER; 735 MG SODIUM.

NUTRITION BONUS: 480% DV VITAMIN A, 110% DV VITAMIN C, 1,445 MG POTASSIUM (72% DV), 38% DV FIBER, 96 MCG FOLATE (24% DV), 4 MG IRON (20% DV), 173 MG CALCIUM (17% DV).

Leek, Barley & Mushroom Packets

PREP TIME: 1 HOUR | START TO FINISH: 1 HOUR 10 MINUTES | TO MAKE AHEAD: PREPARE THROUGH STEP 7. THE PACKETS WILL KEEP, COVERED, IN THE REFRIGERATOR FOR UP TO 2 DAYS. | EASE OF PREPARATION: CHALLENGING

Not your grandma's cabbage rolls; these are decidedly modern, highlighting the individual flavors of the ingredients. The portobello gravy adds an elegant finish.

- 1½ cups Portobello Gravy (*page 289*)
- 1 tablespoon extra-virgin olive oil
- 2 cups thinly sliced leeks (white and pale green parts only), washed (*see Cooking Tip, page 397*)
- 2 cups sliced mushrooms
- ½ cup pearl barley (*see Ingredient Note, page 394*)
- 2½ cups vegetable broth, homemade (*page 67*) *or* canned, divided
- 2 tablespoons dry white wine *or* water
- 1 large head Savoy cabbage
- 3 tablespoons chopped fresh dill, divided, plus 4 sprigs for garnish
- 3 tablespoons chopped fresh parsley, divided
- Salt to taste
- Freshly ground pepper to taste
- ¼ cup reduced-fat sour cream for garnish

1. Put a large pot of salted water on to boil for blanching cabbage.
2. Make Portobello Gravy.
3. Meanwhile, heat oil in a large saucepan over medium heat; add leeks and mushrooms and cook, stirring frequently, until tender, about 5 minutes. Stir in barley. Add 2 cups broth and wine (or water); bring to a boil. Reduce heat to low. Cover and simmer until barley is tender and liquid has been absorbed, 30 to 35 minutes.
4. Remove core from cabbage with a paring knife. Carefully remove 10 to 12 well-formed outer leaves. (You will only need 8 leaves; prepare a few extra in case any tear.) Reserve center of cabbage for another use, such as coleslaw.
5. Place a large bowl of ice water beside the stove and lay some kitchen towels on a work surface. Drop several cabbage leaves into the boiling water. Blanch just until pliable, 2 to 3 minutes. With tongs or a large slotted spoon, remove cabbage leaves from pot and place in ice water until cool. Drain on kitchen towels. Repeat with remaining cabbage leaves. Using a paring knife, remove and discard thick portion of stem, about 2 inches from each leaf.
6. When barley is cooked, stir in 2 tablespoons each of chopped dill and parsley. Season with salt and pepper. Let cool.
7. Overlap the bottom parts of each cabbage leaf where the stem was. Place a scant ⅓ cup of the barley mixture on the inside of a cabbage leaf near the stem end. Fold leafy sides over filling and roll up firmly from the stem end. Repeat with remaining barley mixture and cabbage leaves to make a total of 8 packets.
8. Bring remaining ½ cup broth to a simmer in a large skillet. Reduce heat to low. Place cabbage packets, seam-side down, in broth. Cover and simmer until heated through, 10 to 15 minutes. Meanwhile, heat gravy over low heat.

9. To serve, spread gravy on 4 dinner plates. Set 2 cabbage rolls on each plate and sprinkle with remaining chopped dill and parsley. Top with a dollop of sour cream and garnish with a dill sprig.

MAKES 4 SERVINGS.

PER SERVING: 286 CALORIES; 7 G FAT (1 G SAT, 5 G MONO); 0 MG CHOLESTEROL; 49 G CARBOHYDRATE; 7 G PROTEIN; 9 G FIBER; 1,076 MG SODIUM.

NUTRITION BONUS: 45% DV VITAMIN A, 37% DV FIBER, 461 MG POTASSIUM (23% DV), 13 MG VITAMIN C (20% DV), 75 MCG FOLATE (19% DV).

Fragrant Chickpea Stew

PREP TIME: 10 MINUTES | **START TO FINISH:** 35 MINUTES | **TO MAKE AHEAD:** THE STEW WILL KEEP, COVERED, IN THE REFRIGERATOR FOR UP TO 2 DAYS. REHEAT ON THE STOVETOP OR IN THE MICROWAVE. | **EASE OF PREPARATION:** EASY

When time is of the essence, this hearty stew makes a quick meal. It has a complex, almost beefy flavor that develops when the onion and garlic are cooked until dark brown. Accompany with steamed rice or whole-wheat flatbreads (chapatis).

- **1 tablespoon canola oil**
- **1 teaspoon cumin seeds**
- **1 medium red onion, chopped (1 cup)**
- **5 medium cloves garlic, minced**
- **1 tablespoon coriander seeds, ground (*see Note*)**
- **1 cup water**
- **1 red potato, scrubbed and cut into 1-inch cubes**
- **1 19-ounce *or* 15½-ounce can chickpeas, rinsed**
- **½ teaspoon salt, or to taste**
- **½ teaspoon coarsely ground pepper**
- **2 tablespoons finely chopped fresh cilantro, divided**
- **1 medium tomato, cut into 1-inch cubes**

1. Heat oil in a large saucepan over medium-high heat; cook cumin seeds for 10 seconds. Add onion and garlic; cook, stirring, until dark brown, 5 to 8 minutes. Add coriander; cook, stirring, for 20 seconds. Stir in water, potato, chickpeas, salt, pepper and 1 tablespoon cilantro. Bring to a boil. Reduce heat to low, cover and simmer until the potato is tender, 15 to 20 minutes.

2. Add tomato, increase heat to medium and simmer, uncovered, for 1 to 2 minutes. Sprinkle with remaining 1 tablespoon cilantro and serve.

INGREDIENT NOTE: **Coriander seeds are tiny and yellowish brown; they are produced when cilantro is allowed to seed. They smell slightly citric. Their flavor does not resemble, in any way, that of cilantro.**

MAKES 4 SERVINGS, ABOUT 1 CUP EACH.

PER SERVING: 255 CALORIES; 6 G FAT (0 G SAT, 3 G MONO); 0 MG CHOLESTEROL; 45 G CARBOHYDRATE; 9 G PROTEIN; 8 G FIBER; 703 MG SODIUM.

NUTRITION BONUS: 20 MG VITAMIN C (35% DV), 33% DV FIBER, 579 MG POTASSIUM (29% DV), 110 MCG FOLATE (28% DV).

Braised Squash with Peppers & Hominy

PREP TIME: 15 MINUTES | **START TO FINISH:** 1 HOUR | **EASE OF PREPARATION:** EASY

Hominy is an underused ingredient that adds a distinctive, earthy flavor to dishes like this spice-warmed stew. It's also high in fiber and loaded with vitamins and minerals.

- 1 tablespoon sunflower *or* other vegetable oil
- 2 onions, chopped
- 1 butternut squash (2½ pounds), peeled, seeded and cut into 1¼-inch chunks
- 1 red bell pepper, cored and cut into large dice
- 2 teaspoons sweet paprika
- ½ teaspoon ground cumin
- ¼ teaspoon caraway seeds
- 1½ teaspoons all-purpose flour
- 1 teaspoon salt, plus more to taste
- ¼ teaspoon freshly ground pepper, plus more to taste
- Pinch of cayenne pepper
- 1 15-ounce can hominy (*see Note*), drained and rinsed
- 2½-3 cups water
- 4 tablespoons chopped fresh parsley *or* cilantro, divided
- 2 tablespoons tomato paste
- 6 lime wedges

1. Heat oil in a large deep skillet over high heat. Add onions, squash, bell pepper, paprika, cumin and caraway seeds. Cook, stirring, until onions and squash are browned in places, about 10 minutes. Add flour, 1 teaspoon salt, ¼ teaspoon pepper and cayenne; cook, stirring, for 1 minute more.

2. Stir in hominy, 2½ cups water, 3 tablespoons parsley (or cilantro) and tomato paste. Bring to a boil, reduce heat to low and simmer, covered, until squash is tender, 25 to 30 minutes. (Add remaining ½ cup water if vegetables look dry.) Adjust seasoning with salt and pepper. Garnish with remaining 1 tablespoon parsley (or cilantro). Serve with lime wedges.

INGREDIENT NOTE:
Hominy is made from corn kernels that have been dried, degermed and hulled. You can find canned hominy in the Latin section of many supermarkets, Latin markets and specialty stores.

MAKES 6 SERVINGS, 1⅓ CUPS EACH.

PER SERVING: 196 CALORIES; 3 G FAT (0 G SAT, 2 G MONO); 0 MG CHOLESTEROL; 41 G CARBOHYDRATE; 4 G PROTEIN; 8 G FIBER; 553 MG SODIUM.

NUTRITION BONUS: 430% DV VITAMIN A, 90 MG VITAMIN C (150% DV), 30% DV FIBER.

Vegetarian Enchiladas

PREP TIME: 50 MINUTES | **START TO FINISH:** 1 HOUR 20 MINUTES | **TO MAKE AHEAD:** PREPARE THROUGH STEP 5. THE ENCHILADAS WILL KEEP, COVERED, IN THE REFRIGERATOR FOR UP TO 2 DAYS. | **EASE OF PREPARATION:** CHALLENGING

The secret to this creamy enchilada sauce is pureed toasted corn, enriched with roasted garlic.

CORN SAUCE

- 2 cloves garlic, unpeeled
- 2 10-ounce packages frozen corn
- 1 cup low-fat milk
- ⅛ teaspoon cayenne pepper
- Salt & freshly ground pepper to taste

ENCHILADAS

- 1 teaspoon canola oil
- 8 ounces button mushrooms, wiped clean, stemmed and sliced
- 10 ounces fresh spinach, stemmed and chopped
- 1 small onion, chopped
- ½ teaspoon salt
- Freshly ground pepper to taste
- 12 corn tortillas
- 1 cup grated extra-sharp Cheddar cheese
- Cilantro & Pumpkin Seed Pesto (*page 297*) *and/or* prepared tomato salsa

TEST KITCHEN TIP:
To toast tortillas, place directly on a burner (gas or electric) set at medium heat. Turn frequently with tongs, until golden, 30 to 60 seconds.

1. **To prepare corn sauce:** Roast garlic in a large heavy skillet over medium-high heat, shaking the pan often, until lightly browned, about 8 minutes. Add half the corn and cook, stirring often, until lightly toasted, about 8 minutes. Reserve the garlic; transfer the corn to a blender. Toast the remaining corn. Place all but ½ cup of the corn in the blender. Peel garlic and add to blender along with milk and cayenne. Blend until smooth. Strain through a fine sieve into a bowl. Stir in reserved corn. Season with salt and pepper. Set aside.
2. **To prepare enchiladas:** Preheat oven to 350°F. Coat a 9-by-13-inch or similar baking dish with cooking spray.
3. Heat oil in a large nonstick skillet over medium-high heat. Add mushrooms and cook, stirring often, until softened, about 4 minutes. Add spinach and cook until wilted, about 2 minutes. Drain off excess liquid. Remove from heat and stir in onion, salt and pepper.
4. Toast tortillas (*see Tip*).
5. Sprinkle a generous tablespoon of cheese down the center of a tortilla. Cover the cheese with a scant ¼ cup of the spinach mixture. Fold one side of the tortilla over the filling, then roll up tightly. Place the enchilada seam-side down in the prepared dish. Repeat with the remaining tortillas, cheese and spinach mixture. Spoon corn sauce over the enchiladas, covering completely.
6. Cover baking dish with foil. Bake for 25 minutes, or until heated through. Uncover and bake for 5 minutes more.
7. Meanwhile, make Cilantro & Pumpkin Seed Pesto, if using.
8. Divide enchiladas among 6 plates. Top with the pesto (and/or salsa). Serve immediately.

MAKES 6 SERVINGS, 2 ENCHILADAS EACH.

PER SERVING: 381 CALORIES; 14 G FAT (6 G SAT, 2 G MONO); 24 MG CHOLESTEROL; 58 G CARBOHYDRATE; 16 G PROTEIN; 9 G FIBER; 418 MG SODIUM.

NUTRITION BONUS: 100% DV VITAMIN A, 36% DV FIBER, 22 MG VITAMIN C (35% DV), 135 MCG FOLATE (34% DV), 629 MG POTASSIUM (31% DV), 305 MG CALCIUM (30% DV).

Eggplant-Couscous Rolls

PREP TIME: 50 MINUTES | **START TO FINISH:** 1 HOUR 20 MINUTES | **EASE OF PREPARATION:** CHALLENGING

This meatless entrée has an ample amount of protein from the couscous and feta cheese. Whole-wheat couscous has a nutty flavor and, like regular couscous, requires no actual cooking, just five minutes to plump in hot water. You can find it in health-food stores, but if it is not available, substitute regular couscous.

- **2 eggplants (1 pound each), ends trimmed**
- **4 teaspoons extra-virgin olive oil, divided**
- **9 ripe plum tomatoes (1¼ pounds total)**
- **1½ cups water**
- **1 cup whole-wheat couscous**
- **½ teaspoon dried thyme**
- **½ teaspoon salt**
- **¾ cup crumbled feta cheese plus 2 tablespoons for garnish**
- **2 tablespoons chopped fresh mint**
- **Freshly ground pepper to taste**

1. Preheat oven to 425°F. Coat 2 baking sheets with cooking spray.
2. Standing eggplants on end, remove a thin slice of skin from two opposite sides and discard. Cut eggplants lengthwise into ⅓-inch-thick slices. Brush both sides of the slices with 2 teaspoons oil and arrange in a single layer on the baking sheets. Cut tomatoes in half lengthwise and remove seeds. Place them, cut-side down, in the remaining space on the baking sheets.
3. Bake the vegetables for 10 minutes. Turn eggplant slices over and bake until the eggplant is lightly browned and tender and the tomato skins are blistered, 10 to 15 minutes longer.
4. Meanwhile, in a medium saucepan, bring water to a boil. Stir in couscous, thyme, salt and 1 teaspoon oil. Remove from the heat, cover and let stand until the water is absorbed, 5 minutes. Uncover and let cool for 15 minutes. With a fork, stir in the feta, mint and pepper.
5. Coat a 9-by-13-inch baking dish with cooking spray. Put some of the couscous mixture in the center of each eggplant slice. Roll up the eggplant slices firmly around the filling and place, seam-side down, in the prepared dish. Cover with foil; bake for 15 minutes.
6. Meanwhile, peel the skin away from the roasted tomatoes and put them in a small saucepan. Mash with a fork and add the remaining 1 teaspoon oil, salt and pepper. Heat gently over low heat. To serve, spoon the tomato sauce over the eggplant rolls and sprinkle with the remaining 2 tablespoons feta cheese.

MAKES 4 SERVINGS.

PER SERVING: 304 CALORIES; 12 G FAT (5 G SAT, 4 G MONO); 13 MG CHOLESTEROL; 43 G CARBOHYDRATE; 14 G PROTEIN; 5 G FIBER; 742 MG SODIUM.

NUTRITION BONUS: 870 MG POTASSIUM (44% DV), 23 MG VITAMIN C (40% DV), 30% DV VITAMIN A, 22% DV FIBER, 179 MG CALCIUM (20% DV).

Lower Carbs

High Fiber

Grilled Eggplant Towers with Tomatoes & Feta

PREP TIME: 40 MINUTES | **START TO FINISH:** 1 HOUR 10 MINUTES
EQUIPMENT: SIX 7- TO 10-OUNCE RAMEKINS OR CUSTARD CUPS | **TO MAKE AHEAD:** PREPARE THROUGH STEP 5. COVER AND REFRIGERATE FOR UP TO 8 HOURS. | **EASE OF PREPARATION:** MODERATE

The brief ingredient list belies the complex taste and sophisticated presentation of this vegetarian entrée. The juice that the tomato and eggplant give off while baking becomes the sauce for the dish, perfect for sopping up with crusty bread. This recipe also makes an attractive appetizer.

- **2 1½-pound eggplants, each cut into nine ½-inch-thick rounds**
- **¼ cup plus 6 teaspoons extra-virgin olive oil**
- **2 medium tomatoes, each cut into 6 rounds**
- **Freshly ground pepper to taste**
- **12 large fresh basil leaves, plus 6 sprigs for garnish**
- **1½ cups crumbled feta cheese (6 ounces)**

1. Preheat grill to medium.
2. Spread eggplant slices on 2 baking sheets or trays. Brush ¼ cup oil over both sides of eggplant slices. Coat another baking sheet with cooking spray and arrange tomato slices on it. Season eggplant and tomatoes with pepper.
3. Oil the grill rack (*see Tip, page 130*). Grill the eggplant slices until browned and tender, 5 to 7 minutes per side. Set aside. Place the baking sheet with the tomatoes directly on the grill rack; cover and grill until tomatoes are bubbling and warm, about 7 minutes.
4. Preheat oven to 350°F. Coat six ramekins or custard cups (about the same diameter as an eggplant slice) with cooking spray.
5. Assemble the towers: Using a wide spatula, layer an eggplant slice, a tomato slice and a basil leaf in each ramekin. Sprinkle with about 1 tablespoon feta. Repeat the layering once more, then top with an eggplant slice. Press down lightly.
6. Place ramekins on a baking sheet and bake until heated through and juices are bubbling around the edges, 25 to 35 minutes.
7. To serve, run a paring knife around the sides of each ramekin. Invert a plate on top and, grasping both with oven mitts, carefully invert the ramekin onto the plate. (Use caution: the ramekins and juices are extremely hot.) Remove the ramekins. The juices will form a sauce around the tower. Drizzle each tower with 1 teaspoon oil and garnish with a basil sprig. Serve hot, warm or at room temperature.

MAKES 6 SERVINGS.

PER SERVING: 265 CALORIES; 19 G FAT (5 G SAT, 11 G MONO); 15 MG CHOLESTEROL; 17 G CARBOHYDRATE; 8 G PROTEIN; 7 G FIBER; 283 MG SODIUM.

Savory Bread Pudding with Spinach & Mushrooms

PREP TIME: 50 MINUTES | **START TO FINISH:** 2 HOURS | **EASE OF PREPARATION:** MODERATE

Bread pudding, an economical dish designed to use up stale bread, is most often associated with dessert. It's equally comforting turned savory, enriched with cheese and studded with vegetables.

- 4 large eggs
- 2 cups 1% milk
- ½ teaspoon hot sauce, such as Tabasco
- ¾ teaspoon salt, divided
- ¼ teaspoon freshly ground pepper, divided
- 3½ cups cubed stale whole-wheat country bread
- 1 10-ounce package frozen spinach
- 1 tablespoon extra-virgin olive oil
- 1 cup chopped onion (1 medium)
- 1 cup chopped red bell pepper (1 small)
- 4 cups sliced mushrooms (12 ounces)
- 1 clove garlic, minced
- 1 cup grated Gruyère, Emmentaler *or* Manchego cheese (3 ounces), divided

1. Whisk eggs in a large bowl. Add milk, hot sauce, ½ teaspoon salt and ⅛ teaspoon pepper; whisk until blended. Add bread and stir to coat well. Cover and refrigerate for 30 minutes.

2. Meanwhile, preheat oven to 350°F. Coat an 8-by-8-inch (or similar 8-cup) ceramic or glass baking dish with cooking spray. Put a kettle of water on to boil for the water bath.

3. Cook spinach according to package directions. Drain, refresh with cold water and squeeze out excess moisture. Set aside.

4. Heat oil in a large nonstick skillet over medium heat. Add onion and bell pepper; cook, stirring often, until tender and golden, 4 to 5 minutes. Add mushrooms and garlic; stir to blend. Reduce heat to medium-low, cover and cook until tender, about 5 minutes. Uncover and increase heat to medium. Cook, stirring, until any excess moisture from the mushrooms has evaporated and mushrooms begin to brown, about 5 minutes. Add spinach, remaining ¼ teaspoon salt and ⅛ teaspoon pepper; cook, stirring, 2 minutes.

5. Add the mushroom mixture and ½ cup cheese to the egg mixture; stir until blended. Scrape into the prepared baking dish; sprinkle the remaining ½ cup cheese evenly over the top. Place the baking dish in a larger pan, put in the oven and pour boiling water into the larger pan to about halfway up the sides of the baking dish. Bake until the pudding is set in the center, 50 to 60 minutes. Let cool slightly; serve hot or warm.

MAKES 6 SERVINGS.

PER SERVING: 289 CALORIES; 14 G FAT (6 G SAT, 5 G MONO); 166 MG CHOLESTEROL; 24 G CARBOHYDRATE; 19 G PROTEIN; 4 G FIBER; 562 MG SODIUM.

NUTRITION BONUS: 130% DV VITAMIN A, 39 MG VITAMIN C (60% DV), 390 MG CALCIUM (40% DV), 580 MG POTASSIUM (29% DV), 96 MCG FOLATE (24% DV), 16% DV FIBER.

Classic Spinach Pie (Spanakopita)

PREP TIME: 45 MINUTES | **START TO FINISH:** 1 HOUR 55 MINUTES | **EASE OF PREPARATION:** CHALLENGING

This traditional Greek dish, seasoned with dill and feta, is one of the tastiest ways we know to eat more spinach. Be sure to plan ahead and allow enough time to thaw the phyllo dough according to package directions.

- 2 pounds fresh spinach, trimmed, washed and chopped, *or* 32 ounces frozen leaf spinach, cooked
- 4 tablespoons extra-virgin olive oil, divided
- 2 cups coarsely chopped onion
- 1½ cups chopped fennel bulb
- ½ cup chopped fresh dill
- ⅓ cup crumbled feta cheese
- 1 teaspoon salt
- 1 teaspoon freshly ground pepper
- ¼ teaspoon cayenne pepper
- Pinch of freshly grated nutmeg
- 1 large egg
- 1 large egg white
- 14 sheets phyllo dough

1. Preheat oven to 350°F. Coat a 12-inch tart pan or pizza pan with cooking spray.
2. Heat a large skillet over medium-high heat. Add spinach; cook, stirring, just until wilted. Transfer to a colander to drain and cool.
3. Wipe out the pan. Add 1 tablespoon oil and heat over medium-high heat; add onion and fennel and cook until softened, 5 to 7 minutes.
4. Squeeze out any excess water from cooled spinach. Stir together spinach, onion/fennel mixture, dill, feta, salt, pepper, cayenne and nutmeg in a large bowl. Lightly beat egg and egg white together and stir into the spinach mixture; set aside.
5. Lay a sheet of phyllo on a work surface; brush it lightly with some of the remaining oil. Lay a second sheet on top at a 45° angle. Brush with oil. Repeat with 5 more sheets to form a rough circle. Transfer the stack of phyllo to the prepared pan, pressing it gently into the bottom and sides. Spread filling evenly over the top.
6. To make a top crust, lightly oil and stack the remaining 7 sheets of phyllo in the same manner as for the bottom crust, brushing the top sheet with oil. Set the stack on top of the filling. With scissors, trim the edges, leaving a 2-inch overhang. Roll edges over to form a rim and brush lightly with oil. With a sharp knife, cut 4 short slits in the center of the pie to vent steam.
7. Bake the pie until the crust is golden, 50 to 60 minutes. (If the pie is browning too quickly, cover loosely with foil.) Let cool for about 10 minutes before serving.

MAKES 8 SERVINGS.

PER SERVING: 301 CALORIES; 10 G FAT (2 G SAT, 6 G MONO); 30 MG CHOLESTEROL; 41 G CARBOHYDRATE; 11 G PROTEIN; 5 G FIBER; 779 MG SODIUM.

NUTRITION BONUS: 220% DV VITAMIN A, 37 MG VITAMIN C (60% DV), 778 MG POTASSIUM (39% DV), 236 MCG FOLATE (59% DV), 3 MG IRON (20% DV).

Quinoa & Spinach Stuffed Peppers

PREP TIME: 50 MINUTES (INCLUDING SOAKING TIME) | **START TO FINISH:** 1½ HOURS | **TO MAKE AHEAD:** THE PEPPERS WILL KEEP, COVERED, IN THE REFRIGERATOR FOR UP TO 2 DAYS. | **EASE OF PREPARATION:** MODERATE

A bell pepper's appearance suggests a great way to cook it. Just scrape out the core and you've got a perfect, edible vessel for stuffing, with grains and greens, nuts and herbs providing a savory contrast to the sweet, tender flesh of the pepper.

- 5 large, plump yellow *or* red bell peppers
- ¾ cup quinoa, rinsed
- 1½ cups water
- 1 teaspoon salt, divided
- ¼ cup currants
- ¼ cup pine nuts
- 2 teaspoons extra-virgin olive oil
- 1 cup chopped scallions
- ½ teaspoon ground cumin
- 10 ounces spinach, shredded (8 cups)
- ¼ cup chopped fresh cilantro
- ¼ cup chopped fresh parsley
- 2 tablespoons chopped fresh dill
- 1 tablespoon lemon juice
- 1 teaspoon freshly grated lemon zest
- Freshly ground pepper to taste

1. Preheat oven to 450°F. Coat a baking sheet with cooking spray.

2. Halve peppers lengthwise, leaving stems intact. With a paring knife, remove seeds and ribs. Place peppers, cut-side down, on the prepared baking sheet. Bake for 10 to 15 minutes, or until just tender. Dice 2 halves; set all peppers aside.

3. Combine quinoa, water and ½ teaspoon salt in a medium saucepan; bring to a simmer. Cover and simmer over low heat until tender, 10 to 15 minutes. Drain off any excess water. Set aside.

SUBSTITUTION: Use 2½ cups cooked couscous in place of the quinoa; skip Step 3.

4. Meanwhile, soak currants in hot water until softened, about 20 minutes. Drain.

5. Toast pine nuts in a large dry skillet over medium heat, stirring, until golden and fragrant, about 5 minutes. Transfer to a small bowl.

6. Heat oil in the skillet over medium heat. Add scallions and cumin; cook, stirring, until softened, about 2 minutes. Add spinach and remaining ½ teaspoon salt; cook, turning occasionally, until spinach is wilted, 2 to 3 minutes. Remove from heat. Stir in cilantro, parsley, dill, lemon juice, lemon zest, reserved chopped pepper, quinoa, currants and pine nuts. Adjust seasoning with salt and pepper.

7. Divide mixture among pepper halves. Serve warm or at room temperature.

MAKES 4 SERVINGS.

PER SERVING: 313 CALORIES; 11 G FAT (1 G SAT, 3 G MONO); 0 MG CHOLESTEROL; 49 G CARBOHYDRATE; 12 G PROTEIN; 6 G FIBER; 651 MG SODIUM.

NUTRITION BONUS: 423 MG VITAMIN C (700% DV), 270% DV VITAMIN A, 1,219 MG POTASSIUM (61% DV), 264 MCG FOLATE (51% DV), 6 MG IRON (35% DV), 23% DV FIBER, 138 MG IRON (15% DV).

Roasted Red Peppers Stuffed with Kale & Rice

PREP TIME: 30 MINUTES | **START TO FINISH:** 1 HOUR | **TO MAKE AHEAD:** PREPARE THROUGH STEP 3, COVER AND REFRIGERATE FOR UP TO 2 DAYS. | **EASE OF PREPARATION:** MODERATE

You can vary the filling by substituting robust mustard greens or collards, or milder greens, such as spinach, escarole or Swiss chard. (Cook greens as directed on page 124.)

PEPPERS

- 3 medium red bell peppers
- 1 tablespoon extra-virgin olive oil
- ¼ teaspoon salt
- Freshly ground pepper to taste

FILLING

- ½ pound kale (6 cups lightly packed), trimmed
- 1 tablespoon extra-virgin olive oil
- 1 medium onion, chopped
- ½ cup chopped red bell pepper
- 2 cloves garlic, minced
- ¾ cup cooked short-grain brown rice (*see Cooking Tips, page 101*)
- ½ cup freshly grated Parmesan cheese
- ¼ cup toasted pine nuts, divided
- 1 tablespoon lemon juice
- ¼ teaspoon salt, *or* to taste
- Freshly ground pepper to taste

1. **To prepare peppers:** Preheat oven to 400°F. Halve peppers lengthwise through the stems, leaving them attached. Remove the seeds. Lightly brush the peppers outside and inside with oil; sprinkle the insides with salt and pepper. Place, cut-side down, in a 9-by-13-inch baking dish. Bake until peppers are just tender, 10 to 15 minutes. Let cool slightly. Turn cut-side up.
2. **To prepare filling:** Bring 2 cups salted water to a boil in a large wide pan. Stir in kale, cover and cook until tender, 10 to 12 minutes. Drain, rinse under cold water; squeeze dry. Finely chop.
3. Heat oil in a large nonstick skillet over medium heat. Add onion and chopped bell pepper; cook, stirring often, until onion is golden, 6 to 8 minutes. Add garlic and cook, stirring, for 30 seconds. Stir in the kale. Remove from the heat and let cool slightly. Stir in rice, Parmesan, 2 tablespoons pine nuts and lemon juice. Season with salt and pepper. Divide the filling among the pepper halves. Sprinkle with the remaining 2 tablespoons pine nuts.
4. Add 2 tablespoons water to the baking dish. Cover the peppers with foil and bake until heated through, 15 to 20 minutes. Uncover and bake for 5 minutes more. Serve hot.

TO TOAST PINE NUTS: Heat a small dry skillet over medium-low heat. Add pine nuts and cook, stirring constantly, until golden and fragrant, 2 to 3 minutes. (Or spread in a small baking pan and bake at 400°F for about 5 minutes.)

MAKES 6 SERVINGS.

PER SERVING: 171 CALORIES; 11 G FAT (2 G SAT, 5 G MONO); 6 MG CHOLESTEROL; 15 G CARBOHYDRATE; 5 G PROTEIN; 3 G FIBER; 304 MG SODIUM.

NUTRITION BONUS: 124 MG VITAMIN C (210% DV), 20% DV VITAMIN A.

POULTRY

11

As cooks, we like the way chicken and other members of its clan travel; poultry is a ready vehicle for exploring the world's flavors. One day we take it to Vietnam, another to Jamaica. Some days we take it back to Grandma's house. In one of those wowing statistics, it is reported that North Americans now consume nearly 100 pounds of poultry per capita annually. And with good reason: chicken and turkey—both white and dark meat—are good sources of protein and are low in fat and calories, particularly sans skin and unbreaded. But simple succulence, economy and sheer versatility are the fundamental reasons why poultry is so well loved. No matter how you cook it, it tastes like home to someone.

CHICKEN

TURKEY

Lower Carbs

Quick Thai Chicken & Vegetable Curry

PREP TIME: 20 MINUTES | **START TO FINISH:** 45 MINUTES | **TO MAKE AHEAD:** THE CURRY WILL KEEP, COVERED, IN THE REFRIGERATOR FOR UP TO 2 DAYS. | **EASE OF PREPARATION:** EASY

Curry quick enough for a weeknight supper—especially if you use precut cauliflower and baby spinach.

- 2 teaspoons canola oil
- 1 medium red bell pepper, cut into 1- to 2-inch-long julienne strips
- 1 medium onion, halved and sliced
- 1 clove garlic, minced
- 1 tablespoon minced fresh ginger
- 1-2 teaspoons red curry paste, to taste (*see Note*)
- 1 pound boneless, skinless chicken breasts, cut into 1-inch cubes
- 1 cup reduced-sodium chicken broth
- 1 cup "lite" coconut milk
- 1 tablespoon fish sauce (*see Ingredient Note, page 395*) or reduced-sodium soy sauce
- 1 teaspoon light brown sugar
- 1½ cups cauliflower florets
- 2 cups baby spinach
- 1 tablespoon lime juice
- Lime wedges

Heat oil in a large nonstick skillet over medium-high heat. Add bell pepper and onion; cook, stirring often, until beginning to soften, about 4 minutes. Add garlic, ginger and curry paste; stir to mix. Add chicken and cook, stirring, until fragrant, about 2 minutes. Stir in broth, coconut milk, fish sauce (or soy sauce) and brown sugar; bring to a simmer. Add cauliflower, reduce heat to medium-low and simmer, stirring occasionally, until the chicken is cooked through and the cauliflower is tender, about 10 minutes. Stir in spinach and lime juice; cook just until spinach has wilted. Serve immediately, with lime wedges.

MAKES 4 SERVINGS, 1¼ CUPS EACH.

PER SERVING: 252 CALORIES; 8 G FAT (4 G SAT, 2 G MONO); 67 MG CHOLESTEROL; 14 G CARBOHYDRATE; 31 G PROTEIN; 2 G FIBER; 349 MG SODIUM.

NUTRITION BONUS: 89 MG VITAMIN C (150% DV), 30% DV VITAMIN A, 576 MG POTASSIUM (29% DV).

VEGETARIAN VARIATION: Substitute 1 pound extra-firm tofu (drained) for the chicken and vegetable broth for chicken broth.

PER SERVING: 240 CALORIES; 14 G FAT (4 G SAT, 1 G MONO); 0 MG CHOLESTEROL; 16 G CARBOHYDRATE; 16 G PROTEIN; 4 G FIBER; 376 MG SODIUM.

NUTRITION BONUS: 88 MG VITAMIN C (150% DV), 30% DV VITAMIN A, 3 MG IRON (20% DV), 16% DV FIBER, 161 MG CALCIUM (15% DV).

Red Curry Paste

A BLEND OF CHILE PEPPERS, garlic, lemongrass and galanga (a rhizome with a flavor similar to ginger), commercial Asian curry paste is a convenient way to add heat and complexity to a recipe. Look for it in small jars or cans in the Asian section of the store. Brands differ in spiciness so use sparingly. Once opened, it will keep in the refrigerator for up to 1 month.

Stuffed Chicken Breasts

PREP TIME: 25 MINUTES | **START TO FINISH:** 50 MINUTES | **EASE OF PREPARATION:** EASY

The hard part of making this elegant dish is choosing the filling. Making a pocket in the chicken breast to hold the stuffing is easy, particularly if you use a good, sharp, thin-bladed knife. Browning the chicken in a skillet before baking gives it a beautiful golden color. Finishing it in the oven ensures that it cooks evenly throughout.

- Filling of your choice (*see below*)
- 4 boneless, skinless chicken breast halves (1-1¼ pounds total)
- 1 egg white
- ½ cup plain dry breadcrumbs
- 2 teaspoons extra-virgin olive oil

◆ **CREAM CHEESE-PESTO FILLING:**

- 2 tablespoons reduced-fat cream cheese (Neufchâtel)
- 1 tablespoon basil pesto (store-bought *or* homemade)
- Freshly ground pepper to taste

Blend in a small bowl with a fork.

◆ **GOAT CHEESE-OLIVE FILLING:**

- 2 tablespoons creamy goat cheese
- 1 tablespoon chopped black olives
- Freshly ground pepper to taste

Blend in a small bowl with a fork.

◆ **HAM & CHEESE FILLING:**

- ¼ cup grated Swiss, Monterey Jack *or* part-skim mozzarella cheese
- 2 tablespoons chopped ham
- 2 teaspoons Dijon mustard
- Freshly ground pepper to taste

Mix in a small bowl.

1. Preheat oven to 400°F. Use a baking sheet with sides and lightly coat it with cooking spray.

2. Prepare the filling of your choice: Cream Cheese-Pesto, Goat Cheese-Olive or Ham & Cheese.

3. Cut a horizontal slit along the thin, long edge of a chicken breast half, nearly through to the opposite side. Open up each breast and place one-fourth of the filling in the center. Close the breast over the filling, pressing the edges firmly together to seal. Repeat with the remaining chicken breasts and filling.

4. Lightly beat egg white with a fork in a medium bowl. Place breadcrumbs in a shallow glass dish. Hold each chicken breast half together and dip in egg white, then dredge in breadcrumbs. (Discard leftovers.)

5. Heat oil in a large nonstick skillet over medium-high heat. Add chicken breasts; cook until browned on one side, about 2 minutes. Place the chicken, browned-side up, on the prepared baking sheet. Bake until the chicken is no longer pink in the center or until an instant-read thermometer registers 170°F, about 20 minutes.

MAKES 4 SERVINGS.

CREAM CHEESE-PESTO STUFFED CHICKEN PER SERVING: 233 CALORIES; 7 G FAT (2 G SAT, 3 G MONO); 71 MG CHOLESTEROL; 11 G CARBOHYDRATE; 30 G PROTEIN; 1 G FIBER; 231 MG SODIUM.

GOAT CHEESE-OLIVE STUFFED CHICKEN PER SERVING: 235 CALORIES; 7 G FAT (2 G SAT, 3 G MONO); 72 MG CHOLESTEROL; 10 G CARBOHYDRATE; 31 G PROTEIN; 1 G FIBER; 248 MG SODIUM.

HAM-&-CHEESE STUFFED CHICKEN PER SERVING: 236 CALORIES; 7 G FAT (2 G SAT, 3 G MONO); 74 MG CHOLESTEROL; 10 G CARBOHYDRATE; 31 G PROTEIN; 1 G FIBER; 287 MG SODIUM.

Brined Chicken Breasts Under a Brick

PREP TIME: 15 MINUTES | **START TO FINISH:** 55 MINUTES | **EASE OF PREPARATION:** MODERATE

This method results in uncommonly juicy, flavorful chicken breasts with great grill marks. Weighting the breasts helps them cook more evenly. We like the convenience of brining in a plastic bag, but you can also use a nonreactive bowl.

- ¼ cup packed dark brown sugar
- ¼ cup kosher salt
- 1 cup water
- 2 cloves garlic, crushed
- 2-3 fresh thyme *or* rosemary sprigs *or* 1 teaspoon dried
- 1 bay leaf
- 1 teaspoon crushed peppercorns
- ½ teaspoon ground allspice
- 2 cups ice cubes
- 4 boneless, skinless chicken breast halves (4-5 ounces each), trimmed of fat, tenders removed
- ½ cup Mojo Sauce (*page 293*), optional

1. Combine sugar, salt and water in a medium saucepan. Heat over medium-high heat, stirring until all solids dissolve. Stir in garlic, thyme (or rosemary), bay leaf, peppercorns and allspice. Remove from heat and transfer to a 4-cup glass measure. Add ice cubes and enough cold water to make 4 cups.

2. Place chicken in a large ziplock bag. Set the bag in a large bowl. Pour the brine into the bag, squeeze out air and seal. Refrigerate for 30 minutes, turning bag occasionally. Drain, discarding brine; pat breasts dry with paper towels.

3. Meanwhile, heat grill to high. Wrap 4 bricks (or the bottom of a large cast-iron skillet) with heavy-duty foil. Oil the grill rack by dipping a folded paper towel in a little vegetable oil; holding it with long-handled tongs, rub it over the grill rack.

4. Prepare Mojo Sauce, if using.

5. Place the chicken on the grill rack and weight with the bricks or skillet. Close the cover and grill, turning once (use oven mitts to lift the weight), until the juices run clear, 2 to 4 minutes per side. Serve with the sauce, if desired.

MAKES 4 SERVINGS.

PER SERVING: 128 CALORIES; 3 G FAT (1 G SAT, 1 G MONO); 63 MG CHOLESTEROL; 2 G CARBOHYDRATE; 23 G PROTEIN; 0 G FIBER; 755 MG SODIUM.

NUTRITION NOTE: The sodium analysis is based on an assumption that one-eighth of the total brine is absorbed. The brining technique is not recommended for people on strict low-sodium diets.

Grilled Chicken with Sesame-Ginger Sauce

Lower Carbs

PREP TIME: 20 MINUTES | **START TO FINISH:** 2½ HOURS (INCLUDING MARINATING TIME)
EASE OF PREPARATION: EASY

Beautiful enough for entertaining, but easy enough to make for a weeknight dinner.

> **TEST KITCHEN TIP:**
> For a seriously spicy marinade, don't seed the serrano.

- ¾ cup Sesame-Ginger Sauce (*recipe follows*)
- ¼ cup reduced-sodium soy sauce
- 2 tablespoons lemon juice
- 1 tablespoon canola oil
- 1 clove garlic, minced
- 1 serrano chile *or* jalapeño pepper, seeded and minced
- 2 teaspoons minced fresh ginger
- ½ teaspoon ground cumin
- 6 boneless, skinless chicken breast halves trimmed of fat (1½-1¾ pounds total)

1. Make Sesame-Ginger Sauce.

2. Combine soy sauce, lemon juice, oil, garlic, chile, ginger and cumin in a large plastic bag. Add chicken and seal bag. Place in the refrigerator and marinate, turning once or twice, for at least 2 hours or overnight.

3. Preheat grill.

4. Remove chicken from marinade and discard plastic bag and any remaining marinade. Oil the grill rack (*see Tip, page 130*). Grill chicken until no longer pink in the center, about 5 minutes per side (*see box, page 206*). Thinly slice chicken and top with sauce.

MAKES 6 SERVINGS.

PER SERVING: 202 CALORIES; 7 G FAT (1 G SAT, 3 G MONO); 66 MG CHOLESTEROL; 6 G CARBOHYDRATE; 28 G PROTEIN; 1 G FIBER; 788 MG SODIUM.

SESAME-GINGER SAUCE

PREP TIME: 10 MINUTES | **START TO FINISH:** 2¼ HOURS (INCLUDING 2 HOURS STEEPING TIME)
TO MAKE AHEAD: THE SAUCE WILL KEEP IN THE REFRIGERATOR FOR UP TO 2 DAYS. | **EASE OF PREPARATION:** EASY

This Asian sauce is delicious with grilled chicken, fish, tofu or vegetables. The quantity of ginger may seem generous, but it is strained before serving, leaving a delicate infusion. You can use a food processor or mini processor to speed up the mincing.

- 1 teaspoon canola oil
- ½ cup minced fresh ginger
- 2-3 teaspoons sugar
- ⅓ cup water
- ¼ cup reduced-sodium soy sauce
- ¼ cup rice vinegar
- 1 tablespoon toasted sesame oil
- 2 scallions, trimmed and thinly sliced

1. Heat canola oil in a small saucepan over medium heat. Add ginger and sugar to taste; cook, stirring, until softened, 3 to 5 minutes. (Add a little water if the mixture seems dry.) Remove from heat; add ⅓ cup water, soy sauce, vinegar and sesame oil. Transfer to a bowl, cover and refrigerate for at least 2 hours or overnight.

2. Strain sauce through a fine sieve. Stir in scallions and serve.

MAKES ABOUT ¾ CUP.

PER TABLESPOON: 24 CALORIES; 2 G FAT (0 G SAT, 1 G MONO); 0 MG CHOLESTEROL; 2 G CARBOHYDRATE; 0 G PROTEIN; 0 G FIBER; 179 MG SODIUM.

Vietnamese Grilled Chicken

PREP TIME: 25 MINUTES | **START TO FINISH:** 1 HOUR 10 MINUTES (INCLUDING MARINATING TIME)
EASE OF PREPARATION: EASY

Meaty chicken thighs are well-suited to this intensely flavored Vietnamese marinade.

- ¼ cup lime juice (2 limes)
- 2½ tablespoons fish sauce (*see Ingredient Note, page 395*)
- 4 cloves garlic, minced
- 2 serrano *or* jalapeño peppers, seeded and minced
- 2 tablespoons sugar
- 1 tablespoon canola oil
- 4 bone-in chicken legs (about 2½ pounds total), skin and fat removed, cut in half through the joint
- 1½ cups Papaya Relish (*recipe follows*)

1. Whisk lime juice, fish sauce, garlic, peppers, sugar and oil in a small bowl. Pour about half of this marinade into a shallow glass dish and reserve the remainder for basting. Add chicken pieces to the dish and turn to coat. Cover and marinate in the refrigerator for 20 minutes to 1 hour, turning occasionally.

2. Meanwhile, make Papaya Relish. Preheat grill to medium-high.

3. Oil the grill rack (*see Tip, page 130*). Grill the chicken, covered, turning several times and basting the browned sides with the reserved marinade, until well browned but not charred, and no longer pink inside, 20 to 30 minutes (*see box, page 206*). Serve with Papaya Relish.

MAKES 4 SERVINGS.

PER SERVING: 253 CALORIES; 9 G FAT (2 G SAT, 4 G MONO); 89 MG CHOLESTEROL; 15 G CARBOHYDRATE; 27 G PROTEIN; 1 G FIBER; 606 MG SODIUM.

PAPAYA RELISH

PREP TIME: 10 MINUTES | **START TO FINISH:** 10 MINUTES
EASE OF PREPARATION: EASY

The relish is at its best served shortly after it is prepared.

- 2 cloves garlic, crushed and peeled
- ½ teaspoon kosher salt
- 3 tablespoons rice-wine vinegar
- 2 teaspoons sugar
- 2 teaspoons hot sauce, such as sambal olek *or* Tabasco
- 1 firm papaya, peeled, seeded and diced (1½ cups)
- ½ cup finely diced red onion
- ¼ cup chopped fresh cilantro

With the side of a chef's knife, mash garlic with salt. Transfer to a small bowl and whisk in vinegar, sugar and hot sauce. Add papaya, onion and cilantro; toss gently to mix.

MAKES 4 SERVINGS, ABOUT ⅓ CUP EACH.

PER SERVING: 43 CALORIES; 0 G FAT (0 G SAT, 0 G MONO); 0 MG CHOLESTEROL; 11 G CARBOHYDRATE; 1 G PROTEIN; 1 G FIBER; 254 MG SODIUM.

INGREDIENT NOTE: Sambal olek, a mix of chiles, brown sugar and salt, can be found in the Asian section of some large supermarkets and at Asian markets.

Lower Carbs

Picnic Oven-Fried Chicken

PREP TIME: 20 MINUTES | **START TO FINISH:** 1 HOUR 35 MINUTES (INCLUDING ½ HOUR MARINATING TIME)
EASE OF PREPARATION: EASY

Whether you take it along on a picnic or serve it at home for a family supper, this updated "fried" chicken is a crowd pleaser. Marinating the chicken in buttermilk keeps it juicy, and the light coating of flour, sesame seeds and spices, misted with olive oil, forms an appealing crust during baking.

- ½ cup buttermilk
- 1 tablespoon Dijon mustard
- 2 cloves garlic, minced
- 1 teaspoon hot sauce, such as Tabasco
- 2½-3 pounds chicken legs, skin removed, fat trimmed
- ½ cup whole-wheat flour
- 2 tablespoons sesame seeds
- 1½ teaspoons paprika
- 1 teaspoon dried thyme leaves
- 1 teaspoon baking powder
- ⅛ teaspoon salt, or to taste
- Freshly ground pepper to taste
- Olive oil cooking spray

1. Whisk buttermilk, mustard, garlic and hot sauce in a shallow glass dish until well blended. Add chicken and turn to coat. Cover and marinate in the refrigerator for at least ½ hour or for up to 8 hours.
2. Preheat oven to 425°F. Line a baking sheet with foil. Set a wire rack on the baking sheet and coat it with cooking spray.
3. Whisk flour, sesame seeds, paprika, thyme, baking powder, salt and pepper in a small bowl. Place the flour mixture in a paper bag or large sealable plastic bag. Shaking off excess marinade, place one or two pieces of chicken at a time in the bag and shake to coat. Shake off excess flour and place chicken on the prepared rack. (Discard any leftover flour mixture and marinade.) Spray chicken pieces with cooking spray.
4. Bake the chicken until golden brown and no longer pink in the center, 40 to 50 minutes (*see box, page 206*).

MAKES 4 SERVINGS.

PER SERVING: 227 CALORIES; 7 G FAT (2 G SAT, 2 G MONO); 130 MG CHOLESTEROL; 5 G CARBOHYDRATE; 34 G PROTEIN; 1 G FIBER; 262 MG SODIUM.

ANALYSIS NOTE: A comparable serving of breast meat has 209 calories and 1 gram saturated fat.

NUTRITION BONUS: 423 MG POTASSIUM (21% DV).

RECIPE RX

KFC chicken legs:
439 calories
6 grams saturated fat

EW chicken legs:
227 calories
2 grams saturated fat

What We Did

How can we enjoy the crisp pleasures of fried chicken without excessive calories and saturated fat? The tricks are to use skinless chicken and to bake rather than fry it. Besides being more healthful, this recipe works nicely to keep the interior moist while creating a crust that makes people forget the missing skin and fried breading.

Chicken Adobo Kebabs

PREP TIME: 25 MINUTES | **START TO FINISH:** 35 MINUTES | **EQUIPMENT:** METAL OR BAMBOO SKEWERS
EASE OF PREPARATION: EASY

Serve with Black Beans & Barley (*page 88*) and salsa on the side.

- 3 tablespoons lemon juice, divided
- 2 cloves garlic, peeled and minced
- 2 teaspoons dried oregano
- 1 teaspoon paprika
- 1 teaspoon salt
- ½ teaspoon ground cumin
- ½ teaspoon ground cinnamon
- ½ teaspoon freshly ground pepper
- 1 pound boneless, skinless chicken breasts, trimmed and cut into 1½-inch chunks
- 2 teaspoons extra-virgin olive oil
- 1 red onion, peeled, quartered and separated into layers
- Lemon wedges

1. Blend 1 tablespoon lemon juice, garlic, oregano, paprika, salt, cumin, cinnamon and pepper in a medium bowl. Add chicken and toss to coat. Cover with plastic wrap and marinate in the refrigerator for at least 20 minutes or up to 2 hours.
2. Mix oil and the remaining 2 tablespoons lemon juice in a small bowl. Set aside.
3. Preheat grill to medium-high.
4. Thread chicken and onion pieces alternately onto 4 or 8 skewers.
5. Oil the grill rack (*see Tip, page 130*). Grill the kebabs, turning occasionally, until browned and cooked through, 6 to 7 minutes, basting the cooked side with the reserved lemon-oil mixture. Serve immediately, with lemon wedges.

EQUIPMENT TIP: When using bamboo skewers, wrap the exposed parts with foil to keep the bamboo from burning. (Contrary to popular opinion, soaking skewers in water does not protect them.)

MAKES 4 SERVINGS.

PER SERVING: 171 CALORIES; 4 G FAT (1 G SAT, 2 G MONO); 66 MG CHOLESTEROL; 6 G CARBOHYDRATE; 27 G PROTEIN; 1 G FIBER; 657 MG SODIUM.

NUTRITION BONUS: 13 MG VITAMIN C (20% DV), 385 MG POTASSIUM (19% DV).

Temperature Check

THE BEST WAY to determine if poultry is fully cooked is to use an instant-read thermometer. The internal temperature should register 180°F for a whole chicken (inserted into the thickest part of the thigh), 170°F for bone-in parts and 160°F for boneless parts.

Lower Carbs

Moroccan Chicken Kebabs

PREP TIME: 20 MINUTES | **START TO FINISH:** 55 MINUTES
EQUIPMENT: METAL OR BAMBOO SKEWERS (SEE TIP, PAGE 206) | **EASE OF PREPARATION:** EASY

These North African-inspired kebabs are marinated for just 20 minutes in a vibrant blend of yogurt and spices. Served on a bed of couscous they make a bright, exciting supper.

- ¼ cup nonfat plain yogurt
- ¼ cup chopped fresh parsley, plus extra for garnish
- 2 tablespoons chopped fresh cilantro
- 2 tablespoons lemon juice
- 1 tablespoon extra-virgin olive oil
- 3 cloves garlic, minced
- 1½ teaspoons paprika
- 1 teaspoon ground cumin
- ½ teaspoon salt
- ¼ teaspoon freshly ground pepper
- ⅛ teaspoon cayenne pepper
- 1 pound boneless, skinless chicken breasts, trimmed of fat and cut into 1-inch pieces
- 2 small bell peppers (red *and/or* yellow), cored, seeded and cut into 1½-inch pieces
- 1 medium zucchini, cut into ¼-inch-thick rounds

1. Stir together yogurt, parsley, cilantro, lemon juice, oil, garlic, paprika, cumin, salt, pepper and cayenne in a medium bowl. Add chicken and toss to coat well. Cover with plastic wrap and marinate in the refrigerator for 20 minutes.

2. Meanwhile, preheat grill or broiler. Blanch bell peppers in boiling salted water for 3 minutes. Remove with a slotted spoon and refresh with cold water. Blanch zucchini for 1 minute. Drain and refresh with cold water.

3. Alternate chicken cubes, peppers and zucchini on skewers. Grill or broil the kebabs until the chicken is no longer pink in the center, 3 to 4 minutes per side. Garnish with a sprinkle of chopped parsley.

MAKES 4 SERVINGS.

PER SERVING: 201 CALORIES; 5 G FAT (1 G SAT, 3 G MONO); 66 MG CHOLESTEROL; 10 G CARBOHYDRATE; 29 G PROTEIN; 3 G FIBER; 383 MG SODIUM.

NUTRITION BONUS: 131 MG VITAMIN C (220% DV), 90% DV VITAMIN A, 599 MG POTASSIUM (30% DV).

Curried Chicken with Sweet Potatoes & Cauliflower

PREP TIME: 25 MINUTES | **START TO FINISH:** 5½ HOURS (INCLUDING MARINATING TIME)
EASE OF PREPARATION: MODERATE

Boneless, skinless chicken thighs, with a little help from the well-seasoned yogurt marinade, remain moist and tender when oven-roasted. *Hint:* Soaking the prepared vegetables in ice water for 15 minutes before roasting will hydrate them, making them more moist and tender when cooked.

- ¾ cup nonfat plain yogurt
- 1 teaspoon Madras-style curry powder (*see Ingredient Note, page 394*)
- 1 teaspoon ground coriander
- 1 teaspoon ground ginger
- 1 clove garlic, minced
- ¾ teaspoon salt, divided
- ¼ teaspoon cayenne pepper
- 8 boneless, skinless chicken thighs (about 1½ pounds), trimmed of fat (*see Tip*)
- 1 sweet potato (about 1 pound), peeled and cut into ½-inch cubes
- 3 cups cauliflower florets (1 small head) *or* broccoli florets
- 1 tablespoon extra-virgin olive oil
- Freshly ground pepper to taste
- ¼ cup chopped unsalted dry-roasted peanuts *or* cashews
- ¼ cup loosely packed cilantro leaves

1. Combine yogurt, curry powder, coriander, ginger, garlic, ½ teaspoon salt and cayenne in a shallow glass dish; mix to blend. Reserve ¼ cup of this mixture; cover and refrigerate. Add chicken to the remaining yogurt mixture and turn to coat. Cover and marinate in the refrigerator for at least 4 hours or overnight.

2. Preheat oven to 450°F. Use a large baking sheet with sides and lightly coat it with cooking spray.

3. Remove the chicken from the marinade and place on the prepared baking sheet. Toss sweet potato with the reserved yogurt mixture in a medium bowl and place on the baking sheet. Toss cauliflower with oil in a medium bowl and add to the baking sheet. Season vegetables with the remaining ¼ teaspoon salt and pepper. Roast chicken and vegetables, uncovered, for 15 minutes.

4. Carefully turn the chicken over and stir the vegetables. Roast until the vegetables are tender and chicken is cooked through, 10 to 15 minutes more (*see box, page 206*).

5. Arrange chicken and vegetables on a platter or individual plates and garnish with peanuts (or cashews) and cilantro.

TEST KITCHEN TIP:
Boneless, skinless chicken thighs can be quite fatty, so trim carefully. To substitute bone-in thighs, pull off the skin and in Step 3 roast chicken for 10 minutes before adding vegetables.

MAKES 4 SERVINGS.

PER SERVING: 473 CALORIES; 14 G FAT (3 G SAT, 7 G MONO); 121 MG CHOLESTEROL; 34 G CARBOHYDRATE; 53 G PROTEIN; 8 G FIBER; 478 MG SODIUM.

NUTRITION BONUS: 30% DV FIBER, 440% DV VITAMIN A, 65 MG VITAMIN C (110% DV), 4 MG IRON (20% DV), 80 MCG FOLATE (2% DV).

Multi-Grain Waffles (PAGE 24)

ABOVE: *Mediterranean Burger* (PAGE 134)
OPPOSITE: *Southwestern Tomato & Pinto Bean Soup* (PAGE 57)

(PAGE 134)

ABOVE: *Slow-Cooker Black Bean-Mushroom Chili* (PAGE 186)
OPPOSITE: *Pizza with White Beans, Prosciutto & Rosemary* (LEFT; PAGE 153), *Peperonata & Sausage Pizza* (RIGHT; PAGE 149)

ABOVE: ***Spice-Crusted Tofu*** (PAGE 181)

OPPOSITE: ***Ginger-Orange Glazed Cornish Hens*** (PAGE 230)

ABOVE: *Grilled Pork Chops with Rhubarb Chutney* (PAGE 283)
OPPOSITE: *Halibut Roasted with Red Bell Peppers, Onions & Russet Potatoes* (PAGE 249)

ABOVE: ***Baked Risotto Primavera*** (PAGE 98)
OPPOSITE: ***Braised Lamb with a Garden-Vegetable Medley*** (PAGE 285)

ABOVE: ***Walnut Cake with a Hint of Rosemary*** (PAGE 361)
OPPOSITE: ***Lemon-Almond Polenta Torta*** (PAGE 360)

ABOVE: *Chocolate-Orange Silk Mousse* (PAGE 324)
OPPOSITE: *Honey-Lavender Plum Gratin* (PAGE 330)

Multi-Grain Whole-Wheat Bread (PAGE 315)

Lower Carbs

Ginger-Coconut Chicken

PREP TIME: 10 MINUTES | **START TO FINISH:** 50 MINUTES (INCLUDING MARINATING TIME)
EASE OF PREPARATION: EASY

The wonderful flavors of southern India—coconut milk, dried Thai chiles and coriander seed—provide a pleasant punch to a basic chicken breast. Although the ingredients look exotic, this is a deceptively easy dish you'll be proud to serve to guests. Feel free to use different cuts of chicken, bone-in or boneless; just adjust the cooking time accordingly. You can also grill the chicken.

- 1 tablespoon yellow split peas
- 1 teaspoon coriander seeds
- 1-2 dried red chiles, such as Thai, cayenne *or* chiles de arbol
- ¼ cup "lite" coconut milk (*see Ingredient Note, page 394*)
- 2 tablespoons minced fresh ginger
- 4 medium cloves garlic, minced
- 2 tablespoons finely chopped fresh cilantro
- ½ teaspoon salt, or to taste
- 4 boneless skinless chicken breast halves (1-1¼ pounds total), trimmed

1. Toast split peas, coriander seeds and chiles in a small skillet over medium heat, shaking the pan occasionally, until the split peas turn reddish-brown, the coriander becomes fragrant and the chiles blacken slightly, 2 to 3 minutes. Transfer to a plate to cool for 3 to 5 minutes. Grind in a spice grinder or mortar and pestle until the mixture is the texture of finely ground pepper.

2. Combine coconut milk, ginger, garlic, cilantro, salt and the spice blend in a shallow glass dish. Add chicken and turn to coat. Cover and refrigerate for at least 30 minutes or overnight.

3. Preheat broiler. Coat a broiler-pan rack with cooking spray. Place the chicken (including marinade) on the rack over the broiler pan. Broil chicken 3 to 5 inches from the heat source until it is no longer pink in the center and the juices run clear, 4 to 6 minutes per side (*see box, page 206*).

MAKES 4 SERVINGS.

PER SERVING: 152 CALORIES; 3 G FAT (1 G SAT, 0 G MONO); 66 MG CHOLESTEROL; 4 G CARBOHYDRATE; 27 G PROTEIN; 1 G FIBER; 371 MG SODIUM.

NUTRITION BONUS: 327 MG POTASSIUM (16% DV).

Jerk Chicken & Nectarine Salad

PREP TIME: 15 MINUTES | **START TO FINISH:** 45 MINUTES | **EASE OF PREPARATION:** EASY

Sweet, ripe nectarines offer a cool counterpoint to this spicy jerk chicken salad. Accompany with Wholesome Cornbread (*page 313*) and Beans & Rice (*page 89*).

- 4 tablespoons lime juice, divided
- 1½ tablespoons dried jerk seasoning
- 1 tablespoon steak sauce, such as Pickapeppa *or* A1
- 4 teaspoons honey, divided
- 1 teaspoon canola oil
- 1 pound boneless, skinless chicken thighs, trimmed of fat
- 3 ripe nectarines, pitted and thickly sliced
- 2 scallions, chopped
- Salt & freshly ground pepper to taste
- 8 cups torn or shredded romaine lettuce

1. Mix 1 tablespoon lime juice, jerk seasoning, steak sauce, 2 teaspoons honey and oil in a shallow dish. Add chicken and turn to coat. Cover and marinate in the refrigerator for 20 minutes.
2. Meanwhile, preheat grill to medium-high or preheat broiler.
3. Stir together nectarines, scallions, remaining 3 tablespoons lime juice and remaining 2 teaspoons honey in a small bowl. Season with salt and pepper.
4. Oil grill rack or broiler pan (*see Tip, page 130*). Grill chicken until no longer pink in the center, 3 to 4 minutes per side (*see box, page 206*). (*Alternatively, place thighs on broiler pan. Broil 4 to 6 inches from heat, 4 to 5 minutes per side.*) Transfer chicken to a cutting board. Let stand for 5 minutes, then slice diagonally.
5. Toss romaine with nectarine mixture in a large bowl. Divide among 6 plates and arrange chicken on top. Serve immediately.

INGREDIENT NOTE:
Jerk seasoning is a dry rub available in the spice section of most supermarkets.

MAKES 4 SERVINGS.

PER SERVING: 247 CALORIES; 6 G FAT (1 G SAT, 2 G MONO); 94 MG CHOLESTEROL; 24 G CARBOHYDRATE; 25 G PROTEIN; 4 G FIBER; 549 MG SODIUM.

NUTRITION BONUS: 140% DV VITAMIN A, 40 MG VITAMIN C (70% DV), 820 MG POTASSIUM (41% DV).

The Jive on Jerk

JERK COOKERY, which originated in Jamaica, is a style of grilling foods seasoned with an often fiery blend of spices. While commercial jerk blends vary with the manufacturer, most contain allspice, cinnamon, ginger, cloves, thyme and hot chiles. Look for blends that have no added salt or sugar (you can add those yourself if you want to).

Quick Cassoulet

PREP TIME: 30 MINUTES | **START TO FINISH:** 1 HOUR 5 MINUTES | **TO MAKE AHEAD:** PREPARE THROUGH STEP 2. COVER AND REFRIGERATE FOR UP TO 2 DAYS. | **EASE OF PREPARATION:** EASY

Inspired by the rustic—and time-consuming—French classic, our cassoulet, made with leftover turkey or chicken and canned beans, makes a simple, hearty supper.

- **1 cup fresh whole-wheat breadcrumbs** (*see Cooking Tip, page 396*)
- **2 teaspoons extra-virgin olive oil**
- **2 medium onions, finely chopped**
- **1 medium carrot, finely chopped**
- **2 cloves garlic, minced**
- **¼ pound turkey kielbasa sausage, thinly sliced**
- **1 14½-ounce can diced tomatoes**
- **1 cup reduced-sodium chicken broth**
- **½ cup dry white wine**
- **2 15½-ounce cans great northern or cannellini beans, rinsed**
- **1½ cups diced cooked turkey *or* chicken**
- **1½ teaspoons chopped fresh thyme *or* ½ teaspoon dried**
- **¼ teaspoon salt, or to taste**
- **Freshly ground pepper to taste**
- **2 tablespoons chopped fresh parsley (optional)**

1. Preheat oven to 350°F. Spread breadcrumbs on a baking sheet and bake until crisp and light golden, stirring occasionally, 6 to 10 minutes; set aside.

2. Meanwhile, heat oil in a 4- to 6-quart Dutch oven over medium heat. Add onions, carrot and garlic; cook, stirring often, until just beginning to color, about 5 minutes. Add kielbasa and cook, stirring, until lightly browned, 3 to 5 minutes. Add tomatoes, broth, wine, beans, turkey (or chicken), thyme, salt and pepper; bring to a simmer.

3. Sprinkle the toasted breadcrumbs over the top and transfer the pot to the oven. Bake until browned and bubbling, 25 to 35 minutes. Sprinkle with parsley, if using, and serve.

MAKES 6 SERVINGS, 1⅓ CUPS EACH.

PER SERVING: 353 CALORIES; 5 G FAT (1 G SAT, 1 G MONO); 25 MG CHOLESTEROL; 48 G CARBOHYDRATE; 27 G PROTEIN; 12 G FIBER; 396 MG SODIUM.

NUTRITION BONUS: 48% DV FIBER, 754 MG POTASSIUM (38% DV), 143 MCG FOLATE (36% DV), 30% DV VITAMIN A, 12 MG VITAMIN C (20% DV), 4 MG IRON (20% DV), 169 MG CALCIUM (15% DV).

Lower Carbs

Herb & Lemon Roast Chicken

PREP TIME: 35 MINUTES | **START TO FINISH:** 2 HOURS | **EASE OF PREPARATION:** MODERATE

Even if you're only feeding four, it is a good idea to roast two chickens at once. It takes the same amount of time and then you have leftovers to use for sandwiches, soup or salad or Quick Cassoulet (*page 227*).

- 2 lemons
- 2 cups packed parsley leaves
- ¼ cup fresh thyme leaves
- ¼ cup fresh rosemary leaves
- 3 cloves garlic, peeled
- 1½ tablespoons extra-virgin olive oil
- 2 teaspoons salt
- Freshly ground pepper to taste
- 2 whole chickens (3½-4 pounds each)
- 1 14½-ounce can reduced-sodium chicken broth, divided
- ½ cup dry white wine
- 2 tablespoons water mixed with 1 tablespoon cornstarch

1. Position oven rack in lower third of oven; preheat to 350°F. Coat a large roasting pan with cooking spray.
2. **To prepare chickens:** Zest lemons, then cut in half. Combine lemon zest, parsley, thyme, rosemary, garlic, oil, salt and pepper in a food processor or blender; process until finely chopped. Reserve ¼ cup of the mixture, covered, in the refrigerator for the gravy.
3. Place chicken hearts, necks and gizzards in the prepared pan (reserve livers for another use). Remove excess fat from chickens. Dry insides with a paper towel. With your fingers, loosen skin over breasts and thighs to make pockets, being careful not to tear the skin.
4. Spread ¼ cup herb mixture in the pan; place the chickens on top, at least 1 inch apart. Rub 1 tablespoon herb mixture into each cavity; spread remaining mixture under skin. Place 2 lemon halves in each cavity. Tuck wings behind the back and tie legs together.
5. Roast the chickens for 20 minutes. Drizzle with ¼ cup chicken broth and roast for 40 minutes more, basting with pan drippings every 20 minutes. Tent with foil and continue roasting until cooked through (*see box, page 206*) and juices run clear, about 30 minutes.
6. **To prepare gravy:** Transfer the chickens to a platter; tent with foil. Pour pan juices into a bowl, leaving giblets in the pan. Chill juices in the freezer for 10 minutes. Meanwhile, add wine and remaining broth to the pan; bring to a boil over medium heat, scraping up any browned bits. Add any juices accumulated on the platter.
7. Skim fat from the chilled juices. Add juices to the pan; return to a boil, then strain into a saucepan. Bring to a simmer. Whisk in cornstarch mixture. Simmer, stirring, until slightly thickened, about 1 minute. Stir in reserved herb mixture. Season with pepper.
8. Carve the chickens, discarding skin. Serve with the gravy.

MAKES 8 SERVINGS.

PER 3-OUNCE SERVING: 165 CALORIES; 7 G FAT (2 G SAT, 3 G MONO); 68 MG CHOLESTEROL; 1 G CARBOHYDRATE; 23 G PROTEIN; 0 G FIBER; 216 MG SODIUM.

Honey-Mustard Roast Chicken with Winter Vegetables

PREP TIME: 25 MINUTES | **START TO FINISH:** 1¼ HOURS | **EASE OF PREPARATION:** EASY

Root vegetables and chicken are roasted together for layer upon layer of intense flavor, with very little added fat. If your parsnips are large and have spongy or woody centers, cut out the cores before slicing.

- 6 small all-purpose potatoes, such as Yukon Gold, cut into wedges
- 6 medium carrots, peeled, halved lengthwise and cut into 2-inch slices
- 3 medium parsnips, peeled, quartered lengthwise and cut into 2-inch slices
- 1 head garlic, separated into cloves and peeled
- 1 tablespoon extra-virgin olive oil
- ½ teaspoon kosher salt, divided
- Freshly ground pepper to taste
- 2½-3 pounds bone-in chicken pieces, skin removed
- 3 sprigs fresh rosemary plus 2 teaspoons chopped rosemary
- 2 tablespoons Dijon mustard
- 1 tablespoon honey

1. Preheat oven to 375°F. Coat a large roasting pan with cooking spray.
2. Combine potatoes, carrots, parsnips, garlic and oil in the roasting pan. Season with ¼ teaspoon salt and pepper; toss well. Season chicken with the remaining ¼ teaspoon salt and pepper and place, skinned-side down, in the center of the pan with rosemary sprigs. Sprinkle with chopped rosemary.
3. Bake the chicken and vegetables for 20 minutes.
4. Meanwhile, in a small bowl, combine mustard and honey.
5. Turn chicken over and stir vegetables. Brush chicken with honey-mustard mixture. Continue roasting, stirring vegetables once or twice, until the chicken is cooked through (*see box, page 206*) and vegetables are tender, 25 to 35 minutes more. (If the chicken is done before the vegetables, remove and keep warm while vegetables finish cooking.) Serve immediately.

MAKES 6 SERVINGS.

PER SERVING: 476 CALORIES; 8 G FAT (2 G SAT, 3 G MONO); 130 MG CHOLESTEROL; 55 G CARBOHYDRATE; 46 G PROTEIN; 9 G FIBER; 427 MG SODIUM.

NUTRITION BONUS: 150% DV VITAMIN A, 52 MG VITAMIN C (90% DV), 1,700 MG POTASSIUM (85% DV), 35% DV FIBER, 99 MCG FOLATE (25% DV), 4 MG IRON (20% DV).

Ginger-Orange Glazed Cornish Hens

PREP TIME: 15 MINUTES | **START TO FINISH:** 55 MINUTES | **EASE OF PREPARATION:** MODERATE

When you crave roast chicken but don't have time to roast a whole bird, consider Cornish hens. The split hens cook up—juicy and succulent—in less than 45 minutes. Here, orange marmalade, spiked with ginger, makes an easy and delicious glaze. Serve with wild rice, winter squash and sautéed greens. (*Photo: page 215.*)

- 1 large onion, cut into ½-inch rounds
- 1 large orange, cut into ½-inch rounds
- 2 Cornish game hens, about 1½ pounds each, cut in half, backbone removed (*see Tip*)
- 1 tablespoon extra-virgin olive oil
- ¼ teaspoon salt
- ¼ teaspoon freshly ground pepper
- ¼ cup orange marmalade
- 2 teaspoons minced fresh ginger
- 1 teaspoon dried tarragon
- ⅛ teaspoon cayenne pepper
- 2 tablespoons water

1. Preheat oven to 450°F. Coat a roasting pan or baking sheet with sides with cooking spray. Place onion and orange rounds in the pan. Place hens, skin-side up, on top; rub with oil and sprinkle with salt and pepper. Bake the hens until the juices run clear and an instant-read thermometer inserted in the center of the breast registers 170°F, 30 to 35 minutes.

2. Meanwhile, combine marmalade, ginger, tarragon and cayenne. Remove hens from oven. Set oven to broil and place a rack 6 inches from the heat source. Brush hens with marmalade mixture. Broil until glaze is lightly browned, 2 to 3 minutes.

3. Remove hens to a serving platter or plates. Remove all but one orange slice from the pan and place over medium heat. Add water and bring to a simmer, using the orange slice as a spatula to scrape up any browned bits. Pour this pan sauce over the hens.

TEST KITCHEN TIP:
The bones of a Cornish hen are soft enough to cut easily with poultry shears or a sharp knife. Cut each hen in half through the breast bone. Cut along both sides of the backbone to separate the halves. Discard backbone.

MAKES 4 SERVINGS.

PER SERVING: 522 CALORIES; 32 G FAT (8 G SAT, 15 G MONO); 204 MG CHOLESTEROL; 22 G CARBOHYDRATE; 36 G PROTEIN; 2 G FIBER; 258 MG SODIUM.

NUTRITION BONUS: 28 MG VITAMIN C (45% DV), 543 MG POTASSIUM (27% DV).

Chicken Tagine with Pomegranates

PREP TIME: 25 MINUTES | **START TO FINISH:** 1¼ HOURS | **TO MAKE AHEAD:** PREPARE THROUGH STEP 4. COVER AND REFRIGERATE FOR UP TO 2 DAYS. REHEAT ON THE STOVETOP, IN THE OVEN (350°F, COVERED, FOR 25 TO 30 MINUTES) OR IN THE MICROWAVE. | **EASE OF PREPARATION:** MODERATE

The Moroccan word ***tagine,*** when translated simply as "stew," hardly does justice to this beautifully fragrant, succulent one-dish meal. (*Tagine* is also the name of the distinctive pot in which the meal is traditionally cooked and served.) Pomegranate juice lends a tart depth of flavor to the sauce; use bottled juice and skip the garnish when the fruit is not in season. Serve with whole-wheat couscous to soak up the delicious sauce.

- **1¼ cups fresh pearl onions *or* frozen small whole onions**
- **1 tablespoon extra-virgin olive oil**
- **1 teaspoon ground ginger**
- **⅛ teaspoon freshly ground pepper**
- **1¼ pounds boneless, skinless chicken thighs, trimmed of fat**
- **1½ cups pomegranate juice (*see Ingredient Note, page 396*)**
- **¾ cup pitted prunes**
- **½ cup dried apricots**
- **15 sprigs cilantro, tied with kitchen string**
- **½ teaspoon salt, or to taste**
- **2 tablespoons sesame seeds for garnish**
- **1 cup pomegranate seeds (1 large fruit; *see Cooking Tip, page 397*) for garnish**

1. Preheat oven to 350°F.
2. If using fresh pearl onions, cook in boiling water for 1 minute. Drain. Peel when cool enough to handle. If using frozen onions, rinse under warm water to thaw.
3. Heat oil in a Dutch oven over medium-high heat. Add ginger and pepper; cook, stirring, until fragrant and beginning to foam, about 1 minute. Add chicken and onions; stir to coat. Cook, stirring occasionally, until onions begin to turn golden, 5 to 8 minutes. Add pomegranate juice, prunes, apricots, cilantro and salt; bring to a simmer. Cover tightly with foil and then with a lid. Transfer to the oven and bake for 30 minutes.
4. Remove lid and foil. Discard cilantro. Return to oven and bake, uncovered, until the chicken is cooked through and tender, about 10 minutes longer.
5. Meanwhile, toast sesame seeds in a small dry skillet over medium-low heat, stirring constantly, until light golden and fragrant, 2 to 3 minutes. Transfer to a small bowl to cool.
6. To serve, spoon the tagine into a serving bowl or onto plates. Garnish with sesame seeds and pomegranate seeds.

MAKES 4 SERVINGS, ABOUT 1 CUP EACH.

PER SERVING: 432 CALORIES; 9 G FAT (2 G SAT, 4 G MONO); 118 MG CHOLESTEROL; 55 G CARBOHYDRATE; 30 G PROTEIN; 3 G FIBER; 432 MG SODIUM.

NUTRITION BONUS: 969 MG POTASSIUM (48% DV), 3 MG IRON (15% DV).

Chicken Braised with Lemon, Fennel & Black Olives

PREP TIME: 30 MINUTES | **START TO FINISH:** 1 HOUR 50 MINUTES | **TO MAKE AHEAD:** THE DISH WILL KEEP, COVERED, IN THE REFRIGERATOR FOR UP TO 2 DAYS. TO REHEAT, COVER WITH FOIL AND BAKE AT 350°F UNTIL HEATED THROUGH, 25 TO 30 MINUTES. | **EASE OF PREPARATION:** MODERATE

Sweet, salty and tart flavors dance in this distinctive, Mediterranean-style braise. The recipe is easily doubled (use a 9-by-13-inch baking dish) and made ahead, making it a sophisticated option for a potluck. Meyer lemons, if available, would be excellent here; simply omit the sugar. Serve with couscous.

- 2 teaspoons freshly grated lemon zest, preferably organic, divided
- 3 tablespoons lemon juice, divided
- 2 tablespoons extra-virgin olive oil, divided
- 2 cloves garlic, minced
- 1 teaspoon dried oregano
- ½ teaspoon sugar
- ¼ teaspoon salt
- Freshly ground pepper to taste
- 1¼ pounds boneless, skinless chicken thighs, trimmed and cut into 3 pieces each
- 1 large fennel bulb
- 1 large onion
- ½ cup dry white wine
- ½ cup reduced-sodium chicken broth
- ½ cup oil-cured black olives, pitted

1. Whisk 1 teaspoon lemon zest, 2 tablespoons lemon juice, 1 tablespoon oil, garlic, oregano, sugar, salt and pepper in a 7½-by-11-inch (2-quart) glass or ceramic baking dish. Add chicken and toss to coat. Cover and marinate in the refrigerator for at least 30 minutes or for up to 8 hours.

2. Meanwhile, trim stalks from fennel, reserving the greens for garnish. Slice the fennel bulb lengthwise into ¼-inch-thick slices. Lay slices flat and cut into ¼-inch-thick slivers. Peel onion, cut in half lengthwise and slice.

3. Preheat oven to 350°F. Heat the remaining 1 tablespoon oil in a large nonstick skillet over medium heat. Add fennel and onion; cook, stirring often, until softened and lightly browned, 8 to 10 minutes. (You may need to add a little water to prevent scorching.) Add wine, broth and the remaining 1 tablespoon lemon juice; bring to a simmer, stirring. Cook for 5 minutes, then stir in olives. Spoon this mixture over the chicken. Cover with foil.

4. Bake until the chicken is cooked through and the fennel is very tender, 35 to 40 minutes. Finely chop enough of the fennel fronds to make 2 tablespoons. Combine with the remaining 1 teaspoon lemon zest; sprinkle over the chicken before serving.

INGREDIENT NOTE:
Oil-cured olives are cured with salt rather than a brine, then rubbed with olive oil. They can be identified by their wrinkled skins.

MAKES 4 SERVINGS, 1½ CUPS EACH.

PER SERVING: 293 CALORIES; 15 G FAT (2 G SAT, 7 G MONO); 106 MG CHOLESTEROL; 11 G CARBOHYDRATE; 27 G PROTEIN; 3 G FIBER; 412 MG SODIUM.

NUTRITION BONUS: 630 MG POTASSIUM (32% DV), 16 MG VITAMIN C (25% DV).

Skillet-Braised Chicken Thighs with Chickpeas

PREP TIME: 25 MINUTES | **START TO FINISH:** 1 HOUR 10 MINUTES | **TO MAKE AHEAD:** THE DISH WILL KEEP, COVERED, IN THE REFRIGERATOR FOR UP TO 2 DAYS. REHEAT ON THE STOVETOP, IN THE OVEN (350°F, COVERED, FOR 25-30 MINUTES) OR IN THE MICROWAVE. | **EASE OF PREPARATION:** MODERATE

This full-bodied dish hails from the Catalán region of Spain. The chicken thighs stay moist and juicy when reheated, so it is a good candidate for making ahead.

- ½ cup all-purpose flour for dredging
- 12 bone-in chicken thighs (3½-4 pounds), skinned and trimmed of fat
- Salt & freshly ground pepper to taste
- 1½ tablespoons extra-virgin olive oil, divided
- 2 small dried red chiles, crumbled
- 2 onions, peeled, quartered and thinly sliced
- 2 cloves garlic, minced
- 1 teaspoon paprika
- 1 teaspoon dried marjoram
- 2 large vine-ripened tomatoes, seeded and chopped
- 2 large green bell peppers, cored, seeded and thinly sliced
- 1 cup reduced-sodium chicken broth, divided
- 1 15½-ounce *or* 19-ounce can chickpeas, rinsed
- 2 tablespoons chopped fresh parsley for garnish

1. Place flour in a shallow dish and dredge chicken thighs, shaking off excess flour. Season both sides with salt and pepper. Heat 1 tablespoon oil in a large cast-iron or nonstick skillet over high heat. Add the chicken, partially cover the pan and cook until the chicken is nicely browned, about 2 minutes per side. Transfer to a plate and set aside.

2. Reduce heat to medium and add the remaining ½ tablespoon oil to the pan. Add chiles and cook until they turn dark, about 2 minutes. Remove with a slotted spoon and discard. Add onions and garlic to the pan; cook until soft and lightly browned, 5 to 7 minutes. Add paprika and marjoram and cook, stirring, for 1 minute. Add tomatoes, green peppers and salt and pepper to taste; cook for 5 minutes longer.

3. Return the chicken to the pan, along with ½ cup chicken broth. Cover and simmer until the chicken is tender and no longer pink inside, 20 to 25 minutes (*see box, page 206*).

4. Add chickpeas and the remaining ½ cup chicken broth; simmer for 5 to 8 minutes. Blot any fat that rises to the surface with paper towels. Taste and adjust seasonings. Garnish with parsley.

MAKES 6 SERVINGS.

PER SERVING: 354 CALORIES; 11 G FAT (2 G SAT, 5 G MONO); 126 MG CHOLESTEROL; 26 G CARBOHYDRATE; 37 G PROTEIN; 6 G FIBER; 299 MG SODIUM.

NUTRITION BONUS: 57 MG VITAMIN C (100% DV), 682 MG POTASSIUM (34% DV), 26% DV FIBER, 20% DV VITAMIN A, 4 MG IRON (20% DV).

Stir-Fried Chicken with Wilted Spinach & Tamari Walnuts

PREP TIME: 30 MINUTES | **START TO FINISH:** 50 MINUTES | **EASE OF PREPARATION:** MODERATE

The joy of stir-frying is that an interesting dish like this cooks in mere minutes. The only trick is to have all the ingredients prepped and ready to add. Once you start stir-frying you can't afford to lose time mincing and measuring.

CHICKEN & MARINADE

- 2 teaspoons tamari *or* reduced-sodium soy sauce
- 2 teaspoons Chinese rice wine *or* dry sherry
- 2 teaspoons honey
- ½ teaspoon dark sesame oil
- 1 pound boneless, skinless chicken breasts, cut crosswise into ½-inch slices, then cut into ¼-inch-wide strips

STIR-FRY SAUCE & VEGETABLES

- ½ cup Tamari Walnuts (*page 235*)
- 1 tablespoon cornstarch
- 1 tablespoon tamari *or* reduced-sodium soy sauce
- 1 tablespoon Chinese rice wine *or* dry sherry
- ½ teaspoon dark sesame oil
- 3 teaspoons canola oil, divided
- ½ cup slivered red bell pepper (2-by-¼-inch pieces)
- 2 tablespoons slivered fresh ginger (1-by-⅛-inch pieces)
- 2 cloves garlic, minced
- 8-10 ounces spinach (8-10 cups), trimmed
- ½ cup thinly sliced scallions (1 bunch)

1. **To marinate chicken:** Combine tamari (or soy sauce), rice wine (or sherry), honey and sesame oil in a medium bowl. Add chicken and toss to coat. Cover and refrigerate until ready to cook.
2. Make Tamari Walnuts. Set aside.
3. **To prepare stir-fry:** Stir cornstarch, tamari (or soy sauce), rice wine (or sherry) and sesame oil in a small bowl until smooth; set stir-fry sauce aside.
4. Heat 1 teaspoon canola oil in a large nonstick skillet or wok over medium-high heat. Add half the chicken, a few pieces at a time, and stir-fry, turning up the heat as necessary to maintain a steady sizzle, until the chicken is no longer pink in the center, 2 to 3 minutes. Transfer chicken and any juices in the pan to a plate. Repeat with another teaspoon oil and the remaining chicken; transfer to the plate.
5. Add the remaining 1 teaspoon oil to the hot pan and heat briefly over medium-high heat. Add bell pepper and stir-fry for 1 minute. Add ginger and garlic; stir-fry for 20 seconds. Add spinach, about half at a time, turning to combine with the seasonings. Cover and cook just until wilted, 30 to 60 seconds.
6. Add the reserved chicken (and any accumulated juices) to the pan, along with scallions. Stir the stir-fry sauce and add it to the pan; stir-fry over high heat until the sauce has thickened, 30 to 60 seconds. Serve immediately, sprinkled with Tamari Walnuts.

MAKES 4 SERVINGS, 1 CUP EACH.

PER SERVING: 314 CALORIES; 17 G FAT (2 G SAT, 5 G MONO); 63 MG CHOLESTEROL; 12 G CARBOHYDRATE; 27 G PROTEIN; 3 G FIBER; 399 MG SODIUM.

NUTRITION BONUS: 45 MG VITAMIN C (70% DV), 60% DV VITAMIN A, 565 MG POTASSIUM (28% DV), 79 MCG FOLATE (20% DV), 3 MG IRON (15% DV).

TAMARI WALNUTS

PREP TIME: 2 MINUTES | **START TO FINISH:** 5 MINUTES | **TO MAKE AHEAD:** THE WALNUTS WILL KEEP, COVERED, IN THE REFRIGERATOR FOR UP TO 1 WEEK. | **EASE OF PREPARATION:** EASY

Keep these nuts on hand for stir-fries, salads or snacking.

- **½ cup coarsely chopped walnuts**
- **2 teaspoons tamari *or* reduced-sodium soy sauce**

Place walnuts in a small skillet; heat over medium heat until hot. Drizzle with tamari (or soy sauce) and stir until the nuts are coated and the pan is dry, about 1 minute. Transfer to a bowl to cool.

MAKES ½ CUP.

PER TABLESPOON: 50 CALORIES; 5 G FAT (1 G SAT, 1 G MONO); 0 MG CHOLESTEROL; 1 G CARBOHYDRATE; 1 G PROTEIN; 1 G FIBER; 45 MG SODIUM.

Spicy Yogurt Chicken

PREP TIME: 15 MINUTES | **START TO FINISH:** 1 HOUR 10 MINUTES (INCLUDING ½ HOUR MARINATING TIME)
EASE OF PREPARATION: EASY

Plain yogurt is a magical ingredient in a marinade. It tenderizes chicken while keeping it moist and succulent. Add a little sweetener, something tart and warm spices—and you have a dynamite dish.

- **2 tablespoons hot water**
- **2 pinches saffron threads (½ teaspoon)**
- **½ cup nonfat *or* low-fat plain yogurt**
- **1 onion, very finely chopped**
- **3 cloves garlic, very finely chopped**
- **2 tablespoons harissa *or* 2 teaspoons hot sauce *or* ½ teaspoon cayenne pepper**
- **2 tablespoons lemon juice**
- **1 tablespoon honey**
- **1 tablespoon extra-virgin olive oil**
- **½ teaspoon salt**
- **½ teaspoon ground cumin**
- **¼ teaspoon ground cinnamon**
- **8 chicken drumsticks, skin removed**

1. Place hot water in a small bowl and crumble saffron threads over it. Steep for 5 minutes. Combine yogurt, onion, garlic, harissa (or hot sauce or cayenne), lemon juice, honey, oil, salt, cumin and cinnamon in a shallow dish. Stir in the saffron water. Add drumsticks and coat well. Cover with plastic wrap and marinate in the refrigerator for at least 30 minutes or up to 12 hours.

2. Meanwhile, preheat oven to 450°F. Line a baking sheet with foil and set an oiled rack on top. Place the drumsticks on the rack and bake until the chicken is golden brown on the outside and no longer pink in the center, about 30 minutes.

MAKES 8 DRUMSTICKS, FOR 4 SERVINGS.

PER SERVING: 241 CALORIES; 9 G FAT (2 G SAT, 4 G MONO); 82 MG CHOLESTEROL; 13 G CARBOHYDRATE; 27 G PROTEIN; 1 G FIBER; 484 MG SODIUM.

NUTRITION BONUS: 9 MG VITAMIN C (15% DV), 300 MG POTASSIUM (15% DV).

Essential Chicken Sauté

HERE IS ONE SIMPLE TECHNIQUE that guarantees juicy results every time. First, pound the chicken: making it thinner ensures quick and even cooking. Next, dredge the chicken lightly in seasoned flour, which helps it turn deep golden brown when sautéed. After the chicken is cooked, deglaze the skillet with broth, wine or a little water to make a pan sauce. The liquid loosens the flavor-boosting browned bits from the bottom of the pan, making a tastier sauce.

Once you have mastered the technique, you can finish the dish with a signature touch. It can be as simple as a splash of white wine with a sprinkling of capers and parsley or some orange juice flavored with soy sauce and ginger. Or use one of the vibrant sauce recipes that follow to transform everyday chicken into a masterpiece.

BASIC CHICKEN SAUTÉ

PREP TIME: 20 MINUTES | **START TO FINISH:** 40 MINUTES
EASE OF PREPARATION: EASY

- **4 boneless, skinless chicken breast halves (1-1¼ pounds)**
- **¼ cup all-purpose flour**
- **½ teaspoon salt, or to taste**
- **Freshly ground pepper to taste**
- **1 tablespoon extra-virgin olive oil *or* canola oil**

1. Trim visible fat from chicken breasts. Remove the tenders (the long thin flaps); reserve for another use. Place trimmed chicken breasts between 2 pieces of plastic wrap. Pound with a rolling pin, meat mallet or heavy skillet until flattened to an even thickness, about ½ inch. Combine flour, salt and pepper in a shallow glass dish. Dredge chicken in seasoned flour, shaking off excess. (Discard any leftover flour.)

2. Heat oil in a large nonstick skillet over medium-high heat. Add chicken and cook until well browned and no longer pink in the center (*see box, page 206*), 4 to 5 minutes per side. Transfer to a plate, cover and keep warm.

3. Continue with the sauce of your choice, as directed in Step 3 of the following recipes.

PROVENÇAL SAUCE

Healthy Weight
Lower Carbs

- **1 small onion, finely chopped**
- **3 cloves garlic, minced**
- **½ teaspoon anchovy paste (optional)**
- **½ cup reduced-sodium chicken broth**
- **¼ cup dry white wine**
- **1 14½-ounce can diced tomatoes**
- **¼ cup chopped fresh basil**
- **2 tablespoons chopped black olives**

Prepare and cook chicken as directed in Steps 1 and 2 of Basic Chicken Sauté.

3. Add onion, garlic and anchovy paste, if using, to the skillet; cook over medium heat, stirring, for 1 minute. Add broth, wine and tomatoes; bring to a simmer. Cook until slightly thickened, 6 to 7 minutes. Stir in basil and olives. Return the chicken and juices to the pan; reduce heat to low and heat through. Spoon sauce over the chicken.

MAKES 4 SERVINGS.

PER SERVING: 234 CALORIES; 8 G FAT (1 G SAT, 4 G MONO); 66 MG CHOLESTEROL; 10 G CARBOHYDRATE; 28 G PROTEIN; 1 G FIBER; 472 MG SODIUM.

NUTRITION BONUS: 541 MG POTASSIUM (27% DV), 13 MG VITAMIN C (20% DV).

Lower Carbs

CREAMY MUSHROOM & LEEK SAUCE

- ½ pound cremini or baby bella mushrooms, wiped clean and thinly sliced (2½ cups)
- 1 small leek, trimmed, washed (*see Cooking Tip, page 397*) and thinly sliced (¾ cup)
- ½ cup dry white wine *or* vermouth
- ¾ cup reduced-sodium chicken broth
- 1 teaspoon cornstarch
- ⅓ cup reduced-fat sour cream
- ¾ teaspoon Dijon mustard
- ⅛ teaspoon salt, or to taste
- Freshly ground pepper to taste
- 2 tablespoons chopped fresh parsley

Prepare and cook chicken as directed in Steps 1 and 2 of Basic Chicken Sauté.

3. Add mushrooms and leek to the skillet; cook over medium heat, stirring often, until most of the moisture has evaporated and the mushrooms are beginning to brown, 4 to 6 minutes. Add wine (or vermouth) and deglaze, scraping up any browned bits, for about 1 minute. Mix broth and cornstarch in a small bowl. Add to the skillet and cook until thickened, 2 to 3 minutes. Stir in sour cream and mustard; cook until heated through, about 1 minute. Season with salt and pepper. Spoon over the chicken and sprinkle with parsley.

MAKES 4 SERVINGS.

PER SERVING: 249 CALORIES; 8 G FAT (3 G SAT, 4 G MONO); 74 MG CHOLESTEROL; 10 G CARBOHYDRATE; 30 G PROTEIN; 1 G FIBER; 352 MG SODIUM.

NUTRITION BONUS: 632 MG POTASSIUM (32% DV).

Lower Carbs

MANGO SAUCE

- 1 jalapeño pepper, seeded and minced
- 2 cloves garlic, minced
- 2 teaspoons minced fresh ginger
- ½ cup reduced-sodium chicken broth
- ½ cup orange juice, preferably fresh-squeezed
- 1 tablespoon brown sugar
- ¾ teaspoon cornstarch
- 1 mango, cut into ½-inch dice (1 cup)
- 2 tablespoons lime juice
- 2 tablespoons chopped fresh cilantro *or* mint

Prepare and cook chicken as directed in Steps 1 and 2 of Basic Chicken Sauté.

3. Add jalapeño, garlic and ginger to the skillet; cook over medium heat, stirring, until softened, 1 to 2 minutes. Add broth and deglaze, scraping up any browned bits, for 1 minute. Mix orange juice, brown sugar and cornstarch in a small bowl. Add to the skillet and bring the sauce to a simmer, stirring. Cook, stirring often, until thickened and slightly reduced, about 4 minutes. Stir in mango and cook until heated through, about 1 minute. Remove from heat and stir in lime juice. Spoon over the chicken and sprinkle with cilantro (or mint).

MAKES 4 SERVINGS.

PER SERVING: 243 CALORIES; 5 G FAT (1 G SAT, 3 G MONO); 66 MG CHOLESTEROL; 20 G CARBOHYDRATE; 27 G PROTEIN; 1 G FIBER; 235 MG SODIUM.

NUTRITION BONUS: 26 MG VITAMIN C (45% DV), 25% DV VITAMIN A, 233 MG POTASSIUM (20% DV).

Curried Turkey Cutlets with Dried Apricots

PREP TIME: 15 MINUTES | **START TO FINISH:** 30 MINUTES | **EASE OF PREPARATION:** EASY

Curry-spiced apricot sauce jazzes up lean turkey cutlets in a looks-exotic-but-is-really-easy way. Don't overcook the cutlets in Step 1—they continue to cook while resting.

- 1 pound turkey cutlets, cut into four portions (*see Note*)
- ¼ teaspoon salt, or to taste
- Freshly ground pepper to taste
- 2 teaspoons extra-virgin olive oil
- ½ cup finely chopped onion
- 3 cloves garlic, minced
- 1 tablespoon minced fresh ginger
- 1-2 teaspoons curry powder
- ¾ cup apple *or* pineapple juice
- ½ cup dried apricots, chopped
- 1 teaspoon cornstarch mixed with 1 tablespoon cold water
- 4 scallions, thinly sliced
- 2 tablespoons slivered fresh mint (optional)
- ¼ cup low-fat plain yogurt

1. Pat turkey cutlets dry with paper towels; sprinkle with salt and pepper. Heat oil in a large nonstick skillet over medium-high heat. Add turkey and cook until browned on both sides and no longer pink in the center, 2 to 3 minutes per side. Transfer to a plate and set aside.
2. Add onion to the pan; cook, stirring, for 1 minute. Add garlic, ginger and curry; cook, stirring, until fragrant, about 30 seconds. Add juice and apricots; bring to a simmer. Cook until the apricots are plump and the liquid is slightly reduced, about 3 minutes.
3. Add cornstarch mixture to the pan and cook, stirring constantly, until thickened, about 1 minute. Return the turkey and any accumulated juices to the pan. Cook, turning the cutlets a few times, until coated and heated through, 1 to 2 minutes. Stir in scallions and mint (if using). Serve immediately, with a dollop of yogurt.

SUBSTITUTION NOTE:
You can use boneless skinless chicken breasts in this recipe: cover with plastic wrap and pound with a meat mallet or rolling pin until about ½ inch thick; cook 4 to 5 minutes per side.

MAKES 4 SERVINGS.

PER SERVING: 252 CALORIES; 3 G FAT (1 G SAT, 2 G MONO); 46 MG CHOLESTEROL; 25 G CARBOHYDRATE; 30 G PROTEIN; 2 G FIBER; 264 MG SODIUM.

NUTRITION BONUS: 11 MG VITAMIN C (20% DV), 472 MG POTASSIUM (24% DV), 3 MG IRON (15% DV).

Turkey & Herbed-Biscuit Potpies

PREP TIME: 40 MINUTES | **START TO FINISH:** 1½ HOURS | **TO MAKE AHEAD:** PREPARE THROUGH STEP 3. THE FILLING WILL KEEP, COVERED, IN THE REFRIGERATOR FOR UP TO 1 DAY. | **EASE OF PREPARATION:** MODERATE

The savory comfort of traditional potpies, without the sky-high calorie count.

FILLING

- 1 large egg
- 1 tablespoon cornstarch
- 2 cups 1% milk
- Pinch of freshly grated nutmeg
- Salt & freshly ground pepper to taste
- 1 tablespoon extra-virgin olive oil, divided
- 1 pound mushrooms (preferably a mix of domestic and wild mushrooms), wiped clean and thinly sliced
- 2 cups frozen pearl onions, thawed
- 2½ cups diced cooked turkey *or* chicken
- 1 cup cooked green beans, cut into 1½-inch lengths
- 2 tablespoons chopped fresh parsley

BISCUIT TOPPING

- 1½ cups all-purpose flour
- 1½ cups whole-wheat pastry flour
- 1 tablespoon sugar
- 2 teaspoons baking powder
- 1 teaspoon baking soda
- 1 teaspoon fresh thyme *or* ½ teaspoon dried thyme leaves
- ½ teaspoon salt
- 2 tablespoons cold butter
- 1 cup buttermilk
- 1½ tablespoons canola oil
- 1 tablespoon milk

1. To prepare filling: Whisk egg and cornstarch in a saucepan until smooth. Add milk and whisk to blend. Whisk constantly over medium heat until thick and starting to boil, about 5 minutes. (The cornstarch prevents it from curdling.) Season with nutmeg, salt and and a generous grinding of pepper. Set aside.

2. Heat ½ tablespoon oil in a large skillet over high heat. Add mushrooms and sauté until browned and their liquid has evaporated, 3 to 5 minutes. Transfer to a bowl.

3. Heat the remaining ½ tablespoon oil in the skillet over medium-high heat. Add onions and cook, stirring, until golden brown, about 5 minutes; transfer to the bowl with the mushrooms. Add turkey (or chicken), green beans, parsley and the reserved milk sauce and stir to combine. Taste and adjust the seasonings with salt and pepper. Divide the filling among 6 shallow baking dishes (2-cup capacity). Set aside.

> **BAKING NOTE:** This recipe can also be made as a single pie in a deep 10-inch pie pan or a 2-quart baking dish.

4. To prepare biscuit topping & bake potpies: Preheat oven to 400°F. Whisk all-purpose flour, whole-wheat flour, sugar, baking powder, baking soda, thyme and salt in a mixing bowl. With 2 knives or your fingers, cut in butter until you have lumps the size of small peas. Add buttermilk and oil and stir just until combined.

5. Turn the dough out onto a floured surface. Knead a few times. Roll out ½ inch thick. Cut the dough into circles large enough to fit the baking dishes. Place over the filling. Brush tops with milk.

6. Set potpies on a baking sheet. Bake in the center of the oven until the tops are golden and the filling is bubbling, 25 to 30 minutes.

MAKES 6 SERVINGS.

PER SERVING: 536 CALORIES; 14 G FAT (5 G SAT, 5 G MONO); 92 MG CHOLESTEROL; 67 G CARBOHYDRATE; 32 G PROTEIN; 5 G FIBER; 732 MG SODIUM.

NUTRITION BONUS: 532 MG POTASSIUM (27% DV), 222 MG CALCIUM (20% DV).

Roast Turkey with Madeira Gravy

PREP TIME: 45 MINUTES | **START TO FINISH:** 4 HOURS | **EASE OF PREPARATION:** MODERATE

This gorgeous herb-rubbed turkey—complete with luscious gravy—is the quintessential holiday centerpiece. It is particularly fitting for Thanksgiving because Madeira, a fortified wine from the Portuguese island of the same name, flowed like water through the Colonies, having arrived here as ballast in ships. Sweet and mellow, reminiscent of sherry, Madeira beautifully enhances a turkey gravy.

TURKEY

- ¼ cup chopped fresh parsley
- 2 tablespoons chopped fresh thyme
- 2 tablespoons chopped fresh rosemary
- 2 tablespoons finely chopped shallots
- 1 tablespoons extra-virgin olive oil
- Salt & freshly ground pepper to taste
- 1 12- to 14-pound turkey with giblets
- 1 onion, peeled and quartered

GIBLET STOCK & GRAVY

- ½ tablespoon extra-virgin olive oil
- 1 onion, coarsely chopped
- 2 carrots, chopped
- 2 stalks celery, chopped
- 3 cups reduced-sodium chicken broth
- ¼ cup dry white wine for basting
- ½ cup Madeira
- 1½ tablespoons cornstarch mixed with 2 tablespoons water

1. Set oven rack in the bottom of the oven and preheat to 325°F. Set a wire roasting rack in a large roasting pan and coat the rack with cooking spray.
2. **To prepare turkey:** Combine parsley, thyme, rosemary, shallots and 1 tablespoon oil in a small bowl. Season with salt.
3. Reserve giblets and neck for the stock; discard the liver. Remove any visible fat from the turkey. Rinse it inside and out with cold water and pat dry. Season the cavity with salt and pepper and place onion in cavity.
4. With your fingers, separate the turkey skin from the breast meat, taking care not to tear the skin or pierce the meat. Smear the herb mixture between the flesh and the skin on both sides of the breastbone. Tie the drumsticks together and tuck the wing tips behind the back. Set the turkey, breast-side up, in the prepared roasting pan and tent with foil.
5. Roast the turkey for 2 hours.
6. Meanwhile, **to prepare giblet stock:** Heat ½ tablespoon oil in a large heavy saucepan over medium heat. Add chopped onion, carrots, celery and the turkey neck and giblets. Cook, stirring occasionally, until well browned, about 15 minutes. Pour in chicken broth and bring to a boil. Reduce the heat to low and simmer, partially covered, for 30 minutes. Strain the giblet stock through a fine sieve (you should have about 2 cups). Chill until ready to use.
7. After the turkey has been in the oven for 2 hours, remove the foil and continue roasting, basting with white wine from time to time, until an instant-read thermometer inserted into the thickest part of the thigh registers 180°F, 45 minutes to 1¼ hours longer. Transfer the turkey to a carving board. Cover loosely with foil and let rest for 20 to 30 minutes before carving.

8. To prepare gravy: While the turkey is resting, pour the drippings from the roasting pan through a strainer into a small bowl, then place the bowl in the freezer for 20 minutes to solidify the fat. Add Madeira to the roasting pan and cook, stirring and scraping up any brown bits, for about 1 minute; strain into a medium saucepan. Skim the fat from the giblet stock and add the stock to the pan. Skim the fat from the chilled pan juices and add the juices to the pan as well. Bring to a simmer. Add the cornstarch mixture to the simmering sauce, whisking until the gravy has thickened slightly. Season with pepper.

9. Remove strings from turkey and carve, discarding the skin. Serve with the Madeira gravy.

MAKES 8 SERVINGS, ABOUT 3 OUNCES EACH, WITH LEFTOVERS.

PER SERVING: 129 CALORIES; 4 G FAT (1 G SAT, 2 G MONO); 79 MG CHOLESTEROL; 2 G CARBOHYDRATE; 19 G PROTEIN; 0 G FIBER; 69 MG SODIUM.

Essential Turkey Broth

PREP TIME: 20 MINUTES | **START TO FINISH:** 3½ HOURS
TO MAKE AHEAD: THE BROTH WILL KEEP, COVERED, IN THE REFRIGERATOR FOR UP TO 2 DAYS OR IN THE FREEZER FOR UP TO 3 MONTHS. | **EASE OF PREPARATION:** EASY

ONCE YOU HAVE STRIPPED OFF the meat for sandwiches and casseroles, stew the turkey carcass into a broth for soup, such as Turkey-Barley Soup (*page 65*).

- Carcass and wings from 1 roasted turkey
- 4 quarts cold water
- 1 large onion *or* 2 medium, peeled and cut into chunks
- 2 medium carrots, peeled and cut into chunks
- 2 stalks celery with leaves, cut into chunks
- 2 medium leeks, trimmed, washed (*see Cooking Tip, page 397*) and cut into chunks
- 1 medium tomato, cut into chunks
- 1 head garlic, cloves separated and peeled
- 6 sprigs fresh parsley
- 6 sprigs fresh thyme *or* 1 teaspoon dried
- 2 bay leaves
- 1 teaspoon salt, or to taste
- ½ teaspoon whole black peppercorns

1. Cut or break turkey carcass into 3 or 4 pieces. Place carcass pieces and wings in a stockpot. Cover with water and bring to a simmer. Reduce heat to low. Skim froth. Add remaining ingredients, return to a simmer and skim again. Cook, uncovered, at a bare simmer, skimming occasionally, until broth is well flavored, about 3 hours.

2. Using tongs or a slotted spoon, remove large pieces of carcass and wings from pot. Strain broth into a large bowl. Cover and refrigerate for up to 2 days. Skim off any fat that solidifies on the surface.

MAKES ABOUT 3 QUARTS.

NOTE: AFTER STRAINING AND SKIMMING, BROTH HAS NEGLIGIBLE CALORIES AND NUTRIENTS EXCEPT SODIUM (590 MG PER CUP).

Lower Carbs

Spiral Stuffed Turkey Breast with Cider Gravy

PREP TIME: 40 MINUTES | **START TO FINISH:** 1¾ HOURS | **EQUIPMENT:** KITCHEN STRING, DUTCH OVEN

TO MAKE AHEAD: PREPARE THROUGH STEP 3. WRAP THE ROULADE IN PLASTIC WRAP AND REFRIGERATE FOR UP TO 8 HOURS.

EASE OF PREPARATION: MODERATE

When a whole bird is just too much—time and effort, as well as size—there is a quicker, simpler way: what's known in French cuisine as a *roulade.* Using a boneless turkey breast, butterflied and flattened, you can serve a beautiful spiral of juicy meat and herb-flecked stuffing that cooks in an hour and is a cinch to carve. Here, the turkey braises in thyme-infused apple cider, creating the basis for a savory sweet-tart gravy that gives the dish an elegant finish.

STUFFING

- **2 teaspoons extra-virgin olive oil**
- **1 cup finely chopped onion**
- **½ cup finely chopped celery**
- **2 cloves garlic, minced**
- **½ cup fresh whole-wheat breadcrumbs** (*see Cooking Tip, page 396*)
- **3 tablespoons chopped fresh parsley**
- **1 tablespoon chopped fresh thyme *or* 1 teaspoon dried**
- **1½ teaspoons chopped fresh sage *or* ½ teaspoon crumbled dried (*not* ground)**
- **¼ teaspoon salt, or to taste**
- **Freshly ground pepper to taste**

TURKEY & GRAVY

- **1 2-pound boneless turkey breast half**
- **¼ teaspoon salt, or to taste**
- **Freshly ground pepper to taste**
- **4 teaspoons extra-virgin olive oil, divided**
- **1 cup apple cider** (*see Ingredient Note, page 243*)

1. Preheat oven to 300°F.

2. To prepare stuffing: Heat oil in a medium nonstick skillet over medium heat. Add onion and celery; cook, stirring often, until softened, 2 to 4 minutes. Add garlic and cook, stirring, for 30 seconds. Remove from heat and stir in breadcrumbs, parsley, thyme, sage, ¼ teaspoon salt and pepper.

3. To prepare turkey: Remove skin from turkey breast and trim off fat. Butterfly the turkey breast (*see box, page 243*). Flatten the turkey breast. Spread the stuffing over the breast and roll the breast up into a cylinder. Secure with kitchen string.

4. Sprinkle the turkey roulade with ¼ teaspoon salt and pepper. Heat 2 teaspoons oil in a large cast-iron or nonstick skillet over medium-high heat. Add the roulade and cook, turning from time to time, until browned all over, 5 to 7 minutes. Transfer to a plate. Add cider to the skillet and bring to a simmer, stirring to scrape up any browned bits. Add broth and bring to a simmer. Remove from heat.

5. Heat the remaining 2 teaspoons oil in a Dutch oven over medium heat. Add onion and cook, stirring often, until softened, 2 to 3 minutes. Add garlic and cook, stirring, for 30 seconds. Add the browned turkey roulade. Pour in the cider mixture, then add thyme sprigs (or dried thyme). Cover the pan and transfer it to the oven.

6. Bake the roulade until it is no longer pink inside and an instant-read thermometer inserted in the center registers 170°, 45 minutes to 1 hour. Transfer to a carving board, tent with foil and keep warm.

- ½ cup reduced-sodium chicken broth
- 1 cup coarsely chopped onion
- 2 cloves garlic, crushed and peeled
- 8 sprigs fresh thyme *or* 1 teaspoon dried
- 4 teaspoons cornstarch
- 2 tablespoons water
- ¼ cup reduced-fat sour cream
- 1½ teaspoons Dijon mustard
- 1 teaspoon lemon juice

7. To prepare gravy: Strain the liquid from the Dutch oven into a medium saucepan, pressing on the solids. Bring to a simmer over medium-high heat; cook for 2 to 3 minutes to intensify the flavor. Mix cornstarch and water in a small bowl; add to the simmering gravy, whisking until lightly thickened. Add sour cream, mustard and lemon juice, whisking until smooth. Season with pepper. Heat through.

8. Remove the string from the roulade. Carve into ½-inch-thick slices and serve with gravy.

INGREDIENT NOTE: Sparkling or still apple cider, alcoholic (hard) or nonalcoholic (sweet)—all work well in this recipe. Still cider produces a darker gravy with a slightly sweeter flavor.

MAKES 8 SERVINGS.

PER SERVING: 222 CALORIES; 5 G FAT (1 G SAT, 3 G MONO); 73 MG CHOLESTEROL; 13 G CARBOHYDRATE; 29 G PROTEIN; 2 G FIBER; 246 MG SODIUM.

NUTRITION BONUS: 438 MG POTASSIUM (22% DV).

TECHNIQUE

Making a Roulade

THIS PREPARATION MAY LOOK ADVANCED, but it is actually quite simple and has numerous advantages. The challenge in roasting a whole turkey is that the breast meat tends to dry out before the leg portion is fully cooked. By cooking the breast alone, you eliminate the different roasting times and take advantage of turkey breast's status as one of the leanest, most economical meats available.

Because the breast is braised, a cooking process that involves browning the food and then simmering it gently in liquid, the moist heat ensures that the lean meat does not dry out. In addition, a magical mingling occurs as the cooking liquid takes on flavor from all the ingredients, forming the basis of a delicious, almost effortless gravy.

Just follow this step-by-step cooking lesson for an impressive alternative to the conventional holiday bird.

HOW TO BUTTERFLY, STUFF & ROLL A TURKEY BREAST

1. Place the turkey breast on a cutting board. Starting on the rounded side, make a horizontal cut with a chef's knife, about halfway down, to within 1 inch of the other side.

2. Open up the breast. Cover the breast with plastic wrap. Pound with a rolling pin or meat mallet to an even ½-inch thickness. Remove plastic wrap.

3. Spread the stuffing over the breast, leaving a 1-inch border on all sides. Roll the breast up into a cylinder.

4. Secure the roulade by tying it with kitchen string at 1-inch intervals.

FISH & SEAFOOD

12

The enjoyment of eating fish is immediate—picture sliding a fork into sweet ivory-white halibut drizzled with tangy herb vinaigrette or a buttery salmon redolent of Moroccan spices—but the rewards last a lifetime. Studies show that a meal of fish at least once a week, especially the cold-water species high in omega-3 fatty acids, reduces the risk of heart problems dramatically. Other research suggests that regularly eating omega-3–rich fish may prevent or relieve depression, joint problems, Alzheimer's disease and, perhaps, several cancers. Even seafood less bountiful in omega-3s, like scallops and crab, are rich in other key nutrients and offer a round richness of flavor that belies their lean, healthful nature.

Oven-Fried Flounder

PREP TIME: 10 MINUTES | **START TO FINISH:** 25 MINUTES | **EASE OF PREPARATION:** EASY

For an updated version of fish and chips, serve with Oven-Fried Potatoes & Sweet Potatoes (*page 118*) and a side of steamed broccoli.

- 1/3 cup fine, dry, unseasoned breadcrumbs
- 1/2 teaspoon salt, or to taste
- Freshly ground pepper to taste
- 4 4-to-6-ounce flounder *or* sole fillets
- 1 tablespoon extra-virgin olive oil
- 1/2 cup Tarragon Tartar Sauce (*recipe follows*)
- Lemon wedges

1. Preheat oven to 450°F. Coat a baking sheet with cooking spray.
2. Place breadcrumbs, salt and pepper in a small dry skillet over medium heat. Cook, stirring, until toasted, about 5 minutes. Remove from heat. Brush both sides of each fish fillet with oil and dredge in breadcrumbs. Place on prepared baking sheet.
3. Bake fish until opaque in the center, 5 to 6 minutes.
4. Meanwhile, make Tarragon Tartar Sauce.
5. To serve, carefully transfer fish to plates using a spatula. Garnish with a dollop of sauce and serve with lemon wedges.

MAKES 4 SERVINGS.

PER SERVING: 215 CALORIES; 9 G FAT (1 G SAT, 4 G MONO); 58 MG CHOLESTEROL; 10 G CARBOHYDRATE; 23 G PROTEIN; 1 G FIBER; 605 MG SODIUM.

TARRAGON TARTAR SAUCE

PREP TIME: 15 MINUTES | **START TO FINISH:** 15 MINUTES | **TO MAKE AHEAD:** THE SAUCE WILL KEEP, COVERED, IN THE REFRIGERATOR FOR UP TO 4 DAYS. | **EASE OF PREPARATION:** EASY

EatingWell's version of the classic, this can accompany just about any sautéed, broiled or grilled fish.

- 1/2 cup nonfat *or* low-fat plain yogurt
- 1/2 cup reduced-fat mayonnaise
- 1 teaspoon sugar
- 1/2 teaspoon Dijon mustard
- 1/2 teaspoon lemon juice
- 1/4 cup finely chopped dill pickle
- 1 tablespoon drained capers, minced
- 2 tablespoons chopped fresh parsley
- 2 teaspoons chopped fresh tarragon *or* 1/2 teaspoon dried
- 1 clove garlic, minced

Whisk yogurt, mayonnaise, sugar, mustard and lemon juice in a small bowl. Stir in pickle, capers, parsley, tarragon and garlic.

MAKES ABOUT 1 1/4 CUPS.

PER TABLESPOON: 22 CALORIES; 2 G FAT (0 G SAT, 0 G MONO); 2 MG CHOLESTEROL; 2 G CARBOHYDRATE; 0 G PROTEIN; 0 G FIBER; 78 MG SODIUM.

Sautéed Flounder with Orange-Shallot Sauce

PREP TIME: 15 MINUTES | **START TO FINISH:** 30 MINUTES | **EASE OF PREPARATION:** EASY

Flounder is one of the more readily available Atlantic fish. Its delicate flavor is wonderfully balanced by the sweet and savory combination of orange, shallot and mustard. A large nonstick skillet is highly recommended. Otherwise, cook the fillets in two batches, using 1½ teaspoons oil per batch.

- ⅓ cup all-purpose flour
- ½ teaspoon salt, or to taste
- Freshly ground pepper to taste
- 1 pound flounder, sole *or* haddock fillets
- 1 tablespoon extra-virgin olive oil
- 1 large shallot, finely chopped (about ⅓ cup)
- ½ cup dry white wine
- 1 cup freshly squeezed orange juice
- 2 heaping teaspoons Dijon mustard
- 2 teaspoons butter
- 2 tablespoons chopped fresh parsley

1. Mix flour, salt and pepper in a shallow dish. Thoroughly dredge fish fillets in the mixture.
2. Heat oil in a large nonstick skillet over medium-high heat until shimmering but not smoking. Add the fish and cook until lightly browned and just opaque in the center, 3 to 4 minutes per side. Transfer to a plate and cover loosely with foil.
3. Add shallot to the pan and cook over medium-high heat, stirring often, until softened and beginning to brown, about 3 minutes. Add wine and bring to a simmer, scraping up any browned bits. Cook until most of the liquid has evaporated, 1 to 2 minutes. Add orange juice and mustard; bring to a boil. Reduce heat to low and simmer until the sauce thickens a bit, about 5 minutes. Add butter and parsley; stir until the butter has melted. Transfer fish to individual plates, top with sauce and serve.

MAKES 4 SERVINGS.

PER SERVING: 222 CALORIES; 7 G FAT (2 G SAT, 3 G MONO); 59 MG CHOLESTEROL; 12 G CARBOHYDRATE; 23 G PROTEIN; 0 G FIBER; 237 MG SODIUM.

NUTRITION BONUS: 38 MG VITAMIN C (60% DV), 612 MG POTASSIUM (31% DV), 40 MCG FOLATE (20% DV).

At the Fish Counter

WHEN BUYING FISH, trust your instincts. Look for red gills, bright reflective skin, firm flesh, an undamaged layer of scales and no browning anywhere. The smell should be sweet, like a morning on the beach. The best whole fish look alive, as if they just came out of the water.

Thyme- & Sesame-Crusted Halibut

PREP TIME: 10 MINUTES | **START TO FINISH:** 30 MINUTES | **EASE OF PREPARATION:** EASY

Quickly roasting fish at high heat keeps it moist and succulent. The thyme-and-sesame crust gives this halibut a distinctive finish.

- 2 tablespoons lemon juice
- 2 tablespoons extra-virgin olive oil
- 1 clove garlic, minced
- Freshly ground pepper to taste
- 1¼ pounds halibut *or* mahi-mahi, cut into 4 portions
- 2 tablespoons sesame seeds
- 1½-2 teaspoons dried thyme leaves
- ¼ teaspoon coarse sea salt *or* kosher salt
- Lemon wedges

1. Preheat oven to 450°F. Line a baking sheet with foil.

2. Mix lemon juice, oil, garlic and pepper in a shallow glass dish. Add fish and turn to coat. Cover and marinate in the refrigerator for 15 minutes.

3. Meanwhile, toast sesame seeds in a small dry skillet over medium-low heat, stirring constantly, until golden and fragrant, 2 to 3 minutes. Transfer to a small bowl to cool. Mix in thyme.

4. Sprinkle the fish with salt and coat evenly with the sesame seed mixture, covering the sides as well as the top. Transfer the fish to the prepared baking sheet and roast until just opaque in the center, 10 to 14 minutes. Serve with lemon wedges.

MAKES 4 SERVINGS.

PER SERVING: 252 CALORIES; 13 G FAT (2 G SAT, 6 G MONO); 45 MG CHOLESTEROL; 3 G CARBOHYDRATE; 31 G PROTEIN; 1 G FIBER; 221 MG SODIUM.

NUTRITION BONUS: 682 MG POTASSIUM (34% DV), 119 MG MAGNESIUM (30% DV).

Halibut Roasted with Red Bell Peppers, Onions & Russet Potatoes

PREP TIME: 20 MINUTES | **START TO FINISH:** 1 HOUR | **EASE OF PREPARATION:** MODERATE

The firm flesh of halibut makes it the perfect choice for this dish, but feel free to substitute salmon, cod or any other thick fish. The bell peppers can be varied as well—exchange green for red or use a combination of red, green and yellow. You can also add rosemary, basil or even mint to the gremolata, a classic Italian seasoning of parsley, garlic and lemon zest. Accompany the dish with greens, such as spinach or chard. (*Photo: page 216.*)

- **2 russet potatoes (about 1 pound), scrubbed, halved lengthwise and cut into ½-inch spears**
- **2 tablespoons extra-virgin olive oil**
- **1 large red bell pepper, quartered, seeded and cut into eight ½-inch wedges**
- **1 large white onion, peeled and cut into ¼-inch wedges**
- **½ teaspoon salt, or to taste, divided**
- **Freshly ground pepper to taste**
- **2 tablespoons coarsely chopped fresh flat-leaf parsley**
- **2 teaspoons coarsely chopped fresh lemon zest, preferably organic**
- **1 teaspoon dried oregano**
- **1 clove garlic, crushed**
- **1½ pounds halibut fillet (about ¾ inch thick), skin removed (*see Technique, page 254*), cut into 4 portions**
- **Lemon wedges**

1. Preheat oven to 400°F. Place potatoes in a large roasting pan or on a large baking sheet with sides; drizzle with oil and turn to coat evenly. Add bell pepper and onion. Season with ¼ teaspoon salt and pepper.
2. Roast the vegetables, turning the potatoes once or twice and moving the pepper and onion pieces around so they brown evenly, until the potatoes are starting to brown and are almost tender, about 35 minutes.
3. While the vegetables are roasting, finely chop parsley, lemon zest, oregano and garlic together to make gremolata. Season halibut with remaining ¼ teaspoon salt and pepper, then sprinkle with 2 teaspoons gremolata.
4. Remove the pan from the oven. Increase oven temperature to 450°. Push the vegetables to the sides of the pan and place the halibut in the center. Spoon some of the onions and peppers over the halibut. Arrange the potatoes around the edges, turning the browned sides up.
5. Roast until the vegetables are browned and tender and the halibut is opaque in the center, 10 to 15 minutes more, depending on the thickness of the fish. Sprinkle the remaining gremolata on top. Arrange the halibut and vegetables on a platter or individual plates. Serve with lemon wedges.

MAKES 4 SERVINGS.

PER SERVING: 363 CALORIES; 10 G FAT (1 G SAT, 5 G MONO); 53 MG CHOLESTEROL; 31 G CARBOHYDRATE; 39 G PROTEIN; 3 G FIBER; 392 MG SODIUM.

NUTRITION BONUS: 117 MG VITAMIN C (190% DV), 1,417 MG POTASSIUM (71% DV), 60% DV VITAMIN A, 3 MG IRON (15% DV).

Poached Halibut with Herbed Vinaigrette

PREP TIME: 10 MINUTES | **START TO FINISH:** 50 MINUTES | **TO MAKE AHEAD:** THE BROTH WILL KEEP, COVERED, IN THE REFRIGERATOR, FOR UP TO 2 DAYS OR IN THE FREEZER FOR UP TO 4 MONTHS. | **EASE OF PREPARATION:** EASY

Gently simmering mild fish in a simple, fragrant broth—known in French cooking as a *court-bouillon*—is a wonderful way to impart flavor. Be careful not to overcrowd or overcook the fish, as either will cause it to fall apart.

BROTH

- 8 cups water
- 1 cup red-wine vinegar
- 1 medium onion, halved
- 1 medium carrot, quartered
- 1 stalk celery, quartered
- 3 cloves garlic, unpeeled, halved
- 1 tablespoon salt, or to taste
- 1 teaspoon peppercorns
- 1 bay leaf
- 1 branch fresh thyme

HALIBUT & VINAIGRETTE

- 4 6-ounce halibut steaks, 1 inch thick, skinned
- Salt & freshly ground pepper to taste
- 2 tablespoons lemon juice
- 1 tablespoon Dijon mustard
- 2 teaspoons reduced-fat sour cream
- 2 tablespoons canola oil
- 1 medium shallot, finely chopped
- 1 tablespoon coarsely chopped fresh Italian parsley
- 1 tablespoon coarsely chopped fresh tarragon
- 1 tablespoon chopped fresh chives
- 2 teaspoons coarsely chopped fresh dill, plus sprigs for garnish

1. To prepare broth: Combine all broth ingredients in a large pot. Bring to a boil, reduce heat to low and simmer, uncovered, for 30 minutes. Strain into a large deep skillet, discarding solids.

2. To poach halibut & make vinaigrette: Bring broth just to a simmer. Season halibut with salt and pepper on both sides. Add halibut to broth and poach, uncovered, until opaque in the center, 5 to 10 minutes.

3. Meanwhile, spoon 2 tablespoons of the simmering broth into a small bowl. Add lemon juice, mustard and sour cream. Gradually whisk in oil. Add shallot and season with salt and pepper.

4. Remove halibut from poaching liquid and divide among 4 warmed plates. Stir parsley, tarragon, chives and chopped dill into the vinaigrette and spoon over the fish. Garnish with dill sprigs. Serve immediately.

MAKES 4 SERVINGS.

PER SERVING: 268 CALORIES; 11 G FAT (1 G SAT, 5 G MONO); 55 MG CHOLESTEROL; 4 G CARBOHYDRATE; 37 G PROTEIN; 0 G FIBER; 272 MG SODIUM.

NUTRITION BONUS: 834 MG POTASSIUM (42% DV), 146 MG MAGNESIUM (37% DV).

Asian Halibut & Brown Rice Packets

PREP TIME: 15 MINUTES | **START TO FINISH:** 30 MINUTES | **EASE OF PREPARATION:** MODERATE

Rice on the grill? Absolutely, and by the time it's cooked it's scented with the exotic flavors of plums and Asian sauce. If halibut isn't available, striped bass, sole or even thick cod fillets will work just fine.

- **¾ cup plus 2 tablespoons water**
- **1 cup plus 2 tablespoons orange juice**
- **2 teaspoons reduced-sodium soy sauce**
- **2 cups instant brown rice**
- **4 scallions, sliced, whites and greens separated**
- **2 tablespoons hoisin sauce**
- **1 tablespoon minced fresh ginger**
- **1 tablespoon toasted sesame oil**
- **1 pound halibut fillet, skin removed, cut into 4 portions**
- **1 large ripe plum, cut into 12 wedges**

1. Preheat a gas or charcoal grill.
2. Heat ¾ cup water, 1 cup orange juice and soy sauce in a small saucepan until just simmering. Pour into a medium bowl, stir in rice and scallion whites and set aside, uncovered, for 10 minutes. Whisk hoisin sauce, ginger, sesame oil and the remaining 2 tablespoons each of water and orange juice in a small bowl.
3. Prepare the foil as directed in Packet Step 1 (*below*). Place one-fourth of the rice mixture in the center (Packet Step 2). Set a piece of fish on the rice. Arrange three wedges of plum on the fish. Top with one-fourth of the hoisin mixture and sprinkle with one-fourth of the scallion greens. Seal the packet as directed in Packet Step 3. Make 3 more packets with the remaining ingredients.
4. Grill the packets as directed in Packet Step 4. Cook until the fish is opaque in the center, 8 to 12 minutes, depending on the thickness. (When opening a packet to check for doneness, be careful of steam.) Use a spatula to slide the contents of the packet onto a plate.

MAKES 4 SERVINGS.

PER SERVING: 389 CALORIES; 8 G FAT (1 G SAT, 2 G MONO); 37 MG CHOLESTEROL; 48 G CARBOHYDRATE; 29 G PROTEIN; 3 G FIBER; 294 MG SODIUM.

TECHNIQUE

Packet Steps

Step 1. Stack two 20-inch sheets of foil (the double layers will help protect the ingredients on the bottom from burning). Coat the center of the top layer with cooking spray.

Step 2. Layer your ingredients on the foil. Center everything: it's easier to wrap the food and makes the packet look neat.

Step 3. Bring the short ends of the foil together, leaving enough room in the packet for steam to gather and cook the food. Fold the foil over and pinch to seal. Pinch seams together along the sides. Make sure all the seams are tightly sealed to keep steam from escaping.

Step 4. Place the packets on a gas grill over medium heat or on a charcoal grill 4 to 6 inches from medium coals. Cover the grill and cook just until the packet contents are done. Handle the hot packets with a large spatula or oven mitts. Carefully open both ends of the packet and allow the hot steam to escape.

Roasted Fish with Potatoes

PREP TIME: 15 MINUTES | **START TO FINISH:** 1 HOUR | **EASE OF PREPARATION:** EASY

Choose a firm fish that holds together well and does not dry out when baked, such as mahi-mahi or tilapia. To save time, use a food processor to slice the potatoes.

- 1 pound red potatoes (4-8 potatoes), scrubbed and thinly sliced
- 3 cloves garlic, minced
- 2 tablespoons extra-virgin olive oil
- ½ teaspoon salt, divided
- Freshly ground pepper to taste
- 1¼ pounds fish fillet, cut into 4 portions
- 4 teaspoons lemon juice, plus wedges for garnish
- 1 tablespoon chopped fresh parsley

1. Preheat oven to 400°F. Coat a 9-by-13-inch baking dish with cooking spray.
2. Toss potatoes with garlic, oil, ¼ teaspoon salt and a generous grinding of pepper in the prepared pan. Cover with foil and roast until tender when pierced with a knife, 30 to 40 minutes.
3. Place fish fillets on potatoes, skin-side down; sprinkle with remaining salt, pepper, lemon juice and parsley. Bake until the fish is opaque in the center, 10 to 15 minutes. Serve with lemon wedges.

MAKES 4 SERVINGS.

PER SERVING: 290 CALORIES; 8 G FAT (1 G SAT, 6 G MONO); 103 MG CHOLESTEROL; 24 G CARBOHYDRATE; 29 G PROTEIN; 2 G FIBER; 425 MG SODIUM.

Mustard-Crusted Salmon

PREP TIME: 10 MINUTES | **START TO FINISH:** 20-25 MINUTES | **EASE OF PREPARATION:** EASY

Prepare more salmon than you need, then toss the flaked leftovers into a green salad for lunch the next day.

- 1¼ pounds center-cut salmon fillets, cut into 4 portions
- ¼ teaspoon salt, or to taste
- Freshly ground pepper to taste
- ¼ cup reduced-fat sour cream
- 2 tablespoons coarse-grained mustard
- 2 teaspoons lemon juice
- Lemon wedges for garnish

1. Preheat broiler. Line a broiler pan or baking sheet with foil, then coat it with cooking spray.
2. Place salmon pieces, skin-side down, on the prepared pan. Season with salt and pepper. Combine sour cream, mustard and lemon juice in a small bowl. Spread evenly over the salmon.
3. Broil the salmon 5 inches from the heat source until it is opaque in the center, 10 to 12 minutes. Serve with lemon wedges.

MAKES 4 SERVINGS.

PER SERVING: 290 CALORIES; 18 G FAT (4 G SAT, 6 G MONO); 89 MG CHOLESTEROL; 2 G CARBOHYDRATE; 29 G PROTEIN; 0 G FIBER; 389 MG SODIUM.

Lower Carbs

Broiled Salmon with Miso Glaze

PREP TIME: 15 MINUTES | **START TO FINISH:** 25 MINUTES | **EASE OF PREPARATION:** EASY

Versatile miso (fermented soybean paste) keeps for months in the refrigerator and adds instant flavor to soups, sauces, dips, marinades and salad dressings. In general, the lighter the miso, the milder and sweeter its flavor. Light miso is the key to the wonderful flavor of this salmon.

- **1 tablespoon sesame seeds**
- **2 tablespoons shiro miso (sweet white miso) paste (*see Ingredient Note, page 395*)**
- **2 tablespoons mirin (Japanese rice wine)**
- **1 tablespoon reduced-sodium soy sauce *or* tamari**
- **1 tablespoon minced fresh ginger**
- **A few drops hot pepper sauce**
- **1¼ pounds center-cut salmon fillet, cut into 4 portions**
- **2 tablespoons thinly sliced scallions**
- **2 tablespoons chopped fresh cilantro *or* parsley**

1. Position oven rack in upper third of oven; preheat broiler. Line a small baking pan with foil. Coat foil with cooking spray.
2. Toast sesame seeds in a small dry skillet over low heat, stirring constantly, until fragrant, 3 to 5 minutes. Set aside in a small bowl.
3. Whisk miso, mirin, soy sauce (or tamari), ginger and hot pepper sauce in a small bowl until smooth.
4. Place salmon fillets, skin-side down, in prepared pan. Brush generously with miso mixture. Broil salmon, 3 to 4 inches from the heat source, until opaque in the center, 6 to 8 minutes.
5. Transfer salmon to warmed plates and garnish with reserved sesame seeds, scallions and cilantro (or parsley).

SHOPPING TIP: Miso paste, mirin and tamari are available in health-food stores and Asian markets.

MAKES 4 SERVINGS.

PER SERVING: 252 CALORIES; 10 G FAT (2 G SAT, 3 G MONO); 78 MG CHOLESTEROL; 7 G CARBOHYDRATE; 30 G PROTEIN; 1 G FIBER; 432 MG SODIUM.

NUTRITION BONUS: 730 MG POTASSIUM (37% DV).

Oven-Poached Salmon Fillets

PREP TIME: 20 MINUTES | **START TO FINISH:** 30 MINUTES | **EASE OF PREPARATION:** EASY

Baking salmon fillets, covered, with a little wine and some shallots produces moist, succulent results as long as you remember the two cardinal rules of fish cookery: choose only the freshest fish and don't overcook it.

- **1 pound salmon fillet, cut into 4 portions, skin removed, if desired**
- **2 tablespoons dry white wine**
- **¼ teaspoon salt**
- **Freshly ground pepper to taste**
- **2 tablespoons finely chopped shallot (1 medium)**
- **½ cup Light Lemon Sauce with Herbs (*page 296*), Tarragon Tartar Sauce (*page 246*), Salsa Verde (*page 294*) *or* Creamy Dill Sauce (*page 257*)**
- **Lemon wedges for garnish**

1. Preheat oven to 425°F. Coat a 9-inch glass pie pan or an 8-inch glass baking dish with cooking spray.

2. Place salmon, skin-side (or skinned-side) down, in the prepared pan. Sprinkle with wine. Season with salt and pepper, then sprinkle with shallots. Cover with foil and bake until opaque in the center and starting to flake, 15 to 25 minutes, depending on thickness.

3. Meanwhile, make the sauce of your choice.

4. When the salmon is ready, transfer to dinner plates. Spoon any liquid remaining in the pan over the salmon and serve with sauce and lemon wedges.

MAKES 4 SERVINGS.

PER SERVING (WITHOUT SAUCE): 216 CALORIES; 12 G FAT (2 G SAT, 4 G MONO); 67 MG CHOLESTEROL; 1 G CARBOHYDRATE; 23 G PROTEIN; 0 G FIBER; 213 MG SODIUM.

NUTRITION BONUS: 433 MG POTASSIUM (22% DV).

TECHNIQUE

Skinning Salmon

WHETHER YOU REMOVE THE SKIN from salmon fillets is a matter of personal taste. If the fillet is not cooked in a sauce, it is easy for a diner to slip the skin off at the table. But if the fillets are cooked and served in a sauce, it is more aesthetic to trim the skin before cooking.

To remove skin from a salmon fillet, place it, skin-side down, on a cutting board. Use a thin sharp knife to cut between the skin and flesh at the tip. Grasp the skin with your free hand and ease the knife carefully between skin and flesh, keeping the knife pointed slightly toward the skin.

Is It Done Yet?

TO TEST THE FILLETS FOR DONENESS, use a sharp knife to poke the fish and check the consistency and color in the center. The flesh should be opaque and should flake, but not fall apart, when pressed.

Grilled Salmon with North African Flavors

PREP TIME: 15 MINUTES | **START TO FINISH:** 45 MINUTES | **EASE OF PREPARATION:** MODERATE

Our version of the classic North African herb paste known as *chermoula* serves as both a marinade and a sauce for this richly flavored salmon. If it is too cool to grill outdoors, you can roast the salmon at 450°F for 12 to 15 minutes.

- ¼ cup low-fat *or* nonfat plain yogurt
- ¼ cup chopped fresh parsley
- ¼ cup chopped fresh cilantro
- 2 tablespoons lemon juice
- 1 tablespoon extra-virgin olive oil
- 3 cloves garlic, minced
- 1½ teaspoons paprika
- 1 teaspoon ground cumin
- ¼ teaspoon salt, or to taste
- Freshly ground pepper to taste
- 1 pound center-cut salmon fillet, cut into 4 portions (*see Tip*)
- 1 lemon, cut into wedges

1. Stir together yogurt, parsley, cilantro, lemon juice, oil, garlic, paprika, cumin, salt and pepper in a small bowl. Reserve ¼ cup for sauce; cover and refrigerate. Place salmon fillets in a large sealable plastic bag. Pour in the remaining herb mixture, seal the bag and turn to coat. Refrigerate for 20 to 30 minutes, turning the bag over once.

2. Meanwhile, preheat grill to medium-high.

3. Oil the grill rack (*see Tip, page 130*). Remove the salmon from the marinade, blotting any excess. Grill the salmon until browned and opaque in the center, 4 to 6 minutes per side. To serve, top each piece with a dollop of the reserved sauce and garnish with lemon wedges.

COOKING TIP: Keeping the skin on when grilling salmon helps hold the fish together and protects the delicate flesh from the searing heat. Once cooked, the skin slips off easily.

MAKES 4 SERVINGS.

PER SERVING: 229 CALORIES; 14 G FAT (3 G SAT, 6 G MONO); 67 MG CHOLESTEROL; 1 G CARBOHYDRATE; 23 G PROTEIN; 0 G FIBER; 134 MG SODIUM.

NUTRITION BONUS: 452 MG POTASSIUM (23% DV), 9 MG VITAMIN C (15% DV).

Salmon on a Bed of Lentils

PREP TIME: 15 MINUTES | **START TO FINISH:** 1 HOUR | **EASE OF PREPARATION:** EASY

Simmered with carrots, turnips and thyme, the lentils make a lovely, hearty bed for the salmon fillets, which are gently cooked on top of them for easy one-dish preparation. Green (Le Puy) lentils are smaller and more delicate than other varieties and hold their shape better during cooking.

- 2 teaspoons extra-virgin olive oil
- 1 tablespoon finely chopped shallots
- 2 teaspoons minced garlic
- 2½ cups reduced-sodium chicken broth
- 1 cup green *or* brown lentils, rinsed
- 1 small onion, peeled and studded with a clove
- 1½ teaspoons chopped fresh thyme *or* ½ teaspoon dried thyme leaves
- ¼ teaspoon salt, or to taste
- Freshly ground pepper to taste
- 2 carrots, peeled and finely chopped
- 2 small white turnips, peeled and finely chopped
- 1 pound salmon fillet, skin removed (*see Technique, page 254*), cut into 4 portions
- 2 tablespoons chopped fresh parsley
- 1 lemon, quartered

1. Heat oil in a Dutch oven or deep sauté pan over medium heat. Add shallots and garlic and cook, stirring, until softened, about 30 seconds. Add broth, lentils, onion, thyme, salt and pepper. Bring to a boil, reduce heat to low and simmer, covered, until the lentils are tender, 25 minutes.
2. Add carrots and turnips; simmer until the vegetables are tender, about 10 minutes more. Remove the onion. Add more broth if necessary; the mixture should be slightly soupy. Taste and adjust seasonings. Lay salmon fillets on top, cover the pan and cook until the salmon is opaque in the center, 8 to 10 minutes.
3. Serve in shallow bowls, garnished with parsley and lemon wedges.

MAKES 4 SERVINGS.

PER SERVING: 382 CALORIES; 11 G FAT (2 G SAT, 4 G MONO); 65 MG CHOLESTEROL; 35 G CARBOHYDRATE; 36 G PROTEIN; 9 G FIBER; 332 MG SODIUM.

NUTRITION BONUS: 80% DV VITAMIN A, 1,112 MG POTASSIUM (56% DV), 36% DV FIBER, 13 MG VITAMIN C (20% DV), 4 MG IRON (20% DV).

High Fiber

Easy Salmon Cakes

PREP TIME: 20 MINUTES | **START TO FINISH:** 45 MINUTES | **TO MAKE AHEAD:** PREPARE THROUGH STEP 3. COVER AND REFRIGERATE FOR UP TO 8 HOURS. | **EASE OF PREPARATION:** EASY

If you are trying to boost your intake of omega-3s, try this simple favorite. It is a great way to use convenient canned (or leftover) salmon. The tangy dill sauce provides a tart balance.

- 3 teaspoons extra-virgin olive oil, divided
- 1 small onion, finely chopped
- 1 stalk celery, finely diced
- 2 tablespoons chopped fresh parsley
- 15 ounces canned salmon, drained, *or* 1½ cups cooked salmon
- 1 large egg, lightly beaten
- 1½ teaspoons Dijon mustard
- 1¾ cups fresh whole-wheat breadcrumbs (*see Tip, page 262*)
- ½ teaspoon freshly ground pepper
- Creamy Dill Sauce (*recipe follows*)
- 1 lemon, cut into wedges

1. Preheat oven to 450°F. Coat a baking sheet with cooking spray.
2. Heat 1½ teaspoons oil in a large nonstick skillet over medium-high heat. Add onion and celery; cook, stirring, until softened, about 3 minutes. Stir in parsley; remove from the heat.
3. Place salmon in a medium bowl. Flake apart with a fork; remove any bones and skin. Add egg and mustard; mix well. Add onion mixture, breadcrumbs and pepper; mix well. Shape the mixture into 8 patties, about 2½ inches wide.
4. Heat remaining 1½ teaspoons oil in the skillet over medium heat. Add 4 patties and cook until the undersides are golden, 2 to 3 minutes. Using a wide spatula, turn them over onto the prepared baking sheet. Repeat with the remaining patties.
5. Bake the salmon cakes until golden on top and heated through, 15 to 20 minutes. Meanwhile, prepare Creamy Dill Sauce. Serve salmon cakes with sauce and lemon wedges.

MAKES 4 SERVINGS.

PER SERVING: 324 CALORIES; 13 G FAT (1 G SAT, 4 G MONO); 133 MG CHOLESTEROL; 24 G CARBOHYDRATE; 32 G PROTEIN; 7 G FIBER; 673 MG SODIUM.

NUTRITION BONUS: 27% DV FIBER, 171 MG CALCIUM (15% DV).

CREAMY DILL SAUCE

PREP TIME: 5 MINUTES | **START TO FINISH:** 10 MINUTES | **TO MAKE AHEAD:** THE SAUCE WILL KEEP, COVERED, IN THE REFRIGERATOR FOR UP TO 2 DAYS. | **EASE OF PREPARATION:** EASY

- ¼ cup reduced-fat mayonnaise
- ¼ cup nonfat plain yogurt
- 2 scallions, thinly sliced
- 1 tablespoon lemon juice
- 1 tablespoon finely chopped fresh dill *or* parsley
- Freshly ground pepper to taste

Combine ingredients in a small bowl and mix well.

MAKES ABOUT ½ CUP.

PER TABLESPOON: 28 CALORIES; 2 G FAT (0 G SAT, 0 G MONO); 2 MG CHOLESTEROL; 2 G CARBOHYDRATE; 0 G PROTEIN; 0 G FIBER; 50 MG SODIUM.

Mediterranean Fish Fillets

PREP TIME: 15 MINUTES | **START TO FINISH:** 30 MINUTES | **EASE OF PREPARATION:** EASY

Many coastal countries offer some version of this versatile dish. The firm flesh of the fish is kept moist by an orange-and-olive-accented tomato sauce. You could also flavor the sauce with capers, roasted peppers or sun-dried tomatoes.

- 2 teaspoons extra-virgin olive oil
- 1 large onion, thinly sliced
- ¼ cup dry white wine
- 2 cloves garlic, finely chopped
- 1 14½-ounce can diced tomatoes
- 8 Kalamata olives, pitted and chopped
- ¼ teaspoon dried oregano
- ¼ teaspoon freshly grated orange zest
- Salt & freshly ground pepper to taste
- 1 pound thick-cut, firm-fleshed fish fillets, such as halibut, mahi-mahi *or* monkfish

1. Preheat oven to 450°F.
2. Heat oil in a large nonstick skillet over medium-high heat. Add onion and cook, stirring often, until lightly browned, about 5 minutes. Add wine and garlic and simmer for 30 seconds. Stir in tomatoes, olives, oregano and orange zest. Adjust seasoning with salt and pepper.
3. Cut fish into 4 pieces and season with salt and pepper. Arrange in a single layer in a pie pan or baking dish. Spoon tomato mixture over fish.
4. Bake, uncovered, until opaque in the center, 15 to 25 minutes. Serve immediately.

MAKES 4 SERVINGS.

PER SERVING: 199 CALORIES; 7 G FAT (1 G SAT, 4 G MONO); 36 MG CHOLESTEROL; 6 G CARBOHYDRATE; 25 G PROTEIN; 1 G FIBER; 294 MG SODIUM.

NUTRITION BONUS: 642 MG POTASSIUM (32% DV), 99 MG MAGNESIUM (25% DV).

Ginger-Steamed Tilapia

PREP TIME: 15 MINUTES | **START TO FINISH:** 20 MINUTES | **EASE OF PREPARATION:** EASY

Tilapia, sometimes called Nile perch, is farmed in warm freshwater ponds. It's a mild, meaty fish similar to sole or flounder. Serve the tilapia with stir-fried bok choy and shiitake mushrooms. For a grain accompaniment, add a bowl of brown rice.

- **1 3-inch piece fresh ginger, peeled and cut into julienne strips (about ½ cup; *see Tip*)**
- **1 pound tilapia fillets, cut into 4 portions**
- **⅓ cup Chile-Garlic Dipping Sauce (*page 293*)**
- **1 bunch scallions, white and pale green parts only, thinly sliced**

1. Bring 1 to 2 inches of water to a boil in a pot large enough to hold a bamboo steamer. (If you don't have a steamer, improvise by setting mugs upside down in a large pot and resting a plate on top.)

2. Spread ginger on two heatproof plates that will fit into the steamer baskets while allowing steam to come up around the sides. Place tilapia on the ginger and set a plate in each steamer basket. Stack the baskets, cover and set over boiling water. Steam until the fish is opaque in the center, 8 to 10 minutes.

3. Meanwhile, prepare Chile-Garlic Dipping Sauce.

4. Carefully open the steamer baskets, tilting the lid away from you. With a slotted spatula, transfer the fish to serving plates, leaving the ginger behind. Sprinkle the tilapia with scallions and serve with the dipping sauce.

TEST KITCHEN TIP:
A gadget called a julienne peeler makes short work of cutting ingredients into julienne strips.

MAKES 4 SERVINGS.

PER SERVING: 145 CALORIES; 3 G FAT (0 G SAT, 1 G MONO); 48 MG CHOLESTEROL; 6 G CARBOHYDRATE; 22 G PROTEIN; 1 G FIBER; 359 MG SODIUM.

NUTRITION BONUS: 26 MG VITAMIN C (45% DV), 470 MG POTASSIUM (24% DV).

The Essential EatingWell Seafood Guide

	FISH OR SEAFOOD	MERCURY	OMEGA-3S	HARVEST NOTES
BEST CHOICES	ANCHOVIES	SAFE	RICH	Abundant
	CATFISH (farmed)	SAFE	Modest	Abundant
	CLAMS	SAFE	Modest	Abundant
	COD (Pacific)	[not available]	Modest	Abundant
	CRABS (except king)	1 meal/week	Modest	Abundant
	FLOUNDER (Pacific, Atlantic summer)	SAFE	Modest	Abundant
	HALIBUT (Pacific)	1 meal/month	Good	Abundant
	HERRING	1 meal/week	RICH	Abundant
	MACKERELS (except king)	SAFE	RICH	Abundant
	MAHI-MAHI (dorado)	1 meal/week	Modest	Abundant
	MUSSELS	SAFE	Modest	Abundant
	OYSTERS	SAFE	Very Good	Abundant
	POLLOCK	1 meal/month	Good	Abundant
	SALMON (farmed)	SAFE	RICH	Abundant
	SALMON (wild)	SAFE	RICH	Abundant
	SARDINES	SAFE	Very Good	Abundant
	SHRIMPS (farmed)	SAFE	Good	Abundant
	SOLE (Pacific)	SAFE	Modest	Abundant
	SQUIDS	SAFE	Modest	Abundant
	STRIPED BASS (farmed)	SAFE	Very Good	Abundant
	STURGEON (farmed)	SAFE	RICH	Abundant
	TILAPIA (farmed)	SAFE	Modest	Abundant
	TROUT (rainbow, farmed)	SAFE	Good	Abundant
	TUNA (canned, light)	SAFE	Good	Abundant
	TUNA (yellowfin, farmed)	SAFE	Good	Abundant
CAUTION ADVISED	BLUEFISH	1 meal/month	Very Good	Abundant
	CRABS (king)	1 meal/week	Modest	Regionally overfished
	LOBSTER (Maine)	1 meal/month	Modest	Abundant
	LOBSTER (northern/American)	1 meal/month	Modest	Regionally overfished
	LOBSTER (spiny/rock)	1 meal/week	Modest	Regionally overfished
	MONKFISH	[not available]	Modest	Overfished
	SCALLOPS	SAFE	Modest	Abundant / Regionally overfished
	SEA BASS (wild)	1 meal/month	Very Good	Abundant
	TUNA (canned, white)	1 meal/week	Very Good	Abundant
	TUNA (steaks)	1 meal/month	Very Good	Abundant
WORST CHOICES	CAVIAR (wild sturgeon)	[not available]	RICH	SEVERELY OVERFISHED
	CHILEAN SEA BASS	[not available]	[not available]	SEVERELY OVERFISHED
	COD (Atlantic)	1 meal/week	Modest	SEVERELY OVERFISHED
	FLOUNDER (Atlantic except summer)	SAFE	Modest	SEVERELY OVERFISHED
	GROUPER	1 meal/month	Modest	SEVERELY OVERFISHED
	HADDOCK	1 meal/week	Modest	SEVERELY OVERFISHED
	HALIBUT (Atlantic)	1 meal/month	Good	SEVERELY OVERFISHED
	MACKEREL (king)	AVOID	RICH	Abundant
	MARLIN	1 meal/month	Modest	SEVERELY OVERFISHED
	ORANGE ROUGHY	1 meal/month	[not available]	SEVERELY OVERFISHED / Destructive harvest
	PACIFIC ROCKFISH (Pacific snapper)	[not available]	[not available]	SEVERELY OVERFISHED
	SHARKS	AVOID	RICH	SEVERELY OVERFISHED / Destructive harvest
	SHRIMPS (wild, foreign)	SAFE	Good	Overfished / Destructive harvest
	SNAPPER (red)	1 meal/month	Modest	SEVERELY OVERFISHED
	SOLE (Atlantic)	SAFE	Modest	SEVERELY OVERFISHED
	SWORDFISH	AVOID	Modest	SEVERELY OVERFISHED / Destructive harvest
	TILEFISH	AVOID	[not available]	SEVERELY OVERFISHED
	TUNA (bluefin)	AVOID	RICH	SEVERELY OVERFISHED

Cioppino

PREP TIME: 30 MINUTES | **START TO FINISH:** 1 HOUR 10 MINUTES | **EASE OF PREPARATION:** MODERATE

What bouillabaisse is to Provence, cioppino is to San Francisco. The principle behind both fish stews is much the same: simmer the catch of the day in a rich broth, grab a soup spoon and enjoy. Like many classic cioppino recipes, this calls for red wine in the broth, but feel free to substitute white. The assortment of seafood can vary as well: little clams instead of mussels, scallops in place of shrimp. Serve with sourdough bread.

- 1 tablespoon extra-virgin olive oil
- 1 onion, chopped
- 1 green bell pepper, chopped
- 4 cloves garlic, finely chopped
- 1 cup dry red wine
- 1 14½-ounce can diced tomatoes
- 1 8-ounce bottle clam juice
- ½ cup chopped fresh parsley
- 1 bay leaf
- ½ teaspoon dried oregano
- ¼ teaspoon crushed red pepper
- 1 pound mussels, scrubbed and debearded
- 1 pound crab legs, cut into 4-inch pieces
- 1 pound medium shrimp (30-40 per pound), peeled and deveined
- 1 pound firm white fish fillet, such as cod, haddock or halibut
- ¼ cup chopped fresh basil
- Salt & freshly ground pepper to taste

1. Heat oil in a heavy soup pot or Dutch oven over medium heat. Add onion and green pepper; cook, stirring, until softened, about 5 minutes. Add garlic and cook until aromatic, about 1 minute. Stir in wine and bring to a boil; cook for 3 minutes, then add tomatoes, clam juice, parsley, bay leaf, oregano and crushed red pepper. Cover, leaving the lid slightly ajar; simmer, stirring occasionally, until the broth is rich and thick, 20 to 30 minutes.

2. Add mussels, cover and cook for 2 minutes. Remove the mussels with tongs as they open, reserving them in a large bowl. Discard any mussels that do not open. Add crab legs, return to a simmer and cook, uncovered, until the crab is heated through, about 5 minutes. Remove with tongs and reserve along with the mussels. Add shrimp, fish and chopped basil; cover and simmer until the shrimp turns pink and the fish is opaque, 2 to 3 minutes. Discard the bay leaf. Taste and adjust seasonings with salt and pepper. Return the reserved mussels and crab legs to the pot. Reheat briefly and serve.

MAKES 8 MAIN-DISH SERVINGS, ABOUT 1½ CUPS EACH.

PER SERVING: 308 CALORIES; 7 G FAT (1 G SAT, 2 G MONO); 151 MG CHOLESTEROL; 10 G CARBOHYDRATE; 45 G PROTEIN; 1 G FIBER; 846 MG SODIUM.

NUTRITION BONUS: 30 MG VITAMIN C (50% DV), 6 MG IRON (35% DV), 710 MG POTASSIUM (35% DV), 120 MG MAGNESIUM (30% DV), 79 MCG FOLATE (20% DV), 15% DV VITAMIN A.

Lower Carbs

Maryland Crab Cakes

PREP TIME: 30 MINUTES | **START TO FINISH:** 1¾ HOURS (INCLUDING CHILLING TIME) | **TO MAKE AHEAD:** PREPARE THROUGH STEP 2. COVER AND REFRIGERATE FOR UP TO 8 HOURS. | **EASE OF PREPARATION:** MODERATE

There are a few tricks to making wonderful crab cakes: Use fresh breadcrumbs made from good, solid sandwich bread to bind the patties and dredge them in dry breadcrumbs to create a beautiful crust. Season the cakes with plenty of fresh herbs and let them sit in the fridge for at least an hour before frying, so they hold together better in the skillet. Of course, use the best crab you can afford, but know that even canned crab will make a delectable crab cake.

- **1½ cups fresh white breadcrumbs (*see Tip*)**
- **12 ounces fresh *or* canned crabmeat (about 2 cups)**
- **2 tablespoons chopped fresh dill, plus sprigs for garnish**
- **2 tablespoons chopped fresh flat-leaf parsley**
- **1 scallion, thinly sliced**
- **2 teaspoons seafood seasoning, such as Old Bay**
- **¼ teaspoon salt, or to taste**
- **⅛ teaspoon freshly ground pepper**
- **1 large egg**
- **3 tablespoons reduced-fat mayonnaise**
- **1 tablespoon lemon juice**
- **2 teaspoons Dijon mustard**
- **⅓ cup unseasoned dry breadcrumbs**
- **1¼ cups Tarragon Tartar Sauce (*page 246*)**
- **4 teaspoons extra-virgin olive oil, divided**
- **Lemon wedges for garnish**

1. Mix fresh breadcrumbs and crabmeat in a large bowl. Add dill, parsley, scallion, seafood seasoning, salt and pepper; toss to mix well.

2. Whisk egg, mayonnaise, lemon juice and mustard in a small bowl until smooth. Drizzle over the crab mixture and stir well. Using your hands, form the mixture into six ½- to ¾-inch-thick patties (½ cup each). Dredge the patties in dry breadcrumbs and place on a small baking sheet lined with plastic wrap. Cover and refrigerate for 1 hour.

3. Meanwhile, make Tarragon Tartar Sauce.

4. Preheat oven to 450°F. Coat a baking sheet with cooking spray.

5. Heat 2 teaspoons oil in a large nonstick skillet over medium heat. Add 3 of the crab cakes and cook until the undersides are golden, 2 to 3 minutes. Using a wide spatula, turn cakes over onto the prepared baking sheet. Add the remaining 2 teaspoons oil to the skillet and repeat with the remaining 3 crab cakes. Bake crab cakes until golden on the second side and heated through, 15 to 20 minutes. Garnish with lemon wedges and dill sprigs and serve with Tarragon Tartar Sauce.

TO MAKE FRESH BREADCRUMBS: Trim crusts from firm sandwich bread. Tear bread into pieces and process in a food processor until coarse crumbs form. One slice of bread makes about ⅓ cup crumbs.

MAKES 6 SERVINGS.

PER SERVING: 263 CALORIES; 13 G FAT (2 G SAT, 5 G MONO); 87 MG CHOLESTEROL; 20 G CARBOHYDRATE; 15 G PROTEIN; 1 G FIBER; 979 MG SODIUM.

NUTRITION BONUS: 8 MG VITAMIN C (15% DV), 58 MCG FOLATE (15% DV).

Scallops with Peas & Pancetta

PREP TIME: 10 MINUTES | **START TO FINISH:** 25 MINUTES | **EASE OF PREPARATION:** MODERATE

Fresh peas and savory bacon are a perfect backdrop for delicate scallops. The secret to juicy, delicious scallops is to make sure that they sizzle as they go into the skillet—be sure the scallops are dry and the pan is hot. If you do not have a 12-inch skillet, cook the scallops in two batches, using 1½ teaspoons oil per batch.

- 1 ounce pancetta (*see Note*), finely chopped (about ¼ cup)
- 1 pound large sea scallops (about 15 scallops) (*see box, below*)
- ¼ teaspoon coarse kosher salt, or to taste
- Freshly ground pepper to taste
- 1 tablespoon extra-virgin olive oil
- ½ cup dry white wine
- ½ cup water
- 2 large shallots, finely chopped (about ½ cup)
- 2 cups frozen peas
- 3 tablespoons chopped fresh chives for garnish

1. Cook pancetta in a 12-inch nonstick skillet over medium heat, stirring frequently, until crisp, 3 to 4 minutes. Drain on paper towels. Do not wash the pan.
2. Rinse scallops and remove any tough white muscle attached to the sides. Pat dry and sprinkle both sides with salt and pepper. Heat oil in the pan over medium-high heat until very hot but not smoking; tilt to coat. Add scallops and cook until browned on both sides and opaque in the center, 1 to 1½ minutes per side. Transfer to a plate.
3. Add wine and water to the pan; stir to loosen any browned bits. Add shallots, reduce heat to medium and cook, stirring occasionally, until softened, 2 to 3 minutes. Stir in peas; cook, stirring occasionally, until tender, 2 to 3 minutes. Return the pancetta, the scallops and any accumulated juices to the pan; heat through. Sprinkle with chives and serve immediately.

INGREDIENT NOTE: Pancetta is an unsmoked Italian bacon usually found in the deli section of large supermarkets and specialty food stores. Regular bacon or turkey bacon may be substituted.

MAKES 4 SERVINGS, ABOUT ¾ CUP EACH.

PER SERVING: 231 CALORIES; 5 G FAT (1 G SAT, 3 G MONO); 42 MG CHOLESTEROL; 16 G CARBOHYDRATE; 25 G PROTEIN; 3 G FIBER; 470 MG SODIUM.

NUTRITION BONUS: 45% DV VITAMIN A, 18 MG VITAMIN C (30% DV), 583 MG POTASSIUM (29% DV), 90 MG MAGNESIUM (23% DV).

Buying Scallops

BE SURE TO REQUEST "DRY" scallops (i.e., not treated with sodium tripolyphosphate, or STP) from your fish store. Sea scallops that have been subjected to a chemical bath are not only mushy and less flavorful, but will not brown properly.

Lower Carbs

South Pacific Shrimp

PREP TIME: 25 MINUTES (INCLUDING PEELING SHRIMP) | **START TO FINISH:** 45 MINUTES

EASE OF PREPARATION: EASY

Vibrant Southeast Asian seasonings are a natural with shrimp. Freeze any leftover coconut milk or refrigerate it for several days; you can use it instead of broth or water to cook rice or enrich a curry.

MARINADE & SHRIMP

- ⅓ cup "lite" coconut milk (*see Ingredient Note, page 394*)
- 2 serrano chiles *or* jalapeño peppers, preferably red, seeded and minced
- 1 teaspoon minced fresh ginger
- 1 clove garlic, minced
- 2 teaspoons reduced-sodium soy sauce
- ¼ cup lime juice
- 1 tablespoon brown sugar
- 1 pound medium shrimp (30-40 per pound), peeled and deveined

SAUCE

- 1 teaspoon extra-virgin olive oil
- ½ cup diced seeded tomato
- 4 cups baby spinach

1. Combine coconut milk, chiles, ginger, garlic, soy sauce, lime juice and brown sugar in a medium bowl. Add shrimp and toss to coat. Cover and marinate in the refrigerator for 10 to 15 minutes, tossing occasionally. Drain well, reserving marinade.
2. Heat oil in a 12-inch nonstick skillet over medium-high heat. Add shrimp and cook, turning once, until barely pink, about 30 seconds per side; transfer to a plate. Add tomato and spinach to the pan; cook, stirring, until the spinach starts to wilt, about 30 seconds. Add the reserved marinade; simmer until the sauce thickens slightly, about 2 minutes. Return the shrimp and any accumulated juices to the pan; heat through. Serve immediately.

COOKING WITH FROZEN SHRIMP: Individually quick-frozen shrimp, sold in resealable bags, are convenient to keep in your freezer. Thaw in a covered bowl in the refrigerator. If you're in a hurry, place shrimp in a colander under cold running water for about 5 minutes.

MAKES 4 SERVINGS, 1 GENEROUS CUP EACH.

PER SERVING: 176 CALORIES; 5 G FAT (2 G SAT, 1 G MONO); 172 MG CHOLESTEROL; 9 G CARBOHYDRATE; 24 G PROTEIN; 1 G FIBER; 282 MG SODIUM.

NUTRITION BONUS: 40% DV VITAMIN A, 18 MG VITAMIN C (30% DV), 4 MG IRON (20% DV).

Asian Stir-Fried Shrimp with Snow Peas

PREP TIME: 20 MINUTES (INCLUDING 10 MINUTES TO DEVEIN SHRIMP)
START TO FINISH: 45 MINUTES (INCLUDING 15 MINUTES FOR MARINATING) | **EASE OF PREPARATION:** EASY

If snow peas or sugar snap peas don't look good at the market, feel free to substitute another crisp, mild-flavored green vegetable, such as sliced bok choy, green beans, zucchini or even celery (and in spring, try asparagus). Cooking time will vary with the vegetable, so watch carefully.

MARINADE & SHRIMP

- 2 tablespoons rice wine *or* dry sherry
- 1 tablespoon reduced-sodium soy sauce
- 1 teaspoon toasted sesame oil
- 1 teaspoon sugar
- 1 pound medium shrimp (30-40 per pound), peeled and deveined

STIR-FRY MIX

- 3 teaspoons peanut oil, divided
- 4 scallions, minced
- 1 tablespoon minced fresh ginger
- 2 cloves garlic, minced
- 2 cups snow peas *or* sugar snap peas, trimmed
- 2 tablespoons water
- 1 teaspoon cornstarch, dissolved in 1 tablespoon water
- 1/8-1/4 teaspoon crushed red pepper

1. **To marinate shrimp:** Combine wine (or sherry), soy sauce, sesame oil and sugar in a medium bowl. Add shrimp and toss to coat. Cover and refrigerate for 15 minutes, tossing occasionally. Drain well, reserving marinade. Pat shrimp dry with paper towels.
2. **To stir-fry shrimp & vegetables:** Heat 1 teaspoon peanut oil in a wok or large nonstick skillet over high heat. Add shrimp and stir-fry until barely pink, about 1 minute. Transfer to a plate. Reduce heat to medium-high and add the remaining 2 teaspoons oil to the wok. Add scallions, ginger and garlic; stir-fry until fragrant, about 30 seconds. Add peas; stir-fry until just crisp-tender, 3 to 5 minutes. Add the reserved marinade and water; cook, stirring, until simmering. Stir in the cornstarch mixture. Cook, stirring, until the sauce is slightly thickened, about 1 minute. Return the shrimp and any accumulated juices to the wok. Season to taste with crushed red pepper. Serve immediately.

SIZE MATTERS, SORT OF: There are no official standards for sizing shrimp: one market's "Jumbo" may be smaller than another's "Large." Instead, go by the number of shrimp per pound; a range of 30 to 40 per pound (sometimes labeled "U/40") works best in most recipes.

MAKES 4 SERVINGS, 1 CUP EACH.

PER SERVING: 165 CALORIES; 6 G FAT (1 G SAT, 2 G MONO); 168 MG CHOLESTEROL; 6 G CARBOHYDRATE; 20 G PROTEIN; 1 G FIBER; 331 MG SODIUM.

NUTRITION BONUS: 20 MG VITAMIN C (35% DV), 4 MG IRON (20% DV), 15% DV VITAMIN A.

Margarita Shrimp Salad

PREP TIME: 20 MINUTES | **START TO FINISH:** 30 MINUTES | **EASE OF PREPARATION:** MODERATE

The flavors of a margarita—tequila, orange and lime—are blended in a tossed salad of fresh shrimp, diced avocado and sliced red onion, spiked with a creamy, spicy sour cream dressing. Don't shy away from avocados because they're high in calories—avocados are rich in good, heart-healthy fat, as well as vitamin E, folate, potassium and other important nutrients.

- 1 pound medium shrimp (30-40 per pound), peeled and deveined
- ¼ cup tequila
- 2 teaspoons freshly grated orange zest, preferably organic
- 1 teaspoon freshly grated lime zest
- ½ teaspoon salt, or to taste
- ¼ cup thinly slivered red onion
- ½ cup Creamy Lime-Chile Dressing (*page 267*)
- 4 cups torn romaine lettuce
- 2 medium endives, cored and torn into pieces (2 cups)
- 1 orange, peeled and cut into segments (*see Cooking Tip, page 397*)
- 2 ripe Hass avocados, peeled, pitted and cut into ½-inch cubes
- 1 tablespoon fresh lime juice (*see Tip*)
- 1 tablespoon extra-virgin olive oil
- Lime wedges

1. Toss shrimp, tequila, orange zest, lime zest and salt in a medium bowl. Cover and marinate in the refrigerator for 10 minutes, stirring occasionally. Place onion in a small bowl, cover with cold water and some ice; let stand for 10 minutes, or until ready to use.

2. Meanwhile, make Creamy Lime-Chile Dressing.

3. Toss romaine, endive, orange segments and drained onion in a large bowl. Add dressing and toss to coat. Divide among 4 plates. Toss avocados with lime juice and divide among the servings.

4. Drain the shrimp, reserving the marinade. Heat oil in a large skillet over medium-high heat. Add the shrimp and sauté until pink and firm, 2 to 3 minutes. Divide among the salads. Add the reserved marinade to the skillet and bring to a boil, stirring; spoon over shrimp. Serve with lime wedges for squeezing.

TO JUICE A LIME:
A lime at room temperature gives the most juice (1½-2 tablespoons). Before juicing, roll the lime on the counter, pressing down with your hand. If the recipe calls for both zest and juice, grate the zest before squeezing the juice.

MAKES 4 SERVINGS, ABOUT 2 CUPS EACH.

PER SERVING: 407 CALORIES; 22 G FAT (4 G SAT, 12 G MONO); 181 MG CHOLESTEROL; 22 G CARBOHYDRATE; 27 G PROTEIN; 10 G FIBER; 633 MG SODIUM.

NUTRITION BONUS: 56 MG VITAMIN C (90% DV), 80% DV VITAMIN A, 1,019 MG POTASSIUM (51% DV), 169 MCG FOLATE (42% DV), 39% DV FIBER, 4 MG IRON (25% DV), 89 MG MAGNESIUM (22% DV), 144 MG CALCIUM (15% DV).

CREAMY LIME-CHILE DRESSING

PREP TIME: 5 MINUTES | **START TO FINISH:** 5 MINUTES | **TO MAKE AHEAD:** THE DRESSING WILL KEEP, COVERED, IN THE REFRIGERATOR FOR UP TO 2 DAYS. | **EASE OF PREPARATION:** EASY

In addition to the Margarita Shrimp Salad, you can use this zingy dressing to make low-fat Caesar salad with romaine, croutons and Parmesan shavings. It also works well as a marinade for chicken.

- 6 tablespoons reduced-fat sour cream
- 3 tablespoons fresh lime juice
- 2 teaspoons minced seeded jalapeño *or* serrano pepper
- 1 teaspoon chili powder
- 1 teaspoon sugar
- ¼ teaspoon salt, or to taste

Whisk all ingredients in a small bowl.

MAKES ABOUT ½ CUP.

PER TABLESPOON: 20 CALORIES; 1 G FAT (1 G SAT, 0 G MONO); 4 MG CHOLESTEROL; 2 G CARBOHYDRATE; 0 G PROTEIN; 0 G FIBER; 81 MG SODIUM.

Sizzled Citrus Shrimp

Healthy Weight

Lower Carbs

PREP TIME: 15 MINUTES (INCLUDING PEELING SHRIMP) | **START TO FINISH:** 40 MINUTES | **EASE OF PREPARATION:** EASY

This quick Spanish-inspired sauté is a lesson in simplicity. All shrimp really needs to dazzle is lots of garlic and a splash of lemon. Serve as a main dish or as a *tapa* (appetizer).

MARINADE & SHRIMP

- 3 tablespoons lemon juice
- 3 tablespoons dry white wine
- 2 teaspoons extra-virgin olive oil
- 3 cloves garlic, minced
- 1 pound medium shrimp (30-40 per pound), peeled and deveined

SAUCE

- 1 teaspoon extra-virgin olive oil
- 1 bay leaf
- ¼ teaspoon crushed red pepper
- ¼ teaspoon salt, or to taste
- 2 tablespoons chopped fresh parsley

1. Combine lemon juice, wine, 2 teaspoons oil and garlic in a medium bowl. Add shrimp and toss to coat. Cover and marinate in the refrigerator for 15 minutes, tossing occasionally. Drain well, reserving marinade.

2. Heat 1 teaspoon oil in a 12-inch nonstick skillet over medium-high heat. Add shrimp and cook, turning once, until barely pink, about 30 seconds per side; transfer to a plate. Add bay leaf, crushed red pepper and the reserved marinade to the pan; simmer for 4 minutes. Return the shrimp and any accumulated juices to the pan; heat through. Season with salt, sprinkle with parsley and serve immediately.

MAKES 4 SERVINGS, ABOUT ¾ CUP EACH.

PER SERVING: 171 CALORIES; 6 G FAT (1 G SAT, 3 G MONO); 172 MG CHOLESTEROL; 4 G CARBOHYDRATE; 23 G PROTEIN; 1 G FIBER; 315 MG SODIUM.

NUTRITION BONUS: 15% DV VITAMIN A, 9 MG VITAMIN C (15% DV).

Shrimp & Vegetable Paella

PREP TIME: 30 MINUTES | **START TO FINISH:** 1 HOUR 5 MINUTES | **TO MAKE AHEAD:** PREPARE THROUGH STEP 1; COVER AND REFRIGERATE FOR UP TO 8 HOURS. REHEAT BEFORE PROCEEDING. | **EASE OF PREPARATION:** MODERATE

This easy one-dish meal, made from supermarket ingredients, has a fair amount of flexibility. The shrimp can be small, medium or large, as long as they feel and look fresh. If red peppers are too dear, use all green and garnish the rice with roasted peppers from a jar.

- **4 teaspoons extra-virgin olive oil, divided**
- **½ pound medium shrimp (30-40 per pound), peeled and patted dry**
- **1 large Bermuda *or* Spanish onion, quartered and thinly sliced**
- **1 large red bell pepper, thinly sliced**
- **1 large green bell pepper, thinly sliced**
- **1-2 teaspoons minced seeded jalapeño pepper**
- **4 large tomatoes, peeled, seeded and chopped**
- **1 medium zucchini, diced**
- **2 cloves garlic, minced**
- **1 tablespoon chopped fresh thyme *or* 1 teaspoon dried**
- **1½ teaspoons paprika**
- **Salt & freshly ground pepper to taste**
- **1¼ cups medium-grain white rice, preferably arborio**
- **2 cups reduced-sodium chicken broth**
- **2 tablespoons finely chopped fresh parsley for garnish**
- **1 lemon, cut in wedges, for garnish**

1. Heat 2 teaspoons oil in a 12-inch-wide, deep, heavy skillet over medium-high heat. Add shrimp and sauté until barely pink, 1 to 2 minutes. Transfer to a plate, cover and set aside in the refrigerator.

2. Add the remaining 2 teaspoons oil to the skillet and add onion, bell peppers and jalapeño. Reduce the heat to medium and cook, stirring often, until the vegetables are tender, about 10 minutes. Add tomatoes, zucchini, garlic, thyme and paprika. Season lightly with salt and pepper and simmer, covered, for 10 minutes.

3. Add rice and stir to coat well with the tomato mixture. Add broth and bring to a boil. Reduce the heat to low and simmer, covered, for 20 to 25 minutes, or until the rice is almost tender.

4. Add the reserved shrimp to the paella and simmer for 5 minutes more. Taste and adjust seasonings. Garnish with parsley and lemon wedges and serve hot.

MAKES 5 SERVINGS.

PER SERVING: 328 CALORIES; 5 G FAT (1 G SAT, 3 G MONO); 69 MG CHOLESTEROL; 54 G CARBOHYDRATE; 17 G PROTEIN; 4 G FIBER; 361 MG SODIUM.

NUTRITION BONUS: 118 MG VITAMIN C (200% DV), 80% DV VITAMIN A, 830 MG POTASSIUM (42% DV), 164 MCG FOLATE (41% DV), 5 MG IRON (25% DV), 18% DV FIBER.

Athenian Orzo

PREP TIME: 25 MINUTES | **START TO FINISH:** 50 MINUTES | **EASE OF PREPARATION:** MODERATE

Orzo, a rice-shaped pasta, makes a delightful base for an authentically Greek combination of shrimp, tomatoes and feta. To serve as a side dish, omit the shrimp and drain the tomatoes before adding them.

- 1½ teaspoons extra-virgin olive oil
- 1 small onion, chopped
- 4 cloves garlic, minced
- ¼ cup dry white wine
- 1 28-ounce can diced tomatoes
- 3 tablespoons chopped fresh parsley, divided
- 1 tablespoon drained capers
- ½ teaspoon dried oregano
- ½ teaspoon dried basil
- ½ teaspoon salt, or to taste
- Freshly ground pepper to taste
- Pinch of crushed red pepper
- 1 pound medium shrimp (30-40 per pound), peeled
- 1 cup orzo
- ½ cup crumbled feta cheese

1. Preheat oven to 450°F. Coat a 9-by-13-inch (or other 2-quart) baking dish with cooking spray. Put a large pot of lightly salted water on to boil.
2. Heat oil in a 2-quart saucepan over medium heat. Add onion and garlic and cook, stirring, until softened, 3 to 4 minutes. Add wine and boil for about 1 minute. Stir in tomatoes, 1½ tablespoons parsley, capers, oregano, basil, salt, pepper and crushed red pepper; cook for 5 minutes. Drop in shrimp and cook, stirring, until barely pink, about 2½ minutes.
3. Cook orzo in the boiling water until tender but still firm, 10 minutes. Drain and transfer to the prepared baking dish. Toss with the tomato-shrimp sauce. Sprinkle with feta and the remaining 1½ tablespoons parsley.
4. Bake, uncovered, until the feta is bubbly, about 10 minutes.

MAKES 4 SERVINGS.

PER SERVING: 397 CALORIES; 9 G FAT (4 G SAT, 3 G MONO); 189 MG CHOLESTEROL; 44 G CARBOHYDRATE; 34 G PROTEIN; 4 G FIBER; 991 MG SODIUM.

NUTRITION BONUS: 26 MG VITAMIN C (45% DV), 730 MG POTASSIUM (37% DV), 7 MG IRON (35% DV), 124 MCG FOLATE (31% DV), 243 MG CALCIUM (25% DV), 97 MG MAGNESIUM (24% DV), 15% DV VITAMIN A, 15% DV FIBER.

MEAT

13

Red meat once carried a red flag. Now protein is king. Where will conventional wisdom wander next? It doesn't matter, if you follow a moderate course. A juicy steak, a meaty pork chop or a hearty lamb stew offers easily absorbed iron, zinc and B vitamins along with the sense of satiety that can make maintaining a sensible diet easier. Our approach is to use leaner cuts (which limits health-compromising fat and temper it with healthier monounsaturated fat), watch portions and serve with lots of vegetables. Though purveyors of steak-and-bacon–centered diets are now belatedly warning their customers of the perils of saturated fat, our richly distinctive meat entrees will never create cause for alarm.

Spicy Orange Beef & Broccoli Stir-Fry

PREP TIME: 10 MINUTES | **START TO FINISH:** 30 MINUTES | **EASE OF PREPARATION:** EASY

Hints of orange and a touch of heat dress up a classic combination. Serve with rice.

- **3 oranges**
- **3 tablespoons reduced-sodium soy sauce**
- **1 tablespoon Chinese rice wine *or* dry sherry**
- **1 tablespoon cornstarch**
- **½ teaspoon sugar**
- **3 teaspoons peanut oil *or* canola oil, divided**
- **1 pound beef sirloin, trimmed and sliced against the grain into ⅛-inch-thick slices**
- **2 tablespoons minced garlic**
- **2 tablespoons minced fresh ginger**
- **6-8 small dried red chiles**
- **2 pounds broccoli, cut into small florets (6 cups)**
- **⅓ cup water**
- **1 red bell pepper, seeded and sliced**
- **½ cup sliced scallion greens**

1. With a small sharp knife or vegetable peeler, carefully pare wide strips of zest from one of the oranges. Cut zest into 1-inch strips and set aside. Squeeze juice from all the oranges into a small bowl (for about ¾ cup). Add soy sauce, rice wine (or sherry), cornstarch and sugar and stir to combine; set aside.

2. In a wok or large skillet, heat 1 teaspoon oil over high heat until almost smoking. Add beef and stir-fry just until no longer pink on the outside, about 1 minute. Transfer to a plate lined with paper towels and set aside.

3. Add the remaining 2 teaspoons oil to the pan and heat until very hot. Add garlic, ginger, chiles and the reserved orange zest; stir-fry until fragrant, about 30 seconds. Add broccoli and water. Cover and steam, stirring occasionally, until the water has evaporated and the broccoli sizzles, about 3 minutes. Add bell pepper and stir-fry for 1 minute more.

4. Stir the reserved orange sauce and pour it into the wok. Bring to a boil, stirring; cook until the sauce has thickened slightly, 1 to 2 minutes. Add scallion greens and the reserved beef and toss to coat with sauce; heat through.

TEST KITCHEN TIP

Freezing the beef sirloin for 30 minutes makes it easier to cut into very thin slices.

MAKES 6 SERVINGS, GENEROUS 1 CUP EACH.

PER SERVING: 232 CALORIES; 6 G FAT (2 G SAT, 2 G MONO); 32 MG CHOLESTEROL; 25 G CARBOHYDRATE; 23 G PROTEIN; 9 G FIBER; 353 MG SODIUM.

NUTRITION BONUS: 238 MG VITAMIN C (400% DV), 130% DV VITAMIN A, 36% DV FIBER, 4 MG IRON (20% DV), 138 MG CALCIUM (15% DV).

Lower Carbs

Grilled Sirloin Salad

PREP TIME: 10 MINUTES | **START TO FINISH:** 25 MINUTES | **EASE OF PREPARATION:** EASY

Pepper-crusted steak, grill-charred vegetables and sesame-ginger dressing turn fresh salad greens into an exciting main course.

- **1 clove garlic, minced**
- **2 tablespoons reduced-sodium soy sauce**
- **2 tablespoons balsamic vinegar**
- **2 teaspoons toasted sesame oil**
- **2 teaspoons brown sugar**
- **1 teaspoon chopped fresh ginger**
- **2 teaspoons black peppercorns, crushed**
- **1 12-ounce sirloin steak, trimmed**
- **Salt to taste**
- **16 scallions, white part only**
- **1 red bell pepper, halved lengthwise and seeded**
- **12 cups torn salad greens, such as escarole, curly endive, radicchio *or* watercress**

1. Preheat grill to high.
2. Combine garlic, soy sauce, vinegar, oil, brown sugar and ginger in a blender or food processor; blend until smooth. Set aside.
3. Press peppercorns into both sides of sirloin. Season with salt. Place the sirloin, scallions and bell pepper halves on the grill and cook for 4 minutes. Turn over and cook until the meat is medium-rare and the vegetables are slightly charred, about 4 minutes more.
4. Let sirloin rest for 5 minutes, then slice thinly, against the grain. Cut scallions into 1-inch pieces. Slice the pepper lengthwise into strips.
5. Toss greens with the reserved dressing in a large bowl. Arrange on a platter or 4 plates. Top with sirloin and grilled vegetables. Serve immediately.

MAKES 4 SERVINGS.

PER SERVING: 190 CALORIES; 7 G FAT (2 G SAT, 3 G MONO); 48 MG CHOLESTEROL; 14 G CARBOHYDRATE; 20 G PROTEIN; 5 G FIBER; 416 MG SODIUM.

NUTRITION BONUS: 105 MG VITAMIN C (170% DV), 120% DV VITAMIN A, 805 MG POTASSIUM (40% DV), 156 MCG FOLATE (39% DV), 4 MG ZINC (27% DV), 4 MG IRON (20% DV), 18% DV FIBER.

Japanese-Inspired Beef & Noodle Salad

PREP TIME: 10 MINUTES | **START TO FINISH:** 40 MINUTES | **TO MAKE AHEAD:** PREPARE RECIPE THROUGH STEP 3 UP TO 2 HOURS AHEAD. COVER AND REFRIGERATE. | **EASE OF PREPARATION:** MODERATE

Sirloin steak, soba noodles (Japanese buckwheat noodles) and shredded carrots make this healthful, aromatic salad a sophisticated treat any night of the week.

- **3 tablespoons mirin** (*see Note*)
- **1 teaspoon ground ginger**
- **1 12-ounce sirloin steak, trimmed**
- **⅔ cup Sesame-Soy Dressing** (*page 275*)
- **4 ounces soba noodles** (*see Ingredient Note, page 396*)
- **1 cup finely shredded or julienned carrot (1 large)**
- **4 cups mesclun** *or* **other assorted salad greens**
- **1 tablespoon sesame seeds, toasted** (*see Tip, page 83*)

1. Whisk mirin and ginger in a small bowl. Place steak in a shallow baking dish or pie pan. Pour mirin mixture over the steak; turn to coat. Cover and marinate in the refrigerator for at least 30 minutes or for up to 2 hours, turning occasionally.

2. Put a large pot of salted water on to boil for cooking noodles. Make Sesame-Soy Dressing.

3. Cook noodles in the boiling water until just tender, about 6 minutes. Drain; rinse under cold water. Transfer noodles to a large bowl. Add carrot and ⅓ cup Sesame-Soy Dressing; toss to coat.

4. Prepare a grill. Lightly oil the grill rack by rubbing it with an oil-soaked paper towel (use tongs to hold the paper towel). Grill the steak for 4 to 6 minutes per side for medium-rare, or until it reaches desired doneness. (*Alternatively, brush a little canola oil over a large skillet or ridged grill pan, preferably cast-iron, and heat over high heat. Add steak and cook for 4 to 6 minutes per side.*) Transfer the steak to a cutting board. Let rest for 5 minutes, then slice thinly against the grain.

5. Build the salad on 4 plates starting with about 1 cup mixed greens, one-fourth of the noodle mixture, then one-fourth of the steak slices. Whisk remaining dressing again to combine, then drizzle about 4 teaspoons over each salad. Sprinkle with sesame seeds and serve immediately.

INGREDIENT NOTE:
Mirin is a sweetened rice wine, made from glutinous rice, found in the Asian aisle of many supermarkets and in Asian markets.

MAKES 4 SERVINGS, ABOUT 2¼ CUPS EACH.

PER SERVING: 390 CALORIES; 15 G FAT (3 G SAT, 7 G MONO); 76 MG CHOLESTEROL; 31 G CARBOHYDRATE; 32 G PROTEIN; 2 G FIBER; 714 MG SODIUM.

NUTRITION BONUS: 100% DV VITAMIN A, 7 MG ZINC (47% DV), 710 MG POTASSIUM (36% DV), 5 MG IRON (30% DV), 98 MCG FOLATE (25% DV), 83 MG MAGNESIUM (21% DV), 10 MG VITAMIN C (15% DV).

SESAME-SOY DRESSING

PREP TIME: 5 MINUTES | **START TO FINISH:** 5 MINUTES | **TO MAKE AHEAD:** THE DRESSING WILL KEEP, COVERED, IN THE REFRIGERATOR FOR UP TO 2 DAYS. | **EASE OF PREPARATION:** EASY

Green tea cuts the saltiness in this soy sauce-based dressing. You can also use it as a dipping sauce or as a sauce for fish.

- **3 tablespoons reduced-sodium soy sauce**
- **3 tablespoons strong brewed green tea *or* black tea**
- **2 tablespoons rice vinegar (*see Note*)**
- **1 tablespoon canola oil**
- **1 tablespoon toasted sesame oil**

Whisk all ingredients in a small bowl.

MAKES ABOUT ⅔ CUP.

PER TABLESPOON: 25 CALORIES; 3 G FAT (0 G SAT, 1 G MONO); 0 MG CHOLESTEROL; 0 G CARBOHYDRATE; 0 G PROTEIN; 0 G FIBER; 146 MG SODIUM.

INGREDIENT NOTE: Rice vinegar is a mild vinegar made from glutinous rice; bottlings range from clear to aged (very dark). Clear rice vinegar works best in this recipe. Substitute cider vinegar in a pinch.

Mini Meatloaves

PREP TIME: 10 MINUTES | **START TO FINISH:** 40 MINUTES | **EASE OF PREPARATION:** EASY

Traditional meatloaf is made with ground beef, pork and veal; here we replace the veal with ground turkey for a tender, flavorful and leaner version of the classic. Baking individual portions in muffin tins speeds cooking, standardizes serving size and produces a moist, delicious main dish.

- **8 ounces lean ground beef**
- **8 ounces lean ground pork**
- **8 ounces ground turkey breast**
- **1 large egg, lightly beaten**
- **¼ cup quick-cooking oats**
- **¼ cup chopped fresh parsley**
- **¼ cup ketchup, divided**
- **3 tablespoons 1% milk**
- **1 small onion, chopped (¾ cup)**
- **¾ teaspoon salt, or to taste**
- **⅛ teaspoon freshly ground pepper**
- **1½ teaspoons Worcestershire sauce**

1. Preheat oven to 375°F. Coat 8 muffin cups with cooking spray.
2. Mix beef, pork, turkey, egg, oats, parsley, 2 tablespoons ketchup, milk, onion, salt and pepper in a large bowl.
3. Form the mixture into 8 balls and place in the prepared muffin cups. Combine the remaining 2 tablespoons ketchup and Worcestershire sauce and spread about ½ teaspoon over each mini meatloaf.
4. Place the muffin pan on a baking sheet. Bake the meatloaves until their internal temperature reaches 160°F, 25 to 30 minutes. Pour off fat before serving.

MAKES 8 SERVINGS.

PER SERVING: 184 CALORIES; 10 G FAT (3 G SAT, 4 G MONO); 78 MG CHOLESTEROL; 5 G CARBOHYDRATE; 18 G PROTEIN; 1 G FIBER; 387 MG SODIUM.

NUTRITION BONUS: 31 MCG VITAMIN K (39% DV), 313 MG POTASSIUM (16% DV).

London Broil with Cherry-Balsamic Sauce

PREP TIME: 10 MINUTES | **START TO FINISH:** 50 MINUTES (INCLUDING MARINATING TIME) | **TO MAKE AHEAD:** THE MEAT CAN MARINATE, COVERED, IN THE REFRIGERATOR, FOR UP TO 8 HOURS. | **EASE OF PREPARATION:** EASY

London broil is a thicker cut of steak that benefits from the tenderizing effects of a marinade. Ours does its job and then doubles as a sauce when simmered with some shallots. Use any steak leftovers on top of a salad or in a sandwich with fresh spinach leaves.

- 1/3 cup dry red wine
- 1/4 cup balsamic vinegar
- 2 tablespoons cherry preserves
- 2 cloves garlic, minced
- 1/2 teaspoon salt
- Freshly ground pepper to taste
- 1 1/2 pounds London broil, trimmed
- 3 tablespoons finely chopped shallot
- 1 teaspoon extra-virgin olive oil
- 2 teaspoons butter

1. Whisk wine, vinegar, cherry preserves, garlic, salt and pepper in a small bowl. Place meat in a shallow glass dish. Pour the marinade over the meat and turn to coat. Cover and marinate in the refrigerator, turning several times, for at least 20 minutes or up to 8 hours.
2. Remove the meat from the marinade. Pour the marinade into a small saucepan; add shallot and set aside. Brush a ridged grill pan (*see Note*) or heavy skillet with oil; heat over medium-high heat. Add the meat and cook for 10 to 12 minutes per side for medium-rare, depending on thickness, or until it reaches desired doneness. (It may appear that the meat is burning but don't worry, it will form a pleasant crust.) Transfer the meat to a cutting board; let rest for 5 minutes.
3. While the meat is cooking, bring the marinade to a boil; cook over medium-high heat for 5 to 7 minutes, or until it is reduced to about 1/2 cup. Remove from the heat; add butter and whisk until melted.
4. Slice the meat thinly against the grain. Add any juices on the cutting board to the sauce. Serve the meat with the sauce.

EQUIPMENT NOTE:
A ridged grill pan is great for indoor grilling, but you can use the broiler or, if weather permits, cook the steak on an outdoor grill.

MAKES 6 SERVINGS.

PER SERVING: 216 CALORIES; 8 G FAT (3 G SAT, 3 G MONO); 41 MG CHOLESTEROL; 7 G CARBOHYDRATE; 25 G PROTEIN; 0 G FIBER; 260 MG SODIUM.

NUTRITION BONUS: 5 MG ZINC (33% DV), 429 MG POTASSIUM (21% DV).

Ultimate Beef Chili

PREP TIME: 40 MINUTES | **START TO FINISH:** 3¼ HOURS
TO MAKE AHEAD: THE CHILI WILL KEEP, COVERED, IN THE REFRIGERATOR FOR UP TO 2 DAYS OR IN THE FREEZER FOR UP TO 2 MONTHS. | **EASE OF PREPARATION:** MODERATE

Offer garnishes, such as reduced-fat sour cream and grated Cheddar cheese (about 1 tablespoon each per person), chopped scallions and chopped fresh tomatoes. Serve with warmed corn tortillas and a green salad topped with orange slices.

- 1 pound beef round, trimmed and cut into ½-inch chunks
- Salt & freshly ground pepper to taste
- 1½ tablespoons canola oil, divided
- 3 onions, chopped
- 1 green bell pepper, seeded and chopped
- 1 red bell pepper, seeded and chopped
- 6 cloves garlic, minced
- 2 jalapeño peppers, seeded and finely chopped
- 2 tablespoons ground cumin
- 2 tablespoons chili powder
- 1 tablespoon paprika
- 2 teaspoons dried oregano
- 12 ounces dark *or* light beer
- 1 28-ounce can diced tomatoes
- 8 sun-dried tomatoes (*not* packed in oil), snipped into small pieces
- 2 bay leaves
- 3 19-ounce cans dark kidney beans, rinsed
- ¼ cup chopped fresh cilantro
- 2 tablespoons lime juice

VARIATION: For a hot, smoky chili, add 1 tablespoon chopped chipotle pepper in adobo sauce.

1. Season beef with salt and pepper. In a Dutch oven, heat ½ tablespoon oil over medium-high heat. Add half the beef and sauté until browned on all sides, 2 to 5 minutes. Transfer to a plate lined with paper towels. Repeat with another ½ tablespoon oil and remaining beef; set aside.

2. Reduce heat to medium and add remaining ½ tablespoon oil. Add onions and bell peppers; cook, stirring frequently, until onions are golden brown, 10 to 20 minutes. Add garlic, jalapeños, cumin, chili powder, paprika and oregano. Stir until aromatic, about 2 minutes.

3. Add beer and simmer, scraping up any browned bits, for about 3 minutes. Add diced tomatoes, sun-dried tomatoes, bay leaves and reserved beef. Cover and simmer, stirring occasionally, until beef is very tender, 1½ to 2 hours.

4. Add beans; cook, covered, stirring occasionally, until chili has thickened, 30 to 45 minutes. Remove bay leaves. Stir in cilantro and lime juice. Adjust seasoning with salt and pepper.

MAKES 12 SERVINGS, 1 CUP EACH.

PER SERVING: 235 CALORIES; 4 G FAT (1 G SAT, 2 G MONO); 17 MG CHOLESTEROL; 34 G CARBOHYDRATE; 19 G PROTEIN; 10 G FIBER; 456 MG SODIUM.

NUTRITION BONUS: 52 MG VITAMIN C (90% DV), 38% DV FIBER, 35% DV VITAMIN A, 4 MG IRON (20% DV).

Lower Carbs

The Best Brisket

PREP TIME: 30 MINUTES | **START TO FINISH:** 7¾ HOURS (INCLUDING CHILLING & REHEATING TIME)
TO MAKE AHEAD: PREPARE THROUGH STEP 6; THE BRISKET WILL KEEP, COVERED, IN THE REFRIGERATOR FOR UP TO 2 DAYS. | **EASE OF PREPARATION:** MODERATE

Start early in the morning or plan to make the brisket a day or two ahead. Not only does the flavor improve over time, it's easier to trim the fat and carve the meat while the pan juices and brisket are cold. Just allow time to reheat before serving.

- **3 large onions, chopped**
- **1 clove garlic, peeled and halved**
- **1 4- to 5-pound beef brisket**
- **2 teaspoons salt, or to taste**
- **½ teaspoon freshly ground pepper**
- **1 tablespoon canola *or* extra-virgin olive oil**
- **1 14½-ounce can diced tomatoes**
- **2 cups dry red wine**
- **2 stalks celery with leaves, chopped**
- **1 bay leaf**
- **1 sprig fresh thyme**
- **1 sprig fresh rosemary**
- **8 carrots, peeled and cut into ½-inch diagonal slices**
- **¼ cup chopped fresh parsley**

1. Preheat oven to 325°F.
2. Place onions and garlic in a 5- to 6-quart casserole.
3. Season brisket with salt and pepper. In a large skillet, heat oil over high heat. Sear brisket until browned, 3 to 4 minutes per side. Place fat-side-up on top of onions. Add tomatoes and their juice, breaking them up with a fork. Add wine, celery, bay leaf, thyme and rosemary.
4. Cover casserole and bake for 3 hours, basting with pan juices every ½ hour.
5. Add carrots and parsley. Bake, uncovered, until carrots and brisket are tender, 30 minutes more.
6. Let brisket cool in pan; cover and refrigerate until chilled, for 3 hours or overnight.
7. About an hour before serving, preheat oven to 350°F.
8. Transfer brisket to a cutting board and trim off any visible fat. Slice against the grain into ¼-inch slices.
9. Skim fat from pan juices. Warm juices and vegetables over medium heat. Transfer brisket to a shallow roasting pan or baking dish and spoon juices and vegetables on top. Cover tightly with foil.
10. Bake the brisket until heated through, 40 to 45 minutes.

MAKES 12 SERVINGS, PLUS LEFTOVERS.

PER SERVING: 303 CALORIES; 11 G FAT (3 G SAT, 5 G MONO); 89 MG CHOLESTEROL; 10 G CARBOHYDRATE; 34 G PROTEIN; 2 G FIBER; 579 MG SODIUM.

NUTRITION BONUS: 100% DV VITAMIN A, 843 MG POTASSIUM (42% DV), 4 MG IRON (20% DV).

Slow-Cooker Pot Roast with Caramelized Onion Gravy

PREP TIME: 20 MINUTES | **SLOW-COOKER TIME:** 4½ HOURS | **TO MAKE AHEAD:** POT ROAST WILL KEEP, COVERED, IN THE REFRIGERATOR FOR UP TO 2 DAYS. REHEAT MEAT IN GRAVY. | **EASE OF PREPARATION:** EASY

Soft, sweet onions, coffee and balsamic vinegar make a tantalizing gravy for this tender, succulent pot roast. Serve with roasted carrots and parsnips and mashed potatoes.

- **1 4-pound boneless top *or* bottom round beef roast, trimmed of fat, twine on**
- **Salt & freshly ground pepper to taste**
- **1 tablespoon extra-virgin olive oil, divided**
- **2 large onions, thinly sliced**
- **4 cloves garlic, minced**
- **1 teaspoon dried thyme leaves**
- **½ cup brewed coffee *or* 1 teaspoon instant coffee granules dissolved in ½ cup boiling water**
- **2 tablespoons balsamic vinegar**
- **2 tablespoons cornstarch mixed with 2 tablespoons water**

1. Season beef with salt and pepper. Heat ½ tablespoon oil in a large heavy skillet over medium-high heat. Add beef and sear until well browned on all sides, about 5 minutes. Transfer to a 4-quart slow cooker.

2. Add remaining ½ tablespoon oil to skillet; reduce heat to medium. Add onions and cook, stirring, until softened and golden, 5 to 7 minutes. Add garlic and thyme; cook, stirring, for 1 minute more. Stir in coffee and vinegar; pour onion mixture over beef.

3. Cover and cook on high until beef is tender but not falling apart, about 4½ hours. Transfer beef to a cutting board, tent with foil and let rest for about 10 minutes.

4. Meanwhile, pour juices from slow cooker into a medium saucepan. Skim off fat. Bring to a boil over medium-high heat. Add the cornstarch mixture to the pan. Cook, whisking constantly, until gravy has thickened slightly, about 1 minute. Season with salt and pepper.

5. Remove twine from beef and carve. Serve with gravy.

MAKES ABOUT 12 SERVINGS, WITH 4 CUPS GRAVY.

PER SERVING: 174 CALORIES; 6 G FAT (2 G SAT, 3 G MONO); 67 MG CHOLESTEROL; 4 G CARBOHYDRATE; 32 G PROTEIN; 0 G FIBER; 99 MG SODIUM.

NUTRITION BONUS: 4 MG ZINC (27% DV), 3 MG IRON (15% DV).

Wine-Braised Beef Stew

PREP TIME: 30 MINUTES | **START TO FINISH:** 4¼ HOURS | **TO MAKE AHEAD:** THE STEW WILL KEEP, COVERED, IN THE REFRIGERATOR FOR UP TO 2 DAYS OR IN THE FREEZER FOR UP TO 3 MONTHS. | **EASE OF PREPARATION:** MODERATE

Plenty of rich, slightly soupy gravy makes this vegetable-packed stew perfect for serving with noodles, barley or crusty bread. We like the stovetop-to-oven method, as the slow, even heat of the oven is easy to control. But if you prefer, use the all-stovetop variation given at the end of the recipe; just keep an eye on the pot to make sure the stew doesn't rise above a bare simmer.

- **1 tablespoon extra-virgin olive oil**
- **1½ pounds beef chuck, trimmed and cut into 1½-inch pieces**
- **8 ounces mushrooms, trimmed, wiped clean and quartered**
- **1 medium onion, chopped**
- **2 stalks celery, chopped**
- **¼ teaspoon salt, or to taste**
- **2-3 cloves garlic, minced**
- **4 teaspoons all-purpose flour**
- **¾ cup dry, full-bodied young red wine, such as Beaujolais *or* Chianti**
- **1½ cups reduced-sodium chicken broth**
- **2 tablespoons tomato paste**
- **1½ cups peeled baby carrots *or* 2 large carrots sliced ¼ inch thick**
- **½ pound turnips, peeled and cut into 1-inch cubes**
- **1 cup frozen baby onions, thawed**
- **1 bouquet garni (*see page 396*): 4 sprigs fresh thyme *or* ½ teaspoon dried, 4 sprigs fresh parsley, a 4-inch strip of orange *or* tangerine peel, 1 bay leaf, ½ teaspoon whole peppercorns**
- **¼ cup chopped fresh parsley**

1. Position rack in lower third of oven; preheat to 275°F.
2. Heat oil in a large ovenproof Dutch oven over high heat until shimmering. Add half the beef and cook, turning occasionally, until well browned, 5 minutes. Transfer to a plate. Add remaining beef to the pan and brown in the same manner. Pour off all but a thin film of fat from the drippings remaining in the pan.
3. Add mushrooms, onion and celery to the pan; sprinkle with salt. Sauté until mushrooms have released and reabsorbed most of their juices, about 8 minutes. Stir in garlic and cook for 30 seconds more. Sprinkle in flour and cook, stirring, until it is fully absorbed and heated through, about 1 minute. Stir in wine, scraping up any browned bits.
4. Add broth, tomato paste, carrots, turnips, baby onions and bouquet garni; bring to a simmer. Add beef and its juices; cover the pan tightly and transfer to the oven.
5. Braise, stirring every 30 minutes or so, until the vegetables and meat are tender, 2½ to 3 hours. Remove and discard the bouquet garni. Sprinkle the stew with parsley just before serving.

MAKES 6 SERVINGS, 1 CUP EACH.

PER SERVING: 268 CALORIES; 11 G FAT (4 G SAT, 5 G MONO); 66 MG CHOLESTEROL; 15 G CARBOHYDRATE; 23 G PROTEIN; 3 G FIBER; 266 MG SODIUM.

NUTRITION BONUS: 110% DV VITAMIN A, 617 MG POTASSIUM (31% DV), 17 MG VITAMIN C (30% DV), 4 MG IRON (20% DV).

STOVETOP VARIATION: Omit Step 1. In Step 4, after adding the beef, cover the pan tightly and reduce heat to low. Proceed with Step 5, keeping the pot at a very gentle simmer.

Slow-Cooker Braised Pork with Salsa

PREP TIME: 45 MINUTES | **SLOW-COOKER TIME:** 6-7 HOURS | **TO MAKE AHEAD:** THE STEW WILL KEEP, COVERED, IN THE REFRIGERATOR FOR UP TO 2 DAYS OR IN THE FREEZER FOR UP TO 3 MONTHS. REHEAT ON THE STOVETOP, IN A MICROWAVE OR IN THE OVEN. | **EASE OF PREPARATION:** MODERATE

With just a few ingredients, you can produce a full-flavored, meltingly tender pork stew in your slow cooker. Serve over quinoa or rice.

- **3 pounds boneless pork shoulder *or* butt**
- **1½ cups prepared tomatillo salsa (*see Note*)**
- **1¾ cups reduced-sodium chicken broth**
- **1 medium onion, thinly sliced**
- **1 teaspoon cumin seeds *or* ground cumin**
- **3 plum tomatoes (½ pound), thinly sliced**
- **½ cup chopped fresh cilantro, divided**
- **½ cup reduced-fat sour cream**

1. Trim and discard pork surface fat. Cut meat apart following layers of fat around muscles; trim and discard fat. Cut into 2-inch chunks and rinse with cold water. Place in a 5- or 6-quart slow cooker. Turn heat to high.

2. Combine salsa, broth, onion and cumin seeds in a saucepan and bring to a boil over high heat. Pour over the meat. Add tomatoes and mix gently. Put the lid on and cook until the meat is pull-apart tender, 6 to 7 hours.

3. With a slotted spoon, transfer pork to a large bowl; cover and keep warm. Pour the sauce and vegetables into a large skillet; skim fat. Bring to a boil over high heat. Boil, skimming froth from time to time, for about 20 minutes, to intensify flavors and thicken slightly. Add the pork and ¼ cup cilantro; heat through.

4. To serve, ladle into bowls and garnish each serving with a dollop of sour cream and a sprinkling of the remaining ¼ cup cilantro.

INGREDIENT NOTE: **Tomatillo salsa (sometimes labeled salsa verde or green salsa) is a blend of green chiles, onions and tomatillos.**

MAKES ABOUT 8 SERVINGS, GENEROUS ¾ CUP EACH.

PER SERVING: 252 CALORIES; 12 G FAT (5 G SAT, 5 G MONO); 84 MG CHOLESTEROL; 7 G CARBOHYDRATE; 28 G PROTEIN; 1 G FIBER; 253 MG SODIUM.

NUTRITION BONUS: 4 MG ZINC (27% DV), 487 MG POTASSIUM (24% DV).

◆ **OVEN METHOD:** **START TO FINISH:** 3 HOURS

Preheat oven to 350°F. Combine pork, salsa, ½ cup chicken broth, onion, cumin seeds and tomatoes in a 9-by-13-inch baking dish; cover snugly with foil. Bake until the pork is pull-apart tender, about 2¼ hours. Skim fat. Uncover and bake until the meat begins to brown, about 15 minutes more. Stir in ¼ cup cilantro. Ladle into bowls, garnish with sour cream and remaining cilantro.

Pork Chops with Pear & Ginger Sauce

PREP TIME: 20 MINUTES | **START TO FINISH:** 40 MINUTES | **EASE OF PREPARATION:** MODERATE

In this quick sauté, vinegar and sugar are caramelized in the skillet, forming a deep, richly flavored base for the sauce. Ginger adds a spicy note that plays against the mild tastes of the pork and pear.

- 4 4-ounce boneless pork chops, ½ inch thick, trimmed
- Salt & freshly ground pepper to taste
- 2 teaspoons canola oil
- 3 tablespoons cider vinegar
- 2 tablespoons sugar
- ⅔ cup dry white wine
- 1 cup reduced-sodium chicken broth
- 1 firm, ripe pear, such as Bosc *or* Anjou, peeled, cored and cut lengthwise into eighths
- 1 1½-inch-long piece fresh ginger, peeled and cut into thin julienne strips (¼ cup)
- 6 scallions, trimmed and sliced into ½-inch lengths
- 2 teaspoons cornstarch mixed with 2 teaspoons water

1. Season pork with salt and pepper. Heat oil in a large nonstick skillet over medium-high heat. Add pork and cook until browned and just cooked through, 2 to 3 minutes per side. Transfer to a plate and keep warm.

2. Add vinegar and sugar to the pan; stir to dissolve the sugar. Cook over medium-high heat until the syrup turns dark amber, 10 to 20 seconds. Pour in wine (stand back, as the caramel may sputter) and bring to a simmer, stirring. Add broth, pears and ginger; bring to a simmer. Cook, uncovered, turning the pears occasionally, for 5 minutes. Add scallions and cook until the pears are tender, about 2 minutes more. Add the cornstarch mixture and cook, stirring, until lightly thickened. Reduce heat to low and return the pork and any accumulated juices to the pan; turn to coat with the sauce. Serve immediately.

MAKES 4 SERVINGS.

PER SERVING: 237 CALORIES; 5 G FAT (1 G SAT, 2 G MONO); 52 MG CHOLESTEROL; 20 G CARBOHYDRATE; 22 G PROTEIN; 2 G FIBER; 278 MG SODIUM.

NUTRITION BONUS: 635 MG POTASSIUM (32% DV).

Grilled Pork Chops with Rhubarb Chutney

PREP TIME: 25 MINUTES | **START TO FINISH:** 1 HOUR | **EASE OF PREPARATION:** EASY

This savory-tart-sweet combination takes the classic pairing of pork and fruit to a whole new level. We've used boneless pork chops because they're quick to cook, and given them a boost of flavor with a simple spice rub. (*Photo: page 217.*)

- ½ cup Rhubarb Chutney (*recipe follows*)
- 1 teaspoon ground coriander
- 1 teaspoon paprika
- ¼ teaspoon ground cinnamon
- ½ teaspoon kosher salt, or to taste
- Freshly ground pepper to taste
- 4 4-ounce boneless pork chops, ½ inch thick, trimmed (*see Tip*)

1. Prepare Rhubarb Chutney. Preheat grill to medium-high.

2. Mix coriander, paprika, cinnamon, salt and pepper in a small bowl. Sprinkle evenly on both sides of each pork chop, rubbing to coat the meat evenly.

3. Lightly oil the grill rack (*see Tip, page 130*). Grill pork chops over medium-high heat until browned and just cooked through, 3 to 5 minutes per side. Serve with chutney.

TEST KITCHEN TIP:
If you can't find thin pork chops, slice thick ones in half crosswise.

MAKES 4 SERVINGS.

PER SERVING: 202 CALORIES; 7 G FAT (2 G SAT, 3 G MONO); 72 MG CHOLESTEROL; 10 G CARBOHYDRATE; 24 G PROTEIN; 1 G FIBER; 281 MG SODIUM.

NUTRITION BONUS: 351 MG POTASSIUM (18% DV).

RHUBARB CHUTNEY

PREP TIME: 10 MINUTES | **START TO FINISH:** 35 MINUTES | **TO MAKE AHEAD:** THE CHUTNEY WILL KEEP, IN AN AIRTIGHT CONTAINER, IN THE REFRIGERATOR FOR UP TO 1 WEEK. | **EASE OF PREPARATION:** EASY

This quick, zesty chutney complements almost any meat or poultry. Use fresh or frozen rhubarb.

- 2 cups diced rhubarb
- ¾ cup diced red apple
- ½ cup dried cranberries *or* cherries
- ¼ cup finely chopped red onion
- ¼ cup water
- ¼ cup honey
- 1 tablespoon minced fresh ginger
- 2 teaspoons red-wine vinegar
- ¼ teaspoon crushed red pepper, plus more to taste

Combine all ingredients in a small saucepan. Bring to a boil, stirring occasionally. Reduce heat to medium-low, cover and simmer until rhubarb is tender, 15 to 20 minutes. Uncover and simmer, stirring occasionally, until thickened, about 5 minutes more. Serve warm or cold.

MAKES 2 CUPS, FOR 16 SERVINGS.

PER SERVING: 35 CALORIES; 0 G FAT (0 G SAT, 0 G MONO); 0 MG CHOLESTEROL; 9 G CARBOHYDRATE; 1 G PROTEIN; 1 G FIBER; 1 MG SODIUM.

Lower Carbs

Spice-Rubbed Pork Tenderloin

PREP TIME: 25 MINUTES | **START TO FINISH:** 35 MINUTES | **EASE OF PREPARATION:** EASY

The bright fresh taste of a watermelon and cucumber salad makes a sensational counterpoint to the fiery spice crust on this succulent pork tenderloin. It's important to brown the meat before roasting, since this cut cooks too quickly for the surface to brown and caramelize in the oven. Grill enthusiasts may omit the stovetop browning (Step 3) and grill the tenderloins over medium heat, covered, for 20 to 25 minutes.

- 2 teaspoons brown sugar
- 2 teaspoons ground coriander
- 1½ teaspoons ground cumin
- ¼ teaspoon coarse sea salt *or* kosher salt
- 2 teaspoons chile-garlic sauce (*see Ingredient Note, page 394*)
- 2 teaspoons extra-virgin olive oil, divided
- 1½ pounds pork tenderloin, trimmed
- 4 cups Sweet & Tangy Watermelon Salad (*recipe follows*)

1. Preheat oven to 375°F. Line a baking sheet with foil.
2. Mix sugar, coriander, cumin, salt, chile sauce and 1 teaspoon oil in a small bowl to form a smooth paste. Rub the paste over the pork.
3. Heat remaining 1 teaspoon oil in a large nonstick skillet over medium-high heat. Add the pork; cook, turning occasionally, until browned on all sides, about 3 minutes. Transfer to the baking sheet.
4. Roast the pork until just cooked through, 20 to 25 minutes (an instant-read thermometer inserted in the center should register 155°F). Let stand, loosely covered with foil, for 5 minutes.
5. Meanwhile, make Sweet & Tangy Watermelon Salad. Carve the pork into ½-inch-thick slices. Serve with the watermelon salad.

MAKES 6 SERVINGS.

PER SERVING: 167 CALORIES; 6 G FAT (2 G SAT, 3 G MONO); 63 MG CHOLESTEROL; 4 G CARBOHYDRATE; 23 G PROTEIN; 1 G FIBER; 213 MG SODIUM.

SWEET & TANGY WATERMELON SALAD

PREP TIME: 10 MINUTES | **START TO FINISH:** 10 MINUTES | **EASE OF PREPARATION:** EASY

Looks like tomato—surprise, it's watermelon.

- 2 tablespoons rice vinegar
- 2½ teaspoons sugar
- 2 cups diced seeded watermelon
- 2 cups diced cucumber
- ½ cup chopped fresh cilantro
- ¼ cup unsalted dry-roasted peanuts, toasted (*see Tip, page 397*) and coarsely chopped

Stir together vinegar and sugar in a medium bowl until the sugar almost dissolves. Add watermelon, cucumber and cilantro; toss gently to combine. Just before serving, sprinkle with peanuts.

MAKES ABOUT 4 CUPS.

PER ⅔-CUP SERVING: 63 CALORIES; 3 G FAT (0 G SAT, 2 G MONO); 0 MG CHOLESTEROL; 8 G CARBOHYDRATE; 2 G PROTEIN; 1 G FIBER; 3 MG SODIUM.

High Fiber

Braised Lamb with a Garden-Vegetable Medley

PREP TIME: 25 MINUTES | **START TO FINISH:** 2¼ HOURS | **TO MAKE AHEAD:** PREPARE THROUGH STEP 4. THE STEW WILL KEEP, COVERED, IN THE REFRIGERATOR FOR UP TO 2 DAYS OR IN THE FREEZER FOR UP TO 3 MONTHS. REHEAT ON STOVETOP, IN MICROWAVE OR OVEN. | **EASE OF PREPARATION:** MODERATE

This spring stew, known as a *navarin* or *ragoût* in France, features seasonal lamb and uses tender young vegetables that add a fresh flavor to the hearty mix. While a braised dish like this takes a little time, it can be prepared entirely in advance, making it perfect for entertaining. (*Photo: page 218.*)

- 2½ pounds boneless lamb leg, trimmed of fat and cut into 2-inch cubes
- ½ teaspoon salt, or to taste
- Freshly ground pepper to taste
- 1 tablespoon extra-virgin olive oil
- 1 medium carrot, finely chopped
- 1 small onion, finely chopped
- 1 tablespoon all-purpose flour
- 1¾ cups dry red wine
- 1 cup reduced-sodium beef broth
- 1 14½-ounce can diced tomatoes
- 4 cloves garlic, minced
- 1 tablespoon finely chopped fresh rosemary
- 1 cup pearl onions, peeled (*see Tip*), *or* frozen small onions, rinsed under warm water to thaw
- 1 cup baby turnips, peeled (¼ inch of green left on) and halved, *or* regular turnips cut into ½-inch wedges
- 1½ cups baby carrots
- 1½ cups peas, fresh *or* frozen
- 2 tablespoons chopped fresh parsley

1. Season lamb with salt and pepper. Heat oil in a large deep skillet or Dutch oven. Add lamb and cook, turning from time to time, until browned on all sides, about 6 minutes. Transfer to a plate.
2. Add carrot and onion to the pan; cook, stirring often, until lightly browned, about 3 minutes. Sprinkle flour over the vegetables; stir to coat. Add wine and scrape up any browned bits. Simmer until reduced slightly, 2 to 3 minutes.
3. Add broth, tomatoes, garlic and rosemary; bring to a simmer. Return the lamb to the pan. Reduce heat to low, cover and simmer for 1¼ hours, checking from time to time to make sure it does not boil too rapidly.
4. Stir in pearl onions, turnips and carrots. Simmer, covered, until the lamb and vegetables are tender, about 30 minutes.
5. Add peas and heat through. Sprinkle with parsley and serve.

TO PEEL PEARL ONIONS: Cook in boiling water for 1 minute. Drain. Peel when cool enough to handle.

MAKES 6 SERVINGS, ABOUT 1⅓ CUPS EACH.

PER SERVING: 384 CALORIES; 11 G FAT (4 G SAT, 5 G MONO); 119 MG CHOLESTEROL; 22 G CARBOHYDRATE; 38 G PROTEIN; 5 G FIBER; 388 MG SODIUM.

NUTRITION BONUS: 120% DV VITAMIN A, 32 MG VITAMIN C (50% DV), 586 MG POTASSIUM (29% DV), 4 MG IRON (25% DV), 20% DV FIBER.

Lower Carbs

Tandoori Leg of Lamb with Fresh Mango Chutney

PREP TIME: 20 MINUTES | **START TO FINISH:** 4 HOURS (INCLUDING 2 HOURS MARINATING TIME)
EASE OF PREPARATION: EASY

A spicy, yogurt-based marinade tenderizes the lamb, which is accompanied by a sweet and gingery chutney.

- 1 5-pound bone-in leg of lamb, trimmed
- 1 cup nonfat plain yogurt
- ¼ cup lime juice (2 limes)
- 2 tablespoons minced fresh ginger
- 3 cloves garlic, crushed
- 1½ teaspoons salt, or to taste
- ¼ teaspoon freshly ground pepper
- 1 tablespoon ground coriander
- ½ teaspoon cayenne pepper
- ½ teaspoon ground cinnamon
- ½ teaspoon ground cloves
- ½ teaspoon ground cardamom
- Fresh Mango Chutney (*recipe follows*)

1. With a sharp knife, make ¼-inch to ½-inch-deep gashes on all sides of lamb in a crisscross pattern. Place the lamb in a plastic bag. Combine yogurt, lime juice, ginger, garlic, salt and pepper in a bowl. Pour the yogurt mixture over the lamb, turning to cover. Marinate in the refrigerator for at least 2 hours or overnight.

2. Preheat oven to 450°F. Place the lamb on a lightly oiled rack in a roasting pan. Combine coriander, cayenne, cinnamon, cloves and cardamom in a small bowl. Sprinkle evenly over the lamb.

3. Roast the lamb for 15 minutes. Reduce heat to 325° and continue roasting until a meat thermometer registers 140°F for medium-rare, 55 to 60 minutes. Let stand for 10 minutes before carving.

4. Meanwhile, make Fresh Mango Chutney to serve with the lamb.

MAKES 10 SERVINGS.

PER SERVING: 337 CALORIES; 11 G FAT (4 G SAT, 4 G MONO); 146 MG CHOLESTEROL; 11 G CARBOHYDRATE; 48 G PROTEIN; 1 G FIBER; 737 MG SODIUM.

NUTRITION BONUS: 677 MG POTASSIUM (34% DV), 4 MG IRON (25% DV).

FRESH MANGO CHUTNEY

PREP TIME: 10 MINUTES | **START TO FINISH:** 10 MINUTES | **TO MAKE AHEAD:** THE CHUTNEY WILL KEEP, COVERED, IN THE REFRIGERATOR FOR UP TO 2 HOURS. | **EASE OF PREPARATION:** EASY

- 2 mangoes, diced (*see Cooking Tip, page 397*)
- 2 tablespoons chopped fresh cilantro
- 1 tablespoon minced fresh ginger
- 1 tablespoon unsweetened flaked coconut
- 1 teaspoon salt, or to taste
- ⅛ teaspoon cayenne pepper

Combine all the ingredients in a small bowl and mix well.

MAKES 1½ CUPS.

PER TABLESPOON: 12 CALORIES; 0 G FAT (0 G SAT, 0 G MONO); 0 MG CHOLESTEROL; 3 G CARBOHYDRATE; 0 G PROTEIN; 0 G FIBER; 97 MG SODIUM.

Slow-Cooker Turkish Lamb & Vegetable Stew

PREP TIME: 20 MINUTES | **SLOW-COOKER TIME:** 4 HOURS

TO MAKE AHEAD: THE STEW WILL KEEP, COVERED, IN THE REFRIGERATOR FOR UP TO 2 DAYS. REHEAT ON THE STOVETOP, IN A MICROWAVE OR IN THE OVEN. | **EASE OF PREPARATION:** MODERATE

Layers of fresh Mediterranean vegetables, seasoned with an abundance of bay, garlic and oregano, meld with tender lamb into a luscious harvest-time supper. Serve the stew with rice or warm whole-wheat pita.

- 1½ pounds lean boneless leg of lamb, trimmed and cut into 1¼-inch pieces
- 1¼ teaspoons salt, divided
- Freshly ground pepper to taste
- 1½ tablespoons extra-virgin olive oil, divided
- 2 large onions, thinly sliced
- 4 cloves garlic, minced
- ½ teaspoon dried oregano
- 1 14-ounce can diced tomatoes
- 1 large all-purpose potato, preferably Yukon Gold, peeled and cut into ⅜-inch-thick slices
- ½ pound green beans, trimmed
- 1 small eggplant, cut into ⅜-inch-thick slices
- 1 medium zucchini, cut into ⅜-inch-thick slices
- 6 bay leaves
- 3 tablespoons chopped fresh parsley

1. Season lamb with ¼ teaspoon salt and pepper to taste. Heat ½ tablespoon oil in a large heavy skillet over medium-high heat. Add half the lamb and sear, turning, until well browned, 2 to 4 minutes. Transfer to a 4-quart slow cooker. Add another ½ tablespoon oil to skillet and brown remaining lamb. Add to slow cooker.
2. Add remaining ½ tablespoon oil to skillet and reduce heat to medium. Add onions and cook, stirring, until softened, 3 to 5 minutes. Add garlic and oregano; cook, stirring, for 1 minute more. Add tomatoes and bring to a simmer, mashing with a potato masher or fork. Remove from heat and spoon half the mixture over the lamb.
3. Arrange potatoes in a layer in the pot; season with ¼ teaspoon salt and pepper to taste. Add green beans, followed by eggplant and zucchini, seasoning each layer with ¼ teaspoon salt and pepper to taste. Spread remaining tomato-onion mixture over vegetables. Top with bay leaves.
4. Cover and cook on high until lamb and vegetables are very tender, about 4 hours. Discard bay leaves. Serve hot, garnished with parsley.

MAKES 8 SERVINGS, ABOUT 1 CUP EACH.

PER SERVING: 179 CALORIES; 7 G FAT (2 G SAT, 4 G MONO); 54 MG CHOLESTEROL; 13 G CARBOHYDRATE; 17 G PROTEIN; 3 G FIBER; 457 MG SODIUM.

ANALYSIS NOTE: Lamb cut from the leg is 19 percent leaner than shoulder meat.

NUTRITION BONUS: 25 MG IRON (40% DV), 738 MG POTASSIUM (37% DV), 3 MG IRON (15% DV).

14

SAUCES & CONDIMENTS

If you love the simplicity and healthfulness of putting chicken, fish or lean meats on the grill or in the oven but find that your dinner routine has become a bit too routine, this chapter can bring more flavor into your life. Here are 18 lively sauces that make healthful meals luxurious, transforming the protein *du jour* into a meal with great tastes in every bite. Most of the sauces are ready in 15 minutes or less and do double-duty as sandwich spreads, burger toppings, dips, marinades or dressings. A squeeze of lemon is nice; a nice lemon-herb sauce is a godsend.

Lower Carbs

Portobello Gravy

PREP TIME: 10 MINUTES | **START TO FINISH:** 30 MINUTES
TO MAKE AHEAD: THE GRAVY WILL KEEP, COVERED, IN THE REFRIGERATOR FOR UP TO 2 DAYS. REHEAT ON THE STOVETOP OR IN THE MICROWAVE. | **EASE OF PREPARATION:** EASY

This rich, earthy gravy can be made with fresh shiitakes as well as portobellos. Leave the mushroom pieces in for a chunky-style sauce or strain them out for a velvety consistency. Serve with Mashed Garlicky Potatoes (*page 112*) or Leek, Barley & Mushroom Packets (*page 188*).

- **1 tablespoon extra-virgin olive oil**
- **1 medium onion, finely chopped**
- **2 cloves garlic, minced**
- **1½ cups chopped cleaned portobello mushrooms (2 medium)**
- **2¼ cups vegetable broth (*see Note*)**
- **3 tablespoons tamari *or* reduced-sodium soy sauce**
- **¼ teaspoon dried thyme leaves**
- **⅛ teaspoon crumbled dried sage**
- **1 tablespoon cornstarch**
- **2 tablespoons water**
- **Freshly ground pepper to taste**

1. Heat oil in a medium saucepan over medium heat. Add onion and garlic; cook, stirring often, until softened, about 5 minutes. Add mushrooms and cook, stirring often, until they begin to release their juices, about 10 minutes.

2. Add broth, tamari (or soy sauce), thyme and sage; simmer for 10 minutes. Mix cornstarch and water in a small bowl. Stir into the sauce and simmer, stirring often, until slightly thickened, about 10 minutes more. Season with pepper. If you prefer a smooth gravy, pass it through a fine sieve (discard mushrooms and onions). Serve hot.

MAKES 2 CUPS CHUNKY GRAVY OR 1 CUP SMOOTH GRAVY, FOR 8 SERVINGS.

PER SERVING (CHUNKY): 44 CALORIES; 2 G FAT (0 G SAT, 1 G MONO); 0 MG CHOLESTEROL; 5 G CARBOHYDRATE; 1 G PROTEIN; 1 G FIBER; 510 MG SODIUM.

INGREDIENT NOTE: Commercial vegetable broth is readily available in natural-foods stores and many supermarkets. We especially like the Imagine and Pacific brands, sold in convenient aseptic packages that allow you to use small amounts and keep the rest refrigerated.

Bourbon-Molasses Barbecue Sauce

PREP TIME: 5 MINUTES | **START TO FINISH:** 30 MINUTES | **TO MAKE AHEAD:** THE SAUCE WILL KEEP, COVERED, IN THE REFRIGERATOR FOR UP TO 1 WEEK. | **EASE OF PREPARATION:** EASY

Why buy commercial sauce when you can have the real thing, ready in minutes? Here is the perfect all-purpose barbecue sauce: easy, inexpensive, unbelievably delicious. Slather it on grilled chicken or pork, or mix it with shredded cooked meat for sandwiches.

- ½ cup cider vinegar
- ⅓ cup ketchup
- 2 tablespoons molasses
- 2 tablespoons bourbon *or* apple juice
- 6-10 dashes Tabasco sauce
- 4 dashes Worcestershire sauce

Combine vinegar, ketchup, molasses, bourbon (or apple juice), Tabasco and Worcestershire in a small saucepan. Bring to a simmer over medium-low heat, stirring occasionally. Let cool to room temperature.

MAKES ABOUT 1 CUP.

PER TABLESPOON: 18 CALORIES; 0 G FAT (0 G SAT, 0 G MONO); 0 MG CHOLESTEROL; 4 G CARBOHYDRATE; 0 G PROTEIN; 0 G FIBER; 58 MG SODIUM.

Rouille Sauce

PREP TIME: 10 MINUTES | **START TO FINISH:** 10 MINUTES | **TO MAKE AHEAD:** THE SAUCE WILL KEEP, COVERED, IN THE REFRIGERATOR FOR UP TO 2 DAYS. | **EASE OF PREPARATION:** EASY

Lower Carbs

Traditionally stirred into bouillabaisse, this quick red-pepper sauce turns plain boiled shrimp into a spicy shrimp cocktail. It's also a great dip for fresh vegetables or sauce for grilled fish.

- 3 slices white sandwich bread, crusts removed, torn into pieces
- 2 cloves garlic, crushed and peeled
- 1 7-ounce jar roasted red peppers, rinsed
- 3 tablespoons reduced-sodium chicken broth *or* fish stock (*page 60*)
- 1½ tablespoons extra-virgin olive oil
- 2 teaspoons lemon juice
- Salt & freshly ground pepper to taste
- Cayenne pepper to taste

Combine bread, garlic, peppers, chicken broth (or fish stock), oil and lemon juice in a blender or food processor. Process until smooth. Season with salt, pepper and cayenne. (The mixture should be highly seasoned.)

MAKES ABOUT 1¼ CUPS.

PER TABLESPOON: 27 CALORIES; 1 G FAT (0 G SAT, 1 G MONO); 0 MG CHOLESTEROL; 4 G CARBOHYDRATE; 1 G PROTEIN; 0 G FIBER; 64 MG SODIUM.

Cucumber-Mint Raita

Lower Carbs

PREP TIME: 10 MINUTES | **START TO FINISH:** 10 MINUTES | **EASE OF PREPARATION:** EASY

Tame the heat of curries with this cool sauce, or serve it on Curried Cashew Burgers (*page 133*).

- 1 cup nonfat plain yogurt
- 1 tablespoon fresh lime juice
- 1 tablespoon chopped fresh mint
- 1 teaspoon ground cumin
- 1 medium cucumber, peeled and diced (1 cup)
- Salt & freshly ground pepper to taste

Whisk yogurt, lime juice, mint and cumin in a small bowl. Stir in cucumber; season with salt and pepper.

MAKES ABOUT 1¾ CUPS.

PER TABLESPOON: 7 CALORIES; 0 G FAT (0 G SAT, 0 G MONO); 1 MG CHOLESTEROL; 1 G CARBOHYDRATE; 1 G PROTEIN; 0 G FIBER; 28 MG SODIUM.

Fresh Mint & Chile Sauce

PREP TIME: 10 MINUTES | **START TO FINISH:** 10 MINUTES | **EASE OF PREPARATION:** EASY

This spicy bright green sauce, a traditional Indian condiment, is superb on grilled chicken, lamb or salmon, with basmati rice.

- 2 teaspoons granulated sugar
- ½ teaspoon salt
- 1 tablespoon chopped fresh ginger
- 1 small serrano chile *or* jalapeño pepper, seeded and chopped
- 1 clove garlic, peeled
- 2 cups packed fresh mint leaves
- 2 tablespoons rice-wine vinegar, or to taste

1. Place sugar and salt in a blender or mini food processor. With the motor running, drop ginger, chile and garlic through the feed tube and process until minced.

2. Add mint and vinegar and pulse until finely chopped, stopping to scrape down sides of workbowl as needed. Transfer to a small serving bowl. Serve within 30 minutes.

MAKES ABOUT ½ CUP.

PER TABLESPOON: 15 CALORIES; 0 G FAT (0 G SAT, 0 G MONO); 0 MG CHOLESTEROL; 3 G CARBOHYDRATE; 1 G PROTEIN; 2 G FIBER; 153 MG SODIUM.

NUTRITION BONUS: 20% DV VITAMIN A, 3 MG IRON (15% DV).

Peanut Dipping Sauce

PREP TIME: 10 MINUTES | **START TO FINISH:** 10 MINUTES | **TO MAKE AHEAD:** THE SAUCE WILL KEEP, COVERED, IN THE REFRIGERATOR FOR UP TO 2 DAYS. | **EASE OF PREPARATION:** EASY

For a sure-hit hors d'oeuvre, serve this sauce with crudités and/or skewered grilled chicken, pork or beef. Or use it as a spread for "grown-up" peanut butter sandwiches.

- 2 cloves garlic, minced
- 2 tablespoons natural peanut butter
- 2 tablespoons reduced-sodium soy sauce
- 2 tablespoons reduced-fat mayonnaise
- 1 tablespoon dark brown sugar
- 1 tablespoon lemon juice
- ½ teaspoon crushed red pepper
- 1-2 tablespoons water (optional)

Combine garlic, peanut butter, soy sauce, mayonnaise, brown sugar, lemon juice and crushed red pepper in a bowl; whisk until smooth. If sauce seems too thick, add water.

MAKES ABOUT ¾ CUP.

PER TABLESPOON: 30 CALORIES; 2 G FAT (0 G SAT, 0 G MONO); 1 MG CHOLESTEROL; 2 G CARBOHYDRATE; 1 G PROTEIN; 0 G FIBER; 104 MG SODIUM.

Vietnamese Dipping Sauce

PREP TIME: 10 MINUTES | **START TO FINISH:** 10 MINUTES | **TO MAKE AHEAD:** THE SAUCE WILL KEEP, COVERED, IN THE REFRIGERATOR FOR UP TO 4 DAYS. | **EASE OF PREPARATION:** EASY

A tantalizing balance between salty and sweet, tart and spicy, this makes a versatile dipping sauce that complements a wide range of dishes, from basic rice to grilled shrimp and spring rolls.

- ⅓ cup fish sauce (*see Ingredient Note, page 395*)
- ¼ cup lime *or* lemon juice
- 2 tablespoons sugar
- 3 cloves garlic, minced
- 1 serrano chile with seeds, minced
- ¼ cup grated *or* finely julienned carrot

1. Whisk fish sauce, lime juice (or lemon juice) and sugar in a small bowl. Stir in garlic and chile.
2. Just before serving, place in individual bowls for dipping and add some shreds of carrot.

MAKES ⅔ CUP.

PER TABLESPOON: 23 CALORIES; 0 G FAT (0 G SAT, 0 G MONO); 0 MG CHOLESTEROL; 5 G CARBOHYDRATE; 1 G PROTEIN; 0 G FIBER; 350 MG SODIUM.

Chile-Garlic Dipping Sauce

PREP TIME: 10 MINUTES | **START TO FINISH:** 10 MINUTES | **TO MAKE AHEAD:** THE SAUCE WILL KEEP, COVERED, IN THE REFRIGERATOR FOR UP TO 4 DAYS. | **EASE OF PREPARATION:** EASY

Serve this piquant sauce with Pan-Fried Dumplings (*page 41*) or Ginger-Steamed Tilapia (*page 259*). It also makes a terrific marinade for chicken, fish, pork or beef or dressing for Asian noodles.

- **¼ cup reduced-sodium soy sauce**
- **¼ cup strong brewed green tea**
- **2 tablespoons lemon juice**
- **2 tablespoons rice vinegar**
- **1 fresh red chile pepper, such as Fresno, seeded and minced**
- **2 cloves garlic, minced**
- **1 scallion, minced**
- **2 teaspoons toasted sesame oil**
- **2 teaspoons honey**

Combine soy sauce, tea, lemon juice, vinegar, chile, garlic, scallion, oil and honey in a small bowl. Serve immediately or cover and refrigerate for 30 minutes to allow flavors to blend.

MAKES ¾ CUP.

PER TABLESPOON: 17 CALORIES; 1 G FAT (0 G SAT, 0 G MONO); 0 MG CHOLESTEROL; 2 G CARBOHYDRATE; 0 G PROTEIN; 0 G FIBER; 179 MG SODIUM.

Mojo Sauce

Lower Carbs

PREP TIME: 10 MINUTES | **START TO FINISH:** 10 MINUTES | **TO MAKE AHEAD:** THE SAUCE WILL KEEP, COVERED, IN THE REFRIGERATOR FOR UP TO 3 DAYS. LET IT COME TO ROOM TEMPERATURE BEFORE USING. **EASE OF PREPARATION:** EASY

The vibrant Latin flavors of this sauce make plain grilled tofu, chicken, shrimp or fish sing.

- **1 tablespoon extra-virgin olive oil**
- **2 cloves garlic, minced**
- **¼ teaspoon ground cumin**
- **¼ cup lime juice**
- **¼ cup orange juice**
- **2 tablespoons chopped fresh cilantro *or* mint**
- **½ teaspoon salt**
- **Freshly ground pepper to taste**

Heat oil in a small nonstick skillet over medium heat. Add garlic and cumin; cook, stirring constantly, just until fragrant (do not brown), about 30 seconds. Remove from heat and stir in lime juice, orange juice, cilantro (or mint), salt and pepper. Let cool; serve at room temperature.

MAKES ABOUT ½ CUP.

PER TABLESPOON: 23 CALORIES; 2 G FAT (0 G SAT, 1 G MONO); 0 MG CHOLESTEROL; 2 G CARBOHYDRATE; 0 G PROTEIN; 0 G FIBER; 146 MG SODIUM.

Thai Sauce

PREP TIME: 10 MINUTES | **START TO FINISH:** 15 MINUTES | **TO MAKE AHEAD:** THE SAUCE WILL KEEP, COVERED, IN THE REFRIGERATOR FOR UP TO 4 DAYS. | **EASE OF PREPARATION:** EASY

This is a variation of a popular sauce from Thailand that can be used as a dipping sauce or salad dressing. For a smooth sauce, puree it in a blender. Try it on Shrimp Spring Rolls (*page 40*).

- 2 tablespoons almond butter *or* peanut butter
- ½ cup plain soy milk
- ¼ cup "lite" coconut milk (*see Ingredient Note, page 394*)
- 2 tablespoons fresh lime juice
- 1 tablespoon fish sauce, or to taste (*see Ingredient Note, page 395*)
- 1 tablespoon honey
- 4 cloves garlic, minced
- 1 fresh red chile pepper, such as Fresno, seeded and minced
- 1 scallion, minced
- 1 tablespoon chopped fresh cilantro

Place almond butter (or peanut butter) in a medium bowl. Slowly whisk in soy milk, coconut milk, lime juice, fish sauce and honey until smooth. Stir in garlic, chile pepper, scallion and cilantro. Serve immediately or cover and refrigerate for 30 minutes to allow flavors to blend.

MAKES 1 CUP.

PER TABLESPOON: 25 CALORIES; 1 G FAT (0 G SAT, 1 G MONO); 0 MG CHOLESTEROL; 3 G CARBOHYDRATE; 1 G PROTEIN; 0 G FIBER; 90 MG SODIUM.

Salsa Verde

Lower Carbs

PREP TIME: 10 MINUTES | **START TO FINISH:** 15 MINUTES | **TO MAKE AHEAD:** THE SAUCE WILL KEEP, COVERED, IN THE REFRIGERATOR FOR UP TO 2 DAYS. BRING TO ROOM TEMPERATURE BEFORE SERVING. **EASE OF PREPARATION:** EASY

Serve this versatile Italian green sauce on beef, chicken, fish, pasta or potatoes.

- 1 cup chopped fresh parsley
- 3 tablespoons capers, rinsed
- 2 cloves garlic, crushed and peeled
- 2 tablespoons extra-virgin olive oil
- 2 tablespoons lemon juice
- 2 tablespoons water
- 2 teaspoons anchovy paste
- Freshly ground pepper to taste

Combine parsley, capers and garlic in a blender or food processor; process until finely chopped. Add oil, lemon juice, water and anchovy paste and process until blended. Season with pepper.

MAKES ½ CUP.

PER TABLESPOON: 47 CALORIES; 4 G FAT (1 G SAT, 3 G MONO); 4 MG CHOLESTEROL; 1 G CARBOHYDRATE; 1 G PROTEIN; 0 G FIBER; 325 MG SODIUM.

Plum Ketchup

PREP TIME: 10 MINUTES | **START TO FINISH:** 50 MINUTES | **TO MAKE AHEAD:** THE KETCHUP WILL KEEP, COVERED, IN THE REFRIGERATOR FOR UP TO 1 WEEK OR IN THE FREEZER FOR UP TO 6 MONTHS. | **EASE OF PREPARATION:** EASY

Fresh and flavorful plum ketchup makes a delicious sandwich spread, a sauce for grilled beef, pork or chicken, or an excellent way to add excitement to turkey burgers.

- 1½ pounds red *or* black plums (5-6 medium), pitted and quartered
- 2 cloves garlic, minced
- ⅓ cup packed light brown sugar
- ⅓ cup cider vinegar
- ⅓ cup water
- ½ teaspoon salt, or to taste
- ½ teaspoon ground ginger
- ¼ teaspoon ground allspice
- ¼ teaspoon freshly ground pepper
- ⅛ teaspoon cayenne pepper
- 1 2-inch cinnamon stick

Combine plums, garlic, brown sugar, vinegar, water, salt, ginger, allspice, pepper, cayenne and cinnamon stick in a large heavy saucepan. Bring to a simmer, stirring frequently. Reduce heat to low and simmer, uncovered, stirring occasionally, until the plums have cooked down to a puree, 35 to 45 minutes. Remove from heat and let cool. Discard the cinnamon stick. Transfer to a bowl or storage container.

MAKES ABOUT 2¼ CUPS.

PER TABLESPOON: 19 CALORIES; 0 G FAT (0 G SAT, 0 G MONO); 0 MG CHOLESTEROL; 5 G CARBOHYDRATE; 0 G PROTEIN; 0 G FIBER; 32 MG SODIUM.

Olive Ketchup

Lower Carbs

PREP TIME: 10 MINUTES | **START TO FINISH:** 10 MINUTES | **TO MAKE AHEAD:** THE KETCHUP WILL KEEP, COVERED, IN THE REFRIGERATOR FOR UP TO 4 DAYS. | **EASE OF PREPARATION:** EASY

This makes a great finish for baked or broiled fish, or serve with Mediterranean Burgers (*page 134*).

- ½ cup Kalamata olives, pitted
- ¼ cup chopped fresh parsley
- 2 scallions, coarsely chopped
- 1 clove garlic, crushed and peeled
- 1 tablespoon extra-virgin olive oil
- 1 teaspoon red-wine vinegar
- 2 teaspoons tomato paste

Combine olives, parsley, scallions, garlic, oil and vinegar in a food processor. Pulse until finely chopped. Transfer to a small bowl and mix in tomato paste.

MAKES ABOUT ½ CUP.

PER TABLESPOON: 46 CALORIES; 4 G FAT (1 G SAT, 3 G MONO); 0 MG CHOLESTEROL; 2 G CARBOHYDRATE; 0 G PROTEIN; 0 G FIBER; 155 MG SODIUM.

Blue Cheese Sauce

PREP TIME: 5 MINUTES | **START TO FINISH:** 5 MINUTES | **TO MAKE AHEAD:** THE SAUCE WILL KEEP, COVERED, IN THE REFRIGERATOR FOR UP TO 2 DAYS. | **EASE OF PREPARATION:** EASY

This rich sauce is excellent on burgers and sandwiches, such as Pecan & Mushroom Burgers (*page 132*) and the Grilled Portobello "Steak" Sandwich (*page 130*). To make a dipping sauce, stir in a little extra low-fat mayonnaise or sour cream, then serve with baby carrots, celery sticks and sliced cucumbers.

- **⅓ cup nonfat plain yogurt**
- **3 tablespoons crumbled blue cheese (1 ounce)**
- **½ teaspoon balsamic vinegar**

Combine yogurt, blue cheese and vinegar in a small bowl and blend with a fork to make a chunky sauce.

MAKES ABOUT ½ CUP.

PER TABLESPOON: 18 CALORIES; 1 G FAT (1 G SAT, 0 G MONO); 3 MG CHOLESTEROL; 1 G CARBOHYDRATE; 1 G PROTEIN; 0 G FIBER; 51 MG SODIUM.

Light Lemon Sauce with Herbs

PREP TIME: 10 MINUTES | **START TO FINISH:** 15 MINUTES | **DEGREE OF DIFFICULTY:** EASY

Lower Carbs

Fines herbes, a mixture of parsley, chervil, tarragon and chives, is a classic combo in French cooking. The herbs give this simple sauce, which is similar to hollandaise, a delightful lift.

- **⅓ cup reduced-fat mayonnaise**
- **⅓ cup reduced-sodium chicken broth**
- **1 tablespoon Dijon mustard**
- **1 tablespoon extra-virgin olive oil**
- **1 tablespoon lemon juice**
- **2 teaspoons chopped fresh parsley**
- **2 teaspoons chopped fresh tarragon**
- **2 teaspoons chopped fresh chives**
- **2 teaspoons chopped fresh chervil**
- **Freshly ground pepper to taste**

Place mayonnaise in a small saucepan. Gradually add broth, whisking until smooth. Heat over medium-low heat, whisking constantly, until heated through but not bubbling, about 2 minutes. Remove from heat and stir in mustard, oil, lemon juice, parsley, tarragon, chives, chervil and pepper. Serve warm.

MAKES ABOUT ¾ CUP.

PER TABLESPOON: 25 CALORIES; 2 G TOTAL FAT (0 G SAT, 1 G MONO); 0 MG CHOLESTEROL; 2 G CARBOHYDRATE; 0 G PROTEIN; 0 G FIBER; 97 MG SODIUM.

SUBSTITUTION: If you don't have fresh chervil, use more fresh parsley instead.

Sesame Mayonnaise

PREP TIME: 5 MINUTES | **START TO FINISH:** 5 MINUTES | **TO MAKE AHEAD:** THE MAYONNAISE WILL KEEP, COVERED, IN THE REFRIGERATOR FOR UP TO 2 DAYS. | **EASE OF PREPARATION:** EASY

Use this tangy mayonnaise to enliven a burger (such as Asian Turkey Burgers, *page 137*, or Turkey-Mushroom Burgers, *page 138*) or a chicken sandwich, as a dip for a platter of grilled summer vegetables, or to dress a simple coleslaw of napa cabbage and scallions.

- **2 tablespoons reduced-fat mayonnaise**
- **2 tablespoons nonfat *or* low-fat plain yogurt**
- **½ teaspoon reduced-sodium soy sauce**
- **½ teaspoon toasted sesame oil**

Combine mayonnaise, yogurt, soy sauce and oil in a small bowl; whisk until blended.

MAKES ABOUT ¼ CUP.

PER TABLESPOON: 31 CALORIES; 3 G FAT (0 G SAT, 1 G MONO); 2 MG CHOLESTEROL; 2 G CARBOHYDRATE; 0 G PROTEIN; 0 G FIBER; 71 MG SODIUM.

VARIATION: SCALLION-LEMON MAYONNAISE

Combine 2 tablespoons reduced-fat mayonnaise, 2 tablespoons nonfat plain yogurt, 1 tablespoon chopped scallions, ½ teaspoon freshly grated lemon zest, 1 tablespoon lemon juice, salt and pepper to taste in a small bowl; whisk until blended.

Cilantro & Pumpkin Seed Pesto

PREP TIME: 10 MINUTES | **START TO FINISH:** 10 MINUTES | **TO MAKE AHEAD:** THE PESTO WILL KEEP, COVERED, IN THE REFRIGERATOR FOR UP TO 2 DAYS. | **EASE OF PREPARATION:** EASY

Serve this nutty, spicy pesto with Vegetarian Enchiladas (*page 191*), Blueberry-Beef Burgers (*page 142*), black beans, grilled chicken or fish.

- **⅓ cup hulled pumpkin seeds**
- **2 jalapeño peppers, quartered and seeded**
- **1 cup fresh cilantro leaves**
- **¼ cup reduced-fat sour cream**
- **1 teaspoon fresh lime juice**
- **Salt to taste**

In a small heavy skillet over medium heat, lightly toast pumpkin seeds, about 2 minutes. Place in a blender or food processor; add jalapeños, cilantro, sour cream and lime juice. Blend until smooth. Season with salt.

MAKES ABOUT ⅔ CUP.

PER TABLESPOON: 31 CALORIES; 3 G FAT (1 G SAT, 1 G MONO); 2 MG CHOLESTEROL; 1 G CARBOHYDRATE; 1 G PROTEIN; 0 G FIBER; 17 MG SODIUM.

MUFFINS & BREADS

15

Happiness may well be this: a warm oven fogging the kitchen windows and softening the crystalline winter morning's sunshine, the air thick and sweet with the aroma of batter slowly transforming into bread. Traditional muffins and quick breads, and sometimes even their yeasted cousins, unfortunately often combine excess (of butter, eggs, sugar) with parsimony (of fruit, fiber, nutrients). Never here. Our baking recipes remain light, not leaden, even as they take every opportunity to use whole grains, fiber-rich mix-ins, even omega-3–rich flaxseeds. The result is filling, classic comfort food with a revamped, much-improved nutritional profile—a happy thought indeed.

MUFFINS

QUICK BREADS

YEAST BREADS

Applesauce-Date Muffins

PREP TIME: 20 MINUTES | **START TO FINISH:** 35 MINUTES | **EASE OF PREPARATION:** EASY

These easy, tasty muffins are rich in fiber, low in saturated fat and perfectly portable, making them great for breakfast or snack time.

- ¼ cup chopped walnuts
- 1½ cups whole-wheat flour
- ⅔ cup bran cereal, such as Bran Buds *or* All-Bran
- 1 teaspoon baking soda
- ½ teaspoon ground cinnamon
- ½ teaspoon salt
- ½ cup chopped dates
- 1 large egg, lightly beaten
- 1¾ cups unsweetened applesauce
- ⅓ cup packed dark brown sugar
- 2 tablespoons canola oil

1. Preheat oven to 425°F. Coat 12 muffin cups with cooking spray.
2. Spread walnuts in a shallow pan and bake until fragrant, 3 to 5 minutes. Let cool.
3. Whisk flour, bran cereal, baking soda, cinnamon and salt in a large bowl. Stir in dates and walnuts.
4. Whisk egg, applesauce, brown sugar and oil in another bowl until smooth. Make a well in the dry ingredients; add the wet ingredients and stir with a rubber spatula until just combined. (Do not overmix.) Spoon the batter into the prepared muffin cups.
5. Bake the muffins until the tops are golden brown and spring back when touched lightly, 12 to 15 minutes. Let cool in the pan for 5 minutes. Loosen edges and turn muffins out onto a wire rack to cool.

MAKES 1 DOZEN MUFFINS.

PER MUFFIN: 175 CALORIES; 5 G FAT (0 G SAT, 2 G MONO); 18 MG CHOLESTEROL; 31 G CARBOHYDRATE; 4 G PROTEIN; 6 G FIBER; 245 MG SODIUM.

NUTRITION BONUS: 22% DV FIBER, 82 MCG FOLATE (21% DV).

Muffin Essentials

- These recipes all use standard-size (2½-by-1-inch) **muffin cups**. The cups may seem quite full, but the batter mounds during baking to produce plump, but not oversized, muffins.
- For a healthful **alternative to butter** melting over a warm muffin, try mixing equal parts honey and fruity or mild olive oil. Warm gently in the microwave or on the stovetop to dissolve the honey.
- **To make reduced-calorie muffins**, replace from 50 to 100 percent of the sugar (depending on your preferences) with a no-calorie sweetener, such as Splenda.
- **To freeze muffins**, wrap individually in plastic wrap, then place in a plastic storage bag and freeze for up to 1 month. **To thaw**, remove plastic wrap, wrap in a paper towel and microwave on defrost for 1 to 2 minutes. To thaw muffins in the oven, wrap in foil and bake at 300°F for 25 to 30 minutes.

Banana-Bran Muffins

PREP TIME: 30 MINUTES | **START TO FINISH:** 1 HOUR | **EASE OF PREPARATION:** EASY

By the end of the week, any bananas left in the fruit bowl are past their prime—just right for these moist bran muffins. Add a handful of dark chocolate chips to entice children to enjoy a fiber-rich treat.

- 2 large eggs
- ⅔ cup packed light brown sugar
- 1 cup mashed ripe bananas (2 medium)
- 1 cup buttermilk (*see Tip, page 302*)
- 1 cup unprocessed wheat bran
- ¼ cup canola oil
- 1 teaspoon vanilla extract
- 1 cup whole-wheat flour
- ¾ cup all-purpose flour
- 1½ teaspoons baking powder
- ½ teaspoon baking soda
- ½ teaspoon ground cinnamon
- ¼ teaspoon salt
- ½ cup chocolate chips (optional)
- ⅓ cup chopped walnuts (optional)

1. Preheat oven to 400°F. Coat 12 muffin cups with cooking spray.

2. Whisk eggs and brown sugar in a medium bowl until smooth. Whisk in bananas, buttermilk, wheat bran, oil and vanilla.

3. Whisk whole-wheat flour, all-purpose flour, baking powder, baking soda, cinnamon and salt in a large bowl. Make a well in the dry ingredients; add the wet ingredients and stir with a rubber spatula until just combined. Stir in chocolate chips, if using. Scoop the batter into the prepared muffin cups (they'll be quite full). Sprinkle with walnuts, if using.

4. Bake the muffins until the tops are golden brown and spring back when touched lightly, 15 to 25 minutes. Let cool in the pan for 5 minutes. Loosen edges and turn muffins out onto a wire rack to cool slightly before serving.

INGREDIENT NOTE: Unprocessed wheat bran is the outer layer of the wheat kernel, removed during milling. Also known as miller's bran, it can be found in the baking section. Do not substitute bran cereal in this recipe.

MAKES 1 DOZEN MUFFINS.

PER MUFFIN: 196 CALORIES; 6 G FAT (1 G SAT, 3 G MONO); 36 MG CHOLESTEROL; 32 G CARBOHYDRATE; 5 G PROTEIN; 4 G FIBER; 182 MG SODIUM.

NUTRITION BONUS: 17% DV FIBER.

Blueberry-Maple Muffins

PREP TIME: 30 MINUTES | **START TO FINISH:** 1 HOUR | **EASE OF PREPARATION:** MODERATE

Flaxseeds give these wholesome muffins a nutty taste (although you can substitute ¾ cup rolled oats) and maple syrup provides the subtle sweetening.

- ⅓ cup whole flaxseeds (*see box, page 317*)
- 1 cup whole-wheat flour
- ¾ cup plus 2 tablespoons all-purpose flour
- 1½ teaspoons baking powder
- ½ teaspoon baking soda
- ¼ teaspoon salt
- 1 teaspoon ground cinnamon
- 2 large eggs
- ½ cup pure maple syrup
- 1 cup buttermilk
- ¼ cup canola oil
- 2 teaspoons freshly grated orange zest, preferably organic
- 1 tablespoon orange juice
- 1 teaspoon vanilla extract
- 1½ cups fresh blueberries
- 1 tablespoon granulated sugar

1. Preheat oven to 400°F. Coat 12 muffin cups with cooking spray.
2. Grind flaxseeds in a spice mill (such as a clean coffee grinder) or dry blender. Transfer to a large bowl. Add whole-wheat flour, all-purpose flour, baking powder, baking soda, salt and cinnamon; whisk to blend.
3. Whisk eggs and maple syrup in a medium bowl until smooth. Add buttermilk, oil, orange zest, orange juice and vanilla; whisk until blended. Add to the flour mixture and mix with a rubber spatula just until dry ingredients are moistened. Fold in blueberries. Scoop the batter into the prepared muffin cups. Sprinkle tops with granulated sugar.
4. Bake the muffins until the tops are golden brown and spring back when touched lightly, 15 to 25 minutes. Let cool in the pan for 5 minutes. Loosen edges and turn muffins out onto a wire rack to cool slightly.

SUBSTITUTION TIPS:
You can use buttermilk powder in place of fresh buttermilk. Or make "sour milk": mix 1 tablespoon lemon juice or vinegar to 1 cup milk.

MAKES 1 DOZEN MUFFINS.

PER MUFFIN: 207 CALORIES; 8 G FAT (1 G SAT, 3 G MONO); 36 MG CHOLESTEROL; 29 G CARBOHYDRATE; 5 G PROTEIN; 4 G FIBER; 185 MG SODIUM.

Chocolate-Graham Muffins

PREP TIME: 20 MINUTES | **START TO FINISH:** 1 HOUR | **EASE OF PREPARATION:** MODERATE

Graham cracker crumbs lend a hearty texture to a chocolate treat so it maintains the characteristics of a muffin, rather than an oversized cupcake, perfect to pack in a lunchbox.

- **1 cup chocolate graham cracker crumbs (*see Note*)**
- **¾ cup all-purpose flour**
- **¾ cup whole-wheat flour**
- **⅓ cup unsweetened cocoa powder, preferably Dutch-process, sifted**
- **1½ teaspoons baking powder**
- **½ teaspoon baking soda**
- **¼ teaspoon salt**
- **2 large eggs**
- **½ cup packed light brown sugar**
- **¼ cup granulated sugar**
- **1 cup buttermilk**
- **3 tablespoons canola oil**
- **1 teaspoon instant coffee powder**
- **1 teaspoon vanilla extract**
- **¼ cup semisweet chocolate chips, preferably mini chips**

1. Preheat oven to 400°F. Coat 12 muffin cups with cooking spray.

2. Pulse graham crackers into crumbs in a food processor or place in a large plastic bag and crush with a rolling pin. Whisk all-purpose flour, whole-wheat flour, cocoa, baking powder, baking soda and salt in a large bowl. Stir in graham cracker crumbs.

3. Whisk eggs, brown sugar and granulated sugar in a medium bowl until smooth. Add buttermilk, oil, coffee and vanilla and whisk until blended. Make a well in the dry ingredients; add the wet ingredients and stir with a rubber spatula until just combined. Gently fold in chocolate chips. Spoon the batter into the prepared muffin cups.

4. Bake the muffins until the tops spring back when touched lightly, 15 to 25 minutes. Let cool in the pan for 5 minutes. Loosen edges and turn muffins out onto a wire rack to cool.

INGREDIENT NOTE:
To avoid trans-fatty acids, look for brands that do not contain partially hydrogenated vegetable oil, such as Mi-Del chocolate snaps or Barbara's Chocolate Go-Go Grahams.

MAKES 1 DOZEN MUFFINS.

PER MUFFIN: 215 CALORIES; 7 G FAT (1 G SAT, 3 G MONO); 36 MG CHOLESTEROL; 35 G CARBOHYDRATE; 4 G PROTEIN; 2 G FIBER; 222 MG SODIUM.

Fig Nugget Muffins

PREP TIME: 20 MINUTES | **START TO FINISH:** 40 MINUTES | **EASE OF PREPARATION:** MODERATE

Perfect for a lazy Sunday morning, these not-too-sweet grain-rich muffins have a surprise center "nugget" of gooey honey and figs, eliminating the need for jam or butter. Freeze leftovers for a midweek breakfast treat (*see "Muffin Essentials," page 300*).

FIG NUGGETS

- ½ cup packed dried figs, preferably Calimyrna
- 2 tablespoons chopped hazelnuts *or* walnuts
- ¼ teaspoon ground cinnamon
- 1 tablespoon orange juice
- 1 tablespoon honey

MUFFIN BATTER

- 1 large egg
- 1 large egg white
- ¾ cup packed light brown sugar
- 1 cup nonfat plain yogurt
- ¼ cup canola oil
- 1 tablespoon freshly grated orange zest, preferably organic
- ⅓ cup orange juice
- 1 teaspoon vanilla extract
- 1 cup oat bran
- 1 cup whole-wheat flour
- ¾ cup all-purpose flour
- 1½ teaspoons baking powder
- ½ teaspoon baking soda
- ¼ teaspoon salt
- 2 tablespoons chopped hazelnuts *or* walnuts

1. Preheat oven to 400°F. Coat 12 muffin cups with cooking spray.

2. To prepare fig nuggets: Combine figs, hazelnuts (or walnuts) and cinnamon in a food processor; pulse until the figs are finely chopped. Add orange juice and honey and pulse until the mixture forms a paste. Set aside.

3. To prepare muffin batter: Whisk egg, egg white and brown sugar in a medium bowl until smooth. Add yogurt, oil, orange zest, orange juice and vanilla and whisk until blended. Stir in oat bran.

4. Whisk whole-wheat flour, all-purpose flour, baking powder, baking soda and salt in a large bowl. Make a well in the dry ingredients; add the wet ingredients and stir with a rubber spatula until just combined. Spoon about half the batter into the prepared muffin cups. Place a scant tablespoon of the reserved fig mixture in the center of each muffin. Top with remaining batter. Sprinkle with nuts.

5. Bake the muffins until the tops are golden brown and spring back when touched lightly, 15 to 25 minutes. Let cool in the pan for 5 minutes. Loosen edges and turn muffins out onto a wire rack to cool.

MAKES 1 DOZEN MUFFINS.

PER MUFFIN: 229 CALORIES; 7 G FAT (1 G SAT, 4 G MONO); 18 MG CHOLESTEROL; 40 G CARBOHYDRATE; 5 G PROTEIN; 4 G FIBER; 171 MG SODIUM.

Morning Glory Muffins

PREP TIME: 20 MINUTES | **START TO FINISH:** 1 HOUR | **EASE OF PREPARATION:** MODERATE

Replacing some of the fat with apple butter provides for a moist, dense and hearty muffin. Enjoy one with a low-fat yogurt for a great start to the day.

- 1 cup all-purpose flour
- 1 cup whole-wheat flour
- ¾ cup sugar
- 1 tablespoon ground cinnamon
- 1 teaspoon baking powder
- 1 teaspoon baking soda
- ¼ teaspoon salt
- 2 cups grated carrots (4 medium)
- 1 apple, peeled, cored and finely chopped (about 1¼ cups)
- ½ cup raisins
- 1 large egg
- 2 large egg whites *or* 4 teaspoons dried egg whites (*see Ingredient Note, page 394*), reconstituted according to package directions
- ½ cup apple butter
- ¼ cup canola oil
- 1 tablespoon vanilla extract
- 2 tablespoons finely chopped walnuts *or* pecans
- 2 tablespoons toasted wheat germ

1. Preheat oven to 375°F. Coat 18 muffin cups with cooking spray.

2. Whisk all-purpose flour, whole-wheat flour, sugar, cinnamon, baking powder, baking soda and salt in a large bowl. Stir in carrots, apple and raisins.

3. Whisk egg, egg whites, apple butter, oil and vanilla in a medium bowl. Make a well in the dry ingredients; add the wet ingredients and stir with a rubber spatula until just combined. Spoon the batter into the prepared muffin cups, filling them about ¾ full. Combine walnuts and wheat germ in a small bowl; sprinkle over the muffin tops.

4. Bake the muffins until the tops are golden brown and spring back when touched lightly, 15 to 25 minutes. Let cool in the pans for 5 minutes. Loosen edges and turn muffins out onto a wire rack to cool.

MAKE-AHEAD TIP:
Get a head start on your morning muffins the night before by mixing up the dry and liquid ingredients separately (refrigerate liquids). In the morning, combine the two, scoop and bake.

MAKES 1½ DOZEN MUFFINS.

PER MUFFIN: 161 CALORIES; 4 G FAT (0 G SAT, 2 G MONO); 12 MG CHOLESTEROL; 28 G CARBOHYDRATE; 3 G PROTEIN; 2 G FIBER; 145 MG SODIUM.

NUTRITION BONUS: 35% DV VITAMIN A.

Pineapple Upside-Down Muffins

PREP TIME: 30 MINUTES | **START TO FINISH:** 1 HOUR | **EASE OF PREPARATION:** EASY

Glistening like sticky buns, these unusual muffins are packed with wholesome ingredients—vegetables, fruit and whole grains—so you can feel good about serving them to your family. If you prefer to make simple carrot muffins for lunchboxes or breakfasts-on-the-go, omit the topping; sprinkle 2 tablespoons chopped nuts over the muffins before baking, if desired.

TOPPING

- **2 tablespoons packed light brown sugar**
- **2 tablespoons chopped walnuts *or* pecans (optional)**
- **1 10-ounce can pineapple slices**

MUFFINS

- **¾ cup whole-wheat flour**
- **¾ cup all-purpose flour**
- **2 teaspoons baking powder**
- **½ teaspoon baking soda**
- **¼ teaspoon salt**
- **1 tablespoon ground cinnamon**
- **2 large eggs**
- **½ cup packed light brown sugar**
- **¼ cup canola oil**
- **2 tablespoons pineapple juice *or* orange juice**
- **1 teaspoon vanilla extract**
- **1 8-ounce can crushed pineapple (*not* drained)**
- **1 cup grated carrot (1 large)**
- **½ cup old-fashioned oats**
- **¾ cup raisins, preferably baking raisins (*see Note*)**
- **¼ cup chopped walnuts *or* pecans (optional)**

1. Preheat oven to 400°F. Coat 12 muffin cups with cooking spray.

2. To prepare topping: Sprinkle ½ teaspoon brown sugar into each muffin cup. Sprinkle nuts, if using, over the sugar. Stack pineapple slices and cut into 6 wedges. Place 2 wedges in each muffin cup.

3. To prepare muffins: Whisk whole-wheat flour, all-purpose flour, baking powder, baking soda, salt and cinnamon in a large bowl.

4. Whisk eggs and brown sugar in a medium bowl until smooth. Whisk in oil, juice and vanilla. Stir in crushed pineapple. Make a well in the dry ingredients; add the wet ingredients and stir with a rubber spatula until just combined. Stir in carrot, oats, raisins and nuts, if using. Scoop the batter into the prepared muffin cups (they'll be quite full).

5. Bake the muffins until the tops are golden brown and firm to the touch, 15 to 25 minutes. Immediately loosen edges and turn muffins out onto a baking sheet. Restore any stray pineapple pieces and nuts. Let cool for at least 10 minutes. Serve upside-down, either warm or at room temperature.

INGREDIENT NOTE: Baking raisins, moister than regular ones, ensure a better texture. To substitute regular raisins, plump them first: soak in boiling water for 10 minutes; drain well.

MAKES 1 DOZEN MUFFINS.

PER MUFFIN: 211 CALORIES; 6 G FAT (1 G SAT, 3 G MONO); 35 MG CHOLESTEROL; 36 G CARBOHYDRATE; 4 G PROTEIN; 3 G FIBER; 185 MG SODIUM.

TOPPING VARIATIONS: Replace canned pineapple with ¾ cup sliced fresh pineapple, banana, mango or plums, or with rhubarb cut into ½-inch pieces.

Spiced Apple Cider Muffins

PREP TIME: 30 MINUTES | **START TO FINISH:** 1 HOUR | **EASE OF PREPARATION:** EASY

Cider doughnuts, a New England harvest treat, inspired these spice-happy muffins. A crumbly streusel topping made with a small amount of butter provides a delicious finish.

STREUSEL

- **2 tablespoons packed light brown sugar**
- **4 teaspoons whole-wheat flour**
- **½ teaspoon ground cinnamon**
- **1 tablespoon butter, cut into small pieces**
- **2 tablespoons finely chopped walnuts (optional)**

MUFFINS

- **1 cup whole-wheat flour**
- **1 cup all-purpose flour**
- **1½ teaspoons baking powder**
- **½ teaspoon baking soda**
- **¼ teaspoon salt**
- **1 tablespoon ground cinnamon**
- **½ teaspoon ground nutmeg**
- **1 large egg**
- **⅓ cup packed light brown sugar**
- **½ cup apple butter, such as Smucker's**
- **⅓ cup maple syrup**
- **⅓ cup apple cider**
- **⅓ cup low-fat plain yogurt**
- **¼ cup canola oil**

1. Preheat oven to 400°F. Coat 12 muffin cups with cooking spray.

2. To prepare streusel: Mix brown sugar, whole-wheat flour and cinnamon in a small bowl. With a pastry blender or your fingers, cut in butter until the mixture resembles coarse crumbs. Stir in walnuts, if using. Set aside.

3. To prepare muffins: Whisk whole-wheat flour, all-purpose flour, baking powder, baking soda, salt, cinnamon and nutmeg in a large bowl.

4. Whisk egg and brown sugar in a medium bowl until smooth. Whisk in apple butter, syrup, cider, yogurt and oil. Make a well in the dry ingredients; add the wet ingredients and stir with a rubber spatula until just combined. Scoop the batter into the prepared muffin cups (they'll be quite full). Sprinkle with the streusel.

5. Bake the muffins until the tops are golden brown and spring back when touched lightly, 15 to 25 minutes. Let cool in the pan for 5 minutes. Loosen edges and turn muffins out onto a wire rack to cool slightly before serving.

MAKES 1 DOZEN MUFFINS.

PER MUFFIN: 209 CALORIES; 7 G FAT (1 G SAT, 3 G MONO); 21 MG CHOLESTEROL; 34 G CARBOHYDRATE; 4 G PROTEIN; 2 G FIBER; 162 MG SODIUM.

Lower Carbs

Cranberry-Nut Mini Loaves with Flaxseeds

PREP TIME: 30 MINUTES | **START TO FINISH:** 1¾ HOURS (INCLUDING COOLING TIME)
EQUIPMENT: THREE 6-BY-3-INCH MINI-LOAF PANS | **TO MAKE AHEAD:** THE LOAVES WILL KEEP, WELL WRAPPED, AT ROOM TEMPERATURE FOR UP TO 4 DAYS OR IN THE FREEZER FOR UP TO 1 MONTH. | **EASE OF PREPARATION:** MODERATE

This tender, flavorful version of a holiday staple is made more wholesome with whole-wheat flour and flaxseeds. You can easily double the recipe if you are making these baby loaves as gifts.

- 1½ cups fresh *or* frozen cranberries
- 2 oranges, preferably organic, scrubbed
- Orange juice, if needed
- ⅓ cup whole flaxseeds (*see box, page 317*)
- 1 cup whole-wheat flour
- 1 cup all-purpose flour
- 1½ teaspoons baking powder
- ½ teaspoon baking soda
- ¼ teaspoon salt
- 1 large egg
- ¾ cup sugar
- ¼ cup canola oil
- 1 teaspoon vanilla extract
- ½ cup chopped walnuts *or* pecans (2 ounces), divided

1. Preheat oven to 350°F. Coat three 6-by-3-inch mini-loaf pans (2-cup capacity) with cooking spray.
2. Pulse cranberries in a food processor until coarsely chopped. Grate orange zest to measure 2 tablespoons. Squeeze juice, adding orange juice, if necessary, to measure ¾ cup.
3. Grind flaxseeds into coarse meal in a clean dry coffee grinder or blender. Transfer to a large bowl. Add whole-wheat flour, all-purpose flour, baking powder, baking soda and salt; whisk to blend.
4. Whisk egg, sugar, oil, vanilla and the orange zest and juice in a medium bowl. Add to the flour mixture and mix with a rubber spatula just until the dry ingredients are moistened. Fold in cranberries and ¼ cup nuts. Scrape the batter into the prepared pans, spreading evenly. Sprinkle the loaves with the remaining ¼ cup nuts. Place the pans on a baking sheet.
5. Bake the loaves until the tops are golden and a cake tester inserted in the center comes out clean, 35 to 45 minutes. Cool in the pans on a wire rack for 10 minutes. Loosen edges and turn the loaves out onto the rack to cool completely before slicing or wrapping.

MAKES 3 MINI LOAVES, 8 SLICES EACH.

PER SLICE: 120 CALORIES; 5 G FAT (0 G SAT, 2 G MONO); 9 MG CHOLESTEROL; 16 G CARBOHYDRATE; 3 G PROTEIN; 2 G FIBER; 79 MG SODIUM.

CRANBERRY-NUT LOAVES VARIATIONS

REGULAR LOAF: The batter will make one 9-by-5-inch loaf (12 slices); bake at 350°F for 55 to 60 minutes.

DOUGHNUTS: To make individual loaves that resemble doughnuts, use a mini-Bundt pan. Fold all nuts into the batter in Step 4. Coat 12 mini-Bundt molds with cooking spray and sprinkle each with ½ teaspoon sugar. Divide the batter among the prepared molds and bake at 400°F until the tops spring back when touched lightly, 10 to 12 minutes. Immediately loosen the edges with the tip of a knife and turn the "doughnuts" out onto a rack to cool.

PER SLICE OR DOUGHNUT: 239 CALORIES; 11 G FAT (1 G SAT, 4 G MONO); 18 MG CHOLESTEROL; 33 G CARBOHYDRATE; 5 G PROTEIN; 4 G FIBER; 157 MG SODIUM.

NUTRITION BONUS: 11 MG VITAMIN C (20% DV), 16% DV FIBER.

Chocolate Zucchini Bread

PREP TIME: 45 MINUTES | **START TO FINISH:** 1¾ HOURS
TO MAKE AHEAD: THE BREAD WILL KEEP, WELL WRAPPED, AT ROOM TEMPERATURE FOR 1 TO 2 DAYS OR IN THE FREEZER FOR UP TO 1 MONTH. | **EASE OF PREPARATION:** EASY

In this recipe remake, we replaced much of the oil with fruit-based fat replacement, reduced the amount of unsweetened chocolate but added cocoa powder and used half as many nuts but toasted them for maximum flavor. The result retained the original's tender crumb and rich, chocolaty flavor with only one-third the fat.

- ½ cup chopped walnuts (1¾ ounces)
- 1 cup all-purpose flour
- 1 cup whole-wheat flour
- ¼ cup unsweetened cocoa, preferably Dutch-process
- ½ teaspoon baking powder
- ½ teaspoon baking soda
- ½ teaspoon salt
- 3 large eggs, lightly beaten
- 1½ cups sugar
- ¾ cup fruit-based fat replacement, such as Lighter Bake, *or* unsweetened applesauce
- ¼ cup canola oil
- 1 teaspoon vanilla extract
- 1 ounce unsweetened chocolate, melted
- 2 cups grated zucchini (1 medium)

1. Preheat oven to 325°F. Coat two 8½-by-4½-inch loaf pans with cooking spray.

2. Spread walnuts in a pie pan and bake until fragrant, 5 to 7 minutes. Set aside to cool.

3. Whisk all-purpose flour, whole-wheat flour, cocoa, baking powder, baking soda and salt in a large bowl.

4. Whisk eggs, sugar, fruit-based fat replacement (or applesauce), oil, vanilla and melted chocolate in another large bowl until blended. Add to the dry ingredients and stir with a rubber spatula until just combined. Fold in zucchini and the reserved walnuts. Spoon the batter into the prepared pans, smoothing the tops.

5. Bake the loaves 55 to 60 minutes, or until the tops are golden and a skewer inserted in the center comes out clean. Let cool in pans on a wire rack for 10 minutes. Invert onto rack and cool completely.

RECIPE RX

Original Zucchini Bread:
365 calories
23 grams fat

EW Zucchini Bread:
239 calories
8 grams fat

MAKES 2 LOAVES, 8 SLICES EACH.

PER SLICE: 239 CALORIES; 8 G FAT (1 G SAT, 3 G MONO); 40 MG CHOLESTEROL; 38 G CARBOHYDRATE; 4 G PROTEIN; 3 G FIBER; 143 MG SODIUM.

Blueberry Danish

PREP TIME: 45 MINUTES | **START TO FINISH:** 1 HOUR 20 MINUTES | **TO MAKE AHEAD:** PREPARE THROUGH STEP 3. THE PASTRY WILL KEEP, WRAPPED, IN THE REFRIGERATOR FOR UP TO 2 DAYS. THE FILLING WILL KEEP, COVERED, IN THE REFRIGERATOR OVERNIGHT. | **EASE OF PREPARATION:** MODERATE

For long, lolling summer mornings, make this luscious, cheese-filled Danish. It uses a tender cottage-cheese pastry that's far easier—and more healthful—than any traditional butter-laden dough.

PASTRY

- **1 cup all-purpose flour**
- **1 cup whole-wheat pastry flour**
- **2 teaspoons baking powder**
- **½ teaspoon salt**
- **¾ cup low-fat cottage cheese**
- **⅓ cup sugar**
- **⅓ cup 1% milk**
- **¼ cup canola oil**
- **1 teaspoon vanilla extract**

FILLING

- **4 ounces reduced-fat cream cheese**
- **¼ cup sugar**
- **1 large egg, separated**
- **2 teaspoons freshly grated lemon zest, preferably organic**
- **1 teaspoon vanilla extract**
- **1 cup fresh blueberries**
- **1 tablespoon water**

GLAZE

- **½ cup confectioners' sugar**
- **2-3 teaspoons lemon juice**

1. **To prepare pastry:** Whisk all-purpose flour, whole-wheat flour, baking powder and salt in a medium bowl.
2. In a food processor, puree cottage cheese. Add sugar, milk, oil and vanilla and process until smooth. Add flour mixture and pulse 4 or 5 times, just until the dough clumps together. Turn out onto a lightly floured surface and gently knead several times; do not overwork. Press the dough into a disk, dust with flour and wrap in plastic wrap. Refrigerate until chilled, at least 30 minutes.
3. **To prepare filling & bake Danish:** Using a food processor or an electric mixer, blend cream cheese with sugar until creamy. Blend in egg yolk, lemon zest and vanilla.
4. Preheat oven to 400°F. Cut a piece of parchment paper or foil to fit a large baking sheet. If using foil, spray it with cooking spray. Set aside nearby.
5. On a lightly floured surface, roll the dough into a rectangle about 12 by 16 inches. Roll the dough back over the rolling pin and transfer it to the prepared paper (or foil). Spread the cream cheese mixture down the center of the dough, leaving a margin of 3¼ inches on the long sides and 1 inch at either end. Sprinkle blueberries evenly over the cream cheese mixture.
6. Using a sharp knife, make 3-inch-long cuts at 1-inch intervals along each side of the dough at 45° angles to the filling. Trim off the top corners and fold the top end of the dough over the filling. Crisscross the angled strips over the filling to create a braided effect, tucking in the dough at the bottom end. Carefully lift the paper (or foil) at each end and transfer to the baking sheet.

INGREDIENT NOTE: Use only fresh blueberries in this recipe.

7. Blend egg white and water with a fork in a small bowl. Brush lightly over the pastry. Bake the Danish until golden and firm, 20 to 25 minutes. Transfer to a wire rack and let cool slightly.

8. To prepare glaze & finish Danish: Combine confectioners' sugar and 2 teaspoons lemon juice in a small bowl. Stir until smooth. Add more lemon juice if the glaze is too thick. With a spoon, drizzle the glaze over the Danish. Slice and serve warm or at room temperature.

MAKES 12 SLICES.

PER SLICE: 219 CALORIES; 7 G FAT (2 G SAT, 3 G MONO); 24 MG CHOLESTEROL; 32 G CARBOHYDRATE; 6 G PROTEIN; 2 G FIBER; 255 MG SODIUM.

Buttermilk Biscuits

PREP TIME: 30 MINUTES | **START TO FINISH:** 50 MINUTES | **EASE OF PREPARATION:** EASY

Nothing like a basket of hot, flaky biscuits to accompany a home-cooked dinner. You can also use these biscuits to top a chicken pot pie or for strawberry shortcake.

- ¾ cup buttermilk
- 1 tablespoon canola oil
- 1 cup whole-wheat pastry flour
- 1 cup all-purpose flour
- 1 tablespoon sugar
- 1½ teaspoons baking powder
- ½ teaspoon baking soda
- ½ teaspoon salt
- 1½ tablespoons cold butter, cut into small pieces
- 1 tablespoon milk for brushing

1. Preheat oven to 425°F. Coat a baking sheet with cooking spray.

2. Combine buttermilk and oil. Whisk whole-wheat flour, all-purpose flour, sugar, baking powder, baking soda and salt in a large bowl. Using your fingertips or 2 knives, cut butter into the dry ingredients until crumbly. Make a well in the center and gradually pour in the buttermilk mixture, stirring with a fork until just combined.

3. Transfer the dough to a floured surface and sprinkle with a little flour. Lightly knead the dough 8 times, then pat or roll out to an even ¾-inch thickness. Cut into 2-inch rounds and transfer to the prepared baking sheet. Gather any scraps of dough and cut more rounds. Brush the tops with milk.

4. Bake the biscuits for 12 to 16 minutes, or until golden brown. Transfer to a wire rack and let cool slightly before serving.

MAKES 1 DOZEN BISCUITS.

PER BISCUIT: 104 CALORIES; 3 G FAT (1 G SAT, 1 G MONO); 4 MG CHOLESTEROL; 16 G CARBOHYDRATE; 3 G PROTEIN; 1 G FIBER; 214 MG SODIUM.

Irish Soda Bread

PREP TIME: 15 MINUTES | **START TO FINISH:** 50 MINUTES | **EASE OF PREPARATION:** EASY

Fragrant homemade whole-wheat bread that is ready in less than 1 hour. The recipe is easily doubled.

- ¾ cup whole-wheat flour
- ¾ cup all-purpose flour
- 2 tablespoons sugar
- 1 teaspoon baking soda
- ½ teaspoon salt
- ½ cup currants
- 2 teaspoons caraway seeds
- ¾ cup buttermilk, plus additional for brushing

1. Preheat oven to 400°F. Coat a pie pan with cooking spray.
2. Whisk whole-wheat flour, all-purpose flour, sugar, baking soda and salt in a large bowl. Stir in currants and caraway seeds. Make a well in the center of the dry ingredients. Gradually pour in the buttermilk, stirring with a fork until just combined. (Do not overmix.)
3. Turn the dough out onto a lightly floured surface and knead several times. Form into a ball, flatten slightly and place in the prepared pie pan. Brush the top with buttermilk and dust with flour. With a sharp knife, cut a ½-inch-deep X into the top of the loaf.
4. Bake the loaf until it is brown on top and sounds hollow when tapped on the bottom, 30 to 40 minutes. Let cool slightly before slicing.

MAKES 1 SMALL LOAF, 8 SLICES.

PER SLICE: 131 CALORIES; 1 G FAT (0 G SAT, 0 G MONO); 1 MG CHOLESTEROL; 27 G CARBOHYDRATE; 4 G PROTEIN; 3 G FIBER; 328 MG SODIUM.

Molasses Quick Bread

Lower Carbs

PREP TIME: 15 MINUTES | **START TO FINISH:** 1 HOUR | **EASE OF PREPARATION:** EASY

This recipe also makes great crunchy muffins. Bake at 350°F for 15 minutes.

- 1 cup whole-wheat flour
- ½ cup cornmeal, preferably stone-ground
- ½ cup wheat germ, preferably untoasted
- 1 teaspoon baking powder
- ¾ teaspoon salt
- ½ teaspoon baking soda
- 1 large egg, lightly beaten
- 1 cup buttermilk
- ⅓ cup molasses
- 1 tablespoon canola oil

1. Preheat oven to 350°F. Coat an 8½-by-4½-inch loaf pan with cooking spray.
2. Whisk flour, cornmeal, wheat germ, baking powder, salt and baking soda in a large bowl. Whisk egg, buttermilk, molasses and oil in a medium bowl. Add to the dry ingredients and stir until just combined. Scrape the batter into the prepared pan.
3. Bake the loaf for 35 to 45 minutes, or until a skewer inserted in the center comes out clean. Let cool in the pan on a wire rack for 10 minutes. Invert onto the rack. Serve warm or at room temperature.

MAKES 1 LOAF, 12 SLICES.

PER SLICE: 119 CALORIES; 2 G FAT (0 G SAT, 1 G MONO); 18 MG CHOLESTEROL; 21 G CARBOHYDRATE; 4 G PROTEIN; 2 G FIBER; 260 MG SODIUM.

Wholesome Cornbread

PREP TIME: 15 MINUTES | **START TO FINISH:** 50 MINUTES | **EASE OF PREPARATION:** EASY

An excellent cornbread to serve with chili or turn into Cornbread & Apple Stuffing (*page 103*).

- 1¼ cups yellow cornmeal
- ¾ cup whole-wheat flour
- 3 tablespoons sugar
- 1 teaspoon baking powder
- ½ teaspoon baking soda
- ½ teaspoon salt
- 1 large egg, lightly beaten
- 1¼ cups buttermilk
- 2 tablespoons canola oil

1. Preheat oven to 350°F. Coat an 8-inch-square baking pan with cooking spray.
2. Whisk cornmeal, flour, sugar, baking powder, baking soda and salt in a large bowl. Whisk egg, buttermilk and oil in a separate bowl. Add to the dry ingredients and stir until just combined. Scrape the batter into the prepared pan, spreading evenly.
3. Bake the cornbread until the top springs back when touched lightly, 25 to 30 minutes. Let cool in the pan on a wire rack for at least 5 minutes. Serve warm or at room temperature.

MAKES 9 SERVINGS.

PER SERVING: 161 CALORIES; 5 G FAT (1 G SAT, 2 G MONO); 25 MG CHOLESTEROL; 25 G CARBOHYDRATE; 5 G PROTEIN; 3 G FIBER; 285 MG SODIUM.

Cinnamon-Raisin Bagels

PREP TIME: 40 MINUTES | **START TO FINISH:** 1½ HOURS | **TO MAKE AHEAD:** FREEZE FRESH (AND PROPERLY COOLED) BAGELS IMMEDIATELY UNLESS YOU ARE EATING THEM ALL THAT DAY. | **EASE OF PREPARATION:** MODERATE

If you love to bake, these hearty homemade bagels are well worth the effort. Serve them warm with a little reduced-fat cream cheese.

- 1 cup raisins
- 1½ cups lukewarm water
- ¼ cup packed light brown sugar
- 2 tablespoons honey
- 4 teaspoons active dry yeast
- 1 tablespoon canola oil
- 1¼ cups whole-wheat flour *or* white whole-wheat flour (*see Ingredient Note, page 317*)
- 4 teaspoons ground cinnamon
- 1 tablespoon kosher salt
- 3-4 cups bread flour (*see Ingredient Note, page 395*)
- 1 large egg white, lightly beaten

KETTLE WATER

- 6 quarts water
- 2 tablespoons packed light brown sugar

1. Put raisins in a small bowl and add enough boiling water to cover; let stand for 5 minutes. Drain and blot dry with a paper towel.
2. Whisk lukewarm water, ¼ cup brown sugar, honey, yeast and oil in a large bowl until the yeast dissolves. Stir in whole-wheat flour, cinnamon, salt and the raisins. Stir in enough of the bread flour to make a soft dough, about 2½ cups.
3. Turn the dough out onto a lightly floured surface. Knead, gradually incorporating more flour, until the dough is smooth and quite firm, 10 to 12 minutes. Cover with a clean cloth and let rest for 10 minutes.
4. Divide the dough into 12 pieces. Roll each piece into a 10-inch-long rope. Form bagels by overlapping the ends by 1 inch. Pinch together firmly. Set the bagels aside, uncovered, to rise until slightly puffy, about 20 minutes.
5. **To kettle & bake bagels:** Preheat oven to 450°F. Line 1 large or 2 small baking sheets with parchment paper. In a large pot, bring 6 quarts water and 2 tablespoons brown sugar to a boil.
6. Slip several risen bagels at a time into the pot—the water should be at a lively simmer. Cook for 45 seconds, turn them over with a slotted spoon or tongs and cook for 45 seconds longer. Remove the bagels with a slotted spoon and drain on a clean kitchen towel; place on the prepared baking sheet(s). Brush with egg white.
7. Place the bagels in the oven, reduce heat to 425° and bake for 15 minutes. Turn the bagels over and bake until golden brown, about 5 minutes more.

MAKES 12 THREE-OUNCE BAGELS.

PER BAGEL: 261 CALORIES; 2 G FAT (0 G SAT, 1 G MONO); 0 MG CHOLESTEROL; 54 G CARBOHYDRATE; 7 G PROTEIN; 4 G FIBER; 488 MG SODIUM.

NUTRITION BONUS: 15% DV FIBER, 3 MG IRON (15% DV), 102 MCG FOLATE (26% DV).

Multi-Grain Whole-Wheat Bread

PREP TIME: 10 MINUTES | **START TO FINISH:** 4-4¾ HOURS (INCLUDING COOLING TIME)
EQUIPMENT: 8½-BY-4½-INCH LOAF PAN (A 9-BY-5-INCH PAN CAN BE USED BUT THE LOAF WILL NOT BE AS HIGH.)
EASE OF PREPARATION: MODERATE

Creating delicious multi-grain bread yourself ensures far more whole grains than most commercially prepared products and your kitchen smells marvelous in the process. A food processor can knead the dough in less than a minute. You can also use your bread machine. (*Photo: page 224.*)

- **1¾ cups whole-wheat flour**
- **¾ cup bread flour (*see Ingredient Note, page 395*)**
- **¾ cup 7-grain cereal (*see Note*)**
- **2 tablespoons skim-milk powder**
- **1 package active dry yeast (2¼ teaspoons)**
- **1¼ teaspoons salt**
- **1⅓ cups water**
- **2 tablespoons molasses**
- **1½ tablespoons canola oil**

INGREDIENT NOTE: Seven-grain cereal is sold in supermarkets and natural-food stores. The usual composition is cracked wheat, steel-cut oats, soybean grits, wheat bran, buckwheat grits, yellow corn grits and millet.

1. Combine whole-wheat flour, bread flour, 7-grain cereal, milk powder, yeast and salt in a food processor fitted with a metal chopping blade (not a dough blade); process for 15 seconds.
2. Stir water, molasses and oil in a measuring cup until the molasses is fully dissolved. With the processor running, slowly pour the liquid through the feed tube. When combined, stop processing and let the dough rest in the workbowl for 30 minutes.
3. Process the dough for 45 seconds. (It will be sticky and will not form a ball.) Scrape into a medium bowl coated with cooking spray. Cover with plastic wrap. Let the dough rise until doubled in bulk, 1 to 1¼ hours.
4. Coat an 8½-by-4½-inch loaf pan with cooking spray. Turn the dough out onto a lightly floured surface and sprinkle with flour. Punch down and form into a loaf. Place in the prepared pan. Cover with plastic wrap and let rise until doubled, 50 minutes to 1 hour.
5. Preheat oven to 400°F. Bake the loaf until dark brown and hollow-sounding when tapped, 35 to 40 minutes. Turn it out onto a wire rack to cool before slicing.

MAKES ONE 1½-POUND LOAF, 14 SLICES.

PER SLICE: 127 CALORIES; 2 G FAT (0 G SAT, 1 G MONO); 0 MG CHOLESTEROL; 23 G CARBOHYDRATE; 4 G PROTEIN; 3 G FIBER; 217 MG SODIUM.

VARIATION: Multi-Grain Bread with Dried Fruit & Nuts
Add 1 cup dried fruit, such as raisins, dried cranberries, chopped pitted dates and/or chopped dried apricots, and ½ cup chopped walnuts to the dough after you remove it from the processor in Step 3; knead until mixed in. If using a bread machine, follow the manufacturer's directions for adding solid ingredients to dough.

Whole-Wheat Flax Bread

PREP TIME: 30 MINUTES | **START TO FINISH:** 3 HOURS 25 MINUTES | **EASE OF PREPARATION:** MODERATE

This super high-fiber bread has a nutty whole-grain taste and texture that makes excellent sandwiches.

- ⅓ cup whole flaxseeds (*see box, page 317*)
- 1¾ cups lukewarm water
- 1 tablespoon honey
- 1 package active dry yeast (2¼ teaspoons)
- 1¼ cups bread flour (*see Ingredient Note, page 395*), divided
- ½ cup pumpernickel *or* dark rye flour
- 1½ teaspoons salt
- 2 cups whole-wheat flour *or* white whole-wheat flour (*see Ingredient Note, page 317*)
- 1 egg, lightly beaten with 1 tablespoon water

1. Grind flaxseed into a coarse meal in a spice mill (such as a clean coffee grinder) or dry blender. Set aside 2 teaspoons for topping.
2. Stir lukewarm water and honey in a large bowl until the honey is dissolved. Sprinkle in yeast; let stand until the yeast bubbles, about 5 minutes.
3. Add 1 cup bread flour, pumpernickel (or rye) flour, salt and remaining ground flaxseed. With a wooden spoon, stir vigorously in the same direction until the batter is smooth. Gradually stir in whole-wheat flour until it becomes too difficult to stir. (*Alternatively, mix dough in a stand-up mixer fitted with a paddle attachment.*)
4. Turn the dough out onto a lightly floured surface and knead, adding only enough of the remaining bread flour to keep it from sticking, until smooth and elastic, 10 to 12 minutes. (The dough will be slightly sticky.)
5. Place the dough in a large oiled bowl. Turn to coat and cover with plastic wrap. Let rise until doubled in bulk, about 1½ hours.
6. Coat a 9-by-5-inch loaf pan with cooking spray. Punch the dough down, flatten into a disk and tightly roll into a log. Place seam-side down in the prepared pan. Cover with plastic wrap; let rise until the dough domes over the top of the pan, about 45 minutes.
7. Preheat oven to 400°F. Lightly brush the loaf with egg mixture and sprinkle with the reserved 2 teaspoons ground flaxseed.
8. Bake the bread for 15 minutes. Reduce oven temperature to 350° and continue baking until the bread pulls away from the sides of the pan, 20 to 25 minutes. Turn the bread out onto a wire rack and cool completely before slicing.

MAKES 1 LOAF, 12 SLICES.

PER SLICE: 184 CALORIES; 4 G FAT (0 G SAT, 1 G MONO); 18 MG CHOLESTEROL; 32 G CARBOHYDRATE; 8 G PROTEIN; 6 G FIBER; 300 MG SODIUM.

NUTRITION BONUS: 23% DV FIBER, 3 MG IRON (15% DV), 60 MCG FOLATE (15% DV).

High Fiber

Flaxseeds

FLAXSEEDS ARE ONE OF THE BEST plant sources of omega-3 fatty acids. They provide both soluble fiber, linked to reduced risk of heart disease, and insoluble fiber, which provides valuable roughage. Flaxseeds are perishable, so purchase whole seeds (instead of ground flaxmeal) and store in the refrigerator or freezer. The seeds must be ground for your body to take advantage of the nutrients, so grind in a clean coffee grinder or dry blender just before using. Flaxseeds can be found in the natural-foods section of large supermarkets and in natural-foods stores.

BREAD-MACHINE VARIATION

1. Grind ⅓ cup flaxseed as in Step 1.
2. Combine 1½ cups water and 1 tablespoon honey in the pan of the bread machine. Add 2 cups whole-wheat flour, 1 cup bread flour, the ground flaxseed, ½ cup pumpernickel (or dark rye) flour and 1½ teaspoons salt. Gently tap the side of the baking pan to level ingredients. Make a small indentation in the dry ingredients and sprinkle in 1 package active dry yeast.
3. Secure pan in machine. Program according to manufacturer's directions for whole-grain and medium crust. Press "start." At the end of the baking cycle, remove bread from pan and cool completely on a wire rack before slicing.

INGREDIENT NOTE
White whole-wheat flour, made from a special variety of white wheat, is light in color and flavor but has the same nutritional properties as regular whole-wheat flour.

PER SLICE: 168 CALORIES; 3 G FAT (0 G SAT, 0 G MONO); 0 MG CHOLESTEROL; 30 G CARBOHYDRATE; 7 G PROTEIN; 6 G FIBER; 294 MG SODIUM.

OLD-FASHIONED DESSERTS

16

It's not surprising that some of the most beloved, sought-after recipes from EATINGWELL are desserts. Almost universally, people crave sweets and, almost universally, when people fall off healthy eating plans, cravings are the culprit. So while we've worked lots of nutritious ingredients into these recipes—you'll find cookies made with oats and whole-wheat flour and plenty of fruit desserts here—many are wonderfully gooey, rich treats that are all about pleasure. Well, almost. Unlike most desserts, these are low in saturated fats and the calories are kept within rational bounds. A sweet life demands a little sugar. With these lightened recipes, a little indulgence can be part of the plan.

QUICK FRUIT DESSERTS

Apple-Cinnamon Rice Pudding

PREP TIME: 35 MINUTES | **START TO FINISH:** 1 HOUR 10 MINUTES | **EASE OF PREPARATION:** MODERATE

Whether you're partial to the fragrant maple and apple goodness warm from the oven or prefer it cold and luxuriously creamy, this simple rice pudding is pure comfort. A teakettle makes neat work of the hot water bath.

- 1½ cups water
- ¾ cup short-grain rice, such as arborio
- ½ teaspoon salt
- 3 cups 1% milk, divided
- 2 large egg yolks
- ¼ cup pure maple syrup
- 2 tablespoons packed light brown sugar
- 1 teaspoon vanilla extract
- 2 tart apples, such as Granny Smith
- 1 teaspoon lemon juice
- ½ cup raisins
- Ground cinnamon for garnish

1. Preheat oven to 350°F. Coat an 8-inch-square baking dish with cooking spray.
2. Bring water to a boil in a 2-quart saucepan. Add rice and salt. Reduce heat to low and simmer, uncovered, stirring occasionally, until water is absorbed, 10 to 12 minutes.
3. Add 2 cups milk to rice and simmer, stirring occasionally, for 8 minutes. (Discard any skin that forms on the surface.) Remove from the heat.
4. Whisk remaining 1 cup milk, egg yolks, maple syrup, brown sugar and vanilla in a medium bowl until smooth.
5. Peel and coarsely grate apples. Place in a small bowl and toss with lemon juice.
6. Stirring constantly, add about 1 cup hot rice mixture to the egg mixture. Scrape back into remaining rice mixture, stirring constantly. Add raisins and grated apples.
7. Scrape mixture into prepared baking dish. Place dish in a shallow roasting pan and pour enough simmering water into roasting pan to come halfway up the sides of the baking dish.
8. Bake pudding for 35 to 40 minutes, or until barely set. Serve warm or chilled, dusted with cinnamon.

MAKES 6 SERVINGS.

PER SERVING: 221 CALORIES; 3 G FAT (1 G SAT, 1 G MONO); 76 MG CHOLESTEROL; 44 G CARBOHYDRATE; 7 G PROTEIN; 1 G FIBER; 266 MG SODIUM.

NUTRITION BONUS: 176 MG CALCIUM (20% DV).

Lemon Pudding Cake

PREP TIME: 20 MINUTES | **START TO FINISH:** 1 HOUR 10 MINUTES | **EASE OF PREPARATION:** EASY

The tart fresh taste of lemons makes it easy to create dishes that need little fat to be fabulous: the proof is in this pudding cake.

- **¾ cup sugar, divided**
- **⅓ cup all-purpose flour**
- **⅛ teaspoon salt**
- **1 cup 1% milk**
- **2 teaspoons freshly grated lemon zest, preferably organic**
- **½ cup lemon juice**
- **2 tablespoons butter, melted**
- **3 large eggs, separated**
- **Confectioners' sugar for dusting**

1. Preheat oven to 350°F. Coat a 9½-inch deep-dish glass or ceramic pie pan (6-cup capacity) with cooking spray. Boil water for the water bath.
2. Whisk together ½ cup sugar, flour and salt in a medium bowl. Make a well in dry ingredients. Add milk, lemon zest, lemon juice, butter and egg yolks. Whisk until smooth.
3. Using an electric mixer, beat egg whites until they form soft peaks. Gradually add remaining ¼ cup sugar, beating until glossy. Fold egg whites into batter (it will be thin and a little lumpy). Scrape into the prepared pie pan.
4. Place pie pan inside a larger shallow pan. Add enough boiling water to come almost halfway up the sides of the pie pan.
5. Bake pudding cake until the top is golden and caky with soft lemon pudding underneath, 30 to 40 minutes. Let cool on a wire rack for 15 minutes. Dust with confectioners' sugar and serve warm.

MAKES 8 SERVINGS.

PER SERVING: 162 CALORIES; 5 G FAT (3 G SAT, 3 G MONO); 89 MG CHOLESTEROL; 26 G CARBOHYDRATE; 4 G PROTEIN; 0 G FIBER; 79 MG SODIUM.

NUTRITION BONUS: 8 MG VITAMIN C (15% DV).

Chocolate Bread Pudding with Custard Sauce

PREP TIME: 25 MINUTES | **START TO FINISH:** 2 HOURS 25 MINUTES (INCLUDING CUSTARD CHILLING)
EASE OF PREPARATION: MODERATE

Rich chocolate filling and an orange-scented custard sauce take plain bread to new heights in this lovely combination of decadence and homey comfort.

- Orange-Scented Custard Sauce (*page 323*)
- 1 tablespoon canola oil
- 2 teaspoons butter
- 8 1-inch slices whole-wheat sandwich bread, crusts removed, cut in half on the diagonal
- ⅓ cup unsweetened cocoa powder
- Pinch of salt
- 2½ cups 1% milk
- 2 ounces good-quality bittersweet (*not* unsweetened) chocolate, chopped
- 2 large eggs
- ½ cup packed light brown sugar
- 1 teaspoon vanilla extract

1. Make Orange-Scented Custard Sauce and refrigerate.
2. Preheat oven to 400°F.
3. Heat oil and butter over low heat in a small saucepan just until butter melts. Brush both sides of the bread slices with butter mixture and place on a baking sheet. Bake until golden brown, 5 to 7 minutes per side.
4. Overlap toasted bread slices in an ungreased 9-inch square baking dish. Reduce oven temperature to 325°.
5. Whisk cocoa and salt in a medium saucepan. Gradually whisk in milk. Bring to a bare simmer over low heat. Remove from heat, add chocolate and whisk until it melts.
6. Whisk eggs, brown sugar and vanilla in a medium bowl until blended. Gradually whisk hot chocolate mixture into egg mixture. Pour custard over bread in baking dish. Let stand for 15 minutes. Meanwhile, boil water for the water bath.
7. Set baking dish in a roasting pan and place in the oven. Add boiling water to the roasting pan to reach halfway up sides of baking dish. Bake pudding until just set, 20 to 25 minutes. (It should still jiggle slightly in the center.) Remove baking dish from roasting pan and cool on a wire rack for about 20 minutes. Serve warm with Orange-Scented Custard Sauce.

MAKES 8 SERVINGS.

PER SERVING: 309 CALORIES; 12 G FAT (6 G SAT, 3 G MONO); 94 MG CHOLESTEROL; 44 G CARBOHYDRATE; 11 G PROTEIN; 4 G FIBER; 276 MG SODIUM.

NUTRITION BONUS: 187 MG CALCIUM (20% DV), 15% DV FIBER.

ORANGE-SCENTED CUSTARD SAUCE

PREP TIME: 20 MINUTES | **START TO FINISH:** 2 HOURS 50 MINUTES (INCLUDING CHILLING TIME)
TO MAKE AHEAD: THE SAUCE WILL KEEP, COVERED, IN THE REFRIGERATOR FOR UP TO 2 DAYS.
EASE OF PREPARATION: MODERATE

Steeping orange zest in the milk boosts the flavor of this virtually fat-free sauce, based on a classic *crème anglaise.*

- **1½ cups 1% milk**
- **1 2-by-1-inch strip orange zest, preferably organic**
- **1 large egg**
- **¼ cup sugar**
- **2 teaspoons all-purpose flour**
- **1½ tablespoons Grand Marnier (optional)**

1. Combine milk and orange zest in a small heavy saucepan. Bring almost to a simmer over low heat. Remove pan from heat, cover and let stand for 30 minutes.
2. Whisk egg, sugar and flour in a bowl until smooth.
3. Rewarm milk over low heat until steaming. Gradually add milk to the egg mixture, whisking constantly. Return mixture to saucepan.
4. Cook sauce over low heat, stirring constantly, until thick enough to coat the back of a spoon, 7 to 8 minutes. (Do not allow sauce to come to a simmer.) Remove from heat.
5. Pour sauce through a fine-meshed sieve into a bowl. Discard orange zest. Stir in Grand Marnier, if using. Place plastic wrap directly on the surface of the sauce and refrigerate until cold, about 2 hours.

MAKES ABOUT 1½ CUPS.

PER TABLESPOON: 20 CALORIES; 0 G FAT (0 G SAT, 0 G MONO); 10 MG CHOLESTEROL; 3 G CARBOHYDRATE; 1 G PROTEIN; 0 G FIBER; 11 MG SODIUM.

Chocolate-Orange Silk Mousse

PREP TIME: 30 MINUTES | **START TO FINISH:** 1½ HOURS | **TO MAKE AHEAD:** THE MOUSSE WILL KEEP, COVERED, IN THE REFRIGERATOR FOR UP TO 2 DAYS. | **EASE OF PREPARATION:** EASY

Intense, heavenly chocolate is all you'll think about when you taste this dessert, though it's packed with all the good things found in tofu. Make sure the tofu is gossamer-smooth before adding the chocolate mixture. (*Photo: page 222.*)

- 1 12.3-ounce package reduced-fat silken tofu (1½ cups)
- 3 ounces good-quality bittersweet chocolate (*not* unsweetened), finely chopped
- ⅓ cup unsweetened cocoa powder
- ¼ cup boiling water
- 1 teaspoon vanilla extract
- ½ teaspoon freshly grated orange zest
- ⅔ cup confectioners' sugar
- ⅔ cup chocolate wafer crumbs (3 ounces) (*see Notes*)

NUTRITION NOTE: Many commercial cookies and wafers contain partially hydrogenated oil, a source of trans-fatty acids. Fortunately, brands made without these oils, such as Newman's Own Organics and Mi-Del, are every bit as tasty. Look for them in the natural-foods section of large supermarkets.

1. Puree tofu in a food processor, scraping down the sides as needed, until completely smooth.

2. Combine chocolate and cocoa in a medium bowl. Add boiling water and stir with a wooden spoon until the chocolate has melted and the mixture is smooth. Stir in vanilla and orange zest. Mix in confectioners' sugar, a little at a time, until smooth. Add the chocolate mixture to the processor; puree until smooth and well blended, scraping down the sides as needed.

3. Spoon about 2 teaspoons chocolate crumbs into each of 5 parfait glasses or dessert dishes. Add about ¼ cup mousse, then layer with another 2 teaspoons crumbs. Top with another ¼ cup mousse and finish with a sprinkling of crumbs. Cover and refrigerate for at least 1 hour.

TO MAKE WAFER CRUMBS: Place wafers in a ziplock plastic bag, seal and crush with a rolling pin. Alternatively, pulse wafers in a food processor.

MAKES 5 SERVINGS, ABOUT ½ CUP EACH.

PER SERVING: 266 CALORIES; 9 G FAT (4 G SAT, 0 G MONO); 1 MG CHOLESTEROL; 42 G CARBOHYDRATE; 8 G PROTEIN; 4 G FIBER; 125 MG SODIUM.

NUTRITION BONUS: 16% DV FIBER.

Tiramisù

PREP TIME: 1 HOUR | **START TO FINISH:** 5 HOURS (INCLUDING CHILLING TIME) | **TO MAKE AHEAD:** TIRAMISÙ WILL KEEP, COVERED, IN THE REFRIGERATOR FOR UP TO 2 DAYS. | **EASE OF PREPARATION:** MODERATE

Italian for "pick me up," tiramisù could be considered an Italian trifle. It consists of layers of coffee-and-brandy-soaked ladyfingers and a rich mascarpone cream filling. We have updated this popular classic by replacing the custard with a fat-free meringue and lightening the mascarpone with reduced-fat cream cheese.

- **8 ounces ladyfingers (60 ladyfingers)**
- **4 tablespoons brandy, divided**
- **1 tablespoon instant coffee (preferably espresso) granules**
- **1 cup water**
- **2 tablespoons dried egg whites (*see Ingredient Note, page 394*), reconstituted according to package directions (equivalent to 3 large egg whites)**
- **¾ cup sugar**
- **¼ teaspoon cream of tartar**
- **4 ounces mascarpone cheese (½ cup)**
- **4 ounces reduced-fat cream cheese (½ cup), softened**
- **1 cup chocolate shavings, about 1 ounce (*see page 397*)**
- **Confectioners' sugar, for garnish**

RECIPE RX

Original Tiramisù:
335 calories
25 grams fat

EW Tiramisù:
209 calories
9 grams fat

1. If ladyfingers are soft, toast them in a 350°F oven for 6 to 8 minutes. Stir together 3 tablespoons brandy, coffee granules and water in a small bowl until the granules are dissolved. Brush over the flat side of the ladyfingers. Set aside.
2. Bring about 1 inch of water to a simmer in the bottom of a medium saucepan. Combine reconstituted egg whites, sugar and cream of tartar in a heatproof mixing bowl that will fit over the saucepan. Set the bowl over the simmering water and beat with a hand-held mixer at low speed 4 to 5 minutes. Increase speed to high and continue beating over heat for about 3 minutes longer. (The mixture should form a ribbon trail.) Remove the bowl from the heat and beat until cool and fluffy, 3 to 4 minutes. Set aside.
3. Beat mascarpone and cream cheese in a large bowl until creamy (no need to wash meringue from beaters). Add about 1 cup of the beaten whites and the remaining 1 tablespoon brandy and beat until smooth, scraping down the sides of the bowl. Using a rubber spatula, fold in the remaining whites by hand.
4. Line the bottom and sides of a 3-quart trifle bowl or soufflé dish with ladyfingers, flat sides toward the center. Spoon in one-quarter of the filling and top with a layer of ladyfingers. Repeat with two more layers of filling and ladyfingers, arranging the fourth layer of ladyfingers decoratively over the top, trimming to fit, if necessary. Top with remaining filling. Cover and chill for at least 4 hours or overnight.
5. Before serving, sprinkle with chocolate shavings and dust with confectioners' sugar.

MAKES 12 SERVINGS, ⅔ CUP EACH.

PER SERVING: 209 CALORIES; 9 G FAT (4 G SAT, 1 G MONO); 86 MG CHOLESTEROL; 26 G CARBOHYDRATE; 5 G PROTEIN; 0 G FIBER; 76 MG SODIUM.

Maple-Pumpkin Custards with Crystallized Ginger

PREP TIME: 20 MINUTES | **START TO FINISH:** 3 HOURS (INCLUDING COOLING AND CHILLING)
TO MAKE AHEAD: PREPARE THROUGH STEP 4. COVER AND REFRIGERATE FOR UP TO 2 DAYS.
EASE OF PREPARATION: MODERATE

A Thanksgiving meal wouldn't be complete without pumpkin, and here in Vermont we wouldn't dream of excluding our beloved maple syrup. We've combined the two in these elegant custards, featuring the best part of a pumpkin pie and saving calories for a luscious finish of real whipped cream. If you can find it, use Grade B dark amber syrup to get the best maple flavor.

- **1½ cups 1% milk**
- **4 large eggs**
- **¾ cup maple syrup**
- **¾ cup canned unseasoned pumpkin puree**
- **1 teaspoon ground cinnamon**
- **½ teaspoon ground nutmeg**
- **¼ teaspoon salt**
- **3 tablespoons whipped cream**
- **¼ cup chopped crystallized ginger**

1. Preheat oven to 325°F. Put a kettle of water on to heat for the water bath. Line a roasting pan with a folded kitchen towel.
2. Heat milk over low heat in a small saucepan until barely steaming but not boiling.
3. Whisk eggs and syrup in a large bowl until smooth. Gently whisk in the warm milk (a little bit at a time so the eggs don't cook). Add pumpkin puree, cinnamon, nutmeg and salt; whisk until blended.
4. Divide the mixture among six 6-ounce (¾-cup) custard cups. Skim foam from the surface. Place custard cups in the prepared roasting pan. Pour enough boiling water into the pan to come halfway up the sides of the custard cups. Place the pan in the oven and bake, uncovered, until custards are just set but still quiver in the center when shaken, 45 to 50 minutes. Transfer custards to a wire rack and let cool for 45 minutes. Cover and refrigerate for at least 1 hour, or until chilled.
5. To serve, top each custard with a dollop of whipped cream and a sprinkling of crystallized ginger.

MAKES 6 SERVINGS.

PER SERVING: 212 CALORIES; 5 G FAT (2 G SAT, 2 G MONO); 145 MG CHOLESTEROL; 37 G CARBOHYDRATE; 7 G PROTEIN; 1 G FIBER; 135 MG SODIUM.

NUTRITION BONUS: 100% DV VITAMIN A.

Crème Brulée

PREP TIME: 20 MINUTES | **START TO FINISH:** 2 HOURS 20 MINUTES (INCLUDING CHILLING TIME)
EASE OF PREPARATION: MODERATE

An amazing creation, our creamless Crème Brulée is every bit as delectable as its full-fat counterpart.

- 4 large egg yolks
- ½ cup nonfat sweetened condensed milk
- 1 tablespoon cornstarch
- 2½ cups 1% milk
- 1 tablespoon vanilla extract
- 6 tablespoons packed light brown sugar

RECIPE RX

Original Crème Brulée:
485 calories
42 grams fat
24 grams saturated

EW Crème Brulée:
210 calories
4 grams fat
2 grams saturated

1. Preheat oven to 350°F. Put a kettle of water on to heat for a water bath. Line a roasting pan with a folded kitchen towel. Place six 6-ounce (¾-cup) ramekins (or custard cups) in the roasting pan.
2. Whisk egg yolks, condensed milk and cornstarch in a bowl until smooth. Heat milk over low heat in a medium saucepan until steaming. (*Alternatively, heat milk in a 4-cup glass measure in the microwave.*) Gently whisk hot milk into egg mixture. Stir in vanilla. Skim foam.
3. Divide custard among ramekins. Skim any remaining foam. Pour enough boiling water into the pan to come halfway up the sides of the ramekins.
4. Bake custards until edges are set but centers still quiver, 40 to 50 minutes. Remove from water; let cool on wire racks. Cover and refrigerate until chilled, for at least 2 hours or up to 2 days.
5. About 1 hour before serving, preheat the broiler. Place chilled custards in a roasting pan or shallow baking dish and surround with ice cubes. Using a paper towel, pat surfaces of custards dry. Sprinkle each evenly with 1 tablespoon brown sugar. Broil until sugar has melted and formed a crust, 4 to 8 minutes. (Rearrange custards as needed for even browning and remove individual custards as soon as they are ready.)
6. Refrigerate, uncovered, until chilled, for about 30 minutes or up to 1 hour.

TEST KITCHEN TIP: Surrounding the sugar-topped custards with ice cubes before broiling prevents the delicate custards from overcooking.

MAKES 6 SERVINGS.

PER SERVING: 210 CALORIES; 4 G FAT (2 G SAT, 2 G MONO); 145 MG CHOLESTEROL; 35 G CARBOHYDRATE; 8 G PROTEIN; 0 G FIBER; 87 MG SODIUM.

NUTRITION BONUS: 212 MG CALCIUM (20% DV).

Cornmeal-Pecan Shortcakes with Lemon Curd & Blueberries

PREP TIME: 40 MINUTES | **START TO FINISH:** 3 HOURS (INCLUDING MAKING LEMON CURD) | **TO MAKE AHEAD:** THE BLUEBERRY FILLING WILL KEEP, COVERED, IN THE REFRIGERATOR FOR UP TO 1 DAY. | **EASE OF PREPARATION:** EASY

Cream cheese and buttermilk are the secrets to these tender, scrumptious shortcakes.

Lemon Curd (*page 329*)

BLUEBERRY FILLING

- 4 cups fresh blueberries, divided
- ½ cup water
- ⅓ cup granulated sugar
- 1 teaspoon vanilla extract

SHORTCAKES

- 1 cup all-purpose flour
- 1 cup yellow cornmeal, preferably stone-ground
- ¼ cup plus 1 tablespoon granulated sugar
- 2 teaspoons baking powder
- 1 teaspoon baking soda
- ½ teaspoon salt
- ¼ cup reduced-fat cream cheese
- ¾ cup plus 2 tablespoons buttermilk
- 1 tablespoon canola oil
- 1 teaspoon vanilla extract
- 2 tablespoons chopped pecans

1. Make Lemon Curd and refrigerate.
2. **To prepare blueberry filling:** Combine 2 cups blueberries, water and sugar in a saucepan. Bring to a boil over medium heat. Cook, stirring, until the berries soften into a sauce, 3 to 5 minutes. Remove from heat; stir in remaining 2 cups blueberries and vanilla. Set aside.
3. **To prepare & assemble shortcakes:** Preheat oven to 425°F. Coat a baking sheet with cooking spray.
4. Whisk flour, cornmeal, ¼ cup sugar, baking powder, baking soda and salt in a mixing bowl. Using a pastry blender or your fingers, cut cream cheese into the dry ingredients until the mixture resembles coarse meal. Combine ¾ cup buttermilk, oil and vanilla in a glass measuring cup. Make a well in the dry ingredients. Add the wet ingredients and stir with a fork until just combined. (The dough will be slightly sticky; do not overmix.)
5. Turn the dough out onto a lightly floured surface. Gently pat into a ¾-inch-thick circle. With a floured knife, cut dough into 8 triangles; place on the prepared baking sheet.
6. Combine pecans and the remaining 1 tablespoon sugar in a small bowl. Brush shortcake tops with the remaining 2 tablespoons buttermilk and sprinkle with the pecan mixture.
7. Bake the shortcakes until golden, 10 to 12 minutes. Transfer to a wire rack to cool slightly. To serve, split shortcakes in half with a serrated knife. Set the bottoms on dessert plates. Spoon on blueberry filling and lemon curd. Set the tops on at an angle. Serve immediately.

MAKES 8 SERVINGS.

PER SERVING: 394 CALORIES; 9 G FAT (3 G SAT, 3 G MONO); 39 MG CHOLESTEROL; 74 G CARBOHYDRATE; 7 G PROTEIN; 4 G FIBER; 379 MG SODIUM.

NUTRITION BONUS: 18 MG VITAMIN C (30% DV), 321 MG POTASSIUM (16% DV).

LEMON CURD

PREP TIME: 15 MINUTES | **START TO FINISH:** 2¼ HOURS (INCLUDING CHILLING TIME) | **TO MAKE AHEAD:** THE LEMON CURD WILL KEEP, COVERED, IN THE REFRIGERATOR FOR UP TO 2 DAYS. | **EASE OF PREPARATION:** EASY

With far less butter and fewer yolks than the standard, this lemon curd remains totally delicious.

- 1 large egg
- 2 large egg whites *or* 4 teaspoons dried egg whites (*see Ingredient Note, page 394*), reconstituted according to package directions
- ¾ cup granulated sugar
- ⅔ cup lemon juice
- 2 tablespoons butter
- 1 tablespoon freshly grated lemon zest, preferably organic

1. Whisk egg, egg whites, sugar and lemon juice in a heavy nonreactive saucepan. Add butter and cook over low heat, whisking constantly, until slightly thickened, 7 to 10 minutes. Do not simmer.
2. Pour sauce through a fine-mesh sieve into a bowl. Stir in lemon zest. Cover surface with plastic wrap and refrigerate until chilled, about 2 hours.

MAKES 1⅓ CUPS.

PER TABLESPOON: 42 CALORIES; 1 G FAT (1 G SAT, 0 G MONO); 12 MG CHOLESTEROL; 8 G CARBOHYDRATE; 0 G PROTEIN; 0 G FIBER; 8 MG SODIUM.

Bananas Foster Gratin

PREP TIME: 10 MINUTES | **START TO FINISH:** 20 MINUTES | **TO MAKE AHEAD:** THE SAUCE (STEP 2) WILL KEEP, COVERED, IN THE REFRIGERATOR FOR UP TO 4 DAYS. | **EASE OF PREPARATION:** EASY

The warm, butterscotch thrill of old-fashioned Bananas Foster is baked into a cookie-crusted gratin.

- ¼ cup packed light brown sugar
- 3 tablespoons water
- 1 tablespoon dark rum *or* lemon juice
- ¼ teaspoon ground cinnamon
- 2 teaspoons butter
- 4 medium bananas
- 1 almond *or* hazelnut biscotti, crushed (¼ cup)
- 1 pint nonfat vanilla frozen yogurt *or* low-fat vanilla ice cream

1. Preheat oven to 450°F. Coat four 1-to-1½-cup gratin dishes or a shallow 1-quart baking dish with cooking spray.
2. Combine brown sugar, water, rum (or lemon juice) and cinnamon in a medium saucepan; bring to a simmer, stirring. Remove from heat and stir in butter.
3. Peel bananas and slice diagonally. Add to sauce and toss to coat. Spoon into prepared dish(es). Sprinkle with biscotti crumbs.
4. Bake gratins for about 10 minutes, or until bubbly. Serve hot or warm with a scoop of frozen yogurt (or ice cream).

MAKES 4 SERVINGS.

PER SERVING: 275 CALORIES; 3 G FAT (2 G SAT, 0 G MONO); 11 MG CHOLESTEROL; 66 G CARBOHYDRATE; 6 G PROTEIN; 3 G FIBER; 78 MG SODIUM.

NUTRITION BONUS: 423 MG POTASSIUM (21% DV), 159 MG CALCIUM (16% DV).

Honey-Lavender Plum Gratin

PREP TIME: 25 MINUTES | **START TO FINISH:** 2¼ HOURS (INCLUDING CHILLING TIME) | **TO MAKE AHEAD:** PREPARE CUSTARD THROUGH STEP 3. COVER AND REFRIGERATE FOR UP TO 2 DAYS. | **EASE OF PREPARATION:** MODERATE

Infusing milk with lavender buds perfumes the honey-sweetened custard, creating an unusual, lovely backdrop for juicy plums. A quick pass under the broiler caramelizes the top. NOTE: Because the custard is stabilized with cornstarch, you can let it reach a gentle simmer. (*Photo: page 223.*)

CUSTARD

- ¾ cup 1% milk
- ¾ teaspoon unsprayed fresh lavender buds *or* ¼ teaspoon dried, rinsed (*see Note*)
- 2 large egg yolks
- 2 tablespoons honey
- 1 teaspoon cornstarch
- ½ teaspoon vanilla extract

FRUIT & TOPPING

- 4 medium plums, pitted and cut into eighths
- 2 tablespoons sugar

1. To prepare custard: Heat milk in a small heavy saucepan over medium heat until steaming. Remove from heat. Add lavender, cover and let steep for 30 minutes.

2. Strain milk through a fine sieve into a medium bowl. Return the milk to the saucepan and reheat until steaming.

3. Whisk egg yolks, honey and cornstarch in a medium bowl until smooth. Gradually add the hot milk, whisking until blended. Return the mixture to the saucepan. Cook over medium heat, whisking constantly, until slightly thickened and starting to bubble gently, 1½ to 2 minutes. Transfer to a clean bowl. Whisk in vanilla. Cover loosely and refrigerate until chilled, about 1 hour.

4. To prepare fruit & topping: Preheat broiler. Coat an 11-by-7-inch oval gratin dish or 4 individual gratin dishes with cooking spray. Spoon custard evenly into the dish or dishes. Arrange plums on their sides, slightly overlapping, in a single layer over custard. Sprinkle sugar evenly over plums. Broil until plums are lightly caramelized, 5 to 7 minutes. Serve immediately.

MAKES 4 SERVINGS.

PER SERVING: 137 CALORIES; 3 G FAT (1 G SAT, 1 G MONO); 105 MG CHOLESTEROL; 26 G CARBOHYDRATE; 3 G PROTEIN; 1 G FIBER; 27 MG SODIUM.

TEST KITCHEN TIP: You can also use the custard as a sauce for fresh raspberries or figs.

INGREDIENT NOTE: Lavender flowers impart a delicate fragrance to custards and ice creams. You can find dried culinary lavender in herb stores and specialty stores. If you don't have lavender, just leave it out: in Steps 1 and 2, simply heat the milk until steaming.

VARIATION: If you have a vanilla bean, this is a great opportunity to use it. In Step 1, make a lengthwise slit in a 3-inch-long piece of vanilla bean with the tip of a sharp knife. Scrape the seeds into the hot milk, then drop in the whole bean along with the lavender and let steep. Omit the vanilla extract from Step 3.

Pear-Cranberry Cobbler

PREP TIME: 30 MINUTES | **START TO FINISH:** 1 HOUR 25 MINUTES (INCLUDING COOLING TIME)
EASE OF PREPARATION: EASY

The French-toast-like topping makes this sweet and tart "cobbler" appropriate for breakfast, brunch or dessert. The method can be used for various other fruits, such as peaches and raspberries or apples and cherries.

- ¼ cup maple syrup
- 1 tablespoon cornstarch
- 5 ripe pears, cored, peeled and chopped (4 cups)
- 1 cup fresh *or* frozen cranberries
- 2 large eggs
- ⅓ cup 1% milk
- 1 teaspoon vanilla extract
- 6 slices whole-wheat sandwich bread, crusts trimmed
- 3 tablespoons sugar
- ¼ teaspoon ground nutmeg

1. Preheat oven to 400°F. Coat an 8-inch-square baking dish with cooking spray.
2. Stir together maple syrup and cornstarch in a medium bowl. Add pears and cranberries and toss to coat. Transfer to the prepared baking dish, cover with foil and bake until the fruit is just tender and the juices have begun to thicken, 20 to 30 minutes.
3. Meanwhile, whisk eggs, milk and vanilla in a large shallow dish. Cut each bread slice in half diagonally. Immerse the bread in the egg-milk mixture, carefully turning the slices for even soaking.
4. Remove the pan from the oven and stir the fruit. Arrange the bread in rows on top of the fruit. Combine sugar and nutmeg; sprinkle evenly over the bread. Bake until the fruit is bubbling and the bread is golden, 20 to 30 minutes more. Serve warm.

MAKES 6 SERVINGS.

PER SERVING: 250 CALORIES; 4 G FAT (1 G SAT, 1 G MONO); 71 MG CHOLESTEROL; 52 G CARBOHYDRATE; 6 G PROTEIN; 5 G FIBER; 152 MG SODIUM.

NUTRITION BONUS: 20% DV FIBER.

Essential Fruit Crumble

PREP TIME: 20-40 MINUTES | **START TO FINISH:** 1 HOUR TO 1 HOUR 20 MINUTES
EASE OF PREPARATION: EASY

A fruit crumble offers the luscious flavor of a fresh fruit pie without the fuss of making a crust. Celebrate the arrival of cherries with this rich-tasting crumble, then, as the season progresses, switch to late-summer peaches or plums. During the cooler months, our apple-cranberry variation will provide a warm, sweet finish to your meals. The nut-studded topping works great with other fruit combinations too.

- Fruit filling of your choice (*page 333*)
- ⅔ cup whole-wheat flour
- ½ cup old-fashioned rolled oats (not instant)
- ½ cup packed light brown sugar
- 1 teaspoon ground cinnamon
- Pinch of salt
- 1 tablespoon butter, cut into small pieces
- 1 tablespoon canola oil
- 3 tablespoons frozen orange juice concentrate
- 1 tablespoon chopped slivered almonds *or* walnuts
- 1½ cups reduced-fat vanilla ice cream *or* nonfat vanilla frozen yogurt (optional)

1. Preheat oven to 375°F. Coat an 8-by-8-inch baking dish (or similar 1½- to 2-quart dish) with cooking spray.

2. Prepare fruit filling of your choice. Place filling in the prepared baking dish. Cover with foil and bake for 20 minutes.

3. Meanwhile, make topping. Mix flour, oats, brown sugar, cinnamon and salt in a medium bowl with a fork. Add butter and blend with a pastry blender or your fingertips. Add oil and stir to coat. Add orange juice concentrate and blend with your fingertips until dry ingredients are moistened.

4. When fruit has baked for 20 minutes, stir it and sprinkle topping evenly over the surface. Sprinkle with almonds (or walnuts). Bake, uncovered, until fruit is bubbly and tender and topping is lightly browned, 20 to 25 minutes more. Let cool for at least 10 minutes before serving. Serve warm or at room temperature with ice cream (or frozen yogurt), if desired.

> **TEST KITCHEN TIP:**
> You can purchase gadgets designed for pitting both cherries and olives at kitchenware stores.

MAKES 8 SERVINGS, ½ CUP EACH.

CHERRY CRUMBLE PER SERVING: 248 CALORIES; 5 G FAT (1 G SAT, 2 G MONO); 4 MG CHOLESTEROL; 52 G CARBOHYDRATE; 4 G PROTEIN; 5 G FIBER; 16 MG SODIUM.

PEACH-RASPBERRY CRUMBLE: 252 CALORIES; 6 G FAT (2 G SAT, 2 G MONO); 10 MG CHOLESTEROL; 49 G CARBOHYDRATE; 5 G PROTEIN; 3 G FIBER; 44 MG SODIUM.

PLUM CRUMBLE: 276 CALORIES; 6 G FAT (2 G SAT, 2 G MONO); 10 MG CHOLESTEROL; 55 G CARBOHYDRATE; 5 G PROTEIN; 4 G FIBER; 44 MG SODIUM.

APPLE-CRANBERRY CRUMBLE: 232 CALORIES; 4 G FAT (1 G SAT, 2 G MONO); 4 MG CHOLESTEROL; 49 G CARBOHYDRATE; 3 G PROTEIN; 5 G FIBER; 17 MG SODIUM.

Recipe Rx

FROM A NUTRITIONAL POINT OF VIEW, crumbles lend themselves readily to healthful revisions. Most recipes include rolled oats—a fiber-rich, whole-grain food—in the topping. Refined white flour is standard in crumble recipes, but substituting whole-wheat flour is an easy and effective way to boost fiber and nutrients and enhance the nutty taste of the topping. A sprinkling of nuts on the top provides a healthful finish along with a nice crunch.

The only challenge in creating a healthful crumble recipe is finding a way to replace the butter. A typical crumble calls for about ½ cup. In our updated version, a mixture of frozen orange juice concentrate and a little canola oil moistens the crumbs, while just a tablespoon of butter provides plenty of the characteristic buttery flavor.

FRUIT FILLINGS

CHERRY FILLING

- **1½ pounds sweet cherries (5 cups), rinsed and pitted**
- **1 cup raspberries, rinsed**
- **⅓ cup sugar**
- **1 tablespoon cornstarch**
- **1 tablespoon lemon juice**
- **1 tablespoon kirsch *or* brandy (optional)**

Combine all ingredients in a large bowl. Toss to coat.

MAKES 8 SERVINGS.

NUTRITION BONUS: 21 MG VITAMIN C (35% DV), 371 MG POTASSIUM (19% DV), 19% DV FIBER.

PEACH-RASPBERRY FILLING

- **2 pounds peaches, peeled (*see Tip, page 337*), pitted and sliced (5 cups)**
- **1 cup raspberries**
- **2 tablespoons sugar**
- **1 tablespoon lemon juice**

Combine all ingredients in a large bowl; toss to coat.

MAKES 8 SERVINGS.

NUTRITION BONUS: 21 MG VITAMIN C (35% DV), 438 MG POTASSIUM (22% DV), 19% DV FIBER.

PLUM FILLING

- **2 pounds plums, pitted and cut into eighths (6 cups)**
- **⅓ cup sugar**
- **2 teaspoons freshly grated orange zest, preferably organic**
- **1 tablespoon orange juice**

Combine all ingredients in a large bowl; toss to coat.

MAKES 8 SERVINGS.

NUTRITION BONUS: 22 MG VITAMIN C (35% DV), 391 MG POTASSIUM (20% DV), 15% DV FIBER.

APPLE-CRANBERRY FILLING

- **1½ pounds apples, peeled and sliced (5 cups)**
- **1 cup fresh or frozen cranberries**
- **⅓ cup sugar**

Combine all ingredients in a large bowl; toss to coat.

MAKES 8 SERVINGS.

NUTRITION BONUS: 15 MG VITAMIN C (25% DV), 21% DV FIBER.

Double Raspberry Soufflés

PREP TIME: 35 MINUTES | **START TO FINISH:** 45 MINUTES | **EASE OF PREPARATION:** MODERATE

These picture-perfect individual soufflés make an impressive dessert that is remarkably low in fat and calories. Soufflés are actually quite easy to make; just be sure the egg whites are stiffly beaten and once the soufflés are done, serve them right away.

BERRY LAYER

- 6 teaspoons sugar
- 3 cups fresh *or* frozen unsweetened raspberries
- 6 teaspoons crème de cassis *or* eau-de-vie de framboise *or* blackcurrant *or* blackberry juice *or* nectar

SOUFFLÉ

- 3 cups fresh *or* frozen unsweetened raspberries
- 1 tablespoon crème de cassis *or* eau-de-vie de framboise *or* blackcurrant *or* blackberry juice *or* nectar
- 4 large egg whites, at room temperature (*see page 365*) *or* 2 tablespoons plus 2 teaspoons dried egg whites (*see Ingredient Note, page 394*), reconstituted according to package directions
- Pinch of salt
- ⅓ cup sugar
- Confectioners' sugar for dusting

1. To prepare berry layer: Preheat oven to 375°F. Coat six 8-ounce soufflé cups with cooking spray. Add 1 teaspoon sugar to each cup and swirl to coat the inside. Distribute raspberries in the bottom of the cups and sprinkle each with 1 teaspoon crème de cassis (or eau-de-vie, juice or nectar).

2. To prepare soufflés: Stir raspberries in a saucepan over low heat until they are juicy (for fresh) or thawed (for frozen). Transfer to a fine sieve set over a bowl. With a spoon, press the berries through the sieve, being careful to extract all the pulp. Discard the seeds.

3. Return the puree to the saucepan. Bring to a simmer and stir over medium heat until very thick and reduced to ¼ cup, about 10 minutes. (Reduce the heat as the mixture thickens.) Stir in 1 tablespoon crème de cassis (or eau-de-vie, juice or nectar) and set aside to cool slightly.

4. Beat egg whites and salt in a mixing bowl with an electric mixer on high speed until soft peaks form. Continuing to beat, gradually add sugar and beat until stiff peaks form. With a rubber spatula, fold about a fourth of the beaten whites into the reserved raspberry puree to lighten its texture, then pour the mixture over the remaining whites. Gently fold the puree and whites together until evenly blended. Spoon the soufflé mixture into the cups, spreading to the edges of the cups.

5. Set the cups on a baking sheet and bake for 10 minutes, or until lightly browned on the top. Dust with confectioners' sugar and serve immediately.

MAKES 6 SERVINGS.

PER SERVING: 153 CALORIES; 1 G FAT (0 G SAT, 0 G MONO); 0 MG CHOLESTEROL; 32 G CARBOHYDRATE; 4 G PROTEIN; 8 G FIBER; 38 MG SODIUM.

NUTRITION BONUS: 32 MG VITAMIN C (50% DV), 32% DV FIBER.

Cranberry & Ruby Grapefruit Compote

PREP TIME: 20 MINUTES | **START TO FINISH:** 2 HOURS 35 MINUTES (INCLUDING CHILLING TIME)
TO MAKE AHEAD: THE COMPOTE WILL KEEP, COVERED, IN THE REFRIGERATOR FOR UP TO 2 DAYS.
EASE OF PREPARATION: MODERATE

Light enough to follow even a substantial meal, this pretty compote has a refreshing balance of sweet and tart flavors. Serve with vanilla frozen yogurt for dessert or with plain yogurt for breakfast or brunch.

- 1¾ cups fresh *or* frozen cranberries
- 1¼ cups water
- 2 ¾-by-2½-inch strips orange zest, preferably organic
- ½ cup orange juice
- ½ cup sugar
- 1 cinnamon stick (optional)
- 3 large red grapefruit
- Fresh mint sprigs for garnish

1. Combine cranberries, water, orange zest, orange juice, sugar and cinnamon stick (if using) in a medium saucepan. Bring to a boil over medium-high heat. Cook, stirring often, until the cranberries are tender and begin to pop, 3 to 5 minutes. Transfer to a large bowl. Cover loosely and refrigerate until thoroughly chilled, about 2 hours.

2. An hour or two before serving, prepare grapefruit: With a sharp knife, remove the skin and all the white pith from the fruit. Working over a bowl, cut the segments from their surrounding membranes. Squeeze juice from the membranes into the bowl before discarding. Add segments and juice to the cranberry mixture. To serve, divide the compote among 6 dessert bowls and garnish with mint.

MAKES 6 SERVINGS, ABOUT ¾ CUP EACH.

PER SERVING: 140 CALORIES; 0 G FAT (0 G SAT, 0 G MONO); 0 MG CHOLESTEROL; 36 G CARBOHYDRATE; 1 G PROTEIN; 4 G FIBER; 2 MG SODIUM.

NUTRITION BONUS: 20 MG VITAMIN C (35% DV), 16% DV FIBER.

CRANBERRY & PEAR VARIATION: Instead of grapefruit, peel and core 3 to 4 Bartlett or Anjou pears; cut into ½-inch wedges. In Step 1, after the mixture comes to a boil, add pears and reduce heat to medium-low. Simmer gently until the cranberries and pears are tender, 5 to 10 minutes. Cover loosely and refrigerate until thoroughly chilled, about 2 hours. Omit Step 2.

Honeydew Compote with Lime, Ginger & a Hint of Serrano

PREP TIME: 15 MINUTES | START TO FINISH: 1 HOUR 50 MINUTES | TO MAKE AHEAD: THE COMPOTE WILL KEEP, COVERED, IN THE REFRIGERATOR FOR UP TO 2 DAYS. | EASE OF PREPARATION: MODERATE

Infusing lime juice with hot pepper, lime zest and ginger makes a delightful syrup for a fresh-tasting fruit dessert.

- 2 teaspoons freshly grated lime zest, preferably organic
- ½ cup lime juice (4-5 limes)
- ⅓ cup water
- ⅓ cup sugar
- 1 tablespoon minced fresh ginger
- ½ teaspoon slivered serrano pepper
- 1 large honeydew melon (about 3 pounds), seeded and cut into chunks
- 1½ teaspoons slivered fresh mint, for garnish
- 2 fresh figs, sliced, for garnish

1. Combine lime zest and juice, water, sugar, ginger and serrano in a small saucepan. Bring to a boil. Reduce heat to low and simmer until sugar is dissolved, about 5 minutes. Let cool to room temperature, about 25 minutes.

2. Strain syrup into a large bowl, pressing on solids to extract maximum flavor. Add melon and toss to coat. Cover and refrigerate for at least 1 hour. Sprinkle with mint and garnish with fig slices.

MAKES 6 SERVINGS, 1 CUP EACH.

PER SERVING: 154 CALORIES; 0 G FAT (0 G SAT, 0 G MONO); 0 MG CHOLESTEROL; 41 G CARBOHYDRATE; 2 G PROTEIN; 4 G FIBER; 60 MG SODIUM.

NUTRITION BONUS: 54 MG VITAMIN C (90% DV), 597 MG POTASSIUM (30% DV).

Peach-Blackberry Compote with Basil Syrup

PREP TIME: 20 MINUTES | **START TO FINISH:** 50 MINUTES | **EASE OF PREPARATION:** EASY

Fresh basil, which has a special affinity with peaches, is the secret ingredient in this sophisticated compote. The basil garnish gives guests a clue to the subtle flavor in the syrup.

TEST KITCHEN TIP:
Dip peaches in boiling water for 30 or 40 seconds to loosen their skins. Let cool slightly, then slip off skins with a paring knife.

- **¼ cup sugar**
- **3 tablespoons dry white wine**
- **3 sprigs fresh basil, plus more for garnish**
- **2 2½-inch strips orange zest, preferably organic**
- **3 cups sliced peeled peaches (3-4 medium) (*see Tip*)**
- **1 cup fresh blackberries**
- **1 tablespoon lemon juice**

1. Combine sugar and wine in small saucepan; bring to a simmer. Remove from heat. Add 3 basil sprigs and orange zest; stir to immerse. Cover and let steep for 30 minutes.
2. Strain syrup into a small bowl, pressing on basil and zest to release maximum flavor.
3. Shortly before serving, combine peaches, blackberries, lemon juice and basil-infused syrup in a serving bowl; toss gently to coat. Serve garnished with basil sprigs.

MAKES 4 SERVINGS, 1 CUP EACH.

PER SERVING: 129 CALORIES; 0 G FAT (0 G SAT, 0 G MONO); 0 MG CHOLESTEROL; 30 G CARBOHYDRATE; 2 G PROTEIN; 4 G FIBER; 1 MG SODIUM.

NUTRITION BONUS: 22 MG VITAMIN C (35% DV), 337 MG POTASSIUM (17% DV), 17% DV FIBER.

Calorie and Carb Cutting

TO REDUCE CALORIES and carbohydrates in fruit desserts and sauces, replace sugar with a no-calorie sweetener, such as Splenda; substitute according to package directions. Most of the sweetening comes from the fruit itself, so the flavor of the added sweetener is almost imperceptible.

Chocolate-Dipped Dried Fruit

PREP TIME: 15 MINUTES | **START TO FINISH:** 1 HOUR | **TO MAKE AHEAD:** THE FRUIT WILL KEEP, IN A TIGHTLY COVERED CONTAINER, IN THE REFRIGERATOR FOR UP TO 1 WEEK. | **EASE OF PREPARATION:** MODERATE

Dip an assortment of dried fruits in dark chocolate to make an impressive holiday gift or buffet item. The chocolate is melted in stages, a process called tempering, which prevents a cloudy bloom from forming on the chocolate when it sets. Of the various methods for tempering, this one is quick, easy and reliable.

- **6 ounces good-quality bittersweet (*not* unsweetened) chocolate, finely chopped, divided**
- **1 pound mixed dried fruit, such as apricots, figs, peaches, pears *and/or* pineapple**

1. Melt 4 ounces chocolate in a double boiler over hot water (or in a microwave on low in 30-second bursts). Stir often to ensure even melting.
2. Remove the top pan and wipe dry (or remove the bowl from the microwave). Stir in the remaining 2 ounces chocolate, in 2 additions, until thoroughly melted and smooth.
3. Line a baking sheet with wax paper. Dip each piece of dried fruit halfway into the chocolate, letting the excess drip off, then place on the wax paper. When all the fruit is dipped, refrigerate until the chocolate has set, at least 15 minutes. Serve at room temperature.

MAKES ABOUT 5 DOZEN PIECES.

PER APRICOT: 28 CALORIES; 2 G TOTAL FAT (1 G SAT, 0 G MONO); 0 MG CHOLESTEROL; 5 G CARBOHYDRATE; 0 G PROTEIN; 1 G FIBER; 0 MG SODIUM.

PER FIG: 48 CALORIES; 2 G TOTAL FAT (1 G SAT, 0 G MONO); 0 MG CHOLESTEROL; 10 G CARBOHYDRATE; 1 G PROTEIN; 2 G FIBER; 1 MG SODIUM.

PER PEACH: 85 CALORIES; 3 G TOTAL FAT (2 G SAT, 0 G MONO); 0 MG CHOLESTEROL; 16 G CARBOHYDRATE; 1 G PROTEIN; 2 G FIBER; 0 MG SODIUM.

PER PEAR: 83 CALORIES; 3 G TOTAL FAT (2 G SAT, 0 G MONO); 0 MG CHOLESTEROL; 17 G CARBOHYDRATE; 1 G PROTEIN; 2 G FIBER; 1 MG SODIUM.

PER PINEAPPLE: 125 CALORIES; 3 G TOTAL FAT (2 G SAT, 0 G MONO); 0 MG CHOLESTEROL; 28 G CARBOHYDRATE; 0 G PROTEIN; 2 G FIBER; 13 MG SODIUM.

Why Temper Chocolate?

COCOA BUTTER, a natural part of the cocoa bean, is in all types of chocolate and has four different crystals, each with a different melting point. Tempering stabilizes cocoa butter crystals so they don't rise to the surface and cause a condition called chocolate bloom. The signs of this are unsightly white and gray streaks and dots. Also, untempered chocolate may have a grainy texture and is difficult to unmold. Tempered chocolate has a shiny, even appearance and smooth texture. It also sets up rapidly, releases from molds easily and breaks with a sharp snap.

Fabulous Fruit Finales

Finishing your meals with a fruit dessert is a tasty way to meet the goal of eating at least 5 servings of fruits and vegetables each day. Here are some ideas for easy ways to transform seasonal fruits into satisfying meal endings.

CHOCOLATE- & BISCOTTI-DIPPED STRAWBERRIES

START TO FINISH: 20 MINUTES

Lower Carbs

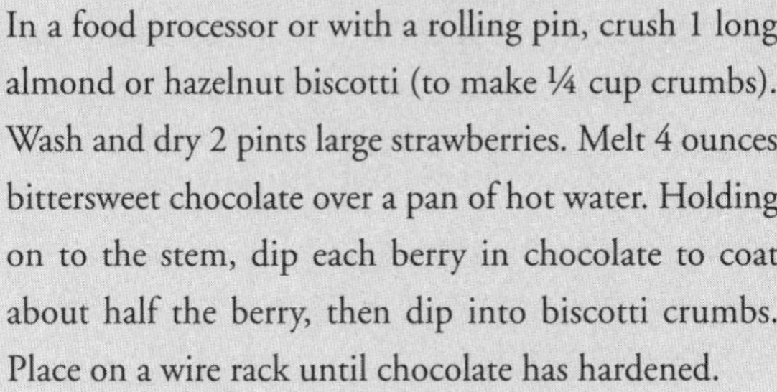

In a food processor or with a rolling pin, crush 1 long almond or hazelnut biscotti (to make ¼ cup crumbs). Wash and dry 2 pints large strawberries. Melt 4 ounces bittersweet chocolate over a pan of hot water. Holding on to the stem, dip each berry in chocolate to coat about half the berry, then dip into biscotti crumbs. Place on a wire rack until chocolate has hardened.

MAKES ABOUT 24 PIECES.

PER PIECE: 28 CALORIES; 2 G FAT (1 G SAT, 0 G MONO); 0 MG CHOLESTEROL; 4 G CARBOHYDRATE; 0 G PROTEIN; 1 G FIBER; 3 MG SODIUM.

NUTRITION BONUS: 14 MG VITAMIN C (25% DV).

BALSAMIC VINEGAR-SPIKED STRAWBERRIES

START TO FINISH: 25 MINUTES

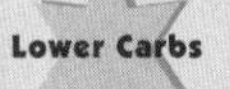

Wash and dry 1 pint strawberries. Hull and slice berries, place in a bowl and toss with 1 to 2 tablespoons sugar. Sprinkle with 2 to 3 teaspoons balsamic vinegar. Let stand for 20 minutes.

MAKES 4 SERVINGS.

PER SERVING: 40 CALORIES; 0 G FAT (0 G SAT, 0 G MONO); 0 MG CHOLESTEROL; 10 G CARBOHYDRATE; 1 G PROTEIN; 2 G FIBER; 1 MG SODIUM.

NUTRITION BONUS: 49 MG VITAMIN C (80% DV).

CHOCOLATE FONDUE

START TO FINISH: 20 MINUTES

Place a bowl of Chocolate-Hazelnut Sauce (*page 393*) in the center of a large platter. Arrange fresh strawberries, sliced kiwi, orange sections or other cut-up fruit (mangoes, star fruit, papayas, bananas, cherries) around the bowl, along with angel food cake or nonfat pound cake cut into cubes. Serve with toothpicks or fondue forks.

MAKES 6 SERVINGS.

PER SERVING: 289 CALORIES; 4 G FAT (1 G SAT, 2 G MONO); 0 MG CHOLESTEROL; 61 G CARBOHYDRATE; 4 G PROTEIN; 6 G FIBER; 176 MG SODIUM.

NUTRITION BONUS: 84 MG VITAMIN C (140% DV), 25% DV FIBER.

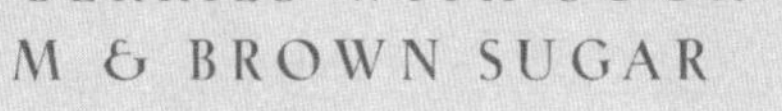

STRAWBERRIES WITH SOUR CREAM & BROWN SUGAR

Healthy Weight

START TO FINISH: 10 MINUTES

Lower Carbs

Wash and dry 2 pints strawberries and arrange on a serving platter. Place ½ cup reduced-fat sour cream and ½ cup light brown sugar in separate small bowls. To eat, dip a berry into sour cream and then into sugar.

MAKES ABOUT 24 PIECES.

PER PIECE: 29 CALORIES; 1 G FAT (0 G SAT, 0 G MONO); 2 MG CHOLESTEROL; 6 G CARBOHYDRATE; 0 G PROTEIN; 0 G FIBER; 2 MG SODIUM.

WINTER FRUIT SALAD

START TO FINISH: 25 MINUTES

With a sharp knife, peel, quarter and core 1 pineapple. Cut into slices. Peel 4 seedless oranges and 3 pink grapefruits, removing white pith; quarter lengthwise and cut into ¼-inch slices. Slice 2 star fruit. Seed 1 pomegranate (*see Cooking Tip, page 397*). Combine the prepared fruit in a large bowl and toss to combine.

MAKES 8 SERVINGS, ABOUT ¾ CUP EACH.

PER SERVING: 111 CALORIES; 0 G FAT (0 G SAT, 0 G MONO); 0 MG CHOLESTEROL; 30 G CARBOHYDRATE; 1 G PROTEIN; 6 G FIBER; 2 MG SODIUM.

NUTRITION BONUS: 97 MG VITAMIN C (160% DV), 23% DV FIBER.

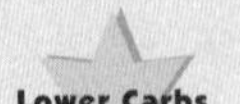

MANGO BRULÉE

START TO FINISH: 15 MINUTES

- **2 mangoes**
- **4 teaspoons brown sugar**
- **4 teaspoons rum *or* orange juice**
- **1 lime, cut into wedges**

Preheat broiler. Place one mango on a cutting board with the narrow side facing you. With a sharp knife, slice off one side, sliding the knife along the flat seed. Repeat on the other side of the mango. With a paring knife, make crisscross cuts through the flesh, cutting up to but not through the skin. Repeat with the second mango. Sprinkle 1 teaspoon brown sugar over each mango half, then drizzle each one with 1 teaspoon rum (or orange juice). Set mango halves on a broiler pan or baking sheet. Broil until tops are light golden, 5 to 7 minutes. Serve with lime wedges.

MAKES 4 SERVINGS.

PER SERVING: 96 CALORIES; 0 G FAT (0 G SAT, 0 G MONO); 0 MG CHOLESTEROL; 22 G CARBOHYDRATE; 1 G PROTEIN; 2 G FIBER; 4 MG SODIUM.

Lower Carbs

BROILED PINEAPPLE

START TO FINISH: 25 MINUTES

Peel a large pineapple. With a sharp knife, cut it crosswise into 1-inch-thick slices. Brush the slices lightly with 1 teaspoon canola oil and place in a single layer on a baking sheet. Broil until lightly browned, about 7 minutes. Turn slices over, brush with 1 teaspoon oil and broil for 5 to 7 minutes longer. Immediately sprinkle pineapple with 2 tablespoons brown sugar. Cut into chunks and serve with lime wedges.

MAKES 6 SERVINGS.

PER SERVING: 68 CALORIES; 2 G FAT (0 G SAT, 1 G MONO); 0 MG CHOLESTEROL; 14 G CARBOHYDRATE; 0 G PROTEIN; 1 G FIBER; 1 MG SODIUM.

NUTRITION BONUS: 30 MG VITAMIN C (50% DV).

Healthy Weight

Lower Carbs

ROASTED APPLES

START TO FINISH: 40 MINUTES

- **2-3 cooking apples, such as Golden Delicious *or* Rome Beauty (about 1 pound)**
- **1 tablespoon lemon juice**
- **2 tablespoons sugar**

Preheat oven to 425°F. Peel, core and cut apples into ½-inch-thick slices. Toss the slices with lemon juice in a large bowl; add sugar and toss once again. Transfer to a baking pan large enough to hold slices in a single layer. Roast, stirring occasionally to prevent scorching, until apples are tender and golden brown, 25 to 30 minutes.

MAKES 4 SERVINGS.

PER SERVING: 80 CALORIES; 0 G FAT (0 G SAT, 0 G MONO); 0 MG CHOLESTEROL; 21 G CARBOHYDRATE; 0 G PROTEIN; 1 G FIBER; 0 MG SODIUM.

Healthy Weight

Lower Carbs

ROASTED PEACHES

START TO FINISH: 30 MINUTES

4 ripe peaches (about 1¼ pounds)
½ tablespoon lemon juice
1 tablespoon sugar

Preheat oven to 425°F. Cut peaches in half and remove pits. In a large bowl, toss the peach halves with lemon juice; add sugar and toss once again. Arrange halves cut-side up in a baking dish. Roast until the peaches are tender, 20 to 25 minutes. If the juices in the pan begin to burn, add a little water and cover the pan loosely with foil.

MAKES 4 SERVINGS.

PER SERVING: 51 CALORIES; 0 G FAT (0 G SAT, 0 G MONO); 0 MG CHOLESTEROL; 13 G CARBOHYDRATE; 1 G PROTEIN; 2 G FIBER; 0 MG SODIUM.

ROASTED PEARS

START TO FINISH: 35 MINUTES

2-3 pears (about 1 pound)
1 tablespoon lemon juice
2 tablespoons sugar

Preheat oven to 425°F. Peel, core and cut pears into ½-inch-thick slices. Toss the pear slices with lemon juice in a large bowl; add sugar and toss once again. Transfer to a baking pan large enough to hold the slices in a single layer. Roast, stirring occasionally to prevent scorching, until the pears are tender and golden brown, 25 to 30 minutes.

MAKES 4 SERVINGS.

PER SERVING: 93 CALORIES; 1 G FAT (0 G SAT, 0 G MONO); 0 MG CHOLESTEROL; 24 G CARBOHYDRATE; 1 G PROTEIN; 3 G FIBER; 0 MG SODIUM.

Lower Carbs

ROASTED PLUMS

START TO FINISH: 35 MINUTES

4-5 ripe plums (about 1 pound)
½ tablespoon lemon juice
1 tablespoon sugar

Preheat oven to 425°F. Slice plums in half and remove pits. Toss the plums with lemon juice in a large bowl; add sugar and toss once again. Arrange the plums cut-side up in a shallow baking dish. Roast until tender, 20 to 25 minutes. If the juices in the pan begin to burn, add a little water and cover the pan loosely with foil. Let cool slightly before serving.

MAKES 4 SERVINGS.

PER SERVING: 65 CALORIES; 0 G FAT (0 G SAT, 0 G MONO); 0 MG CHOLESTEROL; 16 G CARBOHYDRATE; 1 G PROTEIN; 2 G FIBER; 0 MG SODIUM.

NUTRITION BONUS: 12 MG VITAMIN C (20% DV).

High Fiber

FONTINA WITH PEARS & WALNUTS

START TO FINISH: 10 MINUTES

Thinly slice 4 ounces Italian fontina cheese. Set a ripe Comice or Red Bartlett pear, a few slices of cheese and a few walnuts on each of 4 dessert plates. Pass whole-wheat crackers separately and serve a glass of port alongside, if desired.

MAKES 4 SERVINGS.

PER SERVING: 308 CALORIES; 17 G FAT (5 G SAT, 1 G MONO); 25 MG CHOLESTEROL; 34 G CARBOHYDRATE; 10 G PROTEIN; 6 G FIBER; 219 MG SODIUM.

NUTRITION BONUS: 294 MG CALCIUM (30% DV), 24% DV FIBER.

PIES & TARTS

Shades of Autumn Pie

PREP TIME: 1 HOUR | **START TO FINISH:** 4 HOURS (INCLUDING BAKING & COOLING)
EQUIPMENT: 9-INCH PIE PAN | **EASE OF PREPARATION:** MODERATE

The season's best apples—plus a pear for its delicate flavor—fill this wholesome pie. A touch of ginger imparts fragrance and warmth. Serve with low-fat vanilla ice cream or vanilla yogurt.

- **Essential EatingWell Pie Pastry (*page 344*)**
- **6 cups thinly sliced peeled apples (2¼ pounds), such as Northern Spy, Rhode Island Greening *and/or* Gravenstein**
- **1 large firm pear, peeled and thinly sliced**
- **⅓ cup plus 2 tablespoons sugar**
- **2 teaspoons freshly grated lemon zest, preferably organic**
- **1 tablespoon lemon juice**
- **1½ tablespoons cornstarch**
- **½ teaspoon ground ginger**
- **⅛ teaspoon ground nutmeg**

PECAN CRUMB TOPPING

- **¾ cup whole-wheat *or* all-purpose flour**
- **½ cup packed light brown sugar**
- **½ cup pecan halves**
- **¼ teaspoon ground cinnamon**
- **3 tablespoons cold unsalted butter, cut into small pieces**
- **1½ tablespoons milk**

1. Prepare Essential EatingWell Pie Pastry; refrigerate as directed.
2. Coat a 9-inch pie pan with cooking spray. On a lightly floured surface, roll the dough into a 12½-inch circle. Drape the dough over the rolling pin and transfer it to the prepared pan. Press to fit. Trim the pastry, fold the edges under and flute. Cover the pie shell and place in the freezer while you prepare the filling.
3. Combine apples, pear, ⅓ cup sugar, lemon zest and lemon juice in a large bowl; toss to coat. Set aside for 10 minutes. Preheat oven to 400°F.
4. Mix the remaining 2 tablespoons sugar, cornstarch, ginger and nutmeg in a small bowl. Add to the fruit and toss well to combine. Scrape the filling into the cold pie shell, smoothing the top so the slices don't stick up and scorch in the oven.
5. Bake the pie on the center rack for 30 minutes. Cover loosely with foil and bake for 10 minutes more.
6. Meanwhile, **prepare pecan crumb topping:** Put flour, brown sugar, pecans and cinnamon in a food processor; pulse 5 or 6 times to chop the nuts. Scatter butter over the dry ingredients. Pulse again repeatedly until the butter is broken into fine bits. Turn the machine on again and add the milk in a stream. Stop as soon as it has been added. Empty the mixture into a bowl and gently rub it between your fingers until it looks and feels a little like damp sand.
7. After the pie has baked for 40 minutes, reduce oven temperature to 350°F. Place the pie on a baking sheet. Spread the crumb topping evenly over the apples, patting down gently. Bake the pie until the fruit is tender when pierced with the tip of a knife and you can see the juices bubbling at the edge, 20 to 30 minutes more. Keep a close eye on the topping: once it starts to brown, lay

a large sheet of foil over the pie to prevent any further darkening.
8. Transfer the pie to a wire rack and let cool for at least 1 hour before serving.

MAKES 12 SERVINGS.

PER SERVING: 142 CALORIES; 12 G FAT (5 G SAT, 3 G MONO); 35 MG CHOLESTEROL; 46 G CARBOHYDRATE; 4 G PROTEIN; 4 G FIBER; 56 MG SODIUM.

NUTRITION BONUS: 15% DV FIBER.

ESSENTIAL EATINGWELL PIE PASTRY

PREP TIME: 15 MINUTES | **READY TO ROLL:** 1¼ HOURS
TO MAKE AHEAD: THE DOUGH WILL KEEP, WELL WRAPPED, IN THE REFRIGERATOR FOR UP TO 2 DAYS OR IN THE FREEZER FOR UP TO 3 MONTHS. | **EASE OF PREPARATION:** MODERATE (SOME BAKING SKILLS REQUIRED)

Whole-wheat pastry flour contributes a pleasant nutty flavor to an all-purpose pie dough and ensures a tender result.

- **¾ cup whole-wheat pastry flour**
- **¾ cup all-purpose flour**
- **2 tablespoons sugar**
- **¼ teaspoon salt**
- **4 tablespoons cold butter (½ stick), cut into small pieces**
- **1 tablespoon canola oil**
- **¼ cup ice water, plus more as needed**
- **1 large egg yolk**
- **1 teaspoon lemon juice *or* white vinegar**

Whisk whole-wheat flour, all-purpose flour, sugar and salt in a medium bowl. Cut in butter with a pastry blender or your fingers until the mixture resembles coarse crumbs with a few larger pieces. Add oil and stir with a fork to blend. Mix ¼ cup water, egg yolk and lemon juice (or vinegar) in a measuring cup. Make a well in the center of the flour mixture. Add enough of the egg yolk mixture, stirring with a fork, until the dough clumps together. (Add a little water if the dough seems too dry.) Turn the dough out onto a lightly floured surface and knead several times. Form the dough into a ball, then flatten into a disk. Wrap in plastic wrap and refrigerate for at least 1 hour.

MAKES ABOUT 14 OUNCES DOUGH, ENOUGH FOR ONE 9- TO 11-INCH PIE OR TART.

PER 8 SERVINGS: 166 CALORIES; 8 G FAT (4 G SAT, 1 G MONO); 41 MG CHOLESTEROL; 19 G CARBOHYDRATE; 3 G PROTEIN; 1 G FIBER; 82 MG SODIUM.

PER 10 SERVINGS: 133 CALORIES; 6 G FAT (3 G SAT, 1 G MONO); 33 MG CHOLESTEROL; 15 G CARBOHYDRATE; 2 G PROTEIN; 1 G FIBER; 65 MG SODIUM.

PER 12 SERVINGS: 110 CALORIES; 5 G FAT (3 G SAT, 1 G MONO); 28 MG CHOLESTEROL; 13 G CARBOHYDRATE; 2 G PROTEIN; 1 G FIBER; 54 MG SODIUM.

Pear Tart Tatin

PREP TIME: 30 MINUTES | **START TO FINISH:** 2½ HOURS (INCLUDING PASTRY TIME)
EQUIPMENT: 10-INCH OVENPROOF SKILLET | **EASE OF PREPARATION:** MODERATE

Tart Tatin is a classic upside-down tart, traditionally made with apples. It is named after the Tatin sisters of France, who are credited with its creation. The glory of the dessert is the caramelized fruit, in this case pears.

Essential EatingWell Pie Pastry (*page 344*)
5 ripe but firm Bosc pears
3 tablespoons lemon juice, divided
¾ cup water, divided
⅔ cup granulated sugar
1 tablespoon butter

1. Prepare Essential EatingWell Pie Pastry; refrigerate as directed.
2. On a lightly floured surface, roll the dough into a rough circle about ¼ inch thick. With a sharp knife or pastry wheel, cut into a 10-inch circle. (Discard trimmings.) Transfer to a baking sheet lined with parchment or wax paper, cover and freeze until ready to use.
3. Preheat oven to 375°F. Peel pears, cut in half lengthwise and core. Toss with 1 tablespoon lemon juice; set aside.
4. Combine ¼ cup water and sugar in a heavy 10-inch ovenproof skillet. Cook over low heat, stirring, until the sugar dissolves. Increase heat to medium and bring to a simmer. Cover and simmer for 1 minute. Uncover and cook, *without stirring*, until the syrup turns light amber, 6 to 8 minutes. Gently swirl if it is coloring unevenly.
5. Remove from the heat and add the remaining ½ cup water and 2 tablespoons lemon juice. (Stand back, as caramel may sputter.) Return the skillet to low heat and stir until the caramel has dissolved. Add butter and stir until melted.
6. Arrange the pears cut-side down in the caramel in a tight circle, with 1 pear half in the center. Increase heat to medium. Cover and cook for 10 minutes. With tongs, turn pears cut-side up and increase heat to high. Cook, uncovered, until pears are tender and caramel becomes a thick glaze, about 5 minutes. Remove from heat.
7. Lay the pastry over the pears, turning the edges under to fit. (Let the steam from the pears warm the crust until it's pliable.)
8. Bake the tart until the crust is golden, 25 to 30 minutes. Place a large flat serving platter on top of the tart; grasping platter and skillet with oven mitts, quickly invert. Remove the skillet. Let the tart cool for about 20 minutes. Serve warm or at room temperature.

MAKES 8 SERVINGS.

PER SERVING: 307 CALORIES; 10 G FAT (5 G SAT, 1 G MONO); 45 MG CHOLESTEROL; 52 G CARBOHYDRATE; 4 G PROTEIN; 4 G FIBER; 82 MG SODIUM.

Classic Lemon Tart

PREP TIME: 30 MINUTES | **START TO FINISH:** 2¼ HOURS (INCLUDING PASTRY TIME)
EQUIPMENT: 10- OR 11-INCH REMOVABLE-BOTTOM TART PAN | **EASE OF PREPARATION:** MODERATE

When life hands you lemons, make this bright, light lemon tart.

Essential EatingWell Pie Pastry (*page 344*)
2 large eggs
3 large egg whites *or* 6 teaspoons dried egg whites (*see Ingredient Note, page 352*), reconstituted according to package directions
1 cup sugar
2 teaspoons freshly grated lemon zest (*see page 375*), preferably organic
½ cup lemon juice
Confectioners' sugar for dusting

1. Prepare Essential EatingWell Pie Pastry; refrigerate as directed.
2. Position rack in upper third of oven; preheat to 375°F. Coat a 10- or 11-inch removable-bottom tart pan with cooking spray.
3. On a lightly floured surface, roll out the dough into a 12-inch circle. Drape the dough over the rolling pin and transfer it to the prepared pan. Press to fit. Run the rolling pin over the top of the tart pan to trim the edges. Cover the crust with foil or parchment paper and weight with pie weights, dry beans or dry rice. Place the tart pan on a baking sheet.
4. Bake the crust for 10 to 12 minutes, or until the surface is set but not at all browned. Remove the foil and pie weights and set the crust aside on the baking sheet.
5. Whisk eggs, egg whites and sugar in a mixing bowl until smooth. Whisk in lemon zest and lemon juice. Pour the filling into the partially baked crust.
6. Bake the tart in the upper third of the oven until the crust is golden and the filling is set, about 20 minutes. Cool on a wire rack for at least 10 minutes. Dust with confectioners' sugar. Serve warm or at room temperature.

MAKES 8 SERVINGS.

PER SERVING: 294 CALORIES; 9 G FAT (5 G SAT, 2 G MONO); 94 MG CHOLESTEROL; 47 G CARBOHYDRATE; 6 G PROTEIN; 2 G FIBER; 120 MG SODIUM.

NUTRITION BONUS: 8 MG VITAMIN C (15% DV).

Classic Pumpkin Pie

PREP TIME: 30 MINUTES | **START TO FINISH:** 3 HOURS (INCLUDING PASTRY TIME)
EQUIPMENT: 9-INCH PIE PAN | **TO MAKE AHEAD:** THE PIE WILL KEEP, LOOSELY COVERED, IN THE REFRIGERATOR FOR UP TO 1 DAY. | **EASE OF PREPARATION:** MODERATE

Canned evaporated milk—not to be confused with sweetened condensed milk—is a standard ingredient in many pumpkin pie recipes. Making the simple switch from evaporated whole milk to evaporated skim milk lowers the saturated fat of your pie, while maintaining its rich texture.

- **Essential EatingWell Pie Pastry (*page 344*)**
- **1 cup sugar**
- **1½ teaspoons ground cinnamon**
- **¾ teaspoon ground nutmeg**
- **¼ teaspoon salt**
- **2 large eggs**
- **4 large egg whites, *or* 8 teaspoons dried egg whites (*see Ingredient Note, page 352*), reconstituted according to package directions**
- **1 15-ounce can unseasoned pumpkin puree**
- **1 cup evaporated skim milk**
- **1 teaspoon vanilla extract**

1. Prepare Essential EatingWell Pie Pastry; refrigerate as directed.
2. Position rack in lower third of oven; preheat to 425°F. Coat a 9-inch pie pan with cooking spray.
3. Whisk sugar, cinnamon, nutmeg and salt in a large bowl. Add eggs and egg whites; whisk until well blended. Add pumpkin, whisking until smooth. Whisk in milk and vanilla.
4. On a lightly floured surface, roll out the dough into an 11-inch circle. Drape the dough over the rolling pin and fit it into the prepared pie pan. Trim the pastry, fold the edges under and flute. Place the pie pan on a baking sheet. Pour the filling into the crust.
5. Bake the pie for 10 minutes. Cover the edges with strips of foil to prevent overbrowning.
6. Reduce oven temperature to 325°; bake until the center barely jiggles when the pan is tapped, 55 to 60 minutes more. Transfer to a wire rack and let cool.

MAKES 8 SERVINGS.

PER SERVING: 336 CALORIES; 10 G FAT (5 G SAT, 2 G MONO); 96 MG CHOLESTEROL; 53 G CARBOHYDRATE; 9 G PROTEIN; 3 G FIBER; 239 MG SODIUM.

NUTRITION BONUS: 170% DV VITAMIN A.

Rustic Plum-Walnut Tart

PREP TIME: 40 MINUTES | **START TO FINISH:** 2 HOURS (INCLUDING PASTRY TIME)
EASE OF PREPARATION: MODERATE

There is nothing like the sight of late-summer fruit piled high at the farmstand to inspire one to bake. For this French free-form tart, known as a galette, the plums are arranged over a layer of ground walnuts, sugar and flour, which absorbs the delicious plummy juices and helps keep the pastry crust crisp. Serve with Vanilla Cream (*page 390*) or reduced-fat vanilla ice cream.

- Essential EatingWell Pie Pastry (*page 344*)
- 1/3 cup chopped walnuts *or* pecans
- 2 pounds plums, such as Santa Rosa *or* Queen Ann (12-16 plums)
- 1/4 cup all-purpose flour
- 1/2 cup sugar, divided, plus 1 teaspoon for sprinkling
- 1 tablespoon milk
- 3 tablespoons plum jam *or* red currant jelly

1. Prepare Essential EatingWell Pie Pastry; refrigerate as directed.
2. Position oven rack at the lowest level; preheat to 425°F. Coat a baking sheet with cooking spray.
3. On a lightly floured surface, roll the dough into a rough circle, about 14 inches in diameter and slightly less than 1/4 inch thick. Drape the dough over the rolling pin and transfer it to the prepared baking sheet. Cover and refrigerate while you prepare the filling.
4. Spread nuts in a small baking dish and bake until fragrant, about 5 minutes. Let cool.
5. Meanwhile, quarter plums, discarding pits. Place flour, 1/4 cup sugar and the toasted nuts in a food processor or blender; process until the nuts are finely ground.
6. Spread the nut mixture over the crust, leaving a 1 1/2-inch border around the edge. Arrange plums on their sides in concentric circles over the nut mixture. Sprinkle with the remaining 1/4 cup sugar. Fold the crust border over the plums, pleating as necessary. Brush milk over the rim and sprinkle with 1 teaspoon sugar.
7. Bake the tart for 15 minutes, reduce heat to 375°F and bake for 30 to 40 minutes longer, or until the crust is golden and the juices are bubbling. With a long metal spatula, slide the tart onto a serving platter and let cool. Before serving, heat jam (or jelly) over low heat until melted, then brush over the plums.

MAKES 12 SERVINGS.

PER SERVING: 233 CALORIES; 8 G FAT (3 G SAT, 1 G MONO); 28 MG CHOLESTEROL; 38 G CARBOHYDRATE; 3 G PROTEIN; 2 G FIBER; 55 MG SODIUM.

Dessert Pizza

PREP TIME: 35 MINUTES | **START TO FINISH:** 1 HOUR 5 MINUTES
EASE OF PREPARATION: MODERATE (SOME BAKING SKILLS REQUIRED)

Great for a party, this recipe is a *trompe l'oeil.* Raspberry sauce disguises itself as tomato sauce, dried strawberries as pepperoni and white chocolate plays the role of mozzarella cheese in this fruity pizza-style tart. The crust is a clever cottage cheese pastry—easy to make and low in saturated fat yet very rich and tender.

CRUST

- **¾ cup whole-wheat pastry flour** (*see Ingredient Note, page 395*)
- **½ cup all-purpose flour**
- **2 teaspoons baking powder**
- **¼ teaspoon salt**
- **½ cup low-fat cottage cheese**
- **⅓ cup sugar**
- **3 tablespoons canola oil**
- **2 tablespoons milk**
- **1½ teaspoons vanilla extract**
- **Cornmeal for dusting**

TOPPINGS

- **½ cup Raspberry Sauce** (*page 391*)
- **1 cup diced pineapple**
- **1 kiwi fruit, peeled and diced**
- **¼ cup dried strawberries *or* dried cranberries**
- **1 tablespoon milk**
- **2½ teaspoons sugar, divided**
- **1 2-ounce block of white chocolate**

1. **To prepare crust:** Whisk whole-wheat flour, all-purpose flour, baking powder and salt in a small bowl. Puree cottage cheese in a food processor. Add sugar, oil, milk and vanilla and process until smooth. Add the dry ingredients and pulse 4 to 5 times, just until the dough clumps together. Turn out onto a lightly floured work surface and press the dough into a ball. Knead several times, but do not overwork. Dust with flour, wrap in plastic wrap and refrigerate for at least 15 minutes.
2. Meanwhile, make Raspberry Sauce and prepare toppings.
3. **To assemble & bake pie:** Set oven rack at lowest position; preheat oven to 400°F. Spray a 12-inch pizza pan or large baking sheet with cooking spray. Sprinkle with cornmeal, shaking off excess.
4. On a lightly floured work surface, roll the dough into a 12-inch circle about ¼ inch thick. Roll the dough back over a rolling pin and transfer to the prepared pizza pan or baking sheet. Finish the edges by turning them under. To glaze the border, brush it very lightly with a little milk and sprinkle with ½ teaspoon of the sugar.
5. Spread the crust with Raspberry Sauce; scatter pineapple, kiwi and strawberries (or cranberries) on top. Sprinkle with 2 teaspoons sugar. Bake until the crust is golden and crisp, about 20 minutes.
6. Meanwhile, warm white chocolate in the microwave on Defrost until slightly softened but not melted, 20 to 40 seconds. Grate on a vegetable grater. (If the chocolate breaks into fine shreds, rather than large ones, continue to microwave, checking every 10 seconds.)
7. Sprinkle the grated chocolate over the hot pie; let stand until melted. Cut the pie into wedges; serve warm or at room temperature.

MAKES 8 SERVINGS.

PER SERVING: 244 CALORIES; 8 G FAT (2 G SAT, 4 G MONO); 1 MG CHOLESTEROL; 38 G CARBOHYDRATE; 5 G PROTEIN; 2 G FIBER; 234 MG SODIUM.

Ruffled Phyllo Tart with Spring Fruit

PREP TIME: 40 MINUTES | **START TO FINISH:** 3 HOURS (INCLUDING COOLING TIME)
EASE OF PREPARATION: MODERATE (SOME BAKING SKILLS REQUIRED)

Strawberries and rhubarb are a familiar seasonal pairing, but adding apricots to the mix takes it to new heights. The day before you plan to bake the tart, thaw the frozen phyllo in the refrigerator.

FILLING

- **½ cup plus 2 teaspoons sugar**
- **1 tablespoon honey**
- **1 pound fresh rhubarb, trimmed and cut into 1-inch pieces (about 3 cups)**
- **¼ cup cornstarch mixed with 3 tablespoons cold water**
- **½ pound fresh apricots, pitted and quartered (about 4 medium)**
- **1 cup strawberries, hulled and halved**
- **1 teaspoon freshly grated orange zest, preferably organic**
- **¼ teaspoon ground cinnamon**

CRUST

- **3 tablespoons canola oil**
- **2 tablespoons unsalted butter, melted**
- **9 sheets phyllo dough, thawed**
- **1 tablespoon dry unseasoned breadcrumbs**
- **Confectioners' sugar for dusting**

1. Preheat oven to 350°F. Coat a 9-inch pie pan with cooking spray.

2. **To prepare filling:** Combine ½ cup sugar, honey and rhubarb in a large saucepan. Cook over medium-low heat, stirring often, until the rhubarb is juicy and softens slightly, about 5 minutes. Increase heat to medium; gradually add the cornstarch mixture. Cook, stirring constantly, until the juices thicken, 2 to 3 minutes.

3. Combine apricots, strawberries, orange zest and cinnamon in a large bowl. Mix in the rhubarb.

4. **To prepare crust & bake tart:** Mix oil and butter in a small bowl. Cover phyllo with wax paper or plastic wrap and a slightly damp kitchen towel to prevent it from drying out. Center one sheet of phyllo in the pie pan, letting the edges hang over; gently press it into the pan. Dampen a pastry brush with water and lightly brush some of the oil-butter mixture over the phyllo. Sprinkle ½ teaspoon breadcrumbs over the bottom. Repeat with 5 more sheets of phyllo, laying each at a 45° angle to the previous one and sprinkling each with breadcrumbs.

5. Scrape the filling into the crust. Brush one of the remaining phyllo sheets with oil-butter mixture. Place another sheet on top at a 45° angle. Repeat with the last sheet. Place the stack on the filling. Fold the overhanging phyllo up around the tart, creating a ruffled border. Dab any remaining oil-butter mixture on top. Sprinkle with the remaining 2 teaspoons sugar. Cut 4 slits in the center for venting.

6. Place the tart on a baking sheet and bake until nicely browned and bubbling slightly, 45 to 55 minutes. Cool on a wire rack to room temperature (about 1½ hours). Dust with confectioners' sugar.

MAKES 8 SERVINGS.

PER SERVING: 268 CALORIES; 9 G FAT (2 G SAT, 4 G MONO); 8 MG CHOLESTEROL; 44 G CARBOHYDRATE; 4 G PROTEIN; 2 G FIBER; 150 MG SODIUM.

NUTRITION BONUS: 19 MG VITAMIN C (30% DV), 15% DV VITAMIN A.

French Silk Pie

PREP TIME: 30 MINUTES | **START TO FINISH:** 4¼ HOURS (INCLUDING CHILLING TIME) | **TO MAKE AHEAD:** THE PIE WILL KEEP, COVERED, IN THE REFRIGERATOR FOR UP TO 2 DAYS. | **EASE OF PREPARATION:** MODERATE

A creamy meringue is the secret to lightening the filling of this ultra-rich chocolate pie.

CRUST

- 30 chocolate wafers (*see Ingredient Note, page 324*)
- 2 tablespoons chopped pitted dates
- 2 tablespoons water
- 1 tablespoon canola oil

FILLING

- 1 tablespoon brewed coffee
- 1 tablespoon water
- 1½ teaspoons unflavored gelatin
- 1 large egg
- ½ cup 1% milk
- 8 tablespoons packed light brown sugar, divided
- ⅓ cup unsweetened cocoa powder, preferably Dutch-process
- 2 ounces bittersweet (*not* unsweetened) chocolate, chopped
- 1½ teaspoons vanilla extract
- 2 tablespoons dried egg whites (*see Ingredient Note, page 352*), reconstituted according to package directions (equivalent to 3 egg whites)
- ½ teaspoon cream of tartar
- Chocolate shavings (*see Cooking Tip, page 397*), optional

1. Preheat oven to 325°F. Coat a 9-inch pie pan with cooking spray.
2. **To prepare crust:** Combine chocolate wafers and dates in a food processor; process until finely chopped. Add water and oil and process until moistened. Press into the bottom and sides of prepared pan.
3. Bake the crust until crisp, about 10 minutes. Cool completely on a wire rack.
4. **To prepare filling & garnish:** Combine coffee and water in a small bowl. Sprinkle gelatin on top and set aside to soften.
5. Whisk egg, milk, 3 tablespoons brown sugar and cocoa in a small saucepan until smooth. Cook over low heat, whisking constantly, until thickened and an instant-read thermometer registers 160°F, 5 to 7 minutes. Do not let mixture come to a simmer.
6. Remove from the heat. Add the reserved gelatin mixture; stir until dissolved. Add chocolate and vanilla, stirring until melted. Set aside to cool to room temperature, about 30 minutes.
7. Meanwhile, place egg whites and cream of tartar in a large bowl. Beat with an electric mixer on low speed until frothy. Increase speed to high and beat until soft peaks form. Gradually add the remaining 5 tablespoons brown sugar, beating until the meringue is smooth and glossy.
8. Whisk one-fourth of the meringue into the chocolate mixture until smooth. Scrape chocolate mixture into the remaining meringue and use a whisk to incorporate it with a folding motion. Spoon into crust and chill, uncovered, until set, about 3 hours.
9. If desired, garnish with chocolate curls before serving.

RECIPE RX

Original Pie:
470 calories
32 grams fat

EW French Silk Pie:
166 calories
6 grams fat

MAKES 10 SERVINGS.

PER SERVING: 166 CALORIES; 6 G FAT (1 G SAT, 1 G MONO); 22 MG CHOLESTEROL; 28 G CARBOHYDRATE; 4 G PROTEIN; 2 G FIBER; 84 MG SODIUM.

Lemon Chiffon Pie

PREP TIME: 40 MINUTES | **START TO FINISH:** 4½ HOURS (INCLUDING CHILLING TIME) | **TO MAKE AHEAD:** THE PIE WILL KEEP, COVERED, IN THE REFRIGERATOR FOR UP TO 2 DAYS. | **EASE OF PREPARATION:** MODERATE

A light and lively lemon mousse paired with a crisp gingersnap crust makes a refreshing finish to a special meal. Just a little whipped cream gives the mousse a velvety taste and texture.

CRUST

- 30 gingersnap cookies (7½ ounces) (*see Nutrition Note, page 324*)
- 2 tablespoons raisins
- 1 tablespoon canola oil

FILLING

- 3 tablespoons water
- Yellow food coloring (optional)
- 1½ teaspoons unflavored gelatin
- 2 large eggs
- ¼ cup plus ⅔ cup granulated sugar
- 1 tablespoon freshly grated lemon zest, preferably organic
- ½ cup lemon juice
- 2 tablespoons dried egg whites (*see Note*), reconstituted according to package directions (equivalent to 3 egg whites)
- ¼ teaspoon cream of tartar
- ¼ cup whipping cream
- Candied Lemon Zest for garnish (*page 353*), optional

1. Preheat oven to 350°F. Coat a 9-inch pie pan with cooking spray.
2. **To prepare crust:** In a food processor, pulse gingersnaps and raisins until finely chopped. Add oil and process until well combined. Press evenly over bottom and sides of prepared pan.
3. Bake crust for 10 minutes, or until set. Transfer to a wire rack to cool completely.
4. **To prepare filling & garnish:** Place water in a small bowl and add about 3 drops food coloring, if using. Sprinkle gelatin on top and set aside to soften.
5. Whisk whole eggs, ¼ cup sugar, lemon zest and lemon juice in a medium nonreactive saucepan. Place over low heat and cook, whisking constantly, until the mixture thickens slightly and an instant-read thermometer registers 160°F, 8 to 12 minutes. Remove from the heat. Add the reserved gelatin mixture; whisk until blended. Let cool for 20 minutes, whisking occasionally.
6. Meanwhile, place egg whites and cream of tartar in a large bowl. Beat with an electric mixer on low speed until frothy. Increase speed to high and beat until soft peaks form. Gradually add the remaining ⅔ cup sugar, beating until the meringue is stiff and glossy.
7. In a chilled bowl, whip cream until soft peaks form.

INGREDIENT NOTE: Because they are made with pasteurized eggs, dried egg whites are a smart choice for mousses and other uncooked preparations. Just Whites is a common brand. You can find dried egg whites in the baking section of most supermarkets.

TEST KITCHEN TIP: Use a knife dipped in hot water to cut creamy pies into clean slices.

8. Whisk about one-fourth of the meringue into the lemon mixture. Gently whisk in the remaining meringue. With a rubber spatula, fold in the cream. Spoon into the prepared pie shell and chill, loosely covered, until set, about 3 hours.

9. Make Candied Lemon Zest, if desired. Just before serving, decorate the pie.

MAKES 8 SERVINGS.

PER SERVING: 282 CALORIES; 10 G FAT (3 G SAT, 4 G MONO); 61 MG CHOLESTEROL; 46 G CARBOHYDRATE; 4 G PROTEIN; 1 G FIBER; 138 MG SODIUM.

NUTRITION BONUS: 8 MG VITAMIN C (15% DV).

CANDIED LEMON ZEST

PREP TIME: 15 MINUTES | **START TO FINISH:** 45 MINUTES | **TO MAKE AHEAD:** THE ZEST WILL KEEP IN AN AIRTIGHT CONTAINER AT ROOM TEMPERATURE FOR UP TO 2 DAYS OR IN THE REFRIGERATOR FOR UP TO 1 MONTH. | **EASE OF PREPARATION:** EASY

A beautiful—and edible—garnish.

- **1 lemon, preferably organic, scrubbed**
- **½ cup granulated sugar**
- **½ cup water**

1. With a vegetable peeler, remove long strips of zest (without pith) from lemon; cut into julienne strips. Place in a small saucepan and cover with cold water. Bring to a simmer over medium heat. Cook for 7 minutes; drain.

2. Return strips to pan and add sugar and ½ cup water; return to a simmer. Cook over low heat until zest is translucent and syrup is slightly thickened, 10 to 15 minutes. Transfer strips to wax paper with a slotted spoon; let cool.

MAKES ABOUT ⅓ CUP.

PER TABLESPOON: 75 CALORIES; 0 G FAT (0 G SAT, 0 G MONO); 0 MG CHOLESTEROL; 20 G CARBOHYDRATE; 0 G PROTEIN; 0 G FIBER; 1 MG SODIUM.

CAKES & CHEESECAKES

Essential EatingWell Chocolate Bundt Cake

PREP TIME: 25 MINUTES | **START TO FINISH:** 2 HOURS (INCLUDING COOLING TIME)
EQUIPMENT: 12-CUP BUNDT PAN | **EASE OF PREPARATION:** EASY

An adaptation of EATINGWELL's popular Died-and-Went-to-Heaven Chocolate Cake, this recipe is from reader Barr Hogen of San Francisco. "I love chocolate—it has antioxidants—but Americans need more fiber in our diet. So I added prunes, which provide a lot of moisture, and flaxseeds, which have the added benefit of omega-3s," she wrote. "If you can squeeze fiber into your decadent dessert, why not?"

- ½ cup chopped hazelnuts *or* walnuts
- 1½ cups all-purpose flour
- 1 cup granulated sugar
- ¾ cup unsweetened "natural" cocoa powder (*see Ingredient Note, page 394*)
- ⅓ cup whole flaxseeds, ground (*see Ingredient Note, page 395*)
- 1½ teaspoons baking powder
- 1½ teaspoons baking soda
- 1 teaspoon salt
- 1¼ cups buttermilk
- 1 cup packed light brown sugar
- 2 large eggs, lightly beaten
- ¼ cup rice bran oil (*see Ingredient Note, page 395*) *or* canola oil
- 1 teaspoon vanilla extract
- ½ cup hot water
- ½ cup prune puree (*see Tip*), prune pie filling *or* Lighter Bake
- ½ cup chopped bittersweet chocolate *or* chocolate chips
- Confectioners' sugar for dusting

1. Preheat oven to 350°F. Coat a 12-cup Bundt pan with cooking spray and dust with flour (or use cooking spray with flour).

2. Spread nuts in a small baking pan and bake until golden and fragrant, 5 to 7 minutes. Transfer to a plate to cool.

3. Whisk together flour, granulated sugar, cocoa, ground flaxseeds, baking powder, baking soda and salt in a large mixing bowl. Add buttermilk, brown sugar, eggs, oil and vanilla; beat with an electric mixer on medium speed until smooth. Mix hot water and prune puree (or pie filling or Lighter Bake) in a measuring cup; add to the batter and whisk until incorporated. Fold in chocolate and nuts with a rubber spatula. Scrape the batter into the prepared pan, spreading evenly.

4. Bake the cake until the top springs back when touched lightly and a tester inserted in the center comes out clean, 45 to 55 minutes. Cool in pan on a rack for 10 minutes. Turn out onto the rack to cool completely. Dust with confectioners' sugar.

TO MAKE PRUNE PUREE: Combine 6 ounces (1 cup) pitted prunes with 6 tablespoons hot water in a food processor; process until smooth. Makes 1 cup.

MAKES 16 SERVINGS.

PER SERVING: 266 CALORIES; 10 G FAT (2 G SAT, 4 G MONO); 27 MG CHOLESTEROL; 44 G CARBOHYDRATE; 5 G PROTEIN; 2 G FIBER; 342 MG SODIUM.

Chocolate-Hazelnut Cake

PREP TIME: 1 HOUR | **START TO FINISH:** 2½ HOURS | **EQUIPMENT:** 9-INCH ROUND CAKE PAN

TO MAKE AHEAD: PREPARE THROUGH STEP 8. THE CAKE WILL KEEP, WELL WRAPPED, AT ROOM TEMPERATURE FOR UP TO 1 DAY OR IN THE FREEZER FOR UP TO 3 MONTHS.

EASE OF PREPARATION: MODERATE (SOME BAKING SKILLS REQUIRED)

Turn this moist, dense and truly chocolaty cake into an elegant dessert by garnishing each serving with a dollop of whipped cream, some fresh raspberries and a light dusting of cocoa. Note that this cake does not contain any leavening: beaten egg whites alone are used to lighten it.

CAKE

- ½ cup chopped pitted dates
- ½ cup unsweetened cocoa powder, "natural" *or* Dutch-process (*see Ingredient Note, page 394*)
- 1 teaspoon instant coffee granules
- ½ cup boiling water
- ½ cup chopped hazelnuts, plus 2 tablespoons for garnish
- 2 slices firm white sandwich bread, crusts trimmed
- ⅓ cup all-purpose flour
- ¼ teaspoon salt
- ⅔ cup sugar, divided
- 2 tablespoons canola oil
- 1 teaspoon vanilla extract
- 1 large egg
- 3 large egg whites *or* 2 tablespoons dried egg whites (*see Ingredient Note, page 394*), reconstituted according to package directions

1. **To prepare cake:** Preheat oven to 350°F. Coat a 9-inch round cake pan with cooking spray. Line the bottom with parchment or wax paper.

2. Combine dates, cocoa and instant coffee in a small bowl. Add boiling water and stir until cocoa has dissolved. Cover and let stand until dates have softened and mixture has cooled to room temperature, about 20 minutes.

3. Meanwhile, spread hazelnuts in a shallow baking dish and bake until fragrant and lightly toasted, 5 to 10 minutes. Transfer to a plate and let cool.

4. Grind bread into fine crumbs in a food processor. Measure to make sure you have ½ cup. Transfer to a large bowl. (No need to wash the workbowl between steps.)

5. Place ½ cup hazelnuts in the food processor. Add flour and salt; process until nuts are finely ground. Transfer to the bowl with the breadcrumbs.

6. Scrape the cooled date mixture into the food processor. Add ⅓ cup sugar, oil, vanilla and whole egg; process until smooth, stopping several times to scrape down the sides of the workbowl. Scrape the mixture into the bowl with the breadcrumbs and nuts. Mix gently with a rubber spatula.

RECIPE RX

Original Cake:
496 calories
40 grams total fat
19 grams saturated

EW Chocolate-Hazelnut Cake:
234 calories
9 grams total fat
2 grams saturated

GLAZE

- **⅓ cup unsweetened cocoa powder**
- **2 ounces bittersweet (*not* unsweetened) chocolate, finely chopped (⅓ cup)**
- **1 tablespoon corn syrup**
- **1 teaspoon instant coffee granules**
- **¼ cup boiling water**
- **½ teaspoon vanilla extract**
- **1 cup confectioners' sugar**

What We Did

OUR FIRST TACTIC was to establish a rich, complex flavor by relying on nuts, whose fat is primarily the cholesterol-lowering monounsaturated kind. Using a classic French recipe called *Gateau Reine de Saba* (Queen of Sheba Cake) as our model, we were able to reduce the saturated fat significantly by replacing the chocolate in the cake with cocoa and substituting dates for the butter. (Cocoa delivers the same essential flavor as baker's chocolate but without the saturated fat.) Applesauce and prune puree are well-known substitutes for fat in baking, but dates have a remarkable flavor affinity with chocolate and work unexpected magic in this case.

7. In a large clean mixing bowl, beat egg whites with an electric mixer until soft peaks form. Gradually add remaining ⅓ cup sugar, beating until stiff, glossy peaks form. Add one-fourth of the beaten whites to the batter and whisk until blended. Fold in the remaining whites with a rubber spatula just until blended. Scrape the batter into the prepared pan, spreading evenly.

8. Bake until the top springs back when touched lightly, 25 to 35 minutes. Let cool in the pan on a wire rack for 5 minutes. Spray the rack with cooking spray and invert the cake onto it to cool completely.

9. **Meanwhile, to prepare glaze:** Combine cocoa, chocolate, corn syrup and instant coffee in a medium bowl. Add boiling water and stir with a wooden spoon until the chocolate has melted and the mixture is smooth. Stir in vanilla. Gradually add confectioners' sugar to the chocolate mixture, beating with an electric mixer, slowly at first, then gradually increasing speed, until the glaze is smooth and thickened. (The mixture may seem lumpy at first, but it will smooth out.) Cover with plastic wrap and let sit at room temperature until the mixture is set, about 30 minutes.

10. **To finish the cake,** place it bottom-side up on a serving plate. Place several strips of wax paper under the bottom edge to protect the plate from drips. Spoon on glaze and spread it evenly over the top and sides of the cake with an icing spatula or knife. Arrange the remaining 2 tablespoons hazelnuts around the top outside edge. Discard the wax paper before serving.

MAKES 12 SERVINGS.

PER SERVING: 234 CALORIES; 9 G FAT (2 G SAT, 5 G MONO); 18 MG CHOLESTEROL; 38 G CARBOHYDRATE; 5 G PROTEIN; 4 G FIBER; 86 MG SODIUM.

NUTRITION BONUS: 15% DV FIBER.

Ginger-Spice Carrot Cake with Figs

PREP TIME: 50 MINUTES | **START TO FINISH:** 2 HOURS 40 MINUTES (INCLUDING COOLING TIME)
EQUIPMENT: 10-INCH SPRINGFORM PAN | **TO MAKE AHEAD:** THE CAKE WILL KEEP, WELL WRAPPED, IN THE REFRIGERATOR FOR 2 TO 3 DAYS. | **EASE OF PREPARATION:** MODERATE

This new version of a family favorite features a rich blend of dried spices along with crystallized ginger, brandied figs and whole-wheat pastry flour for added nutrition and a tender crumb.

CAKE

- **½ cup brandy**
- **½ cup dried figs, stemmed (about 6 figs)**
- **½ cup chopped walnuts, plus 12 walnut halves for garnish**
- **1 cup whole-wheat pastry flour** (*see Ingredient Note, 395*)
- **1 teaspoon baking powder**
- **½ teaspoon baking soda**
- **1 teaspoon ground cinnamon**
- **1 teaspoon ground ginger**
- **½ teaspoon ground cloves**
- **½ teaspoon ground cardamom**
- **½ teaspoon ground allspice**
- **½ teaspoon nutmeg, preferably freshly grated**
- **¼ teaspoon salt**
- **2 large eggs**
- **1 cup sugar**
- **½ cup mild extra-virgin olive oil**
- **1½ cups grated carrots (2-3 carrots)**
- **¼ cup finely chopped crystallized ginger**

1. Preheat oven to 350°F. Coat a 10-inch springform pan with cooking spray and line the bottom with parchment or wax paper.
2. Combine brandy and figs in a small saucepan; bring to a simmer over low heat. Simmer for 5 minutes, shaking the pan occasionally so all the figs get rehydrated by the brandy. Strain, reserving the brandy. Cool the figs slightly; coarsely chop.
3. Spread chopped walnuts at one end of a baking sheet and walnut halves at the other end. Toast in the oven until fragrant, 5 to 10 minutes. Set aside to cool.
4. Meanwhile, place flour in a large bowl. Sift in baking powder, baking soda, cinnamon, ginger, cloves, cardamom, allspice, nutmeg and salt; whisk to blend.
5. Combine eggs, sugar and oil in a food processor; process until thickened and pale, about 3 minutes. (*Alternatively, combine in a large bowl and beat with an electric mixer on high.*)
6. Add figs, chopped walnuts, carrots and crystallized ginger to flour mixture. Toss to coat well, breaking up any clumps. Add the wet ingredients and stir until just combined. Add enough of the reserved brandy (up to 1 tablespoon) to thin the batter.
7. Scrape the batter into the prepared pan, smoothing the top. Bake until the top is golden and springs back when touched lightly, 45 to 50 minutes. Cool in the pan on a wire rack for 10 minutes. Run a knife around the sides and turn the cake out onto the rack; remove pan and paper. Let cool completely.
8. **To prepare frosting & assemble cake:** Combine cream cheese and butter in a medium bowl; beat with an electric mixer on medium-high until creamy. Add sugar in two batches, beating until smooth and creamy. Add orange zest, vanilla and ginger; blend on low speed. (*Makes 1½ cups.*)

GINGER CREAM CHEESE FROSTING

- 12 ounces reduced-fat cream cheese (Neufchâtel)
- 1 tablespoon unsalted butter, softened
- ½ cup confectioners' sugar
- 1 tablespoon freshly grated orange zest (from 1 orange), preferably organic
- 1½ teaspoons vanilla extract
- ½ teaspoon ground ginger

9. Place the cake right-side up on a serving plate. Put strips of wax paper under the edges to protect the plate from drips. Spread frosting over the top and sides of the cake. Garnish with walnut halves. Discard wax paper before serving.

MAKES 12 SERVINGS.

PER SERVING: 390 CALORIES; 22 G FAT (7 G SAT, 8 G MONO); 58 MG CHOLESTEROL; 39 G CARBOHYDRATE; 7 G PROTEIN; 3 G FIBER; 286 MG SODIUM.

NUTRITION BONUS: 40% DV VITAMIN A.

Old-Fashioned Gingerbread

PREP TIME: 20 MINUTES | **START TO FINISH:** 1 HOUR
EQUIPMENT: 8-BY-11½-INCH BAKING PAN | **EASE OF PREPARATION:** EASY

Ginger, which can be traced as far back as the first century A.D., is an ancient culinary staple. Honor its tradition by baking this moist, spicy cake, served plain or with a spoon of Lemon Curd (*page 329*).

- 1½ cups whole-wheat pastry flour
- 1 cup all-purpose flour
- 2 teaspoons baking soda
- 2 teaspoons ground ginger
- 1½ teaspoons ground cinnamon
- ½ teaspoon salt
- 1 large egg
- ½ cup packed dark brown sugar
- ¼ cup canola oil
- 1 cup molasses
- ½ cup applesauce
- ½ cup buttermilk

1. Preheat oven to 350°F. Coat an 8-by-11½-inch baking pan with cooking spray.

2. Whisk whole-wheat flour, all-purpose flour, baking soda, ginger, cinnamon and salt in a bowl. Set aside.

3. Place egg, sugar and oil in a large bowl. Beat with an electric mixer on high speed until thick and creamy. Reduce speed to low and beat in molasses and applesauce.

4. With a rubber spatula, gently mix reserved dry ingredients and buttermilk into egg mixture, making 3 additions of dry ingredients and 2 additions of buttermilk. (Do not overmix.)

5. Scrape batter into prepared pan. Bake until a skewer inserted in the center comes out clean, 35 to 45 minutes. Let cool slightly in the pan on a wire rack. Serve warm.

MAKES 12 SERVINGS.

PER SERVING: 243 CALORIES; 5 G FAT (1 G SAT, 3 G MONO); 18 MG CHOLESTEROL; 47 G CARBOHYDRATE; 3 G PROTEIN; 2 G FIBER; 128 MG SODIUM.

NUTRITION BONUS: 510 MG POTASSIUM (26% DV), 3 MG IRON (15% DV).

Lemon-Almond Polenta Torta

PREP TIME: 20 MINUTES | **START TO FINISH:** 2 HOURS 20 MINUTES (INCLUDING COOLING TIME)
EQUIPMENT: 9-INCH SPRINGFORM PAN | **TO MAKE AHEAD:** THE CAKE WILL KEEP, WELL WRAPPED, IN THE REFRIGERATOR FOR 2 TO 3 DAYS. | **EASE OF PREPARATION:** MODERATE

Ground whole lemon gives this cake an intense natural flavor; cornmeal gives it a satisfying texture. (*Photo: page 220.*)

- ½ cup coarse yellow cornmeal (*see Note*)
- ½ cup all-purpose flour
- 2 teaspoons baking powder
- ¼ teaspoon salt
- 1½ cups whole almonds (7½ ounces)
- 1 cup sugar
- 1 large lemon, preferably organic, scrubbed
- ¾ cup mild extra-virgin olive oil
- ½ cup 1% milk
- 2 large eggs
- ½ teaspoon almond extract
- 1 cup Raspberry Sauce (*page 391*), optional
- 1 cup Vanilla Cream (*page 390*), optional
- 1 tablespoon confectioners' sugar for dusting
- Fresh berries & mint sprigs for garnish (optional)

1. Preheat oven to 325°F. Coat a 9-inch springform pan with cooking spray; line the bottom with parchment or wax paper.

2. Whisk cornmeal, flour, baking powder and salt in a medium bowl.

3. Pulse almonds and sugar in a food processor for about 30 seconds, aiming for a coarse meal. Cut lemon in half. Juice one half (about 1½ tablespoons); discard rind. Cut the other half into 4 pieces and pick out the seeds. Add the lemon juice and pieces to the food processor; process for 45 seconds. Add oil, milk, eggs and almond extract; process for 1 to 1½ minutes to combine well. Add the cornmeal mixture and pulse very briefly to combine. Scrape the batter into the prepared pan.

INGREDIENT NOTE: Imported varieties of coarsely ground cornmeal may be labeled "polenta." Porridge made from the cornmeal is also called polenta.

4. Bake the cake until golden and firm to the touch, 50 to 60 minutes. It will look quite dark. Cool in the pan on a wire rack for 10 minutes. Run a knife around the sides and turn the cake out onto the rack; remove pan and paper. Let cool completely.

5. Meanwhile, make Raspberry Sauce and Vanilla Cream, if using.

6. Place the cake, right-side up, on a serving plate. Dust with confectioners' sugar. Garnish each slice with berries and mint, if desired. Serve with Raspberry Sauce and Vanilla Cream, if desired.

MAKES 12 SERVINGS.

PER SERVING: 354 CALORIES; 24 G FAT (3 G SAT, 17 G MONO); 36 MG CHOLESTEROL; 30 G CARBOHYDRATE; 6 G PROTEIN; 4 G FIBER; 150 MG SODIUM.

Walnut Cake with a Hint of Rosemary

PREP TIME: 40 MINUTES | **START TO FINISH:** 2 HOURS (INCLUDING COOLING TIME)
EQUIPMENT: 12-CUP BUNDT PAN | **EASE OF PREPARATION:** MODERATE (SOME BAKING SKILL REQUIRED)

Rosemary contributes an ever-so-subtle fragrance to this luxurious cake. Whole-wheat flour blends in seamlessly because its nutty flavor complements the walnuts. (*Photo: page 221.*)

- ¾ cup walnuts
- 1 cup whole-wheat pastry flour (*see page 365*)
- ¾ cup all-purpose flour
- 1½ teaspoons baking powder
- ½ teaspoon baking soda
- ¼ teaspoon salt
- 1 cup buttermilk
- ¼ cup mild olive oil *or* canola oil
- 4 teaspoons very finely chopped fresh rosemary
- 1 teaspoon vanilla extract
- ½ teaspoon freshly grated lemon zest
- 2 large eggs, at room temperature (*see page 365*)
- 2 large egg whites, at room temperature, *or* 4 teaspoons dried egg whites (*see Ingredient Note, page 394*), reconstituted according to package directions
- 1¼ cups sugar
- 1 cup Vanilla Cream (*page 390*)
- Confectioners' sugar for dusting
- 2 cups mixed fresh berries (blueberries, raspberries, blackberries)
- Rosemary sprigs for garnish

1. Position rack in center of oven; preheat to 350°F. Coat a 10-inch (12-cup) Bundt pan, preferably nonstick, with cooking spray.
2. Spread walnuts in a small baking pan and toast in the oven until fragrant, 4 to 6 minutes. Let cool.
3. Place walnuts, whole-wheat flour, all-purpose flour, baking powder, baking soda and salt in a food processor; process until walnuts are finely ground.
4. Combine buttermilk, oil, rosemary, vanilla and lemon zest in a glass measuring cup.
5. Place eggs, egg whites and sugar in a large mixing bowl. Beat with an electric mixer on high speed for 5 minutes. The mixture should be thickened and pale.
6. With a rubber spatula, alternately fold the dry ingredients and buttermilk mixture into the egg mixture, making 3 additions of the dry and 2 additions of liquid. Scrape the batter into the prepared pan, spreading evenly.
7. Bake the cake until the top springs back when touched lightly and a toothpick inserted in the center comes out clean, 35 to 40 minutes. Let cool in the pan on a wire rack for 5 minutes. Loosen the edges and turn the cake out onto the rack to cool completely.
8. Meanwhile, make Vanilla Cream.
9. To serve, set the cake on a platter and dust with confectioners' sugar. Garnish with berries and rosemary sprigs. Serve each piece with a dollop of Vanilla Cream and some berries.

MAKES 16 SERVINGS.

PER SERVING: 230 CALORIES; 10 G FAT (3 G SAT, 4 G MONO); 36 MG CHOLESTEROL; 31 G CARBOHYDRATE; 5 G PROTEIN; 2 G FIBER; 171 MG SODIUM.

Pumpkin-Walnut Cake

PREP TIME: 25 MINUTES | **START TO FINISH:** 2 HOURS (INCLUDING COOLING TIME)
EQUIPMENT: 12-CUP BUNDT PAN OR TUBE PAN | **EASE OF PREPARATION:** MODERATE

A spice-rich autumn treat with a sweet, nutty glaze, this cake travels well for potlucks or bake sales. Pumpkin is the secret to keeping our butterless version exceptionally moist and flavorful.

CAKE

- **½ cup walnuts, divided**
- **1½ cups whole-wheat pastry flour**
- **1 cup all-purpose flour**
- **2 teaspoons baking soda**
- **¾ teaspoon salt**
- **2 teaspoons ground cinnamon**
- **1 teaspoon ground allspice**
- **½ teaspoon ground nutmeg**
- **¼ teaspoon ground cloves**
- **2 large eggs**
- **1 large egg white**
- **1½ cups packed light brown sugar**
- **1 15-ounce can unseasoned pumpkin puree**
- **⅓ cup orange juice**
- **¼ cup canola oil**
- **1 teaspoon vanilla extract**

CARAMEL-WALNUT GLAZE

- **3 tablespoons packed light brown sugar**
- **2 tablespoons 1% milk *or* evaporated skim milk**
- **2 teaspoons butter**

1. To prepare cake: Preheat oven to 350°F. Coat a 12-cup Bundt or tube pan with cooking spray. Dust pan with flour, tilting to coat and tapping out the excess (or use cooking spray with flour).

2. Spread walnuts in a shallow pan and bake until fragrant, about 5 minutes; let cool. Chop walnuts and set aside.

3. Whisk whole-wheat flour, all-purpose flour, baking soda, salt and spices in a medium bowl.

4. Combine eggs, egg white and brown sugar in a large mixing bowl. Beat with an electric mixer until fluffy, 3 to 5 minutes. Add pumpkin, orange juice, oil and vanilla; beat until smooth.

5. Add the dry ingredients to the wet ingredients and stir until just combined. Set aside 2 tablespoons walnuts for the glaze and fold the rest into the batter. Scrape the batter into the prepared pan.

6. Bake the cake for 50 to 60 minutes, or until a skewer inserted in the center comes out clean. Transfer to a wire rack. Let cool in the pan for 10 minutes.

7. To prepare glaze & finish cake: Combine brown sugar, milk and butter in a small saucepan. Bring to a boil over medium heat, stirring frequently. Cook for 1 minute. Remove from heat and stir in the reserved 2 tablespoons walnuts.

8. Turn the cake out onto the rack; place the rack over a baking sheet. Drizzle the warm glaze over the top and sides of the cake. Transfer to a serving plate; spoon any glaze from the baking sheet over the cake. Let cool completely.

RECIPE RX

Original Cake:
370 calories
19 grams total fat

EW Pumpkin-Walnut Cake:
214 calories
7 grams total fat

MAKES 16 SERVINGS.

PER SERVING: 214 CALORIES; 7 G FAT (1 G SAT, 3 G MONO); 28 MG CHOLESTEROL; 36 G CARBOHYDRATE; 4 G PROTEIN; 2 G FIBER; 281 MG SODIUM.

NUTRITION BONUS: 80% DV VITAMIN A.

Banana Cake with Coconut-Cream Frosting

PREP TIME: 20 MINUTES | **START TO FINISH:** 1¾ HOURS | **EQUIPMENT:** TWO 9-INCH ROUND CAKE PANS
TO MAKE AHEAD: PREPARE THROUGH STEP 6. WRAP CAKE LAYERS IN PLASTIC WRAP, THEN FOIL AND FREEZE FOR UP TO 3 MONTHS. | **EASE OF PREPARATION:** MODERATE (SOME BAKING SKILLS REQUIRED)

Combining traditional flavors with modern sensibilities, the creamed butter and sugar have been replaced with a simple meringue in this moist, luscious cake.

- **1 cup whole-wheat pastry flour** (*see page 365*)
- **1 cup all-purpose flour**
- **1½ teaspoons baking powder**
- **1½ teaspoons baking soda**
- **2 teaspoons ground cinnamon**
- **½ teaspoon ground nutmeg**
- **½ teaspoon salt**
- **2 tablespoons butter**
- **1 large egg white**
- **1 large egg, separated**
- **¼ teaspoon cream of tartar**
- **1½ cups sugar, divided**
- **1 cup mashed very ripe bananas (2 large)**
- **3 tablespoons canola oil**
- **1 teaspoon vanilla extract**
- **½ cup buttermilk**

COCONUT-CREAM FROSTING

- **⅓ cup unsweetened coconut chips *or* flaked coconut**
- **12 ounces reduced-fat cream cheese**
- **½ cup confectioners' sugar**
- **½ teaspoon coconut extract**

1. **To prepare cake:** Preheat oven to 350°F. Coat two 9-inch round cake pans with cooking spray. Dust lightly with flour, shaking out excess (or use cooking spray with flour).
2. Whisk whole-wheat flour, all-purpose flour, baking powder, baking soda, cinnamon, nutmeg and salt in a large bowl.
3. Melt butter in a small saucepan over low heat. Cook, swirling, until it turns a nutty brown, 1 to 3 minutes. Transfer to a bowl to cool.
4. Beat egg whites in a large bowl with an electric mixer on low speed until foamy. Add cream of tartar, increase speed to medium-high and beat until soft peaks form. Gradually add ½ cup sugar, beating until stiff but not dry (this can take up to 5 minutes).
5. Combine melted butter, egg yolk, remaining 1 cup sugar, bananas, oil and vanilla in a large bowl. With mixer on low speed, alternately add dry ingredients and buttermilk; beat until just blended. Beat in a heaping spoonful of whites. Using a whisk, fold in remaining whites. Pour batter into prepared pans.
6. Bake the cake until a skewer inserted in the center comes out clean, 30 to 40 minutes. Let cool in the pans on a wire rack for 10 minutes. Invert onto the racks and let cool completely.
7. **To prepare frosting & assemble cake:** Toast coconut in a pie pan at 350°F until lightly browned and fragrant, 2 to 4 minutes.
8. Combine cream cheese, confectioners' sugar and coconut extract in a large bowl; beat with an electric mixer on medium speed until smooth and creamy.
9. Frost the cake, using a little less than half the frosting between layers and the rest on the top. Garnish with toasted coconut.

MAKES 12 SERVINGS.

PER SERVING: 346 CALORIES; 12 G FAT (6 G SAT, 4 G MONO); 39 MG CHOLESTEROL; 53 G CARBOHYDRATE; 7 G PROTEIN; 2 G FIBER; 370 MG SODIUM.

Sugar-on-Snow Cake

PREP TIME: 40 MINUTES | **START TO FINISH:** 3 HOURS 10 MINUTES (INCLUDING CHILLING TIME)
EQUIPMENT: TWO 9-INCH ROUND CAKE PANS | **TO MAKE AHEAD:** THE CAKE LAYERS WILL KEEP, TIGHTLY WRAPPED, AT ROOM TEMPERATURE FOR UP TO 3 DAYS. | **EASE OF PREPARATION:** CHALLENGING

This impressive-looking maple layer cake, with amber syrup drizzled over billowy mounds of frosting, pays homage to a classic early spring New England treat. At maple-sugaring time, snow is scooped up outside the sugarhouse and drizzled with hot maple syrup. The result is a taffy-like confection known as "sugar on snow."

CAKE

- **¾ cup plus ⅓ cup walnuts *or* pecans**
- **¾ cup whole-wheat pastry flour (see *page 365*)**
- **¾ cup all-purpose flour**
- **1½ teaspoons baking powder**
- **½ teaspoon baking soda**
- **¼ teaspoon salt**
- **1 cup buttermilk**
- **1 tablespoon canola oil**
- **1 tablespoon vanilla extract**
- **2 large eggs, at room temperature (*see page 365*)**
- **2 large egg whites, at room temperature**
- **1¼ cups sugar**

MAPLE CREAM FROSTING & DRIZZLE

- **1 tablespoon water**
- **1 teaspoon vanilla extract**
- **1 teaspoon unflavored gelatin**
- **2 tablespoons dried egg whites (*see Ingredient Note, page 394*), reconstituted according to package directions**
- **1 cup maple syrup, divided**
- **¼ teaspoon cream of tartar**
- **Pinch of salt**
- **⅓ cup whipping cream**

1. To prepare cake: Position rack in center of oven; preheat to 325°F. Coat two 9-inch round cake pans with cooking spray. Dust pans with flour, tapping out the excess. Line bottoms with parchment or wax paper and coat it with cooking spray.

2. Spread nuts in a small baking pan and bake until fragrant, 4 to 6 minutes. Let cool. Set aside ⅓ cup.

3. Combine remaining ¾ cup toasted nuts, whole-wheat flour, all-purpose flour, baking powder, baking soda and salt in a food processor; process until nuts are finely ground. Set aside. Combine buttermilk, oil and vanilla in a glass measuring cup; set aside.

4. Combine eggs, egg whites and sugar in a large bowl. Beat with an electric mixer on high speed until thick and pale, about 5 minutes.

5. Alternately fold the dry ingredients and the buttermilk mixture into the egg mixture with a rubber spatula, making 3 additions of dry ingredients and 2 additions of liquid. Divide the batter between the prepared pans, spreading evenly.

6. Bake the cake until the tops spring back when touched lightly and the cake just starts to pull away from the pan, 25 to 30 minutes. Let cool in the pans on a wire rack for 5 minutes. Loosen the edges and invert onto the rack. Remove paper; let cool completely.

7. To prepare frosting: Combine water and vanilla in a small bowl. Sprinkle with gelatin and let soften 1 minute.

8. Bring about 1 inch of water to a bare simmer in a wide pot. Combine reconstituted egg white, ½ cup maple syrup, cream of tartar and salt in a heatproof mixing bowl large enough to fit over the pot. Set the bowl over the water and beat with an electric mixer on low speed, moving the beaters constantly, for 4 minutes.

9. Increase mixer speed to high and continue beating for 3½ minutes longer. Remove the bowl from the heat. Add the gelatin mixture and continue to beat until cooled to room temperature, 4 to 5 minutes longer.

10. In a chilled bowl, beat cream until medium-firm peaks form. Fold in meringue with a rubber spatula.

11. **To assemble & decorate cake:** Frost the cake, using about 1 cup frosting between layers and the rest on the top and sides. Cover loosely and refrigerate for at least 1 hour or up to 8 hours.

12. No more than 1 hour before serving, place a large shallow bowl of water beside the stove. Bring the remaining ½ cup maple syrup to a boil in a small saucepan. Reduce heat to low and boil gently, without stirring, until a little syrup dropped into cold water forms a thread between your fingers, 5 to 10 minutes. Immediately dip the base of the saucepan in water to stop cooking and cool the syrup quickly.

13. When the syrup has cooled and thickened slightly, use a spoon to drizzle it over the cake (rewarm over low heat if the syrup has hardened).

14. Chop the remaining ⅓ cup nuts. Using a flat metal spatula or pastry scraper, press nuts around the bottom half of the cake.

MAKES 16 SERVINGS.

PER SERVING: 246 CALORIES; 9 G FAT (2 G SAT, 2 G MONO); 33 MG CHOLESTEROL; 39 G CARBOHYDRATE; 5 G PROTEIN; 1 G FIBER; 130 MG SODIUM.

Cake Essentials

EGGS

• To bring cold eggs to room temperature quickly, place in a bowl of warm water for a few minutes; they will beat to a greater volume.

• To separate eggs safely: Use an egg separator, an inexpensive gadget found in cookware stores; separating eggs the traditional way, by passing the yolk back and forth between pieces of eggshell or your hands, can expose eggs to bacteria.

FLOUR

• Whole-wheat pastry flour is milled from soft wheat. It contains less gluten than regular whole-wheat flour and helps ensure a tender result in delicate baked goods while providing the nutritional benefits of whole grains. Store in the freezer.

BUTTERMILK

• You can use buttermilk powder in place of fresh buttermilk. Or make "sour milk": mix 1 tablespoon lemon juice or vinegar to 1 cup milk.

MEASURING

• **Dry ingredients:** As in all baking, careful measuring is critical to the success of a recipe. To measure flour, first stir it in the canister to lighten it. Spoon flour into a dry measuring cup until heaping, then level off with the straight edge of a knife. Do not pack or tap.

• **Liquid ingredients:** Place a clear measuring cup on a level surface. Pour in the liquid, then verify the measure by looking at it from eye level, not above.

Rhubarb Upside-Down Cake

PREP TIME: 40 MINUTES | **START TO FINISH:** 1 HOUR 10 MINUTES
EQUIPMENT: 10-INCH OVENPROOF SKILLET | **EASE OF PREPARATION:** MODERATE

Rosy-pink rhubarb makes a particularly pretty upside-down cake. We balanced the fruit's tang with a crunchy nut-and-brown-sugar topping.

TOPPING

- 1 tablespoon dark corn syrup
- 2 teaspoons butter
- ½ cup packed light brown sugar
- 2 tablespoons chopped pecans *or* walnuts
- 1 pound rhubarb, trimmed and cut into 1-inch pieces (3 cups)

CAKE

- ¾ cup whole-wheat pastry flour
- ⅓ cup pecans *or* walnuts
- 1 teaspoon baking powder
- ¼ teaspoon salt
- 2 large egg whites
- ⅔ cup packed light brown sugar, divided
- 2 large eggs
- 2 teaspoons freshly grated orange zest, preferably organic
- 1 teaspoon vanilla extract

EQUIPMENT NOTE: This cake can also be baked in an 8-inch-square glass baking dish. Heat corn syrup and butter in a small pan and brush over the bottom of the baking dish. Bake the cake for 30-35 minutes.

1. **To prepare topping:** Coat a 10-inch ovenproof skillet (such as cast-iron) with cooking spray. Add corn syrup and butter; heat over low heat until butter has melted, swirling the pan to coat the bottom evenly. Remove from the heat; spread brown sugar evenly over the bottom of the pan. Sprinkle nuts over the sugar and arrange rhubarb, rounded sides down, in a circular pattern on top. Set aside.
2. **To prepare cake:** Preheat oven to 375°F. Combine flour, nuts, baking powder and salt in a food processor or blender; process until finely ground.
3. Beat 2 egg whites in a large bowl with an electric mixer on high speed until soft peaks form. Gradually add ⅓ cup brown sugar, beating until stiff and glossy. Set aside. (It is not necessary to wash beaters.) Beat whole eggs with the remaining ⅓ cup brown sugar in another large bowl on high speed until thickened and pale, 3 to 5 minutes. Blend in orange zest and vanilla.
4. Whisk one-fourth of the beaten whites into the whole-egg mixture. Gently fold in half the flour mixture. Fold in the remaining beaten whites, followed by the remaining flour mixture. Spread the batter evenly over the rhubarb.
5. Bake the cake until the top springs back when touched lightly, 25 to 30 minutes. Let cool in the pan on a wire rack for 5 minutes. Loosen the edges with a knife. Invert a serving platter over the cake. Using oven mitts, grasp platter and skillet together and carefully flip them over. Let the skillet sit for a few minutes to allow any caramel clinging to it to drip onto the cake. Remove the skillet. Let the cake cool for at least 20 minutes. Serve warm or at room temperature.

MAKES 10 SERVINGS.

PER SERVING: 195 CALORIES; 6 G FAT (1 G SAT, 3 G MONO); 44 MG CHOLESTEROL; 33 G CARBOHYDRATE; 4 G PROTEIN; 2 G FIBER; 126 MG SODIUM.

Chocolate Truffle Cheesecake

PREP TIME: 30 MINUTES | **START TO FINISH:** 5½ HOURS (INCLUDING COOLING & CHILLING TIMES)
EQUIPMENT: 9-INCH SPRINGFORM PAN | **TO MAKE AHEAD:** THE CHEESECAKE WILL KEEP, COVERED, IN THE REFRIGERATOR FOR UP TO 2 DAYS. | **EASE OF PREPARATION:** MODERATE

Sometimes we even stun ourselves. This ultra-rich and creamy chocolate cheesecake has less than 10 grams of fat per slice, making it one of our all-time best successes. We replaced the full-fat cream cheese in the original with pureed cottage cheese and reduced-fat cream cheese. To achieve a rich chocolate flavor, we used cocoa powder enhanced by a small amount of high-quality chocolate instead of 12 ounces chocolate chips.

CRUST

- 1 cup chocolate wafer crumbs (about 20 wafers; *see page 324*)
- 1 tablespoon brown sugar
- 1 tablespoon canola oil
- 1 teaspoon instant coffee granules dissolved in 2 teaspoons hot water

FILLING

- 24 ounces 1% cottage cheese (3 cups)
- 12 ounces reduced-fat cream cheese (1½ cups), cut into pieces
- 1 cup packed brown sugar
- ½ cup sugar
- ¾ cup unsweetened cocoa powder
- ¼ cup cornstarch
- 1 large egg
- 2 large egg whites
- 2 tablespoons instant coffee granules dissolved in 2 tablespoons hot water
- 2 teaspoons vanilla extract
- ¼ teaspoon salt
- 2 ounces bittersweet (*not* unsweetened) chocolate, melted
- 16 chocolate-covered coffee beans (optional)

RECIPE RX

Original Cheesecake:
420 calories
29 grams total fat

EW Chocolate Truffle Cheesecake:
228 calories
8 grams total fat

1. Preheat oven to 325°F. Put a kettle of water on to heat for the water bath. Spray a 9-inch springform pan with cooking spray. Wrap the outside bottom of the pan with a double thickness of foil.

2. To prepare crust: Blend crumbs, sugar, oil and coffee in a small bowl with a fork or your fingertips. Press into the bottom of the pan.

3. To prepare filling: Puree cottage cheese in a food processor until very smooth, stopping once or twice to scrape down the sides. Add cream cheese, brown and white sugars, cocoa and cornstarch. Process until smooth. Add egg, egg whites, coffee, vanilla, salt and chocolate and blend well. Pour into the crust-lined pan.

4. Place the cheesecake in a roasting pan and pour in enough boiling water to come ½ inch up the side of the springform pan.

5. Bake the cheesecake until the edges are set but the center still jiggles, about 50 minutes. Turn off the oven. Spray a knife with cooking spray and run it around the edge of the cake. Let stand in the oven, with the door ajar, for 1 hour. Transfer from the water bath to a wire rack; remove foil. Let cool to room temperature, about 2 hours. Refrigerate, uncovered, until chilled.

6. Before serving, garnish the cheesecake with chocolate-covered coffee beans, if using.

MAKES 16 SERVINGS.

PER SERVING: 228 CALORIES; 8 G FAT (4 G SAT, 2 G MONO); 27 MG CHOLESTEROL; 33 G CARBOHYDRATE; 10 G PROTEIN; 2 G FIBER; 310 MG SODIUM.

Praline-Crunch Cheesecake

PREP TIME: 25 MINUTES | **START TO FINISH:** 5½ HOURS (INCLUDING COOLING & CHILLING TIMES)
EQUIPMENT: 9-INCH SPRINGFORM PAN | **TO MAKE AHEAD:** THE CHEESECAKE WILL KEEP, COVERED, IN THE REFRIGERATOR FOR UP TO 2 DAYS. | **EASE OF PREPARATION:** EASY

This is the simplest to make of all our cheesecakes but not a bit less extravagant in taste and creamy texture. The indulgence quotient far surpasses its fat and calorie count.

CRUST

- 20 vanilla wafers (2½ ounces)
- 1 tablespoon canola oil

FILLING

- 2½ cups low-fat cottage cheese
- 12 ounces reduced-fat cream cheese (*not* nonfat), softened
- ⅔ cup granulated sugar
- ⅓ cup packed light brown sugar
- ¼ cup cornstarch
- 1 large egg
- 2 large egg whites *or* 4 teaspoons dried egg whites (*see Ingredient Note, page 394*), reconstituted according to package directions
- 1 cup nonfat plain yogurt
- 3 tablespoons bourbon (optional)
- 1½ teaspoons vanilla extract (2½ teaspoons if not using bourbon)
- Pecan Praline Topping (*page 391*)

1. To prepare crust: Preheat oven to 325°F. Put a kettle of water on to heat for the water bath. Coat a 9-inch springform pan with cooking spray. Wrap the outside bottom of the pan with a double thickness of foil.

2. Finely grind vanilla wafers in a food processor. Add oil and process until well combined. Press into the bottom of the pan.

3. To prepare filling: Puree cottage cheese in a food processor until smooth, stopping to scrape down sides of bowl. Add cream cheese, granulated and brown sugars and cornstarch. Process until smooth. Add egg, egg whites, yogurt, bourbon, if using, and vanilla; process until smooth. Pour over crust.

4. Place the cheesecake in a roasting pan and pour in enough boiling water to come ½ inch up the outside of the springform pan.

5. Bake the cheesecake until the edges are set but the center still jiggles, 50 to 60 minutes. Turn off the oven. Spray a knife with cooking spray and run it around the edge of the cake. Let stand in the oven, with the door ajar, for 1 hour. Transfer from the water bath to a wire rack; remove foil. Let cool to room temperature, about 2 hours. Refrigerate, uncovered, until chilled.

6. Just before serving, sprinkle the cheesecake with Pecan Praline Topping.

TEST KITCHEN TIP:
Baking cheesecake in a water bath prevents cracking.

MAKES 16 SERVINGS.

PER SERVING: 209 CALORIES; 7 G FAT (3 G SAT, 3 G MONO); 29 MG CHOLESTEROL; 28 G CARBOHYDRATE; 9 G PROTEIN; 0 G FIBER; 240 MG SODIUM.

Marbled Pumpkin Cheesecake

PREP TIME: 30 MINUTES | **START TO FINISH:** 5½ HOURS (INCLUDING COOLING & CHILLING TIMES)
EQUIPMENT: 9-INCH SPRINGFORM PAN | **TO MAKE AHEAD:** THE CHEESECAKE WILL KEEP, COVERED, IN THE REFRIGERATOR FOR UP TO 2 DAYS. | **EASE OF PREPARATION:** MODERATE

RECIPE RX

Original Cheesecake:
370 calories
27 grams total fat

EW Marbled Pumpkin Cheesecake:
221 calories
8 grams total fat

A spectacular, graceful ending for a holiday feast or any elegant fall or winter meal.

CRUST

- 1 cup gingersnap cookie crumbs (about 20 cookies; *see page 324*)
- 1 tablespoon canola oil

FILLING

- 20 ounces low-fat (1%) cottage cheese (2½ cups)
- 12 ounces reduced-fat cream cheese (1½ cups), softened
- 1 cup sugar
- 4 tablespoons cornstarch, divided
- 1 large egg
- 2 large egg whites *or* 4 teaspoons dried egg whites (*see Ingredient Note, page 394*), reconstituted according to package directions
- 8 ounces reduced-fat sour cream (1 cup)
- 1½ teaspoons vanilla extract
- ¼ teaspoon salt
- 1 teaspoon lemon juice
- ¾ cup unseasoned pumpkin puree
- 3 tablespoons dark brown sugar
- 2 tablespoons unsulfured molasses
- 1 teaspoon ground cinnamon
- 1 teaspoon ground ginger
- ½ teaspoon freshly grated nutmeg
- ⅛ teaspoon ground cloves

1. Preheat oven to 325°F. Put a kettle of water on to heat for the water bath. Coat a 9-inch springform pan with cooking spray. Wrap the outside bottom of the pan with a double thickness of foil.

2. To prepare crust: Combine crumbs and oil in a bowl. Press into the bottom of the pan.

3. To prepare filling & bake cheesecake: Puree cottage cheese in a food processor until very smooth, scraping down the sides of the workbowl once or twice. Add cream cheese, sugar and 3 tablespoons cornstarch; process until smooth. Add egg, egg whites, sour cream, vanilla and salt; blend well. Measure 3½ cups of the batter into a separate bowl; stir in lemon juice. To the remaining filling, add pumpkin, brown sugar, molasses, cinnamon, ginger, nutmeg, cloves and the remaining 1 tablespoon cornstarch; blend well.

4. Pour about 1 cup of the vanilla filling into the center of the crust. Then pour about 1 cup of the pumpkin filling into the center of the vanilla filling. Alternate the remaining fillings in the same manner; concentric circles will form as they spread. To create a marbled effect, gently swirl a knife or skewer through the fillings.

5. Place the cheesecake in a roasting pan and pour in enough boiling water to come ½ inch up the side of the springform pan.

6. Bake the cheesecake until the edges are set but the center still jiggles, about 50 minutes. Turn off the oven. Spray a knife with cooking spray and run it around the edge of the cake. Let stand in the oven, with the door ajar, for 1 hour. Transfer from the water bath to a wire rack; remove foil. Let cool to room temperature, about 2 hours. Refrigerate, uncovered, until chilled.

MAKES 16 SERVINGS.

PER SERVING: 221 CALORIES; 8 G FAT (4 G SAT, 3 G MONO); 32 MG CHOLESTEROL; 29 G CARBOHYDRATE; 9 G PROTEIN; 1 G FIBER; 320 MG SODIUM.

COOKIES
& BARS

Bev's Chocolate Chip Cookies

PREP TIME: 10 MINUTES | **START TO FINISH:** 35 MINUTES
TO MAKE AHEAD: THE COOKIES WILL KEEP IN AN AIRTIGHT CONTAINER FOR UP TO 3 DAYS OR IN THE FREEZER FOR UP TO 2 MONTHS. | **EASE OF PREPARATION:** EASY

EatingWell reader Beverley Rosenber of Santa Barbara, California, contributed this recipe to our *Kitchen to Kitchen* department. She updated a favorite treat by cutting back on sugar and incorporating whole grains. To increase protein, Ms. Rosenber replaces the rolled oats with 1 cup almond meal.

- **¾ cup rolled oats**
- **1 cup whole-wheat flour**
- **½ teaspoon baking soda**
- **½ teaspoon salt**
- **¼ cup butter, softened**
- **¼ cup canola oil**
- **⅓ cup granulated sugar**
- **⅓ cup brown sugar**
- **1 large egg**
- **1 teaspoon vanilla**
- **1 cup chocolate chips**

1. Preheat oven to 350°F. Coat 2 baking sheets with cooking spray.
2. Grind oats in a blender or food processor. Transfer to a bowl and stir in flour, baking soda and salt. Beat butter in a mixing bowl with an electric mixer until fluffy. Add oil, granulated sugar, brown sugar, egg and vanilla; beat until smooth and creamy. With the mixer running, add the dry ingredients, beating on low speed until just combined. Stir in chocolate chips.
3. Drop the dough by heaping teaspoonfuls, at least 1 inch apart, onto the prepared baking sheets. Bake cookies, 1 sheet at a time, until firm around the edges and golden on top, about 15 minutes. Cool cookies for 2 minutes on the baking sheets, then transfer cookies to wire racks to cool completely.

MAKES ABOUT 2½ DOZEN COOKIES.

PER COOKIE: 99 CALORIES; 5 G FAT (2 G SAT, 2 G MONO); 11 MG CHOLESTEROL; 12 G CARBOHYDRATE; 1 G PROTEIN; 1 G FIBER; 64 MG SODIUM.

Chocolate Crinkles

PREP TIME: 30 MINUTES | **START TO FINISH:** 3¼ HOURS (INCLUDING CHILLING TIME)
TO MAKE AHEAD: THE COOKIES WILL KEEP IN AN AIRTIGHT CONTAINER FOR UP TO 3 DAYS OR IN THE FREEZER FOR UP TO 2 MONTHS. SPRINKLE WITH FRESH CONFECTIONERS' SUGAR AFTER THAWING.
EASE OF PREPARATION: MODERATE

Very dark and chocolaty, these sugar-coated rounds are remarkably low in fat—a mere two grams per cookie. A tin of Chocolate Crinkles is the perfect gift for the chocoholic who is trying to cut back on fat.

- 2 cups all-purpose flour
- 2½ cups confectioners' sugar, divided
- ½ cup unsweetened "natural" cocoa powder (*see Ingredient Note, page 394*)
- 2½ teaspoons baking powder
- ¼ teaspoon salt
- 3½ ounces unsweetened chocolate, coarsely chopped
- 3½ tablespoons canola oil
- 1½ cups packed light brown sugar
- ⅓ cup light corn syrup
- 1½ tablespoons vanilla extract
- 4 large egg whites *or* 2 tablespoons plus 2 teaspoons dried egg whites (*see Ingredient Note, page 394*), reconstituted according to package directions

1. Sift flour, 1½ cups of the confectioners' sugar, cocoa, baking powder and salt together into a large bowl.

2. Combine chocolate and oil in a heavy medium saucepan; warm over very low heat, stirring frequently, until just melted and smooth; be very careful that the chocolate does not scorch. Remove from the heat and let cool slightly. Stir in brown sugar, corn syrup and vanilla until well blended. Using a whisk, beat egg whites into the chocolate mixture until no lumps of brown sugar remain. With a wooden spoon, gently stir the chocolate mixture into the dry ingredients just until smooth. Cover the dough and refrigerate until firm enough to shape into balls, at least 2½ hours and up to 8 hours.

3. Preheat oven to 350°F. Coat several baking sheets with cooking spray.

4. Put the remaining 1 cup confectioners' sugar in a shallow bowl. Dusting your hands with additional confectioners' sugar, roll portions of dough into 1-inch balls between your palms. Dredge each ball in confectioners' sugar until heavily coated. Place the balls on baking sheets, about 1½ inches apart.

5. Bake the cookies, 1 sheet at a time, until the tops are almost firm when tapped, 8 to 10 minutes. Cool for 2 minutes on the baking sheets, then transfer to wire racks to cool completely.

MAKES ABOUT 4 DOZEN COOKIES.

PER COOKIE: 96 CALORIES; 2 G FAT (1 G SAT, 1 G MONO); 0 MG CHOLESTEROL; 19 G CARBOHYDRATE; 1 G PROTEIN; 1 G FIBER; 40 MG SODIUM.

Lower Carbs

Apple-Oatmeal Cookies

PREP TIME: 30 MINUTES | **START TO FINISH:** 45 MINUTES
TO MAKE AHEAD: THE COOKIES WILL KEEP IN AN AIRTIGHT CONTAINER FOR UP TO 2 DAYS OR IN THE FREEZER FOR UP TO 2 MONTHS. | **EASE OF PREPARATION:** EASY

Cookies and kids go hand-in-hand, which can be worrisome nutritionally. But these wholesome cinnamon-sugar-crusted treats—without a gram of saturated fat—make snack time happy for everybody.

- **1 cup old-fashioned oats**
- **½ cup chopped pecans *or* walnuts**
- **1 cup whole-wheat pastry flour (*see Note*)**
- **½ teaspoon baking soda**
- **¼ teaspoon baking powder**
- **¼ teaspoon salt**
- **½ teaspoon ground cinnamon, divided**
- **⅛ teaspoon ground nutmeg**
- **2 large egg whites *or* 4 teaspoons dried egg whites (*see Ingredient Note, page 394*), reconstituted according to package directions**
- **½ cup coarsely grated peeled apple, such as McIntosh *or* Cortland (about 1 small apple)**
- **½ cup packed light brown sugar**
- **¼ cup apple butter**
- **4 tablespoons granulated sugar, divided**
- **2 tablespoons canola oil**
- **½ teaspoon vanilla extract**
- **½ cup diced dried apples**

1. Preheat oven to 375°F.
2. Spread oats and nuts on a baking sheet. Bake until fragrant and golden, 5 to 8 minutes; set aside. Coat 2 baking sheets with cooking spray.
3. Whisk together flour, baking soda, baking powder, salt, ¼ teaspoon cinnamon and nutmeg in a medium bowl.
4. Combine egg whites, grated apple, brown sugar, apple butter, 3 tablespoons granulated sugar, oil and vanilla in a large bowl; stir until blended. Add the dry ingredients and stir until just moistened. Stir in dried apples and reserved oats and nuts.
5. Drop the dough by level tablespoonfuls, about 2 inches apart, onto the prepared baking sheets.
6. Combine the remaining 1 tablespoon granulated sugar and ¼ teaspoon cinnamon in a small bowl. Coat the bottom of a glass with cooking spray. Dip the glass into the cinnamon sugar and flatten cookies with it, dipping the glass into the cinnamon sugar for each.
7. Bake the cookies, one sheet at a time, until lightly browned, 10 to 12 minutes. Cool cookies for 2 minutes on the baking sheets, then transfer to wire racks to cool completely.

INGREDIENT NOTE: Look for whole-wheat pastry flour in health-food stores; it gives baked goods a light texture while adding fiber. Store in an airtight container in the freezer.

MAKES ABOUT 3 DOZEN COOKIES.

PER COOKIE: 71 CALORIES; 2 G FAT (0 G SAT, 1 G MONO); 0 MG CHOLESTEROL; 12 G CARBOHYDRATE; 1 G PROTEIN; 1 G FIBER; 55 MG SODIUM.

Jam-Filled Almond Cookies

PREP TIME: 30 MINUTES | **START TO FINISH:** 2 HOURS

TO MAKE AHEAD: PREPARE THROUGH STEP 2. THE DOUGH WILL KEEP, WRAPPED IN PLASTIC, IN THE REFRIGERATOR FOR UP TO 2 DAYS. AFTER BAKING BUT BEFORE ASSEMBLY, THE COOKIES WILL KEEP IN AN AIRTIGHT CONTAINER FOR UP TO 5 DAYS. AFTER ASSEMBLY, FREEZE FOR LONGER STORAGE. | **EASE OF PREPARATION:** MODERATE

Old-fashioned jam-filled sandwich cookies made lighter but no less lovely than you remember.

- 1½ cups sliced almonds
- 1 cup sugar
- 1 cup all-purpose flour
- ⅔ cup cake flour
- 1 teaspoon ground cinnamon
- 2 tablespoons butter, cut into small pieces
- 4 ounces reduced-fat cream cheese, cut into small pieces
- ¼ cup fruit-based fat replacement, such as Sunsweet Lighter Bake (*see Note*) *or* applesauce
- ⅔ cup apricot *or* raspberry jam
- Confectioners' sugar for dusting

INGREDIENT NOTE: A blend of apples and prunes, Lighter Bake can be used as a substitute for fat in baked goods. It can be found in the cooking oil or baking sections of large supermarkets.

1. Pulse almonds, sugar, flours and cinnamon in a food processor until finely ground. Add butter and cream cheese; pulse until the mixture resembles coarse meal. Add fruit-based fat replacement and pulse until the mixture begins to form a ball, about 45 seconds.
2. Lightly sprinkle a work surface with flour; remove the dough from the processor and knead briefly. Divide the dough in half and shape each piece into a disk. Wrap in plastic and refrigerate until firm, at least 1 hour.
3. Position rack in center of oven; preheat to 350°F. Line 3 baking sheets with parchment paper or coat them with cooking spray.
4. Lightly dust the dough with flour. Roll out each piece between sheets of lightly floured wax paper to an even ⅛-inch thickness. Transfer the dough, still in wax paper, to a baking sheet. Chill in the freezer until firm, about 20 minutes.
5. Working with one piece of dough at a time, use a 2½-inch fluted round cutter to cut out cookies. For half of the cookies, use a 1-inch round or star cutter to cut out a hole in the center. Reroll and cut scraps. Place cookies 1 inch apart on prepared baking sheets.
6. Bake the cookies one sheet at a time until set and very lightly browned, 10 to 12 minutes. Set baking sheets on wire racks and cool completely.
7. To assemble cookies, spread a rounded teaspoon of jam in the center of each solid cookie. Heavily dust cookies with cutouts with confectioners' sugar. Place the dusted cookies, sugar-side up, on top of the cookies with jam.

MAKES ABOUT 2½ DOZEN COOKIES.

PER COOKIE: 113 CALORIES; 4 G FAT (1 G SAT, 2 G MONO); 4 MG CHOLESTEROL; 18 G CARBOHYDRATE; 2 G PROTEIN; 1 G FIBER; 15 MG SODIUM.

Lower Carbs

Lemon Cookies

PREP TIME: 25 MINUTES | **START TO FINISH:** 1 HOUR 10 MINUTES (INCLUDING CHILLING TIME)
TO MAKE AHEAD: PREPARE THROUGH STEP 2. THE DOUGH WILL KEEP, WELL WRAPPED, IN THE REFRIGERATOR FOR UP TO 3 DAYS. AFTER BAKING, THE COOKIES WILL KEEP IN AN AIRTIGHT CONTAINER FOR UP TO 3 DAYS; FREEZE FOR LONGER STORAGE. | **EASE OF PREPARATION:** EASY

These crisp lemon cookies are perfect with a cup of afternoon tea.

- **2½ cups whole-wheat pastry flour** (*see Ingredient Note, page 395*)
- **1 teaspoon baking powder**
- **1 teaspoon baking soda**
- **½ teaspoon salt**
- **1¼ cups sugar, divided**
- **½ cup applesauce**
- **¼ cup canola oil**
- **4 teaspoons freshly grated lemon zest, preferably organic**
- **2 tablespoons lemon juice**

1. Whisk flour, baking powder, baking soda and salt in a large bowl.
2. Whisk 1 cup sugar, applesauce, oil, lemon zest and lemon juice in another bowl until smooth. Make a well in the dry ingredients and add wet ingredients. Stir until blended. Cover with plastic wrap and refrigerate until chilled, 30 minutes to 1 hour.
3. Preheat oven to 350°F. Coat 2 baking sheets with cooking spray.
4. Place remaining ¼ cup sugar in a small bowl. Using floured hands, roll dough into 1½-inch balls. Roll balls in sugar to coat and place 2 inches apart on the prepared baking sheets.
5. Bake the cookies, one sheet at a time, until very lightly browned, 12 to 14 minutes. (The longer they bake, the crisper they become.) Cool on the baking sheet for 2 minutes, then transfer to wire racks to cool completely.

MAKES ABOUT 2 DOZEN COOKIES.

PER COOKIE: 97 CALORIES; 3 G FAT (0 G SAT, 1 G MONO); 0 MG CHOLESTEROL; 19 G CARBOHYDRATE; 1 G PROTEIN; 1 G FIBER; 101 MG SODIUM.

Zest Essentials

IF YOU ARE USING A SIGNIFICANT QUANTITY OF ZEST, it is advisable to purchase organic fruit in order to avoid pesticides. A microplane grater is a kitchen gadget that seems to be tailor-made for zesting citrus. To grate zest, first wash and dry the fruit. Set a microplane or old-fashioned box grater on a piece of wax paper to catch the zest; rub the fruit over the small holes with quick downward strokes. Avoid using too much pressure when grating because the white pith below the zest is bitter. Use a pastry brush to sweep off any zest left clinging to the grater. Whatever way you grate it, remember that it is easiest to grate the zest before you squeeze the fruit, so organize your recipe prep accordingly. Grated zest will keep in a plastic bag in the freezer for up to 3 months.

Date-Pecan Bars

PREP TIME: 10 MINUTES | **START TO FINISH:** 45 MINUTES
TO MAKE AHEAD: THE BARS WILL KEEP IN AN AIRTIGHT CONTAINER FOR UP TO 3 DAYS.
EASE OF PREPARATION: EASY

Here, graham cracker crumbs, dates and nuts are folded into beaten eggs and sugar to make a wonderfully chewy bar that's much lighter than traditional recipes.

- **2 teaspoons instant coffee powder**
- **2 teaspoons vanilla extract**
- **¾ cup sugar**
- **2 large eggs**
- **1 large egg white**
- **¼ teaspoon salt**
- **2 cups fine graham cracker crumbs (36 graham cracker squares) (*see Nutrition Note, page 324*)**
- **⅔ cup chopped dates**
- **½ cup chopped pecans (2 ounces)**
- **Confectioners' sugar for dusting (optional)**

1. Preheat oven to 300°F. Coat an 8-by-12-inch or 7-by-11-inch baking pan with cooking spray.

2. Stir together coffee powder and vanilla in a large bowl until the powder dissolves. Add sugar, eggs, egg white and salt and beat with an electric mixer on high speed until thick and pale, about 2 minutes. Fold in graham cracker crumbs, dates and pecans. Transfer the batter to the prepared baking pan; smooth the top.

3. Bake the bars until the top feels dry and a knife inserted in the center comes out clean, 30 to 35 minutes.

4. Let cool in the pan on a wire rack. Cut into bars. If desired, dust lightly with confectioners' sugar.

TEST KITCHEN TIP:
To turn graham crackers into graham crumbs, use a food processor or place the crackers in a large ziplock plastic bag and crush them with a rolling pin.

MAKES 15 BARS.

PER BAR: 147 CALORIES; 5 G FAT (1 G SAT, 2 G MONO); 28 MG CHOLESTEROL; 25 G CARBOHYDRATE; 2 G PROTEIN; 1 G FIBER; 120 MG SODIUM.

Hermits

PREP TIME: 15 MINUTES | **START TO FINISH:** 35 MINUTES
TO MAKE AHEAD: THE BARS WILL KEEP IN AN AIRTIGHT CONTAINER FOR UP TO 3 DAYS.
EASE OF PREPARATION: EASY

These moist, spicy favorites keep well (if they get the chance).

- **⅔ cup whole-wheat pastry flour** (*see Ingredient Note, page 395*)
- **⅔ cup all-purpose flour**
- **1 teaspoon baking powder**
- **½ teaspoon baking soda**
- **½ teaspoon salt**
- **2 teaspoons ground cinnamon**
- **1 teaspoon ground allspice**
- **½ teaspoon freshly grated nutmeg**
- **¼ teaspoon ground cloves**
- **½ cup dark molasses**
- **¾ cup packed light brown sugar**
- **¼ cup canola oil**
- **¼ cup apple butter**
- **2 large eggs**
- **1½ cups raisins**

1. Preheat oven to 350°F. Coat a 9-by-13-inch baking pan with cooking spray.

2. In a small bowl, whisk whole-wheat flour, all-purpose flour, baking powder, baking soda, salt, cinnamon, allspice, nutmeg and cloves. In a large bowl, beat together molasses, brown sugar, oil, apple butter and eggs with an electric mixer until smooth. Add the dry ingredients and beat on low speed just until combined. Stir in raisins. Transfer the batter to the prepared pan; smooth the top.

3. Bake the hermits for 20 to 25 minutes, or until the top feels "set" when lightly pressed in the center. Let cool in the pan on a wire rack. Cut into bars.

MAKES 20 BARS.

PER BAR: 151 CALORIES; 3 G FAT (0 G SAT, 2 G MONO); 21 MG CHOLESTEROL; 30 G CARBOHYDRATE; 2 G PROTEIN; 1 G FIBER; 102 MG SODIUM.

Lebkuchen Bars

PREP TIME: 20 MINUTES | **START TO FINISH:** 1 HOUR

TO MAKE AHEAD: THE BARS WILL KEEP IN AN AIRTIGHT CONTAINER AT ROOM TEMPERATURE FOR UP TO 1 MONTH.

EASE OF PREPARATION: MODERATE

These honey-and-spice bars, based on the traditional German Christmas cookies, get even better as they age.

BARS

- 1 cup all-purpose flour
- ¾ cup whole-wheat pastry flour
- ⅔ cup sliced almonds
- ½ teaspoon baking powder
- ½ teaspoon baking soda
- ⅛ teaspoon salt
- 1 teaspoon ground cinnamon
- ½ teaspoon ground cardamom
- ½ teaspoon ground ginger
- ¼ teaspoon ground nutmeg
- Pinch of ground cloves
- 2 teaspoons freshly grated lemon zest, preferably organic
- ¼ teaspoon aniseed, crushed
- ¼ cup granulated sugar
- ¼ cup packed light brown sugar
- 1 tablespoon butter
- ½ cup honey
- 1 large egg white
- ⅓ cup finely chopped candied orange *or* lemon peel (optional)

GLAZE

- ½ cup confectioners' sugar
- 1 tablespoon lemon juice

1. **To prepare bars:** Position rack in center of oven; preheat to 350°F. Coat an 8-by-11½-inch baking pan with cooking spray.
2. Pulse all-purpose flour, whole-wheat flour, almonds, baking powder, baking soda, salt, cinnamon, cardamom, ginger, nutmeg and cloves in a food processor until ground into a fine powder. Stir in lemon zest and aniseed. Set aside.
3. Combine granulated sugar, brown sugar, butter and honey in a heavy 2-quart saucepan; heat over medium heat, stirring often, until butter is melted and sugar has dissolved. Transfer to a large mixing bowl.
4. Add dry ingredients in 4 additions to the honey mixture, beating with an electric mixer on low speed and scraping down the sides of the bowl after each addition. Add egg white and candied peel (if using); blend on low speed just until mixed. Transfer to prepared pan. With damp fingertips, press dough evenly into pan.
5. Bake lebkuchen until puffed and light golden, about 20 minutes. Cool in the pan on a wire rack for 10 minutes.
6. **To prepare glaze:** Whisk confectioners' sugar and lemon juice in a small bowl until smooth. While lebkuchen is still warm, spread glaze on top. Cool completely. Cut into bars.

MAKES 2 DOZEN BARS.

PER BAR: 99 CALORIES; 2 G FAT (0 G SAT, 1 G MONO); 1 MG CHOLESTEROL; 19 G CARBOHYDRATE; 2 G PROTEIN; 1 G FIBER; 41 MG SODIUM.

Swirled Cheesecake Brownies

PREP TIME: 25 MINUTES | **START TO FINISH:** 2 HOURS (INCLUDING COOLING TIME)
TO MAKE AHEAD: THE BROWNIES WILL KEEP, COVERED, IN THE REFRIGERATOR FOR UP TO 2 DAYS. (ALTERNATIVELY, BAKE BROWNIES IN AN 8½-BY-12½-INCH FOIL PAN, WRAP WELL AND STORE IN THE FREEZER FOR UP TO 3 MONTHS.) BRING TO ROOM TEMPERATURE AND CUT INTO BARS SHORTLY BEFORE SERVING.
EASE OF PREPARATION: MODERATE

Made with whole-wheat flour, these decadent-tasting brownies have a beautiful marbled cheesecake topping. Cutting them into bite-size pieces helps to keep the calorie count in check.

CHEESECAKE TOPPING

- 4 ounces reduced-fat cream cheese (Neufchâtel)
- ¼ cup sugar
- 1 large egg
- 1 tablespoon all-purpose flour
- 1 tablespoon nonfat plain yogurt
- ½ teaspoon vanilla extract

BROWNIE

- ⅔ cup whole-wheat pastry flour
- ½ cup unsweetened cocoa powder
- ¼ teaspoon salt
- 1 large egg
- 2 large egg whites *or* 4 teaspoons dried egg whites (*see Ingredient Note, page 394*), reconstituted according to package directions
- 1¼ cups packed light brown sugar
- ¼ cup canola oil
- ¼ cup strong brewed (*or* prepared instant) coffee *or* black tea
- 2 teaspoons vanilla extract

1. Preheat oven to 350°F. Coat a 7-by-11-inch brownie pan or baking pan with cooking spray.
2. **To prepare topping:** Place cream cheese in a small mixing bowl and beat with an electric mixer until smooth and creamy. Add sugar and beat until smooth. Add egg, flour, yogurt and vanilla; beat until well blended.
3. **To prepare brownies:** Whisk whole-wheat flour, cocoa and salt in a bowl. Place egg, egg whites and brown sugar in a large bowl and beat with the electric mixer on medium speed until smooth. Add oil, coffee (or tea) and vanilla; beat until well blended. Add the dry ingredients and beat on low speed just until well blended, stopping once to scrape down the sides.
4. Scrape about half of the brownie batter into the prepared pan. Slowly pour the topping evenly on top. Drop the remaining brownie batter in large dollops over the topping. Draw the tip of a sharp knife or skewer through the two batters to create a swirled effect.
5. Bake the brownies until the top is just firm to the touch, about 20 minutes. Let cool completely in the pan on a wire rack. Coat a knife with cooking spray and cut into 24 bars.

MAKES 24 BARS.

PER BAR: 105 CALORIES; 4 G FAT (1 G SAT, 2 G MONO); 21 MG CHOLESTEROL; 16 G CARBOHYDRATE; 2 G PROTEIN; 1 G FIBER; 54 MG SODIUM.

FROZEN DESSERTS

Peach-Orange Frozen Yogurt

PREP TIME: 25 MINUTES | **START TO FINISH:** 3½ HOURS (INCLUDING CHILLING TIME)
EQUIPMENT: ICE CREAM MAKER | **TO MAKE AHEAD:** THE FROZEN YOGURT WILL KEEP, IN AN AIRTIGHT CONTAINER, IN THE FREEZER FOR UP TO 1 WEEK. | **EASE OF PREPARATION:** EASY

Peaches and orange juice team up nicely in this cool summer dessert. Leave the peach skins on during poaching: they add flavor, a creamy consistency and color to the yogurt.

- **⅔ cup sugar**
- **5-6 ripe peaches (about 1⅓ pounds), skins on, halved and pitted**
- **½ cup orange juice**
- **2 6-ounce containers custard-style vanilla yogurt (*see Note*)**
- **1-2 tablespoons mild honey**

1. Combine sugar, peach halves and orange juice in 3-quart nonreactive saucepan; bring to a boil over medium-high heat, stirring. Reduce heat to medium-low and cook, uncovered, stirring occasionally, until the skins loosen and the peaches are almost tender when pierced with a fork, 8 to 14 minutes. When they are cool enough to handle, slip off and discard the skins.
2. Cover and refrigerate peaches and poaching liquid until thoroughly chilled, at least 2½ hours. (To speed the process, freeze for 1½ to 2 hours.)
3. Stir yogurt and 1 tablespoon honey into the peach mixture. Transfer the mixture to a food processor or blender and process until completely smooth, 2 to 3 minutes. Taste and add more honey, if desired. Transfer the mixture to an ice cream maker. Freeze according to manufacturer's directions.
4. Serve immediately or transfer to a storage container and let harden in the freezer for 1 to 1½ hours. Serve in chilled dishes.

INGREDIENT NOTE:
Custard-style yogurt contains stabilizers (gelatin, gum), which contribute to a creamy texture when frozen.

MAKES 8 SERVINGS, ½ CUP EACH (1 QUART).

PER SERVING: 214 CALORIES; 1 G FAT (0 G SAT, 0 G MONO); 4 MG CHOLESTEROL; 51 G CARBOHYDRATE; 3 G PROTEIN; 4 G FIBER; 28 MG SODIUM.

NUTRITION BONUS: 21 MG VITAMIN C (35% DV), 515 MG POTASSIUM (26% DV), 25% DV VITAMIN A, 16% DV FIBER.

Ricotta-Pistachio Frozen Yogurt

PREP TIME: 10 MINUTES | **START TO FINISH:** 55 MINUTES
EQUIPMENT: ICE CREAM MAKER | **TO MAKE AHEAD:** THE FROZEN YOGURT WILL KEEP, IN AN AIRTIGHT CONTAINER, IN THE FREEZER FOR UP TO 1 WEEK. | **EASE OF PREPARATION:** EASY

If you love the addictively delicious filling of Italian cannoli, this frozen yogurt is for you. Gild the lily by serving it with dark chocolate sauce, such as Hot Fudge Sauce (*page 393*).

- **2 tablespoons coarsely chopped pistachios**
- **1½ cups part-skim ricotta cheese**
- **1½ cups nonfat plain yogurt**
- **1 14-ounce can nonfat sweetened condensed milk (*not* evaporated milk)**
- **2 teaspoons vanilla extract**
- **¼ teaspoon almond extract**
- **¼ teaspoon ground nutmeg**

1. Toast pistachios in a small dry skillet over low heat, stirring constantly, until fragrant, about 5 minutes. Transfer to a plate to cool.

2. Process ricotta in a food processor until very smooth and creamy, 2 to 3 minutes. Add yogurt, sweetened condensed milk, vanilla and almond extracts and nutmeg. Process until smooth.

3. Pour ricotta mixture into an ice cream maker and freeze according to manufacturer's directions. Stir in pistachios.

4. Serve immediately or transfer to a storage container and let harden in the freezer for 1 to 1½ hours. Serve in chilled dishes.

MAKES 10 SERVINGS, ½ CUP EACH (1¼ QUARTS).

PER SERVING: 195 CALORIES; 4 G FAT (2 G SAT, 1 G MONO); 15 MG CHOLESTEROL; 29 G CARBOHYDRATE; 10 G PROTEIN; 0 G FIBER; 117 MG SODIUM.

NUTRITION BONUS: 288 MG CALCIUM (30% DV), 305 MG POTASSIUM (15% DV).

Sundae Bar

CHOCOLATE-HAZELNUT BANANA SPLITS

START TO FINISH: 10 MINUTES

- **2 tablespoons chopped hazelnuts**
- **4 bananas**
- **1 pint vanilla nonfat frozen yogurt *or* low-fat ice cream, slightly softened (*see box, page 384*)**
- **½ cup Chocolate-Hazelnut Sauce (*page 393*)**

Toast hazelnuts in a small dry skillet over medium-low heat, stirring, until lightly colored and fragrant, 3 to 4 minutes. Peel bananas and cut in half lengthwise. Arrange 2 banana halves on each dessert plate. Place a scoop of frozen yogurt (or ice cream) in the center of each banana split and top with Chocolate-Hazelnut Sauce. Garnish with hazelnuts and serve.

MAKES 4 SERVINGS.

PER SERVING: 317 CALORIES; 5 G FAT (1 G SAT, 3 G MONO); 0 MG CHOLESTEROL; 73 G CARBOHYDRATE; 7 G PROTEIN; 5 G FIBER; 97 MG SODIUM.

NUTRITION BONUS: 487 MG POTASSIUM (24% DV), 184 MG CALCIUM (20% DV), 18% DV FIBER, 10 MG VITAMIN C (15% DV).

PINEAPPLE-CARAMEL SUNDAES

START TO FINISH: 25 MINUTES

- **1 pineapple, peeled and cored**
- **1 tablespoon sugar**
- **¼ cup unsweetened flaked coconut**
- **1 pint vanilla nonfat frozen yogurt *or* low-fat ice cream, slightly softened (*see box, page 384*)**
- **⅔ cup Caramel-Orange Sauce (*page 392*)**

Preheat broiler. Line a baking sheet with foil and coat the foil with cooking spray. Slice pineapple, place on the baking sheet and sprinkle with sugar. Broil until light golden, 5 to 10 minutes. Meanwhile, toast coconut in a small dry skillet over medium-low heat, stirring, until lightly colored and fragrant, 3 to 4 minutes. Arrange several pineapple slices on each dessert plate. Top with a scoop of frozen yogurt (or ice cream). Drizzle with Caramel-Orange Sauce. Garnish with coconut and serve.

MAKES 4 SERVINGS.

PER SERVING: 326 CALORIES; 4 G FAT (1 G SAT, 0 G MONO); 6 MG CHOLESTEROL; 68 G CARBOHYDRATE; 6 G PROTEIN; 2 G FIBER; 73 MG SODIUM.

NUTRITION BONUS: 54 MG VITAMIN C (90% DV), 402 MG POTASSIUM (20% DV), 168 MG CALCIUM (15% DV).

MIXED BERRY SUNDAES

START TO FINISH: 10 MINUTES

- **3 cups mixed fresh berries, such as raspberries, blueberries, blackberries, sliced strawberries**
- **2 tablespoons crème de cassis *or* black currant juice**
- **1 tablespoon lemon juice**
- **1 tablespoon sugar**
- **1 pint nonfat raspberry sorbet *or* lemon sorbet, slightly softened (*see box, page 384*)**

Crush ¼ cup berries in a bowl with a fork. Add crème de cassis (or juice), lemon juice and sugar, stirring until sugar is dissolved. Add the remaining 2¾ cups berries; stir gently to coat. Place a scoop of sorbet in each dish and top with the berry mixture.

MAKES 4 SERVINGS.

PER SERVING: 191 CALORIES; 0 G FAT (0 G SAT, 0 G MONO); 0 MG CHOLESTEROL; 48 G CARBOHYDRATE; 1 G PROTEIN; 6 G FIBER; 3 MG SODIUM.

NUTRITION BONUS: 26 MG VITAMIN C (45% DV), 25% DV FIBER.

Instant Strawberry Frozen Yogurt

PREP TIME: 10 MINUTES | **START TO FINISH:** 10 MINUTES

EQUIPMENT: FOOD PROCESSOR | **TO MAKE AHEAD:** THE FROZEN YOGURT WILL KEEP, IN AN AIRTIGHT CONTAINER, IN THE FREEZER FOR UP TO 1 WEEK. | **EASE OF PREPARATION:** EASY

Even if you don't have an ice cream maker, you can still enjoy homemade frozen yogurt that is better than store-bought. The trick is to start with unsweetened frozen fruit and whirl it in a food processor with yogurt or buttermilk.

- **1 16-ounce package IQF (individually quick-frozen) unsweetened strawberries (about 3½ cups)**
- **½ cup sugar, preferably instant-dissolving**
- **½ cup nonfat plain yogurt *or* buttermilk**
- **1 tablespoon lemon juice**

Combine frozen strawberries and sugar in a food processor. Pulse until coarsely chopped. Combine yogurt (or buttermilk) and lemon juice; with the machine running, gradually pour the mixture through the feed tube. Process until smooth and creamy, scraping down the sides of the workbowl once or twice. (The frozen yogurt should be firm enough to be served directly from the food processor, but if it is a little soft, let it harden in the freezer for about 30 minutes.)

MAKES ABOUT 3 CUPS, FOR 4 SERVINGS.

PER SERVING: 150 CALORIES; 0 G FAT (0 G SAT, 0 G MONO); 1 MG CHOLESTEROL; 38 G CARBOHYDRATE; 2 G PROTEIN; 2 G FIBER; 19 MG SODIUM.

NUTRITION BONUS: 50 MG VITAMIN C (80% DV).

Frozen Essentials

ICE CREAM, frozen the old-fashioned way by churning it in a canister surrounded by ice and salt, used to be a treat reserved for special occasions. But modern ice cream makers with a canister you simply chill in the freezer make it a breeze for home cooks to churn up their own frozen desserts. And by making your own, you can limit the butterfat and focus on fresh fruit flavors. Here are a few pointers for successful frozen-dessert making.

- Allow enough time to thoroughly chill the ice cream, sorbet or frozen yogurt base before churn-freezing. The faster the freezing process, the smoother the final texture.
- To improve the texture of lower-fat frozen ice creams, our recipes often add gelatin or milk solids in the form of nonfat sweetened condensed milk.
- If possible, once the frozen dessert is ready let it harden in the freezer for about 1 hour before scooping. Prechill the storage container and serving dishes; low-fat ice creams and frozen yogurts melt faster than full-fat ones.
- Homemade ice creams, frozen yogurts and sorbets become very hard when stored in the freezer for prolonged periods. To temper them, transfer to the refrigerator for 20 to 30 minutes before scooping. Alternatively, microwave on Defrost or medium-low for 30 to 60 seconds.

Watermelon Slush

PREP TIME: 20 MINUTES | **START TO FINISH:** 3½ HOURS (INCLUDING CHILLING & FREEZING TIMES)
TO MAKE AHEAD: THE SLUSH WILL KEEP, IN AN AIRTIGHT CONTAINER, IN THE FREEZER FOR UP TO 2 DAYS.
EASE OF PREPARATION: EASY

This incredibly refreshing icy dessert is made without using an ice cream maker.

- ½ cup sugar
- ¾ cup water
- 6 cups watermelon chunks (4-pound watermelon), seeded
- 2 tablespoons fresh lime juice

1. Combine sugar and water in a medium saucepan. Bring to a boil over medium-high heat, stirring to dissolve the sugar. Reduce heat to low and simmer for 5 minutes. Remove from heat and let cool to room temperature, about 45 minutes. Cover and refrigerate until chilled, about 1 hour.
2. Place watermelon and lime juice in a food processor; process until smooth. Set a sieve over a large bowl and press the puree through to remove tiny seeds. Whisk in the sugar syrup.
3. Pour the watermelon mixture into a shallow metal pan and freeze until ice crystals form around the edges, about 30 minutes. Stir the ice crystals into the center of the pan and return to the freezer; repeat every 20 minutes until all the liquid is frozen.
4. Serve immediately or transfer to a storage container and let harden in the freezer for 1 to 1½ hours. Serve in chilled dishes.

MAKES 12 SERVINGS, ½ CUP EACH.

PER SERVING: 56 CALORIES; 0 G FAT (0 G SAT, 0 G MONO); 0 MG CHOLESTEROL; 14 G CARBOHYDRATE; 0 G PROTEIN; 0 G FIBER; 1 MG SODIUM.

NUTRITION BONUS: 11 MG VITAMIN C (20% DV), 15% DV VITAMIN A.

Pineapple-Coconut Sorbet

PREP TIME: 20 MINUTES | **START TO FINISH:** 2 HOURS (INCLUDING CHILLING TIME)
EQUIPMENT: ICE CREAM MAKER OR FOOD PROCESSOR | **TO MAKE AHEAD:** THE SORBET WILL KEEP, IN AN AIRTIGHT CONTAINER, IN THE FREEZER FOR UP TO 1 WEEK. | **EASE OF PREPARATION:** EASY

A touch of coconut milk—infused with fresh ginger for a subtle kick—complements sweet pineapple and creates a luxurious consistency in this sorbet.

- **½ cup "lite" coconut milk (*see Ingredient Note, page 394*)**
- **½ cup sugar**
- **3 ¼-inch-thick slices peeled fresh ginger, crushed**
- **1 pineapple (about 3½ pounds), peeled, cored and cut into chunks**
- **2 teaspoons lime juice**

1. Combine coconut milk, sugar and ginger in a small saucepan. Bring to a simmer over medium heat. Simmer for 1½ minutes. Remove from heat and let stand for 20 minutes. Strain into a large bowl.

2. Place pineapple in a food processor and process until smooth. Add pineapple puree to coconut milk mixture and whisk until blended. Whisk in lime juice. Cover and refrigerate until chilled, about 1 hour.

3. Pour the pineapple mixture into an ice cream maker and freeze according to manufacturer's directions. (*Alternatively, freeze mixture in a shallow metal pan until solid, about 6 hours. Break into chunks and process in a food processor until smooth.*)

4. Serve immediately or transfer to a storage container and let harden in the freezer for 1 to 1½ hours. Serve in chilled dishes.

MAKES 8 SERVINGS, ½ CUP EACH (1 QUART).

PER SERVING: 157 CALORIES; 1 G FAT (1 G SAT, 0 G MONO); 0 MG CHOLESTEROL; 38 G CARBOHYDRATE; 1 G PROTEIN; 3 G FIBER; 6 MG SODIUM.

NUTRITION BONUS: 72 MG VITAMIN C (120% DV).

Mango-Lime Sorbet

PREP TIME: 25 MINUTES | **START TO FINISH:** 2 HOURS (INCLUDING CHILLING TIME)
EQUIPMENT: ICE CREAM MAKER OR FOOD PROCESSOR | **TO MAKE AHEAD:** THE SORBET WILL KEEP, IN AN AIRTIGHT CONTAINER, IN THE FREEZER FOR UP TO 1 WEEK. | **EASE OF PREPARATION:** EASY

A stunning golden-orange color, this lively sorbet is even more dramatic served with Raspberry Sauce (*page 391*).

- **1 cup sugar**
- **1½ cups water**
- **3 pounds ripe mangoes (3 large or 4 medium), peeled and cut into chunks (*see Cooking Tip, page 397*)**
- **¼ cup lime juice**

1. Combine sugar and water in a saucepan. Stir over medium heat until the liquid comes to a full boil and the sugar has dissolved. Remove from the heat and let cool to room temperature. Cover with plastic wrap and refrigerate until chilled, about 1 hour.
2. Puree mango in a food processor or blender. Work the puree through a fine sieve. (This will remove any fibers, the amount of which can vary.) Measure out 2 cups of puree (freeze any extra for another use) and stir into the syrup, along with lime juice.
3. Freeze the mixture in an ice cream maker according to the manufacturer's directions. (*Alternatively, freeze the mixture in a shallow metal cake pan or ice cube trays until solid, about 6 hours. Break into chunks and process in a food processor until smooth.*)
4. Serve immediately or transfer to a storage container and let harden in the freezer for 1 to 1½ hours. Serve in chilled dishes.

MAKES 8 SERVINGS, ½ CUP EACH (1 QUART).

PER SERVING: 209 CALORIES; 1 G FAT (0 G SAT, 0 G MONO); 0 MG CHOLESTEROL; 55 G CARBOHYDRATE; 1 G PROTEIN; 3 G FIBER; 4 MG SODIUM.

NUTRITION BONUS: 49 MG VITAMIN C (80% DV), 25% DV VITAMIN A.

Espresso Semifreddo

PREP TIME: 45 MINUTES | **START TO FINISH:** 7 HOURS (INCLUDING FREEZING TIME)
EQUIPMENT: INSTANT-READ THERMOMETER | **TO MAKE AHEAD:** PREPARE THROUGH STEP 6. THE SEMIFREDDO WILL KEEP, WELL WRAPPED, IN THE FREEZER FOR UP TO 1 WEEK. | **EASE OF PREPARATION:** CHALLENGING

Traditional versions of this elegant dessert—which translates as "half cold"—rely on lots of whipped cream for the light texture; here a fluffy cooked meringue does the job equally well.

- 2 large eggs
- ¼ cup plus ⅓ cup sugar
- ⅓ cup strong brewed espresso (*or* dark-roast coffee) *or* 3 tablespoons instant espresso granules dissolved in ⅓ cup boiling water, cooled
- 2 tablespoons hazelnut liqueur, such as Frangelico
- 1 teaspoon vanilla extract
- 2 tablespoons dried egg whites (*see Ingredient Note, page 394*) reconstituted according to package directions (equivalent to 3 large egg whites)
- 3 tablespoons cold water
- ½ teaspoon cream of tartar
- ⅓ cup whipping cream
- 2 tablespoons chopped hazelnuts

TEST KITCHEN TIP:
To successfully unmold the semifreddo, it is important to use metal molds. If you have only glass or ceramic ramekins, simply serve directly from them.

1. Fill a large saucepan or Dutch oven with 1 inch water and bring to a simmer. Place a small mixing bowl in the freezer to chill.
2. Whisk whole eggs and ¼ cup sugar in a heavy, medium, nonreactive saucepan until smooth. Whisk in espresso (or coffee). Cook over low heat, whisking constantly, until slightly thickened and an instant-read thermometer registers 160°F, about 10 minutes. (Do not let mixture come to a simmer.) Remove from heat and whisk in liqueur and vanilla. Transfer to a large bowl and let cool to room temperature, about 20 minutes.
3. Combine reconstituted egg whites, cold water, cream of tartar and remaining ⅓ cup sugar in a large heatproof mixing bowl. Set bowl over (not in) the barely simmering water and beat with a hand-held electric mixer at low speed for 4 to 5 minutes. Increase mixer speed to high and continue beating for 3 minutes more. The meringue should hold firm peaks. Remove from the heat and continue beating until cool and fluffy, 3 to 4 minutes.
4. Whip cream in the chilled mixing bowl (no need to wash meringue from beaters) until soft peaks form.
5. Whisk one-fourth of the meringue into the cooled coffee mixture. Using the whisk, fold in remaining meringue. With a rubber spatula, fold in whipped cream.
6. Divide mixture among six ¾-cup metal molds or spoon into an 8-by-4-inch metal loaf pan. Cover with plastic wrap and freeze until firm, at least 6 hours.

RECIPE RX

Traditional Semifreddo:
430 calories
34 grams fat
19 grams saturated

EW Semifreddo:
185 calories
7 grams fat
3 grams saturated

7. Before serving, toast hazelnuts at 350°F until fragrant, about 5 minutes. (*Alternatively, microwave hazelnuts on high for 4 minutes, stirring twice.*) Let cool. Dip bottoms of molds or pan in hot water for a few seconds, then invert onto chilled dessert plates or a serving platter. Garnish with hazelnuts and serve.

MAKES 6 SERVINGS.

PER SERVING: 185 CALORIES; 7 G FAT (3 G SAT, 3 G MONO); 85 MG CHOLESTEROL; 24 G CARBOHYDRATE; 5 G PROTEIN; 0 G FIBER; 58 MG SODIUM.

Malt Shop Chocolate Ice Cream

PREP TIME: 25 MINUTES | **START TO FINISH:** 2 HOURS (INCLUDING CHILLING TIME)
EQUIPMENT: ICE CREAM MAKER | **TO MAKE AHEAD:** THE ICE CREAM WILL KEEP, IN AN AIRTIGHT CONTAINER, IN THE FREEZER FOR UP TO 1 WEEK. | **EASE OF PREPARATION:** EASY

A favorite flavor from soda-shop days turned into a low-fat ice cream.

- **1½ teaspoons unflavored gelatin**
- **1 tablespoon water**
- **2½ cups 1% milk, divided**
- **1 14-ounce can nonfat sweetened condensed milk (*not* evaporated milk)**
- **¼ cup unsweetened cocoa powder**
- **½ cup malted-milk powder**
- **¼ cup dark corn syrup**
- **1 ounce unsweetened chocolate, coarsely chopped**
- **1 teaspoon vanilla extract**

1. Place gelatin in a small bowl; sprinkle in water and let stand until softened, 1 minute or longer.
2. Combine ½ cup milk, sweetened condensed milk, cocoa, malted-milk powder and corn syrup in a heavy medium saucepan; whisk until smooth. Bring to a simmer over medium heat, whisking constantly. Remove from the heat and add chocolate and the softened gelatin; stir until the chocolate has melted. Transfer the mixture into a bowl. Gradually whisk in the remaining 2 cups milk and vanilla until smooth. Refrigerate until chilled, about 1 hour.
3. Pour into an ice cream maker and freeze according to the manufacturer's directions.
4. Serve immediately or transfer to a storage container and let harden in the freezer for 1 to 1½ hours. Serve in chilled dishes.

MAKES 8 SERVINGS, ½ CUP EACH (1 QUART).

PER SERVING: 318 CALORIES; 5 G FAT (3 G SAT, 1 G MONO); 14 MG CHOLESTEROL; 60 G CARBOHYDRATE; 11 G PROTEIN; 2 G FIBER; 214 MG SODIUM.

NUTRITION BONUS: 301 MG VITAMIN C (30% DV), 419 MG POTASSIUM (21% DV).

DESSERT TOPPINGS

Lower Carbs

Vanilla Cream

PREP TIME: 10 MINUTES | **START TO FINISH:** 1¼ HOURS (INCLUDING 1 HOUR TO DRAIN YOGURT)

TO MAKE AHEAD: THE CREAM WILL KEEP, COVERED, IN THE REFRIGERATOR FOR UP TO 2 DAYS.

EASE OF PREPARATION: EASY

This versatile creamy topping blends the nutritional virtues of yogurt with the luxury of a little whipped cream.

- 1 cup (8 ounces) low-fat *or* nonfat vanilla yogurt
- ¼ cup whipping cream
- 2½ teaspoons confectioners' sugar (optional)

1. Line a sieve or colander with cheesecloth and set over a bowl, leaving at least ½-inch clearance from the bottom. (*Alternatively, use a coffee filter lined with filter paper.*) Spoon in yogurt, cover and let drain in the refrigerator for 1 hour. Discard whey.

2. Whip cream in a small bowl until soft peaks form. Add sugar, if using, and continue whipping until firm peaks form. Fold in drained yogurt.

MAKES ABOUT 1 CUP.

PER TABLESPOON: 24 CALORIES; 1 G FAT (1 G SAT, 0 G MONO); 5 MG CHOLESTEROL; 2 G CARBOHYDRATE; 1 G PROTEIN; 0 G FIBER; 11 MG SODIUM.

Raspberry Sauce

Healthy Weight

Lower Carbs

PREP TIME: 10 MINUTES | **START TO FINISH:** 10 MINUTES | **TO MAKE AHEAD:** THE SAUCE WILL KEEP, COVERED, IN THE REFRIGERATOR FOR UP TO 4 DAYS OR IN THE FREEZER FOR UP TO 4 MONTHS. | **EASE OF PREPARATION:** EASY

Spoon this tart, vivid sauce over vanilla ice cream, yogurt, pancakes or virtually any fruit.

- 1 12-ounce package unsweetened frozen raspberries, thawed (3 cups)
- ¼ cup sugar *or* no-calorie sweetener
- 2 teaspoons lemon juice
- 1 teaspoon balsamic vinegar

Puree raspberries, sugar (or sweetener), lemon juice and balsamic vinegar in a food processor until smooth. Strain through a fine sieve into a bowl.

MAKES ABOUT 1½ CUPS.

PER TABLESPOON: 15 CALORIES; 0 G FAT (0 G SAT, 0 G MONO); 0 MG CHOLESTEROL; 4 G CARBOHYDRATE; 0 G PROTEIN; 0 G FIBER; 0 MG SODIUM.

Pecan Praline Topping

Lower Carbs

PREP TIME: 20 MINUTES | **START TO FINISH:** 45 MINUTES (INCLUDING COOLING TIME)
TO MAKE AHEAD: THE PRALINE WILL KEEP, TIGHTLY COVERED, AT ROOM TEMPERATURE FOR UP TO 3 DAYS.
EASE OF PREPARATION: EASY

A sprinkling of this nutty topping brings a vanilla cheesecake to life (*see Praline-Crunch Cheesecake, page 368*). It is also delicious on reduced-fat ice cream or frozen yogurt.

- ½ cup granulated sugar
- ⅓ cup water
- ¼ cup finely chopped pecans

1. Coat a baking sheet with cooking spray.
2. Combine sugar and water in a small heavy saucepan. Bring to a simmer over low heat, stirring occasionally to dissolve the sugar. Increase heat to medium-high and cook, *without stirring*, until syrup turns medium amber, 3 to 5 minutes. Immediately remove from heat and stir in pecans. Pour onto the prepared baking sheet, spreading in a thin layer. Let stand until praline is cool and brittle.
3. Slide a metal spatula under the praline to loosen it; crack into small pieces. Place in a food processor and pulse until coarsely crushed or ground.

MAKES 1 CUP.

PER TABLESPOON: 37 CALORIES; 1 G FAT (0 G SAT, 1 G MONO); 0 MG CHOLESTEROL; 7 G CARBOHYDRATE; 0 G PROTEIN; 0 G FIBER; 0 MG SODIUM.

Lower Carbs

Blackberry Sauce

PREP TIME: 10 MINUTES | **START TO FINISH:** 1 HOUR (INCLUDING COOLING TIME) | **TO MAKE AHEAD:** THE SAUCE WILL KEEP, COVERED, IN THE REFRIGERATOR FOR UP TO 4 DAYS. | **EASE OF PREPARATION:** EASY

The deep berry flavor of this sauce is a lovely complement to lemon desserts, panna cotta or angel food cake.

- 1 16-ounce package frozen blackberries (3½ cups)
- ¼ cup sugar *or* no-calorie sweetener
- ¼ cup water
- 1 tablespoon lemon juice

1. Combine blackberries, sugar (or sweetener) and water in a medium saucepan. Bring to a simmer over medium-high heat, stirring occasionally. Reduce heat to low and simmer for 5 minutes.
2. Press the berry mixture through a fine sieve (or food mill fitted with a fine grate) into a bowl. Discard seeds. Stir lemon juice into sauce. Cover and refrigerate until chilled, about 50 minutes.

MAKES ABOUT 1 CUP.

PER TABLESPOON: 33 CALORIES; 0 G FAT (0 G SAT, 0 G MONO); 0 MG CHOLESTEROL; 8 G CARBOHYDRATE; 0 G PROTEIN; 2 G FIBER; 0 MG SODIUM.

Caramel-Orange Sauce

PREP TIME: 20 MINUTES | **START TO FINISH:** 20 MINUTES
TO MAKE AHEAD: THE SAUCE WILL KEEP, COVERED, IN THE REFRIGERATOR FOR UP TO 1 WEEK. WARM IN THE MICROWAVE OR ON THE STOVETOP BEFORE SERVING. | **EASE OF PREPARATION:** EASY

Try this sophisticated sauce in our Pineapple-Caramel Sundaes (*page 383*) or over Roasted Pears (*page 341*) with vanilla ice cream.

- 1 cup sugar
- ⅓ cup water
- ¾ cup orange juice
- 2 teaspoons butter
- 1 tablespoon brandy

1. Combine sugar and water in a small heavy saucepan. Bring to a boil over medium-high heat, stirring occasionally to dissolve the sugar. Cook, *without stirring*, until the syrup turns deep amber, 5 to 12 minutes. Remove from the heat and carefully pour in orange juice. Stand back, as the caramel may sputter.
2. Return the saucepan to low heat and stir until all the caramel has dissolved. Remove from the heat and swirl in butter. Stir in brandy and let cool slightly before serving.

MAKES ABOUT 1⅓ CUPS.

PER TABLESPOON: 46 CALORIES; 0 G FAT (0 G SAT, 0 G MONO); 1 MG CHOLESTEROL; 10 G CARBOHYDRATE; 0 G PROTEIN; 0 G FIBER; 0 MG SODIUM.

Chocolate-Hazelnut Sauce

PREP TIME: 5 MINUTES | **START TO FINISH:** 5 MINUTES | **TO MAKE AHEAD:** THE SAUCE WILL KEEP, COVERED, IN THE REFRIGERATOR FOR UP TO 3 WEEKS. | **EASE OF PREPARATION:** EASY

This ultra-quick sauce can make any night a special occasion. We especially like it with strawberries, pears or coffee frozen yogurt.

- **⅔ cup fat-free chocolate syrup**
- **¼ cup chocolate-hazelnut spread, such as Nutella**

Stir ingredients together in a small saucepan over low heat until smooth and warm. Serve warm or at room temperature.

MAKES ABOUT 1 CUP.

PER TABLESPOON: 58 CALORIES; 1 G FAT (0 G SAT, 0 G MONO); 0 MG CHOLESTEROL; 11 G CARBOHYDRATE; 1 G PROTEIN; 1 G FIBER; 15 MG SODIUM.

Hot Fudge Sauce

Lower Carbs

PREP TIME: 20 MINUTES | **START TO FINISH:** 25 MINUTES | **TO MAKE AHEAD:** THE SAUCE WILL KEEP, COVERED, IN THE REFRIGERATOR FOR UP TO 3 WEEKS. WARM IN A DOUBLE BOILER OVER GENTLY SIMMERING WATER OR IN A MICROWAVE ON MEDIUM FOR 2 TO 3 MINUTES. | **EASE OF PREPARATION:** EASY

Hot-fudge fantasy is a reality with this scrumptious low-fat sauce. Serve over ice cream or frozen yogurt or drizzle over fresh fruit.

- **1 12-ounce can evaporated skim milk**
- **1¼ cups sugar**
- **⅓ cup light corn syrup**
- **3 ounces bittersweet (*not* unsweetened) chocolate, coarsely chopped**
- **1 ounce unsweetened chocolate, coarsely chopped**
- **½ cup boiling water**
- **7 tablespoons unsweetened cocoa powder**
- **2½ teaspoons vanilla extract**

1. Stir evaporated skim milk, sugar and corn syrup in a large heavy saucepan until blended. Bring to a boil over high heat, stirring constantly. Cook, stirring, until mixture thickens slightly, about 5 minutes. Reduce heat to low and simmer gently, stirring, until light caramel in color, 6 to 8 minutes more. (Be careful not to scorch the sauce.) Immediately remove from the heat. Add bittersweet and unsweetened chocolate all at once, stirring until melted and smooth.
2. Whisk boiling water and cocoa in a small deep bowl until smooth. Strain through a fine sieve into the sauce. Stir in vanilla. Let cool until warm. If the sauce is too stiff to pour, stir in warm water just until fluid but still fairly thick.

MAKES ABOUT 2 CUPS.

PER TABLESPOON: 69 CALORIES; 1 G FAT (1 G SAT, 0 G MONO); 0 MG CHOLESTEROL; 14 G CARBOHYDRATE; 1 G PROTEIN; 1 G FIBER; 18 MG SODIUM.

INGREDIENT NOTES & COOKING TIPS

Ingredient Notes

ARUGULA Also called "rocket," this aromatic green lends a peppery mustard flavor to salads. It is sold in small bunches in supermarkets or farmers' markets. Watercress is a good substitute.

BALSAMIC VINEGAR Made in Northern Italy from Trebbiano grape juice and aged like wine, balsamic vinegar is dark, sweet and complex. The finest balsamics are a handmade product, and are aged anywhere from 12 to 100 years in a series of smaller and smaller casks made of different woods. This traditional balsamic is extremely expensive. Most of the balsamics sold in the United States are commercially produced; they are less concentrated, less complex and less expensive than the traditionals, but offer a similar balance of sweet and tart.

BARLEY Quick-cooking barley is rolled thinner than traditional pearl barley, so the cooking time is about 20 to 30 minutes shorter. It can be found in supermarkets and health-food stores.

BLUEBERRIES Small wild blueberries, which tend to be more tart than cultivated berries, are wonderful for baking. Forage them yourself or look for them frozen, in supermarkets nationwide.

BRAN Unprocessed wheat bran is the outer layer of the wheat kernel, removed during milling. Also known as miller's bran, it can be found in the baking section. Do not substitute bran cereal.

BULGUR Fiber-rich bulgur is made from whole-wheat kernels that are precooked, dried and cracked. You can find it in natural-foods stores and large markets.

BUTTERMILK Buttermilk powder, such as Saco Buttermilk Blend, is a useful substitute for fresh buttermilk. Look in the baking section or with the powdered milk in most supermarkets. Or make "sour milk": mix 1 tablespoon lemon juice or vinegar to 1 cup milk.

CAPERS The pickled flower buds of a cliff-clinging bush, capers add their piquancy to many Mediterranean dishes. Those labeled "petite nonpareil" come from southern France and are the smallest in size; the larger buds, popular throughout Italy and Spain, may need to be chopped before use.

CHILE-GARLIC SAUCE A thick puree used as a base in many Chinese sauces. Look for this spicy ingredient in the international-foods section of the grocery store or at Asian markets.

COCOA POWDER When most of the cocoa butter is pressed out of the ground cocoa nibs, a dry paste is left. This paste is sifted many times to become cocoa powder. Cocoa powder with nothing added to it is called "natural." (Hershey's and Ghirardelli are two popular brands.) When cocoa powder is treated with alkali it is called "Dutch-processed." This treatment makes the cocoa powder darker in color and gives it a more mellow flavor. When baking with Dutch-processed cocoa powder it's important not to add another alkaline element, such as baking soda, a combination that will produce a murky, soapy taste. Dutch-process cocoa (Van Houten is a popular brand) is available in some supermarkets and in specialty-food stores.

COCONUT MILK We use unsweetened reduced-fat coconut milk, usually identified on the label as "lite."

COUSCOUS Resembling a grain, these granules of semolina meal are actually a type of pasta. A staple throughout North Africa, it is traditionally steamed over broth but is now available in a precooked form that only requires 5 minutes of soaking in hot broth or water. Whole-wheat couscous can be found in natural-foods stores.

CREMINI Cremini mushrooms (sometimes called baby bella) are a strain of button mushrooms prized for their dark hue, firm texture and rich flavor.

CUMIN SEEDS These thin seeds have a deep "earthy" flavor, robust and slightly citrusy. The common, grayish brown cumin seeds are similar in appearance to caraway. The seeds are nutty and highly aromatic, often used in Mexican and Indian cooking.

CURRY Madras-style curry powder, named for a city in southern India, is hotter than standard curry powder. You can find it in specialty stores.

EDAMAME Fresh soybeans (also called "sweet beans"), picked in their fuzzy pods just before they reach full maturity, look like bright green lima beans. Their flavor is sweet and mild, with a touch of "beaniness." They are easy to digest and are exceptionally high in protein (½ cup has 16 grams). There are several kinds available today—frozen and fresh, in the pod and shelled—in large supermarkets, natural-foods stores or Asian markets.

EGG WHITES (DRIED) To alleviate food-safety concerns, we call for dried egg whites, which are pasteurized, in recipes in which the egg whites are not cooked. They are also practical in recipes that use several egg whites, allowing you to avoid wasting yolks. Reconstituted dried egg whites whip up into beautiful meringues. Products, such as Just Whites, can be found in the baking section of most supermarkets.

FISH SAUCE A pungent, soy sauce-like condiment used throughout Southeast Asia, made from fermented, salted fish. It is called *nuoc mam* in Vietnam and *nam pla* in Thailand. A little goes a long way. The typical amount per serving is only ¼ to ½ teaspoon. Sodium content varies considerably. We use Thai Kitchen fish sauce in our analyses; it is available in large supermarkets and Asian markets.

FLAXSEEDS can be found in the natural-foods section of large supermarkets and in natural-foods stores. The seeds must be ground for your body to take advantage of the nutrients. Ground seeds are highly perishable, so grind them just before using. Store whole flaxseeds in the refrigerator or freezer.

FLOURS:

◆ **Bread flour** has a higher gluten and protein content than all-purpose flour. It is generally recommended for bread machines and is valuable when making breads with a high percentage of whole-wheat flour.

◆ **White whole-wheat flour**, made from a special variety of white wheat, is light in color and flavor but has the same nutritional properties as regular whole-wheat flour.

◆ **Whole-wheat pastry flour** is milled from soft wheat. It contains less gluten than regular whole-wheat flour and helps ensure a tender result in delicate baked goods while providing the nutritional benefits of whole grains. Available in large supermarkets and in natural-foods stores. Store in the freezer.

LENTILS Smaller and firmer than brown lentils, French green lentils cook in just 20 minutes. They can be found in natural-foods stores and some larger supermarkets. Red lentils, which can be found in natural-foods stores and Middle Eastern markets, also cook in just 20 minutes.

MILLET A little round yellow grain, native to Africa and Asia; grown in the U.S. mostly for birdseed and animal feed but nutritionally similar to wheat. Look for millet in natural-foods stores.

MISO is fermented soybean paste made by inoculating a mixture of soybeans, salt and grains (usually barley or rice) with koji, a beneficial mold. Aged for up to 3 years, miso is undeniably salty, but a little goes a long way.

OILS:

◆ **Canola:** High in omega-3s, this practical bland oil with a relatively high smoke point can be used for sautéing and baking. Most canola oil is highly refined to extract as much oil as possible from the seed. The resulting inexpensive version has a long shelf life. Some consumers choose to pay more for less refined organic canola oil. The organic designation guarantees that the seed was not from genetically modified plants.

◆ **Extra-Virgin Olive:** This flavorful, heart-healthy oil is unrefined and thus high in antioxidants and polyphenols that are a tonic to cardiovascular health. Less expensive but so-called "pure" olive oil (not extra-virgin) is refined and more tolerant to heat but also less nutrient-dense. Don't bother with "light" olive oil; it has virtually no character and even fewer polyphenols. Use extra-virgin in moderate-heat cooking, baking and dressings.

◆ **Rice Bran Oil:** Made from the nutritious bran and germ layers of rice. It has a high smoke point, 490°F, making it an excellent choice for frying, and a delicate flavor, so it is ideal for baking. Look for it in natural-foods stores. For more information, visit www.californiariceoil.com.

◆ **Sesame:** Made from crushed sesame seeds, this oil is a dark, deeply flavored seasoning used throughout northern Asia. It is usually sprinkled on at the end of cooking or added to marinades and dipping sauces. Keep in the refrigerator.

◆ **Walnut:** This specialty oil sports a higher price tag, but along with a rich, nutty flavor come omega-3s and vitamin E. Close runners-up in this category include toasted sesame, pumpkinseed and almond oils. Walnut oil has a relatively long shelf life: three months when refrigerated. Use it to dress salads, especially those containing flavorful cheese and nuts.

PINE NUTS Also known as pignoli and piñon, these are the small, ivory-colored seeds of various pine trees. Their distinctive light nutty flavor is an important note in many Mediterranean dishes. They can be found in small jars in the international-foods section of the supermarket or in bulk at natural-foods stores. Store pine nuts in an airtight container in the freezer, for they turn rancid quickly.

POBLANO CHILE The dark green poblano turns reddish brown as it ripens. The flavor ranges from mild to pungent. Dried, it is known as an ancho or mulato. Fresh poblanos are sold in Mexican markets and most supermarkets.

POMEGRANATE Cutting open a pomegranate reveals a multitude of crimson kernels. We refer to them as "seeds," but technically they're "arils." These small edible sacks containing the juice and a crunchy seed are the part that is good to eat. Fresh pomegranates appear in September and last through December. They are picked ripe, so the fruit is ready to enjoy when you take it home. A good pomegranate should have a soft, leathery skin that gives slightly when pressed. Look for heavy pomegranates: weight is an indication of juiciness. Some markings do not affect the flavor, but avoid fruit with shriveled skin. When refrigerated, pomegranates will keep for up to 3 months. One large pomegranate yields about 1 cup arils.

POMEGRANATE JUICE Out of season, you can enjoy pomegranate's refreshing flavor if you use bottled juice as a beverage and for cooking. Purchase pomegranate juice in the refrigerated or natural-foods section of most supermarkets. The R.W. Knudsen brand is available in natural-foods stores (www.knudsenjuices.com). The distinctive bottles of Pom Wonderful juice are available in the refrigerated section of many supermarkets (www.pomwonderful.com). (*To make your own, see page 397.*)

POMEGRANATE MOLASSES lends a bright, tangy flavor to many Middle Eastern and Persian dishes. (Do not confuse it with grenadine syrup, which is very sweet and contains little or no pomegranate juice.) Bottled molasses is sold in Middle Eastern markets, specialty-foods stores or by mail order (Adriana's Caravan, www.adrianascaravan.com, (800) 316-0820; Kalustyan's, www.kalustyans.com, (800) 352-3451). (*To make your own, see page 397.*)

PORTOBELLO A mature cremini, the portobello is a large, dark brown mushroom with a wide, flaring, flat cap. While the stems are usually too woody to eat, the caps have an especially rich and meaty texture.

PROSCIUTTO A spiced and salt-cured Italian ham that is air-dried then pressed, resulting in a firm, dense texture. Usually sold very thinly sliced, it can be found in specialty-foods stores, Italian markets, deli counters.

RAISINS Baking raisins, moister than regular, ensure a better texture. To substitute regular raisins, plump them first: soak in boiling water for 10 minutes; drain well.

RICE For cooking instructions, see the "Essential Grain-Cooking Guide," page 101. To achieve the characteristic creamy risotto texture, use short- or medium-grain brown rice, available in natural-foods stores and large supermarkets. Lundberg Family Farms (www.lundberg.com) sells an excellent short-grain brown rice. Another source is dannysorganic.com. Also look for Japanese brands in the Asian section of large supermarkets.

RICE-PAPER WRAPPERS These round or triangular translucent sheets made from rice flour are widely used in Vietnamese and Thai cooking. Dipped in warm water, the delicate sheets become soft and pliable in seconds. It just takes a few times working with them to master the technique. Once opened, store in airtight plastic bags. In a cool, dry place they will keep for a couple of months. You can find them in Asian markets and specialty stores.

RICE VINEGAR (OR RICE-WINE VINEGAR) is a mild vinegar made from glutinous rice; bottlings range from clear to aged (extremely dark). Substitute cider vinegar for clear rice vinegar in a pinch.

SOBA These thin buckwheat noodles from Japan are served both cold with a soy-based dipping sauce or hot in a broth. They should be cooked in simmering, not boiling, water and then rinsed well under cold water. Look for soba in natural-foods stores, Asian markets or the specialty-food section of the supermarket.

TOFU "Soybean curd" is made by heating soymilk and a curdling agent in a process similar to dairy cheesemaking. Allowed to stand and thicken, the curds form silken tofu. When stirred and separated from the whey, the pressed curds, with their spongier texture, are known as "regular" tofu. The longer the pressing, the firmer and denser the tofu—soft, firm or extra-firm.

TORTILLAS Flour tortillas are typically made with refined flour, but whole-wheat varieties are becoming increasingly available in supermarkets. Sizes range from 6 to 10 inches in diameter. Heat tortillas (*see Tip, page 397*) to make them soft and pliable for wrapping around fillings.

VEGETABLE BROTH Commercial vegetable broth is readily available in natural-foods stores and many supermarkets. We especially like the Imagine and Pacific brands, sold in convenient aseptic packages that allow you to use small amounts and keep the rest refrigerated. To make your own, see the recipe on page 67.

WONTON WRAPPERS These square wheat-flour wrappers are used for pan-fried, steamed or boiled Chinese dumplings. Fresh wonton wrappers will keep, well wrapped, in the refrigerator for up to 1 week or for up to 3 months in the freezer. You can find them in large supermarkets and Asian markets.

Cooking Tips

To make a BOUQUET GARNI: Use an oversized teaball or a 4-inch square of clean cheesecloth tied with kitchen string to bundle herbs and aromatics together in a seasoning packet. That way, you can easily remove and discard the packet when finished with it.

To make fresh BREADCRUMBS: Trim crusts from firm sandwich bread. Tear bread into pieces and process in a food processor until coarse crumbs form. One slice of bread makes about ⅓ cup crumbs.

To defat CHICKEN BROTH: If you don't have time to wait for the broth to chill, use a bulb baster to siphon the clear broth from below the surface where the fat collects. (Alternatively, use a fat-separator strainer designed for this purpose.)

To make CHOCOLATE SHAVINGS: Curls of shaved chocolate make a quick, easy and impressive garnish for almost any chocolate dessert. Place a block of chocolate (2 ounces or larger) on wax paper and microwave on Defrost just until slightly softened but not melted, 15 to 30 seconds. Use a swivel-bladed vegetable peeler to shave off curls. If the chocolate gets too hard to shave easily, warm it again.

To segment CITRUS FRUIT: After zesting, use a small sharp knife to remove any remaining peel and all the bitter white pith. To make attractive segments, work over a bowl to catch the juice and slice between each segment and its surrounding membrane.

To separate EGGS safely: Use an egg separator, an inexpensive gadget found in cookware stores; separating eggs by passing the yolk back and forth between pieces of eggshell or your hands can expose the eggs to bacteria.

To clean LEEKS: Trim and discard coarse green tops. Split leeks lengthwise with a sharp knife, beginning about 1 inch from the root end and cutting toward the green end. Leave root end attached. Swish leeks repeatedly in a basin of cold water to remove grit. Alternatively, trim roots and ragged tops. Slice leeks and place in plenty of water, then drain. Repeat a few times. The slices do not absorb water or lose flavor and the process is faster.

To peel a MANGO: Place the mango on a cutting board with the narrow side facing you. With a sharp knife, slice off one side, sliding the knife along the flat seed. Repeat on the other side of the mango. With a paring knife, make crisscross cuts through the flesh, cutting up to but not through the skin. To remove cubes of mango flesh, press the skin so the cut side pops outward, then slice off the cubes.

To MEASURE DRY INGREDIENTS: For all baking, careful measuring is critical to the success of a recipe. To measure flour, first stir it in the canister to lighten it. Spoon flour into a dry measuring cup until heaping, then level off with the straight edge of a knife. Do not pack or tap.

To MEASURE LIQUIDS: Place a clear measuring cup on a level surface. Pour in the liquid, then verify the measure by looking at it from eye level, not above.

To toast NUTS: Whether you are using almonds, pine nuts, walnuts, pecans, hazelnuts or pistachios, toasting brings out their inherently rich flavor. Choose the most convenient method for toasting.

- In the oven: Preheat oven to 350°F. (Alternatively, a toaster oven is convenient if you do not wish to heat your regular oven.) Spread nuts in a small baking pan. Bake, shaking the pan once or twice to ensure even browning, until the nuts are lightly browned and fragrant, 5 to 8 minutes. Transfer to a small bowl to cool.

- In the microwave: Spread nuts on a microwave-safe plate or in a glass pie pan or baking dish. Microwave on high, stirring several times, until the nuts are golden brown and fragrant. Allow 4 to 5 minutes to toast ½ cup nuts.

- On the stovetop: Heat a small dry skillet over medium-low heat. Add nuts and cook, stirring constantly, until the nuts are lightly browned and fragrant, 2 to 3 minutes. Transfer to a small bowl to cool.

To seed a POMEGRANATE: To avoid the enduring stains of pomegranate juice, work under water. Fill a large bowl with water. Hold the pomegranate in the water and slice off the crown. Lightly score the fruit into quarters, from crown to stem end. Keeping the fruit under water, break it apart, gently separating the plump arils from the outer skin and white pith. The seeds will drop to the bottom of the bowl and the pith will float to the surface. Discard the pith. Pour the seeds into a colander. Rinse and pat dry. The seeds can be frozen in an airtight container or sealable plastic bag for up to 3 months.

To make POMEGRANATE JUICE, use pomegranates at room temperature. Roll the fruit on the counter to break up the seed sacks within. Carefully cut the pomegranate in half and extract the juice using a reamer or a juicer (or process the seeds in a blender or food processor). Strain the juice through a fine-meshed sieve, pressing on the pulp to extract as much juice as possible. Discard pulp. You will need at least 6 pomegranates to produce 1 cup juice. The juice will keep, covered, in the refrigerator for up to 2 days or in the freezer for up to 3 months.

To make POMEGRANATE MOLASSES, simmer 4 cups pomegranate juice, uncovered, in a medium nonreactive saucepan over medium heat until thick enough to coat a spoon, 45 to 50 minutes. (Do not let the syrup reduce too much or it will darken and become very sticky.) Makes about ½ cup. The molasses will keep, in an airtight container, in the refrigerator for up to 3 months.

To heat TORTILLAS:

- In the oven: Preheat oven to 300°F. Stack tortillas (about 4 in a batch) and wrap tightly in foil. Place in oven for 5 to 10 minutes, or until warm.

- In the microwave: Stack 4 tortillas between damp paper towels and microwave on high for 30 seconds, or until hot and pliable.

- On the stovetop: Place a tortilla directly on a burner (gas or electric) set at medium heat. Turn frequently with tongs until golden and charred in spots, 30 to 60 seconds.

THE ESSENTIAL EATINGWELL PANTRY

THE CHALLENGE TO GETTING A HEALTHFUL MEAL on the table frequently lies not in the cooking but in the shopping. While you will need to pick up items like fresh salad greens, chicken and fish for weeknight dinners, and specialized ingredients for specific recipes, a well-stocked pantry and freezer can make trying a new (or old favorite) recipe much easier. Here is a list of staples we suggest you keep on hand to prepare many of the recipes in this book.

OILS, VINEGARS & CONDIMENTS

- Extra-virgin olive oil for cooking and salad dressings
- Canola oil for cooking and baking
- Flavorful nut and seed oils for salad dressings and stir-fry seasonings: toasted sesame oil, walnut oil
- Butter, preferably unsalted. It doesn't take much to deliver a buttery finish to a special cake or sauce. Store in the freezer if you use infrequently.
- Reduced-fat mayonnaise
- A selection of vinegars: balsamic, red-wine, white-wine, rice (or rice-wine), apple cider
- Asian condiments and flavorings: reduced-sodium soy sauce, fish sauce, hoisin sauce, oyster sauce, chile-garlic sauce, curry paste
- Kalamata olives and green olives
- Dijon mustard
- Capers (*see Ingredient Note, page 394*)

FLAVORINGS

- Kosher salt or coarse sea salt and fine salt
- Black peppercorns
- Onions
- Fresh garlic
- Fresh ginger
- Anchovies or anchovy paste for flavoring pasta sauces and salad dressings
- Dried herbs: bay leaves, crumbled dried sage (do not use ground sage), dried thyme leaves, oregano, tarragon
- Spices: allspice (whole berries or ground), coriander seeds, caraway seeds, cinnamon sticks, ground cinnamon, chili powder, cumin seeds, ground cumin, paprika, crushed red pepper, nutmeg, ground ginger
- Lemons, limes and oranges. The zest is as valuable as the juice. Organic fruit is recommended when you use a lot of zest.

CANNED GOODS & BOTTLED ITEMS

- Diced tomatoes and tomato paste
- Reduced-sodium chicken broth, beef broth and/or vegetable broth (*see Ingredient Note, page 396*)
- Clam juice
- Light coconut milk for Asian curries and soups (*see Ingredient Note, page 394*)
- Canned beans: cannellini (white kidney) beans, great northern beans, chickpeas (garbanzo beans), black beans and red kidney beans
- Chunk light tuna and salmon

GRAINS & LEGUMES

- Assorted whole-wheat pastas
- Brown rice. Store opened packages in the refrigerator or freezer. Cook a double batch on the weekend because leftovers reheat beautifully in the microwave.
- Pearl barley and quick-cooking barley (*see Ingredient Note, page 394*)
- Rolled oats
- Whole-wheat couscous (*see Ingredient Note, page 394*)
- Bulgur (*see Ingredient Note, page 394*)
- Dried lentils (*see Ingredient Note, page 395*)
- Yellow cornmeal
- Plain dry breadcrumbs

NUTS & SEEDS

- Walnuts
- Pecans
- Almonds
- Hazelnuts
- Dry-roasted unsalted peanuts
- Pine nuts (*see Ingredient Note, page 395*)

- Natural peanut butter
- Sesame seeds
- Flaxseeds (*see Ingredient Note, page 395*)

Store opened packages of nuts and seeds in the refrigerator or freezer.

Baking & Dessert-Making Ingredients

- Whole-wheat flour, regular and pastry flour (*see Ingredient Note, page 395*). Store opened packages in the refrigerator or freezer.
- All-purpose flour
- Granulated sugar
- Brown sugar
- Honey
- Pure maple syrup
- Baking powder
- Baking soda
- Active dry yeast and quick-rising yeast
- Unflavored gelatin
- Cream of tartar
- Dried egg whites (*see Ingredient Note, page 394*)
- Cornstarch
- Vanilla extract. For maximum perfume, be sure to purchase "pure," not imitation.
- Assorted dried fruits, such as apricots, prunes, cherries, cranberries, dates, figs, raisins
- Unsweetened cocoa powder, natural and/or Dutch-processed (*see Ingredient Note, page 394*)
- Bittersweet chocolate and semisweet chocolate chips
- Evaporated low-fat or fat-free milk

Refrigerator Basics

- Low-fat milk or soymilk
- Low-fat or nonfat plain yogurt and/or vanilla yogurt
- Reduced-fat sour cream
- Good-quality Parmesan cheese and/or Romano cheese
- Sharp Cheddar cheese
- Eggs (large). Keep them on hand for fast omelets and frittatas.
- Orange juice
- Dry white wine. If you wish, substitute nonalcoholic wine.

Freezer Basics

- Fruit-juice concentrates (orange, apple, pineapple)
- Frozen vegetables: peas, spinach, broccoli, stir-fry pepper mix, corn, small whole onions, hash browns
- Frozen berries
- Italian turkey sausage and sliced prosciutto to flavor fast pasta sauces
- Low-fat vanilla ice cream or frozen yogurt for impromptu desserts

Ingredient Sources

We strive to feature recipes with easily accessible ingredients, but some ingredients are worth going out of your way to find. Even if you live in a remote area, the Internet and overnight shipping mean that specialty and ethnic ingredients are just a click away. Here are some of the mail-order purveyors we have found to be most useful.

- **Bob's Red Mill**, www.bobsredmill.com, (800) 349-2173. A great resource for a vast array of whole-grain products.
- **Dean & DeLuca**, www.deandeluca.com, (800) 781-9246. The wonders of this Manhattan food shop include lavender buds (*see page 330*) and are delivered to your kitchen.
- **EthnicGrocer.com**: An incredible selection of ingredients from all corners of the world.
- **Kalustyan's**, www.kalustyans.com, (800) 352-3451. A good place to look for Middle Eastern and Indian ingredients.
- **King Arthur Flour**, www.kingarthurflour.com, (800) 827-6836. Wonderful source of whole grains, specialty flours, baking supplies and more.
- **Melissa's**, www.melissas.com, (800) 588-0151. A wide selection of specialty produce.
- **Penzeys Spices**, www.penzeys.com, (800) 741-7787. Specializing in premium spices, herbs and seasonings.

HEALTHY WEIGHT-LOSS INDEX

All the recipes in this special index meet current nutritional guidelines for healthy weight loss, and are identified with ✓. These recipes are reduced in calories, carbohydrates and fats, while providing fiber and abundant flavor. We judged the recipes based on the following specific criteria for each course and nutrient:

COURSE	CALORIES	CARBS (G)	TOTAL FAT (G)	SAT FAT (G)
SOUPS & SALADS	≤ 250	≤ 33	≤ 10	≤ 5
SIDE DISHES	≤ 250	≤ 33	≤ 10	≤ 5
ENTREES	≤ 350	≤ 33	≤ 20	≤ 10
MUFFINS & BREADS	≤ 230	≤ 33	≤ 10	≤ 5
DESSERTS	≤ 230	≤ 33	≤ 10	≤ 5

Recipes identified with ♦♦♦ in the Lower Carbs column are well suited for people following a very-low-carbohydrate weight-loss plan. For weight maintenance on such plans, also choose from the ♦♦ and ♦ listings. High-fiber foods +++ are also well suited for such weight-loss plans and have been evaluated and rated in three categories according to the following scales:

CARBOHYDRATES	
♦♦♦	12 grams and under
♦♦	22 grams and under
♦	33 grams and under

FIBER	
+++	10 grams and over
++	5 to 9.5 grams
+	2.5 to 4.5 grams

SWIFT & SIMPLE INDEX

Entrees ready in 50 minutes or less.

RECIPE INDEX

Page numbers in italics indicate photographs.

H

I, J, K

L

M

N

O

CONTRIBUTORS

Our thanks to the fine food writers whose work was previously published in EATINGWELL *Magazine.*